T0304697

Get the eBook FREE!
(PDF, ePub, Kindle, and liveBook all included)

We believe that once you buy a book from us, you should be able to read it in any format we have available. To get electro versions of this book at no additional cost to you, purchase a then register this book at the Manning website.

Go to https://www.manning.com/freebook and follow the instructions to complete your pBook registration.

That's it!
Thanks from Manning!

Praise for the first edition

This book helped highlight some issues my team was having with EF Core and has become an inva *resource that takes pride of place on our bookshelves.*

—Evan Wallace, senior software Developer at Berkley Insurance Au

The most complete go-to book for anything you need to know about EF Core! The #1 must-have E *reference for your library!*

—Mauro Quercioli, senior independent software architect/developer, Siena I.T. Consulting Corpo

Knowing that EF Core in Action is right there on my desk, I am approaching my latest assignme *build out a new WebAPI application using Entity Framework Core—with complete confidence. Th* *addresses everything we needed to know about EF Core and more!*

—Phil Taffet, senior .NET developer, California Earthquake Aut

Finally a book to learn all about EF Core. It's fun and engaging reading this. Be careful—whether y *beginner or professional, you'll learn something.*

—Raushan Kumar Jha, SE-2, Microsoft India (

This is a solid book dealing well with the topic in hand but also handling the wider concerns around *Entity Framework in real-world applications.*

—Sebastian Rogers, technical director, Simple Innov

Entity Framewor
Core in Actio

SECOND EDITI

JON P SM
FOREWORD BY JULIE LER

MANNI
SHELTER Is

ine information and ordering of this and other Manning books, please visit
anning.com. The publisher offers discounts on this book when ordered in quantity.
re information, please contact

pecial Sales Department
Manning Publications Co.
0 Baldwin Road
O Box 761
helter Island, NY 11964
mail: orders@manning.com

Manning Publications Co.
0 Baldwin Road
O Box 761
helter Island, NY 11964

Development editor: Marina Michaels
Technical development editor: Joel Kotarski
Review editor: Aleksandar Dragosavljević
Production editor: Keri Hales
Copy editor: Keir Simpson
Proofreader: Melody Dolab
Technical proofreader: Julien Pohie
Typesetter: Dennis Dalinnik
Cover designer: Marija Tudor

9781617298363
in the United States of America

conter

PART 1   ●●

v

6   Tips and techniques for reading and writing with EF Core

8 Configuring relationships   226

9 *Handling database migrations*   268

10 Configuring advanced features and handling concurrency conflicts 306

Have you ever worked on an application that doesn't use data and requires some r
of interacting with a data store? In my decades as a software developer, every a
application I have worked on or have helped others with has depended on readin
writing to some type of data store. When I became a solo entrepreneur in the 19
came up with the name The Data Farm for my company. I am definitely a data ne

Over the past few decades, Microsoft has gone through many iterations of
access frameworks. If you've been working in this arena for a while, you might re
ber DAO and RDO, ADO, and ADO.NET. In 2006, Microsoft shared the first
tions of the as-yet-unnamed Entity Framework (EF), based on work done at Micr
Research in a private meeting at TechEd. I was one of the few people invited to
meeting. It was my first time seeing an Object Relational Mapper (ORM), a li
that focuses on relieving developers from the redundant drudgery of building
nections and commands, writing SQL, transforming query results into objects
transforming object changes into SQL to persist back to the database.

Many of us worried that this framework was yet another data access framewor
Microsoft would give up on in short order, forcing us to learn yet another one a
the road. But history has proved us wrong. Fifteen years later, Microsoft is still i
ing in Entity Framework, which has evolved into the cross-platform and open so
Entity Framework Core and continues to be Microsoft's go-to data access libra
.NET developers.

Over the 15 years that EF has been around and evolving, .NET has evolved as
EF and EF Core have grown in capability, but at the same time, the library has be

smarter about getting out of the developer's way when it comes to building modern software systems. We can customize mappings to support persistence with intricate database schema. As a Domain-Driven Design practitioner, I have been extremely happy with the attention that the team has paid to allowing EF Core to persist carefully designed entities, value objects, and aggregates that, by design, are not burdened with knowledge of database schema.

As an early adopter who worked closely with the EF team even before the initial release, I wrote four books on Entity Framework between 2008 and 2011. Though I do love to write, I eventually discovered that I also love creating videos, so I focused my own efforts on creating and publishing courses on EF Core and other topics as a Pluralsight author. I still write articles, but no more books, which is why I'm so happy that Jon P Smith found his way to writing for Manning.

When Jon published the first edition of *Entity Framework Core in Action*, I recognized in him a fellow "curious cat" who left no stone unturned in his quest to understand how EF Core works. Equally, he takes the role of sharing that information seriously, ensuring that his readers are able to follow along and truly gain expertise. His work is meticulous, and his knowledge is deep. As I have continued creating training resources for those who prefer to learn from videos, I've been pleased to recommend Jon's work to those who are looking for a trustworthy book on EF Core. Updating content to reflect the newest version, EF Core 5, is no small task. Jon has once again earned my respect (and the respect of many other people) with the edition you now have in hand.

With this book, you're really getting three books in one. First, Jon handholds you through the basics, even building some simple applications that use EF Core. When you've become comfortable, it's time to dig more deeply into intermediate-level use, with relationships, migrations, and control beyond EF Core's default behavior. Finally, it's time to use EF Core in real-world applications, tackling important topics such as performance and architecture. Jon's meticulous exploration and his own experience working with large software applications make him a skilled and trustworthy guide.

—JULIE LERMAN

Julie Lerman is known as the foremost expert on Entity Framework and EF Core outside Microsoft. She is the author of the Programming Entity Framework *book series and dozens of courses on Pluralsight.com. Julie coaches businesses on modernizing their software. You can find her presenting and keynoting on EF, Domain-Driven Design, and other topics at software conferences around the world.*

Any software developer should be used to having to learn new libraries or langu
but for me, the learning has been a bit extreme. I stopped coding in 1988, when I
into technical management, and I didn't come back to coding until 2009—a 2
gap. To say that the landscape had changed is an understatement; I felt like a ch
Christmas morning with so many lovely presents, I couldn't take them all in.

I made all the rookie mistakes at the beginning, such as thinking that object-ori
programming is about using inheritance, which it isn't. But I learned the new s
and new tools (wow!), and reveled in the amount of information I could get on
chose to focus on Microsoft's stack, mainly because of the wealth of documen
available. That was a good choice at the time, but with the .NET Core initiative
its open source, multiplatform approach, it turns out to be an excellent choice.

The first applications I worked on in 2009 were ones that optimized and disp
healthcare needs geographically, especially around where to locate treatment ce
That task required complex math (which my wife provided) and serious dat
work. I went through ADO.NET, and LINQ to SQL. In 2013, I swapped to Entity F
work (EF), when EF 5 supported SQL's spatial (geographical) types, and then n
to EF Core when it came out.

Over the intervening years, I have used EF Core a lot, both on client project
for building open source libraries. In addition to writing this book, I've written e
sively on EF Core in my own blog (www.thereformedprogrammer.net). It turn
that I like taking complex software ideas and trying to make them easy for othe
ple to understand, which I hope I manage to do in this book.

Entity Framework Core in Action, Second Edition, covers all the features of EF Core 5.0, with plenty of examples and code you can run. I've also included numerous patterns and practices to help you build robust and refactorable code. Part 3 of the book, called "Using Entity Framework Core in real-world applications," shows my focus on building and shipping real applications. And I have not one, but three chapters on performance-tuning EF Core so you have many performance improvement techniques at your fingertips when your application is not performing as well as you need it to.

Some of the most pleasurable chapters to write were ones that delved into how EF Core works inside (chapters 1, 6, and 11) and performance-tuning an application (chapters 14, 15, and 16). Personally, I learned a lot from using a modular monolith architecture (chapter 13) and building a substantial application with Cosmos DB (chapter 16). Along the way, I try to present the pros and cons of each approach I use, as I don't believe there is a "silver bullet" answer in software—only a range of compromises that we as developers need to consider when choosing how to implement something.

acknowledgmer

Although I did most of the work on the book, I had a lot of help along the way, want to say "Thank you" to all those who helped.

Thanks to my wife, Dr. Honora Smith, for putting up with my sitting in front computer for three-fourths of a year and for getting me back into programm love her to bits. Another special mention goes to my great friend JC for his hel support.

Manning Publications has been great, with a robust and comprehensive pr that is hard but thorough, which produces an excellent end product. The te great, and I'm going to list the significant people in chronological order, startin Brian Sawyer, Breckyn Ely, Marina Michaels, Joel Kotarski, Rejhana Markanovic, Maras, Heather Tucker, Aleksandar Dragosavljević, and many others who helpe production of the book. Marina Michaels was my main contact for the first ed and I obviously didn't cause her too many problems, as she kindly agreed to he on the second edition.

I also got a lot of help from the busy EF Core team. As well as answering nt ous issues that were raised on the EF Core GitHub repo, they checked a few c chapters in which their input was valuable. Arthur Vickers and Shay Rojansk special mention for reviewing some chapters. The other people on the tea alphabetical order, are Andriy Svyryd, Brice Lambson, Jeremy Likness, Ma Markowski, and Smit Patel.

I would also like to thank Julien Pohie, technical proofreader, and the reviewe Pezewski, Anne Epstein, Foster Haines, Hari Khalsa, Janek López, Jeff Neumann

ACKNOWLEDGMENTS

Clermont, John Rhodes, Mauro Quercioli, Paul G. Brown, Raushan Jha, Ricardo Peres, Shawn Lam, Stephen Byrne, Sumit K Singh, Thomas Gueth, Thomas Overby Hansen, and Wayne Mather. Your suggestions helped make this a better book.

about this bo

Entity Framework Core in Action, Second Edition, is about writing EF Core database quickly, correctly, and ultimately for fast performance. To help with the "quick rect, fast" aspects, I include a lot of examples with plenty of tips and techniques along the way, I throw in quite a bit on how EF Core works on the inside, becaus information will help you when things don't work the way you think they should

The Microsoft documentation is good but doesn't have room for detailed c ples. In this book, I try to give you at least one example of each feature I cover you'll often find unit tests in the GitHub repo (see the "About the code" sectic links) that test a feature in multiple ways. Sometimes, reading a unit test can cc what's happening much more quickly than reading the text in a book can, so cor the unit tests to be a useful resource.

Who should read this book?

Entity Framework Core in Action, Second Edition, is aimed at both software devel who've never used EF before and seasoned EF Core developers, plus anyonc who wants to know what EF Core is capable of doing. I assume that you're fai with .NET development with C# and that you have at least some idea of what a tional database is. You don't need to be a C# expert, but if you're new to C# might find some of the code hard to read, as I don't explain C#. The book with basic EF Core commands, which should be accessible to most C# program but from part 2 onward, the topics get more complex as the content goes dc into EF Core's features.

How this book is organized

I've tried to build a path that starts with the basics (part 1), goes deep into the details (part 2), and ends with useful tools and techniques (part 3). I try not to assume you'll read the book cover to cover, especially the reference section in part 2, but at least skim-reading the first six chapters will help you understand the basics that I use later in the book.

Part 1: Getting started

- Chapter 1 introduces EF Core with a super-simple console application so you can see all the parts of EF Core in action. I also provide an overview of how EF Core works and why you might like to use it.
- Chapter 2 looks at querying (reading data from) the database. I cover the relationships between data stored in the database and how you can load that related data by using EF Core.
- Chapter 3 moves on to changing the data in a database: adding new data, updating existing data, and deleting data from a database.
- Chapter 4 looks at the different ways you can build robust business logic that uses EF Core to access the database. *Business logic* is the name given to code that implements business rules or workflow that's specific to the business problem your application solves.
- Chapter 5 is about building an ASP.NET Core application that uses EF Core. It pulls together the code developed in chapters 2, 3, and 4 to make a web application. I also talk about deploying the web application and accessing the hosted database.
- Chapter 6 covers a wide range of topics. Most topics contain a description of an aspect of EF Core combined with ways to exploit that feature in your code.

Part 2: Entity Framework Core in depth

- Chapter 7 covers the configuration of nonrelational properties—properties that hold a value, such as int, string, DateTime, and so on.
- Chapter 8 covers the configuration of relationships—the links between classes, such as a Book class linking to one or more Author classes. It also includes special mapping techniques, such as mapping multiple classes to one table.
- Chapter 9 covers all the ways you can change the database structure when using EF Core. It also looks at the issues that arise when you need to change the structure of a database that's being used by a live application.
- Chapter 10 looks at advanced mapping features and the whole area of detecting and handling concurrency conflicts.
- Chapter 11 digs deep into how EF Core's DbContext works, with a blow-by-blow view of what the various methods and properties do inside your application's DbContext.

Part 3: Using Entity Framework Core in real-world applications

- Chapter 12 introduces two approaches that send messages to the enh:
  SaveChanges/SaveChangesAsync methods. These two approaches pr
  another way to combine multiple updates into one transactional database u|
- Chapter 13 looks at applying Domain-Driven Design (DDD) approaches tc
  classes mapped to the database by EF Core. It also describes another arc
  tural approach used in the part 3 Book App.
- Chapter 14 lists all the issues that could affect the performance of your dat
  accesses and discusses what to do about them.
- Chapter 15 is a worked example of performance-tuning an EF Core ap
  tion. I take the original Book App display query, developed in part 1, and
  three levels of performance tuning.
- Chapter 16 uses Cosmos DB to further performance-tune the Book App, •
  uncovers the strengths and weakness of Cosmos DB and its EF Core pro
  The chapter ends with what you need to do when changing from one dat
  type to another.
- Chapter 17 is all about unit testing applications that use EF Core. I've als
  ated a NuGet package that you can use to help in your own unit testing.

Appendix

- Appendix A introduces the LINQ language that EF Core uses. This app•
  is useful for those who are unfamiliar with LINQ or who want a •
  refresher on LINQ.

About the code

I feel that I really know something only if I've written code to use that function c
ture, so the companion GitHub repo at http://mng.bz/XdlG is available to you.

> **NOTE** I strongly recommend cloning the code from the GitHub URL shown
> above. The copy of the repo listed on the Manning book page has problems
> with the Part3 branch because of long directory names.

This repo contains the code for the applications I show in the book and unit test
I ran to make sure that what I said in the book is correct. The repo has
branches:

- master, which covers part 1 of the book (chapters 1–6)
- Part2, which covers part 2 of the book (chapters 7–11)
- Part3, which covers part 3 of the book (chapters 12–17)

To run any of the applications, you should first read the Readme file at http:/,
.bz/yYjG in the GitHub repo. Each branch's Readme file has three main section;

- *What you need to install to run the example applications,* which tells you the c
  opment applications, .NET version, and database requirements to run a

the applications in the GitHub repo. (This information is the same for every branch.)

- *What you can run in this branch,* which tells you what application(s) you can run in the branch of the GitHub repo you have selected.
- *How to find and run the unit tests,* which tells you where the unit tests are and the various ways you can run them.

As you work through the three parts of the book, you can select each Git branch to access the code specifically for that part. Also, look out for the associated unit tests, grouped by chapter and feature.

> **NOTE** For chapter 17, which is about unit testing, I used a library I created. This library, which you can find at https://github.com/JonPSmith/EfCore .TestSupport, is an updated version of the EfCore.TestSupport library I created for the first edition of this book, now using new features available in EF Core 5. This library is an open source (MIT license) library, so you can use the NuGet package called `EfCore.TestSupport` (version 5 and later) in your own unit tests.

Code conventions

The code samples in this book, and their output, appear in a `fixed-width font` and are often accompanied by annotations. The code samples are deliberately kept as simple as possible because they aren't intended to be reusable parts that can be plugged into your code. Instead, the code samples are stripped down so that you can focus on the principle being illustrated.

This book contains many examples of source code, both in numbered listings and inline with normal text. In both cases, source code is formatted in a `fixed-width font` `like this` to separate it from ordinary text. Sometimes, code is also **in bold** to highlight code that has changed from previous steps in the chapter, such as when a new feature adds to an existing line of code.

In many cases, the original source code has been reformatted; we've added line breaks and reworked indentation to accommodate the available page space in the book. In rare cases, even these changes were not enough, so some listings include line-continuation markers (➥). Additionally, some comments in the source code have been removed from the listings when the code is described in the text. Code annotations accompany many of the listings, highlighting important concepts.

Source code for the examples in this book is available for download from the GitHub repo (http://mng.bz/XdlG).

liveBook discussion forum

Purchase of *Entity Framework Core in Action, Second Edition,* includes free access to a private web forum run by Manning Publications where you can make comments about the book, ask technical questions, and receive help from the author and from other

users. To access the forum, go to https://livebook.manning.com/book/entity-f
work-core-in-action-second-edition. You can also learn more about Manning's fc
and the rules of conduct at https://livebook.manning.com/#!/discussion.

Manning's commitment to our readers is to provide a venue where a meani
dialogue between individual readers and between readers and the author car
place. It is not a commitment to any specific amount of participation on the p
the author, whose contribution to the forum remains voluntary (and unpaid). W
gest you try asking the author some challenging questions lest his interest stray
forum and the archives of previous discussions will be accessible from the publi
website as long as the book is in print.

Online resources

Here are useful links to the Microsoft documentation and code:

- *Microsoft's EF Core documentation*—https://docs.microsoft.com/en-us/ef/cc
- *EF Core code*—https://github.com/dotnet/efcore
- *ASP.NET Core, working with EF Core*—https://docs.microsoft.com/en-us/asp
  core/data/
- *Stack Overflow EF Core tag* [entity-framework-core]—https://stackoverflow

about the author

JON P SMITH is a freelance software developer and architect with a special focus on .NET Core and Azure. He works mainly on the backend of client applications, typically using Entity Framework Core (EF Core) and ASP.NET Core web applications. He works remotely for clients around the world, with many of the projects coming from the United States. He typically helps with designing, performance-tuning, and writing sections of the client's application.

Jon is interested in defining patterns and building libraries that improve the speed of development of applications when using EF Core and ASP.NET Core. His libraries were written because he found some repetitive part of a project he was working on that could be turned into a useful library. You can see a summary of his main libraries on his GitHub overview page (https://github.com/JonPSmith).

Jon also writes on his technical blog at http://www.thereformedprogrammer.net, where he has covered topics related to EF Core, ASP.NET Core, and different architectural approaches. The most popular article on his technical blog site is about an improved ASP.NET Core authorization system; see http://mng.bz/ao2z. He has also spoken at a few conferences and at many Meetups in the United Kingdom.

about the cover illustratic

The figure on the cover of *Entity Framework Core in Action, Second Edition,* is capti "The Wife of a Franc Merchant." The illustration is taken from Thomas Jefferys' *lection of the Dresses of Different Nations, Ancient and Modern* (four volumes), Lo published between 1757 and 1772. The title page states that these illustration hand-colored copperplate engravings, heightened with gum arabic.

Thomas Jefferys (1719–71) was called "Geographer to King George III." He w English cartographer and the leading map supplier of his day. He engravec printed maps for government and other official entities, and produced a wide i of commercial maps and atlases, especially of North America. His work as a mapn sparked an interest in the local dress customs of the lands he surveyed and ma which are brilliantly displayed in this collection. Fascination with faraway land travel for pleasure were relatively new phenomena in the late 18th century, and c tions such as this one were popular, introducing both the tourist and the arm traveler to the inhabitants of other countries.

The diversity of the drawings in Jefferys' volumes speaks vividly of the uniqu and individuality of the world's nations some 200 years ago. Dress codes have cha since then, and the diversity by region and country, so rich at the time, has away. Now, it's often hard to tell the inhabitants of one continent from another haps (trying to view things optimistically) we've traded cultural and visual div for more varied personal lives—or more varied and interesting intellectual and nical lives.

At a time when it's difficult to tell one computer book from another, Manning celebrates the inventiveness and initiative of the computer business with book covers based on the rich diversity of the regional life of two centuries ago, brought back to life by Jeffreys' pictures.

Part

Getting start

Data is everywhere, growing by petabytes per year, and a lot of it is stor databases. Millions of applications are also out there—at the beginning of there were 1.2 billion websites—and most of them need to access data in bases. And I haven't started on the Internet of Things yet. So it shouldn' surprise that Gartner, a leading research and advisory company, says that ¿ IT spending will reach \$3.7 trillion in 2021 (http://mng.bz/gonl).

The good news for you is that your skills will be in demand. But the bad is that the pressure to develop applications quickly is unrelenting. This b about one tool that you can use to write database access code quickly: Micro Entity Framework Core (EF Core). EF Core provides an object-oriented v access relational and nonrelational (NoSQL) databases in the .NET env ment. The cool thing about EF Core and the other .NET Core libraries i they can run on the Windows, Linux, and Apple platforms, and they're fast

In part 1, I get you into the code straightaway. In chapter 1, you'll b super-simple console application, and by the end of chapter 5, you'll build sonably sophisticated web application that sells books. Chapters 2 and 3 ex the reading and writing of data to a relational database, respectively, and ter 4 covers writing your business logic. In chapter 5, you'll use Micro ASP.NET Core web framework to build the example book-selling site. Chap expands your knowledge of how EF Core works inside through a series o ful techniques for solving database problems, such as a quick way to copy in the database.

You'll have a lot of learning to do in part 1, even though I skip a few te mainly by relying on a lot of EF Core's default settings. Nevertheless, ¡

should give you a good understanding of what EF Core can do, with later parts growing your knowledge with extra EF Core features, more details on how you can configure EF Core, and chapters devoted to specific areas such as performance tuning.

Introduction to Ent?
Framework C?

This chapter covers

- Understanding the anatomy of an EF Core application
- Accessing and updating a database with EF Core
- Exploring a real-world EF Core application
- Deciding whether to use EF Core in your application

Entity Framework Core, or *EF Core*, is a library that software developers can u access databases. There are many ways to build such a library, but EF C? designed as an *object-relational mapper* (*O/RM*). O/RMs work by mapping bet two worlds: the relational database, with its own API, and the object-oriented ware world of classes and software code. EF Core's main strength is allowing sof developers to write database access code quickly in a language that you may better than SQL.

EF Core is multiplatform-capable: it can run on Windows, Linux, and App does this as part of the .NET Core initiative—hence the *Co?* part of the EF Core ? .NET 5 covers the whole range of desktop, web, cloud, mobile, gaming, Intern Things (IoT), and artificial intelligence (AI), but this book is focused on EF Cor?

EF Core isn't the first version of Entity Framework; an existing, non-Core, Entity Framework library is known as *EF6.x.* EF Core starts with years of experience built into it via feedback from these previous versions, 4 to 6.x. It has kept the same type of interface as EF6.x but has major changes underneath, such as the ability to handle nonrelational databases, which EF6.x wasn't designed to do. I had used EF5 and EF6 in many applications before EF Core came along, which allowed me to see the significant improvements EF Core made over EF6.x in both features and performance.

This book is for software developers who are already using EF Core, as well as developers who've never used Entity Framework, and seasoned EF6.x developers who want to move over to EF Core. I do assume that you're familiar with .NET development using C# and that you have at least some idea of what relational databases are. I don't assume you know how to write Structured Query Language (SQL), the language used by a majority of relational databases, because EF Core can do most of that for you. But I do show the SQL that EF Core produces because it helps you understand what's going on; using some of the EF Core advanced features requires you to have SQL knowledge, but the book provides plenty of diagrams to help you along the way.

> **TIP** If you don't know a lot about SQL and want to learn more, I suggest the W3Schools online resource: https://www.w3schools.com/sql/sql_intro.asp. The SQL set of commands is vast, and EF Core queries use only a small subset (such as SELECT, WHERE, and INNER JOIN), so that resource is a good place to start.

This chapter introduces you to EF Core through the use of a small application that calls into the EF Core library. You'll look under the hood to see how EF Core interprets software commands and accesses the database. Having an overview of what's happening inside EF Core will help you as you read through the rest of the book.

What you'll learn from this book

The book gives you an introduction to EF Core, starting with the basics and advancing to some more complex parts of EF Core. To get the best out of this book, you should be comfortable with developing applications using C#, including creating projects and loading NuGet packages. You will learn

- The fundamentals of using EF Core to access a database
- How to use EF Core in an ASP.NET Core web application
- The many ways you can configure EF Core to work exactly as you need
- Some of the deeper database features you might want to use
- How to handle changes in the database layout as your application grows
- How to improve the performance of your database code
- Most important, how to make sure that your code is working correctly

Throughout the book I build simple but fully featured applications so that you ca
EF Core working in real situations. All these applications are available via the exa
repo, which also includes lots of tips and techniques I have picked up while work
a contract developer and on my own projects.

1.2 *My "lightbulb moment" with Entity Framework*

Before we get into the nitty-gritty, let me tell you about one defining moment
when using Entity Framework that put me on the road to embracing EF. It was m
who got me back into programming after a 21-year gap (that's a story in itself!).

My wife, Dr. Honora Smith, is a lecturer in mathematics at the University of S
ampton, who specializes in the modeling of healthcare systems, especially focusi
where to locate health facilities. I had worked with her to build several applicatio
do geographic modeling and visualization for the UK National Health Servic
worked for South Africa on optimizing HIV/AIDS testing.

At the start of 2013, I decided to build a web application specifically for healt
modeling. I used ASP.NET MVC4 and EF5, which had just come out and supp
SQL spatial types that handle geographic data. The project went okay, but i
hard work. I knew that the frontend was going to be hard; it was a single-page a
cation using Backbone.js, but I was surprised at how long it took me to do the s
side work.

I applied good software practices and made sure that the database and bu
logic were matched to the problem space—that of modeling and optimizing the
tion of health facilities. That was fine, but I spent an inordinate amount of time
ing code to convert the database entries and business logic to a form suitable to
to the user. Also, I was using a Repository/Unit of Work pattern to hide EF5 code
I was continually having to tweak areas to make the repository work properly.

At the end of a project, I always look back and ask, "Could I have done tha
ter?" As a software architect, I'm always looking for parts that (a) worked wel
were repetitious and should be automated, or (c) had ongoing problems. This
the list was as follows:

- *Worked well*—The ServiceLayer, a layer in my application that isolated/ad
  the lower layers of the application from the ASP.NET MVC4 frontend, wo
  well. (I introduce this layered architecture in chapter 2.)

- *Was repetitious*—I used ViewModel classes, also known as *data transfer*
  (DTOs), to represent the data I needed to show to the user. Using a
  Model/DTO worked well, but writing the code to copy the database tab
  the ViewModel/DTO was repetitious and boring. (I also talk about View
  els/DTOs in chapter 2.)

- *Had ongoing problems*—The Repository/Unit of Work pattern didn't wor
  me. Ongoing problems occurred throughout the project. (I cover the Re
  tory pattern and alternatives in chapter 13.)

As a result of my review, I built a library called GenericServices (https://github.com/JonPSmith/GenericServices) to use with EF6.x. This library automated the copying of data between database classes and ViewModels/DTOs, and removed the need for a Repository/Unit of Work pattern. It seemed to be working well, but to stress-test GenericServices, I decided to build a frontend over one of Microsoft's example databases: the AdventureWorks 2012 Lite database. I built the whole application with the help of a frontend UI library in 10 days!

 Entity Framework + the right libraries + the right approach
= quick development of database access code

The site wasn't too pretty, but appearance wasn't the point. By analyzing my use of the Repository/Unit of Work pattern with EF6.x, I found a better approach. Then, by encapsulating this better approach into my GenericServices library, I automated the process of building Create, Read, Update, and Delete (CRUD) database commands. The result allowed me to build applications really quickly—definitely a "lightbulb moment," and I was hooked on EF.

Since then, I've built new libraries that work with EF Core, which I have found to significantly speed the development of 90% of my database accesses. I work as a contract developer, and these libraries, which are open source and available to you too, automate some of the standard requirements, allowing me to concentrate on the harder topics, such as understanding the client's needs, writing custom business logic, and performance-tuning where necessary. I will be talking about these libraries in later chapters.

Some words for existing EF6.x developers

TIME-SAVER If you haven't used Entity Framework 6.x, you can skip this section.

If you know EF6.x, much of EF Core will be familiar to you. To help you navigate this book quickly, I've added EF6 notes.

EF6 Watch for notes like this throughout the book. They point out the places where EF Core is different from EF6.x. Also be sure to look at the summaries at the end of each chapter, which point out the biggest changes between EF6 and EF Core in the chapter.

I'll also give you one tip from my journey of learning EF Core. I know EF6.x well, but that knowledge became a bit of a problem when I started using EF Core. I was using an EF6.x approach to problems and didn't notice that EF Core had new ways to solve them. In most cases, the approaches are similar, but in some areas, they aren't.

My advice to you, as an existing EF6.x developer, is to approach EF Core as a library that someone has written to mimic EF6.x, but understand that it works in ferent way. That way, you'll keep your eyes open for the new and different wa doing things in EF Core.

1.4 An overview of EF Core

You can use EF Core as an O/RM that maps between the relational database an .NET world of classes and software code. Table 1.1 shows how EF Core maps th worlds of the relational database and .NET software.

Table 1.1 EF Core mapping between a database and .NET software

Relational database	.NET software
Table	.NET class
Table columns	Class properties/fields
Rows	Elements in .NET collections—for instance, `List`
Primary keys: unique row	A unique class instance
Foreign keys: define a relationship	Reference to another class
SQL—for instance, `WHERE`	.NET LINQ—for instance, `Where(p => …`

1.4.1 The downsides of O/RMs

Making a good O/RM is complex. Although EF6.x or EF Core can seem easy to u times the EF Core "magic" can catch you by surprise. Let me mention two issues aware of before we dive into how EF Core works.

The first issue is *object-relational impedance mismatch*. Database servers and o oriented software use different principles; databases use primary keys to define i row is unique, whereas .NET class instances are, by default, considered uniqi their reference. EF Core handles much of the impedance mismatch for you, but .NET classes gain primary and foreign keys, which is extra data needed only fc database. Your software-only version of the classes doesn't need those extra prope but the database does.

The second issue is that an O/RM—and especially an O/RM as comprehens EF Core—is the opposite of the first issue. EF Core "hides" the database so wel you can sometimes forget about the database underneath. This problem can you to write code that would work well in C# but doesn't work for a database. example is having an expression body property return the full name of a perso combining the `FirstName` and `LastName` properties in the class, such as

```
public string FullName => $"{FirstName} {LastName}";
```

An expression body property such as the one just shown is the right thing to do in C#, but the same property would throw an exception if you tried to filter or order on that property, because EF Core needs a FullName column in the table so that it can apply an SQL WHERE or ORDER command at the database level.

That's why I spend time in this chapter showing how EF Core works on the inside and the SQL it produces. The more you understand about what EF Core is doing, the better equipped you'll be to write good EF Core code, and—more important—you'll know what to do when your code doesn't work.

> **NOTE** Throughout this book, I use a "Get it working, but be ready to make it faster if I need to" approach to using EF Core. EF Core allows me to develop quickly, but I'm aware that because of EF Core, or my poor use of it, the performance of my database access code might not be good enough for a particular business need. Chapter 5 covers how to isolate your EF Core so you can tune it with minimal side effects, and chapter 15 shows how to find and improve database code that isn't fast enough.

What about NoSQL?

We can't talk about relational databases without mentioning nonrelational databases, also known colloquially as NoSQL (see http://mng.bz/DW63). Both relational and nonrelational databases have a role in modern applications. I've used both SQL Server (relational database) and Azure Tables (nonrelational database) in the same application to handle two business needs.

EF Core handles both relational and nonrelational databases—a departure from EF6.x, which was designed around relational databases only. Most of the EF Core commands covered in this book apply to both types of databases, but there are some differences at the database level between relational databases and NoSQL databases, which leave out some of the more complex database commands in favor of scalability and performance.

EF Core 3.0 added a database provider for the Azure NoSQL database called Cosmos DB, which I cover in chapter 16. In that chapter, I point out the differences between a relational database and Cosmos DB; I was surprised by what I found. Now that EF Core has been altered to handle NoSQL databases, I expect that more NoSQL database providers will be written.

> **NOTE** Cosmos DB and other NoSQL databases have many strengths compared with SQL databases. It's much easier, for example, to have multiple copies of NoSQL databases around the world, which gives the user quicker access, and if a data center goes down, other copies can take over the load. But NoSQL databases also have some limitations compared with SQL databases; read chapter 16 for an in-depth analysis of Cosmos DB's benefits and limitations.

1.6   *Your first EF Core application*

In this chapter, you'll start with a simple example so that we can focus on wh
Core is doing rather than what the code is doing. For this example, you're goi
use a small console application called MyFirstEfCoreApp, which accesses a si
database. The MyFirstEfCoreApp application's job is to list and update books in a
plied database. Figure 1.1 shows the console output.

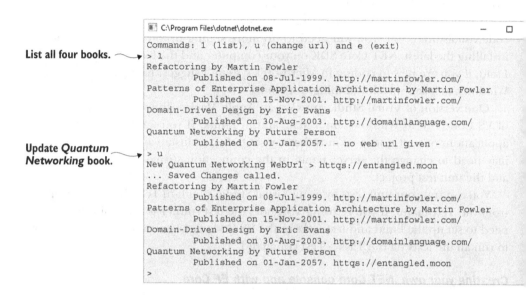

List all four books.

Update *Quantum Networking* book.

**Figure 1.1   The console application provides a command that uses an EF Core query to read and display all
books in your sample database, plus a command to update the database. These two commands show you how
Core works inside.**

This application isn't going to win any prizes for its interface or complexity, but
good place to start, especially because I want to show you how EF Core works i
nally to help you understand what's going on later in this book.

You can download this example application from the Git repo at http://
.bz/XdlG. You can look at the code and run the application. To do this, you need
ware development tools.

1.6.1   *What you need to install*

Microsoft has two development tools for a .NET Core application: Visual Studio
Visual Studio Code (shortened to VS Code). Visual Studio is slightly easier to use
I suggest that newcomers to .NET use Visual Studio. You can download Visual S
from www.visualstudio.com. Numerous versions exist, including a free comm

version, but you need to read the license to make sure that you qualify; see www
.visualstudio.com/vs/community.

When you install Visual Studio on Windows, make sure to include the .NET Core
Cross-Platform Development feature and Data storage and processing, which are in
the Other Toolsets section during the Install Workloads stage. Selecting the .NET
Core Cross-Platform Development feature will also install the .NET Core software
development kit (SDK) on your system; you need this SDK to create applications with
.NET. See http://mng.bz/2x0T for more information.

If you want to use VS Code, which is free, you can download it from https://
code.visualstudio.com. You will need to do more setting up on your system, such as
installing the latest .NET Core SDK on your computer and the localdb SQL Server. As
I said, if you are new to coding in Microsoft's system, I suggest using Visual Studio on
Windows, as it sets up a lot of things for you.

One version of Visual Studio runs on an Apple Macintosh machine, and versions
of VS Code run in Windows, on a Mac, and in Linux. If you want to run any of the
applications or unit tests, you must have an SQL Server instance on your system. You
may need to change the server name in the connection strings for the applications
and the unit-test project.

You can run your unit tests by using Visual Studio's built-in Test Explorer, available
from the Test menu. If you're using VS Code, the test runner is also built in, but you
need to set up the build and test tasks in the VS Code tasks.json file, which allows you
to run all the tests via the Task > Test command.

Creating your own .NET Core console app with EF Core

I know that many developers like to create their own applications, because building
the code yourself means that you know exactly what's involved. This section details
how to create the .NET console application MyFirstEfCoreApp by using Visual Studio.

CREATING A .NET CORE CONSOLE APPLICATION

Visual Studio has a great set of tutorials, and you can find an example of creating a C#
console application at http://mng.bz/e56z.

> **TIP** You can find out which version of .NET your application is using by
> choosing Project > MyFirstEfCoreApp Properties from the main menu; the
> Application tab shows the Target Framework. Some versions of EF Core
> require a certain version of .NET Core.

ADDING THE EF CORE LIBRARY TO YOUR APPLICATION

You can install the NuGet library in various ways. The more visual way is to use the
NuGet Package Manager; you can find a tutorial at http://mng.bz/pVeG. For this
application, you need the EF Core package for the database that your application is
going to access. In this case, you choose the Microsoft.EntityFrameworkCore.SqlServer
NuGet package, because it'll use the development SQL Server that was installed when
you installed Visual Studio.

The other thing you need to look at is the version number of the NuGet pa‹
you are about to install. EF Core has been built such that each major release ‹
own number. A version number of 5.1.3, for example, means EF Core major vers;
with minor release 1 and patch (bug fix) version 3. Often, you need to load diff
EF Core packages in different projects. You might load Microsoft.EntityFrame
Core in your data layer and Microsoft.EntityFrameworkCore.SqlServer in the wel
for example. If you need to do this, you should try to use NuGet packages wit
same Major.Minor.Patch listed in your project's properties. If a match is not f‹
make sure that the NuGet Major.Minor version matches your project's version.

Downloading and running the example application from the Git repo

You have two options for downloading and running the MyFirstEfCoreApp cons‹
application in the Git repo: Visual Studio or VS Code. You can find another Visual S
dio tutorial, "Open a project from a repo," at http://mng.bz/OEOn. The repo assc
ated with this book is http://mng.bz/XdlG.

Be sure to select the right branch. A Git repo has branches that allow you to swi‹
between different versions of the code. For this book, I created three main branch‹
master, which contains the code for part 1 (chapters 1–6); Part2, which contains t
code for part 2 (chapters 7–11); and Part3, which contains the code for part 3 (ch‹
ters 12–17).

By default, the repo will be opened in the master branch, so someone who is not us
to Git can get started straight away. The Readme file in each branch has more in‹
mation about what you need to install and what you can run.

1.7 *The database that MyFirstEfCoreApp will access*

EF Core is about accessing databases, but where does that database come from‹
Core gives you two options: EF Core can create it for you, in what's known as a *co‹*
approach, or you can provide an existing database you built outside EF Core, in ‹
known as a *database-first* approach. The first part of the book uses code-first be‹
it's the approach that many developers use.

> **EF6** In EF6, you could use an EDMX/database designer to design your data-
> base visually, an option known as *design-first.* EF Core doesn't support this
> design-first approach in any form, and there are no plans to add it.

In this chapter, we're not going to learn about how a database is created. To allo‹
MyFirstEfCoreApp application to work, the code will create the database and ad‹
test data if there isn't an existing database.

> **NOTE** In my code, I use a basic EF Core command meant for unit testing to
> create the database, because it's simple and quick. Chapter 5 covers how to get
> EF Core to create a database properly, and chapter 9 presents the whole issue

of creating and changing the structure of the database, known as the database's *schema*.

For this MyFirstEfCoreApp application example, I created a simple database, shown in figure 1.2, with only two tables:

- A Books table holding the book information
- An Author table holding the author of each book

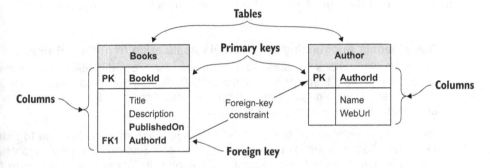

Figure 1.2 Our example relational database with two tables: Books and Author

ADVANCED NOTE In this example, I let EF Core name the tables using its default configuration settings. The Books table name comes from the `DbSet<Book>` `Books` property shown in figure 1.5. The Author table name hasn't got a `DbSet<T>` property in figure 1.5, so EF Core uses the name of the class.

Figure 1.3 shows the content of the database. It holds only four books, the first two of which have the same author: Martin Fowler.

Title	Description	AvailableFrom	Auth		Auth	Name	WebUrl
Refactoring	Improving h	08-Jul-1999	1		1	Martin Fowler	http://ma
Patterns of Enterprise Ap	Written in d	15-Nov-2002	1		2	Eric Evans	http://don
Domain-Driven Design	Linking bus	30-Aug-2003	2		3	Future Person	null
Quantum Networking	Entanged q	01-Jan-2057	3				

1.3 The content of the database, showing four books, two of which have the same author

1.8 Setting up the MyFirstEfCoreApp application

Having created and set up a .NET console application, you can now start writir
Core code. You need to write two fundamental parts before creating any dat.
access code:

- The classes that you want EF Core to map to the tables in your database
- The application's DbContext, which is the primary class that you'll use to
  figure and access the database

1.8.1 The classes that map to the database: Book and Author

EF Core maps classes to database tables. Therefore, you need to create a class tha
define the database table or match a database table if you already have a data
Lots of rules and configurations exist (covered in chapters 7 and 8), but figur
gives the typical format of a class that's mapped to a database table.

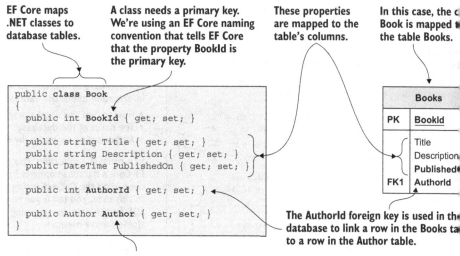

Figure 1.4 contents:

EF Core maps .NET classes to database tables.

A class needs a primary key. We're using an EF Core naming convention that tells EF Core that the property BookId is the primary key.

These properties are mapped to the table's columns.

In this case, the c Book is mapped t the table Books.

```
public class Book
{
    public int BookId { get; set; }

    public string Title { get; set; }
    public string Description { get; set; }
    public DateTime PublishedOn { get; set; }

    public int AuthorId { get; set; }

    public Author Author { get; set; }
}
```

Books	
PK	BookId
	Title
	Description
	Published‹
FK1	AuthorId

The AuthorId foreign key is used in the database to link a row in the Books ta to a row in the Author table.

The Author property is an EF Core navigational property. EF Core uses this on a save to see whether the Book has an Author class attached. If so, it sets the foreign key, AuthorId.

Upon loading a Book class, the method Include will fill this property with the Author class that's linked to this Book class by using the foreign key, AuthorId.

Figure 1.4 The.NET class `Book`**, on the left, maps to a database table called Books, on the right. 1 is a typical way to build your application, with multiple classes that map to database tables.**

Listing 1.1 shows the other class you'll be using: `Author`. This class has the same s
ture as the `Book` class in figure 1.4, with a primary key that follows the EF Core na
conventions of `<ClassName>Id` (see section 7.3.5). The `Book` class also has a n.
tional property of type `Author` and an `int` type property called `AuthorId` that ma
the `Author`'s primary key. These two properties tell EF Core that you want a link

the Book class to the Author class and that the AuthorId property should be used as the foreign key to link the two tables in the database.

Listing 1.1 The Author class from MyFirstEfCoreApp

```
public class Author
{
    public int AuthorId { get; set; }        ◁────  Holds the primary key of the Author row
    public string Name { get; set; }                 in the DB. Note that the foreign key in
    public string WebUrl { get; set; }               the Book class has the same name.
}
```

The application's DbContext

The other important part of the application is DbContext, a class you create that inherits from EF Core's DbContext class. This class holds the information EF Core needs to configure that database mapping and is also the class you use in your code to access the database (see section 1.9.2). Figure 1.5 shows the application's DbContext, called AppDbContext, that the MyFirstEfCoreApp console application uses.

ou must have a class that inherits from the EF Core class DbContext. This
lass holds the information and configuration for accessing your database.

```
public class AppDbContext : DbContext
{
    private const string ConnectionString =
        @"Server=(localdb)\mssqllocaldb;
        Database=MyFirstEfCoreDb;
        Trusted_Connection=True";

    protected override void OnConfiguring(
        DbContextOptionsBuilder optionsBuilder)
    {
        optionsBuilder
            .UseSqlServer(connectionString);
    }

    public DbSet<Book> Books { get; set; }
}
```

The database connection string holds information about the database:
* How to find the database server
* The name of the database
* Authorization to access the database

In a console application, you configure EF Core's database options by overriding the OnConfiguring method. In this case, you tell it you're using an SQL Server database by using the UseSqlServer method.

By creating a property called Books of type DbSet<Book>, you tell EF Core that there's a database table named Books, and it has the columns and keys as found in the Book class.

ur database has a table called Author, but you purposely didn't create a property for that table.
F Core finds that table by finding a navigational property of type Author in the Book class.

igure 1.5 Two main parts of the application's DbContext created for the MyFirstEfCoreApp console
pplication. First, the setting of the database options defines what type of database to use and where it can
e found. Second, the DbSet<T> property (or properties) tell(s) EF Core what classes should be mapped to
he database.

In our small example application, all the decisions on the modeling are done by EF Core, which works things out by using a set of conventions. You have loads of extra ways to tell EF Core what the database model is, and these commands can get plex. It takes chapter 7, chapter 8, and a bit of chapter 10 to cover all the options able to you as a developer.

Also, you're using a standard approach to define the database access in a co application: overriding the OnConfiguring method inside the application's Dl text and providing all the information EF Core needs to define the type and loc of the database. The disadvantage of this approach is that it has a fixed conne string, which makes development and unit testing difficult.

For ASP.NET Core web applications, this problem is bigger because you wa access a local database for testing, and a different hosted database when runni production. In chapter 2, as you start building an ASP.NET Core web applica you'll use a different approach that allows you to change the database string (se tion 2.2.2).

1.9 *Looking under the hood of EF Core*

Having run the MyFirstEfCoreApp application, you can now use it to see how a Core library works. The focus isn't on the application code, but on what hap inside the EF Core library when you read and write data to the database. My aim provide you a mental model of how EF Core accesses a database. This model sh help as you dig into the myriad commands described throughout the rest of this

Do you really need to know how EF Core works inside to use it?

You can use the EF Core library without bothering to learn how it works. But knowi what's happening inside EF Core will help you understand why the various comman work the way they do. You'll also be better armed when you need to debug your da base access code.

The following pages include lots of explanations and diagrams to show you what ha pens inside EF Core. EF Core "hides" the database so that you, as a developer, c write database access code easily—which does work well in practice. But as I stat earlier, knowing how EF Core works can help you if you want to do something mc complex or if things don't work the way you expect.

1.9.1 *Modeling the database*

Before you can do anything with the database, EF Core must go through a pr that I refer to as *modeling the database*. This modeling is EF Core's way of workin what the database looks like by looking at the classes and other EF Core configur data. Then EF Core uses the resulting model in all database accesses.

The modeling process is kicked off the first time you create the applicat DbContext, in this case called AppDbContext (shown in figure 1.5). It has one erty, DbSet<Book>, which is the way that the code accesses the database.

Figure 1.6 provides an overview of the modeling process, which will help understand the process EF Core uses to model the database. Later chapters intro you to a range of commands that allow you to configure your database more precisely, but for now, you'll use the default configurations.

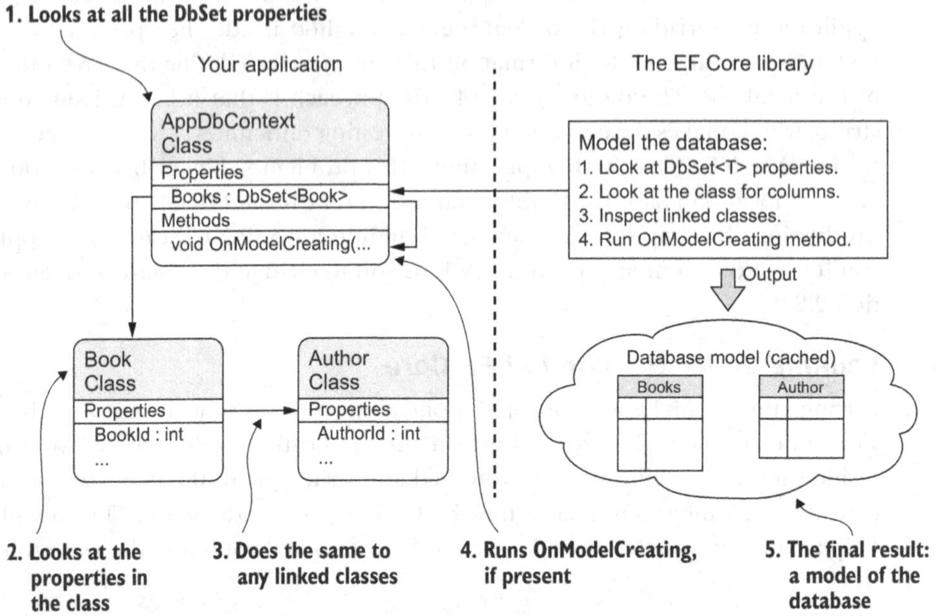

1. Looks at all the DbSet properties

Your application

The EF Core library

AppDbContext Class
Properties
 Books : DbSet<Book>
Methods
 void OnModelCreating(...

Model the database:
1. Look at DbSet<T> properties.
2. Look at the class for columns.
3. Inspect linked classes.
4. Run OnModelCreating method.

Output

Book Class
Properties
 BookId : int
 ...

Author Class
Properties
 AuthorId : int
 ...

Database model (cached)
Books   Author

2. Looks at the properties in the class

3. Does the same to any linked classes

4. Runs OnModelCreating, if present

5. The final result: a model of the database

Figure 1.6   The figure shows how EF Core will create a model of the database your classes map to. First, it looks at the classes you have defined via the DbSet<T> properties; then it looks down all the references to other classes. Using these classes, EF Core can work out the default model of the database. But then it runs the OnModelCreating method in the application's DbContext, which you can override to add your specific commands to configure the database the way you want it.

Figure 1.6 shows the modeling steps that EF Core uses on our AppDbContext, which happens the first time you create an instance of the AppDbContext. (After that, the model is cached, so that subsequent instances are created quickly.) The following text provides a more detailed description of the process:

- EF Core looks at the application's DbContext and finds all the public DbSet<T> properties. From this data, it defines the initial name for the one table it finds: Books.

- EF Core looks through all the classes referred to in DbSet<T> and looks at its properties to work out the column names, types, and so forth. It also looks for special attributes on the class and/or properties that provide extra modeling information.

- EF Core looks for any classes that the DbSet<T> classes refer to. In our case, the Book class has a reference to the Author class, so EF Core scans that class too. It

carries out the same search on the properties of the Author class as it did o
Book class in step 2. It also takes the class name, Author, as the table name

- For the last input to the modeling process, EF Core runs the virtual me
  OnModelCreating inside the application's DbContext. In this simple ap
  tion, you don't override the OnModelCreating method, but if you did
  could provide extra information via a fluent API to do more configurati
  the modeling.

- EF Core creates an internal model of the database based on all the inform
  it gathered. This database model is cached so that later accesses will be qui
  Then this model is used for performing all database accesses.

You might have noticed that figure 1.6 shows no database. This is so because whe
Core is building its internal model, it doesn't look at the database. I emphasize
fact to show how important it is to build a good model of the database you want; o
wise, problems could occur if a mismatch exists between what EF Core thinks the
base looks like and what the actual database is like.

In your application, you may use EF Core to create the database, in which
there's no chance of a mismatch. Even so, if you want a good and efficient data
it's worth taking care to build a good representation of the database you want in
code so that the created database performs well. The options for creating, upd:
and managing the database structure are a big topic, detailed in chapter 9.

1.9.2 Reading data from the database

You're now at the point where you can access the database. The console applic
has a list (l) command, which reads the database and prints the information o
terminal. Figure 1.7 shows the result of running the console application and typi

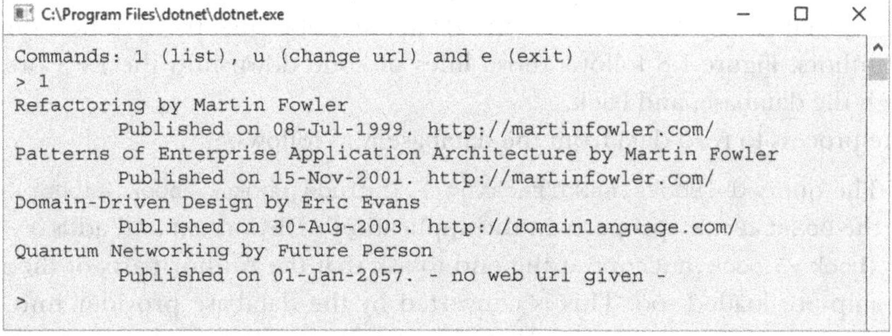

```
C:\Program Files\dotnet\dotnet.exe                                 —    □    ✕

Commands: 1 (list), u (change url) and e (exit)
> 1
Refactoring by Martin Fowler
        Published on 08-Jul-1999. http://martinfowler.com/
Patterns of Enterprise Application Architecture by Martin Fowler
        Published on 15-Nov-2001. http://martinfowler.com/
Domain-Driven Design by Eric Evans
        Published on 30-Aug-2003. http://domainlanguage.com/
Quantum Networking by Future Person
        Published on 01-Jan-2057. - no web url given -
>
```

Figure 1.7 Output of the console application when listing the content of the database

The following listing shows the code that's called to list all the books, with each au
out to the console.

Listing 1.2 The code to read all the books and output them to the console

```
public static void ListAll()                  You create the application's
{                                              DbContext through which all
    using (var db = new AppDbContext())        database accesses are done.
    {
        foreach (var book in                   Reads all the books. AsNoTracking
            db.Books.AsNoTracking()            indicates that this access is read-only.

            .Include(book => book.Author))
        {                                          The include causes the
            var webUrl = book.Author.WebUrl == null    author information to be
                ? "- no web URL given -"       loaded with each book.
                : book.Author.WebUrl;          See chapter 2 for more
            Console.WriteLine(                 information.
                $"{book.Title} by {book.Author.Name}");
            Console.WriteLine("      " +
                "Published on " +
                $"{book.PublishedOn:dd-MMM-yyyy}" +
                $". {webUrl}");
        }
    }
}
```

EF Core uses Microsoft's .NET's Language Integrated Query (LINQ) to carry the commands it wants done, and normal .NET classes to hold the data. Listing 1.2's query doesn't include any LINQ methods, but later in the book, you'll see plenty of LINQ examples.

NOTE *Learning LINQ will be essential to you, as EF Core uses LINQ commands for database accesses.* The appendix provides a brief introduction to LINQ. Plenty of online resources are also available; see http://mng.bz/YqBN.

Two lines of code in bold in listing 1.2 cause the database access. Now let's see how EF Core uses that LINQ code to access the database and return the required books with their authors. Figure 1.8 follows those lines of code down into the EF Core library, through the database, and back.

The process to read data from the database is as follows:

- The query db.Books.AsNoTracking().Include(book => book.Author) accesses the DbSet<Book> property in the application's DbContext and adds a .Include (book => book.Author) at the end to ask that the Author parts of the relationship are loaded too. This is converted by the database provider into an SQL command to access the database. The resulting SQL is cached to avoid the cost of retranslation if the same database access is used again.

EF Core tries to be as efficient as possible on database accesses. In this case, it combines the two tables it needs to read, Books and Author, into one big table so that it can do the job in one database access. The following listing shows the SQL created by EF Core and the database provider.

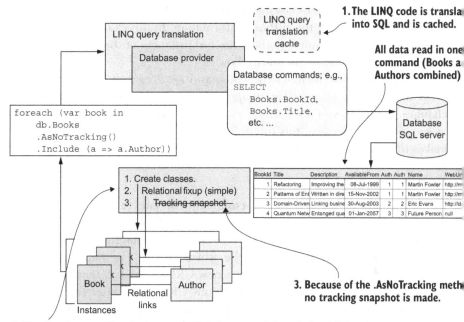

1. The LINQ code is transla
into SQL and is cached.

All data read in one
command (Books a
Authors combined)

3. Because of the .AsNoTracking meth
no tracking snapshot is made.

2. The data is turned into instances of .NET classes, and the relational links are
set up appropriately. (.AsNoTracking uses a simplified fixup for speed reasons.)

Figure 1.8   A look inside EF Core as it executes a database query

Listing 1.3   SQL command produced to read Books and Author

```
SELECT [b].[BookId],
[b].[AuthorId],
[b].[Description],
[b].[PublishedOn],
[b].[Title],
[a].[AuthorId],
[a].[Name],
[a].[WebUrl]
FROM [Books] AS [b]
INNER JOIN [Author] AS [a] ON
[b].[AuthorId] = [a].[AuthorId]
```

After the database provider has read the data, EF Core puts the data through a
cess that (a) creates instances of the .NET classes and (b) uses the database relat
links, called *foreign keys*, to correctly link the .NET classes by reference—called a
tional fixup. Because we added the AsNoTracking method, the relational fixup u
simplified fixup for speed reasons.

NOTE I discuss the differences between the AsNoTracking simplified relational fixup and the normal relational fixup in section 6.1.2.

The result is a set of .NET class instances with the Book's Author property linked to an Author class containing the author's information. In this example, two books have the same author, Martin Fowler, so there are two instances of the Author class, both holding the same information on Martin Fowler.

Because the code includes the command AsNoTracking, EF Core knows to suppress the creation of a *tracking snapshot*. Tracking snapshots are used for spotting changes to data, as you'll see in the example of editing the WebUrl database column in section 1.9.3. Because this query is read-only, suppressing the tracking snapshot makes the command faster.

Updating the database

Now you want to use the second command, update (u), in MyFirstEfCoreApp to update the WebUrl column in the Author table of the book *Quantum Networking*. As shown in figure 1.9, you first list all the books to show that the last book has no author URL set. Then you run the command u, which asks for a new author URL for the last book, *Quantum Networking*. You input a new URL of httqs://entangled.moon (it's a fictitious future book, so why not a fictitious URL!), and after the update, the command lists all the books again, showing that the author's URL has changed (with the two ovals showing you the before and after URLs).

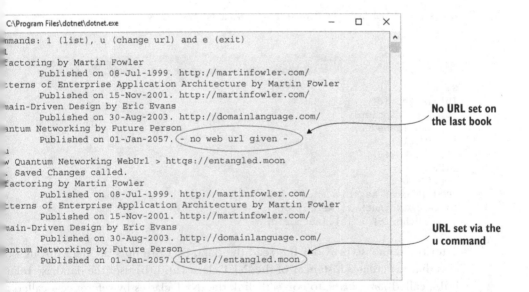

ure 1.9 **This figure shows an update in action. The first command is** 1 **(list), which shows each book with** author's name and URL on the next line. Then you press u (update), which allows you to update the URL he last book's author. The update command called the list command, so that you can see that your update s successful.

The code for updating the WebUrl column in the Author table linked to the with the title *Quantum Networking* is shown here.

Listing 1.4   The code to update the author's WebUrl of the book *Quantum Network...*

```
public static void ChangeWebUrl()
{
    Console.Write("New Quantum Networking WebUrl > ");          Reads in from
    var newWebUrl = Console.ReadLine();                         the console
                                                                the new URL

    using (var db = new AppDbContext())
    {                                                    Loads the author
        var singleBook = db.Books                        information with
            .Include(book => book.Author)                the book
            .Single(book => book.Title == "Quantum Networking");

        singleBook.Author.WebUrl = newWebUrl;                   To update the
        db.SaveChanges();                                       database, you
        Console.WriteLine("... SavedChanges called.");          change the d...
    }                                                           that was read...
                                 SaveChanges tells EF Core
    ListAll();                   to check for any changes to
}               Lists all        the data that has been read
                the book         in and write out those
                information      changes to the database.
```

Selects only the book with the title Quantum Networking

Figure 1.10 shows what is happening inside the EF Core library and follows its ress. This example is a lot more complicated than the previous read example, me give you some pointers on what to look for.

First, the read stage, at the top of the diagram, is similar to the read example so should be familiar. In this case, the query loads a specific book, using the b title as the filter. The important change is point 2: that a tracking snapshot is tak the data.

This change occurs in the update stage, in the bottom half of the diagram. I you can see how EF Core compares the loaded data with the tracking snapshot tc the changes. From this data, it sees that only the WebUrl property has been upd and EF Core creates an SQL command to update only the WebUrl column in the rect row of the Author table.

I've described most of the steps, but here is a blow-by-blow account of how author's WebUrl column is updated:

1 The application uses a LINQ query to find a single book with its author i mation. EF Core turns the LINQ query into an SQL command to read the where the Title is *Quantum Networking*, returning an instance of both the and the Author classes, and checks that only one row was found.

2 The LINQ query doesn't include the .AsNoTracking method you had i previous read versions, so the query is considered to be a *tracked query*. T fore, EF Core creates a tracking snapshot of the data loaded.

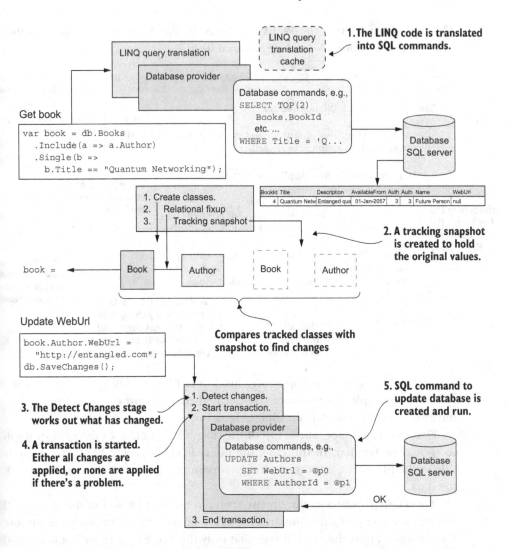

Figure 1.10 This figure shows what **EF Core** does inside when you update an `Author`'s `WebUrl` property and ask EF Core to write it to the database. This figure is quite complex, but if you start at the top and follow the numbered text, it should be easier to understand. It starts with a read to get the required `Book` and `Author`. (Note that in this process, the tracking snapshot is present; see step 2.) Then, when your code updates the `WebUrl` and calls `SaveChanges`, EF Core creates and executes the correct **SQL** command to update the WebUrl column in the correct row.

3   Then the code changes the `WebUrl` property in the `Author` class of the book. When `SaveChanges` is called, the Detect Changes stage compares all the classes that were returned from a tracked query with the tracking snapshot. From this, it can detect what has changed—in this case, only the `WebUrl` property of the `Author` class, which has a primary key of 3.

4 As a change is detected, EF Core starts a *transaction*. Every database upd
done as an *atomic unit*: if multiple changes to the database occur, either th
succeed, or they all fail. This fact is important, because a relational dat
could get into a bad state if only part of an update were applied.

5 The update request is converted by the database provider to an SQL comm
that does the update. If the SQL command is successful, the transaction is
mitted, and the SaveChanges method returns; otherwise, an exception is r

1.10   The stages of development of EF Core

EF Core and .NET Core have come a long way since the first release. Over time,
rosoft has been working hard to improve the native performance of .NET Core
adding more features, to the point that .NET 5 can take over from the existing
Framework 4.8.

Figure 1.11 shows the history of the major releases of EF Core so far. The EF
version numbers follow the NET Core version number. Note that the releases a
top of the figure are *long-term-support* (LTS) releases, meaning that release is
ported for three years after the initial release. Major releases are expected every
with LTS releases coming every two years.

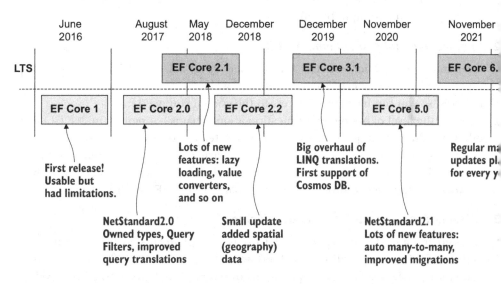

**Figure 1.11   This figure depicts the development of EF Core, which runs alongside the development of the
open source developer platform. The EF Core 5 version is highlighted because this book covers all the EF
features up to and including EF Core 5.**

Should you use EF Core in your next project?

Now that you have a quick overview of what EF Core is and how it works, the next question is whether you should start using EF Core in your project. For anyone who's planning to switch to EF Core, the key question is "Is EF Core sufficiently superior to the data access library I currently use to make it worth using for my next project?" A cost is associated with learning and adopting any new library, especially complex libraries such as EF Core, so this question is a valid one. Here is my take on EF Core and .NET Core in general.

1 .NET is the future software platform, and it's fast!

Over time, Microsoft has been working hard to improve the native performance of .NET Core while adding more features. This focus on performance has propelled Microsoft's ASP.NET Core web application from ~250th for ASP.NET MVC to around the 10th to 40th position for ASP.NET Core (depending on workload); see http://mng.bz/Gxaq. Similar but smaller performance gains have been added to EF Core.

Microsoft did say that .NET 5 would take over from the existing .NET Framework 4.8, but the COVID-19 outbreak derailed that plan a bit, and now .NET 6 will replace .NET Framework 4.8. But the writing on the wall is clear: if you're starting a new project, and .NET 5 and EF Core have the features your project needs, moving to EF Core means you aren't going to be left behind.

2 Open source and open communication

Over many years, Microsoft has transformed itself. All its .NET Core work is open source, with lots of external people getting involved with fixing bugs and adding new features, so you can have direct access to the code if you need it.

Also, the level of open communication about what is happening in .NET Core and other products is impressive. The EF Core team, for example, produces weekly updates on what it is doing, providing lots of early previews of new releases and making nightly builds of EF Core available to all. The team takes feedback seriously, and all work and defects are shown in the issue pages of the EF Core repo.

3 Multiplatform applications and development

As I said at the start of the chapter, EF Core is multiplatform-capable; you can develop and run EF Core applications on Windows, Linux, and Apple. This fact means that you can run Microsoft-based applications on cheap Linux systems. Also, developing different platforms is quite possible. In fact, Arthur Vickers, who is one of the lead engineers on the EF Core team, decided to move from Windows to Linux as his primary development platform. You can read about his experiences at http://mng.bz/zxWa.

1.11.4 Rapid development and good features

I work as a contract developer as my day job. In a typical data-driven applicati
write a lot of database access code, some of it complex. With EF Core, I can write
access code really quickly, and in a way that makes access code easy to understand
refactor if it's too slow. This is the main reason I use EF Core.

At the same time, I need an O/RM that has lots of features so that I can bu
database the way I want without hitting too many barriers in EF Core. Sure,
things are ruled out, such as building SQL Common Table Expressions, but a
raw SQL gets around things like that if I need it to.

1.11.5 Well supported

EF Core has good documentation (https://docs.microsoft.com/en-us/ef/core/in
and of course, you have this book, which brings together the documentation
deeper explanations and examples, plus patterns and practices to make you a
developer. The internet is full of blogs on EF Core, including mine at https://
.thereformedprogrammer.net. And for questions and bugs, there is always Stack
flow; see http://mng.bz/0mDx.

The other part of support is the development tools. Microsoft seems to
changed focus by providing support for multiple platforms, but it has also crea
free cross-platform development environment called VS Code. Microsoft has
made its main development tool, Visual Studio (Windows and Mac), free to indiv
developers and small businesses; the Usage section near the bottom of its web pa
www.visualstudio.com/vs/community details the terms. That's a compelling offe

1.11.6 Always high-performance

Ah, the database performance issue. Look, I'm not going to say that EF Core is
to, out of the box, produce blistering database access performance with beautiful
and fast data ingest. That's the cost you pay for quick development of your data a
code; all that "magic" inside EF Core can't be as good as hand-coded SQL, bu
might be surprised how good it can be. See chapter 15, where I tune up an ap
tion's performance progressively.

But you have lots of options to improve the performance of your application
my applications, I find that only about 5–10% of my queries are the key ones
need hand-tuning. Chapters 14 and 15 are dedicated to performance tuning, as is
of chapter 16. These chapters show that you can do a lot to improve the perform
of EF Core database accesses.

But there is no reason you can't drop down to raw SQL for some of the dat
accesses. That's the great thing: build the application quickly by using EF Core
then convert the (few) places where EF Core isn't delivering good performance t
SQL commands via ADO.NET or Dapper.

When should you not use EF Core?

I'm obviously pro-EF Core, but I won't use it on a client project unless using it makes sense. So let's look at a few blockers that might suggest *not* using EF Core.

The first one is obvious: Does it support the database you want to use? You can find a list of supported databases at https://docs.microsoft.com/en-us/ef/core/providers.

The second factor is the level of performance you need. If you're writing, say, a small RESTful service or Serverless system, I'm not sure that pulling in the whole of EF Core is worthwhile; you could use a fast but development-time-hungry library because there aren't many database accesses to write. But if you have a large application, with lots of boring admin accesses and a few important customer-facing accesses, a hybrid approach could work for you. (See chapter 15 for an example of a mixed EF Core/Dapper application.)

Also, EF Core isn't that good at bulk commands. Normally, tasks such as bulk-loading large amounts of data and deleting all the rows in a table can be implemented quicker by raw SQL. But several EF Core bulk CRUD extensions (some open source and some paid) can help; try searching for *EF Core bulk loading* to find possible libraries.

Summary

- EF Core is an object-relational mapper (O/RM) that uses Microsoft's Language Integrated Query (LINQ) to define database queries and return data to linked instances of .NET classes.
- EF Core is designed to make writing code for accessing a database quick and intuitive. This O/RM has plenty of features to match many requirements.
- You've seen various examples of what's happening inside EF Core. These examples will help you understand what the EF Core commands described in later chapters can do.
- There are many good reasons to consider using EF Core: it's built on a lot of experience, is well supported, and runs on multiple platforms.

For readers who are familiar with EF6.x:

- Look for EF6 notes throughout the book. These notes mark differences between the EF Core approach and EF6.x's approach. Also, check the summaries at the end of each chapter, which will point you to the major EF Core changes in that chapter.
- Think of EF Core as a new library that someone has written to mimic EF6.x but that works in a different way. That mindset will help you spot the EF Core improvements that change the way you access a database.
- EF Core no longer supports the EDMX/database designer approach that earlier forms of EF used.

Querying the databa

This chapter covers

- Modeling three main types of database relationships
- Creating and changing a database via migration
- Defining and creating an application DbContext
- Loading related data
- Splitting complex queries into subqueries

This chapter is all about using EF Core for reading, called *querying*, the data You'll create a database that contains the three main types of database relation found in EF Core. Along the way, you'll learn to create and change a datab structure via EF Core.

Next, you'll learn how to access a database via EF Core, reading data from database tables. You'll explore the basic format of EF Core queries before loc at various approaches to loading related data with the main data, such as loa the author with the book from chapter 1.

After learning the ways to load related data, you'll start to build the more plex queries needed to make a book-selling site work. This task covers sor filtering, and paging, plus approaches that combine these separate query mands to create one composite database query.

TIP I use unit tests to ensure that what I write in this book is correct. You might like to look at/run these unit tests, as they may help you understand what is going on. You can find them in the associated GitHub repo at http://mng.bz/XdlG. Look at the Readme file in the repo for information on where to find the unit tests and how to run them.

Setting the scene: Our book-selling site

In this chapter, you'll start building the example book-selling site, referred to as the *Book App* from now on. This example application provides a good vehicle for looking at relationships in queries. This section introduces the database, the various classes, and EF Core parts that the Book App needs to access the database.

The Book App's relational database

Although we could have created a database with all the data about a book, its author(s), and its reviews in one table, that wouldn't have worked well in a relational database, especially because the reviews are variable in length. The norm for relational databases is to split out any repeated data (such as the authors).

We could have arranged the various parts of the book data in the database in several ways, but for this example, the database has one of each of the main types of relationships you can have in EF Core. These three types are

- *One-to-one relationship*—PriceOffer to a Book
- *One-to-many relationship*—Book with Reviews
- *Many-to-many relationship*—Books linked to Authors and Books linked to Tags

ONE-TO-ONE RELATIONSHIP: PRICEOFFER TO A BOOK

A book can have a promotional price applied to it with an optional row in the Price-Offer, which is an example of a one-to-one relationship. (Technically, the relationship is one-to-zero-or-one, but EF Core handles it the same way.) See figure 2.1.

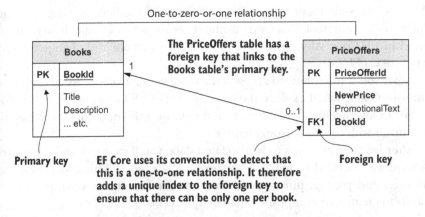

Figure 2.1 The one-to-one relationship between a Book and an optional PriceOffer. If a PriceOffer is linked to a Book, the NewPrice in the PriceOffer overrides the Price in the Book.

To calculate the final price of the book, you need to check for a row in the Price table that's linked to the Books via a foreign key. If such a row is found, the New supersedes the price for the original book, and the PromotionalText is shown onsc as in this example:

$40 $30 Our summertime price special, for this week only!

ADVANCED FEATURE   In this example, I have a primary key and a foreign key to make the relationship easier to understand. But for one-to-one relationships, you can make the foreign key be the primary key too. In the PriceOffer table shown in figure 2.1, you would have a primary key, called BookId, which would also be the foreign key. As a result, you lose the PriceOfferId column, which makes the table slightly more efficient from the database side. I cover this topic later in the book, in section 8.6.1.

ONE-TO-MANY RELATIONSHIP: REVIEWS TO A BOOK

You want to allow customers to review a book; they can give a book a star ratin; optionally leave a comment. Because a book may have no reviews or many (unlim reviews, you need to create a table to hold that data. In this example, you'll ca table Review. The Books table has a one-to-many relationship to the Review tab shown in figure 2.2.

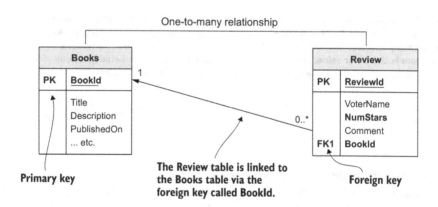

Figure 2.2   The one-to-many relationship between a Book and its zero-to-many Reviews. These Reviews work the same as they do on any e-commerce site, such as Amazon.

In the Summary display, you need to count the number of reviews and work ou average star rating to show a summary. Here's a typical onscreen display you r produce from this one-to-many relationship:

Votes 4.5 by 2 customers

MANY-TO-MANY RELATIONSHIP: MANUALLY CONFIGURED

Books can be written by one or more authors, and an author may write one or more books. Therefore, you need a table called Books to hold the books data and another table called Authors to hold the authors. The link between the Books and Authors tables is called a *many-to-many relationship*, which in this case needs a linking table to achieve this relationship.

In this case, you create your own linking table with an Order value in it because the names of the authors in a book must be displayed in a specific order (figure 2.3).

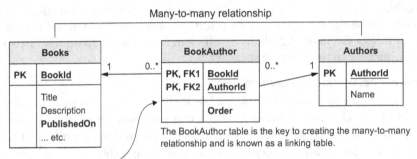

Figure 2.3 The three tables involved in creating the many-to-many relationship between the Books table and the Authors table. I use a many-to-many relationship because books can have many authors, and authors may have written many books. The extra feature needed here is the Order value, because the order in which authors are listed in a book matters, so I use the Order value to display the authors in the correct sequence.

A typical onscreen display from the many-to-many relationship would look like this:

by Dino Esposito, Andrea Saltarello

MANY-TO-MANY RELATIONSHIP: AUTOCONFIGURED BY EF CORE

Books can be tagged with different categories—such as Microsoft .NET, Linux, Web, and so on—to help the customer to find a book on the topic they are interested in. A category might be applied to multiple books, and a book might have one or more categories, so a many-to-many linking table is needed. But unlike in the previous BookAuthor linking table, the tags don't have to be ordered, which makes the linking table simpler.

EF Core 5 and later can automatically create the many-to-many linking table for you. Figure 2.4 shows your database with the automatic BookTag table that provides a many-to-many link between the Books table and the Tags table. The BookTag table is grayed out to represent the fact that EF Core creates it automatically and that it isn't mapped to any of the classes you have created.

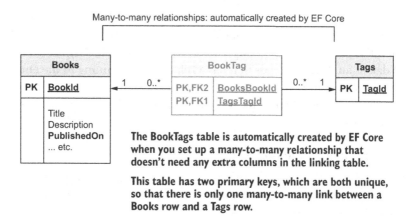

Figure 2.4   **The Books and Tags tables are created by you, and EF Core detects the many-to-many relationship between the Books table and the Tags table. EF Core automatically creates the linking table needed to set up the many-to-many relationships.**

NOTE   Chapter 8 covers the different ways to set up many-to-many relationships.

A typical onscreen display from a many-to-many relationship would look like this

Categories: Microsoft .NET, Web

2.1.2   *Other relationship types not covered in this chapter*

The three types of relationships I covered in section 2.1.1 are the main relation you will be using: one-to-one, one-to-many, and many-to-many. But EF Core does some other variations. Here is a quick rundown on what is coming later in chapt

- *Owned Type class*—Useful for adding grouped data, such as an `Address` cla an entity class. The `Address` class is linked to the main entity, but your cod copy around the `Address` class rather than copying individual `Street`, `State`, and related properties.
- *Table splitting*—Maps multiple classes to one table. You could have a sum class with the basic properties in it and a detailed class containing all the for example, which would give you a quicker load of the summary data.
- *Table per hierarchy (TPH)*—Useful for groups of data that are similar. If you a lot of data with only a few differences, such as a list of animals, you can h base `Animal` class that `Dog`, `Cat`, and `Snake` classes can inherit, with per properties such as `LengthOfTail` for `Dog` and `Cat` and a `Venomous` flag fo `Snake`. EF Core maps all the classes to one table, which can be more efficie
- *Table per type (TPT)*—Useful for groups of data that have dissimilar data. introduced in EF Core 5, is the opposite of TPH, in which each class has its table. Following the `Animal` example for TPH, the TPT version would ma `Dog`, `Cat`, and `Snake` classes to three different tables in the database.

These four relationship patterns are built into EF Core to allow you to optimize the way you handle or store data in the database. But another relationship type doesn't need specific EF Core commands to implement: *hierarchical* data. A typical example of hierarchical data is an `Employee` class that has a relationship pointing to the employee's manager, who in turn is an employee. EF Core uses the same approaches as one-to-one and one-to-many to provide hierarchical relationships; I talk more about this type of relationship in chapters 6 and 8.

The database showing all the tables

Figure 2.5 shows the Book App's database that you'll be using for the examples in this chapter and in chapter 3. It contains all the tables I've described so far, including all the columns and relationships in the Books table.

NOTE The database diagram uses the same layout and terms as in chapter 1: *PK* means *primary key*, and *FK* means *foreign key*.

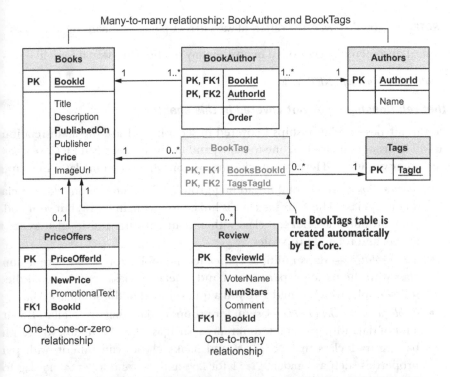

Figure 2.5 **The complete relational database schema for the Book App, showing all the tables and their columns used for holding the book information. You create classes to map to all the tables you see in this figure, apart from the BookTags table (shown as grayed out). EF Core created the BookTags table automatically when it found the direct many-to-many relationship between the Books and Tags tables.**

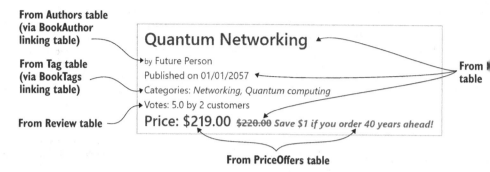

From Authors table
(via BookAuthor
linking table)

From Tag table
(via BookTags
linking table)

From Review table

From PriceOffers table

Figure 2.6 A listing of a single book showing which database table provides each part of the informat
As you can see, the listing requires information from all five of the database tables to create this view
this chapter, you will build the code to produce this display, with various ordering, filtering, and pagi
features to make a proper e-commerce application.

To help you make sense of this database, figure 2.6 shows the onscreen output of th
of books but focuses on only one book. As you can see, the Book App needs to a
every table in the database to build the book list (figure 2.10 in section 2.6). La
show you this same book display, but with the query that supplies each element).

2.1.4 The classes that EF Core maps to the database

I've created five .NET classes to map to the six tables in the database. These classe
called Book, PriceOffer, Review, Tag, Author, and BookAuthor for the many-to-n
linking table, and they are referred to as *entity classes* to show that they're mappe
EF Core to the database. From the software point of view, there's nothing sp
about entity classes. They're normal .NET classes, sometimes referred to as *plai*
CLR objects (POCOs). The term *entity class* identifies the class as one that EF Cor
mapped to the database.

The primary entity class is the Book class, shown in the following listing. You
see that it refers to a single PriceOffer class, a collection of Review class instan
collection of Tag class instances, and finally a collection of BookAuthor classes
links the book data to one or more Author classes containing the author's name.

Listing 2.1 The Book class, mapped to the Books table in the database

```
public class Book
{
```
The Book class contains the
main book information.

```
public int BookId { get; set; }
public string Title { get; set; }
public string Description { get; set; }
public DateTime PublishedOn { get; set; }
public string Publisher { get; set; }
public decimal Price { get; set; }
public string ImageUrl { get; set; }
```

We use EF Core's By Convention configuration to define the primary key of this entity class, so we use <ClassName>Id, and because the property is of type int, EF Core assumes that the database will use the SQL IDENTITY command to create a unique key when a new row is added.

```
//--------------------------------------------------
//relationships

public PriceOffer Promotion { get; set; }
public ICollection<Review> Reviews { get; set; }
public ICollection<Tag> Tags { get; set; }
public ICollection<BookAuthor>
   AuthorsLink { get; set; }
}
```

Link to the optional one-to-one PriceOffer relationship.

There can be zero to many reviews of the book.

EF Core 5's automatic many-to-many relationship to the Tag entity class

Provides a link to the many-to-many linking table that links to the Authors of this book

NOTE In part 1, the entity classes use the default (empty) constructor. If you want to create specific constructors for any of your entity classes, you should be aware that EF Core may use your constructor when reading and creating an instance of an entity class. I cover this topic in section 6.1.11.

For simplicity, we use EF Core's By Convention configuration approach to model the database. We use By Convention naming for the properties that hold the primary key and foreign keys in each of the entity classes. In addition, the .NET type of the navigational properties, such as ICollection<Review> Reviews, defines what sort of relationship we want. Because the Reviews property is of the .NET type ICollection <Review>, for example, the relationship is a one-to-many relationship. Chapters 7 and 8 describe the other approaches for configuring the EF Core database model.

ADVANCED NOTE In the Book App, when I have navigational properties that are collections, I use the type ICollection<T>. I do so because the new eager loading sort capability (see section 2.4.1) can return a sorted collection, and the default HashSet definition says it holds only a collection "whose elements are in no particular order." But there is a performance cost to not using HashSet when your navigational properties contain a large collection. I cover this issue in chapter 14.

What happens if you want to access an existing database?

The examples in this book show how to define and create a database via EF Core because the most complex situation is when you need to understand all the configuration options. But accessing an existing database is much easier, because EF Core can build your application's DbContext class and all your entity classes for you, using a feature called *reverse engineering*, which is covered in section 9.7.

> The other possibility is that you don't want EF Core to change the database structu
> but want to look after that task yourself, such as via an SQL change script or a da
> base deployment tool. I cover that approach in section 9.6.2.

2.2 Creating the application's DbContext

To access the database, you need to do the following:

1. Define your application's DbContext, which you do by creating a class and i iting from EF Core's DbContext class.
2. Create an instance of that class every time you want to access the database.

All the database queries you'll see later in this chapter use these steps, which I des in detail in the following sections.

2.2.1 Defining the application's DbContext: EfCoreContext

The key class you need to use EF Core is the application's DbContext. You d this class by inheriting EF Core's DbContext class and adding various properti allow your software to access the database tables. It also contains methods you override to access other features in EF Core, such as configuring the database eling. Figure 2.7 gives you an overview of the Book App's DbContext, pointin all the important parts.

One point to note about figure 2.7 is that the Book App's DbContext do include DbSet<T> properties for your Review entity class and the BookAuthor lir entity class. In the book app, both entity classes are accessed not directly, but vi Book class navigational properties, as you'll see in section 2.4.

> **NOTE** I skip configuring the database modeling, which is done in the OnModel-
> Creating method of the application's DbContext. Chapters 7 and 8 cover
> how to model the database in detail.

2.2.2 Creating an instance of the application's DbContext

Chapter 1 showed you how to set up the application's DbContext by overridir OnConfiguring method. The downside of that approach is that the connection s is fixed. In this chapter, you'll use another approach, because you'd want to use ferent database for development and unit testing. You'll use a method that pro that database via the application's DbContext constructor.

Listing 2.2 provides the options for the database at the time you create the ap tion DbContext, called EfCoreContext. To be honest, this listing is based on w use in the unit-testing chapter (chapter 17), because it has the benefit of showin each step of creating an instance of the application's DbContext. Chapter 5, wh about using EF Core in an ASP.NET Core application, presents a more powerfu to create the application's DbContext, using a feature called dependency injectic

the name of the DbContext that defines your database.
I be using this in your application to access the database.

Any application DbContext must inherit
from the EF Core's DbContext class.

These public properties of type
DbSet<T> are mapped by EF Core to
tables in your database, using the name
of the property as the table name. You
can query these tables via LINQ methods
on a property.

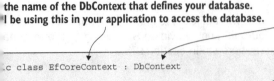

```
.c class EfCoreContext : DbContext

public DbSet<Book>       Books { get; set; }
public DbSet<Author>     Authors { get; set; }
public DbSet<Tag>        Tags { get; set; }
public DbSet<PriceOffer> PriceOffers { get; set; }


public EfCoreContext (
    DbContextOptions<EfCoreContext> options)
    : base(options) {}


protected override void
    OnModelCreating (ModelBuilder modelBuilder)

    //... code left out
```

The classes, such as Book, Author, Tag
and PriceOffer, are entity classes. Their
properties are mapped to columns in
the appropriate database table.

For your ASP.NET Core application, you
need a constructor to set up the
database options. This allows your
application to define what sort of
database it is and where it's located.

The OnModelCreating method
contains configuration information
for EF Core. I explain this in
chapters 7 and 8.

2.7 The application's DbContext is the key class in accessing the database. This figure shows the main
of an application's DbContext, starting with its inheriting EF Core's DbContext, which brings in lots of code
atures. You have to add some properties with the class DbSet<T> that map your classes to a database
with the same name as the property name you use. The other parts are the constructor, which handles
g up the database options, and the OnModelCreating method, which you can override to add your own
uration commands and set up the database the way you want.

Listing 2.2 Creating an instance of the application's DbContext to access the database

```
const string connection =
    "Data Source=(localdb)\\mssqllocaldb;"+
    "Database=EfCoreInActionDb.Chapter02;"+
    "Integrated Security=True;";
var optionsBuilder =
    new DbContextOptionsBuilder
        <EfCoreContext>();

optionsBuilder.UseSqlServer(connection);
var options = optionsBuilder.Options;

using (var context = new EfCoreContext(options))
{

    var bookCount = context.Books.Count();
    //... etc.
```

The connection string, with its format
dictated by the sort of database
provider and hosting you're using

You need an EF Core DbContextOptionsBuilder<>
instance to set the options you need.

You're accessing an SQL
Server database and using the
UseSqlServer method from
the Microsoft.EntityFramework-
Core.SqlServer library, and this
method needs the database
connection string.

Creates the all-important
EfCoreContext, using the options you've
set up. You use a using statement
because the DbContext is disposable.

Uses the DbContext to
find out the number of
books in the database

At the end of this listing, you create an instance of EfCoreContext inside a u statement because DbContext has an IDisposable interface and therefore shou disposed after you've used it. So from now on, if you see a variable called conte was created by using the code in listing 2.2 or a similar approach.

2.2.3 *Creating a database for your own application*

You have a few ways to create a database using EF Core, but the normal way is t EF Core's migration feature. This feature uses your application's DbContext an entity classes, like the ones I've described, as the model for the database struc The Add-Migration command first models your database and then, using that m builds commands to create a database that fits that model.

> **TIP** If you have cloned the Git repo that goes with this book (http://mng.bz/ XdlG), you can see what a migration looks like by looking at the Migration folder in the DataLayer project. Also, all the correct NuGet packages are added to the DataLayer and BookApp projects to allow migrations to be created and applied to an SQL Server database.

The great thing about migrations, besides handling database creation, is the fac they can update the database with any changes you make in the software. I change your entity classes or any of your application's DbContext configuration Add-Migration command will build a set of commands to update the existing base. Here are the steps you need to go through to add a migration and crea migrate a database. This process is based on a ASP.NET Core application (see ch. 5 for more on ASP.NET Core) with your DbContext in a separate project an developing with Visual Studio. (I cover other options in chapter 9.)

1. The project that contains your DbContext needs the NuGet package M soft.EntityFrameworkCore.SqlServer or another database provider if you using a different database.
2. The ASP.NET Core project needs the following NuGet packages:
   a. Microsoft.EntityFrameworkCore.SqlServer (or same database provider step 1)
   b. Microsoft.EntityFrameworkCore.Tools
3. The ASP.NET Core's Startup class contains the commands to add an EF database provider, and the appsettings.json file contains the connection s for the database you want to create/migrate. (EF Core uses the ASP.NET C CreateHostBuilder(args).Build() methods to obtain a valid instance of DbContext.)
4. In Visual Studio, open the Package Manager Console (PMC) by choosing ? > NuGet Package Manager > Package Manager Console.
5. In the PMC window, make sure that the default project is your ASP.NET project.

6 In PMC, run the command `Add-Migration MyMigrationName -Project Data-Layer`. This command creates a set of classes that migrate the database from its current state to a state that matches your application's DbContext and the entity classes at the time that you run your command. (The `MyMigrationName` shown in the command is the name that will be used for the migration.)

7 Run the command `Update-Database` to apply the commands created by the `Add-Migration` command to your database. If no database exists, `Update-Database` will create one. If a database exists, the command checks whether that database has this database migration applied to it, and if any database migrations are missing, this command applies them to the database. (See chapter 9 for more on migration commands.)

> **NOTE** You can also use EF Core's .NET Core command-line interface (CLI) to run these commands (see http://mng.bz/454w). Chapter 9 lists both the Visual Studio and CLI versions of the migration commands.

An alternative to using the `Update-Database` command is to call the `context.Database.Migrate` method in the startup code of your application. This approach is especially useful for an ASP.NET Core web application that's hosted; chapter 5 covers this option, including some of its limitations.

> **NOTE** Chapter 9 provides a detailed look at EF Core's migrations feature as well as other ways to alter the structure of your database (referred to as the database's *schema*).

Understanding database queries

Now you can start looking at how to query a database by using EF Core. Figure 2.8 shows an example EF Core database query, with the three main parts of the query highlighted.

```
context.Books.Where(p => p.Title.StartsWith("Quantum").ToList();
```

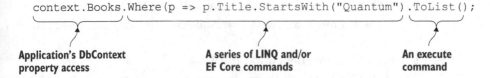

| Application's DbContext property access | A series of LINQ and/or EF Core commands | An execute command |

Figure 2.8 The three parts of an EF Core database query, with example code. You will become familiar with this type of LINQ statement, which is the basic building block of all queries.

> **TIME-SAVER** If you're familiar with EF and/or LINQ, you can skip this section.

The command shown in figure 2.8 consists of several methods, one after the other. This structure is known as a *fluent interface*. Fluent interfaces like this one flow logically and intuitively, which makes them easy to read. The three parts of this command are described in the following sections.

NOTE The LINQ command in figure 2.8 is known as the LINQ method, or lambda syntax. You can use another format for writing LINQ commands with EF Core: the query syntax. I describe the two LINQ syntaxes in appendix A.

2.3.1 Application's DbContext property access

The first part of the command is connected to the database via EF Corea. The common way to refer to a database table is via a `DbSet<T>` property in the applica DbContext, as shown in figure 2.7.

You'll use this DbContext property access throughout this chapter, but later ters introduce other ways to get to a class or property. The basic idea is the same need to start with something that's connected to the database via EF Core.

2.3.2 A series of LINQ/EF Core commands

The major part of a command is a set of LINQ and/or EF Core methods that c the type of query you need. The LINQ query can range from being super-simp quite complicated. This chapter starts with simple examples of queries, but by the of this chapter, you'll learn how to build complex queries.

NOTE *Learning LINQ will be essential to you, as EF Core uses LINQ commands for database accesses.* The appendix gives you a brief overview of LINQ. Plenty of online resources are available too; see http://mng.bz/j4Qx.

2.3.3 The execute command

The last part of the command reveals something about LINQ. Until a final exe command is applied at the end of the sequence of LINQ commands, the LINQ is as a series of commands in what is called an *expression tree* (see section A.2.2), v means that it hasn't been executed on the data yet. EF Core can translate an ex sion tree into the correct commands for the database you're using. In EF Co query is executed against the database when

- It's enumerated by a `foreach` statement.
- It's enumerated by a collection operation such as `ToArray`, `ToDictio` `ToList`, `ToListAsync`, and so forth.
- LINQ operators such as `First` or `Any` are specified in the outermost part c query.

You'll use certain EF Core commands, such as `Load`, in the explicit loading of a tionship later in this chapter.

At this point, your LINQ query will be converted to database commands and to the database. If you want to build high-performance database queries, you wai your LINQ commands for filtering, sorting, paging, and so on to come before yo an execute command. Therefore, your filter, sort, and other LINQ commands w run inside the database, which improves the performance of your query. You wi this approach in action in section 2.8, when you build a query to filter, sort, and page the books in the database to display to your user.

The two types of database queries

The database query in figure 2.8 is what I call a *normal* query, also known as a *read-write* query. This query reads in data from the database in such a way that you can update that data (see chapter 3) or use it as an existing relationship for a new entry, such as creating a new book with an existing Author (see section 6.2.2).

The other type of query is an AsNoTracking query, also known as a read-only query. This query has the EF Core's AsNoTracking method added to the LINQ query (see the following code snippet). As well as making the query read-only, the AsNo-Tracking method improves the performance of the query by turning off certain EF Core features; see section 6.12 for more information:

```
context.Books.AsNoTracking()
        .Where(p => p.Title.StartsWith("Quantum")).ToList();
```

> **NOTE** Section 6.1.2 provides a detailed list of the differences between the normal, read-write query and the AsNoTracking, read-only query.

Loading related data

I've shown you the Book entity class, which has links to three other entity classes: PriceOffer, Review, and BookAuthor. Now I want to explain how you, as a developer, can access the data behind these relationships. You can load data in four ways: eager loading, explicit loading, select loading, and lazy loading. Before I cover these approaches, however, you need to be aware that EF Core won't load any relationships in an entity class unless you ask it to. If you load a Book class, each of the relationship properties in the Book entity class (Promotion, Reviews, and AuthorsLink) will be null by default.

This default behavior of not loading relationships is correct, because it means that EF Core minimizes the database accesses. If you want to load a relationship, you need to add code to tell EF Core to do that. The following sections describe the four approaches that get EF Core to load a relationship.

Eager loading: Loading relationships with the primary entity class

The first approach to loading related data is *eager loading*, which entails telling EF Core to load the relationship in the same query that loads the primary entity class. Eager loading is specified via two fluent methods, Include and ThenInclude. The next listing shows the loading of the first row of the Books table as an instance of the Book entity class and the eager loading of the single relationship, Reviews.

Listing 2.3   Eager loading of first book with the corresponding `Reviews` relationsh

```
var firstBook = context.Books
    .Include(book => book.Reviews)
    .FirstOrDefault();
```

> Gets a collection of Review class instances, which may be an empty collection

> Takes the first book or null if there are no books in the database

If you look at the SQL command that this EF Core query creates, shown in the fo ing snippet, you'll see two SQL commands. The first command loads the first r the Books table. The second loads the reviews, where the foreign key, BookId, ha same value as the first Books row primary key:

```
SELECT "t"."BookId", "t"."Description", "t"."ImageUrl",
    "t"."Price", "t"."PublishedOn", "t"."Publisher",
        "t"."Title", "r"."ReviewId", "r"."BookId",
            "r"."Comment", "r"."NumStars", "r"."VoterName"
FROM (
    SELECT "b"."BookId", "b"."Description", "b"."ImageUrl",
        "b"."Price", "b"."PublishedOn", "b"."Publisher", "b"."Title"
    FROM "Books" AS "b"
    LIMIT 1
) AS "t"
LEFT JOIN "Review" AS "r" ON "t"."BookId" = "r"."BookId"
ORDER BY "t"."BookId", "r"."ReviewId"
```

Now let's look at a more complex example. The following listing shows a query t the first Book, with eager loading of all its relationships—in this case, Authors and the second-level Author table, the Reviews, and the optional Promotion class

---

Listing 2.4   Eager loading of the `Book` class and all the related data

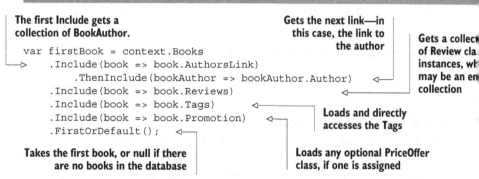

The first Include gets a collection of BookAuthor.

Gets the next link—in this case, the link to the author

Gets a collect of Review cla instances, wh may be an er collection

```
var firstBook = context.Books
    .Include(book => book.AuthorsLink)
        .ThenInclude(bookAuthor => bookAuthor.Author)
    .Include(book => book.Reviews)
    .Include(book => book.Tags)
    .Include(book => book.Promotion)
    .FirstOrDefault();
```

Takes the first book, or null if there are no books in the database

Loads and directly accesses the Tags

Loads any optional PriceOffer class, if one is assigned

The listing shows the use of the eager-loading method Include to get the Auth Link relationship. This relationship is a first-level relationship, referred to din from the entity class you're loading. That Include is followed by ThenInclude to the second-level relationship—in this case, the Author table at the other end o linking table, BookAuthor. This pattern, Include followed by ThenInclude, i standard way of accessing relationships that go deeper than a first-level relationship. You can go to any depth with multiple `ThenIncludes`, one after the other.

If you use the direct linking of many-to-many relationships introduced in EF Core 5, you don't need `ThenInclude` to load the second-level relationship because the property directly accesses the other end of the many-to-many relationship via the `Tags` property, which is of type `ICollection<Tag>`. This approach can simplify the use of a many-to-many relationship as long you don't need some data in the linking table, such as the `Order` property in the `BookAuthor` linking entity class used to order the `Book`'s `Authors` correctly.

> **EF6** Eager loading in EF Core is similar to that in EF6.x, but EF6.x doesn't have a `ThenInclude` method. As a result, the `Include/ThenInclude` code used in listing 2.4 would be written in EF6.x as `context.Books.Include(book => book.AuthorLink.Select(bookAuthor => bookAuthor.Author)`.

If the relationship doesn't exist (such as the optional `PriceOffer` class pointed to by the Promotion property in the `Book` class), `Include` doesn't fail; it simply doesn't load anything, or in the case of collections, it returns an empty collection (a valid collection with zero entries). The same rule applies to `ThenInclude`: if the previous `Include` or `ThenInclude` was empty, subsequent `ThenIncludes` are ignored. If you don't `Include` a collection, it is null by default.

The advantage of eager loading is that EF Core will load all the data referred to by the `Include` and `ThenInclude` in an efficient manner, using a minimum of database accesses, or *database round-trips*. I find this type of loading to be useful in relational updates in which I need to update an existing relationship; chapter 3 covers this topic. I also find eager loading to be useful in business logic; chapter 4 covers this topic in much more detail.

The downside is that eager loading loads *all* the data, even when you don't need part of it. The book list display, for example, doesn't need the book description, which could be quite large.

SORTING AND FILTERING WHEN USING INCLUDE AND/OR THENINCLUDE

EF Core 5 added the ability to sort or filter the related entities when you use the `Include` or `ThenInclude` methods. This capability is helpful if you want to load only a subset of the related data (such as only `Reviews` with five stars) and/or to order the included entities (such as ordering the `AuthorsLink` collection against the `Order` property). The only LINQ commands you can use in the `Include` or `ThenInclude` methods are `Where`, `OrderBy`, `OrderByDescending`, `ThenBy`, `ThenByDescending`, `Skip`, and `Take`, but those commands are all you need for sorting and filtering.

The next listing shows the same code as listing 2.4, but with the `AuthorsLink` collection being sorted on the `Order` property and with the `Reviews` collection being filtered to load only `Reviews` in which `NumStars` is 5.

Listing 2.5 Sorting and filtering when using `Include` or `ThenInclude`

```
var firstBook = context.Books
    .Include(book => book.AuthorsLink
        .OrderBy(bookAuthor => bookAuthor.Order))
        .ThenInclude(bookAuthor => bookAuthor.Author)
    .Include(book => book.Reviews
        .Where(review => review.NumStars == 5))
    .Include(book => book.Promotion)
    .First();
```

Sort example: On the loading of the Author collection, you sort the BookAuthors so that Authors will be in the correct order to disp…

Filter example. Here, you loa… the Reviews with a star ratin…

2.4.2 Explicit loading: Loading relationships after the primary entity class

The second approach to loading data is *explicit loading*. After you've loaded the mary entity class, you can explicitly load any other relationships you want. Listin… does the same job as listing 2.4 with explicit loading. First, it loads the Book; th… uses explicit-loading commands to read all the relationships.

Listing 2.6 Explicit loading of the `Book` class and related data

```
var firstBook = context.Books.First();
context.Entry(firstBook)
    .Collection(book => book.AuthorsLink).Load();
foreach (var authorLink in firstBook.AuthorsLink)
{
    context.Entry(authorLink)
        .Reference(bookAuthor =>
            bookAuthor.Author).Load();
}

context.Entry(firstBook)
    .Collection(book => book.Tags).Load();
context.Entry(firstBook)
    .Reference(book => book.Promotion).Load();
```

Reads in the first book on its own

Explicity load… the linking ta… BookAuthor

To load all the possibl… authors, the code has… loop through all the BookAuthor entries…

…and load each linked Author class.

Loads all the reviews

Loads the Tags

Loads the optional PriceOffer class

Alternatively, explicit loading can be used to apply a query to the relationship in… of loading the relationship. Listing 2.7 shows the use of the explicit-loading me… Query to obtain the count of reviews and to load the star ratings of each review… can use any standard LINQ command after the Query method, such as Wher… OrderBy.

Listing 2.7 Explicit loading of the `Book` class with a refined set of related data

```
var firstBook = context.Books.First();
var numReviews = context.Entry(firstBook)
    .Collection(book => book.Reviews)
    .Query().Count();
```

Reads in the first book on its own

Executes a query to count reviews for this book

```
var starRatings = context.Entry(firstBook)     |  Executes a query to
    .Collection(book => book.Reviews)           |  get all the star ratings
    .Query().Select(review => review.NumStars)  |  for the book
    .ToList();
```

The advantage of explicit loading is that you can load a relationship of an entity class later. I've found this technique useful when I'm using a library that loads only the primary entity class, and need one of its relationships. Explicit loading can also be useful when you need that related data in only some circumstances. You might also find explicit loading to be useful in complex business logic because you can leave the job of loading the specific relationships to the parts of the business logic that need it.

The downside of explicit loading is more database round trips, which can be inefficient. If you know up front the data you need, eager loading the data is usually more efficient because it takes fewer database round trips to load the relationships.

Select loading: Loading specific parts of primary entity class and any relationships

The third approach to loading data is using the LINQ Select method to pick out the data you want, which I call *select loading*. The next listing shows the use of the Select method to select a few standard properties from the Book class and execute specific code inside the query to get the count of customer reviews for this book.

> **Listing 2.8** Select of the Book class picking specific properties and one calculation

```
var books = context.Books
    .Select(book => new     ◁──┐  Uses the LINQ Select keyword
        {                      │  and creates an anonymous
                           ◁──┘  type to hold the results
ple copies of a  |       book.Title,
e of properties  |       book.Price,
                         NumReviews              |  Runs a query that counts
                             = book.Reviews.Count, |  the number of reviews
        }
    ).ToList();
```

The advantage of this approach is that only the data you need is loaded, which can be more efficient if you don't need all the data. For listing 2.8, only one SQL SELECT command is required to get all that data, which is also efficient in terms of database round trips. EF Core turns the p.Reviews.Count part of the query into an SQL command, so that count is done inside the database, as you can see in the following snippet of the SQL created by EF Core:

```
SELECT "b"."Title", "b"."Price", (
    SELECT COUNT(*)
    FROM "Review" AS "r"
    WHERE "b"."BookId" = "r"."BookId") AS "NumReviews"
FROM "Books" AS "b"
```

The downside to the select-loading approach is that you need to write code for property/calculation you want. In section 7.15.4, I show a way to automate this pro

NOTE Section 2.6 contains a much more complex select-loading example, which you'll use to build the high-performance book list query for the Book App.

2.4.4 *Lazy loading: Loading relationships as required*

Lazy loading makes writing queries easy, but it has a bad effect on database p mance. Lazy loading does require some changes to your DbContext or your classes, but after you make those changes, reading is easy; if you access a navigat property that isn't loaded, EF Core will execute a database query to load that n tional property.

You can set up lazy loading in either of two ways:

- Adding the Microsoft.EntityFrameworkCore.Proxies library when config your DbContext
- Injecting a lazy loading method into the entity class via its constructor

The first option is simple but locks you into setting up lazy loading for all the rel ships. The second option requires you to write more code but allows you to pick v relationships use lazy loading. I'm going to explain only the first option in this ter because it is simple, and leave the second option for chapter 6 (section 6. because it uses concepts that I haven't covered yet, such as dependency injection

NOTE If you want to see all the lazy-loading options now, access Microsoft's EF Core documentation at https://docs.microsoft.com/en-us/ef/core/querying/related-data/lazy.

To configure the simple lazy loading approach, you must do two things:

- Add the keyword `virtual` before *every* property that is a relationship.
- Add the method `UseLazyLoadingProxies` when setting up your DbContex

So the converted Book entity type to the simple lazy loading approach would like the following code snippet, with the virtual keyword added to the navigati properties:

```
public class BookLazy
{
    public int BookLazyId { get; set; }
    //… Other properties left out for clarity

    public virtual PriceOffer Promotion { get; set; }
    public virtual ICollection<Review> Reviews { get; set; }
    public virtual ICollection<BookAuthor> AuthorsLink { get; set; }
}
```

Using the EF Core's Proxy library has a limitation: you must make every relational erty virtual; otherwise, EF Core will throw an exception when you use the DbConte

The second part is adding the EF Core's Proxy library to the application that sets up the DbContext and then adding the `UseLazyLoadingProxies` to the configuring of the DbContext. The following code snippet shows the added method to the DbContext shown in listing 2.2 (`UseLazyLoadingProxies`):

```
var optionsBuilder =
    new DbContextOptionsBuilder<EfCoreContext>();
optionsBuilder
    .UseLazyLoadingProxies()
    .UseSqlServer(connection);
var options = optionsBuilder.Options;

using (var context = new EfCoreContext(options))
```

When you have configured lazy loading in your entity classes and in the way you create the DbContext, reading relationships is simple; you don't need extra `Include` methods in your query because the data is loaded from the database when your code accesses that relationship property. Listing 2.9 shows the lazy loading of the `Book`'s `Reviews` property.

Listing 2.9   Lazy loading of `BookLazy`'s `Reviews` navigational property

Gets an instance of the BookLazy entity class that has configured its Reviews property to use lazy loading

When the Reviews property is accessed, EF Core will read in the reviews from the database.

```
var book = context.BookLazy.Single();
var reviews = book.Reviews.ToList();
```

Listing 2.9 creates two database accesses. The first access loads the `BookLazy` data without any properties, and the second happens when you access `BookLazy`'s `Reviews` property.

Many developers find lazy loading to be useful, but I avoid it because of its performance issues. There is time overhead for every access to the database server, so the best approach is to minimize the number of calls to the database server. But lazy loading (and explicit loading) can create lots of database accesses, making the query slow and causing the database server to work harder. See section 14.5.1 for a side-by-side comparison of the four types of loading of related data.

TIP   Even if you have set up a relational property for lazy loading, you can get better performance by adding an `Include` on a virtual relational property. The lazy loading will see that the property has been loaded and not load it again. Changing the first line of listing 2.9 to `context.BookLazy.Include (book => book.Reviews).Single()`, for example, would reduce the two database accesses to one access.

2.5 Using client vs. server evaluation: Adapting data at the last stage of a query

All the queries you've seen so far are ones that EF Core can convert to command can be run on the database server. But EF Core has a feature called *client vs. serve uation*, which allows you to run code at the last stage of the query (that is, the Select part in your query) that can't be converted to database commands. EF runs these non-server-runnable commands after the data has come back fron database.

> **EF6** Client vs. server evaluation is a new feature in EF Core, and a useful one too.

The client vs. server evaluation feature gives you the opportunity to adapt/chang data within the last part of the query, which can save you from having to apply an step after the query. In section 2.6, you use client vs. server evaluation to cre comma-delimited list of the authors of a book. If you didn't use client vs. server e ation for that task, you would need to (a) send back a list of all the Author name (b) add an extra step after the query, using a foreach section to apply a string. to each book's authors.

> **Warning: EF Core will throw an exception if it cannot convert your LINQ**
>
> Before EF Core 3, any LINQ that couldn't be translated to a database command wou be run in software using the client vs. server evaluation. In some cases, th approach would produce extremely poor-performing queries. (I wrote about this su ject in the first edition of this book.) EF Core 3 changed this situation so that the ent vs. server evaluation is used in only the final stage of your LINQ queries, stoppi client vs. server evaluation from producing poor-performing queries.
>
> But that change creates a different problem: if your LINQ queries can't be convert to database commands, EF Core will throw an InvalidOperationException, w a message containing the words could not be translated. The trouble is that y get that error only when you try that query—and you don't want that error to happe in production!
>
> Throughout this book, I will guide you to write queries that will work, but with comp queries, it's easy to get something not quite right in your LINQ, causing the Invali OperationException to be thrown. This still happens to me, even though I know Core well, which is why I recommend in chapter 17 that you unit-test your databa accesses with a real database and/or have a set of integration tests.

For the list display of the books in the Book App, you need to (a) extract al authors' names, in order, from the Authors table and (b) turn them into one s with commas between names. Here's an example that loads two properties, Bo and Title, in the normal manner, and a third property, AuthorsString, that use ent vs. server evaluation.

Listing 2.10 `Select query that includes a non-SQL command,` `string.Join`

```
var firstBook = context.Books
    .Select(book => new
    {
        book.BookId,
        book.Title,
        AuthorsString = string.Join(", ",
            book.AuthorsLink
            .OrderBy(ba => ba.Order)
            .Select(ba => ba.Author.Name))
    }
    ).First();
```

These parts of the select can be converted to SQL and run on the server.

Running this code on a book that has two authors, Jack and Jill, would cause `AuthorsString` to contain Jack, Jill, and the `BookId`, and `Title` would be set to the value of the corresponding columns in the Books table. Figure 2.9 shows how listing 2.10 would be processed through four stages. I want to focus on stage 3, where EF Core runs the client-side code that it couldn't convert to SQL.

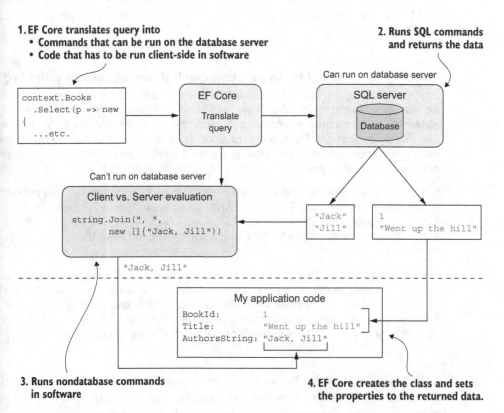

Figure 2.9 Some parts of the query are converted to SQL and run in SQL Server; another part, `string.Join`, has to be done client-side by EF Core before the combined result is handed back to the application code.

The example in listing 2.10 is fairly simple, but you need to be careful how you property created by client vs. server evaluation. Using client vs. server evaluatic a property means that you cannot use that property in any LINQ command would produce database commands, such as any commands that sort or filter property. If you do, you will get an `InvalidOperationException`, with a me that contains the words `could not be translated`. In figure 2.9, for example, i tried to sort or filter on the `AuthorsString`, you would get the `could not be tr lated` exception.

2.6 Building complex queries

Having covered the basics of querying the database, let's look at examples tha more common in real applications. You're going to build a query to list all the l in the Book App, with a range of features including sorting, filtering, and paging

You could build the book display by using eager loading. First, you'd load a data; then, in the code, you'd combine the authors, calculate the price, calc the average votes, and so on. The problem with that approach is that (a) you are ing data you don't need and (b) sorting and filtering have to be done in software this chapter's Book App, which has approximately 50 books, you could eager-loa the books and relationships into memory and then sort or filter them in software that approach wouldn't work for Amazon!

The better solution is to calculate the values inside SQL Server so that sorting filtering can be done before the data is returned to the application. In the rest o chapter, you'll use a select-loading approach that combines the select, sort, filter paging parts into one big query. You start in this section with the select part. Bef show you the select query that loads the book data, however, let's go back to the list display of *Quantum Networking* from the beginning of this chapter. This time ure 2.10 shows each individual LINQ query needed to get each piece of data.

This figure is complicated because the queries needed to get all the data are plicated. With this diagram in mind, let's look at how to build the book select q You start with the class you're going to put the data in. This type of class, which e only to bring together the exact data you want, is referred to in various way ASP.NET, it is referred to as a ViewModel, but that term also has other connota and uses; therefore, I refer to this type of class as a *Data Transfer Object* (*DTO*). ing 2.11 shows you the DTO class `BookListDto`.

> **DEFINITION** There are lots of definitions of a Data Transfer Object (DTO), but the one that fits my use of DTOs is "object that is used to encapsulate data, and send it from one subsystem of an application to another" (Stack Overflow, https://stackoverflow.com/a/1058186/1434764).

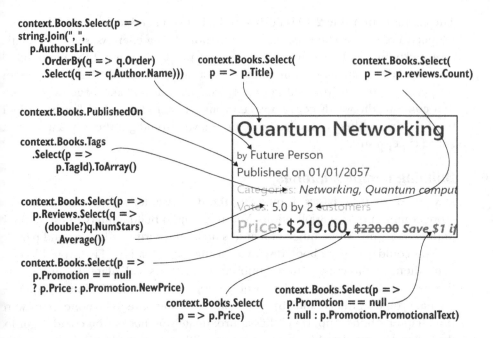

```
context.Books.Select(p =>
string.Join(", ",
    p.AuthorsLink
    .OrderBy(q => q.Order)
    .Select(q => q.Author.Name)))
```

```
context.Books.Select(
    p => p.Title)
```

```
context.Books.Select(
    p => p.reviews.Count)
```

```
context.Books.PublishedOn
```

```
context.Books.Tags
    .Select(p =>
        p.TagId).ToArray()
```

```
context.Books.Select(p =>
    p.Reviews.Select(q =>
        (double?)q.NumStars)
        .Average())
```

```
context.Books.Select(p =>
    p.Promotion == null
    ? p.Price : p.Promotion.NewPrice)
```

```
context.Books.Select(
    p => p.Price)
```

```
context.Books.Select(p =>
    p.Promotion == null
    ? null : p.Promotion.PromotionalText)
```

Quantum Networking

by Future Person

Published on 01/01/2057

Categories: *Networking, Quantum comput*

Votes: 5.0 by 2 customers

Price: **$219.00** $220.00 *Save $1 i*

Figure 2.10 Each individual query needed to build the book list display, with each part of the query that's used to provide the value needed for that part of the book display. Some queries are easy, such as getting the title of the book, but others aren't so obvious, such as working out the average votes from the reviews.

Listing 2.11 The DTO `BookListDto`

You need the primary key if the customer clicks the entry to buy the book.

```
public class BookListDto
{
    public int BookId { get; set; }
    public string Title { get; set; }
    public DateTime PublishedOn { get; set; }
    public decimal Price { get; set; }
    public decimal
        ActualPrice { get; set; }
    public string
        PromotionPromotionalText { get; set; }
    public string AuthorsOrdered { get; set; }

    public int ReviewsCount { get; set; }
    public double?
        ReviewsAverageVotes { get; set; }
    public string[] TagStrings { get; set; }
}
```

Although the publication date isn't shown, you'll want to sort by it, so you have to include it.

Selling price—either the normal price or the promotional.NewPrice if present

Promotional text to show whether there's a new price

String to hold the comma-delimited list of authors' names

Number of people who reviewed the book

Average of all the votes, null if no votes

The Tag names (that is the categories) for this book

To work with EF Core's select loading, the class that's going to receive the data must[ ]
a default constructor (which you can create without providing any properties to the[ ]
structor), the class must not be static, and the properties must have public setters.

Next, you'll build a select query that fills in every property in BookLis[ ]
Because you want to use this query with other query parts, such as sort, filter, and[ ]
ing, you'll use the IQueryable<T> type to create a method called MapBookToDt[ ]
takes in IQueryable<Book> and returns IQueryable<BookListDto>. The follc[ ]
listing shows this method. As you can see, the LINQ Select pulls together all the[ ]
vidual queries you saw in figure 2.10.

Listing 2.12 The Select query to fill BookListDto

```
public static IQueryable<BookListDto>                          Takes in IQueryable<Book> a
    MapBookToDto(this IQueryable<Book> books)                  returns IQueryable<BookList
{
    return books.Select(book => new BookListDto
    {
        BookId = book.BookId,                                  Simple copies of
        Title = book.Title,                                    existing columns in
        Price = book.Price,                                    the Books table
        PublishedOn = book.PublishedOn,
        ActualPrice = book.Promotion == null                   Calculates the selling price, which
            ? book.Price                                       the normal price, or the promoti
            : book.Promotion.NewPrice,                         price if that relationship exists
        PromotionPromotionalText =
            book.Promotion == null
                ? null                                         Obtains an array of author
                : book.Promotion.PromotionalText,              names, in the right order.
        AuthorsOrdered = string.Join(", ",                     using client vs. server eval
            book.AuthorsLink                                   because you want the auth
                .OrderBy(ba => ba.Order)                       names combined into one
                .Select(ba => ba.Author.Name)),
        ReviewsCount = book.Reviews.Count,                     To get EF Core to t
        ReviewsAverageVotes =                                  LINQ average into t
            book.Reviews.Select(review =>                      command, you nee
                (double?) review.NumStars).Average(),          the NumStars to (d
        TagStrings = book.Tags
            .Select(x => x.TagId).ToArray(),                   Array of Tag names
    });                                                        (categories) for this book
}
```

PromotionalText depends on whether a PriceOffer exists for this book — annotation for `PromotionPromotionalText = book.Promotion == null`

You need to calculate the number of reviews. — annotation for `ReviewsCount = book.Reviews.Count`

NOTE The individual parts of the Select query in listing 2.12 are the repetitive code I mention in my lightbulb moment in chapter 1. Chapter 6 introduces mappers that automate much of this coding, but in part 1 of this book,
I list all the code in full so that you see the whole picture. Be assured that
there's a way to automate the select-loading approach of querying that will
improve your productivity.

The MapBookToDto method uses the Query Object pattern; the method take[ ]
IQueryable<T> and outputs IQueryable<T>, which allows you to encapsulate a q[ ]

or part of a query, in a method. That way, the query is isolated in one place, which makes it easier to find, debug, and performance-tune. You'll use the Query Object pattern for the sort, filter, and paging parts of the query too.

NOTE   Query Objects are useful for building queries such as the book list in this example, but alternative approaches exist, such as the Repository pattern.

The `MapBookToDto` method is also what .NET calls an *extension method*. Extension methods allow you to chain Query Objects together. You'll see this chaining used in section 2.9, when you combine each part of the book list query to create the final, composite query.

NOTE   A method can become an extension method if (a) it's declared in a static class, (b) the method is static, and (c) the first parameter has the keyword `this` in front of it.

Query Objects take in a `IQueryable<T1>` input and return `IQueryable<T2>`, so you're adding LINQ commands to the original `IQueryable<T1>` input. You can add another Query Object to the end, or if you want to execute the query, add an execute command (see figure 2.8) such as `ToList` to execute the query. You'll see this approach in action in section 2.9, when you combine the Book's Select, Sort, Filter, and Paging Query Objects, which EF Core turns into a fairly efficient database query. In chapter 15, you'll work through a series of performance tunes to make the book list query even faster.

NOTE   You can see the results of this query by cloning the code from the Git repo and then running the Book App web application locally. A Logs menu feature will show you the SQL used to load the book list with the specific sorting, filtering, and paging setting you've selected.

Introducing the architecture of the Book App

I've waited until this point to talk about the design of the Book App, because it should make more sense now that you've created the `BookListDto` class. At this stage, you have the entity classes (`Book`, `Author`, and so on) that map to the database via EF Core. You also have a `BookListDto` class, which holds the data in the form that the presentation side needs—in this case, an ASP.NET Core web server.

In a simple example application, you might put the entity classes in one folder, the DTOs in another, and so on. But even in a small application, such as the Book App, this practice can be confusing, because the approach you use with the database is different from the approach you use when displaying data to the customer. The Separation of Concerns (SoC) principle (see http://mng.bz/7Vom) says that your software should be broken down into separate parts. The book display database query, for example, shouldn't contain the code that creates the HTML to show to the books to the user.

You could split the parts of the Book App in numerous ways, but we'll use a com design called *layered architecture*. This approach works well for small to medium-size applications. Figure 2.11 shows the architecture of the Book App for this chapter.

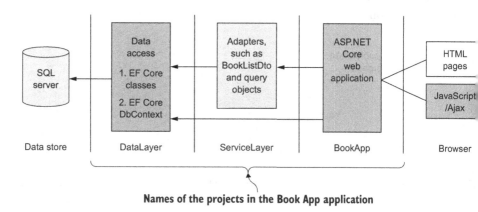

Names of the projects in the Book App application

Figure 2.11 The layered architectural approach for the Book App. Placing the parts of the code i discrete projects separates what the code in each project does. The DataLayer, for example, has worry only about the database and doesn't need to know how the data is going to be used; this is tl SoC principle in action. The arrows always point to the left because the lower (left) projects can't access the higher (right) projects.

The three large rectangles are .NET projects, with their names at the bottom o figure. The classes and code of these three projects are split in the following way:

- *DataLayer*—This layer's focus is the database access. The entity classes an application's DbContext are in this project. This layer doesn't know anyt about the layers above it.
- *ServiceLayer*—This layer acts as an adapter between the DataLayer and ASP.NET Core web application by using DTOs, Query Objects, and va classes to run the commands. The idea is that the frontend ASP.NET Core has so much to do that the ServiceLayer hands its premade data for displa
- *BookApp*—The focus of this layer, called the *presentation layer*, is on prese data in a way that's convenient and applicable to the user. The present layer should focus only on the interaction with the user, which is why we as much as possible of the database and data adapting out of the present layer. In the Book App, you'll use an ASP.NET Core web application se mainly HTML pages, with a small amount of JavaScript running in the bro

Using a layered architecture makes the Book App a little more complex to u stand, but it's one way to build real applications. Using layers also enables you to more easily what each bit of the code is supposed to be doing in the associate repo, because the code isn't all tangled up.

Adding sorting, filtering, and paging

With the project structure out of the way, you can push on more quickly and build the remaining Query Objects to create the final book list display. I'll start by showing you a screenshot (figure 2.12) of the Book App's sort, filter, and page controls to give you an idea of what you're implementing.

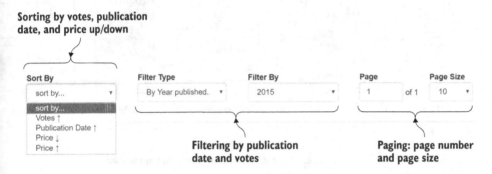

Sorting by votes, publication date, and price up/down

Filtering by publication date and votes

Paging: page number and page size

Figure 2.12 The three commands—sorting, filtering, and paging—as shown on the Book App's home page. You can see this page in action if you run the Book App in the accompanying Git repo.

Sorting books by price, publication date, and customer ratings

Sorting in LINQ is done by the methods `OrderBy` and `OrderByDescending`. You create a Query Object called `OrderBooksBy` as an extension method, as shown in the next listing. You'll see that in addition to the `IQueryable<BookListDto>` parameter, this method takes in an enum parameter that defines the type of sort the user wants.

Listing 2.13 The `OrderBooksBy` Query Object method

```
public static IQueryable<BookListDto> OrderBooksBy
    (this IQueryable<BookListDto> books,
     OrderByOptions orderByOptions)
{
    switch (orderByOptions)
    {
        case OrderByOptions.SimpleOrder:
            return books.OrderByDescending(
                x => x.BookId);
        case OrderByOptions.ByVotes:
            return books.OrderByDescending(x =>
                x.ReviewsAverageVotes);
        case OrderByOptions.ByPublicationDate:
            return books.OrderByDescending(
                x => x.PublishedOn);
        case OrderByOptions.ByPriceLowestFirst:
            return books.OrderBy(x => x.ActualPrice);
        case OrderByOptions.ByPriceHighestFirst:
            return books.OrderByDescending(
                x => x.ActualPrice);
```

Because of paging, you always need to sort. You default-sort on the primary key, which is fast.

Orders the book by votes. Books without any votes (null return) go at the bottom.

Orders by publication date, with the latest books at the top

Orders by actual price, which takes into account any promotional price—both lowest first and highest first

```
        default:
            throw new ArgumentOutOfRangeException(
                nameof(orderByOptions), orderByOptions, null);
    }
}
```

Calling the `OrderBooksBy` method returns the original query with the appropriate LINQ sort command added to the end. You pass this query on to the next query Object, or if you've finished, you call a command to execute the code, such as To.

> **NOTE** Even if the user doesn't select a sort, you'll still sort (see the `Simple-Order` switch statement) because you'll be using paging, providing only a page at a time rather than all the data, and SQL requires the data to be sorted to handle paging. The most efficient sort is on the primary key, so you sort on that key.

2.8.2 Filtering books by publication year, categories, and customer ratings

The filtering created for the Book App is a bit more complex than the sorting cov in section 2.8.1 because you get the customer to first select the type of filter they and then select the actual filter value. The filter value for `Votes` is easy: it's a s fixed values (4 or higher, 3 or higher, and so on), and the categories are the `TagId`. But to filter by Date, you need to find the dates of the publications to put i drop-down list.

It's instructive to look at the code for working out the years that have b because that code is a nice example of combining LINQ commands to create the drop-down list. Here's a snippet of code taken from the `GetFilterDropDownVa` method.

Listing 2.14   The code to produce a list of the years when books are published

Loads books while filtering out the future books; then selects
the years when the books were published

The Distinct
method retur
a list of each
year a book w
published.

Orders the
years, with
newest year
at the top

```
var result = _db.Books
    .Where(x => x.PublishedOn <= DateTime.UtcNow.Date)
    .Select(x => x.PublishedOn.Year)
    .Distinct()
    .OrderByDescending(x => x.PublishedOn)
    .Select(x => new DropdownTuple
    {
        Value = x.ToString(),
        Text = x.ToString()
    }).ToList();
var comingSoon = _db.Books.
    Any(x => x.PublishedOn > DateTime.Today);
if (comingSoon)
    result.Insert(0, new DropdownTuple
    {
        Value = BookListDtoFilter.AllBooksNotPublishedString,
```

I finally use two client/server
evaluations to turn the
values into strings.

Returns true if a book in the
list is not yet published

Adds a "coming soon" filter
for all the future books

```
        Text = BookListDtoFilter.AllBooksNotPublishedString
    });

return result;
```

The result of this code is a list of Value/Text pairs holding each year that books are published, plus a Coming Soon section for books yet to be published. This data is turned into an HTML drop-down list by ASP.NET Core and sent to the browser.

The following listing shows the filter Query Object called FilterBooksBy, which takes as an input the Value part of the drop-down list created in listing 2.14, plus whatever type of filtering the customer has asked for.

Listing 2.15 The FilterBooksBy Query Object method

```
public static IQueryable<BookListDto> FilterBooksBy(        The method is given both
    this IQueryable<BookListDto> books,                     the type of filter and the
    BooksFilterBy filterBy, string filterValue)  ◁─┘        user-selected filter value.
{
    if (string.IsNullOrEmpty(filterValue))       If the filter value isn't set, returns
        return books;                            IQueryable with no change

    switch (filterBy)
    {
        case BooksFilterBy.NoFilter:        For no filter selected, returns
            return books;                   IQueryable with no change
        case BooksFilterBy.ByVotes:
            var filterVote = int.Parse(filterValue);        The filter by votes returns
            return books.Where(x =>                         only books with an average
                x.ReviewsAverageVotes > filterVote);        vote above the filterVote value.
        case BooksFilterBy.ByTags:                          If there are no reviews for a
            return books.Where(x => x.TagStrings             book, the ReviewsAverageVotes
                .Any(y => y == filterValue));               property will be null, and the
        case BooksFilterBy.ByPublicationYear:               test always returns false.
            if (filterValue == AllBooksNotPublishedString)   If Coming Soon was
                return books.Where(                          picked, returns only
                    x => x.PublishedOn > DateTime.UtcNow);   books not yet published

            var filterYear = int.Parse(filterValue);         If we have a specific
            return books.Where(                              year, we filter on that.
                x => x.PublishedOn.Year == filterYear        Note that we also
                    && x.PublishedOn <= DateTime.UtcNow);    remove future books
        default:                                             (in case the user chose
            throw new ArgumentOutOfRangeException            this year's date).
                (nameof(filterBy), filterBy, null);
    }
}
```

(left margin annotation: ny books category tches the filterValue — pointing to the ByTags case)

Other filtering options: Searching text for a specific string

We could've created loads of other types of filters/searches of books, and searching by title is an obvious one. But you want to make sure that the LINQ commands you use to search a string are executed in the database, because they'll perform much better than

loading all the data and filtering in software. EF Core converts the following C#
in a LINQ query to a database command: ==, Equal, StartsWith, EndsWith, Cont
and IndexOf. Table 2.1 shows some of these commands in action.

Table 2.1 Example .NET string commands in an SQL Server database

String command	Example (finds a title with the string "The Cat sat on the mat.")

StartsWith	```var books = context.Books```
	``` .Where(p => p.Title.StartsWith("The"))```
	``` .ToList();```

EndsWith	```var books = context.Books```
	``` .Where(p => p.Title.EndsWith("MAT."))```
	``` .ToList();```

Contains	```var books = context.Books``` ``` .Where(p => p.Title.Contains("cat"))```

The other important thing to know is that the case sensitivity of a string search
cuted by SQL commands depends on the type of database, and in some datab
the rule is called *collation*. A default SQL Server database default collation uses
insensitive searches, so searching for Cat would find cat and Cat. Many SQL data
are case-insensitive by default, but Sqlite has a mix of case-sensitive/case-insensitive
unit test Ch02_StringSearch class in the repo for more details), and Cosmos DB
default case-sensitive.

EF Core 5 provides various ways to set the collation in a database. Typically
configure the collation for the database or a specific column (covered in section
but you can also define the collation in a query by using the EF.Functions.Col
method. The following code snippet sets an SQL Server collation, which means
this query will compare the string using the Latin1_General_CS_AS (case-sens
collation for this query:

```
context.Books.Where( x =>
    EF.Functions.Collate(x.Title, "Latin1_General_CS_AS")
        == "HELP" //This does not match "help"
```

NOTE Defining what is uppercase and what is lowercase over many languages
with many scripts is a complex issue! Fortunately, relational databases have
been performing this task for many years, and SQL Server has more than 200
collations.

Another string command is the SQL command LIKE, which you can access thr
the EF.Function.Like method. This command provides a simple pattern-matc
approach using _ (underscore) to match any letter and % to match zero-to-many
acters. The following code snippet would match "The Cat sat on the mat." and

dog sat on the step." but not "The rabbit sat on the hutch." because rabbit isn't three letters long:

```
var books = context.Books
    .Where(p => EF.Functions.Like(p.Title, "The ___ sat on the %."))
    .ToList();
```

OTHER QUERY OPTIONS: COMPLEX QUERIES (GROUPBY, SUM, MAX, AND SO ON)
This chapter has covered a wide range of query commands, but EF Core can translate many more commands to most databases. Section 6.1.8 covers the commands that need a bit more explanation or special coding.

Paging the books in the list

If you've used Google search, you've used paging. Google presents the first dozen or so results, and you can *page* through the rest. Our Book App uses paging, which is simple to implement by using the LINQ commands' Skip and Take methods.

Although the other Query Objects were tied to the BookListDto class because the LINQ paging commands are so simple, you can create a generic paging Query Object that will work with any IQueryable<T> query. This Query Object is shown in the following listing. The object does rely on getting a page number in the right range, but another part of the application has to do that anyway to show the correct paging information onscreen.

Listing 2.16 A generic Page Query Object method

```
public static IQueryable<T> Page<T>(
    this IQueryable<T> query,
    int pageNumZeroStart, int pageSize)
{
    if (pageSize == 0)
        throw new ArgumentOutOfRangeException
            (nameof(pageSize), "pageSize cannot be zero.");

    if (pageNumZeroStart != 0)
        query = query
            .Skip(pageNumZeroStart * pageSize);          ◁── Skips the correct
                                                              number of pages
    return query.Take(pageSize);           ◁── Takes the number
}                                              for this page size
```

As I said earlier, paging works only if the data is ordered. Otherwise, SQL Server will throw an exception because relational databases don't guarantee the order in which data is handed back; there's no default row order in a relational database.

Putting it all together: Combining Query Objects

We've covered each Query Object you need to build a book list for the Book App. Now it's time to see how to combine these Query Objects to create a composite query to work with the website. The benefit of building a complex query in separate parts is

that this approach makes writing and testing the overall query simpler, becaus[e]
can test each part on its own.

Listing 2.17 shows a class called ListBooksService, which has one method, [s]
FilterPage, which uses all the Query Objects (select, sort, filter, and page) to
the composite query. It also needs the application's DbContext to access the [B]
property, which you provide via the constructor.

> **TIP** Listing 2.17 highlights in bold the AsNoTracking method. This method
> stops EF Core from taking a tracking snapshot (see figure 1.6) on read-only
> queries, which makes the query slightly quicker. You should use the AsNo-
> Tracking method in any read-only queries (queries in which you read the
> data, but don't ever update it). In this case, we are not loading any entity classes,
> so it's redundant, but I put it there to remind us that the query is read-only.

Listing 2.17 The ListBookService class providing a sorted, filtered, and paged

```
public class ListBooksService
{                                                    Starts by selecting the
    private readonly EfCoreContext _context;         Books property in the
                                                     Application's DbContext
    public ListBooksService(EfCoreContext context)
    {                                                Because this query is rea
        _context = context;                          only, you add .AsNoTrack[
    }
                                                     Uses the Select Query C
    public IQueryable<BookListDto> SortFilterPage    which picks out/calcula
        (SortFilterPageOptions options)              the data it needs
    {
        var booksQuery = _context.Books    ◄──┘
            .AsNoTracking()                ◄────┘     Adds the commands
            .MapBookToDto()                ◄────┘     order the data by us[
            .OrderBooksBy(options.OrderByOptions) ◄──┘ the given options
            .FilterBooksBy(options.FilterBy,
                        options.FilterValue);         Adds the commands
                                                      to filter the data
        options.SetupRestOfDto(booksQuery);   ◄───
                                                     This stage sets up the
```
Applies the paging   `return booksQuery.Page(options.PageNum-1,`   number of pages and
commands   `options.PageSize);`   makes sure that PageNum
                                         is in the right range.

```
    }
}
```

As you can see, the four Query Objects—select, sort, filter, and page—are added in[
(called *chaining*) to form the final composite query. Note that the options.Se[
RestOfDto(booksQuery) code before the Page Query Object sorts out things su[
how many pages there are, ensures that the PageNum is in the right range, and[
forms a few other housekeeping items. Chapter 5 shows how the ListBooksServi[
called in our ASP.NET Core web application.

Summary

- To access a database in any way via EF Core, you need to define an application DbContext.
- An EF Core query consists of three parts: the application's DbContext property, a series of LINQ/EF Core commands, and a command to execute the query.
- Using EF Core, you can model three primary database relationships: one-to-one, one-to-many, and many-to-many. Other relationships are covered in chapter 8.
- The classes that EF Core maps to the database are referred to as *entity classes*. I use this term to highlight the fact that the class I'm referring to is mapped by EF Core to the database.
- If you load an entity class, it won't load any of its relationships by default. Querying the Book entity class, for example, won't load its relationship properties (Reviews, AuthorsLink, and Promotion); it leaves them as null.
- You can load related data that's attached to an entity class in four ways: eager loading, explicit loading, select loading, and lazy loading.
- EF Core's client vs. server evaluation feature allows the last stage of a query to contain commands, such as string.Join, that can't be converted to SQL commands.
- I use the term *Query Object* to refer to an encapsulated query or a section of a query. These Query Objects are often built as .NET extension methods, which means that they can easily be chained together, similar to the way LINQ is written.
- Selecting, sorting, filtering, and paging are common query uses that can be encapsulated in a Query Object.
- If you write your LINQ queries carefully, you can move the aggregate calculations, such as Count, Sum, and Average, into the relational database, improving performance.

For readers who are familiar with EF6.x:

- Many of the concepts in this chapter are the same as in EF6.x. In some cases (such as eager loading), the EF Core commands and/or configuration have changed slightly, but often for the better.

Changir
the database conte

This chapter covers

- Creating a new row in a database table
- Updating existing rows in a database table for two types of applications
- Updating entities with one-to-one, one-to-many, and many-to-many relationships
- Deleting single entities, and entities with relationships, from a database

---

Chapter 2 covered querying a database. This chapter moves on to changing content of a database. Changing data has three distinct parts—creating new row a database table, updating existing rows in a database table, and deleting rows database table—and I cover them in that order. *Create*, *update*, and *delete*, along *read* (which is *query* in EF Core terms) are database terms for what's happening the foursome is often shortened to *CRUD*.

You'll use the same database as in chapter 2, which has the Book, PriceO Review, BookAuthor, and Author entity classes. These classes provide a good s tion of property types and relationships that you can use to learn the various i and approaches to changing data in a database via EF Core.

Introducing EF Core's entity State

Before I start describing the methods to add, update, or delete entities, I want to introduce you to EF Core's entity property, called State. This property provides another look under the hood at the way EF Core does things, which helps you understand what's going on when you add, update, or delete entities.

Any entity class instance has a State, which can be accessed via the following EF Core command: context.Entry(someEntityInstance).State. The State tells EF Core what to do with this instance when SaveChanges is called. Here's a list of the possible states and what happens if SaveChanges is called:

- Added—The entity needs to be created in the database. SaveChanges inserts it.
- Unchanged—The entity exists in the database and hasn't been modified on the client. SaveChanges ignores it.
- Modified—The entity exists in the database and has been modified on the client. SaveChanges updates it.
- Deleted—The entity exists in the database but should be deleted. SaveChanges deletes it.
- Detached—The entity you provided isn't tracked. SaveChanges doesn't see it.

Normally, you don't look at or alter the State directly. You use the various commands listed in this chapter to add, update, or delete entities. These commands make sure the State is set in a *tracked entity* (see definition below). When SaveChanges is called, it looks at all the tracked entities and their State to decide what type of database changes it needs to apply to the database. I refer to the entity's State in the rest of the chapter to show you how EF Core decides what type of change to apply to the database.

> **DEFINITION** *Tracked entities* are entity instances that have been read in from the database by using a query that didn't include the AsNoTracking method. Alternatively, after an entity instance has been used as a parameter to EF Core methods (such as Add, Update, or Delete), it becomes tracked.

Creating new rows in a table

Creating new data in a database is about adding (via the SQL command INSERT in a relational database) a new row to a table. If you want to add a new author to our Book App, for example, that addition would be referred to as a create operation on the database.

In EF Core terms, creating new data in a database is the simplest of the update operations because EF Core can take a set of linked entity classes, save them to the database, and sort out the foreign keys needed to link things. In this section, you'll start with a simple example and then build up to more complex creates.

3.2.1 Creating a single entity on its own

Let's start with an entity class that has no navigational properties—that is, rela
ships to other tables in your database. This example is rare but shows the two ste
a create operation:

   1 Add the entity to the application's DbContext.
   2 Call the application's DbContext's SaveChanges method.

This listing creates an ExampleEntity entity class and adds a new row to the table
the entity is mapped to—in this case, the ExampleEntities table.

Listing 3.1 An example of creating a single entity

```
var itemToAdd = new ExampleEntity          Uses the Add method to add SingleEntity to the
{                                          application's DbContext. The DbContext determin
    MyMessage = "Hello World"              the table to add it to, based on its parameter typ
};
context.Add(itemToAdd);                    Calls the SaveChanges method from the
context.SaveChanges();                     application's DbContext to update the database
```

Because you add the entity instance itemToAdd that wasn't originally tracked, EF
starts to track it and sets its State to Added. After SaveChanges is called, EF Core
a tracked entity of type ExampleEntity with a State of Added, so it's added as a
row in the database table associated with the ExampleEntity class.

> **EF6** In EF6.x, you'd need to add the itemToAdd to a DbSet<ExampleEntity>
> property in the application's DbContext—for example, context.Example-
> Entities.Add(itemToAdd). That approach is still valid, but EF Core has intro-
> duced the shorthand shown in listing 3.1, which applies to the Add, Remove,
> Update, and Attach methods. (See chapter 11 for more on the last two com-
> mands.) EF Core works out which entity you're altering by looking at the type
> of the instance you provide.

EF Core creates the SQL command to update an SQL Server–based database.

Listing 3.2 SQL commands created to insert a new row into the SingleEntities t

```
SET NOCOUNT ON;
INSERT INTO ExampleEntities]          Inserts (creates) a new row into
    ([MyMessage]) VALUES (@p0);       the ExampleEntities table

SELECT [ExampleEntityId]
FROM [ExampleEntities]                Reads back the
WHERE @@ROWCOUNT = 1 AND             primary key in the
    [ExampleEntityId] = scope_identity();   newly created row
```

The second SQL command produced by EF Core reads back the primary key o
row that was created by the database server. This command ensures that the c
nal ExampleEntity instance is updated with the primary key so that the in-mei

version of the entity is the same as the version in the database. Reading back the primary key is important, as you might update the entity later, and the update will need the primary key.

EF6 In EF6.x, when you call `SaveChanges`, EF6.x by default validates the data by using the standard .NET validation approach; it looks for data validation attributes and, if they are present, runs `IValidatableObject.Validate` on entity classes. EF Core doesn't include this feature because a lot of validation is done in the frontend, but it's not hard to add a validation feature if you need it. Chapter 4 shows you how.

Creating a book with a review

Next, you'll look at a create that includes relationships—in this case, adding a new book with a review. Although the setup of the entity classes is a bit more complex, the process has the same steps as our earlier, nonrelational create:

- It adds the entity class(es) in some way to EF Core's tracked entities with the `State` of `Add`.
- It calls `SaveChanges`, which looks at the `State` of all the tracked entities and runs the SQL `INSERT` command for all entities with the `State` set to `Added`.

This example uses the Book App's database with its Books and Review tables. Figure 3.1 shows a partial database diagram of these tables.

A Book entity with one Review

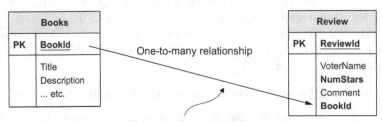

When EF Core writes this new Book entity and
its related Review entity to the database, it copies
the Book's database-generated primary key into
the foreign key in the Review entity.

Figure 3.1   The Books and Review tables. The Review row has a foreign key that
EF Core fills with the primary key value from the new Books row that's created.

In the next listing, you create a new `Book` entity and fill the `Reviews` collection property with a single `Review` entity. Then you call the `context.Add` method, followed by the `SaveChanges` method, which writes both entities to the database.

Listing 3.3 Adding a Book entity class also adds any linked entity classes

Creates
a new
collection
of reviews

Creates the book
with the title
"Test Book"

```
var book = new Book
{
    Title = "Test Book",
    PublishedOn = DateTime.Today,
    Reviews = new List<Review>()
    {
        new Review
        {
            NumStars = 5,
            Comment = "Great test book!",
            VoterName = "Mr U Test"
        }
    }
};
context.Add(book);
context.SaveChanges();
```

Adds one review
with its content

Uses the Add method to add
the book to the application's
DbContext property, Books

Calls the SaveChanges method from the application's
DbContext to update the database. It finds a new Book,
which has a collection containing one new Review, and
then adds both to the database.

The thing to note from this listing is that you add only the Book entity class, bu
related Review entity class is also written to the database. This happens becaus
Core follows all the relational links and finds the new Review instance, and bec
that Review isn't tracked, EF Core knows that the Review needs to be added t
database.

As you saw in the simple example in listing 3.1, EF Core works out what to do
the linked entity classes by accessing their EF Core State values. If the li
instances are new (not already known to EF Core), EF Core will start tracking
and set their State to Added. In all other cases, EF Core will obey the State link
the entity instance. In listing 3.3, the Review entity instance isn't already known
Core, which means that its State is Detached, but when the Add call is made, its S
is set to Added. That instance will be INSERTed into the database as a new row.

WHAT HAPPENS AFTER THE SAVECHANGES RETURNS SUCCESSFULLY?

When the Add and SaveChanges have finished successfully, a few things happen
entity instances that have been inserted into the database are now tracked by EF (
and their State is set to Unchanged. Because we are using a relational database,
because the two entity classes, Book and Review, have primary keys that are of type
EF Core by default will expect the database to create the primary keys by usin
SQL IDENTITY keyword. Therefore, the SQL commands created by EF Core read
the primary keys into the appropriate primary keys in the entity class instanc
make sure that the entity classes match the database.

NOTE The Cosmos DB database doesn't have an equivalent to SQL's IDENTITY,
so you need to provide a unique key, such as GUIDs (globally unique identifiers).

Unique GUIDs are generated by what EF Core calls a `ValueGenerator` (see chapter 10). GUIDs are also useful for primary keys in relational databases when you need a unique key that won't change when you copy/duplicate the data to another database.

Also, EF Core knows about the relationships by the navigational properties in the entity classes. In listing 3.3, the `Book` entity's `Reviews` collection property has a new `Review` entity instance in it. As part of the `SaveChanges` process, any foreign key will be set by copying the primary keys into the foreign keys in each of the new relationships. Then the entity instance matches the database. That's useful in case you want to read the primary or foreign keys, and EF Core can detect any subsequent changes you make to the primary or foreign keys if you call `SaveChanges` again.

> ### Why you should call `SaveChanges` only once at the end of your changes
>
> In listing 3.3. you see that the `SaveChanges` method is called at the end of create, and you see the same pattern—the `SaveChanges` method is called at the end—in the update and delete examples too. In fact, even for complex database change containing a mixture of creates, updates, and deletes, you should still call the `SaveChanges` method only once at the end. You do that because EF Core will save all your changes (creates, updates and deletes) and apply them to the database together, and if the database rejects any of your changes, all your changes are rejected (by means of a database feature called a *transaction*; see section 4.7.2).
>
> This pattern is called a *Unit Of Work* and means that your database changes can't be half-applied to the database. If you created a new `Book` with a `BookAuthor` reference to an `Author` that wasn't in the database, for example, you wouldn't want the `Book` instance to be saved. Saving it might break the book display, which expects every `Book` to have at least one `Author`.
>
> Sometimes, you may think that you need to call `SaveChanges` twice—say, when you need the primary key of a new entity class to fill in the foreign key of entity class, but there is always a way around that situation with EF Core. In fact, listing 3.3 gets around it by creating a new `Book` and a new `Review` at the same time. Have a read through section 6.2.1 and 6.2.2 to get an "under the hood" look at how EF Core achieves this task.

EXAMPLE THAT HAS ONE INSTANCE ALREADY IN THE DATABASE

The other situation you may need to deal with is creating a new entity containing a navigational property that uses another entity already in the database. If you want to create a new `Book` entity that has an `Author` that already exists in the database, you need to obtain a tracked instance of the `Author` entity that you want to add to your new `Book` entity. The following listing gives you one example. Note that the database already contains an author called "Mr. A."

Listing 3.4 Adding a Book with an existing Author

```
var foundAuthor = context.Authors
    .SingleOrDefault(author => author.Name == "Mr. A");
if (foundAuthor == null)
    throw new Exception("Author not found");
```
Reads in the Autho◼
with a check that t◼
Author was found

```
var book = new Book
{
    Title = "Test Book",
    PublishedOn = DateTime.Today
};
```
Creates a Book in
the same way as the
previous example

```
book.AuthorsLink = new List<BookAuthor>
{
    new BookAuthor
    {
        Book = book,
        Author = foundAuthor
    }
};
```
Adds an AuthorBook
linking entry, but
uses the Author that
is already in the
database

```
context.Add(book);
context.SaveChanges();
```
Adds the new Book to the DbContext
Books property and calls SaveChanges

The first four lines load an `Author` entity with some checks to make sure that i◼ found; this `Author` class instance is tracked, so EF Core knows that it is already i◼ database. You create a new `Book` entity and add a new `BookAuthor` linking entity instead of creating a new `Author` entity instance, you use the `Author` entity tha◼ read in from the database. Because EF Core is tracking the `Author` instance and k◼ that it's in the database, EF Core won't try to add it again to the database ◼ `SaveChanges` is called at the end of listing 3.4.

3.3 Updating database rows

Updating a database row is achieved in three stages:

1 Read the data (database row), possibly with some relationships.
2 Change one or more properties (database columns).
3 Write the changes back to the database (update the row).

In this section, you'll ignore any relationships and focus on the three stages. I◼ next section, you'll learn how to update relationships by adding more comman◼ each stage.

Listing 3.5 changes the publication date of an existing book. Through this ◼ you can see the standard flow of an update:

1 You load the entity class(es) you want to change as a tracked entity.
2 You change the property/properties in your entity class(es).
3 You call `SaveChanges` to update the database.

Listing 3.5 Updating *Quantum Networking*'s publication date

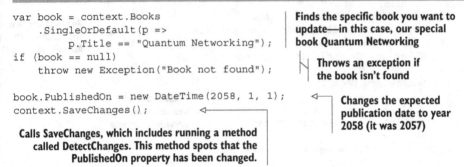

```
var book = context.Books
    .SingleOrDefault(p =>
        p.Title == "Quantum Networking");
if (book == null)
    throw new Exception("Book not found");

book.PublishedOn = new DateTime(2058, 1, 1);
context.SaveChanges();
```

Finds the specific book you want to update—in this case, our special book Quantum Networking

Throws an exception if the book isn't found

Changes the expected publication date to year 2058 (it was 2057)

Calls SaveChanges, which includes running a method called DetectChanges. This method spots that the PublishedOn property has been changed.

When the SaveChanges method is called, it runs a method called DetectChanges, which compares the tracking snapshot against the entity class instance that it handed to the application when the query was originally executed. From this example, EF Core decides that only the PublishedOn property has been changed, and EF Core builds the SQL to update that property.

NOTE Using the tracking snapshot is the normal way that DetectChanges finds the changed properties. But chapter 11 describes an alternative to the tracking snapshot, such as INotifyPropertyChanging. This topic is advanced, so I use the tracked-entities approach throughout part 1 of this book.

The following listing shows the two SQL commands that EF Core produces for the code in listing 3.5. One SQL command finds and loads the Book entity class, and a second command updates the PublishedOn column.

Listing 3.6 SQL generated by EF Core for the query and update in listing 3.5

```
SELECT TOP(2)
    [p].[BookId],
    [p].[Description],
    [p].[ImageUrl],
    [p].[Price],
    [p].[PublishedOn],
    [p].[Publisher],
    [p].[Title]
FROM [Books] AS [p]
WHERE [p].[Title] = N'Quantum Networking'

SET NOCOUNT ON;
UPDATE [Books]
    SET [PublishedOn] = @p0

WHERE [BookId] = @p1;
SELECT @@ROWCOUNT;
```

Reads up to two rows from the Books table. You asked for a single item, but this code makes sure that it fails if more than one row fits.

Your LINQ Where method, which picks out the correct row by its title

SQL UPDATE command—in this case, on the Books table

Because EF Core's DetectChanges method finds that only the PublishedOn property has changed, it can target that column in the table.

...s back the number of rows that were inserted ...nto this transaction. SaveChanges returns this integer, but normally, you can ignore it.

EF Core uses the primary key from the original book to uniquely select the row it wants to update.

3.3.1 *Handling disconnected updates in a web application*

As you learned in section 3.3, an update is a three-stage process, needing a rea
update, and a SaveChanges call to be executed by the same instance of the ap
tion's DbContext. The problem is that for certain applications, such as website
RESTful APIs, using the same instance of the application's DbContext isn't po:
because in web applications, each HTTP request typically is a new request, wit
data held over from the last HTTP request. In these types of applications, an uj
consists of two stages:

- The first stage is an initial read, done in one instance of the applica
  DbContext.
- The second stage applies the update by using a new instance of the ap]
  tion's DbContext.

In EF Core, this type of update is called a *disconnected* update because the first
and the second stage use two different instances of the application's DbContext
the preceding list). You can handle a disconnected update in several ways.
method you should use depends a lot on your application. Here are the two main
of handling disconnected updates:

- *You send only the data you need to update back from the first stage.* If you were u
  ing the published date for a book, you would send back only the BookId an
  PublishedOn properties. In the second stage, you use the primary key to r(
  the original entity with tracking and update the specific properties you wa
  change. In this example, the primary key is the BookId, and the proper
  update is the PublishedOn property of the Book entity (see figure 3.2). V
  you call SaveChanges, EF Core can work out which properties you've cha
  and update only those columns in the database.
- *You send all the data needed to re-create the entity class back from the first stage.* I]
  second stage, you rebuild the entity class, and maybe relationships, by usin;
  data from the first stage and tell EF Core to update the whole entity (see fi
  3.3). When you call SaveChanges, EF Core will know, because you told it, tl
  must update all the columns in the table row(s) affected with the substitute
  that the first stage provided.

NOTE Another way of handling the partial update of an entity described in
option 1 is to create a new entity instance and manipulate the State of each
property. Chapter 11 covers this option, when we look at how to alter the
entity's State in more detail.

That's a lot of words! Now I'll give you an example of each approach for handlin;
connected updates.

DISCONNECTED UPDATE, WITH RELOAD

Figure 3.2 shows an example of a disconnected update in a web application. In this case, you're providing a feature to allow an admin user to update the publication date of a book. The figure shows that you send only the BookId and the PublicationDate data back from the first stage.

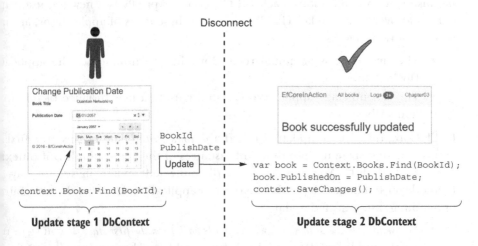

Figure 3.2 The two stages in a disconnected update on a website using EF Core. The thick, dashed line in the middle represents the point where the data held in the application in the first stage is lost, and the second stage starts with no knowledge of what stage 1 did. Only the BookId and PublishDate information is returned when the user clicks the Update button that bridges the gap.

For web applications, the approach of returning only a limited amount of data to the web server is a common way of handling EF Core updates. This approach makes the request faster, but a big reason for it is security. You wouldn't want the Price of a Book to be returned, for example, as that information would allow hackers to alter the price of the book they want to buy.

There are several ways of controlling what data is returned/accepted by the web server. In ASP.NET Core, for example, you have the attribute BindNever, which allows you to define named properties that won't be returned to the second stage. But a more general approach, and one I prefer, is to use a special class that contains only properties that should be sent/received. This class is referred to as a DTO or View-Model. It's similar in nature to the DTO used in the select-loading query in chapter 2, but in this case it's used not only in the query, but also to receive the specific data you need back from the user, via a browser. For our example that updates the publication date, you need three parts. The first part, a DTO to send/receive the data to/from the user, is shown here.

Listing 3.7 `ChangePubDateDto` **sends data to and receives it from the user**

```
public class ChangePubDateDto
{
    public int BookId { get; set; }

    public string Title { get; set; }

    [DataType(DataType.Date)]
    public DateTime PublishedOn { get; set; }
}
```

Holds the primary key of the row you want to update, which makes finding the right row quick and accurate

You send over the title to show the user so that they can be sure they are altering the right book.

The property you want to alter. You send out the current publication date and get back the changed publication date.

The quickest way to read an entity class using its primary key(s)

When you want to update a specific entity and need to read it in using its primary ke you have a few options. I used to use the `Find` command, but after some digging now recommend `SingleOrDefault` because it's quicker than the `Find` commar But I should point out two useful things about the `Find` method:

- The `Find` method checks the current application's DbContext to see wheth the required entity instance has already been loaded, which can save access to the database. But if the entity isn't in the application's DbConte the load will be slower because of this extra check.
- The `Find` method is simpler and quicker to type because it's shorter th the `SingleOrDefault` version, such as `context.Find<Book>(key)` vers `context.SingleOrDefault(p => p.Bookid == key)`.

The upside of using the `SingleOrDefault` method is that you can add it to the e of a query with methods such as `Include`, which you can't do with `Find`.

Second, you need a method to get the initial data for stage 1. Third, you ne method to receive the data back from the browser and then reload/update the I This listing shows the `ChangePubDateService` class that contains two methods to dle these two stages.

Listing 3.8 **The** `ChangePubDateService` **class to handle the disconnected upda**

This interface is needed when registering this class in DI. You use DI in chapter 5 when building the ASP.NET Core BookApp.

```
public class ChangePubDateService : IChangePubDateService
{
    private readonly EfCoreContext _context;

    public ChangePubDateService(EfCoreContext context)
    {
        _context = context;
    }
```

The application's DbContext is provid a class constructor- normal way of buil classes that you wil a service in ASP.NE

```
    public ChangePubDateDto GetOriginal(int id)
    {
        return _context.Books
            .Select(p => new ChangePubDateDto
            {
                BookId = p.BookId,
                Title = p.Title,
                PublishedOn = p.PublishedOn
            })
            .Single(k => k.BookId == id);
    }

    public Book UpdateBook(ChangePubDateDto dto)
    {
        var book = _context.Books.SingleOrDefault(
            x => x.BookId == dto.BookId);
        if (book == null)
            throw new ArgumentException(
                "Book not found");
        book.PublishedOn = dto.PublishedOn;
        _context.SaveChanges();
        return book;
    }
}
```

thod handles t part of the such as by the data from sen book to the user.

A select load query that returns only three properties

the key the ow t to ate

This method handles the second part of the update, such as performing a selective update of the chosen book.

Loads the book. I use SingleOrDefault because it's slightly quicker than the Find method.

se where a found and exception.

Selective update of the PublishedOn property of the loaded book

SaveChanges uses its DetectChanges method to find out what has changed and then updates the database.

Returns the updated book

The advantages of this reload-then-update approach is that it's more secure (in our example, sending/returning the price of the book over HTTP would allow someone to alter it) and faster because of less data. The downside is that you have to write code to copy over the specific properties you want to update. Chapter 6 covers a few tricks to automate this process.

> **NOTE** You can see this code and try updating the publication date on the example Book App. If you download the code from the Git repo and run it locally, you'll see an Admin button for each book. This button contains a link called Change Pub Date, which will step you through this process. You can also see the SQL commands that EF Core uses to carry out this update via the Logs menu item.

DISCONNECTED UPDATE, SENDING ALL THE DATA

In some cases, all the data may be sent back, so there's no reason to reload the original data. This can happen for simple entity classes, in some RESTful APIs, or process-to-process communication. A lot depends on how closely the given API format matches the database format and how much you trust the other system.

Figure 3.3 shows an example of a RESTful API in which an external system first queries the system for books with a given title. In the update stage, the external system sends back an update on the author of the book it received.

Listing 3.9 simulates the RESTful API by having a first stage that reads in the `Author` entity class you want to update and then serializes it into a JSON string.

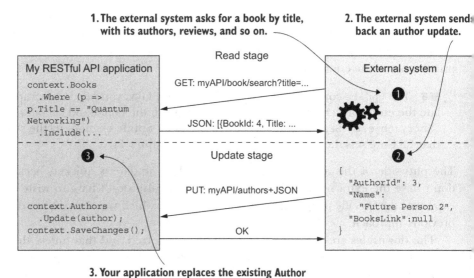

1. The external system asks for a book by title, with its authors, reviews, and so on.

2. The external system sends back an author update.

3. Your application replaces the existing Author data with the data from the external system.

Figure 3.3 An example of a disconnected update, in which you replace all the database information with the new data. Unlike the one in the previous example, this process doesn't need to reload the original data before performing the update.

(Figure 3.3, step 2 shows what that JSON looks like.) Then you decode that JSON use the EF Core Update command, which replaces all the information in the defined by the primary key—in this case, the AuthorId.

Listing 3.9   Simulating an update/replace request from an external system

```
string json;
using (var context = new EfCoreContext(options))
{
    var author = context.Books
        .Where(p => p.Title == "Quantum Networking")
        .Select(p => p.AuthorsLink.First().Author)
        .Single();
    author.Name = "Future Person 2";
    json = JsonConvert.SerializeObject(author);
}
using (var context = new EfCoreContext(options))
{
    var author = JsonConvert
        .DeserializeObject<Author>(json);

    context.Authors.Update(author);
    context.SaveChanges();
}
```

Simulates an external system returning a modified Author entity class as a JSON string

Provides a link to the many-to-many linking table that links to the authors of this book

Simulates receiving a JSON str from an external system and decoding it into an Author cla

Update command, which replaces all the row data for the given primary key—in this case, AuthorId

You call the EF Core Update command with the Author entity instance as a parameter, which marks as modified all the properties of the Author entity. When the Save-Changes command is called, it'll update all the columns in the row that have the same primary key as the entity class.

> **EF6** The Update command is new in EF Core. In EF6.x, you need to manipulate the entity object state directly, such as by using the command DbContext .Entry(object).State = EntityState.Modified. Subtle changes in the way that EF Core sets the entity state are covered in chapter 11.

The plus side of this approach is that the database update is quicker, because you don't have the extra read of the original data. You also don't have to write code to copy over the specific properties you want to update, which you did need to do in the previous approach.

The downsides are that more data can be transferred and that unless the API is carefully designed, it can be difficult to reconcile the data you receive with the data already in the database. Also, you're trusting the external system to remember all the data correctly, especially the primary keys of your system.

> **NOTE** Listing 3.9 covers only a single class with no relationship, but in many RESTful APIs and process-to-process communications, a lot of linked data might be sent over. In the example, the API might expect the whole book with all its relationships to be sent back only for an update of the author's name. This process gets complicated, so I cover it in chapter 11, which shows how to manage the state of each property and introduces EF Core's TrackGraph method, which helps handle partial updates of classes with relationships.

Handling relationships in updates

Now that we've established the three basic steps for updating the database, it's time to look at updating relationships between entity classes—adding a new review to a book, for example. Updating relationships adds another level of complexity to the code, especially in the disconnected state, which is why I put this content in a separate section.

This section covers updates for the three types of relational linking that EF Core uses and gives examples of both connected and disconnected updates. In all cases, you'll use the Book entity class, which has three relationship links. The following listing shows the Book entity class, but with the focus on the relationships at the end. (I've removed some nonrelational properties to keep the focus on the relationships.)

Listing 3.10 The Book entity class, showing the relationships to update

```
public class Book              ◄─────────┐   Book class contains the
{                                        │   main book information.
    public int BookId { get; set; }
    //... other nonrelational properties removed for clarity
```

```
//------------------------------------------------
//relationships

public PriceOffer Promotion { get; set; }
public ICollection<Review> Reviews { get; set; }
public ICollection<Tag> Tags { get; set; }
public ICollection<BookAuthor>
    AuthorsLink { get; set; }
}
```

Links to the optional PriceOffer

Can be zero to n reviews of the b

EF Core 5's automati many-to-many relati to the Tag entity clas

Provides a link to the many-to-many linking table that links to the authors of this book

3.4.1 Principal and dependent relationships

The terms *principal* and *dependent* are used in EF to define parts of a relationship:

- *Principal entity*—Contains a primary key that the dependent relationship to via a foreign key
- *Dependent entity*—Contains the foreign key that refers to the principal en primary key

In the Book App example, the Book entity class is the principal entity. The Pr Offer, Review, and BookAuthor entity classes are the dependent entities. I finc terms *principal* and *dependent* to be helpful, because they define what's in charge principal entity. I use these terms throughout this book where applicable.

> **NOTE** An entity class can be both a principal and a dependent entity at the same time. In a hierarchical relationship of, say, libraries with books that have reviews, the book would be a dependent relationship of the library entity class.

CAN THE DEPENDENT PART OF A RELATIONSHIP EXIST WITHOUT THE PRINCIPAL?

The other aspect of a dependent relationship is whether it can exist on its own. I principal relationship is deleted, is there a business case for the dependent rela ship to still exist? In many cases, the dependent part of a relationship doesn't r sense without the principal relationship. A book review has no meaning if the bc links to is deleted from the database, for example.

In a few cases, a dependent relationship should exist even if the principal p deleted. Suppose that you want to have a log of all the changes that happen book in its lifetime. If you delete a book, you wouldn't want that set of logs t deleted too.

This task is handled in databases by handling the nullability of the foreign k the foreign key in the dependent relationship is non-nullable, the dependent rela ship can't exist without the principal. In the example Book App database, the Pr Offer, Review, and BookAuthor entities are all dependent on the principal, Book e so their foreign keys are of type int. If the book is deleted or the link to the bo removed, the dependent entities will be deleted.

But if you define a class for logging—let's call it BookLog—you want this cla exist even if the book is deleted. To make this happen, you'd make its BookId fo key of type `Nullable<int>`. Then, if you delete the book that the `BookLog` entity is linked to, you could configure that the `BookLog`'s `BookId` foreign key would be set to null.

> **NOTE** In the preceding `BookLog` example, if you delete a `Book` entity that a `BookLog` is linked to, the default action is to set the `BookLog`'s foreign key to null because EF Core defaults to a `ClientSetNull` setting for the `OnDelete` property of optional relationships. Section 8.8.1 covers this topic in more detail.

I mention this situation now because as we go through updating the relationships, in some cases, a dependent relationship is removed from its principal. I'll give an example of replacing all the dependent relationships with new ones. What happens to the old relationships we remove depends on the nullability of the foreign key: if the foreign key is non-nullable, the dependent relationships are deleted, and if the foreign key is nullable, it's set to null. I talk more about this topic and how EF Core handles deletion in section 3.5.

Updating one-to-one relationships: Adding a PriceOffer to a book

In our example Book App database, we have an optional, dependent relationship property called `Promotion` from the `Book` entity class to the `PriceOffer` entity class. This subsection covers how to add a `PriceOffer` class to an existing book. This listing shows you the content of the `PriceOffer` entity class, which links to the Books table via the foreign key called `BookId`.

Listing 3.11 `PriceOffer` **entity class, showing the foreign key back to the Book entity**

```
public class PriceOffer                          ◁──  PriceOffer, if present, is
{                                                     designed to override
    public int PriceOfferId { get; set; }             the normal price.
    public decimal NewPrice { get; set; }
    public string PromotionalText { get; set; }

    //-------------------------------------------------
    //Relationships
                                                  ┌──  Foreign key back to the book
    public int BookId { get; set; }         ◁─────┘    it should be applied to
}
```

CONNECTED STATE UPDATE

The connected state update assumes that you're using the same context for both the read and the update. Listing 3.12 shows an example of the code, which has three stages:

1 Load the `Book` entity with any existing `PriceOffer` relationship.
2 Set the relationship to the new `PriceOffer` entity you want to apply to this book.
3 Call `SaveChanges` to update the database.

Listing 3.12 Adding a new promotional price to an existing book that doesn't have

Finds a book. In this example, the book doesn't
have an existing promotion, but it would also
work if there were an existing promotion.

Although the include isn't needed because y
loading something without a Promotion, us
the include is good practice, as you should
any relationships if you're going to change
relationship.

```
var book = context.Books
    .Include(p => p.Promotion)
    .First(p => p.Promotion == null);

book.Promotion = new PriceOffer
{
    NewPrice = book.Price / 2,
    PromotionalText = "Half price today!"
};
context.SaveChanges();
```

Adds a new
PriceOffer to
this book

The SaveChanges method calls DetectChanges, which
finds that the Promotion property has changed, so it
adds that entity to the PriceOffers table.

As you can see, the update of the relationship is like the basic update you mac
change the book's published date. In this case, EF Core has to do extra work becau
the relationship. EF Core creates a new row in the PriceOffers table, which you ca
in the SQL snippet that EF Core produces for the code in listing 3.12:

```
INSERT INTO [PriceOffers]
    ([BookId], [NewPrice], [PromotionalText])
    VALUES (@p0, @p1, @p2);
```

Now, what happens if there's an existing promotion on the book (that is, the Pr
tion property in the Book entity class isn't null)? That case is why the Include
p.Promotion) command in the query that loaded the Book entity class is so impor
Because of that Include method, EF Core will know that an existing PriceOff
assigned to this book and will delete it before adding the new version.

To be clear, in this case you must use some form of loading of the relationsh
eager, explicit, select, or *lazy* loading of the relationship—so that EF Core knows abc
before the update. If you don't, and if there's an existing relationship, EF Core
throw an exception on a duplicate foreign key BookId, which EF Core has plac
unique index on, and another row in the PriceOffers table will have the same va

DISCONNECTED STATE UPDATE

In the disconnected state, the information to define which book to update and
to put in the PriceOffer entity class would be passed back from stage 1 to sta
That situation happened in the update of the book's publication date (figure
where the BookId and the PublishedOn values were fed back.

In the case of adding a promotion to a book, you need to pass in the BookId, w
uniquely defines the book you want, plus the NewPrice and the Promotional
values that make up the PriceOffer entity class. The next listing shows you
ChangePriceOfferService class, which contains the two methods to show the d

the user and update the promotion on the Book entity class when the user submits a request.

Listing 3.13 `ChangePriceOfferService` class with a method to handle each stage

```
public class ChangePriceOfferService : IChangePriceOfferService
{
    private readonly EfCoreContext _context;

    public Book OrgBook { get; private set; }

    public ChangePriceOfferService(EfCoreContext context)
    {
        _context = context;
    }

    public PriceOffer GetOriginal(int id)
    {
        OrgBook = _context.Books
            .Include(r => r.Promotion)
            .Single(k => k.BookId == id);

        return OrgBook?.Promotion
            ?? new PriceOffer
            {
                BookId = id,
                NewPrice = OrgBook.Price
            };
    }

    public Book AddUpdatePriceOffer(PriceOffer promotion)
    {
        var book = _context.Books
            .Include(r => r.Promotion)
            .Single(k => k.BookId
                == promotion.BookId);

        if (book.Promotion == null)
        {
            book.Promotion = promotion;
        }
        else
        {
            book.Promotion.NewPrice
                = promotion.NewPrice;
            book.Promotion.PromotionalText
                = promotion.PromotionalText;
        }
        _context.SaveChanges();
        return book;
    }
}
```

Gets a PriceOffer class to send to the user to update

Loads the book with any existing Promotion

You return either the existing Promotion for editing or create a new one. The important point is to set the BookId, as you need to pass it through to the second stage.

Loads the book with any existing promotion, which is important because otherwise, your new PriceOffer will clash and throw an error

whether should a new ffer or ate the xisting eOffer

You need to add a new PriceOffer, so you assign the promotion to the relational link. EF Core will see it and add a new row in the PriceOffer table.

You need to do an update, so you copy over only the parts that you want to change. EF Core will see this update and produce code to update only these two columns.

SaveChanges uses its DetectChanges method, which sees what changes—either adding a new PriceOffer or updating an existing one.

Returns the updated book

This code either updates an existing PriceOffer or adds a new PriceOffer if none exists. When SaveChanges is called, it can work out, via EF Core's DetectChanges method, what type of update is needed and create the correct SQL to update the base. This is different from the connected version shown in listing 3.12, where replaced any PriceOffer with a new version. Both versions work, but if you are ging who last created/updated an entity (see section 11.4.3), updating an exi entity gives you a bit more information about what changed.

ALTERNATIVE WAY OF UPDATING THE RELATIONSHIP: CREATING A NEW ROW DIRECTLY
We've approached this update as changing a relationship in the Book entity class you can also approach it as creating/deleting a row in the PriceOffers table. Thi ing finds the first Book in the database that doesn't have a Promotion linked to it then adds a new PriceOffer entity to that book.

Listing 3.14 Creating a `PriceOffer` row to go with an existing book

```
var book = context.Books
    .First(p => p.Promotion == null);

context.Add( new PriceOffer
{
    BookId = book.BookId,
    NewPrice = book.Price / 2,
    PromotionalText = "Half price today!"
});
context.SaveChanges();
```

> You find the book that you want to add the new PriceOffer to, which must not be an existing PriceOffer.

Adds the new PriceOffer to the PriceOffers table

> Defines the PriceOffer. You must include the BookId (which EF Core filled in previously).

> SaveChanges adds the PriceOffer to the PriceOffers table.

You should note that previously, you didn't have to set the BookId property in PriceOffer entity class, because EF Core did that for you. But when you're creat relationship this way, you do need to set the foreign key. Having done so, if you the Book entity class with its Promotion relationship after the previous create you'll find that the Book has gained a Promotion relationship.

> **NOTE** The PriceOffer entity class doesn't have a relational property link back to the Book class (public Book BookLink {get; set;}). If it did, you could set the BookLink to the Book entity class instead of setting the foreign key. Either setting the foreign key(s) or setting a relational link back to the principal entity will tell EF Core to set up the relationship.

The advantage of creating the dependent entity class is that it saves you from nee to reload the principal entity class (in this case, Book) in a disconnected state. downside is that EF Core doesn't help you with the relationships. In this case, if t were an existing PriceOffer on the book and you added another, SaveChanges w fail because you'd have two PriceOffer rows with the same foreign key.

When EF Core can't help you with the relationships, you need to use the cre delete approach with care. Sometimes, this approach can make handling a com relationship easier, so it's worth keeping in mind, but I prefer updating the prin entity class's relationship in most one-to-one cases.

NOTE Later, in section 3.4.5, you'll learn another way of updating relationships by changing foreign keys.

Updating one-to-many relationships: Adding a review to a book

You've learned the basic steps in updating a relationship by looking at a one-to-one relationship. I'll move a bit quicker with the remaining relationships, as you've seen the basic pattern. But I'll also point out some differences in the *many* side of a relationship.

The one-to-many relationship in the Book App database is represented by Book's Reviews; a user of the site can add a review to a book. There can be any number of reviews, from none to a lot. This listing shows the Review-dependent entity class, which links to the Books table via the foreign key called BookId.

Listing 3.15 The Review class, showing the foreign key back to the Book entity class

```
public class Review          ◁─┤  Holds customer reviews
{                                with their ratings
    public int ReviewId { get; set; }
    public string VoterName { get; set; }
    public int NumStars { get; set; }
    public string Comment { get; set; }

    //-------------------------------------------
    //Relationships

    public int BookId { get; set; }   ◁─┤  Foreign key holds the key of the
}                                          book this review belongs to.
```

CONNECTED STATE UPDATE

Listing 3.16 adds a new Review to a Book. This code follows the same pattern as the one-to-one connected update: load the Book entity class and the Reviews relationship via the Include method. But in this case, you add the Review entity to the Book's Reviews collection. Because you used the Include method, the Reviews property will be an empty collection if there are no reviews or a collection of the reviews linked to this book. In this example, the database already contains some Book entities, and I take the first.

Listing 3.16 Adding a review to a book in the connected state

```
var book = context.Books          Finds the first book
    .Include(p => p.Reviews)       and loads it with any
    .First();                      reviews it might have

book.Reviews.Add(new Review
{                                  Adds a new      SaveChanges calls DetectChanges,
    VoterName = "Unit Test",       review to       which finds that the Reviews property
    NumStars = 5,                  this book       has changed, and from there finds the
    Comment = "Great book!"                        new Review, which it adds to the
});                                                 Review table.
context.SaveChanges();         ◁────────────────
```

As with the `PriceOffer` example, you don't fill in the foreign key (the `BookId` | erty) in the `Review`, because EF Core knows that the `Review` is being added to a entity class and sets up the foreign key to the right value.

ALTERING/REPLACING ALL THE ONE-TO-MANY RELATIONSHIPS

Before moving on to the disconnected state update, I want to consider the ca which you want to alter or replace the whole collection, rather than add to the c tion, as you did with the review.

If the books had categories (say, Software Design, Software Languages, and so you might allow an admin user to change the categories. One way to implemen change would be to show the current categories in a multiselect list, allow the a user to change them, and then replace *all* the categories on the book with the selection.

EF Core makes replacing the whole collection easy. If you assign a new colle to a one-to-many relationship that has been loaded with tracking (such as by usin; `Include` method), EF Core will replace the existing collection with the new collec If the items in the collection can be linked to only the principal class (the depen class has a non-nullable foreign key), by default, EF Core will delete the items were in the collection that have been removed.

Next is an example of replacing the whole collection of existing book reviews a new collection. The effect is to remove the original reviews and replace them with one new review.

Listing 3.17 Replacing a whole collection of reviews with another collection

```
var book = context.Books
    .Include(p => p.Reviews)
    .Single(p => p.BookId == twoReviewBookId);

book.Reviews = new List<Review>
{
    new Review
    {
        VoterName = "Unit Test",
        NumStars = 5,
    }
};
context.SaveChanges();
```

This include is important; creates a collection with existing reviews in it or a empty collection if there no existing reviews.

This book you're loading has two reviews.

You replace the whole collection.

SaveChanges, via DetectChanges, knows that the old collection should be deleted and that the new collection should be written to the database.

Because you're using test data in the example, you know that the book with the pri key `twoReviewBookId` has two reviews and that the book is the only one with rev hence, there are only two reviews in the whole database. After the `SaveChanges` me is called, the book has only one review, and the two old reviews have been delete now the database has only one review in it.

Removing a single row is as simple as removing the entity from the list. EF Cor see the change and delete the row that's linked to that entity. Similarly, if you a new Review to the Book's Reviews collection property, EF Core will see that change to that collection and add the new Review to the database.

The loading of the existing collection is important for these changes: if you don't load them, EF Core can't remove, update, or replace them. The old versions will still be in the database after the update because EF Core didn't know about them at the time of the update. You haven't replaced the existing two Reviews with your single Review. In fact, you now have three Reviews—the two that were originally in the database and your new one—which is not what you intended to do.

DISCONNECTED-STATE UPDATE

In the disconnected state, you create an empty Review entity class but fill in its foreign key, BookId, with the book the user wants to provide a review for. Then the user votes on the book, and you add that review to the book that they referred to. The following listing shows the AddReviewService class, which has methods for the setup and update of the book, to add a new review from a user.

Listing 3.18 Adding a new review to a book in the example Book App

```
public class AddReviewService
{
    private readonly EfCoreContext _context;

    public string BookTitle { get; private set; }

    public AddReviewService(EfCoreContext context)
    {
        _context = context;
    }

    public Review GetBlankReview(int id)        ⟵── Forms a review to be filled in by the user
    {
        BookTitle = _context.Books
            .Where(p => p.BookId == id)          You read the book title to
            .Select(p => p.Title)                show to the user when they're
            .Single();                           filling in their review.
        return new Review
        {                                        Creates a review with
            BookId = id                          the BookId foreign
        };                                       key filled in
    }
                                                 Updates the book
    public Book AddReviewToBook(Review review)  ⟵── with the new review
    {
        var book = _context.Books                Loads the correct book by using the value in
            .Include(r => r.Reviews)             the review's foreign key, and includes any
            .Single(k => k.BookId                existing reviews (or an empty collection if
                == review.BookId);               there are no reviews yet)
        book.Reviews.Add(review);
        _context.SaveChanges();        ⟵──┐     SaveChanges uses its DetectChanges method, which
        return book;                       │     sees that the Book Review property has changed,
    }                                            and creates a new row in the Review table.
}
```

Margin annotations (left side): ...s the ...eview ...o the ...views ...ction ⟶ book.Reviews.Add(review);   the ...ook ⟶ return book;

This code has a simpler first part than the previous disconnected-state exam
because you're adding a new review, so you don't have to load the existing data fo
user. But overall, the code takes the same approach that the ChangePriceOf
Service class used.

ALTERNATIVE WAY OF UPDATING THE RELATIONSHIP: CREATING A NEW ROW DIRECTLY
As with the PriceOffer, you can add a one-to-many relationship directly to the
base. But again, you take on the role of managing the relationship. If you wa
replace the entire reviews collection, for example, you'd have to delete all the
that the reviews linked to the book in question before adding your new collectior

Adding a row directly to the database has some advantages, because loadin
the one-to-many relationships might turn out to be a lot of data if you have lc
items and/or they're big. Therefore, keep this approach in mind if you have pe
mance issues.

> **NOTE** My experiments show that not loading the relationship and then
> assigning a new collection to a one-to-many relationship is equivalent to creat-
> ing a new row directly. But I don't recommend doing this because it's not the
> normal update pattern; someone else (or even you) might come back later
> and misread your intentions.

3.4.4 Updating a many-to-many relationship

In EF Core, we talk about many-to-many relationships, but a relational database do
directly implement many-to-many relationships. Instead, we're dealing with two
to-many relationships, as shown in figure 3.4.

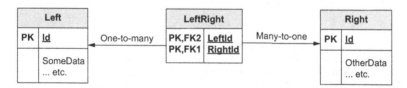

**Figure 3.4 A many-to-many relationship in the database is created by a linking
table that contains the primary keys of the two tables that need a many-to-many
relationship.**

In EF Core, you have two ways to create many-to-many relationships between
entity classes:

- You link to a linking table in each entity—that is, you have an ICollec
  <LeftRight> property in your Left entity class. You need to create an e
  class to act as the linking table (such as LeftRight in figure 3.4), but that e
  class lets you add extra data in the linking table so that you can sort/filte
  many-to-many relationships.

- You link directly between the two entity classes you want to have a many-to-many relationship—that is, you have an ICollection<Right> property in your Left entity class. This link is much easier to code because EF Core handles the creation of the linking table, but then you can't access the linking table in a normal Include method to sort/filter.

NOTE This chapter uses EF Core default settings for a many-to-many relationship. Chapter 8 covers the configuration options for many-to-many relationships.

UPDATING A MANY-TO-MANY RELATIONSHIP VIA A LINKING ENTITY CLASS

In the Book entity class, you need a many-to-many link to the Authors of the book. But in a book, the order of the authors' names matters. Therefore, you create a linking table with an Order (byte) property that allows you to display the Author's Name properties in the correct order, which means that you

- Create an entity class called BookAuthor, which contains both the primary key of the Book entity class (BookId) and the primary key of the Author entity class (AuthorId). You also add an Order property, which contains a number setting the order in which the Authors should be displayed for this book. The Book-Author linking entity class also contains two one-to-one relationships to the Author and the Book.
- You add a navigational property called AuthorsLink of type ICollection <BookAuthor> to your Book entity class.
- You also add a navigational property called BooksLink of type ICollection <BookAuthor> to your Author entity class.

These three entity classes are shown in figure 3.5, with only the Book to BookAuthor and BookAuthor to Author links shown.

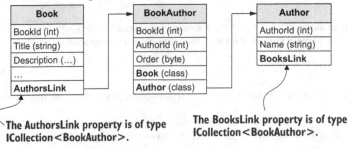

This sort of many-to-many relationship allows you access the BookAuthor linking table in an Include or query. This allows you to access sort/filter data in the linking table, in this example sorting on the Order property.

Book	BookAuthor	Author
BookId (int)	BookId (int)	AuthorId (int)
Title (string)	AuthorId (int)	Name (string)
Description (...)	Order (byte)	**BooksLink**
...	**Book** (class)	
AuthorsLink	**Author** (class)	

The AuthorsLink property is of type ICollection<BookAuthor>.

The BooksLink property is of type ICollection<BookAuthor>.

Figure 3.5 The Book to its Authors many-to-many relationship, which uses a BookAuthor linking table. Because you create a one-to-many link to the BookAuthor entity class, you can access the Order property to sort the order in which the Author names should be shown to the customer.

The `BookAuthor` entity class, shown in figure 3.5, has two properties: `BookId` `AuthorId`. These properties are foreign keys to the Books table and the Authors t respectively. Together, they also form the primary key (known as a *composit* because it has more than one part) for the `BookAuthor` row. The composite ke the effect of ensuring that there's only one link between the `Book` and the `Aut` Chapter 7 covers composite keys in more detail. In addition, the `BookAuthor` e class also has an `Order` property, which allows you to define the order of the Au entity classes so that the `Author`'s `Name` property will be shown in the Book book list.

As an example, you will add the author Martin Fowler as an extra author to *Quantum Networking book* via the `BookAuthor` linking entity class. (I'm sure that M Fowler would love to collaborate on this book if he's around when quantum netv ing is perfected.) You set the `Order` property to `1` to make Martin Fowler the se author. (The existing `BookAuthor` entity for the current `Author` has the `Order` erty set to `0`.) The next listing shows the resulting code.

Listing 3.19 Adding a new `Author` to the book *Quantum Networking*

```
var book = context.Books
    .Include(p => p.AuthorsLink)
    .Single(p => p.Title == "Quantum Networking");
```
This code finds the book w title "Quantum Networkin; current author is "Future

```
var existingAuthor = context.Authors
    .Single(p => p.Name == "Martin Fowler");
```
You find an existing author—in this case, "Martin Fowler."

```
book.AuthorsLink.Add(new BookAuthor
{
    Book = book,
    Author = existingAuthor,
    Order = (byte) book.AuthorsLink.Count
});
context.SaveChanges();
```
You add a new BookAutho linking entity to the Book' AuthorsLink collection.

You fill in the two navigational properties that are in the many-to-many relationship.

You set the Order to the old count of AuthorsLink—in this case, 1 (because the first author has a value of 0).

The SaveChanges will create a new row in the BookAuthor table.

The thing to understand is that the `BookAuthor` entity class is the *many* side o relationship. This listing, which adds another author to one of the books, sh look familiar because it's similar to the one-to-many update methods I've alr explained.

One thing to note is that when you load the Book's `AuthorsLink`, you don't to load the corresponding `BooksLink` in the `Author` entity class. The reason is when you update the `AuthorsLink` collection, EF Core knows that there is a link t `Book`, and during the update, EF Core will fill in that link automatically. The next someone loads the `Author` entity class and its `BooksLink` relationship, they'll see a to the *Quantum Networking* book in that collection. (See section 6.2.2 for a det review of what links are filled in when.)

Also be aware that deleting an `AuthorsLink` entry won't delete the `Book` or `Author` entities they link to because that entry is the *one* end of a one-to-many relationship, which isn't dependent on the `Book` or `Author`. In fact, the `Book` and `Author` entity classes are *principal entities*, with the `BookAuthor` classes being dependent on both of the principal entity classes.

UPDATING A MANY-TO-MANY RELATIONSHIP WITH DIRECT ACCESS TO THE OTHER ENTITY

EF Core 5 added the ability to access another entity class directly in a many-to-many relationship. This ability makes it much easier to set up and use the many-to-many relationship, but you won't be able to access the linking table in an `Include` method.

> **EF6** In EF6.x, you can define a many-to-many relationship, and EF6.x will create a hidden linking table for you and handle all the creation/deletion of the rows in that table. EF Core 5 adds that ability, but now you have much better control of configuration of the linking table.

In the Book App, a book can have zero to many categories, such as Linux, Databases, and Microsoft .NET, to help a customer find the right book. These categories are held in a `Tag` entity (the `TagId` holds the category name) with a direct many-to-many relationship to a `Book`. This allows the `Book` to show its categories in the Book App's book list display and also allows the Book App to provide a feature to filter the book list display by a category. Figure 3.6 shows the `Book` and `Tag` entity classes with their properties that link directly to one another.

This sort of many-to-many relationship is much easier to use because you can access the other side of the relationship (Tags, in this example) directly, and EF Core handles creating the linking entity class and its table.

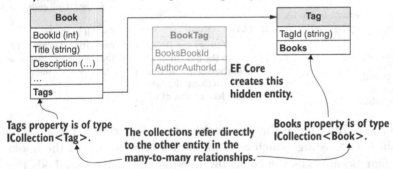

Figure 3.6 A direct many-to-many relationship between the `Book` entity class and the `Tag` entity class. You can access each end of the many-to-many relationship. EF Core builds a hidden entity class when it sees this sort of many-to-many relationship and creates the correct database code to use the associated linking table.

This direct-access many-to-many feature makes adding/deleting links between the `Book` entity and the `Tag` entities simple. The following listing shows how you would add another `Tag` to the *Quantum Networking* Book.

You add the Tag to the Books Tags collection.

```
var book = context.Books                        Finds the book with the
    .Include(p => p.Tags)                        "Quantum Networking"
    .Single(p => p.Title == "Quantum Networking"); loads it with its Tags

var existingTag = context.Tags                   You find the Tag called "Edit
    .Single(p => p.TagId == "Editor's Choice");  Choice" to add this book.

book.Tags.Add(existingTag);      When SaveChanges is called, EF Core creates
context.SaveChanges();           a new row in the hidden BookTags table.
```

If you compare the previous listing (listing 3.20) with adding another `Author`
`Book` in listing 3.19, you'll see that it's much easier to add a new entry to a direct n
to-many relationship. EF Core takes on the work of creating the necessary row in
BooksTag table. And if you removed an entry in the `Tags` collection, you would d
the corresponding row in the BooksTag table.

ALTERNATIVE WAY OF UPDATING THE RELATIONSHIP: CREATING A NEW ROW DIRECTLY
Having described how to update the two types of many-to-many relationships, no
discuss another approach: creating the linking table row directly. The benefit of
approach is better performance when you have lots of entries in the collection.

Rather than having to read in the collection, you can create a new entry in the
ing table. You could create a `BookAuthor` entity class and fill in the `Book` and Au
one-to-one relationships in that class, for example. Then you `Add` that new BookAu
entity instance to the database and call `SaveChanges`. For the `AuthorsLink` collec
which is likely to be small, this technique is most likely not worth the extra effort
for many-to-many relationships that contain lots of linking entries, it can signific
improve performance.

3.4.5 Advanced feature: Updating relationships via foreign keys

Up to this point, I've shown you how to update relationships by using the entity c
themselves. When you added a review to a book, for example, you loaded the
entity with all its `Reviews`. That's fine, but in a disconnected state, you have to loa
`Book` and all its `Reviews` from the book's primary key that came back from
browser/RESTful API. In many situations, you can cut out the loading of the e
classes and set the foreign keys instead.

This technique applies to most of the disconnected updates I've shown so far
let me give you an example of moving a review from one book to another. (I kno
this scenario is unlikely in the real world. But it makes for a simple example.) The
lowing listing carries out the update after the user types the request. The
assumes that the `ReviewId` of the `Review` the user wants to change and the new Bo
that they want to attach the review to are returned in a variable called `dto`.

Listing 3.21   Updating the foreign key to change a relationship

```
var reviewToChange = context
    .Find<Review>(dto.ReviewId);
reviewToChange.BookId = dto.NewBookId;
context.SaveChanges();
```

Finds the review that you want to move by using the primary key returned from the browser

Changes the foreign key in the review to point to the book it should be linked to

Calls SaveChanges, which finds the foreign key in the review changed, so it updates that column in the database

The benefit of this technique is that you don't have to load the Book entity class or use an Include command to load all the Reviews associated with this book. In our example Book App, these entities aren't too big, but in a real application, the principal and dependent entities could be quite large. (Some Amazon products have thousands of reviews, for example.) In disconnected systems, in which we often send only the primary keys over the disconnect, this approach can be useful for cutting down on database accesses and, hence, improving performance.

> **NOTE** When updating relationships via foreign keys, you may need to access entities that don't have a DbSet<T> property in the application's DbContext, so how can you read in the data? Listing 3.21 uses the Find<T> method, but if you need a more complex query, you can access any entity via the Set<T> method, such as context.Set<Review>().Where(p => p.NumVotes > 5).

Deleting entities

The final way to change the data in the database is to delete a row from a table. Deleting data is easier than making the updates we've already discussed, but it does have a few points to be aware of. Before I describe how to delete entities from the database, I want to introduce an approach called *soft delete*, in which an entity is hidden instead of deleted.

> **NOTE** I have some extra information about using soft delete in section 6.1.7, which covers certain situations in real applications.

Soft-delete approach: Using a global query filter to hide entities

One school of thought says that you shouldn't delete anything from a database but use a status to hide it, known as a soft delete. (See Udi Dahan's post "Don't Delete—Just Don't" at http://mng.bz/6glD.) I think this approach is a sensible one, and EF Core provides a feature called global query filter that allows a soft delete to be implemented simply.

The thinking behind a soft delete is that in real-world applications, data doesn't stop being data; it transforms into another state. In the case of our books example, a book may not still be on sale, but the fact that the book existed isn't in doubt, so why delete it? Instead, you set a flag to say that the entity is to be hidden in all queries and

relationship. To see how this process works, you'll add the soft-delete feature to th
of Book entities. To do so, you need to do two things:

- *Add a* boolean *property called* SoftDeleted *to the* Book *entity class.* If that pro
  is true, the Book entity instance is soft-deleted; it shouldn't be found in a
  mal query.
- *Add a global query filter via EF Core's fluent configuration commands.* The effect
  apply an extra Where filter to any access to the Books table.

Adding the SoftDeleted property to a Book entity instance is straightforward.
code snippet shows the Book entity class with the SoftDeleted property:

```
public class Book
{
    //… other properties left out for clarity
    public bool SoftDeleted { get; set; }
}
```

Adding the global query filter to the DbSet<Book>Books property means adding a
Core configuration command to the application's DbContext. Chapter 7 covers
configuration command, but it's shown in bold in the following listing so that
have an idea of what's going on.

Listing 3.22   Adding a global query filter to the DbSet<Book>Books property

```
public class EfCoreContext : DbContext
{
    //… Other parts removed for clarity

    protected override void
        OnModelCreating(ModelBuilder modelBuilder)
    {
        //… other configration parts removed for clarity

        modelBuilder.Entity<Book>()                          ◁─┐  Adds a filter to all accesse
            .HasQueryFilter(p => !p.SoftDeleted);            ◁─┘  the Book entities. You can
    }                                                             bypass this filter by using
}                                                                 IgnoreQueryFilters operat
```

To soft-delete a Book entity, you need to set the SoftDeleted property to true and
SaveChanges. Then any query on the Book entities will exclude the Book entities
have the SoftDeleted property set to true.

   If you want to access all the entities that have a model-level filter, you add
IgnoreQueryFilters method to the query, such as context.Books.IgnoreQu
Filters(). This method bypasses any query filter on that entity.

> **NOTE** I have built a library called EfCore.SoftDeleteServices that provides
> a code for both configuring and using this form of soft delete. See http://
> mng.bz/op7r for more information.

Now that we've covered the soft-delete approach, let's cover the ways to truly delete an entity from the database. We'll start with a straightforward example and work up to deleting an entity that has relationships.

Deleting a dependent-only entity with no relationships

I've chosen the `PriceOffer` entity class to show a basic delete because it's a dependent entity. Therefore, you can delete it without affecting other entities. This listing finds a `PriceOffer` and then deletes it.

> **Listing 3.23 Removing (deleting) an entity from the database**

```
var promotion = context.PriceOffers          Finds the first
    .First();                                 PriceOffer

context.Remove(promotion);          ◄──    Removes that PriceOffer from the
context.SaveChanges();              ◄──┐    application's DbContext. The DbContext
SaveChanges calls DetectChanges, which finds   works out what to remove based on its
a tracked PriceOffer entity marked as deleted   parameter type.
     and then deletes it from the database.
```

Calling the `Remove` method sets the `State` of the entity provided as the parameter to `Deleted`. Then, when you call `SaveChanges`, EF Core finds the entity marked as `Deleted` and creates the correct database commands to delete the appropriate row from the table the entity referred to (in this case, a row in the PriceOffers table). The SQL command that EF Core produces for SQL Server is shown in the following snippet:

```
SET NOCOUNT ON;
DELETE FROM [PriceOffers]
WHERE [PriceOfferId] = @p0;
SELECT @@ROWCOUNT;
```

Deleting a principal entity that has relationships

Section 3.3.1 discussed principal and dependent relationships and the nullability of the foreign key. Relational databases need to keep *referential integrity*, so if you delete a row in a table that other rows are pointing to via a foreign key, something has to happen to stop referential integrity from being lost.

> **DEFINITION** *Referential integrity* is a relational database concept indicating that table relationships must always be consistent. Any foreign-key field must agree with the primary key referenced by the foreign key (see http://mng.bz/XY0M).

Following are three ways that you can set a database to keep referential integrity when you delete a principal entity with dependent entities:

- You can tell the database server to delete the dependent entities that rely on the principal entity, known as *cascade deletes*.

- You can tell the database server to set the foreign keys of the dependent en‌ to null, if the column allows that.
- If neither of those rules is set up, the database server will raise an error if yo‌ to delete a principal entity with dependent entities.

3.5.4 Deleting a book with its dependent relationships

In this section, you're going to delete a Book entity, which is a principal entity‌ three dependent relationships: Promotion, Reviews, and AuthorsLink. These ‌ dependent entities can't exist without the Book entity; a non-nullable foreign key‌ these dependent entities to a specific Book row.

By default, EF Core uses cascade deletes for dependent relationships with‌ nullable foreign keys. Cascade deletes make deleting principal entities easier fron‌ developer's point of view, because the other two rules need extra code to handle c‌ ing the dependent entities. But in many business applications, this approach ma‌ be appropriate. This chapter uses the cascade delete approach because it's EF C‌ default for non-nullable foreign keys.

With that caveat in mind, let's see cascade delete in action by using the de‌ cascade-delete setting to delete a Book that has relationships. This listing load‌ Promotion (PriceOffer entity class), Reviews, AuthorsLink, and Tags relation‌ with the Book entity class before deleting that Book.

Listing 3.24 Deleting a book that has three dependent entity classes

```
var book = context.Books
    .Include(p => p.Promotion)
    .Include(p => p.Reviews)
    .Include(p => p.AuthorsLink)
    .Include(p => p.Tags)
    .Single(p => p.Title
            == "Quantum Networking");

context.Books.Remove(book);
context.SaveChanges();
```

The four Includes make sure that the four dependent relationships are loaded with the Book.

Finds the Quantum Networking book, which you know has a promotion, two reviews, one BookAuthor link, and one BookTag

Deletes that book

SaveChanges calls DetectChanges, which finds a tracked Book entity marked as deleted, deletes its dependent relationships, and then deletes the book.

My test data contains a book with the title *Quantum Networking*, which has one Pr‌ Offer, two Reviews, and a BookAuthor entity associated with it. The foreign keys ‌ those dependent entities I mentioned point to the *Quantum Networking* book. ‌ the code in listing 3.24 has run, EF Core deletes the Book, the PriceOffer, the‌ Reviews, the single BookAuthor link, and the single (hidden) BookTag.

That last statement, indicating that all are deleted by EF Core, is an impor‌ point. Because you put in the four Includes, EF Core knew about the dependent‌ ties and performed the delete. If you didn't incorporate the Includes in your c‌ EF Core wouldn't know about the dependent entities and couldn't delete the t‌ dependent entities. In that case, the problem of keeping referential integrity w‌

fall to the database server, and its response would depend on how the DELETE ON part of the foreign-key constraint was set up. Databases created by EF Core for these entity classes would, by default, be set to use cascade deletes.

NOTE The Author and Tag linked to the Book aren't deleted because they are not dependent entities of the Book; only the BookAuthor and BookTag linking entities are deleted. This arrangement makes sense because the Author and Tag might be used on other Books.

Section 8.8.1 shows how to configure the way that EF Core handles the deletion of a dependent entity in a relationship. Sometimes, it's useful to stop a principal entity from being deleted if a certain dependent entity is linked to it. In our example Book App, for example, if a customer orders a book, you want to keep that order information even if the book is no longer for sale. In this case, you change the EF Core's on-delete action to Restrict and remove the ON DELETE CASCADE from the foreign-key constraint in the database so that an error will be raised if an attempt to delete the book is made.

NOTE When you're deleting a principal entity with a dependent entity that has a nullable foreign key (known as an *optional dependent relationship*), subtle differences exist between the way that EF Core handles the delete and the way that the database handles the delete. I explain this situation in section 8.8.1 via a useful table 8.1.

Summary

- Entity instances have a State, whose values can be Added, Unchanged, Modified, Deleted, or Detached. This State defines what happens to the entity when SaveChanges is called.
- If you Add an entity, its State is set to Added. When you call SaveChanges, that entity is written out to the database as a new row.
- You can update a property, or properties, in an entity class by loading the entity class as a tracked entity, changing the property/properties, and calling SaveChanges.
- Real-world applications use two types of update scenarios—connected and disconnected state—that affect the way you perform the update.
- EF Core has an Update method, which marks the whole of the entity class as updated. You can use this method when you want to update the entity class and have all the data already available to you.
- When you're updating a relationship, you have two options, with different advantages and disadvantages:
  - You can load the existing relationship with the primary entity and update that relationship in the primary entity. EF Core will sort things out from there. This option is easier to use but can create performance issues when you're dealing with large collections.

- You can create, update, or delete the dependent entity. This approa⟩ harder to get right but typically is faster because you don't need to loa⟨ existing relationships.

- To delete an entity from the database, you use the Remove method, followe⟨ the SaveChanges method.

For EF6.x readers:

- The Update method is a welcome new command in EF Core. In EF6.x, you to use DbContext.Entry(object).State to achieve that feature.

- EF Core provides shorthand for Add, Update, and Remove. You can apply a these commands to the context itself, as in context.Add(book).

- In EF6.x, by default, SaveChanges validates the data before adding an ent⟩ or updating an entity in the database. EF Core doesn't run any validatio⟨ SaveChanges, but it's easy to add back (see chapter 4).

- EF6.x allows you to define many-to-many relationships directly and looks creating the linking table and managing the rows to make that process ⟨ NET Core 5 adds this feature to EF Core; section 3.4.4 covers this topic.

Using EF Core in business logic

This chapter covers

- Understanding business logic and its use of EF Core
- Looking at three types of business logic, from the easy to the complex
- Reviewing each type of business logic, with pros and cons
- Adding a step that validates the data before it's written to the database
- Using transactions to daisy-chain code sequences

Real-world applications are built to supply a set of services, ranging from holding a simple list of things on your computer to managing a nuclear reactor. Every real-world problem has a set of rules, often referred to as *business rules*, or by the more generic name *domain rules*. (This book uses *business rules*.)

The code you write to implement a business rule is known as *business logic* or *domain logic*. Because business rules can be complex, the business logic you write can also be complex. Just think about all the checks and steps that should be done when you order something online.

Business logic can range from a simple check of status to massive artificial ir
gence (AI) code, but in nearly all cases, business logic needs access to a data
Although all the approaches in chapters 2 and 3 come into play, the way you z
those EF Core commands in business logic can be a little different, which is wh
written this chapter.

This chapter describes a pattern for handling business logic that compartme
izes some of the complexity to reduce the load on you, the developer. You'll also l
several techniques for writing different types of business logic that use EF Co
access the database. These techniques range from using software classes for valid
to standardizing your business logic's interface to make frontend code simpler.
overall aim is to help you quickly write accurate, understandable, and well-perfori
business logic.

4.1 The questions to ask and the decisions you need to make before you start coding

Our CRUD code in chapters 2 and 3 adapted and transformed data as it moved
and out of the database. Some of that code was complex, and I showed you the Ç
Object pattern to make a large query more manageable. Similarly, business logic
range from the simple to the complex.

> **DEFINITION** In this chapter, I use the term *business rule* to represent a human-
> readable statement of some logic that needs to be implemented, such as "The
> price of a book cannot be negative." I also use the term *business logic,* which is
> the code that implements all the business rules needed for a particular fea-
> ture in the application.

Before you start working on your business logic, you should think about the answe
some questions:

- Do you understand the business rules for the feature you're implementing
- Do the business rules make sense, or are they incomplete?
- Are there any edge cases or exceptions that you need to cover?
- How can you prove that your implementation matches the business rules?
- How easy will it be to change your code if the business rules change?

4.1.1 The three levels of complexity of your business logic code

When you have some grasp of the business rules you need to implement, you sh
have some idea of how complex the business logic is. Most of the rules are going t
simple to write, but a few are going to be really complex. The trick is to implemen
simple business logic quickly but use a more structured approach for the more
plex business logic.

Based on my experiences, I created a list of three levels of complexity of
ness logic with different patterns for each level: validation, simple, and comp

The following three sections describe these three levels of complexity and how they will affect the code you write. But be aware that these three patterns aren't strict rules. Some business rules may be simple, but you may decide to use a more complex pattern because it's easier to unit-test. Nevertheless, this list is useful for discussing the types and patterns you can use for writing business logic.

VALIDATION CODE TO CHECK THE DATA USED TO CHANGE AN ENTITY CLASS

When you work with CUD (create, update, and delete) code, as in chapter 3, you may need to check whether the data is in a certain range. The Review's NumStars property must be in the range 0 to 5, for example. This sort of test is known as *validation*. For me, validation is the starting point for calling the code *business logic* instead of *CRUD code*.

This type of business logic is common; you see it everywhere (see the nearby sidebar "Does all the business logic code live in a specific business logic layer?" before section 4.2). The simplest validation business logic normally uses if-then statements that test data values, but a useful set of attributes called Data Annotations can automate some of the validation code you need to write. (You will see Data Annotations later, in section 4.7.1.)

But there are lots of levels of validation, from simple range checking to validating that a person's driving license is valid via some sort of checking service, which makes defining this starting level of business logic more difficult. But as I said at the start, these levels are guidelines, and the "check person's driving license" validation example would elevate that code to the next level of business logic.

SIMPLE BUSINESS LOGIC (THAT IS, LITTLE OR NO BRANCHING AND EASY TO UNDERSTAND)

The next type is business logic that has little or no branching—that is, few or no if-then branching statements and no calling out to other business code. The code is easy to understand because you can read it and see every step that has to be executed in order. A good example would be code to create a book with its authors—that needs code to create the Book, then find or create the Authors, and finally add the Book-Author linking entity classes. The code is simple, with no branching, but it still takes many lines of code to create a book with its authors.

I am always surprised by how much "simple" business logic like this there is in a real application; typically, I find that a lot of admin functions fall into this category. Therefore, having a simple pattern for building and checking this type of business logic is crucial to you for building your code quickly.

COMPLEX BUSINESS LOGIC (THAT IS, CODE THAT NEEDS SERIOUS EFFORT TO WRITE CORRECTLY)

I call the hardest business logic to write *complex*. There isn't a good definition of this term, but for this type of code, you need to think hard about the problem before you can implement it. Here's a quote from one of the leading books on writing business logic, which portrays the challenge of writing complex business code:

> *The heart of software is its ability to solve domain (business)-related problems for its users.*
> *All other features, vital though they may be, support this basic purpose. When the domain*

is complex, this is a difficult task, calling for the concentrated effort of talented and skilled people.

—Eric Evans, *Domain-Driven Design*[1]

This type of business logic is complex enough that I have developed a struct approach that isolates the business logic from the database and the frontend. way, I can concentrate on the pure business problem—another application of the aration of Concerns principle (which I talk about in detail in section 5.5.2).

Does all the business logic code live in a specific business logic layer?

No. In real-world applications, especially ones that interact with a human being, y want the user experience to be as good as possible. For that reason, some busine logic lives in the presentation layer.

The obvious logic to go into the presentation layer is validation business log because the earlier you can give feedback to the user, the better. Most frontend sy tems have built-in features that facilitate validation and good feedback of errors the user.

Another area is business logic that has many steps. Often, it's better for the us when complex business logic flows are shown as a sequence of pages or steps ir wizard.

Even in the backend of an application, I spread my business logic over several laye (that is, projects) in my Book App. I explain how and why I do that in this chapter.

4.2 Complex business logic example: Processing an order for books

I start with the complex business logic because that logic will introduce you to a erful approach to handling business—an approach taken from Eric Evan's Domain-Driven design, which I quote in the preceding section. First, though, ta look at a complex business feature that you'll want to implement in the Book The example you'll build is handling a user's order for books. Figure 4.1 show checkout page of the Book App. You're going to implement the code that runs v the user clicks the Purchase button.

NOTE You can try the checkout process by downloading the Book App code from the associated Git repo and running it locally. The Book App uses an HTTP cookie to hold your basket and your identity (which saves you from having to log in). No money is needed; as the terms and conditions text says, you aren't actually going to buy a book.

---

[1] *Domain-Driven Design: Tackling Complexity in the Heart of Software* (Addison-Wesley Professional, 2003)

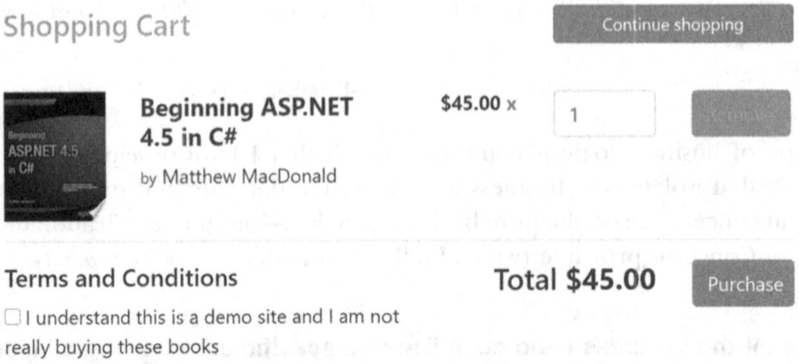

Shopping Cart

Continue shopping

Beginning ASP.NET 4.5 in C#

by Matthew MacDonald

$45.00 × 1

Terms and Conditions

☐ I understand this is a demo site and I am not really buying these books

Total $45.00   Purchase

Figure 4.1 The checkout page of the Book App. When the user clicks the Buy Book button next to a book, the app adds the book to their basket and then displays the Checkout page, which shows all the books in the user's basket. Clicking the Purchase button calls the business logic that creates the order, which is the code we are going to write.

Using a design pattern to implement complex business logic

Before you start writing code to process an order, take a look at a pattern that will help you write, test, and performance-tune your business logic. The pattern is based on the Domain-Driven Design (DDD) concepts expounded by Eric Evans, but the business logic code isn't inside the entity classes. This pattern is known as a *transactions script* or *procedural* pattern of business logic because the code is contained in a standalone method.

This procedural pattern is easy to understand and uses the basic EF Core commands you have already seen. But many people see the procedural approach as being a DDD antipattern, known as an *anemic domain model* (see http://mng.bz/nM7g). Later, in part 3 of this book, you will extend this approach to a fully DDD design.

This section and chapter 13 present my interpretation of Evans' DDD approach and plenty of other ways to apply DDD with EF. Although I offer my approach, which I hope will help you, don't be afraid to look for other approaches.

Five guidelines for building business logic that uses EF Core

The following list explains the five guidelines that make up the business logic pattern you'll be using in this chapter. Most of the pattern comes from DDD concepts, but some is the result of writing lots of complex business logic and seeing areas to improve:

- *The business logic has first call on how the database structure is defined.* Because the problem you're trying to solve (which Evans calls the *domain model*) is the heart of the problem, the logic should define the way the whole application is designed.

Therefore, you try to make the database structure and the entity classes m your business logic data needs as much as you can.

- *The business logic should have no distractions.* Writing the business logic is dif enough in itself, so you isolate it from all the other application layers other the entity classes. When you write the business logic, you must think only a the business problem you're trying to fix. You leave the task of adapting data for presentation to the service layer in your application.

- *Business logic should think that it's working on in-memory data.* Evans taught n write business logic as though the data is in memory. You need to have some and *save* parts, of course, but for the core of your business logic, treat the da much as is practical) as though it's a normal, in-memory class or collection.

- *Isolate the database access code into a separate project.* This rule came out of wr an e-commerce application with complex pricing and delivery rules. Before used EF directly in my business logic, but I found that it was hard to mai and difficult to performance-tune. Instead, you should use another proje companion to the business logic, to hold all the database access code.

- *The business logic shouldn't call EF Core's* SaveChanges *directly.* You should ha class in the service layer (or a custom library) whose job it is to run the bus logic. If there are no errors, this class calls SaveChanges. The main reaso this rule is to have control of whether to write out the data, but it has other efits, which I'll describe in section 4.4.5.

Figure 4.2 shows the application structure you'll create to help you apply these g lines when implementing business logic. In this case, you'll add two new projec the original Book App structure described in chapter 2:

- The pure business logic project, which holds the business logic classes work on the in-memory data provided by the companion business data access methods.

- The business database access project, which provides a companion clas each pure business logic class that needs database access. Each companion makes the pure business logic class think that it's working on an in-memo of data.

Figure 4.2 has five numbers, with comments, that match the five guidelines.

4.4 Implementing the business logic for processing an order

Now that I've described the business need, with its business rules, and the pa you're going to use, you're ready to write code. The aim is to break the impleme tion into smaller steps that focus on specific parts of the problem at hand. You' how this business logic pattern helps you to focus on each part of the implement in turn.

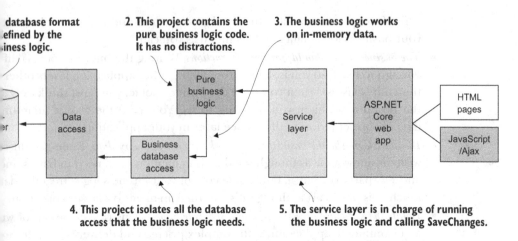

database format | **2. This project contains the** | **3. The business logic works**
efined by the | **pure business logic code.** | **on in-memory data.**
iness logic. | **It has no distractions.**

4. This project isolates all the database | **5. The service layer is in charge of running**
access that the business logic needs. | **the business logic and calling SaveChanges.**

4.2 The projects inside our Book App, with two new projects for handling complex business logic. The
business logic" project contains the isolated business logic, which thinks it is working on an in-memory
classes. The "Business database access" project provides an interface that the pure business logic can
access the database. The service layer's job is to adapt the data from the ASP.NET Core application to
o the pure business logic in the form it wants that data to be in and call the final SaveChanges to save
usiness logic doesn't report any errors.

You're going to implement the code in sections that match the five guidelines listed in
section 4.3.1. At the end, you'll see how this combined code is called from the
ASP.NET Core application that the Book App is using.

Guideline 1: Business logic has first call on defining the database structure

This guideline says that the design of the database should follow the business needs—
in this case, represented by six business rules. Only three of these rules are relevant to
the database design:

- An order must include at least one book (implying that there can be more).
- The price of the book must be copied to the order, because the price could
  change later.
- The order must remember the person who ordered the books.

These three rules dictates an Order entity class that has a collection of LineItem entity
classes—a one-to-many relationship. The Order entity class holds the information
about the person placing the order, and each LineItem entity class holds a reference
to the book order, how many, and at what price.

Figure 4.3 shows what these two tables, LineItem and Orders, look like in the database. To make the image more understandable, I show the Books table (in gray) that
each LineItem row references.

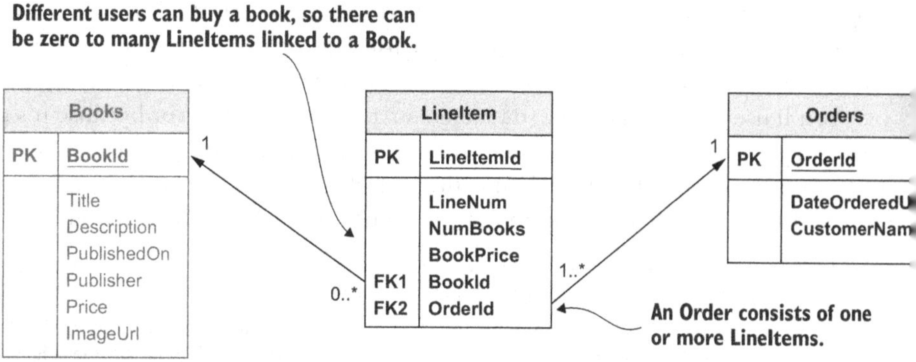

Different users can buy a book, so there can be zero to many LineItems linked to a Book.

Books			LineItem			Orders	
PK	BookId		PK	LineItemId		PK	OrderId
	Title			LineNum			DateOrderedU
	Description			NumBooks			CustomerNam
	PublishedOn			BookPrice			
	Publisher		FK1	BookId			
	Price		FK2	OrderId			
	ImageUrl						

Figure 4.3   The new LineItem and Orders tables added to allow orders for books to be taken. There one Orders row per purchase, with a lineItem row for each Book in the order.

> **NOTE**   The Orders table name is plural because you added a DbSet<Order>
> Orders property to the application's DbContext, and by default, EF Core uses
> the property name, Orders, as the table name. You haven't added a property
> for the LineItem entity class because it's accessed via the Order's relational
> link. In that case, EF Core, by default, uses the class name, LineItem, as the
> table name. You can set the table name to a specific name; see section 7.11.1.

4.4.2   Guideline 2: Business logic should have no distractions

Now you're at the heart of the business logic code, and the code here will do m
the work. This code is going to be the hardest part of the implementation tha
write, but you want to help yourself by cutting off any distractions. That way, you
stay focused on the problem.

To do so, write the pure business code with reference to only two other parts o
system: the entity classes shown in figure 4.3 (Order, LineItem, and Book) and
companion class that will handle all the database accesses. Even with this minim
tion of scope, you're still going to break the job into a few parts.

CHECKING FOR ERRORS AND FEEDING THEM BACK TO THE USER: VALIDATION

The business rules contain several checks, such as "The Terms and Conditions
must be ticked." The rules also say that you need to give good feedback to the us
that they can fix any problems and complete their purchase. These sorts of ch
called *validation*, are common throughout an application.

You have two main approaches to handling the passing of errors back up to hi
levels. One is to throw an exception when an error occurs, and the other is to
back the errors to the caller via a status interface. Each option has its own advan
and disadvantages. This example uses the second approach: passing the errors ba
some form of status class to the higher level to check.

To help, you'll create a small abstract class called BizActionErrors, shown in
ing 4.1. This class provides a common error-handling interface for all your bus

logic. The class contains a C# method called `AddError` that the business logic can call to add an error and an *immutable list* (a list that can't be changed) called `Errors`, which holds all the validation errors found while running the business logic.

You'll use a class called `ValidationResult` to store each error because it's the standard way of returning errors with optional, additional information on the exact property the error was related to. Using the `ValidationResult` class instead of a simple string fits with another validation method you'll add later in this chapter.

Listing 4.1   Abstract base class providing error handling for your business logic

```
public abstract class BizActionErrors          ◁——  Abstract class that provides
{                                                     error handling for business logic

    private readonly List<ValidationResult> _errors       Holds the list of validation
        = new List<ValidationResult>();                   errors privately

    public IImmutableList<ValidationResult>        Provides a public,
        Errors => _errors.ToImmutableList();       immutable list of errors

    public bool HasErrors => _errors.Any();        ◁——  Creates a bool
                                                         HasErrors to
    protected void AddError(string errorMessage,         make checking
        params string[] propertyNames)                   for errors easier
    {
        _errors.Add( new ValidationResult              Allows a simple error
            (errorMessage, propertyNames));            message, or an error
    }                                                  message with properties
}                          Validation result has an error    linked to it, to be added
                           message and a possibly empty list  to the errors list
                           of properties it's linked to
```

Using this abstract class means that your business logic is easier to write and all your business logic has a consistent way of handling errors. The other advantage is that you can change the way errors are handled internally without having to change any of your business logic code.

Your business logic for handling an order does a lot of validation, which is typical for an order, because it often involves money. Other business logic may not do any validation, but the base class `BizActionErrors` will automatically return a `HasErrors` of `false`, which means that all business logic can be dealt with in the same way.

Guideline 3: Business logic should think that it's working on in-memory data

Now you'll start on the main class: `PlaceOrderAction`, which contains the pure business logic. This class relies on the companion class `PlaceOrderDbAccess` to present the data as an in-memory set (in this case, a dictionary) and to write the created order to the database. Although you're not trying to hide the database from the pure business logic, you do want it to work as though the data is normal .NET classes.

Listing 4.2 shows the `PlaceOrderAction` class, which inherits the abstract `BizActionErrors` to handle returning error messages to the user. It also use methods that the companion `PlaceOrderDbAccess` class provides:

- `FindBooksByIdsWithPriceOffers`—Takes the list of `BookIds` and returns ; tionary with the `BookId` as the key and the `Book` entity class as the value and associated `PriceOffers`
- `Add`—Adds the `Order` entity class with its `LineItem` collection to the databa

Listing 4.2 `PlaceOrderAction` class with build-a-new-order business logic

```
public class PlaceOrderAction :            The BizActionErrors class provides
   BizActionErrors,          ◄────         error handling for the business logic.
   IBizAction<PlaceOrderInDto,Order>   ◄────────
{                                                   The IBizAction interface
                                                    the business logic confo
   private readonly IPlaceOrderDbAccess _dbAccess;  standard interface.

   public PlaceOrderAction(IPlaceOrderDbAccess dbAccess)   ◄──    The Place●
   {                                                              uses Place
       _dbAccess = dbAccess;                                      DbAccess ●
   }                                                              handle da●
                                                                  accesses.
   public Order Action(PlaceOrderInDto dto)   ◄─
   {                                                    This method is called●
       if (!dto.AcceptTAndCs)                           the BizRunner to exe●
       {                                                this business logic.
           AddError(
"You must accept the T&Cs to place an order.");
           return null;
       }                                        Some basic
       if (!dto.LineItems.Any())                validation
       {
           AddError("No items in your basket.");
           return null;
       }

       var booksDict =                                      The PlaceOrderDb●
           _dbAccess.FindBooksByIdsWithPriceOffers          finds all the bough●
               (dto.LineItems.Select(x => x.BookId));       with optional Pric●
       var order = new Order
       {                                           Creates the Order, using
           CustomerId = dto.UserId,                FormLineItemsWithError
           LineItems =                             Checking to create the
               FormLineItemsWithErrorChecking      LineItems
                   (dto.LineItems, booksDict)
       };

       if (!HasErrors)                  Adds the order to the database
           _dbAccess.Add(order);        only if there are no errors

       return HasErrors ? null : order;   ◄──   If there are errors, returns nu●
   }                                            otherwise, returns the order
}
```

```
    private List<LineItem>  FormLineItemsWithErrorChecking       This private method
        (IEnumerable<OrderLineItem> lineItems,                   handles the creation
         IDictionary<int,Book> booksDict)                        of each LineItem for
                                                                 each book ordered.
    {
        var result = new List<LineItem>();
        var i = 1;                                            Goes through each
                                                              book type that the
        foreach (var lineItem in lineItems)                   person ordered
        {
            if (!booksDict.
                ContainsKey(lineItem.BookId))                  Treats a missing book
                    throw new InvalidOperationException       as a system error and
  ("An order failed because book, " +                          throws an exception
  $"id = {lineItem.BookId} was missing.");

            var book = booksDict[lineItem.BookId];           Calculates the
            var bookPrice =                                   price at the time
                book.Promotion?.NewPrice ?? book.Price;       of the order
            if (bookPrice <= 0)                               More validation that
                AddError(                                     checks whether the
  $"Sorry, the book '{book.Title}' is not for sale.");        book can be sold
            else
            {
                //Valid, so add to the order
                result.Add(new LineItem
                {                                             Everything is OK, so
                    BookPrice = bookPrice,                    create the LineItem
                    ChosenBook = book,                        entity class with the
                    LineNum = (byte)(i++),                    details.
                    NumBooks = lineItem.NumBooks
                });
            }
        }
        return result;                                        Returns all
    }                                                         the LineItems
}                                                             for this order
```

You'll notice that you add another validation check to ensure that the book the user selected is still in the database. This check wasn't in the business rules, but it could occur, especially if malicious inputs were provided. In this case, you make a distinction between errors that the user can correct, which are returned by the `Errors` property, and system errors (in this case, a missing book), for which you throw an exception that the system should log.

You may have seen at the top of the class that you apply an interface in the form of `IBizAction<PlaceOrderInDto,Order>`. This interface ensures that this business logic class conforms to a standard interface that you use across all your business logic. You'll see this in section 4.7.1, when you create a generic class to run and check the business logic.

4.4.4 Guideline 4: Isolate the database access code into a separate project

Our guideline says to put all the database access code that the business logic nee a separate, companion class. This technique ensures that all the database accesse in one place, making testing, refactoring, and performance tuning much easier.

Another benefit that a reader of my blog noted is that this guideline can h you're working with an existing, older database. In this case, the database entities not be a good match for the business logic you want to write. If so, you can us BizDbAccess methods as an *Adapter pattern* that converts the older database stru to a form more easily processed by your business logic.

> **DEFINITION** The *Adapter pattern* converts the interface of a class to another interface that the client expects. This pattern lets classes work together that couldn't otherwise do so because of incompatible interfaces. See https:// sourcemaking.com/design_patterns/adapter.

You make sure that your pure business logic, class PlaceOrderAction, and bus database access class PlaceOrderDbAccess are in separate projects. That appr allows you to exclude any EF Core libraries from the pure business logic pr ensuring that all database access is done via the companion class, PlaceOrde Access. In my own projects, I split the entity classes into a separate project fron EF code. Then my pure business logic project doesn't have the Microsoft.Ent FrameworkCore NuGet library, so my business logic can't execute any database mands directly; it has to rely on the PlaceOrderDbAccess class for any data acces

For simplicity, the example code holds the entity classes in the same project a application's DbContext. Listing 4.3 shows our PlaceOrderDbAccess class, which in ments two methods to provide the database accesses that the pure business logic ne

- The FindBooksByIdsWithPriceOffers method, which finds and loads Book entity class, with any optional PriceOffer.
- The Add method, which adds the finished Order entity class to the applicat DbContext property, Orders, so that it can be saved to the database afte Core's SaveChanges method is called.

Listing 4.3 PlaceOrderDbAccess, which handles all the database accesses

```
public class PlaceOrderDbAccess : IPlaceOrderDbAccess
{
    private readonly EfCoreContext _context;

    public PlaceOrderDbAccess(EfCoreContext context)
    {
        _context = context;
    }

    public IDictionary<int, Book>
        FindBooksByIdsWithPriceOffers
```

All the BizDbAc need the applica DbContext to ac the database.

This method finds all the books that the user wants to buy.

```
                  (IEnumerable<int> bookIds)
    {
        return _context.Books
            .Where(x => bookIds.Contains(x.BookId))
            .Include(r => r.Promotion)
            .ToDictionary(key => key.BookId);
    }
}

public void Add(Order newOrder)
{
    _context.Add(newOrder);
}
}
```

Finds a book for each Id, using the LINQ Contains method to find all the keys

Includes any optional promotion, which the BizLogic needs for working out the price

Returns the result as a dictionary to make it easier for the BizLogic to look them up

The `PlaceOrderDbAccess` class implements an interface called `IPlaceOrderDbAccess`, which is how the `PlaceOrderAction` class accesses this class. In addition to helping with dependency injection, which is covered in chapter 5, using an interface allows you to replace the `PlaceOrderDbAccess` class with a test version—a process called *stubbing* or *mocking*—when you're unit-testing the `PlaceOrderAction` class. Section 17.7 covers this topic in more detail.

Guideline 5: Business logic shouldn't call EF Core's SaveChanges

The final rule says that the business logic doesn't call EF Core's `SaveChanges`, which would update the database directly. There are a few reasons for this rule:

- You consider the service layer to be the main orchestrator of database accesses: it's in command of what gets written to the database.
- The service layer calls `SaveChanges` only if the business logic returns no errors.

To help you run your business logic, I've built a series of simple classes that I use to run any business logic; I call these classes `BizRunners`. They're generic classes, able to run business logic with different input and output types. Different variants of the `Biz-Runner` can handle different input/output combinations and async methods (chapter 5 covers async/await with EF Core), as well as some with extra features, which are `PlaceOrderAction` (covered in section 4.7.3).

Each `BizRunner` works by defining a generic interface that the business logic must implement. Your class in the `BizLogic` project runs an action that expects a single input parameter of type `PlaceOrderInDto` and returns an object of type `Order`. Therefore, the `PlaceOrderAction` class implements the interface as shown in the following listing, but with its input and output types (`IBizAction<PlaceOrderInDto,Order>`).

Listing 4.4   The interface that allows the `BizRunner` to execute business logic

The BizAction uses the TIn and a TOut to define the input and output of the Action method.

```
public interface IBizAction<in TIn, out TOut>
{
    IImmutableList<ValidationResult>
        Errors { get; }
    bool HasErrors { get; }
```

Returns the error information from the business logic

```
    TOut Action(TIn dto);          ◄─────┐  The action that the
}                                         │  BizRunner will call
```

When you have the business logic class implement this interface, the BizR
knows how to run that code. The BizRunner itself is small, as you'll see in the fo
ing listing, which shows that it's called RunnerWriteDb<TIn, TOut>. This BizR
variant is designed to work with business logic that has an input, provides an ou
and writes to the database.

Listing 4.5 The `BizRunner` that runs the business logic and returns a result or er

```
public class RunnerWriteDb<TIn, TOut>
{
    private readonly IBizAction<TIn, TOut> _actionClass;
    private readonly EfCoreContext _context;

    public IImmutableList<ValidationResult>          Error information from
        \ Errors => _actionClass.Errors;             business logic is passe
    public bool HasErrors => _actionClass.HasErrors; to the user of the Biz▌

    public RunnerWriteDb(                            Handles business logic that conform
        IBizAction<TIn, TOut> actionClass,           to the IBizAction<TIn, TOut>
        EfCoreContext context)                       interface
    {
        _context = context;
        _actionClass = actionClass;
    }                                                Calls RunAction in your service lay
                                                     or in your presentation layer if the
    public TOut RunAction(TIn dataIn)       ◄──────┘ data comes back in the right form
    {
        var result = _actionClass.Action(dataIn);  ◄──────┤  Runs the business
        if (!HasErrors)                                    │  logic you gave it
            _context.SaveChanges();         ┐
        return result;          ◄───┐        │  If there are no errors, calls
    }                               │        │  SaveChanges to execute any
}                           Returns the result  add, update, or delete methods
                            that the business
                            logic returned
```

The BizRunner pattern hides the business logic and presents a common i
face/API that other classes can use. The caller of the BizRunner doesn't need to v
about EF Core, because all the calls to EF Core are in the BizDbAccess code or i
BizRunner. That fact in itself is reason enough to use the BizRunner pattern, b
you'll see later, this pattern allows you to create other forms of BizRunner that
extra features.

> **NOTE** You may want to check out an open-source library I created, called
> EfCore.GenericBizRunner, which provides the same features as the Biz-
> Runner but in a library. It uses generic classes that run your business logic
> without requiring you to write extra code. See http://mng.bz/vz7J for more
> information.

One important point about the BizRunner is that it should be the only method allowed to call SaveChanges during the lifetime of the application's DbContext. Why? The business logic isn't thinking about the database, so it's quite normal for the business logic to add or update an entity class at any time, and an error may be found later. To stop the changes made before the error was found from being written to the database, you're relying on SaveChanges to *not* be called during the lifetime of the application's DbContext.

In an ASP.NET application, controlling the lifetime of the application's DbContext is fairly easy to manage, because a new instance of the application's DbContext is created for each HTTP request. In longer-running applications, this situation is a problem. In the past, I've avoided it by making the BizRunner create a new, hidden instance of the application's DbContext so that I can be sure no other code is going to call SaveChanges on that DbContext instance.

Putting it all together: Calling the order-processing business logic

Now that you've learned all the parts of this complex business logic pattern, you're ready to see how to call this code. Listing 4.6 shows the PlaceOrderService class in the service layer, which calls the BizRunner to execute the PlaceOrderAction that does the order processing.

> **NOTE** I use an HTTP cookie to hold the user's selection of what books they want to buy. I refer to this cookie as the *basket cookie.* This cookie works because an HTTP cookie can store a small amount of data on the user's computer. I use ASP.NET Core's cookie features to access the user's basket cookie. For more information, see http://mng.bz/4ZNa.

If the business logic is successful, the code clears the basket cookie and returns the Order entity class key so that a confirmation page can be shown to the user. If the order fails, it doesn't clear the basket cookie, and the checkout page is shown again, with the error messages, so that the user can correct any problems and retry.

Listing 4.6 The `PlaceOrderService` class that calls the business logic

```
public class PlaceOrderService
{
    private readonly BasketCookie _basketCookie;      ◁── This class handles the basket cookie, which contains the user-selected books.

    private readonly
        RunnerWriteDb<PlaceOrderInDto, Order> _runner;
    public IImmutableList<ValidationResult>
        Errors => _runner.Errors;                     Defines the input, PlaceOrderInDto, and output, Order, of this business logic

    public PlaceOrderService(                          The constructor takes in
        IRequestCookieCollection cookiesIn,            the cookie in/out data,
        IResponseCookies cookiesOut,                   plus the application's
        EfCoreContext context)                         DbContext.
    {
```

Creates a
BasketCookie
using the cookie
in/out data from
ASP.NET Core

```
_basketCookie = new BasketCookie(
    cookiesIn, cookiesOut);
_runner =
    new RunnerWriteDb<PlaceOrderInDto, Order>(
        new PlaceOrderAction(
            new PlaceOrderDbAccess(context)),
        context);
}
```

Creates the BizRunn⬛
with the business lo⬛
that is to be run

Checkout-
CookieService
is a class that
encodes/decodes
the basket data.

```
public int PlaceOrder(bool acceptTAndCs)
{
    var checkoutService = new CheckoutCookieService(
        _basketCookie.GetValue());
```

This method is th⬛
call when the use⬛
the Purchase butt⬛

```
    var order = _runner.RunAction(
        new PlaceOrderInDto(acceptTAndCs,
        checkoutService.UserId,
        checkoutService.LineItems));
```

Runs the business logic
with the data it needs
from the basket cookie

If the business
logic has errors,
it returns
immediately. The
basket cookie is
not cleared.

```
    if (_runner.HasErrors) return 0;

    checkoutService.ClearAllLineItems();
    _basketCookie.AddOrUpdateCookie(
        checkoutService.EncodeForCookie());
```

The order was placed
successfully, so it clears
the basket cookie.

```
    return order.OrderId;
    }
}
```

Returns the OrderId, which
allows ASP.NET to confirm the
order details to the user

In addition to running the business logic, this class acts as an Adapter pattern; it ⬛
forms the data from the basket cookie into a form that the business logic accepts⬛
on a successful completion, it extracts the Order entity class's primary key, Order⬛
send back to the ASP.NET Core presentation layer.

This Adapter-pattern role is typical of the code that calls the business logic be⬛
a mismatch often occurs between the presentation layer format and the business
format. This mismatch can be small, as in this example, but you're likely to need
some form of adaptation in all but the simplest calls to your business logic. That⬛
tion is why my more-sophisticated EfCore.GenericBizRunner library has a bu⬛
Adapter pattern feature.

4.4.7 Placing an order in the Book App

Now that we've covered the business logic for processing an order, the BizRunner⬛
the PlaceOrderService that executes the business logic, let's see how to use this⬛
in the context of the Book App. Figure 4.4 shows the process, from the user cli⬛
the Purchase button through running the business logic and returning a res⬛
don't go into the presentation code in detail here, as this chapter is about usin⬛
Core in business logic, but I do cover some of it in chapter 5, which is about ⬛
EF Core in ASP.NET Core applications.

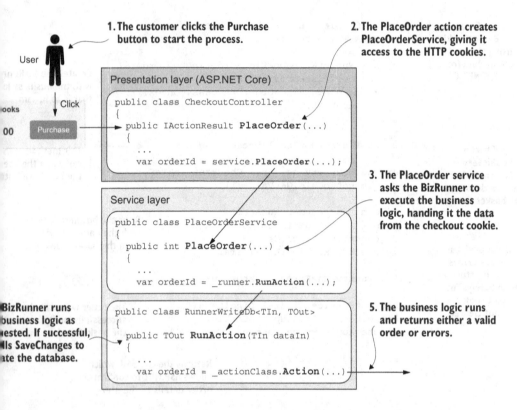

1. The customer clicks the Purchase button to start the process.

2. The PlaceOrder action creates PlaceOrderService, giving it access to the HTTP cookies.

User

ooks

00

Click

Purchase

Presentation layer (ASP.NET Core)

```
public class CheckoutController
{
    public IActionResult PlaceOrder(...)
    {
        ...
        var orderId = service.PlaceOrder(...);
```

3. The PlaceOrder service asks the BizRunner to execute the business logic, handing it the data from the checkout cookie.

Service layer

```
public class PlaceOrderService
{
    public int PlaceOrder(...)
    {
        ...
        var orderId = _runner.RunAction(...);
```

```
public class RunnerWriteDb<TIn, TOut>
{
    public TOut RunAction(TIn dataIn)
    {
        ...
        var orderId = _actionClass.Action(...)
```

BizRunner runs business logic as requested. If successful, calls SaveChanges to update the database.

5. The business logic runs and returns either a valid order or errors.

4.4 The series of steps from the user's clicking the Purchase button to the service layer, where the runner executes the business logic to process the order

From the click of the Purchase button in figure 4.4, the ASP.NET Core action, Place-Order, in the CheckoutController is executed. This action creates a class called PlaceOrderService in the service layer, which holds most of the Adapter pattern logic. The caller provides that class with read/write access to the cookies, as the checkout data is held in an HTTP cookie on the user's device.

You saw the PlaceOrderService class in listing 4.6. Its PlaceOrder method extracts the checkout data from the HTTP cookie and creates a DTO in the form that the business logic needs. Then it calls the generic BizRunner to run the business logic that it needs to execute. When the BizRunner has returned from the business logic, two routes are possible:

- *The order was successfully placed (no errors).* In this case, the PlaceOrder method cleared the basket cookie and returned the OrderId of the placed order, so the ASP.NET Core code could show a confirmation page with a summary of the order.
- *The order was unsuccessful (errors present).* In this case, the PlaceOrder method returned immediately to the ASP.NET Core code, which detected errors,

redisplayed the checkout page, and added the error messages so that the
could rectify the errors and try again.

NOTE You can try the checkout process by downloading the book app code
and running it locally to see the results. To try the error path, don't check the
Terms and Conditions (T&C) box.

4.4.8 *The pros and cons of the complex business logic pattern*

I have used this pattern for complex business logic for years. I think that it's an e
lent approach overall, but it's code-heavy, by which I mean that you have to write
structural code to implement it. Therefore, I use it only for complex business]
The following sections cover the pros and cons in detail.

ADVANTAGES OF THIS PATTERN

This pattern follows the DDD approach, which is well respected and widely use
keeps the business logic "pure" in that it doesn't know about the database, whic
been hidden via the `BizDbAccess` methods that provide a per-business logic re
tory. Also, the `BizDbAccess` class allows you to test your business logic without us
database, as your unit tests can provide a replacement class (known as a stub or m
that can provide test data as required.

DISADVANTAGES OF THIS PATTERN

The key disadvantage is you have to write more code to separate the business
from the database accesses, which takes more time and effort. If the business lo
simple, or if most of the code works on the database, the effort of creating a sep
class to handle database accesses isn't worthwhile.

4.5 *Simple business logic example: ChangePriceOfferService*

For my example of my simple business logic, you are going to build business log
handle the addition or removal of a price promotion for a book. This exampl
business rules, but as you will see, those rules are bound up with a lot of data
accesses. The rules are

- If the `Book` has a `PriceOffer`, the code should delete the current `PriceO`
  (remove the price promotion).
- If the `Book` doesn't have a `PriceOffer`, we add a new price promotion.
- If the code is adding a price promotion, the `PromotionalText` must not be
  or empty.

As you'll see in section 4.5.2, the code is a mixture of business rules and data
accesses, which I define as a simple business logic type.

My design approach for simple business logic

For simple business logic, I want to have minimal extra structure because I have deemed that the business logic is simple enough and/or so interlinked with the database accesses that it doesn't need to be isolated. As a result, the five guidelines stated in section 4.3.1 are not used, making the code quicker to build. The downside is that the business logic is mixed with other code, which can make the business logic difficult to understand and harder to unit-test—trade-offs that you have to manage for faster development.

Typically, I place simple business logic in the service layer, not the BizLogic layer, because my simple business logic needs access to the application's DbContext, and the BizLogic layer does not allow that access. I generally place my simple business logic with CRUD classes that work on the same feature. In the `ChangePriceOfferService` example, I place the `ChangePriceOfferService` class in the `AdminServices` folder alongside the other CRUD services.

Writing the ChangePriceOfferService code

The `ChangePriceOfferService` class contains two methods: a `GetOriginal` method, which is a simple CRUD command to load the `PriceOffer`, and an `AddRemovePrice-Offer` method that handles the creation or removal of the `PriceOffer` class for a `Book`. The second method contains business logic and is shown in the following listing.

Listing 4.7   `AddRemovePriceOffer` method in `ChangePriceOfferService`

This method deletes a PriceOffer if present;
otherwise, it adds a new PriceOffer.

```
public ValidationResult AddRemovePriceOffer(PriceOffer promotion)
{
    var book = _context.Books                         Loads the book,
        .Include(r => r.Promotion)                    with any existing
        .Single(k => k.BookId                         promotion
                     == promotion.BookId);

    if (book.Promotion != null)
    {
        _context.Remove(book.promotion);       Deletes the PriceOffer entry that
        _context.SaveChanges();                was linked to the chosen book
        return null;                  ←────
    }                                          Returns null, which means that
                                               the method finished successfully
    if (string.IsNullOrEmpty(promotion.PromotionalText))
    {
        return new ValidationResult(                   Returns an error message,
            "This field cannot be empty",              with the property name
            new []{ nameof(PriceOffer.PromotionalText)});   that was incorrect
    }
                                        Assigns the new PriceOffer
    book.Promotion = promotion;    ←──┘  to the selected book
```

```
_context.SaveChanges();                    The SaveChanges method
return null;                               updates the database.
}
                                           The addition of a new price promotion was
                                           successful, so the method returns null.
```

4.5.3 The pros and cons of this business logic pattern

You have written some business logic implemented in a different way from the complex business logic for processing an order, which I have described as simple ness logic. The major differences between the simple business logic and the con business logic are

- The simple business logic didn't follow the DDD-inspired guidelines from se 4.3.1. In particular, it didn't isolate the database access from the business log
- The simple business logic was placed in the service layer (instead of in the Logic layer) alongside the CRUD services related to the basket.

This pattern has the following pros and cons.

ADVANTAGES OF THIS PATTERN

This pattern has little or no set structure, so you can write the code in the simplest v archive the required business goal. Normally, the code will be shorter than the cor business pattern, which has extra classes to isolate the business logic from the datab

The business logic is also self-contained, with all the code in one place. Unlik complex business logic example, this business logic handles everything. It dc need a `BizRunner` to execute it, for example, because the code calls `SaveCha` itself, making it easier to alter, move, and test because it doesn't rely on anything

Also, by putting the business logic classes in the service layer, I can group simple business logic services in the same folder as the CRUD services related to business feature. As a result, I can find all the basic code for a feature quickly, be the complex business code is in another project.

DISADVANTAGES OF THIS PATTERN

You don't have the DDD-inspired approach of the complex business logic patte guide you, so the onus is on you to design the business logic in a sound way. experience will aid you in picking the best pattern to use and writing the correct Simplicity is the key here. If the code is easy to follow, you got it right; otherwise code is too complex and needs to follow the complex business logic pattern.

4.6 Validation business logic example: Adding review to a book, with checks

The final example is an upgrade to a CRUD example in chapter 3. In that cha you added a `Review` to a `Book`. But that version was missing some vital business ru

- The `NumStars` property must be between 0 and 5.
- The `Comment` property should have some text in it.

In this section, you are going to update the CRUD code to add a validation check. The following listing shows you the improved AddReviewWithChecks method but concentrates on the validation part.

> **Listing 4.8 The improved CRUD code with business validation checks added**

This method adds a review to a book, with validation checks on the data.

Creates a status class to hold any errors

```
public IStatusGeneric AddReviewWithChecks(Review review)
{
    var status = new StatusGenericHandler();        ←
    if (review.NumStars < 0 || review.NumStars > 5)
        status.AddError("This must be between 0 and 5.",
            nameof(Review.NumStars));
    if (string.IsNullOrWhiteSpace(review.Comment))
        status.AddError("Please provide a comment with your review.",
            nameof(Review.Comment));
    if (!status.IsValid)
        return status;

    var book = _context.Books
        .Include(r => r.Reviews)
        .Single(k => k.BookId
                == review.BookId);
    book.Reviews.Add(review);
    _context.SaveChanges();
    return status;
}
```

Adds an error to the status if the star rating is in the correct range

If there are any errors, the method returns immediately with those errors.

The CRUD code that adds a review to a book

Returns the status, which will be valid if no errors were found

NOTE The IStatusGeneric interface and StatusGenericHandler class used in listing 4.8 come from a NuGet package called GenericServices.Status-Generic. This library provides a simple but comprehensive way to return a good/bad status that matches the .NET Core validation approach. The companion NuGet package, called EfCore.GenericServices.AspNetCore, provides ways to convert the IStatusGeneric status to ASP.NET Core's ModelState Razor-based pages or to HTTP returns for Web API Controllers.

This method is a CRUD method with business validation added, which is typical of this type of business logic. In this case, you used if-then code to check the property, but you could use DataAnnotations instead. As I said earlier, this type of validation is typically done in the frontend, but duplicating the validation of sensitive data in the backend code can make the application more robust. Later, in section 4.7.1, I show you how you can validate data before it's written to the database, which gives you another option.

The pros and cons of this business logic pattern

The validation business logic is the CRUD services you saw in chapter 3, enhanced by adding validation checks. Therefore, I place validation business logic classes in the service layer alongside the other CRUD services.

ADVANTAGES OF THIS PATTERN

You are already aware of the CRUD services from chapter 3, so you don't need to
another pattern—only add validation checks and return a status. Like many
people, however, I consider these validation business logic classes to be the sa▪
CRUD services with some extra checks in them.

DISADVANTAGES OF THIS PATTERN

The only disadvantage is that you need to do something with the status that the p▪
returns, such as redisplaying the input form with an error message. But that's the ▪
side of providing extra validation rather than the validation business logic design.

4.7 Adding extra features to your business logic handling

This pattern for handling business logic makes it easier to add extra features to▪
business logic handling. In this section, you'll add two features:

- Entity class validation to `SaveChanges`
- Transactions that daisy-chain a series of business logic code

These features use EF Core commands that aren't limited to business logic. Bot▪
tures could be used in other areas, so you might want to keep them in mind ▪
you're working on your application.

4.7.1 Validating the data that you write to the database

I have already talked about validating data before it gets to the database, but thi▪
tion shows you how to add validation when writing to the database. NET cont▪
whole ecosystem to validate data, to check the value of a property against ce▪
rules (such as checking whether an integer is within the range of 1 to 10 or a s▪
isn't longer than 20 characters). This ecosystem is used by many of Microsoft's
tend systems.

> **EF6** If you're scanning for EF6.x changes, read the next paragraph. EF
> Core's `SaveChanges` doesn't validate the data before writing to the database,
> but this section shows how to add it back.

In the previous version of EF (EF6.x), data that was being added or updated wa▪
dated by default before being written to the database. In EF Core, which is desi▪
to be more lightweight and faster, no validation occurs when adding data to or u▪
ing the database. The idea is that the validation is often done at the frontend, s▪
repeat the validation?

As you've seen, the business logic contains lots of validation code, and it's ▪
useful to move this code into the entity classes as a validation check, especially ▪
error is related to a specific property in the entity class. This example is anothe▪
of breaking a complex set of rules into several parts.

Listing 4.9 moves the test to check that the book is for sale into the valid▪
code, rather than having to do it in the business logic. The listing also adds tw▪

validation checks to show you the various forms that validation checks can take, making the example more comprehensive.

Figure 4.5 shows the LineItem entity class with two types of validation added. The first type is a [Range(min,max)] attribute, known as Data Annotations (see section 7.4), which is added to the LineNum property. The second validation method to apply is the IValidatableObject interface. This interface requires you to add a method called IValidatableObject.Validate, in which you can write your own validation rules and return errors if those rules are violated.

Listing 4.9 Validation rules applied to the LineNum entity class

```
public class LineItem : IValidatableObject        ◁──┐   The IValidatableObject interface adds
{                                                     │   a IValidatableObject.Validate method.
    public int LineItemId { get; set; }

    [Range(1,5, ErrorMessage =                         ⊢   Adds an error message if
        "This order is over the limit of 5 books.")]       the LineNum property is
    public byte LineNum { get; set; }                      not in range

    public short NumBooks { get; set; }

    public decimal BookPrice { get; set; }

    // relationships

    public int OrderId { get; set; }
    public int BookId { get; set; }
                                                              The
    public Book ChosenBook { get; set; }                      IValidatableObject
                                                              interface requires
    IEnumerable<ValidationResult> IValidatableObject.Validate   this method to be
        (ValidationContext validationContext)                 created.
    {
        var currContext =
            validationContext.GetService(typeof(DbContext));

        if (ChosenBook.Price < 0)                          Moves the Price check
            yield return new ValidationResult(             out of the business logic
$"Sorry, the book '{ChosenBook.Title}' is not for sale.");  into this validation

        if (NumBooks > 100)                        Extra validation rule: an order
            yield return new ValidationResult(     for more than 100 books
    "If you want to order a 100 or more books"+    needs to phone in an order.
" please phone us on 01234-5678-90",
                new[] { nameof(NumBooks) });  ◁──┐  Returns the name of the
        }                                         property with the error to
}                                                 provide a better error message
```

I should point out that in the IValidatableObject.Validate method, you access a property outside the LineNum class: the Title of the ChosenBook. ChosenBook is a navigational property, and when the DetectChanges method is called, the *relational fixup*

feature (see figure 1.10, stage 3) will ensure that the ChosenBook property isn't
As a result, the validation code in listing 4.9 can access navigational properties th:
business logic might not have.

> **NOTE** In addition to using the extensive list of built-in validation attributes,
> you can create your own validation attributes by inheriting the Validation-
> Attribute class on your own class. See http://mng.bz/9cec for more on
> the standard validation attributes that are available and for how to use the
> ValidationAttribute class.

After adding the validation rule code to your LineItem entity class, you need to
validation stage to EF Core's SaveChanges method, called SaveChanges\
Validation. Although the obvious place to put this stage is inside the applica\
DbContext, you'll create an extension method instead. This method will allow S
ChangesWithValidation to be used on any DbContext, which means that you
copy this class and use it in your application.

The following listing shows this SaveChangesWithValidation extension me\
and listing 4.11 shows the private method ExecuteValidation that SaveChanges\
Validation calls to handle the validation.

Listing 4.10 `SaveChangesWithValidation` added to the application's DbCon\

SaveChangesWithValidation returns a
list of ValidationResults.

SaveChangesWit\
is an extension n\
takes the DbCon\
its input.

```
public static ImmutableList<ValidationResult>
    SaveChangesWithValidation(this DbContext context)
{
    var result = context.ExecuteValidation();

    if (result.Any()) return result;

    context.SaveChanges();

    return result;
}
```

The ExecuteValidation is u
SaveChangesWithCheckin\
ChangesWithCheckingAsy\

If there are errors, return
them immediately and don't
call SaveChanges.

Returns the empty set of
errors to signify that
there are no errors

There aren't any errors, so I am
going to call SaveChanges.

Listing 4.11 `SaveChangesWithValidation` calls `ExecuteValidation` met\

```
private static ImmutableList<ValidationResult>
    ExecuteValidation(this DbContext context)
{
    var result = new List<ValidationResult>();
    foreach (var entry in
        context.ChangeTracker.Entries()
            .Where(e =>
                (e.State == EntityState.Added) ||
                (e.State == EntityState.Modified)))
    {
```

Uses EF Core's ChangeTracker
to get access to all the entity
classes it is tracking

Filters the entities that
will be added or update\
in the database

```
        var entity = entry.Entity;
        var valProvider = new
            ValidationDbContextServiceProvider(context);
        var valContext = new
            ValidationContext(entity, valProvider, null);
        var entityErrors = new List<ValidationResult>();
        if (!Validator.TryValidateObject(
            entity, valContext, entityErrors, true))
        {
            result.AddRange(entityErrors);
        }
    }
}
return result.ToImmutableList();
}
```

> **Implements the IServiceProvider interface and passes the DbContext to the Validate method**

> **The Validator.TryValidateObject is the method that validates each class.**

> y errors dded to the list.

> **Returns the list of all the errors found (empty if there are no errors)**

The main code is in the ExecuteValidation method, because you need to use it in sync and async versions of SaveChangesWithValidation. The call to context.Change-Tracker.Entries calls the DbContext's DetectChanges to ensure that all the changes you've made are found before the validation is run. Then the code looks at all the entities that have been added or modified (updated) and validates them all.

One piece of code I want to point out in listing 4.11 is a class called ValidationDb-ContextServiceProvider, which implements the IServiceProvider interface. This class is used when you create ValidationContext, so it is available in any entity classes that have the IValidatableObject interface, allowing the Validate method to access the current application's DbContext if necessary. Having access to the current DbContext allows you to create better error messages by obtaining extra information from the database.

You design the SaveChangesWithValidation method to return the errors rather than throw an exception. You do this to fit in with the business logic, which returns errors as a list, not an exception. You can create a new BizRunner variant, Runner-WriteDbWithValidation, that uses SaveChangesWithValidation instead of the normal SaveChanges and returns errors from the business logic or any validation errors found when writing to the database. The next listing shows the BizRunner class Runner-WriteDbWithValidation.

Listing 4.12   BizRunner variant `RunnerWriteDbWithValidation`

```
public class RunnerWriteDbWithValidation<TIn, TOut>
{
    private readonly IBizAction<TIn, TOut> _actionClass;
    private readonly EfCoreContext _context;

    public IImmutableList<ValidationResult>
        Errors { get; private set; }
    public bool HasErrors => Errors.Any();

    public RunnerWriteDbWithValidation(
        IBizAction<TIn, TOut> actionClass,
        EfCoreContext context)
```

> **This version needs its own Errors/HasErrors properties, as errors come from two sources.**

> **Handles business logic that conforms to the IBizAction<TIn, TOut> interface**

```
{
    _context = context;
    _actionClass = actionClass;
}

public TOut RunAction(TIn dataIn)
{
    var result = _actionClass.Action(dataIn);
    Errors = _actionClass.Errors;
    if (!HasErrors)
    {
        Errors =
            _context.SaveChangesWithValidation()
                .ToImmutableList();
    }
    return result;
}
```

Runs the business logic I gave it

If no errors, calls SaveChanges-WithChecking

This method is called to execute the business logic and handle any errors.

Any errors from the business logic are assigned to the local errors list.

Any validation errors are assigned to the Errors list.

Returns the result that the business logic returned

The nice thing about this new variant of the `BizRunner` pattern is that it has ex the same interface as the original, nonvalidating `BizRunner`. You can substitute Rur `WriteDbWithValidation<TIn, TOut>` for the original `BizRunner` without needi change the business logic or the way that the calling method executes the `BizRur`

In section 4.7.2, you'll produce yet another variant of the `BizRunner` that car multiple business logic classes in such a way that they look like a single business method. This is possible because of the business logic pattern described at the st this chapter.

4.7.2 Using transactions to daisy-chain a sequence of business logic code

As I said earlier, business logic can get complex. When it comes to designing implementing a large or complex piece of business logic, you have three options

- *Option 1*—Write one big method that does everything.
- *Option 2*—Write a few smaller methods, with one overarching method to them in sequence.
- *Option 3*—Write a few smaller methods, each of which updates the database combine them into one Unit Of Work (see sidebar in section 3.2.2).

Option 1 normally isn't a good idea because the method will be so hard to under and refactor. It also has problems if parts of the business logic are used elsew because you could break the DRY (don't repeat yourself) software principle.

Option 2 can work but can have problems if later stages rely on database item: ten by earlier stages, which could break the atomic unit rule mentioned in chap when there are multiple changes to the database, they all succeed, or they all fail.

This leaves option 3, which is possible because of a feature of EF Core (and relational databases) called *transactions*. In section 3.2.2, the sidebar "Why you sh call `SaveChanges` only once at the end of your changes" introduced the Unit Of and showed how SaveChanges saves all the changes inside a transaction to make sure that all the changes were saved or, if the database rejected any part of the change, that no changes were saved to the database.

In this case, you want to spread the Unit Of Work over several smaller methods; let's call them Biz1, Biz2, and Biz3. You don't have to change Biz methods; they still think that they are working on their own and will expect SaveChanges to be called when each Biz method finishes. But when you create an overarching transaction, all three Biz methods, with their SaveChanges call, will work as one Unit Of Work. As a result, a database rejection/error in Biz3 will reject any database changes made by Biz1, Biz2, and Biz3.

This database rejection works because when you use EF Core to create an explicit relational database transaction, it has two effects:

- Any writes to the database are hidden from other database users until you call the transaction's Commit method.
- If you decide that you don't want the database writes (say, because the business logic has an error), you can discard all database writes done in the transaction by calling the transaction RollBack command.

Figure 4.5 shows three separate pieces of business logic, each expecting a call to Save-Changes to update the database but being run by a class called the *transactional* Biz-Runner. After each piece of business logic has run, the BizRunner calls SaveChanges, which means that anything the business logic writes out is now available for subsequent

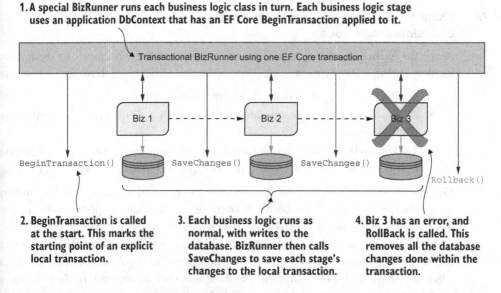

1. A special BizRunner runs each business logic class in turn. Each business logic stage uses an application DbContext that has an EF Core BeginTransaction applied to it.

2. **BeginTransaction is called at the start. This marks the starting point of an explicit local transaction.**

3. **Each business logic runs as normal, with writes to the database. BizRunner then calls SaveChanges to save each stage's changes to the local transaction.**

4. **Biz 3 has an error, and RollBack is called. This removes all the database changes done within the transaction.**

Figure 4.5   An example of executing three separate business logic stages under one transaction. When the last business logic stage returns an error, the other database changes applied by the first two business logic stages are rolled back.

business logic stages via the local transaction. In the final stage, the business logic, ▮
returns errors, which causes the BizRunner to call the RollBack command, whic▮
the effect of removing any database writes done by Biz 1 and Biz 2.

The next listing shows the code for the new transactional BizRunner, which st▮
transaction on the application's DbContext before calling any of the business lo▮

Listing 4.13 `RunnerTransact2WriteDb` running two business logic stages in se▮

The three types are input, class passed
from Part1 to Part2, and output.

The BizRunner can
return null if there
are errors, so it has
to be a class.

```
public class RunnerTransact2WriteDb<TIn, TPass, TOut>
    where TOut : class
{
    private readonly IBizAction<TIn, TPass>
        _actionPart1;
    private readonly IBizAction<TPass, TOut>
        _actionPart2;
    private readonly EfCoreContext _context;

    public IImmutableList<ValidationResult>
        Errors { get; private set; }
    public bool HasErrors => Errors.Any();

    public RunnerTransact2WriteDb(
        EfCoreContext context,
        IBizAction<TIn, TPass> actionPart1,
        IBizAction<TPass, TOut> actionPart2)
    {
        _context = context;
        _actionPart1 = actionPart1;
        _actionPart2 = actionPart2;
    }

    public TOut RunAction(TIn dataIn)
    {
        using (var transaction =
            _context.Database.BeginTransaction())
        {
            var passResult = RunPart(
                _actionPart1, dataIn);
            if (HasErrors) return null;
            var result = RunPart(
                _actionPart2, passResult);

            if (!HasErrors)
            {
                transaction.Commit();
            }
            return result;
        }
    }
}
```

Defines the generic
BizAction for the two
business logic parts

Holds any error
information returned
by the business logic

The constructor takes
both business classes and
the application DbContext.

If there are errors,
returns null. (The
rollback is handled
by the dispose.)

Starts the transaction
within a using statement

The private method, RunPart,
runs the first business part.

If the first part of the business logic
successful, runs the second business▮

If there are no errors,
commits the transaction
to the database

Returns the result
from the last
business logic

If commit is not called before the using
end, RollBack undoes all the changes.

```
private TPartOut RunPart<TPartIn, TPartOut>(        This private method
    IBizAction<TPartIn, TPartOut> bizPart,          handles running each part
    TPartIn dataIn)                                 of the business logic.
    where TPartOut : class
{
    var result = bizPart.Action(dataIn);           Runs the business logic and copies
    Errors = bizPart.Errors;                        the business logic's Errors
    if (!HasErrors)
    {                                               If the business logic was
        _context.SaveChanges();                     successful, calls SaveChanges
    }
    return result;        ⟵──┐ Returns the result from
}                                the business logic it ran
}
```

In your `RunnerTransact2WriteDb` class, you execute each part of the business logic in turn, and at the end of each execution, you do one of the following:

- *No errors*—You call `SaveChanges` to save to the transaction any changes that business logic has run. That save is within a local transaction, so other methods accessing the database won't see those changes yet. Then you call the next part of the business logic, if there is one.
- *Has errors*—You copy the errors found by the business logic that just finished to the `BizRunner` error list and exit the `BizRunner`. At that point, the code steps outside the using clause that holds the transaction, which causes disposal of the transaction. Because no transaction `Commit` has been called, the disposal will cause the transaction to execute its `RollBack` method, which discards the database writes to the transaction. Those writes are never written to the database.

If you've run all the business logic with no errors, you call the `Commit` command on the transaction. This command does an atomic update of the database to reflect all the changes to the database that are contained in the local transaction.

Using the RunnerTransact2WriteDb class

To test the `RunnerTransact2WriteDb` class, you'll split the order-processing code you used earlier into two parts:

- `PlaceOrderPart1`—Creates the `Order` entity, with no `LineItems`
- `PlaceOrderPart2`—Adds the `LineItems` for each book bought to the `Order` entity that was created by the `PlaceOrderPart1` class

`PlaceOrderPart1` and `PlaceOrderPart2` are based on the `PlaceOrderAction` code you've already seen, so I don't repeat the business code here.

Listing 4.14 shows you the code changes that are required for `PlaceOrderService` (shown in listing 4.6) to change over to use the `RunnerTransact2WriteDb` BizRunner. The listing focuses on the part that creates and runs the two stages, `Part1` and `Part2`, with the unchanged parts of the code left out so you can see the changes easily.

Listing 4.14 The `PlaceOrderServiceTransact` class showing the changed p.

```
public class PlaceOrderServiceTransact
{
    //... code removed as the same as in listing 4.5

    public PlaceOrderServiceTransact(
        IRequestCookieCollection cookiesIn,
        IResponseCookies cookiesOut,
        EfCoreContext context)
    {
        _checkoutCookie = new CheckoutCookie(
            cookiesIn, cookiesOut);
        _runner = new RunnerTransact2WriteDb
            <PlaceOrderInDto, Part1ToPart2Dto, Order>(
            context,
            new PlaceOrderPart1(
                new PlaceOrderDbAccess(context)),
            new PlaceOrderPart2(
                new PlaceOrderDbAccess(context)));
    }

    public int PlaceOrder(bool tsAndCsAccepted)
    {
        //... code removed as the same as in listing 4.6
    }
}
```

This version of PlaceOrde uses transactions to exe two business logic classe PlaceOrderPart1 and PlaceOrderPart2.

The BizRunner needs the input, the class passed from Part1 to Part2, and the output.

The BizRunner needs the application's DbContext.

This BizRunner handles multiple business logic inside a transaction.

Provides an instance of first part of the busine

Provides an instance of the second part of the business logic

The important thing to note is that the business logic has no idea whether it's run in a transaction. You can use a piece of business logic on its own or as part of a tra tion. Similarly, listing 4.14 shows that only the caller of transaction-based bus logic, which I call the BizRunner, needs to change. Using a transaction makes it e: combine multiple business logic classes under one transaction without needi change any of your business logic code.

The advantage of using transactions like this one is that you can split and/or : parts of your business logic while making these multiple business logic calls lo your application, especially its database, like one call. I've used this approach wi needed to create and then immediately update a complex, multipart entity. Be I needed the Update business logic for other cases, I used a transaction to call the ate business logic followed by the Update business logic, which saved me develop effort and kept my code DRY.

The disadvantage of this approach is that it adds complexity to the database a which can make debugging a little more difficult, or the use of database transac could cause a performance issue. Also, be aware that if you use the EnableRetr Failure option (see section 11.8) to retry database accessed on errors, you ne handle possible multiple calls to your business logic.

Summary

- The term *business logic* describes code written to implement real-world business rules. The business logic code can range from the simple to the complex.
- Depending on the complexity of your business logic, you need to choose an approach that balances how easy it is to solve the business problem against the time it takes you to develop and test your solution.
- Isolating the database access part of your business logic into another class/project can make the pure business logic simpler to write but take longer to develop.
- Putting all the business logic for a feature in one class is quick and easy but can make the code harder to understand and test.
- Creating a standardized interface for your business logic makes calling and running the business logic much simpler for the frontend.
- Sometimes, it's easier to move some of the validation logic into the entity classes and run the checks when that data is being written to the database.
- For business logic that's complex or being reused, it might be simpler to use a database transaction to allow a sequence of business logic parts to be run in sequence but, from the database point of view, look like one atomic unit.

For readers who are familiar with EF6.x:

- Unlike EF6.x, EF Core's SaveChanges method doesn't validate data before it's written to the database. But it's easy to implement a method that provides this feature in EF Core.

Using EF Core in ASP.NET Core web applications

In this chapter, you'll pull everything together by using ASP.NET Core to b[u]
real web application. Using ASP.NET Core brings in issues that are outsid[e]
Core, such as dependency injection (covered in section 5.4) and async/await [cov]
ered in section 5.10). But they're necessary if you're going to use EF Core i[n]
type of application.

This chapter assumes that you've read chapters 2–4 and know about que[ries]
and updating the database and what business logic is. This chapter is about w[here]
to place your database access code and how to call it in a real application. I[t]
covers the specific issues of using EF Core in an ASP.NET Core (including B[lazor]
Server) applications. For that reason, this chapter includes quite a bit [of]
ASP.NET Core, but it's all focused on using EF Core well in this type of applic[ation.]

I end with more general information on various ways to obtain an instance of the application's DbContext for cases such as background tasks.

Introducing ASP.NET Core

The ASP.NET Core website states that "ASP.NET Core is a cross-platform, high-performance, open-source framework for building modern, cloud-based, Internet-connected applications" (http://mng.bz/QmOw). This summary is a good one, but ASP.NET Core has so many great features that it's hard to pick which ones to comment on.

> **NOTE**   I recommend Andrew Lock's book *ASP.NET Core in Action* (Manning, 2020) for a detailed description of ASP.NET Core's many features.

I've been using ASP.NET MVC5, the precursor of ASP.NET Core, for years. I thought it was a good framework, if a bit slow in performance. But for me, ASP.NET Core blows ASP.NET MVC5 out of the water, with a phenomenal improvement in performance and new ways to show data, such as Razor Pages and Blazor.

> **TIP**   When I first tried ASP.NET Core, I was disappointed by its performance; it turns out that the default logging slows things down in development mode. When I replaced the normal loggers with my quicker, in-memory logging, the Book App page that was listing the book was three times faster! So watch out for too much logging slowing your application.

In this book, you will build the Book App, which is a web application, using ASP.NET Core to show how EF Core works with a real application. ASP.NET Core can be used in a number of ways, but for the Book App examples. we will use ASP.NET Core's Model-View-Controller (MVC) pattern.

Understanding the architecture of the Book App

Chapter 2 presented a diagram of the Book App, and chapter 4 extended it with two more projects to handle the business logic. Figure 5.1 shows you the combined architecture after chapter 4, with all the projects in the application. As you go through this chapter, you'll learn how and why we split the database access code across the various projects. One reason is to make your web application easier to write, refactor, and test.

This layered architecture, which creates a single executable containing all the code, works well with many cloud providers that can spin up more instances of the web application if it's under a heavy load; your host will run multiple copies of a web application and place a load balancer to spread the load over all the copies. This process is known as *scaling out* in Microsoft Azure and *auto scaling* in Amazon Web Services (AWS).

> **NOTE**   In part 3, I update the architecture of the Book App to use the modular monolith, Domain-Driven Design, and clean architecture. See the useful Microsoft document about layered and clean architectures at http://mng .bz/5jD1.

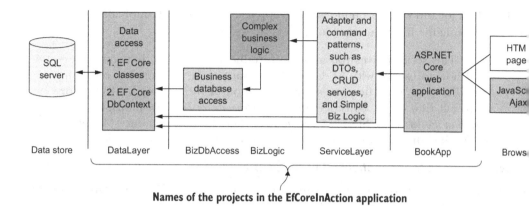

Names of the projects in the EfCoreInAction application

Figure 5.1 All the projects in the Book App. The arrows show the main routes by which EF Core data move **and down the layers.**

5.3 Understanding dependency injection

ASP.NET Core uses *dependency injection* (DI) extensively, as does .NET in general
need to understand DI because it's the method used in ASP.NET Core to g
instance of the application's DbContext.

> **DEFINITION** *Dependency injection* is a way to link together your application
> dynamically. Normally, you'd write var myClass = new MyClass() to create a
> new instance of MyClass. That code works, but you've hardcoded the creation
> of that class, and you can change it only by changing your code. With DI, you
> can *register* your MyClass with a DI provider, using, say, an interface such as
> IMyClass. Then, when you need the class, you use IMyClass myClass, and the
> DI provider will dynamically create an instance and *inject* it into the IMyClass
> myClass parameter/property.

Using DI has lots of benefits, and here are the main ones:

- DI allows your application to link itself dynamically. The DI provider will
  out what classes you need and create them in the right order. If one of
  classes needs the application's DbContext, for example, the DI can provid
- Using interfaces and DI together means that your application is more lo
  coupled; you can replace a class with another class that matches the same
  face. This technique is especially useful in unit testing: you can prov
  replacement version of the service with another, simpler class that implen
  the interface (called *stubbing* or *mocking* in unit tests).
- Other, more advanced features exist, such as using DI to select which cl
  return based on certain settings. If you're building an e-commerce applica
  in development mode, you might want to use a dummy credit card ha
  instead of the normal credit card system.

I use DI a lot and wouldn't build any real application without it, but I admit that it can be confusing the first time you see it.

> **NOTE** This section gives you a quick introduction to DI so that you understand how to use DI with EF Core. If you want more information on DI in ASP.NET Core, see Microsoft's documentation at http://mng.bz/Kv16. For an overall view of DI, consider the book *Dependency Injection Principles, Practices, and Patterns,* by Steven Van Deursen and Mark Seemann (Manning, 2019), which has a whole chapter on NET Core DI (http://mng.bz/XdjG).

Why you need to learn about DI in ASP.NET Core

Chapter 2 showed you how to create an instance of the application's DbContext by using the following snippet of code:

```
const string connection =
    "Data Source=(localdb)\\mssqllocaldb;" +
    "Database=EfCoreInActionDb.Chapter02;" +
    "Integrated Security=True;";
var optionsBuilder =
    new DbContextOptionsBuilder
        <EfCoreContext>();

optionsBuilder.UseSqlServer(connection);
var options = optionsBuilder.Options;

using (var context = new EfCoreContext(options))
{...
```

That code works but has a few problems. First, you're going to have to repeat this code for each database access you make. Second, this code uses a fixed database access string, referred to as a *connection string,* which isn't going to work when you want to deploy your site to a host, because the database location for the hosted database will be different from the database you use for development.

You can work around these two problems in several ways, such as by overriding the OnConfiguration method in the application's DbContext (covered in section 5.11.1). But DI is a better way to handle this situation and is what ASP.NET Core uses. Using a slightly different set of commands, you can tell the DI provider how to create your application's DbContext—a process called *registering a service*—and then ask the DI for an instance of your application's DbContext anywhere in ASP.NET Core's system that supports DI.

A basic example of dependency injection in ASP.NET Core

Setting up the code to configure the application's DbContext is a little complicated and can hide the DI part. My first example of DI in ASP.NET Core, shown in figure 5.2, uses a simple class called Demo, which you'll use in an ASP.NET controller. This example will be useful in section 5.7, when I show you how to use DI to make your code simpler to call.

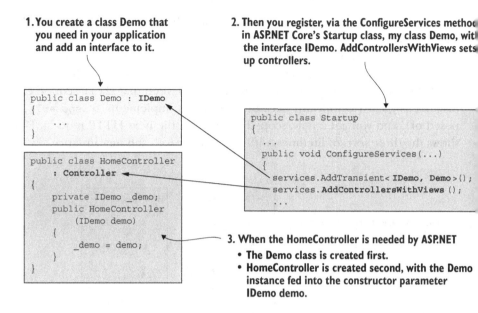

1. You create a class Demo that you need in your application and add an interface to it.

2. Then you register, via the ConfigureServices method in ASP.NET Core's Startup class, my class Demo, with the interface IDemo. AddControllersWithViews sets up controllers.

```
public class Demo : IDemo
{
    ...
}
```

```
public class HomeController
    : Controller
{
    private IDemo _demo;
    public HomeController
        (IDemo demo)
    {
        _demo = demo;
    }
}
```

```
public class Startup
{
    ...
    public void ConfigureServices(...)
    {
        services.AddTransient< IDemo, Demo >();
        services.AddControllersWithViews();
        ...
    }
}
```

3. When the HomeController is needed by ASP.NET
   • The Demo class is created first.
   • HomeController is created second, with the Demo instance fed into the constructor parameter IDemo demo.

Figure 5.2   An example of a class called Demo being inserted via DI into a controller's constructor. code on the right registers your IDemo/Demo pair, and the AddControllersWithViews comm registers all the ASP.NET Core controllers. When ASP.NET Core needs the HomeController (use showing HTML pages), DI will create the HomeController. Because the HomeController ne an IDemo instance, DI will create one and inject it into the HomeController's constructor.

Figure 5.2 shows that by registering the IDemo/Demo pair with ASP.NET Core's DI can access it in your HomeController class. Classes that are registered are referr as *services*.

The rule is that any DI service can be referenced, or *injected*, in any other DI se In figure 5.2, you register your IDemo/Demo class and call the AddControllersWith configuration method to register the ASP.NET Core's controller classes—specifica this example, the HomeController class. This allows you to use the IDemo interfa the HomeController's constructor, and the DI provides an instance on the Demo In DI terms, you use *constructor injection* to create an instance of the class that you've istered. You'll use DI in various ways in this chapter, but the rules and terms de here will help you make sense of these later examples.

5.3.3   The lifetime of a service created by DI

One feature of DI that's important when talking about EF Core is the *lifetime* instance created by DI—how long the instance exists before being lost or dispose In our IDemo/Demo example, you registered the instance as *transient*; every time ask for an instance of Demo, it creates a new one. If you want to use your own cl with DI, you most likely declare a *transient* lifetime; that's what I use for all my ser as it means that each instance starts with its default setup. For simple, valuelike cl such as data setup at startup, you may declare them as *singleton* (you get the same instance every time).

The application's DbContext is different. It has its lifetime set to *scoped*, which means that however many instances of the application's DbContext you ask for during one HTTP request, you get the same instance. But when that HTTP request ends, that instance is gone (technically, because DbContext implements IDisposable, it's disposed of), and you get a new, scoped instance in the next HTTP request. Figure 5.3 shows the three sorts of lifetimes, with a new letter for each new instance.

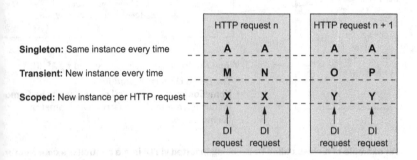

Figure 5.3   Instances produced by DI have three types of lifetimes: singleton, transient, and scoped. This figure shows those three types with four injections for each, two per HTTP request. The letters represent each instance. If a letter is used multiple times, all those injections are the same instance of the class.

You need to use a scoped lifetime for the application's DbContext in case you inject the application's DbContext into multiple classes. Sometimes, for example, it's good to break a complex update into multiple classes. If you do, you need the application's DbContext to be the same in all the classes; otherwise, changes made in one class would not appear in another class.

Let's break a complex update into a Main class and a SubPart class, where the Main class obtains an instance of the SubPart via an ISubPart interface in its constructor. Now the Main part calls a method in the ISubPart interface, and the SubPart code loads an entity class and changes a property. At the end of the whole update, the Main code calls SaveChanges. If the two applications' DbContext injected into Main and SubPart classes are different, the change that the SubPart class made is lost.

This situation may sound obscure or unusual, but in even medium-size applications, it can happen a lot. I often break complex code into separate classes, either because the whole code is so big or because I want to unit-test different parts of the code separately.

Conversely, each HTTP request must have its own instance of the application's DbContext, because EF Core's DbContext isn't *thread-safe* (see section 5.11.1). This

fact is why the application's DbContext has a scoped lifetime for each HTTP re
and is one of the reasons why DI is so useful.

5.3.4 Special considerations for Blazor Server applications

If you are using a Blazor frontend talking to a ASP.NET Core backend, known
Blazor Server hosting model, you need to change your approach to registering ar
obtaining an instance of your application's DbContext. The problem is that w
Blazor frontend, you can send calls for a database access in parallel, which mean
multiple threads will try to use one instance of your application's DbContext, v
isn't allowed.

You have a few ways to get around this problem, but the simplest is to create a
instance of your application's DbContext for every database access. EF Core 5 has
vided a DbContext factory method that creates a new instance every time you
(see section 5.4.3). The DbContext factory method prevents multiple threads
trying to use the same instance of your application's DbContext.

The downside of using the DbContext factory method is that different classe
istered to DI won't use the same DbContext instance. The scoped lifetime DbCo
instance example in section 5.3.3, for example, would cause problems becaus
Main class and a SubPart class would have different instances of your applica
DbContext. One solution to this problem is to have the Main class obtain an ins
of the application's DbContext and pass that instance to the SubPart class, eith
creating the SubPart itself or via a method parameter.

Even the DbContext factory approach can have problems with services tha
long-lived. The EF Core team has written guidance on using EF Core with a B
Server application with an example application that shows some of the technique
http://mng.bz/yY7G.

5.4 Making the application's DbContext available via DI

Now that you understand DI, you're ready to set up your application's DbContex
service so that you can access it later via DI. You do this at the startup of the ASP
Core web application by registering the application's DbContext with the DI prov
using information that tells EF Core what sort of database you're accessing and v
it's located.

5.4.1 Providing information on the database's location

When developing your application, you'll want to run it on your development mac
and access a local database for testing. The type of the database will be defined b
business need, but the location of the database on your development machine is
you and whatever database server you're using.

For web applications, the location of the database normally isn't hardcoded
the application because it'll change when the web application is moved to its host, v
real users can access it. Therefore, the location and various database configur

settings are typically stored as a *connection string*. This string is stored in an application setting file that ASP.NET reads when it starts. ASP.NET Core has a range of application setting files, but for now, you'll concentrate on the three standard ones:

- *appsetting.json*—Holds the settings that are common to development and production
- *appsettings.Development.json*—Holds the settings for the development build
- *appsettings.Production.json*—Holds the settings for the production build (when the web application is deployed to a host for users to access it)

NOTE   There's a lot more to application setting files in ASP.NET Core that we haven't covered. Please look at the APS.NET Core documentation for a more complete description.

Typically, the development connection string is stored in the appsettings.Development .json file. Listing 5.1 shows a connection string suitable for running an SQL database locally on a Windows PC.

NOTE   The Visual Studio installation includes a feature called *SQL Server Express*, which allows you to use SQL Server for development.

Listing 5.1   `appsettings.Development.json` file with database connection string

```
{
  "ConnectionStrings": {
    "DefaultConnection":
"Server=(localdb)\\mssqllocaldb;Database=EfCoreInActionDb
;Trusted_Connection=True"
  },
  … other parts removed as not relevant to database access
}
```

You need to edit your appsettings.Development.json file to add the connection string for your local, development database. This file may or may not have a `Connection-Strings` section, depending on whether you set Authentication to Individual User Accounts. (The Individual User Accounts option needs its own database, so Visual Studio adds a connection string for the authorization database to the appsetting.json file.) You can call your connection string anything you like; this example uses the name `DefaultConnection` in our application.

Registering your application's DbContext with the DI provider

The next step is registering your application's DbContext with the DI provider at startup. Any configuration to be done when ASP.NET Core starts up is done in the aptly named `Startup` class. This class is executed when the ASP.NET Core application starts and contains several methods to set up/configure the web application.

The application's DbContext for ASP.NET Core has a constructor that ta
DbContextOptions<T> parameter defining the database options. That way, the dat
connection string can change when you deploy your web application (see section
As a reminder, here's what the Book App's DbContext constructor looks like, sho
bold in this code snippet:

```
public class EfCoreContext : DbContext
{
    //... properties removed for clarity

    public EfCoreContext(
        DbContextOptions<EfCoreContext> options)
        : base(options) {}

    //... other code removed for clarity
}
```

The following listing shows how the application's DbContext is registered as a se
in an ASP.NET Core application. This registration is done in the ConfigureSer
method in the Startup class of your ASP.NET Core application, along with all t
services you need to register.

Listing 5.2 Registering your DbContext in ASP.NET Core's Startup class

**Sets up a series of services to use
with controllers and Views**

**This method in the Startup
class sets up services.**

```
public void ConfigureServices(IServiceCollection services)
{
    services.AddControllersWithViews();

    var connection = Configuration
        .GetConnectionString("DefaultConnection");

    services.AddDbContext<EfCoreContext>(
        options => options.UseSqlServer(connection));

    //... other service registrations removed
}
```

**You get the connection
from the appsettings.j
which can be changed
you deploy.**

**Configures the app
DbContext to use S
Server and provide
connection**

Your first step is getting the connection string from the application's Configura
class. In ASP.NET Core, the Configuration class is set up during the Startup
constructor, which reads the appsetting files. Getting the connection string tha
allows you to change the database connection string when you deploy the code
host. Section 5.8.1, which is about deploying an ASP.NET Core application that
a database, covers how this process works.

The second step—making the application's DbContext available via DI—is
by the AddDbContext method, which registers the application's DbContext, EfC
Context, and the DbContextOptions<EfCoreContext> instances as services. Whe
use the type EfCoreContext in places where DI intercepts, the DI provider will c

an instance of the application's DbContext, using the DbContextOptions<EfCore-Context> options. Or if you ask for multiple instances in the same HTTP request, the DI provider will return the same instances. You'll see this process in action when you start using the application's DbContext to do database queries and updates in section 5.6.

Registering a DbContext Factory with the DI provider

As stated in section 5.3.4, Blazor Server applications need careful managing of the instances of your application's DbContext, as do some other application types. In EF Core 5, the IDbContextFactory<TContext> interface was added along with a method to register the DbContext factory, as shown in the following listing.

Listing 5.3 Registering a DbContext factory in ASP.NET Core's Startup class

Sets up a series of services to use with controllers and Views

This method in the Startup class sets up services.

```
public void ConfigureServices(IServiceCollection services)    ⟵┘
{
    services.AddControllersWithViews();

    var connection = Configuration
        .GetConnectionString("DefaultConnection");

    services.AddDbContextFactory<EfCoreContext>(
        options => options.UseSqlServer(connection));

    //… other service registrations removed
}
```

You get the connection string from the appsettings.json file, which can be changed when you deploy.

Configures the DbContext factory to use SQL Server and provide the connection

---

Typically, you use the AddDbContextFactory method only with Blazor in the frontend or in applications where you cannot control the parallel access to the same application's DbContext, which breaks the thread-safe rule (see section 5.11.1). Many other applications, such as ASP.NET Core, manage parallel accesses for you, so you can obtain an instance of the application's DbContext via DI.

Calling your database access code from ASP.NET Core

Having configured the application DbContext and registered it as a DI service, you're ready to access the database. In these examples, you're going to run a query to display the books and run commands that update the database. You'll focus on how to execute these methods from ASP.NET Core; I assume that you've already grasped how to query and update the database from previous chapters.

> **NOTE** The example code is mainly about using ASP.NET Core MVC, but all the examples of using DI also apply to all forms of ASP.NET Core: Razor Pages, MVC, and Web API. A few sections also cover the Blazor Server applications, because the handling of obtaining an instance of the application's DbContext by DI is different.

5.5.1 A summary of how ASP.NET Core MVC works and the terms it uses

First, here's a quick summary of how to use ASP.NET Core to implement our App. To display the various HTML pages, you'll use an ASP.NET Core *controller,* \ is the class that handles delivering HTML pages via Razor Views. To do this, you' ate a class called HomeController, which inherits from ASP.NET Core's Contro class. This controller has several Razor Views linked to its methods, which in ASP Core are known as *action methods.*

Our Book App's HomeController has an action method called Index, which s the book list, and one called About, which provides a summary page for the site have other controllers to handle checkout, existing orders, admin actions, and s Although you could put all your database access code inside each action meth each controller, I rarely do because I use a software design principle called Separ of Concerns (SoC), which the next subsection explains.

5.5.2 Where does the EF Core code live in the Book App?

As you learned in section 5.2, our Book App is built using a layered architec which is meant to represent an architecture that could be used in a real-world ap tion. In this section, you'll see where to place the various pieces of EF Core's dat access code and why.

> DEFINITION *Separation of Concerns* is the idea that a software system must be decomposed into parts that overlap in functionality as little as possible. It's linked to two other principles: coupling and cohesion. With *coupling,* you want each project in your application to be as self-contained as possible, and with *cohesion,* each project in your application should have code that provides similar or strongly related functions. See http://mng.bz/wHJS for more information.

Figure 5.4 maps where the database access code is located in your application, the earlier architecture diagram (figure 5.1). The bubbles show what type of dat code you'll find in each layer. Notice that the ASP.NET Core project and the business logic (BizLogic) project have no EF Core query/update code in them.

Applying SoC principles has benefits throughout the application. You lea about the reason for splitting out the complex business logic in chapter 4. But i chapter, you'll see the benefits for the ASP.NET Core project:

- The ASP.NET Core frontend is all about displaying data, and doing that we big task that needs lots of concentration. Therefore, you'll use the service to handle both the EF Core commands and the transformation of the dat data into a form that the ASP.NET Core frontend can easily use—ofte DTOs, also known as ViewModels in ASP.NET Core. Then you can concen on making the best user experience rather than think about whether you the database query right.

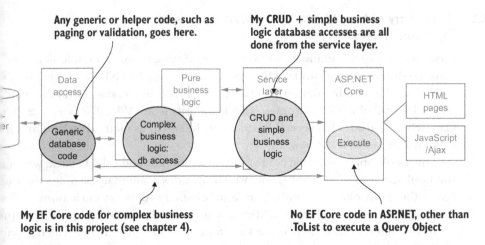

Any generic or helper code, such as paging or validation, goes here.

My CRUD + simple business logic database accesses are all done from the service layer.

My EF Core code for complex business logic is in this project (see chapter 4).

No EF Core code in ASP.NET, other than .ToList to execute a Query Object

5.4   Locations of the database access code (the EF Core code) in the Book App. Separating the EF code in this way makes it easier to find, understand, refactor, and test.

- ASP.NET controllers often have multiple pages/actions (say, one to list items, one to add a new item, one to edit an item, and so on), each of which would need its own database code. By moving the database code out to the service layer, you can create individual classes for each database access rather than have the code spread throughout a controller.
- It's much easier to unit-test your database code if it's in the service layer rather than when it's in an ASP.NET Core controller. You can test ASP.NET Core controllers, but testing can get complicated if your code accesses properties such as HtppRequest (which it does), because it's hard to replicate some of these features to get your unit test to work.

NOTE   You can run tests against your full ASP.NET Core application by using the Microsoft.AspNetCore.Mvc.Testing NuGet package. This testing is known as integration testing when you are testing the whole application, whereas unit testing focuses on testing small parts of the application. You can find more about integration testing at http://mng.bz/MXa7.

Implementing the book list query page

Now that I've set the scene, you're going to implement the ASP.NET Core part of the list of books in our Book App. To remind you what the site looks like, figure 5.5 shows a screenshot of the Book App, with the list of books and the local admin update features.

In chapter 2, you wrote a class called ListBooksService that handled the complexities of transforming, sorting, filtering, and paging the books to display. You'll want to use this class in an ASP.NET Core action called Index in the controller

BookApp   All Books   Logs **7+**   Bg-logs   Your Orders   Privacy   About

Sort By	Filter Type	Filter By	Page	Page
Price 1 ∨	By Categories... ∨	Quantum Entanç ∨	1 of 1	10

Quantum Networking

by Future Person
Published on 01/01/2057
Categories: *Quantum Entanglement*   Admin ▾   Buy Book ▾
Votes: 5.0 by 2 customers
Price: **$219.00** ~~$220.00~~ *Save $1 if you order 40 years ahead!*   Change Pub Date
                                                               Remove Promotion
                                                               Add Review

Figure 5.5 The home page of the Book App, showing the list of books and the admin features, including th
Change Pub(lication) Date of a book

HomeController. The main issue is that to create an instance of the ListBooksSer
class, you need an instance of the application's DbContext.

5.6.1 Injecting an instance of the application's DbContext via DI

The standard way of providing an instance of the application's DbContext i
ASP.NET Core application (and other types of hosted applications) is via DI inje
via a class's constructor (see section 5.3.2). For an ASP.NET Core application
might add a constructor in the controller that has the application's DbContext cl.
a parameter (dependency injection by constructor).

Listing 5.4 shows the start of the ASP.NET Core HomeController, where y.
added a constructor and copied the injected EfCoreContext class to a local field
can be used to create an instance of the BookListService class that you need i
the books. This code uses the DI approach from section 5.3.2 and figure 5.!
replaces the Demo class with the application's DbContext class, EfCoreContext.

Listing 5.4 The Index action in the HomeController displays the list of books

```
public class HomeController : Controller
{
    private readonly EfCoreContext _context;

    public HomeController(EfCoreContext context)          The application's
    {                                                     DbContext is provided
        _context = context;                               by ASP.NET Core via DI.
    }

    public IActionResult Index                            The options parameter is filled wi
        (SortFilterPageOptions options)                   filter, and page options via the UF
```

ASP.NET action,
called when the
home page is
called up by
the user

```
{
    var listService =
        new ListBooksService(_context);

    var bookList = listService
        .SortFilterPage(options)
        .ToList();

    return View(new BookListCombinedDto
        (options, bookList));
}
```

ListBooksService is created by using the application's DbContext from the private field _context.

The SortFilterPage method is called with the sort, filter, and page options provided.

Sends the options (to fill in the controls at the top of the page) and the list of BookListDtos to display as an HTML table

The ToList() method executes the LINQ commands, causing EF Core to translate the LINQ into the appropriate SQL to access the database and return the result as a list.

After you've used the local copy of the application's DbContext to create your List-BooksService, you can call its SortFilterPage method. This method takes the parameters returned from the various controls on the list page and returns an IQueryable<BookListDto> result. Then you add the ToList method to the end of the result, which causes EF Core to execute that IQueryable result against the database and return the list of book information the user has asked for. This result is given to an ASP.NET Core view to display.

You could've had the SortFilterPage method return a List<BookListDto> result, but that approach would've limited you to using a synchronous database access. As you'll see in section 5.10 on async/await, by returning an IQueryable<BookListDto> result, you can choose to use a normal (synchronous) or an async version of the final command that executes the query.

Using the DbContext Factory to create an instance of a DbContext

In some applications, such as a Blazor Server app (see section 5.3.4), the normal scoping of your application's DbContext doesn't work. In this case, you can inject EF Core's IDbContextFactory<TContext> by using DI. This decoupling is useful for Blazor applications, in which EF Core recommends using the IDbContextFactory, and may be useful in other scenarios.

Here is an example taken from the BlazorServerEFCoreSample provided by the EF Core team. In this example, the DbContext Factory is injected into a Blazor Razor page, as shown in the following listing. Only the use of the DbContext Factory and the creation of the DbContext have comments.

Listing 5.5   Example of injecting the DbContext Factory into a Razor page

```
@page "/add"

@inject IDbContextFactory<ContactContext> DbFactory
@inject NavigationManager Nav
@inject IPageHelper PageHelper
```

The DbContext Factory is injected into the Razor page.

```
@if (Contact != null)
{
    <ContactForm Busy="@Busy"
                 Contact="@Contact"
                 IsAdd="true"
                 CancelRequest="Cancel"
                 ValidationResult=
"@(async (success) => await ValidationResultAsync(success))" />
}
@if (Success)
{
    <br />
    <div class="alert alert-success">The contact was successfully
    added.</div>
}
@if (Error)
{
    <br />
    <div class="alert alert-danger">Failed to update the contact
    (@ErrorMessage).</div>
}

@code {
    //… various fields left out
    private async Task ValidationResultAsync(bool success)
    {
        if (Busy)
            return;

        if (!success)
        {
            Success = false;
            Error = false;
            return;
        }

        Busy = true;

        using var context = DbFactory.CreateDbContext();
        context.Contacts.Add(Contact);

        try
        {
            await context.SaveChangesAsync();
            Success = true;
            Error = false;
            // ready for the next
            Contact = new Contact();
            Busy = false;
        }
        catch (Exception ex)
        {
            Success = false;
            Error = true;
            ErrorMessage = ex.Message;
```

Annotations:

- **Another technique to handle Blazor Server apps. It won't handle extra requests until the first request has finished.** (points to `if (Busy) return;`)

- **Creates a ne instance of application' DbContext. the use of v for disposin** (points to `using var context = DbFactory.CreateDbContext();`)

- **The new Contact information is added to the DbContext.** (points to `context.Contacts.Add(Contact);`)

- **Saves the Contact to the database** (points to `await context.SaveChangesAsync();`)

```
        Busy = false;
    }
}

private void Cancel()
{
    Nav.NavigateTo($"/{PageHelper.Page}");
}
}
```

Note that the DbContext instances that created the DbContext Factory are not managed by the application's service provider and therefore must be disposed by the application. In the Blazor Razor page shown in listing 5.5, the using var context = ... will dispose the DbContext instance when the scope of the local context variable is exited.

NOTE   You can find the Razor page shown in listing 5.5 at http://mng.bz/aorz.

Implementing your database methods as a DI service

Although the constructor injection approach you used in the preceding section works, there's another way to use DI that provides better isolation of the database access code: *parameter injection.* In ASP.NET Core, you can arrange for a service to be injected into an *action* method via a parameter marked with the attribute [From-Services]. You can provide a specific service that each action method in your controller needs; this approach is both more efficient and simpler to unit-test. To see how it works, you're going to use a class called ChangePubDateService that's in your service layer to update the publication date of a book. This class allows the admin user to change the publication date of a book, as shown in figure 5.6.

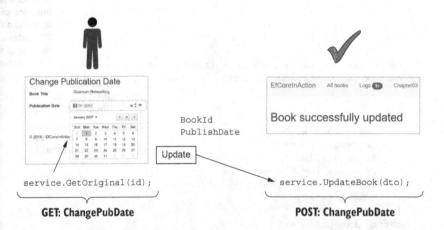

Figure 5.6   The two stages in changing the publication date of a book. The GET stage calls the GetOriginal method to show the user the book and its current publication date. Then the POST stage calls the UpdateBook method with the user set date.

You can see that the process has two stages:

- You show the admin user the current publication date and allow the change it.
- The update is applied to the database, and you tell the user that it was succe

To use parameter injection of your ChangePubDateService class, you need to d things:

- Register your class, ChangePubDateService, with the DI so that it becomes vice you can inject by using DI.
- Use parameter injection to inject the class instance, ChangePubDate, int two ASP.NET action methods that need it (GET and POST).

This approach works well for building ASP.NET Core applications, and I've usec all my ASP.NET MVC projects for many years. In addition to providing good isol and making testing easier, this approach makes the ASP.NET Core controller a methods much easier to write. You'll see in section 5.7.2 that the code insid ChangePubDate action method is simple and short.

5.7.1 Registering your class as a DI service

You can register a class with DI in ASP.NET in numerous ways. The standard wa add an IChangePubDateService interface to the class. Technically, you don't ne interface, but using one is good practice and can be helpful in unit-testing. You use the interface in section 5.7.3 to make registering your classes simpler.

The following listing shows the IChangePubDateService interface. Don't f that the ASP.NET Core controller will be dealing with something of type IChange DateService, so you need to make sure that all the public methods and propertie available in the interface.

Listing 5.6 The IChangePubDateService interface needed to register the class i

```
public interface IChangePubDateService
{
    ChangePubDateDto GetOriginal(int id);
    Book UpdateBook(ChangePubDateDto dto);
}
```

Then you register this interface/class with the DI service. The default way to do t ASP.NET Core is to add a line to the ConfigureServices method in the Startup This listing shows the updated method, with the new code in bold. You add ChangePubDateService as a transient, because you want a new version created time you ask for it.

Listing 5.7 The ASP.NET Core ConfigureService method in the Startup clas

```
public void ConfigureServices (IServiceCollection services)
{
```

```
// Add framework services.
services.AddControllersWithViews();
var connection = Configuration
    .GetConnectionString("DefaultConnection");
services.AddDbContext<EfCoreContext>(
    options => options.UseSqlServer(connection))

services.AddTransient
    <IChangePubDateService, ChangePubDateService>();    ⟵
}
```

Registers the Change-PubDateService class as a service, with the IChangePubDateService interface as the way to access it

Injecting ChangePubDateService into the ASP.NET action method

Having set up the ChangePubDateService class as a service that can be injected via DI, now you need to create an instance in your ASP.NET Core AdminController. The two ASP.NET Core action methods are both called ChangePubDate; one is a GET to fill in the edit page, and one is a POST to do the update.

Figure 5.7 shows how DI creates the ChangePubDateService service, which has an instance of EfCoreDbContext injected via its constructor. Then the ChangePubDate-Service is injected into the AdminController's GET action via parameter injection. As

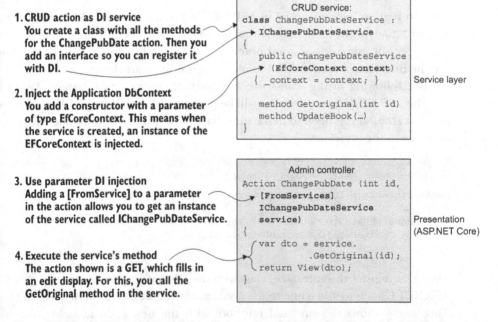

1. CRUD action as DI service
You create a class with all the methods for the ChangePubDate action. Then you add an interface so you can register it with DI.

2. Inject the Application DbContext
You add a constructor with a parameter of type EfCoreContext. This means when the service is created, an instance of the EFCoreContext is injected.

3. Use parameter DI injection
Adding a [FromService] to a parameter in the action allows you to get an instance of the service called IChangePubDateService.

4. Execute the service's method
The action shown is a GET, which fills in an edit display. For this, you call the GetOriginal method in the service.

CRUD service:
```
class ChangePubDateService :
    IChangePubDateService
{
    public ChangePubDateService
        (EfCoreContext context)
    { _context = context; }

    method GetOriginal(int id)
    method UpdateBook(...)
}
```
Service layer

Admin controller
```
Action ChangePubDate (int id,
    [FromServices]
    IChangePubDateService
    service)
{
    var dto = service.
            .GetOriginal(id);
    return View(dto);
}
```
Presentation (ASP.NET Core)

Figure 5.7   Using DI to provide a service often requires the DI provider to create other classes first. In this fairly simple case, there are at least four levels of DI. The AdminController's ChangePubDate is called (bottom rectangle); then the [FromServices] attribute on one of the method's parameters tells the DI provider to create an instance of the ChangePubDateService class. The ChangePubDateService (top rectangle) class requires an instance of the EfCoreDbContext class, so the DI provider must create that instance too, which in turn requires the DbContextOptions<EfCoreContext> to be created so that the EfCoreDbContext class can be created.

you will see, the DI provider is called numerous times to create all the classes ne to handle the HTTP request.

You could have provided an instance of the ChangePubDateService class via structor injection, as you did with the application's DbContext, but that approac a downside. AdminController contains several other database update comm such as adding a review to a book, adding a promotion to a book, and so on. Usir constructor injection would mean you were needlessly creating an instance of Cha PubDateService class when one of these other commands is being called. By usir parameter injection into each action, you take only the time and memory cost o ating the single service you need. The following listing shows the ChangePut ASP.NET GET action that's called when someone clicks the Admin > Change Pub link, wanting to change the publication date.

Listing 5.8 The ChangePubDate **action method in** AdminController

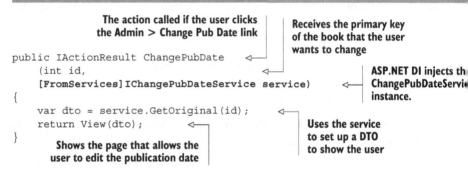

Line 3 (in bold) in this listing is the important one. You've used parameter inje to inject, via DI, an instance of the ChangePubDateService class. The same line i in the POST version of the ChangePubDate action.

Note that the ChangePubDateService class needs the EfCoreContext class the application's DbContext, in its constructor. That's fine because DI is recursive keep filling in parameters, or other DI injections, as long as each class that's ne has been registered.

5.7.3 *Improving registering your database access classes as services*

Before leaving the topic of DI, I want to introduce a better way of registering classes as services via DI. The previous example, in which you made your Change DateService class into a service, required you to add code to register that class service in ASP.NET Core's ConfigureServices. This process works, but it's consuming and error-prone, as you need to add a line of code to register each that you want to use as a service.

In the first edition of this book, I suggested using a DI library called Au (https://autofaccn.readthedocs.io/en/latest) because it has a command that reg all the classes with interfaces in an assembly (also known as a *project*). Since then come across a tweet by David Fowler that links to a set of dependency injection container benchmarks; see http://mng.bz/go2l. From that page, I found out that the ASP.NET Core DI container is a lot faster than AutoFac! At that point, I built a library called NetCore.AutoRegisterDi (see http://mng.bz/5jDz), which has only one job: to register all classes with interfaces in an assembly by using the .NET Core DI Provider.

> **NOTE** After I created my NetCore.AutoRegisterDi library, Andrew Lock pointed me to an existing library called Scrutor; see his article at http://mng .bz/6gly. Scrutor has more features for selecting classes to register than my NetCore.AutoRegisterDi does, so do have a look at Scrutor.

HOW I ORGANIZE THE REGISTERING OF SERVICES WITH THE NET CORE DI CONTAINER

The NetCore.AutoRegisterDi library is simple: it scans one or more assembles; looks for standard public, nongeneric classes that have public interfaces; and registers them with NET Core's DI provider. It has some simple filtering and some lifetime-setting capabilities, but not much more (it's only ~80 lines of code). But this simple piece of code gives you two benefits over manually registering your classes/interfaces with the DI provider:

- It saves you time because you don't have to register every interface/class manually.
- More important, it automatically registers your interfaces/classes so that you don't forget.

The second reason is why I find this library to be so useful: I can't forget to register a service. The following listing shows you a typical call to the NetCore.AutoRegisterDi library.

Listing 5.9   Using NetCore.AutoRegisterDi to register classes as DI services

This method takes zero to many assemblies to scan. If no assembly is provided, it will scan the calling assembly.

You can get references to the assemblies by providing a class that is in that assembly.

```
var assembly1ToScan = Assembly.GetAssembly(typeof(ass1Class));
var assembly2ToScan = Assembly.GetAssembly(typeof(ass2Class));

service.RegisterAssemblyPublicNonGenericClasses(
        assembly1ToScan, assembly2ToScan)
    .Where(c => c.Name.EndsWith("Service"))
    .AsPublicImplementedInterfaces();
```

This optional filter system allows you to filter the classes that you want to register.

Registers all the classes that have public interfaces. By default, the services are registered as transient, but you can change that registration by adding a ServiceLifetime parameter or attributes.

I could put a call like the one shown in listing 5.9 in the Configure method in ASP.NET Core's Startup class that registers all the assemblies, but I don't. I prefer to add an extension method in every project that has classes that need to register as a DI service. That way, I have isolated the setup of each project into one class in each project that needs it.

Each extension method uses the `NetCore.AutoRegisterDi` library to registe standard classes/services in the project. The extension method also has spac additional code, such as handcoded registration of classes/services that can't be tered automatically, such as generic classes/services.

The following listing shows an example of the extension method in the se layer. This code needs the `NetCore.AutoRegisterDi` NuGet package to be add that project.

Listing 5.10   Extension method in ServiceLayer that handles all the DI service registe

The NetCore.AutoRegisterDi library
understands NET Core DI, so you can
access the IServiceCollection interface.

Creates a static
class to hold my
extension

```
public static class NetCoreDiSetupExtensions
{
    public static void RegisterServiceLayerDi
        (this IServiceCollection services)
    {
        services.RegisterAssemblyPublicNonGenericClasses()
            .AsPublicImplementedInterfaces();
    }
}
```

This class is in the
ServiceLayer, so I give
method a name with th
Assembly name in it.

Calling th
Assembly
GenericCl
without a
means th
the callin

For handcoded
registrations that
NetCore.AutoRegisterDi
can't do, such as
generic classes

This method will
register all the
public classes with
interfaces with a
Transient lifetime.

The Book App in part 1 of the book has classes/services that need registering i ServiceLayer, BizDbAccess, and BizLogic projects. To do so, you copy the code i ing 5.10 into the other projects and change the name of the method so that each can be identified. A call to each method automatically registers the standard ser because by default, the `RegisterAssemblyPublicNonGenericClasses` scans the as bly that it's called from.

Now that you have individual versions of listing 5.8 in each of the three pro that need them, you need to call each one to set up each project. You do so by ad the following code to the `Configure` method in ASP.NET Core's `Startup` class.

Listing 5.11   Calling all your registration methods in the projects that need them

```
public void ConfigureServices(IServiceCollection services)
{
    //… other registrations left out

    services.RegisterBizDbAccessDi();
    services.RegisterBizLogicDi();
    services.RegisterServiceLayerDi();
}
```

This meth
the Start
sets up s
for ASP.N

You add your
registration extension
methods here.

The result is that all the classes you have written with public interfaces in the Se Layer, BizDbAccess, and BizLogic projects will automatically be registered as DI ser

Deploying an ASP.NET Core application with a database

After developing your ASP.NET Core application with a database, at some point you'll want to copy it to a web server so that others can use it. This process is called *deploying* your application to a *host*. This section shows how.

> **NOTE**   For more information on ASP.NET Core deployment, Andrew Lock's book *ASP.NET Core in Action*, 2nd ed. (Manning, 2020; see https://www .manning.com/books/asp-net-core-in-action-second-edition) has a chapter on deployment; or see Microsoft's online documentation at http://mng.bz/op7M.

Knowing where the database is on the web server

When you run your ASP.NET Core application locally during development, it accesses a database server on your development computer. This example uses Visual Studio, which comes with a local SQL server for development that's available via the reference (localdb)\mssqllocaldb. As explained in section 5.4.1, the connection string for that database is held in the appsettings.Development.json file.

When you deploy your application to a web server, Visual Studio by default rebuilds your application with the ASPNETCORE_ENVIRONMENT variable set to Production. This setting causes your application to try to load the appsetting.json file, followed by the appsettings.Production.json file. The appsettings.Production.json file is the place where you (or the publishing system) put the connection string for your host database.

> **TIP**   At startup, appsettings.Production.json is read last and overrides any setting with the same name in the appsetting.json file. Therefore, you can put your development connection string setting in the appsetting.json file if you want to, but best practice is to put it in the appsettings.Development.json file.

You can set your hosted database's connection string manually with Visual Studio's Publish feature; right-click the ASP.NET Core project in Solution Explorer view and select Publish. When you publish your application, Visual Studio creates/updates the appsettings.Production.json file with the connection string you provided and deploys that file with the application. On startup, the constructor of the ASP.NET Core's Startup class reads both files, and the appsettings.Production.json connection string is used.

Most Windows hosting systems provide a Visual Studio publish profile that you can import to the Publish feature. That profile makes setting up deployment much easier, as it not only details where the ASP.NET Core application should be written to, but also provides the connection string for the hosted database.

Cloud systems such as Azure Web App service have a feature that can override properties in your appsettings.json file on deployment. This means you can set your database connection, which contains the database username and password, within Azure; your username and password never exist on your development system and, hence, are more secure.

5.8.2 Creating and migrating the database

When your application and its database are running on a web server, control o
database changes. On your development machine, you can do pretty much any
to the database, but after you deploy to a web server, the rules can change. Dep
ing on the host or your company's business rules, what you can do to the data
will vary.

A version of the Book App from the first edition of this book, for example
hosted on a cost-effective (cheap!) shared hosting platform (WebWiz in the U
Kingdom), which doesn't allow your application to create or delete the database
also used Microsoft's Azure cloud system, on which I can delete and create a data
but creating a database takes a long time.

The simplest approach, which works on all the systems I've come across, is ge
the hosting system to create an empty database and then applying the comman
alter the database structure. The easiest way is via EF Core migrations, which
about to describe, but there are other ways.

> **WARNING** Before I start, I need to warn you that changing the database struc-
> ture of a website needs to be approached carefully, especially for 24/7 web-
> sites that need to keep working during a database change. Lots of things can
> go wrong, and the effect could be lost data or a broken website.

This chapter describes EF Core migrations, which are a good system but has their
itations. Chapter 9 presents ways of handling database migrations, including m
sophisticated techniques, and discusses the pros and cons of each approach.

5.9 Using EF Core's migration feature to change the database's structure

This section describes how to use EF Core's migration feature to update a data
You can use migrations on both your development machine and your host, b
explained in section 5.8.2, the challenging one is the database on your web host.
book has is a whole chapter (chapter 9) on migrations, but this section gives yo
overview of using migrations in ASP.NET Core applications.

5.9.1 Updating your production database

As you may remember from chapter 2, which briefly introduced EF Core migrat
you can type two commands into Visual Studio's Package Manager Console (PMC

- `Add-Migration`—Creates migration code in your application to create/up
  your database structure
- `Update-Database`—Applies the migration code to the database referred
  the application's DbContext

The first command is fine, but the second command will update only the de
database, which is likely to be on your development machine, not your produ

database. What happens when you want to deploy your web application to some sort of web host, and the database isn't at the right level to match the code? You have four ways to update your production database if you're using EF Core's migration feature:

- You can have your application check and migrate the database during startup.
- You can migrate the database in a continuous integration (CI) and continuous delivery (CD) pipeline.
- You can have a standalone application migrate your database.
- You can extract the SQL commands needed to update your database and then use a tool to apply those SQL commands to your production database.

The simplest option is the first one, which I'm going to describe here. It does have limitations, such as not being designed to work in multiple-instance web hosting (called *scaling out* in Azure). But having the application do the migration is simple and is a good first step in using EF Core's migrations in an ASP.NET Core application.

> **WARNING** Microsoft recommends that you update a production database by using SQL commands, which is the most robust approach. But it requires quite a few steps and tools that you may not have on hand, so I cover the simpler `Database.Migrate` approach. Chapter 9 covers every aspect of database migrations, including the advantages and limitations of each approach.

Having your application migrate your database on startup

The advantage of having your application apply any outstanding database migrations at startup is that you can't forget to do it: deploying a new application will stop the old application and then start the new application. By adding code that's run when the application starts, you can call the `context.Database.Migrate` method, which applies any missing migrations to the database before the main application starts—simple, until it goes wrong, which is why chapter 9, dedicated to database migrations, discusses all these issues. But for now, let's keep to the simple approach.

Having decided to apply the migration on startup, you need to decide where to call your migration code. The recommended approach to adding any startup code to an ASP.NET Core application is to append your code to the end of the `Main` method in ASP.NET Core's `Program` class. The normal code in the `Main` method is shown in this code snippet:

```
public static void Main(string[] args)
{
    CreateHostBuilder(args).Build().Run();
}
```

The best way to add the migration code is to build an extension method holding the EF Core code you want to run and append it after the `CreateHostBuilder(args)` `.Build()` call. The following listing shows the ASP.NET Core's `Program` class with one new line (in bold) added to call your extension method, called `MigrateDatabaseAsync`.

NOTE I will be using async/await commands in this section. I cover async/await in section 5.10.

Listing 5.12 ASP.NET Core `Program` class, including a method to migrate the datab

```
public class Program
{
    public static async Task Main(string[] args)
    {
        var host = CreateHostBuilder(args).Build();
        await host.MigrateDatabaseAsync();
        await host.RunAsync();
    }
    //… other code not shown
}
```

You change the Main me
being async so that you
async/await commands i
SetupDatabaseAsync me

Calls your extension method to migrate your database

This call runs the
Startup.Configure
which sets up the **▮**
you need to setup/
your database.

At the end, you
start the ASP.NET
Core application.

The `MigrateDatabaseAsync` method should contain all the code you want to r
startup to migrate, and possibly seed, your database. The following listing show
example of how you might use this method to migrate your database.

Listing 5.13 The `MigrateDatabaseAsync` extension method to migrate the datab

Creates a scoped service provider. After the using block is left, all the services will be unavailable. This approach is the recommended way to obtain services outside an HTTP request.

```
public static async Task MigrateDatabaseAsync
    (this IHost webHost)
{
    using (var scope = webHost.Services.CreateScope())
    {
        var services = scope.ServiceProvider;
        using (var context = services
            .GetRequiredService<EfCoreContext>())
        {
            try
            {
                await context.Database.MigrateAsync();
                //Put any complex database seeding here
            }
            catch (Exception ex)
            {
                var logger = services
                    .GetRequiredService<ILogger<Program>>();
                logger.LogError(ex,
                "An error occurred while migrating the database.");

                throw;
            }
        }
    }
}
```

Creates an extension
method that takes in IHos**▮**

Creates an instance of t
application's DbContext
that has a lifetime of on
the outer using stateme

Calls EF Core's MigrateAsync command to apply any outstanding migrations at startup

You can add a method here to handle complex seeding of the database if required.

If an exception occurs, you
log the information so that
you can diagnose it.

Rethrows the exception because
you don't want the application
to carry on if a problem with
migrating the database occurs

The series of calls at the start of the listing is the recommended way to get a copy of the application's DbContext inside the Configure method in the ASP.NET Core Startup class. This code creates a scoped lifetime instance (see section 5.3.3) of the application's DbContext that can be safely used to access the database.

The key commands in listing 5.13, inside the try block (in bold), call EF Core's MigrateAsync command. This command applies any database migration that exists but hasn't already been applied to the database.

> **EF6**   The EF Core approach to database setup is different from that of EF6.x. On first use of the DbContext, EF6.x runs various checks by using *database initializers*, whereas EF Core does nothing at all to the database on initialization. Therefore, you need to add your own code to handle migrations. The downside is that you need to write some code, but the upside is that you have total control of what happens.

SETTING UP INITIAL DATABASE CONTENT DURING STARTUP

In addition to migrating the database, you may want to add default data to the database at the same time, especially if it's empty. This process, called *seeding* the database, covers adding initial data to the database or maybe updating data in an existing database. The main way to seed your database with static data is via migrations, which I cover in chapter 9. The other option is to run some code when the migration has finished. This option is useful if you have dynamic data or complex updates that the migration seeding can't handle.

An example of running code after the migration is adding example Books, with Authors, Reviews, and so on to the Book App if no books are already present. To do this, you create an extension method, SeedDatabaseAsync, which is shown in the following listing. The code is added after the call to the Database.MigrateAsync method in listing 5.13.

Listing 5.14   Our example MigrateAndSeed extension method

```
public static async Task SeedDatabaseAsync          Extension method that takes in
    (this EfCoreContext context)                    the application's DbContext
{
    if (context.Books.Any()) return;         ◁─┤  If there are existing books, you
                                                    return, as you don't need to add any.

    context.Books.AddRange(                       Database has no books, so you seed it;
        EfTestData.CreateFourBooks());            in this case, you add the default books.
    await context.SaveChangesAsync();      ◁─
}                                                    SaveChangesAsync is called
                                                     to update the database.
```

In this example SeedDatabaseAsync method, you check whether any books are in the database and then add them only if the database is empty (has just been created, for example). This example is a simple one, and here are others:

- Loading data from a file on startup (see the SetupHelpers class in the Service-Layer in the associated GitHub repo)

- Filling in extra data after a specific migration—if you added a `FullName` erty/column, for example, and wanted to fill it in from the `FirstName` `LastName` columns

> **WARNING** I tried doing a database update like the previous `FullName` example on a large database with tens of thousands of rows to update, and it failed. The failure occurred because the update was done via EF Core on startup, and it took so long for the ASP.NET Core application to start that Azure timed out the web application. I now know that I should have done the update by using SQL in the migration (see the example in section 9.5.2), which would have been a lot faster.

If you want to run your seed database method only when a new migration has applied, you can use the DbContext method `Database.GetPendingMigrations` t the list of migrations that are about to be applied. If this method returns an empt lection, there is no pending migration in the current database. You must call `PendingMigrations` before you execute the `Database.Migrate` method, becaus pending migrations collection is empty when the `Migrate` method has finished.

> **EF6** In EF6.x, the `Add-Migration` command adds a class called `Configuration`, which contains a method called `Seed` that's run every time the application starts. EF Core uses the `HasData` configuration method, which allows you to define data to be added during a migration (chapter 9).

5.10 *Using async/await for better scalability*

Async/await is a feature that allows a developer to easily use *asynchronous program* running tasks in parallel. Up to this point in this book, I have not used async/ because I hadn't explained this feature. But you need to know that in real applica that have multiple requests happening at the same time, such as ASP.NET Core, of your database commands will use async/await.

Async/await is a big topic, but in this section, you'll look only at how using as await can benefit an ASP.NET Core's application scalability. It does this by rele resources while waiting for the database server to carry out the command(s) th Core has asked it to do.

> **NOTE** If you want to find out more about async/await's other features, such as running tasks in parallel, have a look at the Microsoft documentation at http://mng.bz/nM7K.

5.10.1 *Why async/await is useful in a web application using EF Core*

When EF Core accesses the database, it needs to wait for the database server to ru commands and return the result. For large datasets and/or complex queries, this cess can take hundreds of milliseconds or even seconds. During that time, a web ap tion is holding on to a thread from the application's thread pool. Each access to the application needs a thread from the thread pool, and there's an upper limit.

Using an async/await version of an EF Core command means that the user's current thread is released until the database access finishes, so someone else can use that thread. Figure 5.8 shows two cases. In case A, two users are simultaneously accessing the website by using normal synchronous accesses, and they clash, so two threads are needed from the thread pool. In case B, user 1's access is a long-running database access that uses an async command to release the thread while it's waiting for the database. This allows user 2 to reuse the thread that the async command released while user 2 is waiting for the database.

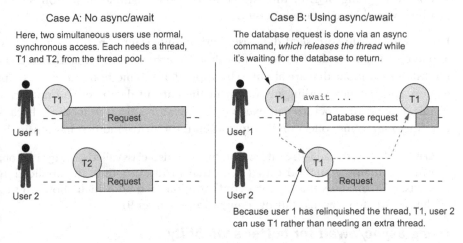

Figure 5.8 Differences in database access. In the normal, synchronous database access in case A, two threads are needed to handle the two users. In case B, user 1's database access is accomplished with an async command, which frees the thread, T1, making it available for user 2.

NOTE You can read a more in-depth explanation of what async/await does in an ASP.NET web application at http://mng.bz/vz7M.

The use of async/await improves the scalability of your website: your web server will be able to handle more concurrent users. The downside is that async/await commands take slightly longer to execute because they run more code. A bit of analysis is needed to get the right balance of scalability and performance.

2 Where should you use async/await with database accesses?

The general advice from Microsoft is to use async methods wherever possible in a web application because they give you better scalability. In real applications, that's what I do. I haven't done it in the part 1 (and 2) Book App, because it's a little easier to understand the code without await statements everywhere, but the part 3 Book App, which is significantly enhanced, uses async throughout.

Sync commands are slightly faster than the equivalent async command (see table 14.5 for the actual differences), but the time difference is so small that sticking

to Microsoft's guideline "Always use async commands in ASP.NET applicatio
the right choice.

5.10.3 Changing over to async/await versions of EF Core commands

Let me start by showing you a method that calls an async version of an EF Core
mand; then I'll explain it. Figure 5.9 shows an async method that returns the
number of books in the database.

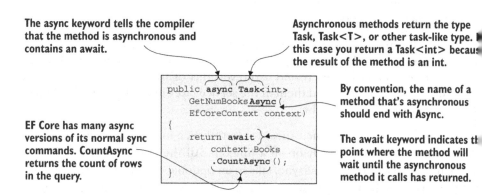

The async keyword tells the compiler that the method is asynchronous and contains an await.

Asynchronous methods return the type Task, Task<T>, or other task-like type. this case you return a Task<int> becaus the result of the method is an int.

```
public async Task<int>
    GetNumBooksAsync (
    EfCoreContext context)
{
    return await
        context.Books
        .CountAsync();
}
```

EF Core has many async versions of its normal sync commands. CountAsync returns the count of rows in the query.

By convention, the name of a method that's asynchronous should end with Async.

The await keyword indicates th point where the method will wait until the asynchronous method it calls has returned.

Figure 5.9   The anatomy of an asynchronous method, highlighting the parts of the code that are different from a normal synchronous method

EF Core contains an async version of all the applicable commands, all of which h
method name that ends with Async. As you saw in the preceding async method e
ple, you need to carry the "async-ness" to the method in which you call the asyn
Core command.

The rule is that after you use an async command, every caller must either b
async method or should pass on the task directly until it gets to the top-level c
which must handle it asynchronously. ASP.NET Core supports async for all the
commands, such as controller actions, so this situation isn't a problem in suc
application.

The next listing shows an async version of your Index action method from
HomeController, with the parts you have to change to make this command us
async database access, with the async parts in bold.

Listing 5.15   The async Index action method from the `HomeController`

```
public async Task<IActionResult> Index
    (SortFilterPageOptions options)
{
    var listService =
        new ListBooksService(_context);
```

You make the Index action method async by using the async keyword, and the returned type has to be wrapped in a generic task.

```
var bookList = await listService
    .SortFilterPage(options)
    .ToListAsync();

return View(new BookListCombinedDto
    (options, bookList));
}
```

◄─── **You must await the result of the ToListAsync method, which is an async command.**

◄─── **You can change SortFilterPage to async by replacing .ToList() with .ToListAsync().**

Because you design your SortFilterPage method to return IQueryable<T>, it's simple to change database access to async by replacing the ToList method with the ToListAsync method.

> **TIP** Business logic code is often a good candidate for using async databases' access methods because their database accesses often contain complex read/write commands. I've created async versions of the BizRunners in case you need them. You can find them in the service layer in the BizRunners directory (see http://mng.bz/PPlw).

Another part of async is the CancellationToken, a mechanism that allows you to stop an async method manually or on a timeout. All the async LINQ and EF Core commands, such as SavChangesAsync, take in an optional CancellationToken. Section 5.11 demonstrates the use of a CancellationToken to stop any recurring background tasks when ASP.NET Core is stopped.

Running parallel tasks: How to provide the DbContext

In some situations, running more than one thread of code is useful. By this, I mean that running a separate *task*—a parallel set of code that runs "at the same time" as the main application. I put "at the same time" in quotes because if there's only one CPU, the two tasks need to share it.

Parallel tasks are useful in various scenarios. Say you're accessing multiple, external sources that you need to wait for before they return a result. By using multiple tasks running in parallel, you gain performance improvements. In another scenario, you might have a long-running task, such as processing order fulfillment in the background. You use parallel tasks to avoid blocking the normal flow and making your website look slow and unresponsive. Figure 5.10 shows an example background task in which a long-running process is run on another thread so that the user isn't held up.

Running parallel tasks isn't specific to ASP.NET Core; it can occur in any application. But larger web applications often use this feature, so I explain it in this chapter. The solution you will build is a background service that runs every hour and logs how many Reviews are in the database. This simple example will show you how to do two things:

- Obtain an instance of your application's DbContext to run in parallel
- Use the ASP.NET Core's IHostedService feature to run your background task

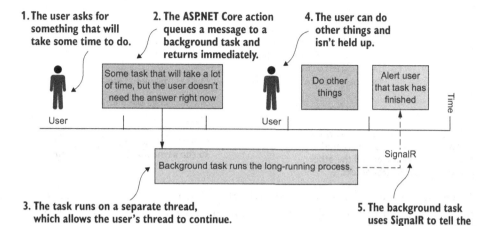

1. The user asks for something that will take some time to do.
2. The ASP.NET Core action queues a message to a background task and returns immediately.
4. The user can do other things and isn't held up.

3. The task runs on a separate thread, which allows the user's thread to continue.

5. The background task uses SignalR to tell the user the task is finished

Figure 5.10 Moving long-running processes to a background task that runs in parallel to the main website, which makes the website feel more responsive. In this example, I use an ASP.NET Core `backgroundService` to run the long-running task. When the task is finished, it uses `SignalR` to update the user's screen with a message saying that the long-running task has finished successfully. (`SignalR` is a library that allows an ASP.NET Core app to send messages to the user's screen.)

5.11.1 Obtaining an instance of your application's DbContext to run in parallel

If you want to run any code that uses EF Core in parallel, you can't use the nor approach of getting the application's DbContext because EF Core's DbContext thread-safe; you can't use the same instance in multiple tasks. EF Core will throw exception if it finds that the same DbContext instance is used in two tasks.

In ASP.NET Core, the correct way to get a DbContext to run in the background by using a DI scoped service. This scoped service allows you to create, via DI, a DbCo that's unique to the task that you're running. To do this, you need to do three th

- Get an instance of the `IServiceScopeFactory` via constructor injection.
- Use the `IServiceScopeFactory` to a *scoped DI service.*
- Use the scoped DI service to obtain an instance of the application's DbCo that is unique to this scope.

The following listing shows the method in your background task that uses the `IServ ScopeFactory` to obtain a unique instance of your application's DbContext. method counts the number of `Reviews` in the database and logs that number.

> Listing 5.16 The method inside the background service that accesses the database

```
private async Task DoWorkAsync(CancellationToken stoppingToken)
{
    using (var scope = _scopeFactory.CreateScope())
    {
```

The IHo will call when the has ela

Uses the ScopeProviderFactory to create a new DI scoped provider

```
var context = scope.ServiceProvider
    .GetRequiredService<EfCoreContext>();
var numReviews = await context.Set<Review>()
    .CountAsync(stoppingToken);
_logger.LogInformation(
    "Number of reviews: {numReviews}", numReviews);
}
}
```

Because of the scoped DI provider, the DbContext instance created will be different from all the other instances of the DbContext.

Logs the information

Counts the reviews, using an async method. You pass the stoppingToken to the async method because doing so is good practice.

The important point of the code is that you provide `ServiceScopeFactory` to each task so that it can use DI to get a unique instance of the DbContext (and any other scoped services). In addition to solving the DbContext thread-safe issue, if you are running the method repeatedly, it's best to have a new instance of the application's DbContext so that data from the last run doesn't affect your next run.

2 *Running a background service in ASP.NET Core*

Earlier, I described how to get a thread-safe version of the application's DbContext; now you'll use it in a background service. The following background example isn't as complex as the one show in figure 5.10, but it covers how to write and run background services.

ASP.NET Core has a feature that allows you to run tasks in the background. This situation isn't really a database issue, but I show you the code for completeness. (I recommend that you look at Microsoft's ASP.NET Core documentation on background tasks at http://mng.bz/QmOj.) This listing shows the code that runs in another thread and calls the `DoWorkAsync` method shown in listing 5.16 every hour.

Listing 5.17   An ASP.NET Core background service that calls `DoWorkAsync` every hour

Inheriting the BackgroundService class means that this class can run continuously in the background.

```
public class BackgroundServiceCountReviews : BackgroundService
{
    private static TimeSpan _period =
        new TimeSpan(0,1,0,0);
```

Holds the delay between each call to the code to log the number of reviews

```
    private readonly IServiceScopeFactory _scopeFactory;
    private readonly ILogger<BackgroundServiceCountReviews> _logger;

    public BackgroundServiceCountReviews(
        IServiceScopeFactory scopeFactory,
        ILogger<BackgroundServiceCountReviews> logger)
    {
        _scopeFactory = scopeFactory;
        _logger = logger;
    }
```

This loop repeatedly calls the DoWorkAsync method, with a delay until the next call is made.

```
protected override async Task ExecuteAsync
    (CancellationToken stoppingToken)
{
    while (!stoppingToken.IsCancellationRequested)
    {
        await DoWorkAsync(stoppingToken);
        await Task.Delay(_period, stoppingToken);
    }
}

private async Task DoWorkAsync...
//see listing 5.16
}
```

**The BackgroundS‹
class has a Execut‹
method that you o
to add your own c**

You need to register your background class with the NET DI provider, usin‹ AddHostedService method. When the Book App starts, your background task w run first, but when your background task gets to a place where it calls an ‹ method and uses the await statement, control goes back to the ASP.NET Core ‹ which starts up the web application.

5.11.3 Other ways of obtaining a new instance of the application's DbContext

Although DI is the recommended method to get the application's DbConte› some cases, such as a console application, DI may not be configured or availab‹ these cases, you have two other options that allow you to obtain an instance o application's DbContext:

- Move your configuration of the application's DbContext by overridin‹ OnConfiguring method in the DbContext and placing the code to se the DbContext there.
- Use the same constructor used for ASP.NET Core and manually inject the base options and connection string, as you do in unit tests (see chapter 17`

The downside of the first option is it uses a fixed connection string, so it a accesses the same database, which could make deployment to another system dif‹ if the database name or options change. The second option—providing the dat‹ options manually—allows you to read in a connection string from the appsetting‹ or a file inside your code.

Another issue to be aware of is that each call will give you a new instance o application's DbContext. From the discussions of lifetime scopes in section 5.3 times you might want to have the same instance of the application's DbConte‹ ensure that tracking changes works. You can work around this issue by designing application so that one instance of the application's DbContext is passed betwee‹ the code that needs to collaborate on database updates.

Summary

- ASP.NET Core uses dependency injection (DI) to provide the application's DbContext. With DI, you can dynamically link parts of your application by letting DI create class instances as required.

- The ConfigureServices method in ASP.NET Core's Startup class is the place to configure and register your version of the application's DbContext by using a connection string that you place in an ASP.NET Core application setting file.

- To get an instance of the application's DbContext to use with your code via DI, you can use constructor injection. DI will look at the type of each of the constructor's parameters and attempt to find a service for which it can provide an instance.

- Your database access code can be built as a service and registered with the DI. Then you can inject your services into the ASP.NET Core action methods via parameter injection: the DI will find a service that finds the type of an ASP.NET Core action method's parameter that's marked with the attribute [FromServices].

- Deploying an ASP.NET Core application that uses a database requires you to define a database connection string that has the location and name of the database on the host.

- EF Core's migration feature provides one way to change your database if your entity classes and/or the EF Core configuration change. The Migrate method has some limitations when used on cloud hosting sites that run multiple instances of your web application.

- Async/await tasking methods on database access code can make your website handle more simultaneous users, but performance could suffer, especially on simple database accesses.

- If you want to use parallel tasks, you need to provide a unique instance of the application's DbContext by creating a new scoped DI provider.

For readers who are familiar with EF6.x:

- The way you obtain an instance of the application's DbContext in ASP.NET Core is via DI.

- Compared with EF6.x, EF Core has a different approach to creating the first instance of a DbContext. EF6.x has database initializers and can run a Seed method. EF Core has none of these EF6.x features but leaves you to write the specific code you want to run at startup.

- Seeding the database in EF Core is different from the way EF6.x works. The EF Core approach adds seeding to migrations, so they are run only if a migration is applied to the database; see chapter 9 for more information.

Tips and techniqu
for reading an
writing with EF Co

This chapter covers

- Selecting the right approach to read data from the database
- Writing queries that perform well on the database side
- Avoiding problems when you use Query Filters and special LINQ commands
- Using AutoMapper to write `Select` queries more quickly
- Writing code to quickly copy and delete entities in the database

---

The first four chapters cover different ways to read/write to a database, an chapter 5, you used that information to build the Book App—an ASP.NET web application. This chapter brings together lots of different tips and techni for reading and writing data with EF Core.

The chapter is split into two sections: reading from the database and writi the database. Each section covers certain read/write issues you may come ac but at the same time explains how EF Core achieves the solutions. The aim give you lots of practical tips by solving different problems and, at the same time, deepen your knowledge of how EF Core works. The tips are useful, but in the long run, becoming an expert on EF Core is going to make you a better developer.

> **TIP** Don't forget that the companion Git repo (http://mng.bz/XdlG) contains unit tests for every chapter of the book. For this chapter, look in the Test project in the master branch for classes starting with Ch06_. Sometimes, seeing the code is quicker than reading the words.

Reading from the database

This section covers different aspects and examples of reading data from a database. The aim is to expose you to some of the inner working of EF Core by looking at different problems and issues. On the way, you will pick up various tips that may be useful as you build applications with EF Core. Here is the list of topics on reading from the database via EF Core:

- Exploring the relational fixup stage in a query
- Understanding what AsNoTracking and its variant do
- Reading in hierarchical data efficiently
- Understanding how the Include method works
- Making loading navigational collections fail-safe
- Using Query Filters in real-world situations
- Considering LINQ commands that need special attention
- Using AutoMapper to automate building Select queries
- Evaluating how EF Core creates an entity class when reading data in

Exploring the relational fixup stage in a query

When you query the database by using EF Core, a stage called relational fixup runs to fill in the navigational properties of other entity classes included in the query. I described this process in section 1.9.2, where the Book entity was linked to its Author. Up to this point, all the queries you have seen link only the entity classes read in by the current query. But in fact, the relational fixup on a normal, read-write query can link outside a single query to any tracked entities, as described in this section.

Whenever you read in entity classes as tracked entities (your query didn't include the command AsNoTracking), the relation fixup stage will run to link up navigational properties. The important point is that the relation fixup stage doesn't only look at the data in your query; it also looks at all the existing tracked entities when it's filling in the navigational properties. Figure 6.1 shows two ways to load a Book with its Reviews, both of which fill in the Book's Reviews navigational property.

As this simple example shows, the relational fixup that is run when a query has finished will fill in any navigational links based on the database key constraints, and it's pretty powerful, If you loaded all the Books, Reviews, BookAuthor, and Authors in four separate queries, for example, EF Core would correctly link up all the navigational

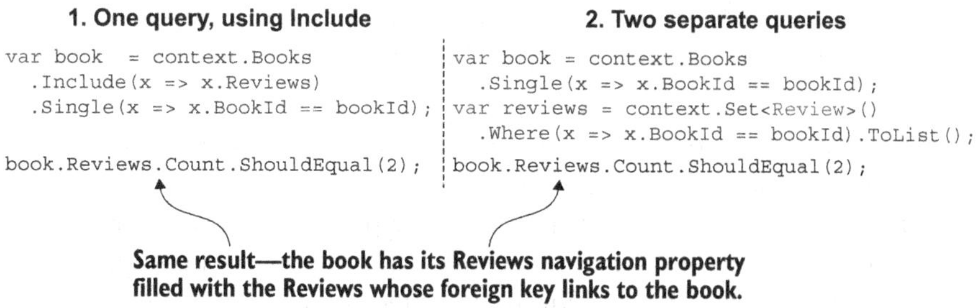

1. One query, using Include

```
var book  = context.Books
   .Include(x => x.Reviews)
   .Single(x => x.BookId == bookId);

book.Reviews.Count.ShouldEqual(2);
```

2. Two separate queries

```
var book = context.Books
   .Single(x => x.BookId == bookId);
var reviews = context.Set<Review>()
   .Where(x => x.BookId == bookId).ToList();
book.Reviews.Count.ShouldEqual(2);
```

Same result—the book has its Reviews navigation property
filled with the Reviews whose foreign key links to the book.

Figure 6.1 This figure shows a single query that loads a `Book` with its `Reviews`, using the
`Include` method to load the `Reviews` (see code on the left). The query on the right loads the
book without its `Reviews`; then it does a second query that loads the `Reviews` separately.
Both versions of the code produce the same result: a `Book` entity is loaded, and its `Reviews`
navigational property is also loaded, with the `Reviews` linked to that `Book`.

properties. The following code snippet does just that: the books read in the firs
start with no relationships filled in, but by the end of the four lines of code, the b
`Reviews` and `AuthorsLink` navigational properties are filled in, and the `BookAut`
`Book` and `Author` navigational properties are also filled in:

```
var books = context.Books.ToList();
var reviews = context.Set<Review>().ToList();
var authorsLinks = context.Set<BookAuthor>().ToList();
var authors = context.Authors.ToList();
```

This feature of EF Core allows you to do some useful things. In section 6.1.3, y
learn how to read hierarchical data efficiently by using this technique.

6.1.2 *Understanding what AsNoTracking and its variant do*

When you query the database via EF Core, you are doing so for a reason: to alte
data read in, such as changing the `Title` property in the `Book` entity, or to perfo
read-only query, such as displaying the `Books` with their prices, authors, and so on.
section covers how the `AsNoTracking` and `AsNoTrackingWithIdentityResolu`
methods improve the performance of a read-only query and affect the data rea
The following code snippet from chapter 1 uses `AsNoTracking` to display a list of F
and their `Authors` on the console:

```
var books = context.Books
         .AsNoTracking()
         .Include(a => a.Author)
         .ToList();
```

A normal query without either of two `AsNoTracking` methods will track the e
classes loaded by the query, allowing you to update or delete the entity classes yc
loaded. But if you need only a read-only version, you can include two methods in

query. Both methods improve performance and ensure that changes to the data won't be written back to the database, but there are slight differences in the relationships returned:

- `AsNoTracking` produces a quicker query time but doesn't always represent the exact database relationships.
- `AsNoTrackingWithIdentityResolution` typically is quicker than a normal query but slower than the same query with `AsNoTracking`. The improvement is that the database relationships are represented correctly, with a entity class instance for each row in the database.

Let's start by looking at the differences in the data returned by a query that uses the two `AsNoTracking` variants. To give you the best performance, the `AsNoTracking` method doesn't execute the feature called identity resolution that ensures that there is only one instance of an entity per row in the database. Not applying the identity resolution feature to the query means that you might get an extra instances of entity classes.

Figure 6.2 shows what happens when you use the `AsNoTracking` and `AsNoTrackingWithIdentityResolution` methods on the super-simple database in chapter 1. That example has four books, but the first two books have the same author. As the figure shows, the `AsNoTracking` query creates four `Author` class instances, but the database has only three rows in the Author table.

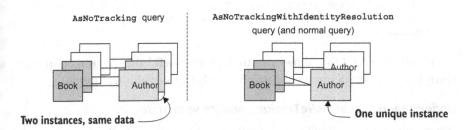

Figure 6.2 The first two books have the same author, Martin Fowler. In the `AsNoTracking` query on the left, EF Core creates four instances of the `Author` class, two of which contain the same data. A query containing `AsNoTrackingWithIdentityResolution` (or a normal query) on the right creates only three instances of the `Author` class, and the first two books point to the same instance.

In most read-only situations, such as displaying each book with the author's name, having four `Author` class instances doesn't matter because the duplicate classes contain the same data. In these types of read-only queries, you should use the `AsNoTracking` method because it produces the fastest query.

But if you are using the relationships in some way, such as to create a report of books which linked to other books by the same author, the `AsNoTracking` method might cause a problem. In a case like that one, you should use the `AsNoTrackingWithIdentityResolution` method.

HISTORY Some history: before EF Core 3.0, the AsNoTracking method included the identity resolution stage, but in EF Core 3.0, which had a big focus on performance, the identity resolution was removed from the AsNoTracking method. Removing the identity-resolution call produced some problems with existing applications, so EF Core 5 added the AsNoTrackingWithIdentity-Resolution method to fix the problems.

To give you an idea of the performance differences, I did a simple test of three ries, loading a hundred Books with their Reviews, BookAuthor, and Author en Table 6.1 shows the timings (second query).

Table 6.1 Result of running the same query using a normal, read-write query and queries that c the AsNoTracking and AsNoTrackingWithIdentityResolution methods

AsNoTracking variants	Time (ms)	Percentage differe
- no AsNoTracking (normal query)	95	100%
AsNoTracking	40	42%
AsNoTrackingWithIdentityResolution	85	90%

As you can see, AsNoTracking is fastest in this (unscientific) test and something twice as fast as a normal query, so it's worth using. The AsNoTrackingWithIdent Resolution method is only slightly faster (in this case) than the normal read query, but as in the AsNoTracking version, the entities aren't tracked, which imp the performance of SaveChanges when it's looking for updated data.

Another feature of the AsNoTracking and AsNoTrackingWithIdentityResolu methods is that the relational fixup stage (see section 6.1.1) works only withir query. As a result, two queries using AsNoTracking or AsNoTrackingWithIdent Resolution will create new instances of each entity even if the first query loade same data. With normal queries, two separate queries would return the same e class instances, because the relational fixup stage works across all tracked entities

6.1.3 Reading in hierarchical data efficiently

I once worked for a client that had a lot of *hierarchical data*—data that has a seri linked entity classes with an indeterminate depth. The problem was that I had to the whole hierarchy before I could display it. I initially did this by eager loadin the first two levels; then I used explicit loading for deeper levels. This techr worked, but performance was slow, and the database was overloaded with lots of s database accesses.

This situation got me thinking: If the normal query relational fixup is so cl could it help me improve the performance of the query? It could! Let me give yc example, using employees of a company. Figure 6.3 shows you the hierarchical s ture of a company we want to load.

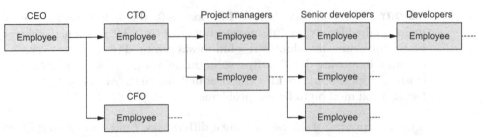

Hierarchical data can have an unknown level of depth—that is, you don't know how many .Include(x => x.WorksForMe) but need to load all the data.

Figure 6.3   One example of hierarchical data. The problem with this sort of data is that you don't know how deep it goes. But it turns out that one `.Include(x => x.WorksForMe)` is all you need. Then the relational fixup stage of the query will link the hierarchical data in the correct manner.

You could use `.Include(x => x.WorksForMe).ThenInclude(x => x.WorksForMe)` and so on, but a single `.Include(x => x.WorksForMe)` is enough, as the relational fixup can work out the rest. The next listing provides an example in which you want a list of all the employees working in development, with their relationships. The LINQ in this query is translated into one SQL query.

Listing 6.1   Loading all the employees working in development, with their relationships

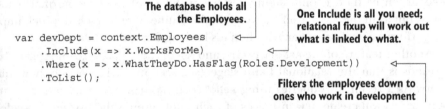

Listing 6.1 provides a tracked version of the hierarchical data, but if you want a read-only version, you can add the `AsNoTrackingWithIdentityResolution` method to the query. Note that `AsNoTracking` won't work, because the linking of the relationships relies on EF Core's relational fixup feature, which is turned off in the `AsNoTracking` method.

Before I found this approach, I was using explicit loading, which produced poor-performing queries. Swapping to this approach improved the time the single query took and also reduced the load on the database server.

NOTE   You do need to work out which relationship to `Include`. In this case, I have a `Manager` navigational property (single) and a `WorksForMe` navigational property (collection). It turns out that including the `WorksForMe` property fills in both the `WorksForMe` collection and the `Manager` property. But including the `Manager` navigational property means that the `WorksForMe` collection is created only if there are entities to link to; otherwise, the

WorksForMe collection is null. I don't know why the two difference Include usages are different; that's why I test everything to make sure that I know how EF Core works.

6.1.4 Understanding how the Include method works

The simplest way to load an entity class with its relationships is to use the Inc method, which is easy to use and normally produces an efficient database access it is worth knowing how the Include method works and what to watch out for.

The way that the Include method was converted to SQL changed when EF 3.0 came along. The EF Core 3.0 change provides performance improvemen many situations, but for some complex queries, it has a negative effect on perform. Take an example from the Book App database, and look at loading a Book wi Reviews and Authors. The following code snippet shows the query:

```
var query = context.Books
    .Include(x => x.Reviews)
    .Include(x => x.AuthorsLink)
        .ThenInclude(x => x.Author);
```

Figure 6.4 shows the different SQL queries produced by EF Core 2.2 and EF Cor for a Book that has four Reviews and two Authors.

The benefit of the EF Core 3.0 way of handling loading collections relationsh performance, which in many situations is quicker. I did a simple experiment, loa Books with ten Reviews and two Authors in EF Core 2.1 and EF Core 3.0, and th

Before EF Core 3   **The LINQ query become three separate SQL queries; the total rows are 1 + 4 + 2**

Query 1

BookId	Title	Descriptio	ImageUr	Price	PublishedOn	Publisher
1	My book	This is a	http://boo	40	10/12/2020	Manning

Query 2

ReviewId	BookId	Comment	NumStars	VoterName
1	1	Great!	5	Person1
2	1	Good	4	Person2
3	1	Average	3	Person3
4	1	Rubbish!	0	Person4

Query 3

BookId	AuthorId	Order	AuthorId	Name
1	1	0	1	Author1
1	2	1	2	Author2

After EF Core 3   **The LINQ query becomes one SQL query with joined data; the total rows are 1 * 4 * 2 = 8.**

Single query

BookId	Title	Descriptio	ImageUr	Price	PublishedOn	Publisher	ReviewId	BookId	Comment	NumStars	VoterNa	BookId	AuthorId	Order	AuthorId	Name
1	My book	This is a	http://boo	40	10/12/2020	Manning	1	1	Great!	5	Person1	1	1	0	1	Author1
1	My book	This is a	http://boo	40	10/12/2020	Manning	2	1	Good	4	Person2	1	1	0	1	Author1
1	My book	This is a	http://boo	40	10/12/2020	Manning	3	1	Average	3	Person3	1	1	0	1	Author1
1	My book	This is a	http://boo	40	10/12/2020	Manning	4	1	Rubbish!	0	Person4	1	1	0	1	Author1
1	My book	This is a	http://boo	40	10/12/2020	Manning	1	1	Great!	5	Person1	1	2	1	2	Author2
1	My book	This is a	http://boo	40	10/12/2020	Manning	2	1	Good	4	Person2	1	2	1	2	Author2
1	My book	This is a	http://boo	40	10/12/2020	Manning	3	1	Average	3	Person3	1	2	1	2	Author2
1	My book	This is a	http://boo	40	10/12/2020	Manning	4	1	Rubbish!	0	Person4	1	2	1	2	Author2

Figure 6.4 Comparing the way that EF Core loads data before and after EF Core 3 was released. The to version is how EF Core worked prior to EF Core 3—it used separate database queries to read in any collecti The lower version is what EF Core 3 and above do—it combines all the data into one big query.

Core 3.0 version was approximately 20% faster. But in some specific situations, it can be very slow indeed, as I cover next.

Performance problems occur if you have multiple collection relationships that you want to include in the query, and some of those relationships have a large number of entries in the collection. You can see the problem by looking at the two calculations on the far-right side of figure 6.4. This figure shows that the number of rows read in via EF Core versions before 3.0 is calculated by *adding* the rows. But in EF Core 3.0 and later, the number of rows read is calculated by *multiplying* the rows. Suppose that you are loading 3 relationships, each of which has 100 rows. The pre-3.0 version of EF Core would read in 100+100+100 = 300 rows, but EF Core 3.0 and later would use 100 * 100 * 100 = 1 million rows.

To see the performance issues, I created a test in which an entity had three one-to-many relationships, each of which had 100 rows in the database. The following snippet shows the normal Include approach to loading relationships in a query, which took 3500 milliseconds (a terrible result!):

```
var result = context.ManyTops
    .Include(x => x.Collection1)
    .Include(x => x.Collection2)
    .Include(x => x.Collection3)
    .Single(x => x.Id == id);
```

Fortunately, EF Core 5 provides a method called AsSplitQuery that tells EF Core to read each Include separately, as in the following listing. This operation took only 100 milliseconds, which is about 50 times faster.

Listing 6.2 Reading relationships separately and letting relational fixup join them up

```
var result = context.ManyTops
    .AsSplitQuery()          ◁——  Causes each Include to be
    .Include(x => x.Collection1)   loaded separately, thus
    .Include(x => x.Collection2)   stopping the multiplication
    .Include(x => x.Collection3)   problem
    .Single(x => x.Id == id)
```

If you find that a query that uses multiple Includes is slow, it could be because two or more included collections contain a lot of entries. In this case, add the AsSplit-Query method before your Includes to swap to the separate load of every included collection.

Making loading navigational collections fail-safe

I always try to make any code fail-safe, by which I mean that if I make a mistake in my code, I'd rather it fail with an exception than do the wrong thing silently. One area I worry about is forgetting to add the correct set of Includes when I'm loading an entity with relationships. It seems that I would never forget to do that, but in applications with lots of relationships, it can easily happen. In fact, I have done it many times,

including in my clients' applications, which is why I use a fail-safe approach. Le
explain the problem and then my solution.

For any navigational property that uses a collection, I often see developers a
an empty collection to a collection navigational property, either in the construct
via an assignment to the property (see the following listing).

Listing 6.3 A entity class with navigational collections set to an empty collection

```
public class BookNotSafe
{
    public int Id { get; set; }
    public ICollection<ReviewNotSafe> Reviews { get; set; }

    public BookNotSafe()
    {
        Reviews = new List<ReviewNotSafe>();
    }
}
```

This navigational property called
Reviews has many entries—that is,
a one-to-many relationship.

The navigational property calle
is preloaded with an empty col
making it easier to add Review
to the navigational property wl
primary entity, BookNotSafe, is

Developers do this to make it easier to add entries to a navigational collection
newly created instance of an entity class. The downside is that if you forget the Inc
to load a navigational property collection, you get an empty collection when the
base might have data that should fill that collection.

You have another problem if you want to replace the whole collection. If you c
have the `Include`, the old entries in the database aren't removed, so you get a cc
nation of new and old entities, which is the wrong answer. In the following code
pet (adapted from listing 3.17), instead of replacing the two existing `Reviews`,
database ends up with three `Reviews`:

```
var book = context.Books
        //missing .Include(x => x.Reviews)
        .Single(p => p.BookId == twoReviewBookId);

book.Reviews = new List<Review>{ new Review{ NumStars = 1}};
context.SaveChanges();
```

Another good reason not to assign an empty collection to a collection is performa
If you need to use explicit loading of a collection, for example, and you know tha
already loaded because it's not null, you can skip doing the (redundant) explicit
ing. Also, in chapter 13, I select the best-performing way to add a new `Review` e
class to a `Book` entity class, depending on whether the `Book`'s `Reviews` collection p
erty is already loaded.

So in my code (and throughout this book), I don't preload any navigational pr
ties with a collection. Instead of failing silently when I leave out the `Include` meth
get a `NullReferenceException` when the code accesses the navigational colle
property. To my mind, that result is much better than getting the wrong data.

Using Global Query Filters in real-world situations

Global Query Filters (shortened to Query Filter) were introduced in section 3.5 to implement a soft-delete feature. In this section, you'll look at some of the issues involved in using soft delete in real applications. You will also look at using Query Filters to produce multitenant systems.

SOFT DELETE IN REAL-WORLD APPLICATIONS

The soft-delete feature is useful because the users of the application get a second chance when they delete something. Two of my clients both had applications that used the soft-delete feature on nearly every entity class. Typically, a normal user would delete something, which in fact meant soft-deleting it, and an admin person could undelete the item. Both applications were complex and quite different, so I learned a lot about implementing soft delete.

First, soft delete doesn't work like the normal database delete command. With database deletes, if you delete a `Book`, you would also delete all the `PriceOffer`, `Reviews`, and `AuthorLinks` linked to the `Book` you deleted (see section 3.5.3). That situation doesn't happen with soft delete, which has some interesting issues.

If you soft-delete a `Book`, for example, the `PriceOffer`, `Reviews`, and `AuthorLinks` are still there, which can cause problems if you don't think things through. In section 5.11.1, you built a background process that logged the number of `Reviews` in the database on every hour. If you soft-deleted a `Book` that had ten `Reviews`, you might expect the number of `Reviews` to go down, but with the code in listing 5.14, it wouldn't. You need a way to handle this problem.

A pattern in Domain-Driven Design (DDD) called Root and Aggregates helps you in this situation. In this pattern, the `Book` entity class is the Root, and the `PriceOffer`, `Reviews`, and `AuthorLinks` are Aggregates. (See the principal and dependent descriptions in section 3.1.1.) This pattern goes on to say you should access Aggregates only via the Root. This process works well with soft deletes because if the `Book` (Root) is soft-deleted, you can't access its Aggregates. So the correct code for counting all the `Reviews`, taking the soft delete into account, is

```
var numReviews = context.Books.SelectMany(x => x.Reviews).Count();
```

> **NOTE**   Another way to solve the Root/Aggregate problem with soft deletes is to mimic the cascade delete behavior when setting soft deletes, which is quite complex to do. But I have built a library called `EfCore.SoftDeleteServices` that mimics cascade-delete behavior but uses soft deletes; see https://github.com/JonPSmith/EfCore.SoftDeleteServices.

The second thing to consider is that you shouldn't apply soft deletes to a one-to-one relationship. You will have problems if you try to add a new one-to-one entity when an existing but soft-deleted entity is already there. If you had a soft-deleted `PriceOffer`, which has a one-to-one relationship with the `Book`, and tried to add another `PriceOffer`

to the Book, you would get a database exception. A one-to-one relationship has a ur
index on the foreign key BookId, and a (soft-deleted) PriceOffer was taking that s

As my clients have found, the soft-delete feature is useful because users can m
enly delete the wrong data. But being aware of the issues allows you to plan hc
handle them in your applications. I usually use the Root/Aggregate approach
don't allow soft deletes of one-to-one dependent entities.

USING QUERY FILTERS TO CREATE MULTITENANT SYSTEMS

A *multitenant system* is one in which different users or groups of users have data
should be accessed only by certain users. You can find many examples, suc
Office365 and GitHub. The Query Filters feature isn't enough to build Office36
its own, but you can use Query Filters to build complex multitenant application.

In the soft-delete use of the Query Filter, you used a Boolean as the filter, but
multitenant system, you need a more elaborate key, which I refer to as the Data
Each tenant has a unique DataKey. A tenant might be an individual user or, r
likely, a group of users. Figure 6.5 shows an example Software as a Service (S
application that provides stock control for lots of retail companies. In this case
works for Dress4U and has the DataKey on login.

In the Book App, no one needs to log in, so you can't implement the exact appr
shown in figure 6.5, but it does have a basket cookie with a pseudo UserId tha
can use. When a user selects a book to buy in the Book App, a basket cookie is cre

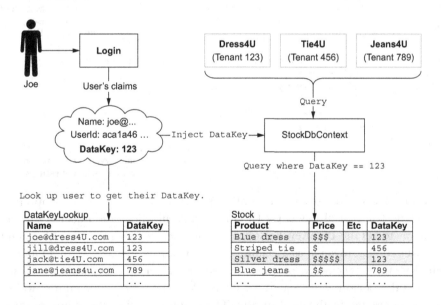

Figure 6.5 When Joe logs in, his name and `UserId` are looked up in the DataKeyLookup
table, and the appropriate DataKey (123) is added to his user claims. When Joe asks for a
list of stock, the DataKey from the user's claims is extracted and given to the application's
DbContext when it is created. Then the DataKey is used in a Global Query Filter applied to
the Stock table. Therefore, Joe sees only the Blue dress and the Silver dress.

to hold each book in the user's basket, plus a UserId. This basket cookie is used if the user clicks the My Orders menu item to show only the Orders from this user. The following code takes the UserId from the basket cookie and uses a Query Filter to return only the Orders that the user created. Two main parts make this code work:

- A UserIdService gets the UserId from the basket cookie.
- The IUserIdService is injected via the application's DbContext constructor and used to access the current user.

The following listing shows the UserIdService code, which relies on the IHttpContext-Accessor to access the current HTTP request.

Listing 6.4 UserIdService that extracts the UserId from the basket cookie

```
public class UserIdService : IUserIdService
{
    private readonly IHttpContextAccessor _httpAccessor;

    public UserIdService(IHttpContextAccessor httpAccessor)
    {
        _httpAccessor = httpAccessor;
    }

    public Guid GetUserId()
    {
        var httpContext = _httpAccessor.HttpContext;
        if (httpContext == null)
            return Guid.Empty;

        var cookie = new BasketCookie(httpContext.Request.Cookies);
        if (!cookie.Exists())
            return Guid.Empty;

        var service = new CheckoutCookieService(cookie.GetValue());
        return service.UserId;
    }
}
```

> The IHttpContextAccessor is a way to access the current HTTP context. To use it, you need to register it in the Startup class, using the command services.AddHttpContext-Accessor().

> In some cases, the HTTPContext could be null, such as a background task. In such a case, you provide an empty GUID.

> s existing look for cookie. If o cookie, eturns an ty GUID.

> If there is a basket cookie, creates the CheckoutCookieService, which extracts the UserId and returns it

When you have a value to act as a DataKey, you need to provide it to the application's DbContext. The typical way is via DI constructor injection; the injected service provides a way to get the DataKey. For our example, we are using the UserId, taken from the basket cookie, to serve as a DataKey. Then you use that UserId in a Query Filter applied to the CustomerId property in the Order entity class, which contains the UserId of the person who created the Order. Any query for Order entities will return only Orders created by the current user. The following listing shows how to inject the UserIdService service into the application's DbContext and then use that UserId in a Query Filter.

Listing 6.5 Book App's DbContext with injection of `UserId` and Query Filter

This property holds the UserId used in the Query Filter on the Order entity class.

Sets the UserIdService. Note that this parameter is optional, which makes it much easier to use in unit tests that don't use the Query Filter.

Normal options for setting up the application's DbContext

Sets the UserId. If the UserId is null, a simple replacement version provides the default Guid.Empty value.

The method where you configure EF Core and put your Query Filter

Soft-delete Query Filter

Order query filter, which matches the current UserId obtained from the cookie basket with the CustomerId in the Order entity class

```csharp
public class EfCoreContext : DbContext
{
    private readonly Guid _userId;

    public EfCoreContext(DbContextOptions<EfCoreContext> options,
        IUserIdService userIdService = null)
        : base(options)
    {
        _userId = userIdService?.GetUserId()
                ?? new ReplacementUserIdService().GetUserId();
    }

    public DbSet<Book> Books { get; set; }
    //… rest of DbSet<T> left out

    protected override void OnModelCreating(ModelBuilder modelBuilder)
    {
        //… other configuration left out for clarity

        modelBuilder.Entity<Book>()
            .HasQueryFilter(p => !p.SoftDeleted);
        modelBuilder.Entity<Order>()
            .HasQueryFilter(x => x.CustomerName == _userId);
    }
}
```

To be clear, every instance of the application's DbContext gets the UserId of the current user, or an empty GUID if they never "bought" a book. Whereas the DbContext configuration is set up on first use and cached, the lambda Query Filter is linked to a live field called _userId. The query filter is fixed, but the _userId is dynamic and can change on every instance of the DbContext.

But it's important that the Query Filter not be put in a separate configuration class (see section 7.5.1), because the _userId would become fixed to the UserId provided on first use. You must put the lambda query somewhere that it can get the dynamic _userId variable. In this case, I place it in the OnModelCreating method inside the application's DbContext, which is fine. In chapter 7, I show you a way to automate the configuration of the Query Filters that keep the _userId dynamic; see section 7.1.5.

If you have an ASP.NET Core application that users log in to, you can use IHttpContextAccessor to access the current ClaimPrincipal. The ClaimPrincipal contains a list of Claims for the logged-in user, including their UserId, which is stored in a claim with the name defined by the system constant ClaimTypes.NameIdentifier. But as shown in figure 6.5, you could add a new Claim to the user on login to provide a DataKey that is used in the Query Filter.

> **NOTE** For an example of a full multitenant system in which a user's Id is used to find a tenant's DataKey at login time and a DataKey Claim is added to the user Claims, see the article at http://mng.bz/yY7q.

Considering LINQ commands that need special attention

EF Core does a great job of mapping LINQ methods to SQL, the language of most relational databases. But three types of LINQ methods need special handling:

- Some LINQ commands need extra code to make them fit the way that the database works, such as the LINQ Average, Sum, Max, and other aggregate commands needed to handle a return of null. Just about the only aggregate that won't return null is Count.
- Some LINQ commands can work with a database, but only within rigid boundaries because the database doesn't support all the possibilities of the command. An example is the GroupBy LINQ command; the database can have only a simple key, and there are significant limitations on the IGrouping part.
- Some LINQ commands have a good match to a database feature, but with some limitations on what the database can return. Examples are Join and GroupJoin.

The EF Core documentation has a great page called Complex Query Operators (see http://mng.bz/MXan) with good descriptions of many of these commands, so I'm not going to go through them all. But I do want to warn you about the feared InvalidOperationException exception, with a message containing the words could not be translated, and tell you what to do when you get it.

The problem is that if you get your LINQ slightly wrong, you will get the could not be translated exception. The message might not be too helpful in diagnosing the problem (but see the following note), other than saying that you should switch to client evaluation explicitly by inserting a call to AsEnumerable . . ." Although you could switch to client evaluation, you might take a (big) performance hit.

> **NOTE** The EF Core team is refining the messages returned from a could not be translated exception and adding specific messages for common situations, such as trying to use the String.Equal method with a StringComparison parameter (which can't be converted to SQL).

The following section provides some tips for making the more mainstream complex commands work with a relational database. I also suggest that you test any complex queries, as they are easy to get wrong.

AGGREGATES NEED A NULL (APART FROM COUNT)

You are likely to use the LINQ aggregates Max, Min, Sum, Average, Count, and CountLong, so here are some pointers on what to do to get them to work:

- The Count and CountLong methods work fine if you count something sensible in the database, such as a row or relational links such as the number of Reviews for a Book.

- The LINQ aggregates Max, Min, Sum, and Average need a nullable result, su
  context.Books.Max(x => (decimal?)x.Price). If the source (Price in
  example) isn't nullable, you must have cast to the nullable version of the so
  Also, if you are using Sqlite for unit testing, remember that it doesn't sup
  decimal, so you would get an error even if you used the nullable version.
- You can't use the LINQ Aggregate method directly on the database becaw
  does a per-row calculation.

GROUPBY LINQ COMMAND

The other LINQ method that can be useful is GroupBy. When GroupBy is used c
SQL database, the Key part needs to be a scalar value (or values) because that's
the SQL GROUP BY supports. The IGrouping part can be a selection of data, inclu
some LINQ commands. My experience is that you need to follow a GroupBy comr
with an execute command (see section 2.3.3) such as ToList. Anything else seer
cause the could not be translated exception.

Here is a real example taken from a client's application, with some of the n
changed to keep the client's secrets. Notice that the Key can be a combination o
lar columns and the IGrouping part:

```
var something = await _context.SomeComplexEntity
    .GroupBy(x => new { x.ItemID, x.Item.Name })
    .Select(x => new
    {
        Id = x.Key.ItemID,
        Name = x.Key.Name,
        MaxPrice = x.Max(o => (decimal?)o.Price)
    })
    .ToListAsync();
```

6.1.8 Using AutoMapper to automate building Select queries

In chapter 2, you learned that Select queries allow you to build one query that re
exactly the data you need, and these queries are often quite efficient from the pe
mance side too. The problem is that they take a bit more time to write—only a few 1
lines, but real applications can be thousands of queries, so each Select query ad
development time. I'm always looking for ways to automate things, and AutoMa
(https://automapper.org) can help you automate the building of Select querie

I am not going to describe all the features of AutoMapper, which might ta
whole book in itself! But I'll give you an overview of how to set up and use A
Mapper, because I don't think those topics are covered well elsewhere. Let's sta
comparing a simple Select query that is handcoded against an AutoMapper-
Select query, as shown in figure 6.6.

Although the example in figure 6.6 is simple, it shows that you can collapse a Se
query to one line by using AutoMapper's ProjectTo method. Figure 6.6 uses A
Mapper's By Convention configuration, where it maps properties in the source—
class, in this case—to the DTO properties by matching them by the type and nam
each property. AutoMapper can automatically map some relationships. A prope

Handcoded version	AutoMapper version
| ```
ar dto = context.Books
.Select(p => new ChangePubDateDto
{
    BookId = p.BookId,
    Title = p.Title,
    PublishedOn = p.PublishedOn
})
.Single(k => k.BookId == lastBook.BookId);
``` | ```
var dto = context.Books
    .ProjectTo<ChangePubDateDtoAm>(config)
    .Single(x => x.BookId == lastBook.BookId);
``` |

gure 6.6   Both versions of the Select query produce the same results and the same SQL code. This query
super simple, with only three properties copied over, but it gives you an idea of how AutoMapper works. In
is case, the DTO has properties of the same type and name as the properties we want to copy over, which
eans AutoMapper will automatically build the LINQ code to copy those three properties.

type decimal and called PromotionNewPrice would map the Book's Promotion.NewPrice relationship, for example. (This AutoMapper feature is called *flattening*; see http://mng .bz/aorB.)

Figure 6.7 shows four by-convention configurations of using AutoMapper:

- *Same type and same name mapping*—Properties are mapped from the entity class to DTO properties by having the same type and same name.

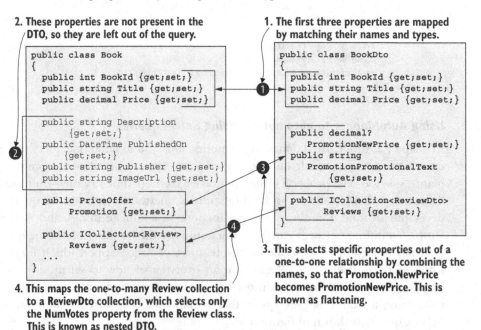

2. These properties are not present in the DTO, so they are left out of the query.

1. The first three properties are mapped by matching their names and types.

3. This selects specific properties out of a one-to-one relationship by combining the names, so that Promotion.NewPrice becomes PromotionNewPrice. This is known as flattening.

4. This maps the one-to-many Review collection to a ReviewDto collection, which selects only the NumVotes property from the Review class. This is known as nested DTO.

Figure 6.7   Four ways that AutoMapper maps the Book entity class to the BookDto class. The default convention is to map via similar names and types, including handling relationships by having a name equivalent to the property access but without the dot. The DTO property PromotionNewPrice, for example, is mapped automatically to the Promotion.NewPrice property in the source. Mappings also can be nested; a collection in the entity class can be mapped to a collection with a DTO.

- *Trimming properties*—By leaving out properties that are in the entity class the DTO, the Select query won't load those columns.
- *Flattening relationships*—The name in the DTO is a combination of the na tional property name and the property in the navigational property type. Book entity reference of Promotion.NewPrice, for example, is mapped t DTO's PromotionNewPrice property.
- *Nested DTOs*—This configuration allows you to map collections from the e class to a DTO class, so you can copy specific properties from the entity cl a navigational collection property.

Now that you have an idea of what AutoMapper can do, I want to give you som on how to use and configure it.

FOR SIMPLE MAPPINGS, USE THE [AUTOMAP] ATTRIBUTE

Using AutoMapper's ProjectTo method is straightforward, but it relies on the cc uration of AutoMapper, which is more complex. In release 8.1 of AutoMapper, Ji Bogart added the AutoMap attribute, which allows by convention configuration of ple mappings. The following code snippet shows the [AutoMap] attribute in the line (in bold), where you define what entity class this DTO should map from:

```
[AutoMap(typeof(Book))]
public class ChangePubDateDtoAm
{
    public int BookId { get; set; }
    public string Title { get; set; }
    public DateTime PublishedOn { get; set; }
}
```

Classes mapped via AutoMap attribute use AutoMapper's By Convention confi tion, with a few parameters and attributes to allow some tweaking. As you saw in f 6.7, by convention can do quite a lot, but certainly not all that you might need that, you need AutoMapper's Profile class.

COMPLEX MAPPINGS NEED A PROFILE CLASS

When AutoMapper's By Convention approach isn't enough, you need to buil AutoMapper Profile class, which allows you to define the mapping for prope that aren't covered by the By Convention approach. To map a Book to the BookL Dto described in listings 2.10 and 2.11, for example, three of the nine DTO prope need special handling. You have to create a MappingConfiguration. You have ways to do this, but typically, you use AutoMapper's Profile class, which is easy to and register. The following listing shows a class that inherits the Profile class an up the mappings that are too complex for AutoMapper to deduce.

> **Listing 6.6 AutoMapper Profile class configuring special mappings for some proper**

```
public class BookListDtoProfile : Profile
{
    public BookListDtoProfile()
```

Your class must inherit the Auto Profile class. You can have multi classes that inherit Profile.

```
{
    CreateMap<Book, BookListDto>()
        .ForMember(p => p.ActualPrice,
            m => m.MapFrom(s => s.Promotion == null
                ? s.Price : s.Promotion.NewPrice))
        .ForMember(p => p.AuthorsOrdered,
            m => m.MapFrom(s => string.Join(", ",
                s.AuthorsLink.Select(x => x.Author.Name))))
        .ForMember(p => p.ReviewsAverageVotes,
            m => m.MapFrom(s =>
                s.Reviews.Select(y =>
                    (double?)y.NumStars).Average()));
    }
}
```

Map the from entity to the stDto

The Actual price depends on whether the Promotion has a PriceOffer.

the special code make the Average in the database

Gets the list of Author names as a comma-delimited string

This code sets up three of the nine properties, with the other six properties using Auto-Mapper's By Convention approach, which is why some of the names of the properties in the ListBookDto class are long. The DTO property called PromotionPromotionalText, for example, has that name because it maps by convention to the navigational property Promotion and then to the PromotionalText property in the PriceOffer entity class.

You can add lots of CreateMap calls in one Profile, or you can have multiple Profiles. Profiles can get complex, and managing them is the main pain point involved in using AutoMapper. One of my clients had a single Profile that was 1,000 lines long.

REGISTER AUTOMAPPER CONFIGURATIONS

The last stage is registering all the mapping with dependency injection. Fortunately, AutoMapper has a NuGet package called AutoMapper.Extensions.Microsoft .DependencyInjection containing the method AddAutoMapper, which scans the assemblies you provide and registers an IMapper interface as a service. You use the IMapper interface to inject the configuration for all your classes that have the [AutoMap] attribute and all the classes that inherit AutoMapper's Profile class. In an ASP.NET Core application, the following code snippet would be added to the Configure method of the Startup class:

```
public void ConfigureServices(IServiceCollection services)
{
    services.AddControllersWithViews();
    // … other code removed for clarity

    services.AddAutoMapper( MyAssemblyToScan1, MyAssemblyToScan2…);
}
```

Evaluating how EF Core creates an entity class when reading data in

Up until now, the entity classes in this book haven't had user-defined constructors, so if you read in that entity class, EF Core uses the default parameterless constructor and then updates the properties and backing fields directly. (Chapter 7 describes backing

fields.) But sometimes, it's useful to have a constructor with parameters, becau
makes it easier to create an instance or because you want to make sure that the c
created in the correct way.

> **NOTE** Using constructors to create a class is a good approach, because you
> can define what parameters you must set to create a valid instance. When
> you're using the DDD approach with EF Core (see chapter 13), the only way
> to create an entity class is via some form of constructor or static factory.

Since EF Core 2.1, EF Core has used an entity class's constructor when it needs to
ate an entity class instance, typically when reading in data. If you use EF Core
Convention pattern for your constructor—that is, the constructor's parameters m
the properties by type and name (with camel/Pascal casing) and don't include na
tional properties, as shown in the following listing—EF Core will use it too.

Listing 6.7 An entity class with a constructor that works with EF Core

```
public class ReviewGood
{
    public int Id { get; private set; }
    public string VoterName { get; private set; }
    public int NumStars { get; set; }

    public ReviewGood
        (string voterName)
    {
        VoterName = voterName;
        NumStars = 2;
    }
}
```

You can set your properti
to have a private setter. E
Core can still set them.

The constructor doesn't need parameters
for all the properties in the class. Also, the
constructor can be any type of accessibility
public, private, and so on.

EF Core will look for a parameter with the
same type and a name that matches the
property (with matching of Pascal/camel
case versions of the name).

Any assignment to a property
that doesn't have a parameter is
fine. EF Core will set that property
after the constructor to the data
read back from the database.

The assignment should not include any
changing of the data; otherwise, you won't
get the exact data that was in the database.

I could have added a constructor to the `ReviewGood` class that set all the non-navigat
properties, but I wanted to point out that EF Core can use a constructor to create
entity instance and then fill in any properties that weren't in the constructor's pa
eters. Now, having looked at a constructor that works, let's look at constructors tha
Core can't or won't use and how to handle each problem.

CONSTRUCTORS THAT CAN CAUSE YOU PROBLEMS WITH EF CORE

The first type of constructor that EF Core can't use is one with a parameter whose
or name doesn't match. The following listing shows an example with a param
called `starRating`, which assigns to the property called `NumStars`. If this construc
the only one, EF Core will throw an exception the first time you use the applicat
DbContext.

Listing 6.8 Class with constructor that EF Core can't use, causing an exception

```
public class ReviewBadCtor
{
    public int Id { get; set; }
    public string VoterName { get; set; }
    public int NumStars { get; set; }

    public ReviewBadCtor(          ◄────── The only constructor
        string voterName,                  in this class
        int starRating)        ◄────┐  This parameter's name doesn't
    {                                │  match the name of any property in
        VoterName = voterName;       │  this class, so EF Core can't use it to
        NumStars = starRating;       │  create an instance of the class when
    }                                │  it is reading in data.
}
```

Another example of a constructor that EF Core can't use is one with a parameter that sets a navigational property. If the Book entity class had a constructor that included a parameter to set the PriceOffer Promotion navigational property, for example, EF Core couldn't use it either. A constructor that EF Core can use can have only nonrelational properties.

If your constructor doesn't match EF Core's By Convention pattern, you need to provide a constructor that EF Core can use. The standard solution is to add a private parameterless constructor, which EF Core can use to create the class instance and use its normal parameter/field setting.

> **NOTE** EF Core can use constructors with access modifiers. It uses any level of access from private to public constructors, for example. As you have already seen, it can also write to a property with a private setter, such as public int Id {get; private set;}. EF Core can handle read-only properties (such as instance public int Id {get;}), but with some limitations; see http://mng .bz/go2E.

Another, more subtle problem occurs if you alter the parameter data when you assign it to the matching property. The following code snippet would cause problems because the data read in would be altered in the assignment:

```
public ReviewBad(string voterName)
{
    VoterName = "Name: "+voterName; //alter the parameter before assign to
    property
    //… other code left out
}
```

The result of the assignment in the ReviewBad constructor means that if the data in the database was XXX, after the read, it would be Name: XXX, which is not what you want. The solution is to change the name of the parameter so that it doesn't match the property name. In this case, you might call it voterNameNeedingPrefix.

Finally, be aware that checks and validations you apply to your parameters in constructor are going to be applied when EF Core uses the constructor. If you h test to make sure that a string is not null, then you should configure the databas umn to be non-null (see chapter 7) to make sure that some rogue data in your base doesn't return a null value.

EF CORE CAN INJECT CERTAIN SERVICES VIA THE ENTITY CONSTRUCTOR

While we are talking about entity class constructors, we should look at EF Core's ity to inject some services via the entity class's constructor. EF Core can inject types of services, the most useful of which injects a method to allow lazy loadi relationships, which I describe in full. The other two uses are advanced featu summarize what they do and provide a link to the Microsoft EF Core document for more information.

In section 2.4.4, you learned how to configure lazy loading of relationships vi `Microsoft.EntityFrameworkCore.Proxies` NuGet package. That package is the plest way to configure lazy loading, but it has the drawback that all the navigat properties must be set up to use lazy loading—that is, every navigational pro must have the keyword `virtual` added to its property definition.

If you want to limit what relationships use lazy loading, you can obtain a lazy ing service via an entity class's constructor. Then you change the navigational pr ties to use this service in the property's getter method. The following listing sho `BookLazy` entity class that has two relationships: a `PriceOffer` relationship doesn't use lazy loading and a `Reviews` relationship that does.

Listing 6.9 Showing how lazy loading works via an injected lazy loader method

```
public class BookLazy                    You need a public constructor
{                                        so that you can create this
    public BookLazy() { }                book in your code.

    private BookLazy(ILazyLoader lazyLoader)
    {                                            This private constructor
        _lazyLoader = lazyLoader;                is used by EF Core to
    }                                            inject the LazyLoader.
    private readonly ILazyLoader _lazyLoader;

    public int Id { get; set; }                  A normal relational
                                                 link that isn't loaded
    public PriceOffer Promotion { get; set; }    via lazy loading

    private ICollection<LazyReview> _reviews;    A read of the prop
    public ICollection<LazyReview> Reviews       will trigger a lazy
    {                                            loading of the data
        get => _lazyLoader.Load(this, ref _reviews);   (if not already loa
        set => _reviews = value;
    }                                The set simply updates
}                                    the backing field.
```

The actual reviews are held in a backing field (see section 8.7).

The list that you will access

Injecting the service via the ILazyLoader interface requires the NuGet package Microsoft.EntityFrameworkCore.Abstractions to be added to the project. This package has a minimal set of types and no dependencies, so it doesn't "pollute" the project with references to the DbContext and other data-access types.

But if you are enforcing an architecture that doesn't allow any external packages in it, you can add a parameter by using the type Action<object, string> in the entity's constructor. EF Core will fill the parameter of type Action<object, string> with an action that takes the entity instance as its first parameter and the name of the field as the second parameter. When this action is invoked, it loads the relationship data into the named field in the given entity class instance.

> **NOTE** By providing a small extension method, you can make the Action <object, string> option work similarly to ILazyLoader. You can see this effect in the extension method at the end of the "Lazy loading without proxies" section of the EF Core documentation page at http://mng.bz/e5Zv in the class LazyBook2 in the Test project in the GitHub repo associated with this book.

The other two ways of injecting a service into the entity class via a constructor are as follows:

- Injecting the DbContext instance that the entity class is linked to is useful if you want to run database accesses inside your entity class. In chapter 13, I cover the pros and cons of executing database accesses inside your entity class. In a nutshell, you shouldn't use this technique unless you have a serious performance or business logic problem that can't be solved any other way.
- The IEntityType for this entity class instance gives you access to the configuration, State, EF Core information about this entity, and so on associated with this entity type.

These two techniques are advanced features, and I won't cover these in detail. The EF Core documentation on entity class constructors has more information on this topic; see http://mng.bz/pV78.

Writing to the database with EF Core

The first part of this chapter was about querying the database. Now you'll turn your mind to writing to the database: creating, updating, and deleting entity classes. As in section 6.1, the aim is to expose you to how EF Core works inside when writing to the database. Some subsections of section 6.1 are about learning what is happening when you write to the database, and some are neat techniques for copying or deleting data quickly. Here is the list of topics that I will cover:

- Evaluating how EF Core writes entities with relationships to the database
- Evaluating how DbContext handles writing out entities with relationships
- Copying data with relationships quickly
- Deleting an entity quickly

6.2.1 Evaluating how EF Core writes entities/relationships to the database

When you are creating a new entity with new relationship(s), navigational prope
are your friends because EF Core takes on the problem of filling the foreign ke
you. The next listing shows a simple example: adding a new `Book` that has a new Rev

---

Listing 6.10 Adding a new `Book` entity with a new `Review`

```
var book = new Book
{
    Title = "Test",                          Creates a
    Reviews = new List<Review>()             new Book
};
book.Reviews.Add(
    new Review { NumStars = 1 });            Adds a new Review to the Book's
                                             Reviews navigational property
context.Add(book);
context.SaveChanges();        ◄             The Add method says that the entity instance
                                            should be added to the appropriate row, with
        SaveChanges carries out the         any relationships added or updated.
            database update.
```

To add these two linked entities to the database, EF Core has to do the following.

- *Work out the order in which it should create these new rows*—In this case, it has to
  ate a row in the Books table so that it has the primary key of the `Book`.
- *Copy any primary keys into the foreign key of any relationships*—In this ca
  copies the Books row's primary key, `BookId`, into the foreign key in the
  Review row.
- *Copy back any new data created in the database so that the entity classes properly rep
  the database*—In this case, it must copy back the `BookId` and update the Bo
  property in both the `Book` and `Review` entity classes and the `ReviewId` for
  `Review` entity class.

The following listing shows the SQL for this create.

Listing 6.11 The SQL commands to create the two rows, with return of primary key

Because EF Core wants to return the primary key, it
turns off the return of the database changes.

```
       -- first database access                        Inserts a new row into the
─ ▷   SET NOCOUNT ON;                                   table. The database gener.
       INSERT INTO [Books] ([Description], [Title], ...)   Book's primary key.
       VALUES (@p0, @p1, @p2, @p3, @p4, @p5, @p6);

                                                        Returns the primar
       SELECT [BookId] FROM [Books]                     with checks to ensu
       WHERE @@ROWCOUNT = 1 AND [BookId] = scope_identity();   the new row was ac

       -- second database access                        Inserts a new row into the Re
─ ▷   SET NOCOUNT ON;                                   table. The database generates
       INSERT INTO [Review] ([BookId], [Comment], ...)  Review's primary key.
       VALUES (@p7, @p8, @p9, @p10);
```

```
SELECT [ReviewId] FROM [Review]
WHERE @@ROWCOUNT = 1 AND [ReviewId] = scope_identity();
```

> **Returns the primary key, with checks to ensure that the new row was added**

This example is simple, but it covers all the main parts. What you need to understand is that you can create complex data with relationships and relationships of those relationships, and EF Core will work out how to add them to the database.

I have seen EF Core code in which the developer used multiple calls to the SaveChanges method to obtain the primary key from the first create to set the foreign key for the related entity. You don't need to do that if you have navigational properties that link the different entities. So if you think that you need to call SaveChanges twice, normally you haven't set up the right navigational properties to handle that case.

> **WARNING** Calling SaveChanges multiple times to create an entity with relationships isn't recommended because if the second SaveChanges fails for some reason, you have an incomplete set of data in your database, which could cause problems. See the sidebar called "Why you should call SaveChanges only once at the end of your changes" in section 3.2.2 for more information.

Evaluating how DbContext handles writing out entities/relationships

In section 6.2.1, you saw what EF Core does at the database end, but now we are going to look at what happens inside EF Core. Most of the time, you don't need this information, but sometimes, knowing it is important. If you are catching changes during a call to SaveChanges, for example, you get its State only before SaveChanges is called, but you have the primary key of a newly created entity only after the call to SaveChanges.

> **NOTE** I bumped into the before/after SaveChanges problem when I wrote the first edition of this book. I needed to detect changes to a Book entity class and changes to any of its related entity classes, such as Review, BookAuthor, and PriceOffer. At that point, I needed to catch the State of each entity at the start, but I might not have had the right foreign key until SaveChanges had finished.

Even if you aren't trying something as complex as the before/after SaveChanges issue, it is good to understand how EF Core works. This example is a little more complex than the last one because I want to show you the different ways that EF Core handles new instances of an entity class over an instance of an entity that has been read from the database. The code in the next listing creates a new Book, but with an Author that is already in the database. The code has comments STAGE 1, STAGE 2, and STAGE 3, and I describe what happens after each stage.

Listing 6.12   Creating a new `Book` with a new many-to-many link to an existing `Aut...`

Each of the three stages starts with a comment.

Reads in an existing Author for the new book

Creates a new BookAuthor linking row, ready to link the Book to the Author

```
//STAGE1
var author = context.Authors.First();
var bookAuthor = new BookAuthor { Author = author };
var book = new Book
{
    Title = "Test Book",
    AuthorsLink = new List<BookAuthor> { bookAuthor }
};

//STAGE2
context.Add(book);

//STAGE3
context.SaveChanges();
```

Creates a Book and in the AuthorsLink navigational property a single entry, linking to the existing Author

Calls the Add method, which tells EF Core that the Book needs to be added to the database

SaveChanges looks at all the tracked entities and works out how to update the database to achieve what you have asked it to do.

Figures 6.8, 6.9, and 6.10 show you what is happening inside the entity classes their tracked data at each stage. Each of the three figures shows the following da the end of its stage:

- The `State` of each entity instance at each stage of the process (shown a each entity class)
- The primary and foreign keys with the current value in brackets. If a key is it hasn't been set yet.
- The navigational links are shown as connections from the navigational pro to the appropriate entity class that it is linked to.
- Changes between each stage, shown by bold text or thicker lines for the na tional links.

Figure 6.8 shows the situation after Stage 1 has finished. This initial code sets up a Book entity class (left) with a new `BookAuthor` entity class (middle) that links the to an existing `Author` entity class (right).

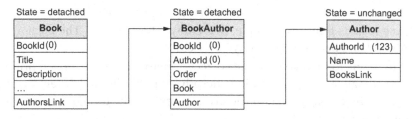

Figure 6.8   End of stage 1. This figure shows that the new `Book` with a new `BookAuthor` linking to the `Book` has a `State` of `Detached`, and the existing `Author`, which was read in from the database, has a `State` of `Unchanged`. The figure also shows the two navigational links that the code set up to link the `Book` entity to the `Author` entity. Finally, the primary and foreign keys of the `Book` and `BookAuthor` are unset—that is, zero—whereas the `Author` entity has an existing primary key (123) because it is already in the database.

Figure 6.8 is a pictorial version of the three entity classes after Stage 1 has finished in listing 6.12. This figure is the starting point before you call any EF Core methods. Figure 6.9 shows the situation after the line `context.Add(book)` is executed. The changes are shown in bold and with thick lines for the added navigational links.

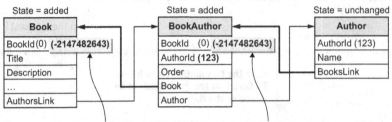

The two rectangles containing (-2147482643) represent the CurrentValue property in the tracking data for the two entity classes where EF Core stores a pseudo key.

Figure 6.9   End of Stage 2. Lots of things have happened here. The `State` of the two new entities, `Book` and `BookAuthor`, has changed to `Added`. At the same time, the `Add` method tries to set up the foreign keys: It knows the `Author`'s primary key, so it can set the `AuthorId` in the `BookAuthor` entity. It doesn't know the `Book`'s primary key (`BookId`), so it puts a unique negative number in the hidden tracking values, acting as a pseudo key. The `Add` also has a relational fixup stage that fills in any other navigational properties.

You may be surprised by how much happened when the `Add` method was executed. (I was!) It seems to be getting the entities as close as possible to the positions they will be after `SaveChanges` is called. Here are the things that happen when the `Add` method is called in Stage 2.

The `Add` method sets the `State` of the entity provided as a parameter to `Added`—in this example, the `Book` entity. Then it looks at all entities linked to the entity provided as a parameter, either by navigational properties or by foreign-key values. For each linked entity, it does the following:

- If the entity is not tracked—that is, its current `State` is `Detached`—it sets its `State` to `Added`. In this example, that entity is `BookAuthor`. The `Author`'s `State` isn't updated because that entity is tracked.
- It fills in any foreign keys for the correct primary keys. If the linked primary key isn't yet available, it puts a unique negative number in the `CurrentValue` properties of the tracking data for the primary key and the foreign key, as you see in figure 6.9.
- It fills in any navigational properties that aren't currently set up by running a version of the relational fixup described in section 6.1.1. The relationships are shown as thick lines in figure 6.9.

In this example, the only entities to link to are set by your code, but Add's relat[ion]
fixup stage can link to any tracked entity. The call to the Add method can take [a]
time to execute if you have a lot of relationships and/or lots of tracked entity c[lasses]
in the current DbContext. I cover this performance issue in detail in chapter 14.

The final stage, Stage 3, is what happens when the SaveChanges method is ca[lled]
as shown in figure 6.10.

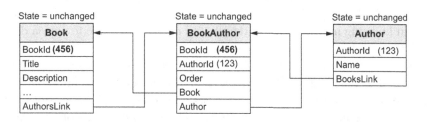

Figure 6.10 **End of Stage 3. After SaveChanges has finished, the Book and
BookAuthor entities have been added to the database: two new rows have been
inserted into the Books and BookAuthors tables. Creating the Book row means that
its primary key is generated by the database, which is copied back into the Book's
BookId and also into the BookAuthor's BookId foreign key. On return, the State
of the Book and BookAuthor are set to Unchanged.**

You saw in section 6.2.1 that any columns set or changed by the database are co[pied]
back into the entity class so that the entity matches the database. In this example[,]
Book's BookId and the BookAuthor's BookId were updated to have the key value [cre-]
ated in the database. Also, now that all the entities involved in this database [now]
match the database, their States are set to Unchanged.

That example may have seemed to be a long explanation of something that [just]
works," and many times, you don't need to know why. But when something do[esn't]
work correctly, or when you want to do something complex, such as logging e[ntity]
class changes, this information is useful.

Which wins if they are different: navigational links or foreign key values?

I stated in Stage 2 of section 6.2.2 that the add method "looks at all entities link[ed]
to the entity provided as a parameter, either by navigational properties or by forei[gn]
key values." Which wins if a navigational link links to one entity and the foreign k[ey]
links to a different entity? My tests say that the navigational link wins. But that res[ult]
is not defined in the EF Core documentation. I have asked for clarification (se[e]
https://github.com/dotnet/efcore/issues/21105), but until there is an answer [to]
this issue, you must test your code to ensure the "navigational properties win ov[er]
foreign key values" feature hasn't changed.

A quick way to copy data with relationships

Sometimes, you want to copy an entity class with all its relationships. One of my clients needed different versions of a custom-designed structure to send to a customer so they could pick the version they liked. These designs had many common parts, and the designers didn't want to type that data for each design; they wanted to build the first design and copy it as a starting point for the next design.

One solution would be to clone each entity class and its relationships, but that's hard work. (My client's designs could have hundreds of items, each with ~25 relationships.) But knowing how EF Core works allowed me to write code to copy a design by using EF Core itself.

As an example, you are going to use your knowledge of EF Core to copy a user's Book App Order, which has a collection of LineItems, which in turn links to Books. You want to copy the Order only with the LineItems, but you do *not* want to copy the Books that the LineItems links to; two copies of a Book would cause all sorts of problems. Let's start by looking at the Order that we want to copy, shown in the following listing.

Listing 6.13   Creating an Order with two LineItems ready to be copied

```
var books = context.SeedDatabaseFourBooks();
var order = new Order
{
    CustomerId = Guid.Empty,
    LineItems = new List<LineItem>
    {
        new LineItem
        {
            LineNum = 1, ChosenBook = books[0], NumBooks = 1
        },
        new LineItem
        {
            LineNum = 2, ChosenBook = books[1], NumBooks = 2
        },
    }
};
context.Add(order);
context.SaveChanges();
```

For this test, add four books to use as test data.

Creates an Order with two LineItems to copy

Sets CustomerId to the default value so that the query filter reads the order back

The first linked book

Adds the second LineNum linked to the second book

Writes this Order to the database

To copy that Order properly, you need to know three things (and you know the first two from section 6.2.2):

- If you Add an entity that has linked entities that are not tracked—that is, with a State of Detached—they will be set to the State Added.
- EF Core can find linked entities via the navigational links.
- If you try to Add an entity class to the database, and the primary key is already in the database, you will get a database exception because the primary key must be unique.

When you know those three things, you can get EF Core to copy the Order wi
LineItems, but not the Books that the LineItems link to. Here is the code that c
the Order and its LineItems but doesn't copy the Book linked to the LineItems.

Listing 6.14 Copying an Order with its LineItems

This code is going
to query the
Orders table.

AsNoTracking means that
the entities are read-only;
their State will be Detached.

Include the LineItems, as
you want to copy them too.

```
var order = context.Orders
    .AsNoTracking()
    .Include(x => x.LineItems)
    .Single(x => x.OrderId == id);
```

Takes the Order
that you want
to copy

You do not add .ThenInclude(x =>
x.ChosenBook) to the query. If you did,
the query would copy the Book entities,
which is not what you want.

```
order.OrderId = default;
order.LineItems.First().LineItemId = default;
order.LineItems.Last().LineItemId = default;
context.Add(order);
context.SaveChanges();
```

Writes out the order
and creates a copy

Resets the primary keys (Ord
and LineItem) to their defaul
value, telling the database to
generate new primary keys

Note that you haven't reset the foreign keys because you are relying on the fact
the navigational properties override any foreign key values. (See the earlier sid
"Which wins if they are different: navigational links or foreign key values?")
because you are careful, you build a unit test to check that the relationships are
ied properly.

6.2.4 A quick way to delete an entity

Now you can copy an entity with its relationships. What about deleting an e
quickly? It turns out that there is a quick way to delete an entity that works well
disconnected state delete when you're working with a web application.

Chapter 3 covered deleting an entity by reading in the entity you want to d
and then calling EF Core's Remove method with that entity instance. That appr
works, but it requires two database accesses—one to read in the entity you wa
delete and another when the SaveChanges is called to delete the entity. As it turns
though, all that the Remove method needs is the appropriate entity class with it
mary key(s) set. The following listing shows the deletion of a Book entity by provi
the Book's primary key value, BookId.

Listing 6.15 Deleting an entity from the database by setting its primary key

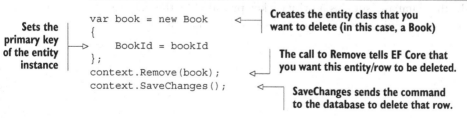

Sets the
primary key
of the entity
instance

```
var book = new Book
{
    BookId = bookId
};
context.Remove(book);
context.SaveChanges();
```

Creates the entity class that you
want to delete (in this case, a Book)

The call to Remove tells EF Core that
you want this entity/row to be deleted.

SaveChanges sends the command
to the database to delete that row.

In a disconnected situation, such as some form of web application, the command to delete returns only the type and primary key value(s), making the delete code simpler and quicker. Some minor things are different from the read/remove approach to relationships:

- If there is no row for the primary key you gave, EF Core throws a `DbUpdate-ConcurrencyException`, saying that nothing was deleted.
- The database is in command of which other linked entities are deleted; EF Core has no say in that. (See the discussion of `OnDelete` in chapter 8 for more information.)

Summary

- When reading in entity classes as tracked entities, EF Core uses a process called relational fixup that sets up all the navigational properties to any other tracked entities.
- The normal tracking query uses identity resolution, producing the best representation of the database structure with one entity class instance for each unique primary key.
- The `AsNoTracking` query is quicker than a normal tracking query because it doesn't use identity resolution, but it can create duplicate entity classes with the same data.
- If your query loads multiple collections of relationships by using the `Include` method, it creates one big database query, which can be slow in some circumstances.
- If your query is missing an `Include` method, you will get the wrong result, but there is a way to set up your navigational collections so that your code will fail instead of returning incorrect data.
- Using Global Query Filters to implement a soft-delete feature works well, but watch how you handle relationships that rely on the soft-deleted entity.
- Select queries are efficient from the database side but can take more lines of code to write. The AutoMapper library can automate the building of `Select` queries.
- EF Core creates an entity class when reading in data. It does this via the default parameterless constructor or any other constructors you write if you follow the normal pattern.
- When EF Core creates an entity in the database, it reads back any data generated by the database, such as a primary key provided by the database, so that it can update the entity class instance to match the database.

Part 2

Entity Framework in dep

Part 1 showed how you might build an application by using EF Core. P
covers how to configure EF Core exactly the way you need it and the diff
ways you can change (EF Core term: *migrate*) your database. It also introd
you to advanced features that can make your software more efficient in
development and performance terms. Part 2 is more of a reference section
covers each part of EF Core in detail, but (I hope) not in a boring way.

Chapter 7 introduces the way that EF Core configures itself when it's
used so that you know where and how to apply any of your own EF Core con
rations. The chapter focuses on nonrelational properties, with types such as
string, and DateTime.

Chapter 8 shows how EF Core finds and configures relationships. EF
does a good job of configuring most relationships for you, but it does need
on some, and you'll want to configure others because EF Core's default set
don't suit your needs.

Chapter 9 covers the important issue of matching the database to you
Core configuration, with either the software or the database SQL in contr
deals with different ways to safely alter—that is, migrate—a database as
application evolves.

Chapter 10 covers more-advanced configurable features, such as defi
computed columns in your database and catching and handling concu
updates of the database. You'll use these features only in certain circumsta
but you should know that they're there in case you need them.

Chapter 11 looks at methods inside the EF Core's DbContext class, especially how SaveChanges works out what to write to the database and how you can influence that. This chapter covers other diverse topics, such as raw SQL access to the database, database connection resiliency, and the DbContext's Model property.

Configurir
nonrelational properti

This chapter covers

- Configuring EF Core three ways
- Focusing on nonrelational properties
- Defining the database structure
- Introducing value converters, shadow properties, and backing fields
- Deciding which type of configuration works best in different situations

This chapter introduces configuring EF Core in general but concentrates on conf
ing the nonrelational properties in an entity class; these properties are known as
properties. Chapter 8 covers configuring relational properties, and chapter 10 c
configuring more-advanced features, such as DbFunctions, computed columns,
so on.

This chapter starts with an overview of the configuration process that EF
runs when the application's DbContext is used for the first time. Then you'll
how to configure the mapping between the .NET classes and their associated
base tables, with features such as setting the name, SQL type, and nullability o
columns in a table.

This chapter also introduces three EF Core features—*value converters, shadow properties,* and *backing fields*—that enable you to control how the data is stored and controlled by the rest of your non-EF Core code. Value converters, for example, allow you to transform data when it is written/read from the database, allowing you to make the database representation easier to understand and debug; shadow properties and backing fields allow you to "hide," or control access to, database data at the software level. These features can help you write better, less fragile applications that are easier to debug and refactor.

Three ways of configuring EF Core

Chapter 1 covered how EF Core models the database and presented a figure to show what EF Core is doing, with the focus on the database. Figure 7.1 has a more detailed depiction of the configuration process that happens the first time you use the application's DbContext. This figure shows the entire process, with the three configuration approaches: By Convention, Data Annotations, and the Fluent API. This example focuses on the configuration of scalar properties, but the process is the same for all configurations of EF Core.

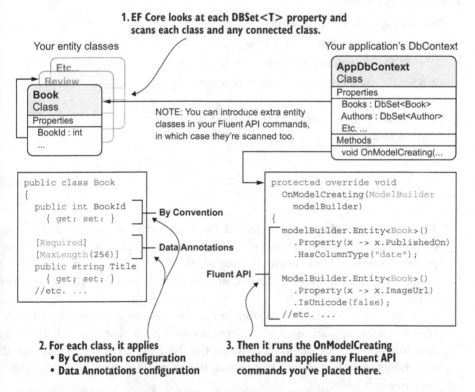

Figure 7.1 When the application's DbContext is first used, EF Core sets off a process to configure itself and build a model of the database it's supposed to access. You can use three approaches to configure EF Core: By Convention, Data Annotations, and Fluent API. Most real applications need a mixture of all three approaches to configure EF Core in exactly the way your application needs.

This list summarizes the three approaches to configuring EF Core:

- *By Convention*—When you follow simple rules on property types and name
  Core will autoconfigure many of the software and database features. Th
  Convention approach is quick and easy, but it can't handle every eventuali
- *Data Annotations*—A range of .NET attributes known as *Data Annotations* ca
  added to entity classes and/or properties to provide extra configuration infc
  tion. These attributes can also be useful for data validation, covered in chap
- *Fluent API*—EF Core has a method called `OnModelCreating` that's run whe
  EF context is first used. You can override this method and add comm;
  known as the *Fluent API*, to provide extra information to EF Core in its m
  ing stage. The Fluent API is the most comprehensive form of configur;
  information, and some features are available only via that API.

> **NOTE** Most real applications need to use all three approaches to configure
> EF Core and the database in exactly the way they need. Some configuration
> features are available via two or even all three approaches (such as defining
> the primary key in an entity class). Section 7.16 gives you my recommenda-
> tions on which approach to use for certain features, plus a way to automate
> some of your configurations.

7.2 A worked example of configuring EF Core

For anything beyond a Hello World version of using EF Core, you're likely to
some form of Data Annotations or Fluent API configuration. In part 1, you need
set up the key for the many-to-many link table. In this chapter, you'll see an exa
of applying the three configuration approaches introduced in section 7.1 to b
match the database to the needs of our Book App.

In this example, you're going to remodel the `Book` entity class used in chapter
and change the size and type of some of the columns from the defaults that EF
uses via a EF Core migration. These changes make your database smaller, make
ing or searching on some columns faster, and check that some columns aren't r
It's always good practice to define the correct size, type, and nullability for your
base columns based on the business needs.

To do this, you'll use a combination of all three configuration approaches. Th
Convention configuration has a major part to play, as it defines the table and col
names, but you'll add specific Data Annotations and Fluent API configuration n
ods to change a few of the columns from the default By Convention settings. Figur
shows how each configuration approach affects EF Core's internal model of data
table structure. Because of space limitations, the figure doesn't show all the
Annotations and Fluent API configuration methods applied to the table, but you
see them in listings 7.1 and 7.2, respectively.

> **NOTE** Figure 7.2 uses arrows to link different EF Core configuration code to
> the parts of the database table's columns. To be completely clear, changing

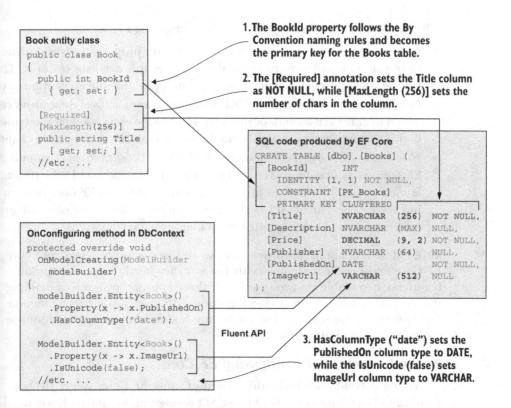

Figure 7.2   To configure the Books table in the exact format you want, you must use all three configuration approaches. A large part is done with By Convention (all the parts not in bold), but then you use Data Annotations to set the size and nullability of the Title column and the Fluent API to change the type of the PublishedOn and ImageUrl columns.

EF Core configurations doesn't magically change the database. Chapter 9, which is about changing the database structure (known as the schema) covers several ways in which the EF Core configurations alter the database or the database alters the EF Core configurations in your code.

You will see more detailed explanations of these settings as you read this chapter, but this part gives you an overall view of different ways you can configure your application's DbContext. It's also interesting to think about how some of these configurations could be useful in your own projects. Here are a few EF Core configurations that I use in most projects I work on:

- [Required] *attribute*—This attribute tells EF Core that the Title column can't be SQL NULL, which means that the database will return an error if you try to insert/update a book with a null Title property.
- [MaxLength(256)] *attribute*—This attribute tells EF Core that the number of characters stored in the database should 256 rather than defaulting to the database's

maximum size (2 GB in SQL Server). Having fixed-length strings of the right
2-byte Unicode or 1-byte ASCII, makes the database access slightly more effi
and allows an SQL index to be applied to these fixed-size columns.

DEFINITION An *SQL index* is a feature that improves the performance of sorting and searching. Section 7.10 covers this topic in more detail.

- HasColumnType("date") *Fluent API*—By making the PublishedOn column
  only the date (which is all you need) rather than the default datetime2
  reduce the column size from 8 bytes to 3 bytes, which makes searching and
  ing on the PublishedOn column faster.
- IsUnicode(false) *Fluent API*—The ImageUrl property contains only 8-bit A
  characters, so you tell EF Core so, which means that the string will be st
  that way. So if the ImageUrl property has a [MaxLength(512)] attribut
  shown in listing 7.1), the IsUnicode(false) method would reduce the si
  the ImageUrl column from 1024 bytes (Unicode takes 2 bytes per characte
  512 bytes (ASCII takes 1 byte per character).

This listing shows you the updated Book entity class code, with the new Data An
tions in bold. (The Fluent API commands are described in section 7.5.)

Listing 7.1 The Book entity class with added Data Annotations

```
public class Book
{
    public int BookId { get; set; }            Tells EF Core
                                               that the string
    [Required]                                 is non-nullable
    [MaxLength(256)]
    public string Title { get; set; }
    public string Description { get; set; }
    public DateTime PublishedOn { get; set; }   Defines the size
    [MaxLength(64)]                              of the string
    public string Publisher { get; set; }       column in the
    public decimal Price { get; set; }          database

    [MaxLength(512)]
    public string ImageUrl { get; set; }
    public bool SoftDeleted { get; set; }

    //-------------------------------------------------
    //relationships

    public PriceOffer Promotion { get; set; }
    public IList<Review> Reviews { get; set; }
    public IList<BookAuthor> AuthorsLink { get; set; }
}
```

TIP You'd normally set the size parameter in the [MaxLength(nn)] attribute by using a constant so that if you create a DTO, it will use the same

constant. If you change the size of one property, you change all the associated properties.

Now that you've seen an example that uses all three configuration approaches, let's explore each approach in detail.

Configuring by convention

By Convention is the default configuration, which can be overridden by the other two approaches, Data Annotations and the Fluent API. The By Convention approach relies on the developer to use the By Convention naming standards and type mappings, which allow EF Core to find and configure entity classes and their relationships, as well as define much of the database model. This approach provides a quick way to configure much of your database mapping, so it's worth learning.

Conventions for entity classes

Classes that EF Core maps to the database are called *entity classes*. As stated in chapter 2, entity classes are normal .NET classes, sometimes referred to as POCOs (plain old CLR objects). EF Core requires entity classes to have the following features:

- The class must be of public access: the keyword `public` should be before the class.
- The class can't be a `static` class, as EF Core must be able to create a new instance of the class.
- The class must have a constructor that EF Core can use. The default, parameterless constructor works, and other constructors with parameters can work. See section 6.1.10 for the detailed rules on how EF Core uses constructors.

Conventions for parameters in an entity class

By convention, EF Core will look for `public` properties in an entity class that have a `public` getter and a setter of any access mode (`public`, `internal`, `protected`, or `private`). The typical, all-public property is

```
public int MyProp { get; set; }
```

Although the all-public property is the norm, in some places having a property with a more localized access setting (such as `public int MyProp { get; private set; }`) gives you more control of how it's set. One example would be a method in the entity class that also does some checks before setting the property; see chapter 13 for more information.

> **NOTE** EF Core can handle read-only properties—properties with only a getter, such as `public int MyProp { get; }`. But in that case, the By Convention approach won't work; you need to use Fluent API to tell EF Core that those properties are mapped to the database.

7.3.3 *Conventions for name, type, and size*

Here are the rules for the name, type, and size of a relational column:

- The name of the property is used as the name of the column in the table.
- The .NET type is translated by the database provider to the corresponding type. Many basic .NET types have a one-to-one mapping to a correspon database type. These basic .NET types are mostly .NET *primitive* types bool, and so on), with some special cases (such as string, DateTime, and G
- The size is defined by the .NET type; for instance, the 32-bit int type is stor the corresponding SQL's 32-bit INT type. String and byte[] types take size of max, which will be different for each database type.

EF6 One change in the default mapping conventions is that EF Core maps a .NET DateTime type to SQL datetime2(7), whereas EF6 maps .NET DateTime to SQL datetime. Microsoft recommends using datetime2(7) because it follows the ANSI and ISO SQL standard. Also, datetime2(7) is more accurate: SQL datetime's resolution is about 0.004 seconds, whereas datetime2(7) has a resolution of 100 nanoseconds.

7.3.4 *By convention, the nullability of a property is based on .NET type*

In relational databases, NULL represents missing or unknown data. Whether a co can be NULL is defined by the .NET type:

- If the type is string, the column can be NULL, because a string can be null.
- Primitive types (such as int) or struct types (such as DateTime) are non-nu default.
- Primitive or struct types can be made nullable by using either the ? suffix (as int?) or the generic Nullable<T> (such as Nullable<int>). In these c the column can be NULL.

Figure 7.3 shows the name, type, size, and nullability conventions applied to a prop

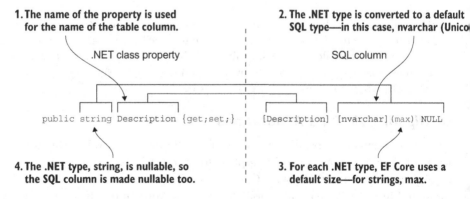

1. The name of the property is used for the name of the table column.

2. The .NET type is converted to a default SQL type—in this case, nvarchar (Unico

.NET class property

SQL column

```
public string Description {get;set;}      [Description] [nvarchar] (max) NULL
```

4. The .NET type, string, is nullable, so the SQL column is made nullable too.

3. For each .NET type, EF Core uses a default size—for strings, max.

Figure 7.3 The application of the By Convention rules to define an SQL column. The type of the property is converted by the database provider to the equivalent SQL type, whereas the name of t property is used for the name of the column.

An EF Core naming convention identifies primary keys

The other rule is about defining the database table's primary key. The EF Core conventions for designating a primary key are as follows:

- EF Core expects one primary-key property. (The By Convention approach doesn't handle keys made up of multiple properties/columns, called *composite keys*.)
- The property is called Id or <class name>id (such as BookId).
- The type of the property defines what assigns a unique value to the key. Chapter 8 covers key generation.

Figure 7.4 shows an example of a database-generated primary key with By Convention mapping for the Book's BookId property and the Books table's SQL column BookId.

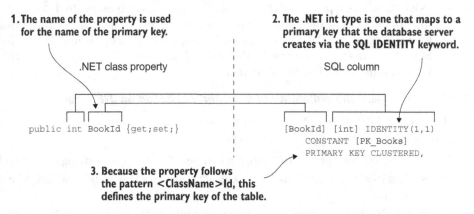

Figure 7.4 The mapping between the .NET class property BookId and the SQL primary column BookId, using the By Convention approach. The name of the property tells EF Core that this property is the primary key. Also, the database provider knows that a type of int means that it should create a unique value for each row added to the table.

TIP Although you have the option of using the short name, Id, for a primary key, I recommend that you use the longer name: <class name> followed by Id (BookId, for example). Understanding what's going on in your code is easier if you use Where(p => BookId == 1) rather than the shorter Where(p => Id == 1), especially when you have lots of entity classes.

Configuring via Data Annotations

Data Annotations are a specific type of .NET attribute used for validation and database features. These attributes can be applied to an entity class or property and provide configuration information to EF Core. This section introduces where you can find them and how they're typically applied. The Data Annotation attributes that are relevant to EF Core configuration come from two namespaces.

7.4.1 Using annotations from System.ComponentModel.DataAnnotations

The attributes in the System.ComponentModel.DataAnnotations namespace are mainly for data validation at the frontend, such as ASP.NET, but EF Core uses sor them for creating the mapping model. Attributes such as [Required] and [Length] are the main ones, with many of the other Data Annotations having no e on EF Core. Figure 7.5 shows how the main attributes, [Required] and [MaxLeng affect the database column definition.

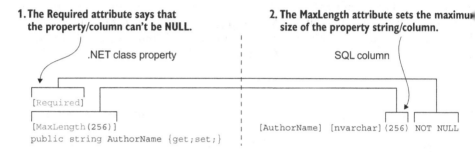

1. The Required attribute says that the property/column can't be **NULL**.

2. The MaxLength attribute sets the maximum size of the property string/column.

.NET class property

SQL column

[Required]

[MaxLength(256)]
public string AuthorName {get;set;}

[AuthorName] [nvarchar](256) NOT NULL

Figure 7.5 The [Required] and [MaxLength] attributes affect the mapping to a database column. The [Required] attribute indicates that the column shouldn't be null, and the [MaxLength] attribute sets the size of the nvarchar.

7.4.2 Using annotations from System.ComponentModel.DataAnnotations.Schema

The attributes in the System.ComponentModel.DataAnnotations.Schema names are more specific to database configuration. This namespace was added in Framework 4.5, well before EF Core was written, but EF Core uses its attributes, as [Table], [Column], and so on, to set the table name and column name/typ described in section 7.11.

7.5 Configuring via the Fluent API

The third approach to configuring EF Core, called the *Fluent API*, is a set of met that works on the ModelBuilder class that's available in the OnModelCreating me inside your application's DbContext. As you will see, the Fluent API works by e sion methods that can be chained together, as LINQ commands are chained toge to set a configuration setting. The Fluent API provides the most comprehensive l configuration commands, with many configurations available only via that API.

But before defining the Fluent API relationship commands, I want to introdu different approach that segregates your Fluent API commands into per-entity sized groups. This approach is useful because as your application grows, puttin Fluent API commands in the OnModelCreating method (as shown in figure makes finding a specific Fluent API hard work. The solution is to move the Fluen for an entity class into a separate configuration class that's then called from the OnModelCreating method.

EF Core provides a method to facilitate this process in the shape of the IEntity-TypeConfiguration<T> interface. Listing 7.2 shows your new application DbContext, EfCoreContext, where you move the Fluent API setup of the various classes into separate configuration classes. The benefit of this approach is that the Fluent API for an entity class is all in one place, not mixed with Fluent API commands for other entity classes.

> **EF6** EF6.x has an EntityTypeConfiguration<T> class that you can inherit to encapsulate the Fluent API configuration for a given entity class. EF Core's implementation achieves the same result but uses an IEntityType-Configuration<T> interface that you apply to your configuration class.

Listing 7.2 Application's DbContext for database with relationships

```
public class EfCoreContext : DbContext          ←——| UserId of the user who
{                                                   | has bought some books

    public EfCoreContext(DbContextOptions<EfCoreContext> options)
        : base(options)
    { }

    public DbSet<Book> Books { get; set; }          The entity classes
    public DbSet<Author> Authors { get; set; }      that your code
    public DbSet<PriceOffer> PriceOffers { get; set; }   will access
    public DbSet<Order> Orders { get; set; }

    protected override void                         The method in which your
        OnModelCreating(ModelBuilder modelBuilder)  Fluent API commands run
    {
        modelBuilder.ApplyConfiguration(new BookConfig());
        modelBuilder.ApplyConfiguration(new BookAuthorConfig());
        modelBuilder.ApplyConfiguration(new PriceOfferConfig());
        modelBuilder.ApplyConfiguration(new LineItemConfig());
    }
}
```

Let's look at the BookConfig class used in listing 7.2 to see how you would construct a per-type configuration class. Listing 7.3 shows a configuration class that implements the IEntityTypeConfiguration<T> interface and contains the Fluent API methods for the Book entity class.

> **NOTE** I am not describing the Fluent APIs in listing 7.3 because it is an example of the use of the IEntityTypeConfiguration<T> interface. The Fluent APIs are covered in section 7.7 (database type) and section 7.10 (indexes).

Listing 7.3 `BookConfig` extension class configures `Book` entity class

```
internal class BookConfig : IEntityTypeConfiguration<Book>
{
    public void Configure
        (EntityTypeBuilder<Book> entity)
    {
        entity.Property(p => p.PublishedOn)
            .HasColumnType("date");

        entity.Property(p => p.Price)
            . HasPrecision(9,2);

        entity.Property(x => x.ImageUrl)
            .IsUnicode(false);

        entity.HasIndex(x => x.PublishedOn);
    }
}
```

The convention-based mapping for .NET string is SQL nvarchar (16 bit Unicode). This command changes the SQL column type to varchar (8-bit ASCII).

Convention-based mapping for .NET DateTime is SQL datetime2. This command changes the SQL column type to date, which hold only the date, not the time.

The precision of (9,2) sets a max price of 9,999,999.99 (9 digits, 2 after decimal point), which takes up the smallest size in the database.

Adds an index to the Publishe property because you sort ar filter on this property

In listing 7.2, I list each of the separate `modelBuilder.ApplyConfiguration` calls so you can see them in action. But a time-saving method called `ApplyConfigurati FromAssembly` can find all your configuration classes that inherit `IEntityT Configuration<T>` and run them all for you. See the following code snippet, w finds and runs all your configuration classes in the same assembly as the DbConto

```
modelBuilder.ApplyConfigurationsFromAssembly(
    Assembly.GetExecutingAssembly());
```

Listing 7.3 shows a typical use of the Fluent API, but please remember that the ent nature of the API allows chaining of multiple commands, as shown in this snippet:

```
modelBuilder.Entity<Book>()
    .Property(x => x.ImageUrl)
    .IsUnicode(false)
    .HasColumnName("DifferentName")
    .HasMaxLength(123)
    .IsRequired(false);
```

EF6 The Fluent API works the same in EF6.x, but with lots of new features and substantial changes in setting up relationships (covered in chapter 8) and subtle changes in data types.

`OnModelCreating` is called when the application first accesses the applicat DbContext. At that stage, EF Core configures itself by using all three approache Convention, Data Annotations, and any Fluent API you've added in the `OnMo Creating` method.

What if Data Annotations and the Fluent API say different things?

The Data Annotations and the Fluent API modeling methods always override convention-based modeling. But what happens if a Data Annotation and the Fluent API both provide a mapping of the same property and setting?

I tried setting the SQL type and length of the WebUrl property to different values via Data Annotations and via the Fluent API. The Fluent API values were used. That test wasn't a definitive one, but it makes sense that the Fluent API was the final arbitrator.

Now that you've learned about the Data Annotations and Fluent API configuration approaches, let's detail the configuration of specific parts of the database model.

Excluding properties and classes from the database

Section 7.3.2 described how EF Core finds properties. But at times, you'll want to exclude data in your entity classes from being in the database. You might want to have local data for a calculation used during the lifetime of the class instance, for example, but you don't want it saved to the database. You can exclude a class or a property in two ways: via Data Annotations or via the Fluent API.

Excluding a class or property via Data Annotations

EF Core will exclude a property or a class that has a [NotMapped] data attribute applied to it. The following listing shows the application of the [NotMapped] data attribute to both a property and a class.

Listing 7.4 Excluding three properties, two by using [NotMapped]

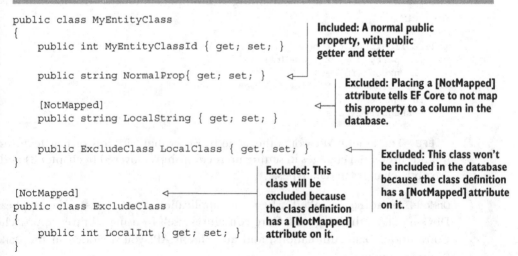

```
public class MyEntityClass
{
    public int MyEntityClassId { get; set; }          Included: A normal public
                                                       property, with public
                                                       getter and setter
    public string NormalProp{ get; set; }
                                                       Excluded: Placing a [NotMapped]
                                                       attribute tells EF Core to not map
    [NotMapped]                                        this property to a column in the
    public string LocalString { get; set; }           database.

    public ExcludeClass LocalClass { get; set; }       Excluded: This class won't
}                                                       be included in the database
                                            Excluded: This  because the class definition
                                            class will be   has a [NotMapped] attribute
[NotMapped]                                 excluded because on it.
public class ExcludeClass                   the class definition
{                                           has a [NotMapped]
    public int LocalInt { get; set; }       attribute on it.
}
```

7.6.2 *Excluding a class or property via the Fluent API*

In addition, you can exclude properties and classes by using the Fluent API confi
tion command `Ignore`, as shown in listing 7.5.

> **NOTE** For simplicity, I show the Fluent API inside the `OnModelCreating` method
> rather than in a separate configuration class.

Listing 7.5 Excluding a property and a class by using the Fluent API

```
public class ExcludeDbContext : DbContext
{
    public DbSet<MyEntityClass> MyEntities { get; set; }

    protected override void OnModelCreating          The Ignore method is used to exc
        (ModelBuilder modelBuilder)                  the LocalString property in the e
    {                                                class, MyEntityClass, from being .
        modelBuilder.Entity<MyEntityClass>()         to the database.
            .Ignore(b => b.LocalString);      ◄───┐
                                                    A different Ignore method ca
        modelBuilder.Ignore<ExcludeClass>();  ◄──── exclude a class such that if yo
    }                                               a property in an entity class
}                                                   Ignored type, that property i
                                                    added to the database.
```

As I said in section 7.3.2, by default, EF Core will ignore read-only properties—th
a property with only a getter (such as `public int MyProp { get; }`).

7.7 *Setting database column type, size, and nullability*

As described earlier, the convention-based modeling uses default values for the
type, size/precision, and nullability based on the .NET type. A common require
is to set one or more of these attributes manually, either because you're using an
ing database or because you have performance or business reasons to do so.

In the introduction to configuring (section 7.3), you worked through an exa
that changed the type and size of various columns. Table 7.1 provides a full list o
commands that are available to perform this task.

Table 7.1 Setting nullability and SQL type/size for a column

Setting	Data Annotations	Fluent API
Set not null (Default is nullable.)	`[Required]` `public string MyProp` `{ get; set; }`	`modelBuilder.Entity<MyClass>` `.Property(p => p.MyProp)` `.IsRequired();`
Set size (string) (Default is MAX length.)	`[MaxLength(123)]` `public string MyProp` `{ get; set; }`	`modelBuilder.Entity<MyClass>` `.Property(p => p.MyProp)` `.HasMaxLength(123);`
Set SQL type/size (Each type has a default precision and size.)	`[Column(TypeName =` `"date")]` `public DateTime` `PublishedOn` `{ get; set; }`	`modelBuilder.Entity<MyClass>` `.Property(p =>` `p.PublishedOn)` `.HasColumnType("date");`

Some specific SQL types have their own Fluent API commands, which are shown in the following list. You can see the first Fluent API commands in use in listing 7.3:

- `IsUnicode(false)`—Sets the SQL type to `varchar(nnn)` (1-byte character, known as ASCII) rather than the default of `nvarchar(nnn)` (2-byte character, known as Unicode).
- `HasPrecision(precision, scale)`—Sets the number of digits (`precision` parameter) and how many of the digits are after the decimal point (`scale` parameter). This Fluent command is new in EF Core 5. The default setting of the SQL decimal is (18,2).
- `HasCollation("collation name")`—Another EF Core 5 feature that allows you to define the collation on a property—that is, the sorting rules, case, and accent sensitivity properties of `char` and `string` types. (See section 2.8.3 for more about collations.)

I recommend using the `IsUnicode(false)` method to tell EF Core that a string property contains only single-byte ASCII-format characters, because using the `IsUnicode` method allows you to set the string size separately.

EF6   EF Core has a slightly different approach to setting the SQL data type of a column. If you provide the data type, you need to give the whole definition, both type and length/precision—as in `[Column(TypeName = "varchar(nnn)")]`, where nnn is an integer number. In EF6, you can use `[Column(TypeName = "varchar")]` and then define the length by using `[MaxLength(nnn)]`, but that technique doesn't work in EF Core. See https://github.com/dotnet/efcore/issues/3985 for more information.

Value conversions: Changing data to/from the database

EF Core's value conversions feature allows you to change data when reading and writing a property to the database. Typical uses are

- Saving `Enum` type properties as a string (instead of a number) so that it's easier to understand when you're looking at the data in the database
- Fixing the problem of `DateTime` losing its UTC (Coordinated Universal Time) setting when read back from the database
- (Advanced) Encrypting a property written to the database and decrypting on reading back

The value conversions have two parts:

- Code that transforms the data as it is written out to the database
- Code that transforms the database column back to the original type when read back

The first example of value conversions deals with a limitation of the SQL database in storing `DateTime` types, in that it doesn't save the `DateTimeKind` part of the `DateTime`

struct that tells us whether the DateTime is local time or UTC. This situation can c
problems. If you send that DateTime to your frontend using JSON, for example
DateTime won't contain the Z suffix character that tells JavaScript that the tir
UTC, so your frontend code may display the wrong time. The following listing s
how to configure a property to have a value conversion that sets the DateTimeKir
the return from the database.

Listing 7.6   Configuring a DateTime property to replace the lost DateTimeKind set

```
protected override void OnModelCreating                    Creates a
    (ModelBuilder modelBuilder)                       ValueConverter from
{                                                       DateTime to DateTime
    var utcConverter = new ValueConverter<DateTime, DateTime>(
        toDb => toDb,
        fromDb =>                                                    Saves the Dat
            DateTime.SpecifyKind(fromDb, DateTimeKind.Utc));         to the databa
                                                                     the normal w
    modelBuilder.Entity<ValueConversionExample>()                    as no convers
        .Property(e => e.DateTimeUtcUtcOnReturn)
        .HasConversion(utcConverter);
    //… other configurations left out
}
```

On reading from the database, you add the UTC setting to the DateTime.

Selects the property you want to configure

Adds the utcConverter to that property

In this case, you had to create your own value converter, but about 20 built-in v
converters are available. (See http://mng.bz/mgYP.) In fact, one value converter
popular that it has a predefined Fluent API method or an attribute—a conversic
store an Enum as a string in the database. Let me explain.

Enums are normally stored in the database as numbers, which is an efficient for
but it does make things harder if you need to delve into the database to work out
happened. So some developers like to save Enums in the database as a string. You
configure a conversion of an Enum type to a string by using the HasConver
<string>() command, as in the following code snippet:

```
modelBuilder.Entity<ValueConversionExample>()
    .Property(e => e.Stage)
    .HasConversion<string>();
```

Following are some rules and limitations on using value conversions:

- A null value will never be passed to a value converter. You need to write a v
  converter to handle only the non-null value, as your converter will be c.
  only if the value isn't a null.
- Watch out for queries that contain sorting on a converted value. If you
  verted your Enums to a string, for example, the sorting will sort by the
  name, not by the Enum value.
- The converter can only map a single property to a single column in the datal
- You can create some complex value converters, such as serializing a list of
  to a JSON string. At this point, EF Core cannot compare the List<int> pro

with the JSON in the database, so it won't update the database. To solve this problem, you need to add what is called a *value comparer*. See the EF Core doc at http://mng.bz/5j5z for more information on this topic.

Later, in section 7.16.4, you will learn a way to automatically apply value converters to certain property types/names to make your life easier.

The different ways of configuring the primary key

You've already seen the By Convention approach of setting up the primary key of an entity. This section covers the normal primary-key setting—one key for which the .NET property defines the name and type. You need to configure the primary key explicitly in two situations:

- When the key name doesn't fit the By Convention naming rules
- When the primary key is made up of more than one property/column, called a *composite key*

A many-to-many relationship-linking table is an example of where the By Convention approach doesn't work. You can use two alternative approaches to define primary keys.

NOTE   Chapter 8 deals with configuring foreign keys, because they define relationships even though they're of a scalar type.

Configuring a primary key via Data Annotations

The [Key] attribute allows you to designate one property as the primary key in a class. Use this annotation when you don't use the By Convention primary key name, as shown in the following listing. This code is simple and clearly marks the primary key.

Listing 7.7   Defining a property as the primary key by using the [Key] annotation

```
private class SomeEntity             [Key] attribute tells EF
{                                    Core that the property
    [Key]                            is a primary key.
    public int NonStandardKeyName { get; set; }

    public string MyString { get; set; }
}
```

Note that the [Key] attribute can't be used for composite keys. In earlier versions of EF Core, you could define composite keys by using [Key] and [Column] attributes, but that feature has been removed.

Configuring a primary key via the Fluent API

You can also configure a primary key via the Fluent API, which is useful for primary keys that don't fit the By Convention patterns. The following listing shows two primary keys being configured by the Fluent API's HasKey method. The first primary key is a single primary key with a nonstandard name in the SomeEntity entity class, and second is a composite primary key, consisting of two columns, in the BookAuthor ing table.

Listing 7.8   Using the Fluent API to configure primary keys on two entity classes

```
protected override void
    OnModelCreating(ModelBuilder modelBuilder)
{
    modelBuilder.Entity<SomeEntity>()
        .HasKey(x => x.NonStandardKeyName);

    modelBuilder.Entity<BookAuthor>()
        .HasKey(x => new {x.BookId, x.AuthorId});

    //… other configuration settings removed
}
```

Defines a normal, single-column primary key. Use HasKey when your key name doesn't match the By Convention defaults.

Uses an anonymous o define two (or more) to form a composite k order in which the pr appear in the anonym object defines their or

---

There is no By Convention version for composite keys, so you must use the Fl API's HasKey method.

7.9.3   Configuring an entity as read-only

In some advanced situations, your entity class might not have a primary key. Here three examples:

- *You want to define an entity class as read-only.* If an entity class hasn't got a pri key, then EF Core will treat it as read-only.
- *You want to map an entity class to a read-only SQL View. SQL Views* are SQL qu that work like SQL tables. See this article for more information: http:// .bz/6g6y.
- *You want to map an entity class to an SQL query by using the* ToSqlQuery *Fluen command.* The ToSqlQuery method allows you to define an SQL comm string that will be executed when you read in that entity class.

To set an entity class explicitly as read-only, you can use the fluent API HasNoK command or apply the attribute [Keyless] to the entity class. And if your entity doesn't have a primary key, you must mark it as read-only, using either of the approaches. Any attempt to change the database via an entity class with no pri key will fail with an exception. EF Core does this because it can't execute the up without a key, which is one way you can define an entity class as read-only. The c way to mark an entity as read-only is to map an entity to an SQL View by using the ent API method ToView("ViewNameString") command, as shown in the follo code snippet:

```
modelBuilder.Entity<MyEntityClass>()
    .ToView("MyView");
```

EF Core will throw an exception if you try to change the database via an entity class that is mapped to a View. If you want to map an entity class to an updatable view—an SQL View that can be updated—you should use the `ToTable` command instead.

Adding indexes to database columns

Relational databases have a feature called an *index,* which provides quicker searching and sorting of rows based on the column, or columns, in the index. In addition, an index may have a constraint, which ensures that each entry in the index is unique. A primary key is given a unique index, for example, to ensure that the primary key is different for each row in the table.

You can add an index to a column via Fluent API and attributes, as shown in table 7.2. An index will speed quick searching and sorting, and if you add the unique constraint, the database will ensure that the column value in each row will be different.

Table 7.2 Adding an index to a column

Action	Fluent API
Add index, Fluent	```modelBuilder.Entity<MyClass>()``` ``` .HasIndex(p => p.MyProp);```
Add index, Attribute	```[Index(nameof(MyProp))]``` ```public class MyClass …```
Add index, multiple columns	```modelBuilder.Entity<Person>()``` ``` .HasIndex(p => new {p.First, p.Surname});```
Add index, multiple columns, Attribute	```[Index(nameof(First), nameof(Surname)]``` ```public class MyClass …```

Add unique index, Fluent	```modelBuilder.Entity<MyClass>()```
	``` .HasIndex(p => p.BookISBN)```
	``` .IsUnique();```

Add unique index, Attribute	```[Index(nameof(MyProp), IsUnique = true)]``` ```public class MyClass …```

Add named index, Fluent	```modelBuilder.Entity<MyClass>()```
	``` .HasIndex(p => p.MyProp)```
	``` .HasDatabaseName("Index_MyProp");```

TIP Don't forget that you can chain the Fluent API commands together to mix and match these methods.

Some databases allow you to specify a filtered or partial index to ignore certain situations by using a WHERE clause. You could set a unique filtered index that ignored any soft-deleted items, for example. To set up a filtered index, you use the `HasFilter` Fluent API method containing an SQL expression to define whether the index should be updated with the value. The following code snippet gives an example of enforcing

that the property `MyProp` will contain a unique value unless the SoftDeleted colum
the table is `true`:

```
modelBuilder.Entity<MyClass>()
    .HasIndex(p => p.MyProp)
    .IsUnique()
    .HasFilter("NOT SoftDeleted");
```

> **NOTE** When you're using the SQL Server provider, EF adds an `IS NOT NULL`
> filter for all nullable columns that are part of a unique index. You can over-
> ride this convention by providing `null` to the `HasFilter` parameter—that is
> `HasFilter(null)`.

7.11 Configuring the naming on the database side

If you're building a new database, using the default names for the various parts o
database is fine. But if you have an existing database, or if your database needs
accessed by an existing system you can't change, you most likely need to use spe
names for the *schema* name, the table names, and the column names of the datab

> **DEFINITION** *Schema* refers to the organization of data inside a database—the
> way the data is organized as tables, columns, constraints, and so on. In some
> databases, such as SQL Server, *schema* is also used to give a namespace to a
> particular grouping of data that the database designer uses to partition the
> database into logical groups.

7.11.1 Configuring table names

By convention, the name of a table is set by the name of the `DbSet<T>` property in
application's DbContext, or if no `DbSet<T>` property is defined, the table uses the
name. In the application's DbContext of our Book App, for example, you defin
`DbSet<Book>` Books property, so the database table name is set to Books. Conver
you haven't defined a `DbSet<T>` property for the `Review` entity class in the app
tion's DbContext, so its table name used the class name and is, therefore, Review.

If your database has specific table names that don't fit the By Convention nam
rules—for example, if the table name can't be converted to a valid .NET var
name because it has a space in it—you can use either Data Annotations or the Fl
API to set the table name specifically. Table 7.3 summarizes the two approaches to
ting the table name.

Table 7.3 Two ways to configure a table name explicitly for an entity class

Configuration method	Example: Setting the table name of the Book class to "XXX"
Data Annotations	`[Table("XXX")]` `public class Book … etc.`
Fluent API	`modelBuilder.Entity<Book>().ToTable("XXX");`

2 Configuring the schema name and schema groupings

Some databases, such as SQL Server, allow you to group your tables by using what is called a schema name. You could have two tables with the same name but different schema names: a table called Books with a schema name Display, for example, would be different from a table called Books with a schema name Order.

By convention, the schema name is set by the database provider because some databases, such as SQLite and MySQL, don't support schemas. In the case of SQL Server, which does support schemas, the default schema name is *dbo*, which is the SQL Server default name. You can change the default schema name only via the Fluent API, using the following snippet in the OnModelCreating method of your application's DbContext:

```
modelBuilder.HasDefaultSchema("NewSchemaName");
```

Table 7.4 shows how to set the schema name for a table. You use this approach if your database is split into logical groups such as sales, production, accounts, and so on, and a table needs to be specifically assigned to a schema.

Table 7.4 Setting the schema name on a specific table

Configuration method	Example: Setting the schema name "sales" on a table
Data Annotations	`[Table("SpecialOrder", Schema = "sales")]` `class MyClass … etc.`
Fluent API	`modelBuilder.Entity<MyClass>()` `        .ToTable("SpecialOrder", schema: "sales");`

3 Configuring the database column names in a table

By convention, the column in a table has the same name as the property name. If your database has a name that can't be represented as a valid .NET variable name or doesn't fit the software use, you can set the column names by using Data Annotations or the Fluent API. Table 7.5 shows the two approaches.

Table 7.5 The two ways to configure a column name

Configuration method	Setting the column name of the `BookId` property to `SpecialCol`
Data Annotations	`[Column("SpecialCol")]` `public int BookId { get; set; }`

Fluent API	`modelBuilder.Entity<MyClass>()`
	`        .Property(b => b.BookId)`
	`        .HasColumnName("SpecialCol");`

7.12 Configuring Global Query Filters

Many applications, such as ASP.NET Core, have security features that control
views and controls the user can access. EF Core has a similar security feature c
Global Query Filters (shortened to *Query Filters*). You can use Query Filters to bu
multitenant application. This type of application holds data for different users in
database, but each user can see only the data they are allowed to access. Another v
to implement a soft-delete feature; instead of deleting data in the database, you n
use a Query Filter to make the soft-deleted row disappear, but the data will sti
there if you need to undelete it later.

I have found Query Filters to be useful in many client jobs, so I included a det
section called "Using Global Query Filters in real-world situations" in chapter 6
tion 6.1.6). That section contains information on how to configure Query Filter
please look there for that information. In section 7.16.4 of this chapter, I show
you can automate the configuration of Query Filters, which ensures that you v
forget to add an important Query Filter to one of your entity classes.

7.13 Applying Fluent API commands based on the database provider type

The EF Core database providers provide a way to detect what database provid
being used when an instance of an application DbContext is created. This appr
is useful for situations such as using, say, an SQLite database for your unit tests
the production database is on an SQL Server, and you want to change some thin
make your unit tests work.

SQLite, for example, doesn't fully support a few NET types, such as decimal,
you try to sort on a decimal property in an SQLite database, you'll get an excep
saying that you won't get the right result from an SQLite database. One way to
around this issue is to convert the decimal type to a double type when using SQLi
won't be accurate, but it might be OK for a controlled set of unit tests.

Each database provider provides an extension method to return true if the v
base matches that provider. The SQL Server database provider, for example, h
method called IsSqlServer(); the SQLite database provider has a method ca
IsSqlite(); and so on. Another approach is to use the ActiveProvider proper
the ModelBuilder class, which returns a string that is the NuGet package name o
database provider, such as "Microsoft.EntityFrameworkCore.SqlServer".

The following listing is an example of applying the decimal to double type ch
if the database is SQLite. This code allows the Book App's OrderBooksBy query o
method to use an in-memory SQLite database.

Listing 7.9   Using database-provider commands to set a column name

```
protected override void OnModelCreating
    (ModelBuilder modelBuilder)
{
    //… put your normal configuration here
```

```
if (Database.IsSqlite())
{
    modelBuilder.Entity<Book>()
        .Property(e => e.Price)
        .HasConversion<double>();
    modelBuilder.Entity<PriceOffer>()
        .Property(e => e.NewPrice)
        .HasConversion<double>();
}
```

> You set the two decimal values to double so that a unit test that sorts on these values doesn't throw an exception.

EF Core 5 added the `IsRelational()` method, which returns `false` for database providers that aren't relational, such as Cosmos Db. You can find a few database-specific Fluent API commands, such as the SQL Server provider method `IsMemoryOptimized`, in the EF Core documentation for each database provider.

> **NOTE** Although you could use this approach to create migrations for different production database types, it's not recommended. The EF Core team suggests that you create a migration for each database type and store each migration in separate directories. For more information, see chapter 9.

Shadow properties: Hiding column data inside EF Core

> **EF6** EF6.x had the concept of shadow properties, but they were used only internally to handle missing foreign keys. In EF Core, shadow properties become a proper feature that you can use.

Shadow properties allow you to access database columns without having them appear in the entity class as a property. Shadow properties allow you to "hide" data that you consider not to be part of the normal use of the entity class. This is all about good software practice: you let upper layers access only the data they need, and you hide anything that those layers don't need to know about. Let me give you two examples that show when you might use shadow properties:

- A common need is to track by whom and when data was changed, maybe for auditing purposes or to understand customer behavior. The tracking data you receive is separate from the primary use of the class, so you may decide to implement that data by using shadow properties, which can be picked up outside the entity class.
- When you're setting up relationships in which you don't define the foreign-key properties in your entity class, EF Core must add those properties to make the relationship work, and it does this via shadow properties. Chapter 8 covers this topic.

1 Configuring shadow properties

There's a By Convention approach to configuring shadow properties, but because it relates only to relationships, I explain it in chapter 8. The other method is to use the Fluent API. You can introduce a new property by using the Fluent API method

Property<T>. Because you're setting up a shadow property, there won't be a prope
that name in the entity class, so you need to use the Fluent API's Property<T> me
which takes a .NET Type and the name of the shadow property. The following li
shows the setup of a shadow property called UpdatedOn that's of type DateTime.

Listing 7.10 Creating the UpdatedOn shadow property by using the Fluent API

```
public class Chapter06DbContext : DbContext
{
    ...

    protected override void
        OnModelCreating(ModelBuilder modelBuilder)
    {
        modelBuilder.Entity<MyEntityClass>()
            .Property<DateTime>("UpdatedOn");        ◁——— Uses the Property<T>
        ...                                                method to define the
    }                                                      shadow property type
}
```

Under By Convention, the name of the table column the shadow property is map
to is the same as the name of the shadow property. You can override this settin
adding the HasColumnName method on to the end of the property method.

WARNING If a property of that name already exists in the entity class, the configuration will use that property instead of creating a shadow property.

7.14.2 Accessing shadow properties

Because the shadow properties don't map to a class property, you need to access t
directly via EF Core. For this purpose, you have to use the EF Core comm
Entry(myEntity).Property("MyPropertyName").CurrentValue, which is a read/
property, as shown in the following listing.

Listing 7.11 Using Entry(inst).Property(name) to set the shadow property

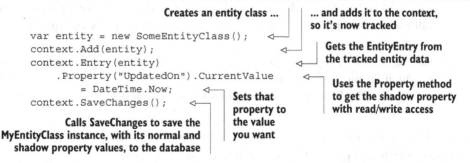

If you want to read a shadow property in an entity that has been loaded, use
context.Entry(entityInstance).Property("PropertyName").CurrentValue c
mand. But you must read the entity as a tracked entity; you should read the e

without the AsNoTracking method being used in the query. The Entry(<entity-Instance>).Property method uses the tracked entity data inside EF Core to hold the value, as it's not held in the entity class instance.

In LINQ queries, you use another technique to access a shadow property: the EF.Property command. You could sort by the UpdatedOn shadow property, for example, by using the following query snippet, with the EF.Property method in bold:

```
context.MyEntities
    .OrderBy(b => EF.Property<DateTime>(b, "UpdatedOn"))
    .ToList();
```

Backing fields: Controlling access to data in an entity class

> **EF6**   Backing fields aren't available in EF6. This EF Core feature provides a level of control over access to data that EF6.x users have been after for some time.

As you saw earlier, columns in a database table are normally mapped to an entity class property with normal getters and setters—public int MyProp { get ; set; }. But you can also map a private field to your database. This feature is called a *backing field*, and it gives you more control of the way that database data is read or set by the software.

Like shadow properties, backing fields hide data, but they do the hiding in another way. For shadow properties, the data is hidden inside EF Core's data, but backing fields hide the data inside the entity class, so it's easier for the entity class to access the backing field inside the class. Here are some examples of situations in which you might use backing fields:

- *Hiding sensitive data*—Hiding a person's date of birth in a private field and making their age in years available to the rest of the software.
- *Catching changes*—Detecting an update of a property by storing the data in a private field and adding code in the setter to detect the update of a property. You will use this technique in chapter 12, when you use property change to trigger an event.
- *Creating Domain-Driven Design (DDD) entity classes*—Creating DDD entity classes in which all the entity classes' properties need to be read-only. Backing fields allow you to lock down navigational collection properties, as described in section 8.7.

But before you get into the complex versions, let's start with the simplest form of backing fields, in which a property getter/setter accesses the field.

7.15.1 Creating a simple backing field accessed by a read/write property

The following code snippet shows you a string property called MyProperty, in w
the string data is stored in a private field. This form of backing field doesn't do
thing particularly different from using a normal property, but this example show
concept of a property linked to a private field:

```
public class MyClass
{
    private string _myProperty;
    public string MyProperty
    {
        get { return _myProperty; }
        set { _myProperty = value; }
    }
}
```

EF Core's By Convention configuration will find the type of backing field and co
ure it as a backing field (see section 7.15.4 for backing-field configuration opti
and by default, EF Core will read/write the database data to this private field.

7.15.2 Creating a read-only column

Creating a read-only column is the most obvious use, although it can also be i
mented via a private setting property (see section 7.3.2). If you have a column i
database that you need to read but don't want the software to write, a backing
is a great solution. In this case, you can create a private field and use a public
erty, with a getter only, to retrieve the value. The following code snippet gives
an example:

```
public class MyClass
{
    private string _readOnlyCol;
    public string ReadOnlyCol => _readOnlyCol;
}
```

Something must set the column property, such as setting a default value in the dat
column (covered in chapter 9) or through some sort of internal database method.

7.15.3 Concealing a person's date of birth: Hiding data inside a class

Hiding a person's date of birth is a possible use of backing fields. In this case,
deem for security reasons that a person's date of birth can be set, but only thei
can be read from the entity class. The following listing shows how to do this i
Person class by using a private _dateOfBirth field and then providing a method t
it and a property to calculate the person's age.

Listing 7.12 Using a backing field to hide sensitive data from normal access

```
public class Person                             The private backing field, which
{                                               can't be accessed directly via
    private DateTime _dateOfBirth;      ◄──┘    normal .NET software

    public void SetDateOfBirth(DateTime dateOfBirth)   ◄──┐ Allows the
    {                                                      │ backing field
        _dateOfBirth = dateOfBirth;                        │ to be set
    }

    public int AgeYears =>                      ◄──┐ You can access the
        Years(_dateOfBirth, DateTime.Today);        │ person's age but not
                                                     │ their exact date of birth.
    //Thanks to dana on stackoverflow
    //see http://stackoverflow.com/a/4127477/1434764
    private static int Years(DateTime start, DateTime end)
    {
        return (end.Year - start.Year - 1) +
               (((end.Month > start.Month) ||
                 ((end.Month == start.Month)
                  && (end.Day >= start.Day)))
                   ? 1 : 0);
}}
```

NOTE In the preceding example, you need to use the Fluent API to create a backing-field-only variable (covered in section 7.15.2), because EF Core can't find this backing field by using the By Convention approach.

From the class point of view, the _dateOfBirth field is hidden, but you can still access the table column via various EF Core commands in the same way that you accessed the shadow properties: by using the EF.Property<DateTime>(entity, "_dateOfBirth") method.

The backing field, _dateOfBirth, isn't totally secure from the developer, but that's not the aim. The idea is to remove the date-of-birth data from the normal properties so that it doesn't get displayed unintentionally in any user-visible view.

4 Configuring backing fields

Having seen backing fields in action, you can configure them By Convention, via Fluent API, and now in EF Core 5 via Data Annotations. The By Convention approach works well but relies on the class to have a property that matches a field by type and a naming convention. If a field doesn't match the property name/type or doesn't have a matching property such as in the _dateOfBirth example, you need to configure your backing fields with Data Annotations or by using the Fluent API. The following sections describe the various configuration approaches.

CONFIGURING BACKING FIELDS BY CONVENTION

If your backing field is linked to a valid property (see section 7.3.2), the field ca
configured by convention. The rules for By Convention configuration state
the private field must have one of the following names that match a property i
same class:

- _<property name> (for example, _MyProperty)
- _<camel-cased property name > (for example, _myProperty)
- m_<property name> (for example, m_MyProperty)
- m_<camel-cased property name> (for example, m_myProperty)

> **DEFINITION** *Camel case* is a convention in which a variable name starts with a
> lowercase letter but uses an uppercase letter to start each subsequent word in
> the name—as in thisIsCamelCase.

CONFIGURING BACKING FIELDS VIA DATA ANNOTATIONS

New in EF Core 5 is the BackingField attribute, which allows you to link a prope
a private field in the entity class. This attribute is useful if you aren't using the By
vention backing field naming style, as in this example:

```
private string _fieldName;
[BackingField(nameof(_fieldName))]
public string PropertyName
{
    get { return _fieldName; }
}

public void SetPropertyNameValue(string someString)
{
    _fieldName = someString;
}
```

CONFIGURING BACKING FIELDS VIA THE FLUENT API

You have several ways of configuring backing fields via the Fluent API. We'll start
the simplest and work up to the more complex. Each example shows you the OnMo
Creating method inside the application's DbContext, with only the field part b
configured:

- *Setting the name of the backing field*—If your backing field name doesn't fc
  EF Core's conventions, you need to specify the field name via the Fluent
  Here's an example:

  ```
  protected override void OnModelCreating
      (ModelBuilder modelBuilder)
  {
      modelBuilder.Entity<Person>()
          .Property(b => b.MyProperty)
          .HasField("_differentName");
      ...
  }
  ```

- *Supplying only the field name*—In this case, if there's a property with the correct name, by convention EF Core will refer to the property, and the property name will be used for the database column. Here's an example:

```
protected override void OnModelCreating
    (ModelBuilder modelBuilder)
{
    modelBuilder.Entity<Person>()
        .Property("_dateOfBirth")
        .HasColumnName("DateOfBirth");
    …
}
```

If no property getter or setter is found, the field will still be mapped to the column, using its name, which in this example is _dateOfBirth, but that's most likely not the name you want for the column. So you add the HasColumnName Fluent API method to get a better column name. The downside is that you'd still need to refer to the data in a query by its field name (in this case, _dateOfBirth), which isn't too friendly or obvious.

ADVANCED: CONFIGURING HOW DATA IS READ/WRITTEN TO THE BACKING FIELD

Since the release of EF Core 3, the default database access mode for backing fields is for EF Core to read and write to the field. This mode works in nearly all cases, but if you want to change the database access mode, you can do so via the Fluent API UsePropertyAccessMode method. The following code snippet tells EF Core to try to use the property for read/write, but if the property is missing a setter, EF Core will fill in the field on a database read:

```
protected override void
    OnModelCreating(ModelBuilder modelBuilder)
{
    modelBuilder.Entity<Person>()
        .Property(b => b.MyProperty)
                .HasField("_differentName")
        .UsePropertyAccessMode(PropertyAccessMode.PreferProperty);
    …
}
```

TIP To see the various access modes for a backing field, use Visual Studio's intellisense feature to look at the comments on each of the PropertyAccessMode Enum values.

Recommendations for using EF Core's configuration

You have so many ways to configure EF Core, some of which duplicate each other, that it isn't always obvious which of the three approaches you should use for each part of the configuration. Here are suggested approaches to use for each part of EF Core configuration:

- Start by using the By Convention approach wherever possible, because it's c and easy.
- Use the validation attributes—MaxLength, Required, and so on—from the Annotations approach, as they're useful for validation.
- For everything else, use the Fluent API approach, because it has the most prehensive set of commands. But consider writing code to automate com settings, such as applying the DateTime "UTC fix" to all DateTime prope whose Name ends with "Utc".

The following sections provide more-detailed explanations of my recommenda for configuring EF Core.

7.16.1 Use By Convention configuration first

EF Core does a respectable job of configuring most standard properties, so a start with that approach. In part 1, you built the whole of this initial database by t the By Convention approach, apart from the composite key in the BookAuthor n to-many linking entity class.

The By Convention approach is quick and easy. You'll see in chapter 8 that relationships can be set up purely by using the By Convention naming rules, w can save you a lot of time. Learning what By Convention can configure will dra cally reduce the amount of configuration code you need to write.

7.16.2 Use validation Data Annotations wherever possible

Although you can do things such as limit the size of a string property with either Annotations or the Fluent API, I recommend using Data Annotations for the fo ing reasons:

- *Frontend validation can use them.* Although EF Core doesn't validate the e class before saving it to the database, other parts of the system may use Annotations for validation. ASP.NET Core uses Data Annotations to vali input, for example, so if you input directly into an entity class, the valida attributes will be useful. Or if you use separate ASP.NET ViewModel or I classes, you can cut and paste the properties with their validation attributes
- *You may want to add validation to EF Core's* SaveChanges. Using data validatic move checks out of your business logic can make your business logic sim Chapter 4 showed you how to add validation of entity classes when SaveCha is called.
- *Data Annotations make great comments.* Attributes, which include Data An tions, are compile-time constants; they're easy to see and easy to understan

3 Use the Fluent API for anything else

Typically, I use the Fluent API for setting up the database column mapping (column name, column data type, and so on) when it differs from the conventional values. You could use the schema Data Annotations to do that, but I try to hide things like these inside the OnModelCreating method because they're database implementation issues rather than software structure issues. That practice is more a preference than a rule, though, so make your own decision. Section 7.16.4 describes how to automate some of your Fluent API configurations, which saves you time and also ensures that all your configuration rules are applied to every matching class/property.

4 Automate adding Fluent API commands by class/property signatures

One useful feature of the Fluent API commands allows you to write code to find and configure certain configurations based on the class/property type, name, and so on. In a real application, you might have hundreds of DateTime properties that need the UTC fix you used in listing 7.6. Rather than add the configuration for each property by hand, wouldn't it be nice to find each property that needs the UTC fix and apply it automatically? You're going to do exactly that.

Automating finding/adding configurations relies on a type called IMutableModel, which you can access in the OnModelCreating method. This type gives you access to all the classes mapped by EF Core to the database, and each IMutableEntityType allows you to access the properties. Most configuration options can be applied via methods in these two interfaces, but a few, such as Query Filters, need a bit more work.

To start, you will build the code that will iterate through each entity class and its properties, and add one configuration, as shown in listing 7.13. This iteration approach defines the way to automate configurations, and in later examples, you will add extra commands to do more configurations.

The following example adds a value converter to a DateTime that applies the UTC fix shown in listing 7.6. But in the following listing, the UTC fix value converter is applied to every property that is a DateTime with a Name that ends with "Utc".

Listing 7.13 Applying value converter to any DateTime property ending in "Utc"

```
protected override void
    OnModelCreating(ModelBuilder modelBuilder)           The Fluent API commands
{                                                         are applied in the
                                                          OnModelCreating method.
    var utcConverter = new ValueConverter<DateTime, DateTime>(      Defines a value
        toDb => toDb,                                               converter to set the
        fromDb =>                                                   UTC setting to the
            DateTime.SpecifyKind(fromDb, DateTimeKind.Utc));        returned DateTime

    foreach (var entityType in modelBuilder.Model.GetEntityTypes())
    {
```

<table>
<tr>
<td>

Loops through all the properties in an entity class that are mapped to the database

</td>
<td>

```
foreach (var entityProperty in entityType.GetProperties())
{
    if (entityProperty.ClrType == typeof(DateTime)
        && entityProperty.Name.EndsWith("Utc"))
    {
        entityProperty.SetValueConverter(utcConverter);
    }
    //… other examples left out for clarity
}
```

</td>
<td>

Adds the converte properti DateTim ending i

</td>
</tr>
</table>

```
}
//… rest of configration code left out
```

Listing 7.13 showed the setup of only one Type/Named property, but normally, you w have lots of Fluent API settings. In this example, you are going to do the following:

1 Add the UTC fix value converter to properties of type DateTime whose N end with "Utc".
2 Set the decimal precision/scale where the property's Name contains "Price
3 Set any string properties whose Name ends in "Url" to be stored as ASCII— is, varchar(nnn).

The following code snippet shows the code inside the OnModelCreating methc the Book App DbContext to add these three configuration settings:

```
foreach (var entityType in modelBuilder.Model.GetEntityTypes())
{
    foreach (var entityProperty in entityType.GetProperties())
    {
        if (entityProperty.ClrType == typeof(DateTime)
            && entityProperty.Name.EndsWith("Utc"))
        {
            entityProperty.SetValueConverter(utcConverter);
        }

        if (entityProperty.ClrType == typeof(decimal)
            && entityProperty.Name.Contains("Price"))
        {
            entityProperty.SetPrecision(9);
            entityProperty.SetScale(2);
        }

        if (entityProperty.ClrType == typeof(string)
            && entityProperty.Name.EndsWith("Url"))
        {
            entityProperty.SetIsUnicode(false);
        }
    }
}
```

A few Fluent APIs configurations need class-specific code, however. The Query Fi for example, need a query that accesses entity classes. For this case, you need to an interface to the entity class you want to add a Query Filter to and create the correct filter query dynamically.

As an example, you are going to build code that allows you to add automatically the SoftDelete Query Filter described in section 3.5.1 and the UserId Query Filter shown in section 6.1.7. Of these two Query Filters, UserId is more complex because it needs to get the current UserId, which changes on every instance of the Book App's DbContext. You can do this in a couple of ways, but you decide to provide the current instance of the DbContext to the query. The following listing shows the extension class, called SoftDeleteQueryExtensions, with its MyQueryFilterTypes enum.

Listing 7.14 The enum/class to use to set up Query Filters on every compatible class

Third optional property holds a copy of the current DbContext instance so that the UserId will be the current one

Defines the different type of LINQ query to put in the Query Filter

A static extension class

Second parameter allows you to pick which type of query filter to add

Call this method to set up the query filter.

```
public enum MyQueryFilterTypes { SoftDelete, UserId }

public static class SoftDeleteQueryExtensions
{
    public static void AddSoftDeleteQueryFilter(
        this IMutableEntityType entityData,
        MyQueryFilterTypes queryFilterType,
        IUserId userIdProvider = null)
    {
        var methodName = $"Get{queryFilterType}Filter";
        var methodToCall = typeof(SoftDeleteQueryExtensions)
            .GetMethod(methodName,
                BindingFlags.NonPublic | BindingFlags.Static)
            .MakeGenericMethod(entityData.ClrType);
        var filter = methodToCall
            .Invoke(null, new object[] { userIdProvider });
        entityData.SetQueryFilter((LambdaExpression)filter);
        if (queryFilterType == MyQueryFilterTypes.SoftDelete)
            entityData.AddIndex(entityData.FindProperty(
                nameof(ISoftDelete.SoftDeleted)));
        if (queryFilterType == MyQueryFilterTypes.UserId)
            entityData.AddIndex(entityData.FindProperty(
                nameof(IUserId.UserId)));
    }

    private static LambdaExpression GetUserIdFilter<TEntity>(
        IUserId userIdProvider)
        where TEntity : class, IUserId
    {
        Expression<Func<TEntity, bool>> filter =
            x => x.UserId == userIdProvider.UserId;
        return filter;
    }
}
```

First parameter comes from EF Core and allows you to add a query filter

The filter by the d type in the Filter ethod

Creates the correctly typed method to create the Where LINQ expression to use in the Query Filter

on the rty for mance

Adds an index on the SoftDeleted property for better performance

Creates a query that is true only if the _userId matches the UserID in the entity class

<table>
<tr>
<td>**Creates a query that is true only if the SoftDeleted property is false**</td>
<td>

```
private static LambdaExpression GetSoftDeleteFilter<TEntity>(
    IUserId userIdProvider)
    where TEntity : class, ISoftDelete
{
    Expression<Func<TEntity, bool>> filter =
        x => !x.SoftDeleted;
    return filter;
}
```

</td>
</tr>
</table>

```
}
```

Because every query of an entity that has a Query Filter will contain a filter on property, the code automatically adds an index on every property that is used Query Filter. That technique improves performance on that entity. Finally, the fo ing listing shows how to use the code shown in listing 7.14 within the Book A DbContext to automate the configuration of the Query Filters.

Listing 7.15 Adding code to the DbContext to automate setting up Query Filters

**Holds the UserId, which is used in the
Query Filter that uses the IUserId interface**

**Adding the IUserId to
DbContext means that
can pass the DbConte:
the UserId query filter**

```
public class EfCoreContext : DbContext, IUserId
{
    public Guid UserId { get; private set; }
```

**Sets up the UserId.
If the userIdService
is null, or if it
returns null for the
UserId, we set a
replacement UserId.**

```
    public EfCoreContext(DbContextOptions<EfCoreContext> options,
        IUserIdService userIdService = null)
        : base(options)
    {
        UserId = userIdService?.GetUserId()
                ?? new ReplacementUserIdService().GetUserId();
    }

    //DbSets removed for clarity
```

**Loops through
all the classes
that EF Core has
currently found
mapped to the
database**

**The automate code goes i
OnModelCreating method**

```
    protected override void
        OnModelCreating(ModelBuilder modelBuilder)
    {
        //other configuration code removed for clarity

        foreach (var entityType in modelBuilder.Model.GetEntityTypes()
        {
            //other property code removed for clarity
```

**If the class inher
ISoftDelete inter
needs the SoftDe
Query Filter.**

**Adds a Query Filter
to this class, with a
query suitable for
SoftDelete**

```
            if (typeof(ISoftDelete)
                .IsAssignableFrom(entityType.ClrType))
            {
                entityType.AddSoftDeleteQueryFilter(
                    MyQueryFilterTypes.SoftDelete);
            }
            if (typeof(IUserId)
                .IsAssignableFrom(entityType.ClrType))
            {
```

**If the class inher
IUserId interface
needs the IUser
Query Filter.**

```
                    entityType.AddSoftDeleteQueryFilter(
                        MyQueryFilterTypes.UserId, this);
            }
        }
}
```

> **Adds the UserId Query Filter to this class. Passing 'this' allows access to the current UserId.**

For the Book App, all this automation is overkill, but in bigger applications, it can save you a great deal of time; more important, it ensures that you have set everything up correctly. To end this section, here are some recommendations and limitations that you should know about if you are going to use this approach:

- If you run the automatic Fluent API code before your handcoded configurations, your handcoded configurations will override any of the automatic Fluent API settings. But be aware that if there is an entity class that is registered only via manually written Fluent API, that entity class won't be seen by the automatic Fluent API code.

- The configuration commands must apply the same configurations every time because the EF Core configures the application's DbContext only once—on first use—and then works from a cache version.

Summary

- The first time you create the application's DbContext, EF Core configures itself by using a combination of three approaches: By Convention, Data Annotations, and the Fluent API.

- Value converters allow you to transform the software type/value when writing and reading back from the database.

- Two EF Core features, shadow properties and backing fields, allow you to hide data from higher levels of your code and/or control access to data in an entity class. Use the By Convention approach to set up as much as you can, because it's simple and quick to code.

- When the By Convention approach doesn't fit your needs, Data Annotations and/or EF Core's Fluent API can provide extra commands to configure both the way EF Core maps the entity classes to the database and the way EF Core will handle that data.

- In addition to writing configuration code manually, you can also add code to configure entity classes and/or properties automatically based on the class/ properties signature.

For readers who are familiar with EF6:

- The basic process of configuring EF Core is, on the surface, similar to the way EF6 works, but there is a significant number of changed or new commands.

- EF Core can use configuration classes to hold the Fluent API commands for a given entity class. The Fluent API commands provide a feature similar to the

EF6.x `EntityType-Configuration<T>` class, but EF Core uses an `IEntityT`
`Configuration<T>` interface instead.

- EF Core has introduced many extra features that are not available in EF6,
  as value converters, shadow properties, and backing fields, all of which are
  come additions to EF.

Configuring relationships

This chapter covers

- Configuring relationships with By Convention
- Configuring relationships with Data Annotations
- Configuring relationships with the Fluent API
- Mapping entities to database tables in five other ways

Chapter 7 described how to configure scalar (nonrelational) properties. This chapter covers how to configure database relationships. I assume that you've read at least the first part of chapter 7, because configuring relationships uses the same three approaches—By Convention, Data Annotations, and the Fluent API—to map the database relationships.

This chapter covers how EF Core finds and configures relationships between entity classes, with pointers and examples showing how to configure each type of relationship: one-to-one, one-to-many, and many-to-many. EF Core's By Convention relationship rules can configure many relationships quickly, but you'll also learn about all the Data Annotations and Fluent API configuration options, which allow you to define precisely the way you want a relationship to behave. You'll also look at features that allow you to enhance your relationships with extra keys and alternative table-mapping approaches. Finally, you'll consider five ways to map classes to the database.

8.1 Defining some relationship terms

This chapter refers to the various parts of a relationship, and you need clear term that you know exactly what part of the relationship we're talking about. Figur shows those terms, using the Book and Review entity classes from our Book App. low this figure with a more detailed description so the terms will make sense to when I use them in this chapter.

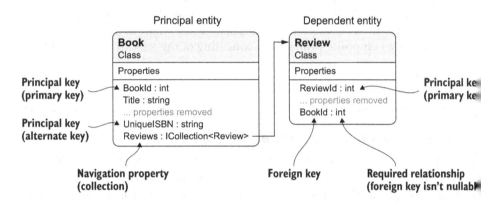

Figure 8.1 The Book and Review entity classes show six of the terms used in this chapter to discuss relationships: *principal entity, dependent entity, principal key, navigational property, foreig key,* and *required relationship*. Not shown is *optional relationship,* which is described in section 2.1.

To ensure that these terms are clear, here are detailed descriptions:

- *Principal key*—A new term, taken from EF Core's documentation, that refe either the primary key, defined in part 1, or the new *alternate key,* which l unique value per row and isn't the primary key (see section 8.8.3)

NOTE Figure 8.1 provides an example of an alternate key called UniqueISBN, which represents a unique value per entity. (*ISBN* stands for *International Standard Book Number,* which is unique for every book.)

- *Principal entity*—The entity that contains the principal-key properties, which dependent relationship refer to via a foreign key(s) (covered in chapter 3)
- *Dependent entity*—The entity that contains the foreign-key properties that to the principal entity (covered in chapter 3)
- *Principal key*—The entity has a principal key, also known as the *primary key,* w is unique for each entity stored in the database

- *Navigational property*—A term taken from EF Core's documentation that refers to the property containing a single entity class, or a collection of entity classes, that EF Core uses to link entity classes
- *Foreign key*—Defined in section 2.1.3, holds the principal key value(s) of the database row it's linked to (or could be null)
- *Required relationship*—A relationship in which the foreign key is non-nullable (and principal entity must exist)
- *Optional relationship*—A relationship in which the foreign key is nullable (and principal entity can be missing)

NOTE A principal key and a foreign key can consist of more than one property/column. These keys are called *composite keys.* You've already seen one of these keys in section 3.4.4, as the BookAuthor many-to-many linking entity class has a composite primary key consisting of the BookId and the AuthorId.

You'll see in section 8.4 that EF Core can find and configure most relationships By Convention. In some cases, EF Core needs help, but generally, it can find and configure your navigational properties for you if you use the By Convention naming rules.

What navigational properties do you need?

The configuring of relationships between entity classes should be guided by the business needs of your project. You could add navigational properties at both ends of a relationship, but that suggests that every navigational property is useful, and some navigational properties aren't. It is good practice to provide only navigational properties that make sense from the business or software design point of view.

In our Book App, for example, the Book entity class has many Review entity classes, and each Review class is linked, via a foreign key, to one Book. Therefore, you could have a navigational property of type ICollection<Review> in the Book class and a navigational property of type Book in the Review class. In that case, you'd have a *fully defined relationship*: a relationship with navigational properties at both ends.

But do you need a fully defined relationship? From the software design point of view, there are two questions about the Book/Review navigational relationships. The answers to these questions define which navigational relationship you need to include:

- Does the Book entity class need to know about the Review entity classes? I say yes, because we want to calculate the average review score.
- Does the Review entity class need to know about the Book entity class? I say no, because in this example application, we don't do anything with that relationship.

Our solution, therefore, is to have only the ICollection<Review> navigational property in the Book class, which is what figure 8.1 portrays.

My experience is you should add a navigational property only when it makes sense from a business point of view or when you need a navigational property to create (EF Core's Add) an entity class with a relationship (see section 6.2.1). Minimizing

navigational properties will help make the entity classes easier to understand,
more-junior developers won't be tempted to use relationships that aren't righ
your project.

8.3   Configuring relationships

In the same way as in chapter 7, which covered configuring nonrelational prope
EF Core has three ways to configure relationships. Here are the three approache
configuring properties, but focused on relationships:

- *By Convention*—EF Core finds and configures relationships by looking for r
  ences to classes that have a primary key in them.
- *Data Annotations*—These annotations can be used to mark foreign keys
  relationship references.
- *Fluent API*—This API provides the richest set of commands to configure
  relationship fully.

The next three sections detail each of these approaches in turn. As you'll see, th
Convention approach can autoconfigure many relationships for you if you follo
naming standards. At the other end of the scale, the Fluent API allows you to d
every part of a relationship manually, which can be useful if you have a relatior
that falls outside the By Convention approach.

8.4   Configuring relationships By Convention

The By Convention approach is a real time-saver when it comes to configuring
tionships. In EF6.x, I used to define my relationships laboriously because I d
fully understand the power of the By Convention approach to relationships.
that I understand the conventions, I let EF Core set up most of my relations
other than in the few cases in which By Convention doesn't work. (Section 8.4.6
those exceptions.)

The rules are straightforward, but the ways that the property name, type, and
lability work together to define a relationship take a bit of time to absorb. I hope
reading this section will save you time when you're developing your next applic
that uses EF Core.

8.4.1   What makes a class an entity class?

Chapter 2 defined the term *entity class* as a normal .NET class that has been ma
by EF Core to the database. Here, you want to define how EF Core finds and iden
a class as an entity class by using the By Convention approach.

Figure 7.1 showed the three ways that EF Core configures itself. Following is a r
of that process, now focused on finding the relationships and navigational properti

1 EF Core scans the application's DbContext, looking for any public DbSe
   properties. It assumes that the classes, T, in the DbSet<T> properties are e
   classes.

2 EF Core also looks at every public property in the classes found in step 1 and looks at properties that could be navigational properties. The properties whose type contains a class that isn't defined as being scalar properties (string is a class, but it's defined as a scalar property) are assumed to be navigational properties. These properties may appear as a single link (such as public PriceOffer Promotion (get; set; }) or a type that implements the IEnumerable<T> interface (such as public ICollection<Review> Reviews { get; set; }).

3 EF Core checks whether each of these entity classes has a primary key (see section 7.9). If the class doesn't have a primary key and hasn't been configured as not having a key (see section 7.9.3), or if the class isn't excluded, EF Core will throw an exception.

An example of an entity class with navigational properties

Listing 8.1 shows the entity class Book, which is defined in the application's DbContext. In this case, you have a public property of type DbSet<Book>, which passed the "must have a valid primary key" test in that it has a public property called BookId.

What you're interested in is how EF Core's By Convention configuration handles the three navigational properties at the bottom of the class. As you'll see in this section, EF Core can work out which sort of relationship it is by the type of the navigational property and the foreign key in the class that the navigational property refers to.

Listing 8.1   The Book entity class, with the relationships at the bottom

```
public class Book
{
    public int BookId { get; set; }
    //other scalar properties removed as not relevant…

    public PriceOffer Promotion { get; set; }

    public ICollection<Tag> Tags { get; set; }

    public ICollection<BookAuthor> AuthorsLink { get; set; }

    public ICollection<Review> Reviews { get; set; }
}
```

Links to a PriceOffer, which is one-to-zero-or-one relationship

Links directly to a list of Tag entities, using EF Core 5's automatic many-to-many relationship

Links to one side of the many-to-many relationship of authors via a linking table

Links to any reviews for this book: one-to-many relationship

If two navigational properties exist between the two entity classes, the relationship is known as *fully defined*, and EF Core can work out By Convention whether it's a one-to-one or a one-to-many relationship. If only one navigational property exists, EF Core can't be sure, so it assumes a one-to-many relationship.

Certain one-to-one relationships may need configuration via the Fluent API if you have only one navigational property or if you want to change the default By Convention setting, such as when you're deleting an entity class with a relationship.

8.4.3 *How EF Core finds foreign keys By Convention*

A foreign key must match the principal key (defined in section 8.1) in type an
name, but to handle a few scenarios, foreign-key name matching has three opt
shown in figure 8.2. The figure shows all three options for a foreign-key name u
the entity class `Review` that references the primary key, `BookId`, in the entity class B

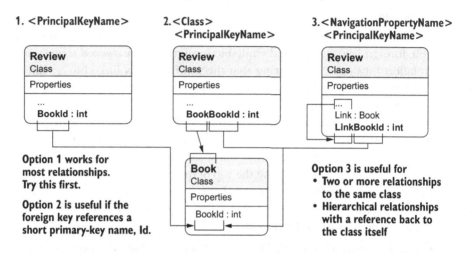

**Figure 8.2   Three By Convention options for a foreign key referring to the `Book` entity class's
primary key. These options allow you to use a unique name for your foreign key, from which EF
Core can work out which primary key this relationship refers to.**

Option 1 is the one I use most; it's depicted in figure 8.1. Option 2 is for develo
who use the short, By Convention primary-key name, `Id`, as it makes the foreign
unique to the class it's linking to. Option 3 helps with specific cases in which you'r
duplicate named properties if you used option 1. The following listing shows an ex
ple of using option 3 to handle a hierarchical relationship.

Listing 8.2   A hierarchical relationship with an option-3 foreign key

```
public class Employee
{
    public int EmployeeId { get; set; }

    public string Name { get; set; }

    //-----------------------------
    //Relationships

    public int? ManagerEmployeeId { get; set; }       Foreign key uses the
    public Employee Manager { get; set; }             <NavigationalPropertyN
}                                                     <PrimaryKeyName> pa
```

The entity class called Employee has a navigational property called Manager that links to the employee's manager, who is an employee as well. You can't use a foreign key of EmployeeId (option 1), because it's already used for the primary key. Therefore, you use option 3 and call the foreign key ManagerEmployeeId by using the navigational property name at the start.

Nullability of foreign keys: Required or optional dependent relationships

The nullability of the foreign key defines whether the relationship is required (non-nullable foreign key) or optional (nullable foreign key). A *required relationship* ensures that relationships exist by ensuring that the foreign key is linked to a valid principal key. Section 8.6.1 describes an Attendee entity that has a required relationship to a Ticket entity class.

An *optional* relationship allows there to be no link between the principal entity and the dependent entity by having the foreign-key value(s) set to null. The Manager navigational property in the Employee entity class, shown in listing 8.2, is an example of an optional relationship, as someone at the top of the business hierarchy won't have a boss.

The required or optional status of the relationship also affects what happens to dependent entities when the principal entity is deleted. The default setting of the OnDelete action for each relationship type is as follows:

- For a *required relationship,* EF Core sets the OnDelete action to Cascade. If the principal entity is deleted, the dependent entity will be deleted too.
- For a *optional relationship,* EF Core sets the OnDelete action to ClientSetNull. If the dependent entity is being tracked, the foreign key will be set to null when the principal entity is deleted. But if the dependent entity *isn't* being tracked, the database constraint delete setting takes over, and the ClientSetNull setting sets the database rules as though the Restrict setting were in place. The result is that the delete fails at the database level, and an exception is thrown.

NOTE The ClientSetNull delete behavior is rather unusual, and section 8.8.1 explains why. That section also describes how to configure the delete behavior of a relationship.

Foreign keys: What happens if you leave them out?

If EF Core finds a relationship via a navigational property or through a relationship you configured via the Fluent API, it needs a foreign key to set up the relationship in the relational database. Including foreign keys in your entity classes is good practice, giving you better control of the nullability of the foreign key. Also, access to foreign keys can be useful when you're handling relationships in a disconnected update (see section 3.3.1).

But if you do leave out a foreign key (on purpose or by accident), EF Core configuration will add a foreign key as a shadow property. *Shadow properties*, which were introduced in chapter 7, are hidden properties that can be accessed only via specific EF

Core commands. Having foreign keys added automatically as shadow propertie:
be useful. One of my clients, for example, had a general Note entity class tha
added to a Notes collection in many entities.

Figure 8.3 shows a one-to-many relationship in which the Note entity class is
in a collection navigational property in two entity classes: Customer and Job. Note
the primary-key names of the Customer and Job entity classes use different By Cor
tion naming approaches to show how the shadow properties are named.

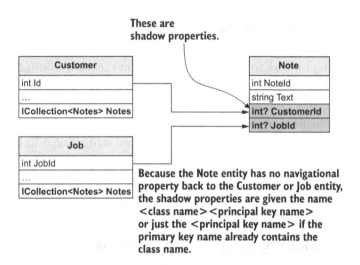

Because the Note entity has no navigational
property back to the Customer or Job entity,
the shadow properties are given the name
<class name> <principal key name>
or just the <principal key name> if the
primary key name already contains the
class name.

**Figure 8.3   EF Core's By Convention configuration will add nullable
(that is, optional relationship) foreign keys as shadow properties if you
don't provide your own foreign keys in the Notes entity class.**

If the entity class that gains a shadow property foreign key has a navigational lii
the other end of the relationship, the name of that shadow property would be <n.
gation property name><principal key property name>. If the Note entity in fi
8.3 has a navigational link back to the Customer entity called LinkBack, the sh<
property foreign key's name would be LinkBackId.

> **NOTE**   My unit tests show that one-to-one relationships are rejected if there is
> no foreign key to link the two entities. Therefore, EF Core's By Convention
> won't set up shadow property foreign keys on one-to-one relationships auto-
> matically.

If you want to add a foreign key as a shadow property, you can do that via the F.
API HasForeignKey, shown in section 8.6, but with the name of the shadow pro|
name provided via a string. Be careful not to use the name of an existing proper
that will not add a shadow property but will use the existing property.

The shadow foreign-key property will be nullable, which has the effect described in section 8.4.4 on nullability of foreign keys. If this effect isn't what you want, you can alter the shadow property's nullability by using the Fluent API `IsRequired` method, as described in section 8.8.2.

EF6   EF6.x uses a similar approach to adding foreign keys if you left them out of your entity classes, but in EF6.x, you can't configure the nullability or access the content. EF Core's shadow properties make leaving out foreign keys more controllable.

When does By Convention configuration not work?

If you're going to use the By Convention configuration approach, you need to know when it's not going to work so that you can use other means to configure your relationship. Here's my list of scenarios that won't work, with the most common listed first:

- You have composite foreign keys (see section 8.6 or section 8.5.1).
- You want to create a one-to-one relationship without navigational links going both ways (see section 8.6.1).
- You want to override the default delete-behavior setting (see section 8.8.1).
- You have two navigational properties going to the same class (see section 8.5.2).
- You want to define a specific database constraint (see section 8.8.4).

Configuring relationships by using Data Annotations

Only two Data Annotations relate to relationships, as most of the navigational configuration is done via the Fluent API: the `ForeignKey` and `InverseProperty` annotations.

The ForeignKey Data Annotation

The `ForeignKey` Data Annotation allows you to define the foreign key for a navigational property in the class. Taking the hierarchical example of the `Employee` class, you can use this annotation to define the foreign key for the `Manager` navigational property. The following listing shows an updated `Employee` entity class with a new, shorter foreign-key name for the `Manager` navigational property that doesn't fit By Convention naming: `ManagerEmployeeId`.

Listing 8.3   Using the `ForeignKey` data annotation to set the foreign-key name

```
public class Employee
{
    public int EmployeeId { get; set; }
    public string Name { get; set; }

    public int? ManagerId { get; set; }          Defines which property is the
    [ForeignKey(nameof(ManagerId))]              foreign key for the Manager
    public Employee Manager { get; set; }        navigational property
}
```

NOTE You've applied the ForeignKey data annotation to the Manager navigational property, giving the name of the foreign key, ManagerId. But the ForeignKey data annotation also works the other way around. You could've applied the ForeignKey data annotation to the foreign-key property, ManagerId, giving the name of the navigational property, Manager—such as [ForeignKey(nameof(Manager))].

The ForeignKey data annotation takes one parameter, which is a string. This s should hold the name of the foreign-key property. If the foreign key is a comp key (has more than one property), it should be comma-delimited—as in [Fore Key("Property1, Property2")].

TIP I suggest that you use the nameof keyword to provide the property name string. That's safer, because if you change the name of the foreign-key property, nameof will either be updated at the same time or throw a compile error if you forgot to change all the references.

8.5.2 *The InverseProperty Data Annotation*

The InverseProperty Data Annotation is a rather specialized Data Annotatio use when you have two navigational properties going to the same class. At that p EF Core can't work out which foreign keys relate to which navigational property. situation is best shown in code. The following listing shows an example Person e class with two lists: one for books owned by the librarian and one for Books o loan to a specific person.

Listing 8.4 LibraryBook entity class with two relationships to Person class

```csharp
public class LibraryBook
{
    public int LibraryBookId { get; set; }
    public string Title { get; set; }

    public int LibrarianPersonId { get; set; }
    public Person Librarian { get; set; }

    public int? OnLoanToPersonId { get; set; }
    public Person OnLoanTo { get; set; }
}
```

The Librarian and the borrower of the book (OnLoanTo navigational property both represented by the Person entity class. The Librarian navigational property the OnLoanTo navigational property both link to the same class, and EF Core can up the navigational linking without help. The InverseProperty Data Annota shown in the following listing provides the information to EF Core when it's conf ing the navigational links.

Listing 8.5 The `Person` entity class, which uses the `InverseProperty` annotation

```
public class Person
{
    public int PersonId { get; set; }
    public string Name { get; set; }

    [InverseProperty("Librarian")]
    public ICollection<LibraryBook>
        LibrarianBooks { get; set; }

    [InverseProperty("OnLoanTo")]
    public ICollection<LibraryBook>
        BooksBorrowedByMe { get; set; }
}
```

Links LibrarianBooks to the
Librarian navigational property
in the LibraryBook class

Links the BooksBorrowedByMe
list to the OnLoanTo navigational
property in the LibraryBook class

This code is one of those configuration options that you rarely use, but if you have this situation, you must either use it or define the relationship with the Fluent API. Otherwise, EF Core will throw an exception when it starts, as it can't work out how to configure the relationships.

Fluent API relationship configuration commands

As I said in section 8.4, you can configure most of your relationships by using EF Core's By Convention approach. But if you want to configure a relationship, the Fluent API has a well-designed set of commands that cover all the possible combinations of relationships. It also has extra commands that allow you to define other database constraints. Figure 8.4 shows the format for defining a relationship with the Fluent API. All Fluent API relationship configuration commands follow this pattern.

EF6 EF Core's Fluent API command names have changed from EF6, and for me, they're much clearer. I found EF6's `WithRequired` and `WithRequired-Principal/WithRequiredDependent` commands to be a bit confusing, whereas

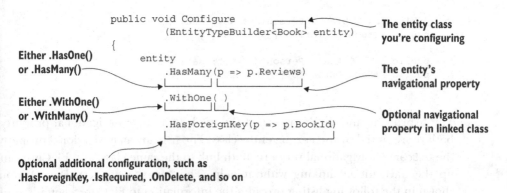

Figure 8.4 The Fluent API allows you to define a relationship between two entity classes.
`HasOne/HasMany` and `WithOne/WithMany` are the two main parts, followed by other commands to specify other parts or set certain features.

the EF Core Fluent API commands have a clearer `HasOne`/`HasMany` followed by `WithOne`/`WithMany` syntax.

Next, we'll define one-to-one, one-to-many, and many-to-many relationships to trate the use of these Fluent API relationships.

8.6.1 Creating a one-to-one relationship

One-to-one relationships can get a little complicated because there are three wa build them in a relational database. To understand these options, you'll look . example in which you have attendees (entity class `Attendee`) at a software conven and each attendee has a unique ticket (entity class `Ticket`).

Chapter 3 showed how to create, update, and delete relationships. To recap, h a code snippet showing how to create a one-to-one relationship:

```
var attendee = new Attendee
{
    Name = "Person1",
    Ticket = new Ticket{ TicketType = TicketTypes.VIP}
};
context.Add(attendee);
context.SaveChanges();
```

Figure 8.5 shows the three options for building this sort of one-to-one relation. The principal entities are at the top of the diagram, and the dependent entities a the bottom. Note that option 1 has the `Attendee` as the dependent entity, wh options 2 and 3 have the `Ticket` as the dependent entity.

Each option has advantages and disadvantages. You should use the one that's for your business needs.

Option 1 is the standard approach to building one-to-one relationships, bec it allows you to define that the one-to-one dependent entity is required (mu present). In our example, an exception will be thrown if you try to save an `Atte` entity instance without a unique `Ticket` attached to it. Figure 8.6 shows option more detail.

With the option-1 one-to-one arrangement, you can make the dependent e optional by making the foreign key nullable. Also, in figure 8.6, you can see the `WithOne` method has a parameter that picks out the `Attendee` navigati property in the `Ticket` entity class that links back to the `Attendee` entity Because the `Attendee` class is the dependent part of the relationship, if you d the `Attendee` entity, the linked `Ticket` won't be deleted, because the `Ticket` i principal entity in the relationship. The downside of option 1 in this example is t allows one `Ticket` to be used for multiple `Attendees`, which doesn't match the ness rules I stated at the start. Finally, this option allows you to replace `Ticket` another `Ticket` instance by assigning a new `Ticket` to the Attendee's Ticket na tional property.

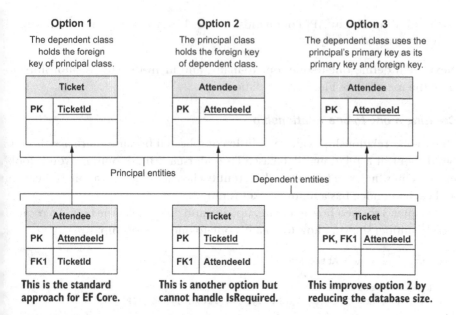

Figure 8.5 The three ways of defining a one-to-one relationship in a relational database; comments at the bottom indicate EF Core's handling of each approach. Option 1 is different from options 2 and 3 in that the order of the two ends of the one-to-one relationship are swapped, which changes which part can be forced to exist. In option 1, the Attendee must have a Ticket, whereas in options 2 and 3, the Ticket is optional for the Attendee. Also, if the principal entity (top row) is deleted, the dependent entity (bottom row) will be deleted too.

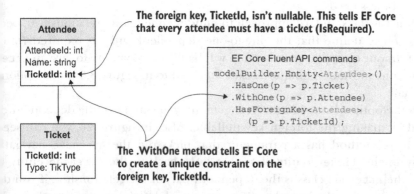

Figure 8.6 The non-nullable foreign key ensures that the principal entity (in this case, Attendee) must have a dependent, one-to-one entity, Ticket. Also, configuring the relationship as one-to-one ensures that each dependent entity, Ticket, is unique. Notice that the Fluent API on the right has navigational properties going both ways; each entity has a navigational property going to the other.

Options 2 and 3 in figure 8.5 turn the principal/dependent relationship around, the Attendee becoming the principal entity in the relationship. This situation s the required/optional nature of the relationship. Now the Attendee can exist wi the Ticket, but the Ticket can't exist without the Attendee. Options 2 and enforce the assignment of a Ticket to only one Attendee, but replacing Ticket another Ticket instance requires you to delete the old ticket first. Figure 8.7 s this relationship.

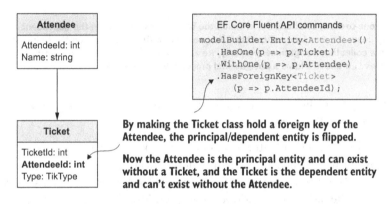

Figure 8.7 Option 2: The Ticket entity holds the foreign key of the Attendee entity, changing which entity is the principal and which is the dependent entity. In this case, the Attendee is now the principal entity, and the Ticket is the dependent entity.

Option 2 and 3 are useful because they form optional one-to-one relationships, referred to as *one-to-zero-or-one relationships*. Option 3 is a more efficient way to d option 2, with the primary key and the foreign key combined. I would've used opt for the PriceOffer entity class in the Book App, but I wanted to start with the sin option-2 approach. Another, even better version uses an Owned type (see section 8 because it is automatically loaded from the same table, which is safer (I can't forg add the Include) and more efficient.

8.6.2 *Creating a one-to-many relationship*

One-to-many relationships are simpler, because there's one format: the many en contain the foreign-key value. You can define most one-to-many relationships wit By Convention approach simply by giving the foreign key in the many entities a r that follows the By Convention approach (see section 8.4.3). But if you want to d a relationship, you can use the Fluent API, which gives you complete control of the relationship is set up. Figure 8.8 provides an example of the Fluent API co create a "one Book has many Reviews" relationship in the Book App.

In this case, the Review entity class doesn't have a navigational link back to Book, so the WithOne method has no parameter.

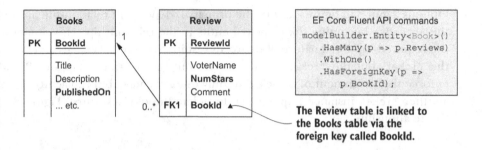

Figure 8.8 A one-to-many relationship, in which the foreign key must be in the dependent entity—in this case, the `Review` entity class. You can see in the Fluent API on the right that the `Book` has a collection navigational property, `Reviews`, linked to the `Review` entity classes, but `Review` doesn't have a navigational property back to `Book`.

NOTE Listing 3.16 shows how to add a `Review` to the `Book`'s one-to-many collection navigational property, `Reviews`.

Collections have a couple of features that are worth knowing about. First, you can use any generic type for a collection that implements the `IEnumerable<T>` interface, such as `IList<T>`, `Collection<T>`, `HashSet<T>`, `List<T>`, and so on. `IEnumerable<T>` on its own is a special case, as you can't add to that collection.

For performance reasons, you should use `HashSet<T>` for navigational collections, because it improves certain parts of EF Core's query and update processes. (See chapter 14 for more on this topic.) But `HashSet` doesn't guarantee the order of entries, which could cause problems if you add sorting to your `Includes` (see section 2.4.1, listing 2.5). That's why I recommend in part 1 and 2 using `ICollection<T>` if you might sort your `Include` methods, as `ICollection` preserves the order in which entries are added. But in part 3, which is about performance, you don't use sort in `Includes` so that you can use `HashSet<T>` for better performance.

Second, although you typically define a collection navigational property with a getter and a setter (such as `public ICollection<Review> Reviews { get; set; }`), doing so isn't necessary. You can provide a getter only if you initialize the backing field with an empty collection. The following is also valid:

```
public ICollection<Review> Reviews { get; } = new List<Review>();
```

Although initializing the collection might make things easier in this case, I don't recommend initializing a navigational collection property. I have given my reasons for not initializing collection navigational properties in section 6.1.6.

.3 *Creating a many-to-many relationship*

Many-to-many relationships are described in chapters 2 and 3; in this section, you learn how to configure them. In those chapters, you learned about the two types of many-to-many relationships:

- *Your linking table contains information that you want to access when reading in th*
  on the other side of the many-to-many relationship. An example is the Book to A\
  many-to-many relationship, in which the linking table contains the ord
  which the Author Names should be shown.
- *You directly access the other side of the many-to-many relationship.* An example i
  Book to Tag many-to-many relationship, in which you can directly access the
  collection in the Book entity class without ever needing to access the linking

CONFIGURING A MANY-TO-MANY RELATIONSHIP USING A LINKING ENTITY CLASS

You start with the many-to-many relationship in which you access the other end o
relationship via the linking table. This relationship takes more work but allows you t
extra data to the linking table, which you can sort/filter on. You saw how to do this i
tion 3.4.4. Figure 8.9 looks at the configuration parts of this many-to-many relations

The By Convention configuration stage can find and configure the four relationships.
But the composite key in the BookAuthor class has to be configured manually.

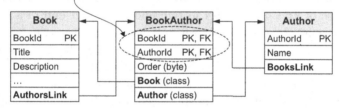

Figure 8.9 The three entity classes involved in a many-to-many relationship, using
a linking table. This type of many-to-many relationship is used only if you have extra
data in the linking table entity class. In this case, the BookAuthor class contains
an Order property that defines the order in which the Author Names should be
displayed alongside a Book.

In the Book/Author example, the By Convention configuration can find and lir
the scalar and navigational properties so that the only configuration required i
ting up the primary key. The following code snippet uses Fluent API in the ap
tion's DbContext's OnModelCreating method:

```
protected override void OnModelCreating(ModelBuilder modelBuilder)
{
    modelBuilder.Entity<BookAuthor>()
        .HasKey(x => new {x.BookId, x.AuthorId});
}
```

You can configure the four relationships in the many-to-many relationship by \
the Fluent API with the code in the following listing. Note that the HasOne/With
Fluent API commands in the listing aren't needed because the BookAuthor entity
follows the By Convention naming and typing rules.

Listing 8.6 Configuring a many-to-many relationship via two one-to-many relationships

```
public static void Configure
    (this EntityTypeBuilder<BookAuthor> entity)
{
    entity.HasKey(p =>
        new { p.BookId, p.AuthorId });

    //-----------------------------
    //Relationships

    entity.HasOne(p => p.Book)
        .WithMany(p => p.AuthorsLink)
        .HasForeignKey(p => p.BookId);

    entity.HasOne(p => p.Author)
        .WithMany(p => p.BooksLink)
        .HasForeignKey(p => p.AuthorId);
}
```

> Uses the names of the Book and Author primary keys to form its own composite key

> Configures the one-to-many relationship from the Book to BookAuthor entity class

> Configures the one-to-many relationship from the Author to the BookAuthor entity class

CONFIGURING A MANY-TO-MANY RELATIONSHIP WITH DIRECT ACCESS TO THE OTHER ENTITY

With the release of EF Core 5, you can reference the other end of a many-to-many relationship directly. The example shown in chapter 2 and 3 was the Book entity class, which has an ICollection<Tag> Tags navigation property that holds a series of Tag entity classes. The Tag entity class contains a category (Microsoft .NET, Web, and so on), which helps the customer find the book they are looking for.

The By Convention configuration works well for a direct many-to-many relationship. If the entity classes at the two ends are valid, the By Convention configuration will set up the relationships and keys for you, as shown in figure 8.10. By Convention will also create the linking entity for you by using a property bag (see section 8.9.5).

This sort of many-to-many relationship is much easier to use because you can access the other side of the relationship (Tags, in this example) directly. EF Core handles creating the linking entity class and its table.

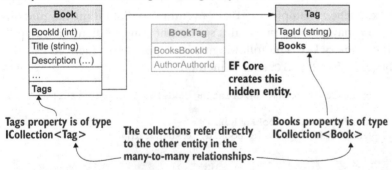

Figure 8.10 EF Core 5's direct many-to-many relationship works because (a) EF Core creates the linking entity class for you and (b) when it sees a query containing a direct many-to-many relationship, it adds the SQL commands to use the hidden linking entity class. Not having to create the linking entity class or perform configuration makes these sorts of many-to-many relationships much easier to set up.

But if you want to add your own linking table and configuration, you can do th Fluent API configuration. The entity class for the linking table is similar to the F Author linked entity class shown in figure 8.9. The difference is that the Au key/relationship is replaced by the Tag key/relationship. The following listing s the Book configuration class setting up the BookTag entity class to link the two pa

---

Listing 8.7 Configuring direct many-to-many relationships using Fluent API

```
public void Configure
    (EntityTypeBuilder<Book> entity)
{
    //… other configrations left out for clarity

    entity.HasMany(x => x.Tags)              The HasMany/WithMany sets up a
        .WithMany(x => x.Books)              direct many-to-many relationship.
        .UsingEntity<BookTag>(
            bookTag => bookTag.HasOne(x => x.Tag)              Defined Tag side
                .WithMany().HasForeignKey(x => x.TagId),       many-to-many re
            bookTag => bookTag.HasOne(x => x.Book)
                .WithMany().HasForeignKey(x => x.BookId));     Defined Book
}                                                             of the many-
                                                              many relatio
```

The UsingEntity<T> method allows you to
define an entity class for the linking table.

The code shown in listing 8.7 does nothing but replace the linking entity that EF would have added, so it isn't worth doing. But it would be useful if you wanted to extra properties to the BookTag entity class, such as a SoftDeleted property that Query Filter to soft-delete a link.

> **MORE INFO** When EF Core 5 was released, a useful video offered good coverage of direct-access many-to-many relationships, including adding your own linking table (and TPH and TPT). See http://mng.bz/opzM.

8.7 *Controlling updates to collection navigational properties*

Sometimes, you need to control access to collection navigational properties. Alth you can control access to a one-to-one navigational by making the setter private approach doesn't work for a collection, as most collection types allow you to ad remove entries. To control collection navigational properties fully, you need to u. Core backing fields, described in section 7.14.

> **EF6** EF6.x didn't have a way to control access to collection navigational properties, which meant that some patterns, such as DDD, were hard to implement successfully. EF Core's backing fields allow you to build entity classes that follow DDD principles.

Storing the collection of linked entities classes in a field allows you to intercept any attempt to update a collection. Here are some business/software design reasons why this feature is useful:

- Triggering some business logic on a change, such as calling a method if a collection contains more than ten entries.
- Building a local cached value for performance reasons, such as holding a cached ReviewsAverageVotes property whenever a Review is added to or removed from your Book entity class.
- Applying a DDD to your entity classes. Any change to data should be done via a method (see chapter 13).

For the example of controlling collection navigational properties, you are going to add a cached ReviewsAverageVotes property to the Book class. This property will hold the average of the votes in all the Reviews linked to this Book. To do so, you need to

- Add a backing field called _reviews to hold the Reviews collection and change the property to return a read-only copy of the collection held in the _reviews backing field.
- Add a read-only property called ReviewsAverageVotes to hold the cached average votes from the Reviews linked to this Book.
- Add methods to Add Reviews to and Remove Reviews from the _reviews backing field. Each method recalculates the average votes, using the current list of Reviews.

The following listing shows the updated Book class showing the code related to the Reviews and the cached ReviewsAverageVotes property.

Listing 8.8 **Book class with a read-only Reviews collection navigational property**

```
public class Book
{
    private readonly ICollection<Review> _reviews
        = new List<Review>();

    public int BookId { get; set; }
    public string Title { get; set; }
    //… other properties/relationships left out

    public double? ReviewsAverageVotes { get; private set; }

    public IReadOnlyCollection<Review> Reviews =>
        _reviews.ToList();

    public void AddReview(Review review)
    {
        _reviews.Add(review);
        ReviewsAverageVotes =
            _reviews.Average(x => x.NumStars);
    }
```

You add a backing field, which is a list. By default, EF Core will read and write to this field.

Holds a precalculated average of the reviews and is read-only

Returns a copy of the reviews in the _reviews backing field

Adds the new review to the backing field _reviews and updates the database on the call to SaveChanges

Recalculates the average votes for the book

```
public void RemoveReview(Review review)                    ◁─────── Adds a method to
{                                                                   remove a review from
    _reviews.Remove(review);                        ◁─────         the _reviews collectio
    ReviewsAverageVotes = _reviews.Any()
        ? _reviews.Average(x => x.NumStars)    ◁──┐              Removes the review from
        : (double?)null;            ◁───┐                        list and updates the data
}                                                               on the call to SaveChange
}
                                  If there are no
                                  reviews, sets the
                                  value to null                 If there are any reviews, re
                                                                the average votes for the b
```

You didn't have to configure the backing field because you were using By Conve
naming, and by default, EF Core reads and writes data to the _reviews field.

This example shows how to make your collection navigational properties
only, but it's not perfect because concurrent updates could make the Revi
AverageVotes cache property out of date. In part 3, you will build an applic
using DDD throughout and implement a robust caching approach that handles
currency issues.

8.8 Additional methods available in Fluent API relationships

We have covered all the ways to configure standard relationships, but some o
most detailed parts of a relationship require adding extra commands to your F
API configuration of a relationship. In this section, we'll go through four me
that define some of the deeper parts of a relationship:

- OnDelete—Changes the delete action of a dependent entity
- IsRequired—Defines the nullability of the foreign key
- HasPrincipalKey—Uses an alternate unique key
- HasConstraintName—Sets the foreign-key constraint name and MetaData a
  to the relationship data

8.8.1 OnDelete: Changing the delete action of a dependent entity

Section 8.4.4 described the default action on the deletion of a principal entity, v
is based on the nullability of the dependent's foreign key(s). The OnDelete Fluen
method allows you to alter what EF Core does when a deletion that affects a de
dent entity occurs.

You can add the OnDelete method to the end of a Fluent API relationship cor
ration. This listing shows the code added in chapter 4 to stop a Book entity from l
deleted if it was referred to in a customer order, via the LineItem entity class.

Listing 8.9 Changing the default OnDelete action on a dependent entity

```
public static void Configure
    (this EntityTypeBuilder<LineItem> entity)
{
    entity.HasOne(p => p.ChosenBook)
```

```
    .WithMany()
    .OnDelete(DeleteBehavior.Restrict);
```
⟵| **Adds the OnDelete method to the end of defining a relationship**

```
}
```

This code causes an exception to be thrown if someone tries to delete a Book entity that a LineItem's foreign key links to that Book. You do this because you want a customer's order to not be changed. Table 8.1 explains the possible DeleteBehavior settings.

Table 8.1 Delete behaviors available in EF Core. The middle column highlights the delete behavior that will be used if you don't apply the OnDelete option.

Name	Effect of the delete behavior on the dependent entity	Default for
Restrict	The delete operation isn't applied to dependent entities. The dependent entities remain unchanged, which may cause the delete to fail, either in EF Core or in the relational database.	
SetNull	The dependent entity isn't deleted, but its foreign-key property is set to null. If any of the dependent entity foreign-key properties isn't nullable, an exception is thrown when SaveChanges is called.	
ClientSetNull	If EF Core is tracking the dependent entity, its foreign key is set to null, and the dependent entity isn't deleted. But if EF Core isn't tracking the dependent entity, the database rules apply. In a database created by EF Core, this DeleteBehavior will set the SQL DELETE constraint to NO ACTION, which causes the delete to fail with an exception.	Optional relationships
Cascade	The dependent entity is deleted.	Required relationships
ClientCascade	For entities being tracked by the DbContext, dependent entities will be deleted when the related principal is deleted. But if EF Core isn't tracking the dependent entity, the database rules apply. In a database created by EF Core, this will be set to Restrict, which causes the delete to fail with an exception.	

Two delete behaviors whose names start with Client are ClientSetNull (added in EF Core 2.0) and ClientCascade (added in EF Core 3.0). These two delete behaviors move some of the handling of deletion actions from the database to the client—that is, the EF Core code. I believe that these two settings have been added to prevent the problems you can get in some databases, such as SQL Server, when your entities have navigational links that loop back to themselves. In these cases, you would get an error from the database server when you try to create your database, which can be hard to diagnose and fix.

In both cases, these commands execute code inside EF Core that does the same job that the database would do with the SetNull and Cascade delete behaviors, respectively. But—and it's a big *but*—EF Core can apply these changes only if you have

loaded all the relevant dependent entities linked to the principal entity that yo
going to delete. If you don't, the database applies its delete rules, which normal
throw an exception.

The `ClientSetNull` delete setting is the default for optional relationships, ar
Core will set the foreign key of the loaded dependent entity class to `null`. If yo
EF Core to create/migrate the database, EF Core sets the database delete rules
DELETE NO ACTION (SQL Server). The database server won't throw an exception if
entities have a circular loop (referred to as possible cyclic delete paths by
Server). The `SetNull` delete setting would set the database delete rules to ON DI
SET NULL (SQL Server), which would cause the database server to throw a poss
cyclic delete paths exception.

The `ClientCascade` delete setting does the same thing for the database's cas
delete feature, in that it will delete any loaded dependent entity class(es). Aga
you use EF Core to create/migrate the database, EF Core sets the database c
rules to ON DELETE NO ACTION (SQL Server). The `Cascade` delete setting would se
database delete rules to ON DELETE CASCADE (SQL Server), which would cause the
base server to throw a possible cyclic delete paths exception.

> **NOTE** The EF Core documentation has a page on cascade delete with some
> worked examples; see http://mng.bz/nMGK. Also, the Part2 branch of the
> associated GitHub repo has a unit test called Ch08_DeleteBehaviour, with
> tests of each of the settings.

Listing 8.10 shows the correct way to use the `ClientSetNull` and `ClientCas`
when you delete a principal entity. The entity in this listing is loaded with an opt
dependent entity, which (by default) has the default delete behavior of `Client`
`Null`. But the same code would work for the `ClientCascade` as long as you loa
correct dependent entity or entities.

Listing 8.10 Deleting a principal entity with an optional dependent entity

```
var entity = context.DeletePrincipals          ⟵── Reads in the
    .Include(p => p.DependentDefault)                principal entity
    .Single(p => p.DeletePrincipalId == 1);    ⟵┐  Includes the
                                                    dependent entity
context.Remove(entity);        ⟵┐                   that has the default
context.SaveChanges();       ⟵─┤ Sets the           delete behavior of
                                 principal           ClientSetNull
    Calls SaveChanges, which     entity for
    sets its foreign key to null deletion
```

Note that if you don't include the `Include` method or another way of loadin
optional dependent entity, `SaveChanges` will throw a `DbUpdateException` bec
the database server will have reported a foreign-key constraint violation. One w
align EF Core's approach to an optional relationship with the database se
approach is to set the delete behavior to `SetNull` instead of the default `ClientSet`

making the foreign-key constraint in the database ON DELETE SET NULL (SQL Server) and putting the database in charge of setting the foreign key to null. Whether or not you load the optional dependent entity, the outcome of the called SaveChanges will be the same: the foreign key on the optional dependent entity will be set to null.

But be aware that some database servers may return an error on database creation if you have a delete-behavior setting of SetNull or Cascade and the servers detect a possible circular relationship, such as hierarchical data. That's why EF Core has the ClientSetNull and ClientCascade delete behaviors.

> **NOTE** If you're managing the database creation/migration outside EF Core, it's important to ensure that the relational database foreign-key constraint is in line with EF Core's OnDelete setting. Otherwise, you'll get inconsistent behavior, depending on whether the dependent entity is being tracked.

IsRequired: Defining the nullability of the foreign key

Chapter 6 describes how the Fluent API method IsRequired allows you to set the nullability of a scalar property, such as a string. In a relationship, the same command sets the nullability of the foreign key—which, as I've already said, defines whether the relationship is required or optional.

The IsRequired method is most useful in shadow properties because EF Core makes shadow properties nullable by default, and the IsRequired method can change them to non-nullable. The next listing depicts the Attendee entity class, used previously to show a one-to-one relationship, but showing two other one-to-one relationships that use shadow properties for their foreign keys.

Listing 8.11 The Attendee entity class showing all its relationships

```
public class Attendee
{
    public int AttendeeId { get; set; }
    public string Name { get; set; }

    public int TicketId { get; set; }
    public Ticket Ticket { get; set; }

    public MyOptionalTrack Optional { get; set; }
    public MyRequiredTrack Required { get; set; }
}
```

Foreign key for the one-to-one relationship, Ticket

One-to-one navigational property that accesses the Ticket entity

One-to-one navigational property using a shadow property for the foreign key. By default, the foreign key is nullable, so the relationship is optional.

One-to-one navigational property using a shadow property for the foreign key. You use Fluent API commands to say that the foreign key isn't nullable, so the relationship is required.

The Optional navigational property, which uses a shadow property for its foreign key, is configured by convention, which means that the shadow property is left as a nullable value. Therefore, it's optional, and if the Attendee entity is deleted, the MyOptionalTrack entity isn't deleted.

For the Required navigational property, the following listing presents the Fluent API configuration. Here, you use the IsRequired method to make the Required one-to-one navigational property as required. Each `Attendee` entity must have a N quiredTrack entity assigned to the `Required` property.

Listing 8.12 The Fluent API configuration of the `Attendee` entity class

```
public void Configure
    (EntityTypeBuilder<Attendee> entity)
{
    entity.HasOne(attendee => attendee.Ticket)
        .WithOne(attendee => attendee.Attendee)
        .HasForeignKey<Attendee>
            (attendee => attendee.TicketId)
        .IsRequired();

    entity.HasOne(attendee => attendee.Required)
        .WithOne(attendee => attendee.Attend)
        .HasForeignKey<Attendee>(
            "MyShadowFk")
        .IsRequired();
}
```

Sets up the one-to-one navigational relationship, Ticket, which has a foreig defined in the Attendee cl.

Specifies the property that's t key. You need to provide the type, as the foreign key could principal or dependent entity

Sets up the one-to-navigational relatio Required, which do have a foreign key

Uses IsRequired to say the foreign key should not be nullable

Uses the HasForeignKey<T> method, which takes a string because it's a shadow property and can be referred to only via a name. Note that you use your own name.

You could've left out the configuration of the `Ticket` navigational property, would be configured correctly under the By Convention rules, but you leave it that you can compare it with the configuration of the `Required` navigational prop which uses a shadow property for its foreign key. The configuration of the Req navigational property is necessary because the `IsRequired` method change: shadow foreign-key property from nullable to non-nullable, which in turn make relationship required.

TYPE AND NAMING CONVENTIONS FOR SHADOW PROPERTY FOREIGN KEYS
Notice how listing 8.12 refers to the shadow foreign-key property: you need to the `HasForeignKey<T>(string)` method. The `<T>` class tells EF Core where to the shadow foreign-key property, which can be either end of the relationshi one-to-one relationships or the many entity class of a one-to-many relationship.

The string parameter of the `HasForeignKey<T>(string)` method allows yo define the shadow foreign-key property name. You can use any name; you don't to stick with the By Convention name listed in figure 8.3. But you need to be ca not to use a name of any existing property in the entity class you're targeting, be that approach can lead to strange behaviors. (There's no warning if you sele existing property, as you might be trying to define a nonshadow foreign key.)

8.8.3 HasPrincipalKey: Using an alternate unique key

I mentioned the term *alternate key* at the beginning of this chapter, saying that i unique value but not the primary key. I gave an example of an alternate key c `UniqueISBN`, which represents a unique key that isn't the primary key. (Reme:

that *ISBN* stands for *International Standard Book Number,* which is a unique number for every book.)

Now let's look at a different example. The following listing creates a Person entity class, which uses a normal int primary key, but you'll use the UserId as an alternate key when linking to the person's contact information, shown in listing 8.14.

Listing 8.13 Person class, with Name taken from ASP.NET authorization

```
public class Person
{
    public int PersonId { get; set; }

    public string Name { get; set; }                    Holds the
                                                        person's
    public Guid UserId { get; set; }        ◄─┐        unique Id

    public ContactInfo ContactInfo { get; set; }   ◄──┐  Navigational
                                                         property linking
}                                                        to the ContactInfo
```

Listing 8.14 ContactInfo class with EmailAddress as a foreign key

```
public class ContactInfo
{
    public int ContactInfoId { get; set; }

    public string MobileNumber { get; set; }        The UserIdentifier is used
    public string LandlineNumber { get; set; }      as a foreign key for the
                                                    Person entity to link to
    public Guid UserIdentifier { get; set; }   ◄──  this contact info.
}
```

Figure 8.11 shows the Fluent API configuration commands, which use the alternate key in the Person entity class as a foreign key in the ContactInfo entity class.

Here are a few notes on alternate keys:

- You can have composite alternate keys, which are made up of two or more properties. You handle them in the same way that you do composite keys: by using an anonymous Type, such as HasPrincipalKey<MyClass>(c => new {c.Part1, c.Part2}).
- Unique keys (see section 7.10) and alternate keys are different, and you should choose the correct one for your business case. Here are some of the differences:
  - Unique keys ensure that each entry is unique; they can't be used in a foreign key.
  - Unique keys can be null, but alternate keys can't.
  - Unique key values can be updated, but alternate keys can't. (See EF Core issue #4073 at http://mng.bz/vzEM).
- You can define a property as a standalone alternate key by using the Fluent API command modelBuilder.Entity<Car>().HasAlternateKey(c => c.License-Plate), but you don't need to do that, because using the HasPrincipalKey

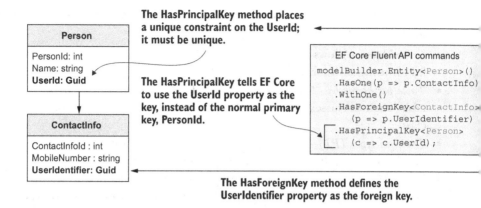

Figure 8.11 The Fluent API sets up a one-to-one relationship by using the `UserId` property, whi contains the person's unique `Id`, as the foreign key to link to the `ContactInfo`. The command `HasPrincipalKey` both defines the `UserId` property as an alternate key and creates the forei key constraint link between the `UserIdentifier` property in the `ContactInfo` entity and the `UserId` in the `Person` entity.

method to set up a relationship automatically registers the property as an nate key.

8.8.4 Less-used options in Fluent API relationships

This section briefly mentions—but doesn't cover in detail—two Fluent API comm that can be used for setting up relationships.

HASCONSTRAINTNAME: SETTING THE FOREIGN-KEY CONSTRAINT NAME

The method `HasConstraintName` allows you to set the name of the foreign-key straint, which can be useful if you want to catch the exception on foreign-key e and use the constraint name to form a more user-friendly error message. This a shows how: http://mng.bz/4ZwV.

METADATA: ACCESS TO THE RELATIONSHIP INFORMATION

The `MetaData` property provides access to the relationship data, some of whi read/write. Much of what the `MetaData` property exposes can be accessed via sp commands, such as `IsRequired`, but if you need something out of the ordinary, through the various methods/properties supported by the `MetaData` property.

8.9 Alternative ways of mapping entities to database tables

Sometimes, it's useful to not have a one-to-one mapping from an entity class to a base table. Instead of having a relationship between two classes, you might wa combine both classes into one table. This approach allows you to load only part c table when you use one of the entities, which will improve the query's perform

This section describes five alternative ways to map classes to the database, each with advantages in certain situations:

- *Owned types*—Allows a class to be merged into the entity class's table and is useful for using normal classes to group data.
- *Table per hierarchy (TPH)*—Allows a set of inherited classes to be saved in one table, such as classes called Dog, Cat, and Rabbit that inherit from the Animal class.
- *Table per type (TPT)*—Maps each class to a different table. This approach works like TPH except that each class is mapped to a separate table.
- *Table splitting*—Allows multiple entity classes to be mapped to the same table and is useful when some columns in a table are read more often than all the table columns.
- *Property bags*—Allows you to create an entity class via a Dictionary, which gives you the option to create the mapping on startup. Property bags also use two other features: mapping the same type to multiple tables and using an indexer in your entity classes.

Owned types: Adding a normal class into an entity class

EF Core has *owned types*, which allow you to define a class that holds a common grouping of data, such as an address or audit data, that you want to use in multiple places in your database. The owned type class doesn't have its own primary key, so it doesn't have an identity of its own; it relies on the entity class that "owns" it for its identity. In DDD terms, owned types are known as *value objects*.

> **EF6** EF Core's owned types are similar to EF6.x's complex types. The biggest change is that you must specifically configure an owned type, whereas EF6.x considers any class without a primary key to be a complex type (which could cause bugs). EF Core's owned types have an extra feature over EF6.x's implementation: the data in an owned type can be configured to be saved in a separate, hidden table.

Here are two ways of using owned types:

- The owned type data is held in the same table that the entity class is mapped to.
- The owned type data is held in a separate table from the entity class.

OWNED TYPE DATA IS HELD IN THE SAME TABLE AS THE ENTITY CLASS

As an example of an owned type, you'll create an entity class called OrderInfo that needs two addresses: BillingAddress and DeliveryAddress. These addresses are provided by the Address class, shown in the following listing. You can mark an Address class as an owned type by adding the attribute [Owned] to the class. An owned type has no primary key, as shown at the bottom of the listing.

Listing 8.15 The `Address` owned type, followed by the `OrderInfo` entity class

```
public class OrderInfo                          ◄──┐  The entity class OrderInfo,
{                                                   │  with a primary key and
    public int OrderInfoId { get; set; }           │  two addresses
    public string OrderNumber { get; set; }

    public Address BillingAddress { get; set; }     ┐  Two distinct Address clas:
    public Address DeliveryAddress { get; set; }    ├  The data for each Addres:
}                                                   │  will be included in the tab:
                                                       the OrderInfo is mapped

[Owned]                                         ◄───────  The attribute [Owned]
public class Address                            ◄────┐    tells EF Core that it is
{                                                    │    an owned type.
    public string NumberAndStreet { get; set; }      │
    public string City { get; set; }                 │  An owned type has
    public string ZipPostCode { get; set; }          │  no primary key.
    [Required]
    [MaxLength(2)]
    public string CountryCodeIso2 { get; set; }
}
```

Because you added the attribute `[Owned]` to the `Address` class, and because you⁺
using the owned type within the same table, you don't need use the Fluent API to
figure the owned type. This approach saves you time, especially if your owned ty
used in many places, because you don't have to write the Fluent API configura
But if you don't want to use the `[Owned]` attribute, the next listing shows you the
ent API to tell EF Core that the `BillingAddress` and the `DeliveryAddress` prope
in the `OrderInfo` entity class are owned types, not relationships.

Listing 8.16 The Fluent API to configure the owned types within `OrderInfo`

```
public class SplitOwnDbContext: DbContext
{                                                         Selects the owner of
    public DbSet<OrderInfo> Orders { get; set; }          the owned type
    //… other code removed for clarity

    protected override void OnModelCreating               Uses the OwnsOne method
       (ModelBuilder modelBuilder)                        EF Core that property Billin:
    {                                                      is an owned type and that t
        modelBuilder.Entity<OrderInfo>()        ◄──┐      should be added to the colt
           .OwnsOne(p => p.BillingAddress);     ◄──┘      the table that the OrderInfc
        modelBuilder.Entity<OrderInfo>()
           .OwnsOne(p => p.DeliveryAddress);    ┐  Repeats the process for
    }                                           ├  the second property,
}                                                  DeliveryAddress
```

The result is a table containing the two scalar properties in the `OrderInfo` entity
followed by two sets of `Address` class properties, one prefixed by `BillingAddress`
another prefixed by `DeliveryAddress_`. Because an owned type property can be

all the properties are held in the database as nullable columns. The CountryCodeIso2 property in listing 8.15, for example, is marked as [Required], so it should be non-nullable, but to allow for a null property value for the BillingAddress or Delivery-Address, it is stored in a nullable column. EF Core does this to tell whether an instance of the owned type should be created when the entity containing an owned type is read in.

The fact that the owned type property can be null means that owned types within an entity class are a good fit for what DDD calls a *value object*. A value object has no key, and two value objects with the same properties are considered to be equal. The fact that they can be null allows for an "empty" value object.

NOTE Nullable owned types were introduced in EF Core 3.0 but had some performance issues. (The SQL uses a LEFT JOIN.) EF Core 5 has fixed those performance issues.

The following listing shows part of the SQL Server CREATE TABLE command that EF Core produces for the OrderInfo entity class with the naming convention.

Listing 8.17 The SQL CREATE TABLE command showing the column names

```
CREATE TABLE [Orders] (
    [OrderInfoId] int NOT NULL IDENTITY,
    [OrderNumber] nvarchar(max) NULL,
    [BillingAddress_City] nvarchar(max) NULL,
    [BillingAddress_NumberAndStreet] nvarchar(max) NULL,
    [BillingAddress_ZipPostCode] nvarchar(max) NULL,
    [BillingAddress_CountryCodeIso2] [nvarchar](2) NULL        ⟵─┐ Property has a
    [DeliveryAddress_City] nvarchar(max) NULL,                     [Required] attribute
    [DeliveryAddress_CountryCodeIso2] nvarchar(max) NULL,          but is stored as a
    [DeliveryAddress_NumberAndStreet] nvarchar(max) NULL,          nullable value to handle
    [DeliveryAddress_CountryCodeIso2] [nvarchar](2) NULL,     ⟵─┘ the billing/delivery
    CONSTRAINT [PK_Orders] PRIMARY KEY ([OrderInfoId])             address being null.
);
```

By default, every property or field in an owned type is stored in a nullable column, even if they are non-nullable. EF Core does this to allow you to not assign an instance to an owned type, at which point all the columns that the owned type uses are set to NULL. And if an entity with an owned type is read in, and all the columns for an owned type are NULL, the owned type property is set to null.

But EF Core 5 added a feature to allow you to say that an owned type is required—that is, must always be present. To do so, you add the Fluent API IsRequired method to the OrderInfo's DeliveryAddress navigational property mapped to the owned type (see the next listing). In addition, this feature allows the individual nullability of columns to follow normal rules. The DeliveryAddress_CountryCodeIso2 column shown in listing 8.17, for example, is now NOT NULL.

Listing 8.18 The Fluent API to configure the owned types within `OrderInfo`

```
protected override void OnModelCreating
    (ModelBuilder modelBuilder)
{
    modelBulder.Entity<OrderInfo>()
       .OwnsOne(p => p.BillingAddress);
    modelBulder.Entity<OrderInfo>()
       .OwnsOne(p => p.DeliveryAddress);

    modelBulder.Entity<OrderInfo>()          Selects the DeliveryAddress
    .Navigation(p => p.DeliveryAddress)      navigational property
       .IsRequired();            <┄┐
}                                    Applying the IsRequired method means
                                     that the DeliveryAddress must not be null.
```

Using owned types can help you organize your database by turning common gr
of data into owned types, making it easier to handle common data groups, su
Address and so on, in your code. Here are some final points on owned types he
an entity class:

- The owned type navigation properties, such as `BillingAddress`, are auto
  cally created and filled with data when you read the entity. There's no nee
  an `Include` method or any other form of relationship loading.
- Julie Lerman (@julielerman on Twitter) pointed out that owned types can re
  one-to-zero-or-one relationships, especially if an owned type is small. O
  types have better performance and are automatically loaded, which mean
  they would be better implementations of the zero-or-one `PriceOffer` us
  the Book App.
- Owned types can be nested. You could create a `CustomerContact` owned
  which in turn contains an `Address` owned type, for example. If you use
  `CustomerContact` owned type in another entity class—let's call it `SuperOrc`
  all the `CustomerContact` properties and the `Address` properties woul
  added to the `SuperOrder`'s table.

OWNED TYPE DATA IS HELD IN A SEPARATE TABLE FROM THE ENTITY CLASS

The other way that EF Core can save the data inside an owned type is in a sep
table rather than the entity class. In this example, you'll create a `User` entity clas
has a property called `HomeAddress` of type `Address`. In this case, you add a `ToT`
method after the `OwnsOne` method in your configuration code.

Listing 8.19 Configuring the owned table data to be stored in a separate table

```
public class SplitOwnDbContext: DbContext
{
    public DbSet<OrderInfo> Orders { get; set; }
    //… other code removed for clarity

    protected override void OnModelCreating
        (ModelBuilder modelBuilder)
```

```
    {
        modelBulder.Entity<User>()
            .OwnsOne(p => p.HomeAddress);
            .ToTable("Addresses");
    }
}
```

Adding ToTable to OwnsOne tells EF Core to store the owned type, Address, in a separate table, with a primary key equal to the primary key of the User entity that was saved to the database.

EF Core sets up a one-to-one relationship in which the primary key is also the foreign key (see section 8.6.1, option 3), and the OnDelete state is set to Cascade so that the owned type entry of the primary entity, User, is deleted. Therefore, the database has two tables: Users and Addresses.

Listing 8.20 The Users and Addresses tables in the database

```
CREATE TABLE [Users] (
    [UserId] int NOT NULL IDENTITY,
    [Name] nvarchar(max) NULL,
    CONSTRAINT [PK_Orders] PRIMARY KEY ([UserId])
);
CREATE TABLE [Addresses] (
    [UserId] int NOT NULL IDENTITY,
    [City] nvarchar(max) NULL,
    [CountryCodeIso2] nvarchar(2) NOT NULL,
    [NumberAndStreet] nvarchar(max) NULL,
    [ZipPostCode] nvarchar(max) NULL,
    CONSTRAINT [PK_Orders] PRIMARY KEY ([UserId]),
    CONSTRAINT "FK_Addresses_Users_UserId" FOREIGN KEY ("UserId")
        REFERENCES "Users" ("UserId") ON DELETE CASCADE
);
```

Notice that non-nullable properties, or nullable properties with the Required setting, are now stored in non-nullable columns.

This use of owned types differs from the first use, in which the data is stored in the entity class table, because you can save a User entity instance without an address. But the same rules apply on querying: the HomeAddress property will be read in on a query of the User entity without the need for an Include method.

The Addresses table used to hold the HomeAddress data is hidden; you can't access it via EF Core. This situation could be a good thing or a bad thing, depending on your business needs. But if you want to access the Address part, you can implement the same feature by using two entity classes with a one-to-many relationship between them.

Table per hierarchy (TPH): Placing inherited classes into one table

Table per hierarchy (TPH) stores all the classes that inherit from one another in a single database table. If you want to save a payment in a shop, for example, that payment could be cash (PaymentCash) or credit card (PaymentCard). Each option contains the amount (say, $10), but the credit card option has extra information, such as an online-transaction receipt. In this case, TPH uses a single table to store all the versions of the inherited classes and return the correct entity type, PaymentCash or Payment-Card, depending on what was saved.

TIP I have used TPH classes in a couple of projects for my clients, and I find TPH to be a good solution for storing sets of data that are similar when some sets need extra properties. Suppose that you had a lot of product types with common Name, Price, ProductCode, Weight, and other properties, but the Sealant products needs MinTemp and MaxTemp properties, which TPH could implement by using one table rather than lots of tables.

TPH can be configured By Convention, which will combine all the versions o
inherited classes into one table. This approach has the benefit of keeping com
data in one table, but accessing that data is a little cumbersome because each i
ited type has its own DbSet<T> property. But when you add the Fluent API, al
inherited classes can be accessed via one DbSet<T> property, which in our exa
makes the PaymentCash / PaymentCard example much more useful.

The first example uses multiple DbSet<T>s, one for each class, and is configure
Convention. The second example uses one DbSet<T> mapped to the base class, v
I find to be the more useful version, and shows the TPH Fluent API commands.

CONFIGURING TPH BY CONVENTION

To apply the By Convention approach to the PaymentCash/PaymentCard exa
you create a class called PaymentCash and then a class called PaymentCard that i
its from PaymentCash, as shown in the following listing. As you can see, Payment
inherits from PaymentCash and adds an extra ReceiptCode property.

Listing 8.21 The two classes: PaymentCash and PaymentCard

```
public class PaymentCash
{
    [Key]
    public int PaymentId { get; set; }
    public decimal Amount { get; set; }
}

//PaymentCredit - inherits from PaymentCash
public class PaymentCard : PaymentCash
{
    public string ReceiptCode { get; set; }
}
```

Listing 8.22, which uses the By Convention approach, shows your applicat
DbContext with two DbSet<T> properties, one for each of the two classes. Because
include both classes, and PaymentCard inherits from PaymentCash, EF Core will
both classes in one table.

Listing 8.22 The updated application's DbContext with the two DbSet<T> proper

```
public class Chapter08DbContext : DbContext
{
    //… other DbSet<T> properties removed
```

```
//Table-per-hierarchy
public DbSet<PaymentCash> CashPayments { get; set; }
public DbSet<PaymentCard> CreditPayments { get; set; }

public Chapter08DbContext(
    DbContextOptions<Chapter08DbContext> options)
    : base(options)
{ }

protected override void OnModelCreating
    (ModelBuilder modelBuilder)
{
    //no configuration needed for PaymentCash or PaymentCard
}
}
```

Finally, this listing shows the code that EF Core produces to create the table that will store both the PaymentCash and PaymentCard entity classes.

Listing 8.23   The SQL produced by EF Core to build the CashPayment table

```
CREATE TABLE [CashPayments] (                          The Discriminator column holds
    [PaymentId] int NOT NULL IDENTITY,                 the name of the class, which EF
    [Amount] decimal(18, 2) NOT NULL,                  Core uses to define what sort
    [Discriminator] nvarchar(max) NOT NULL,       ◄─── of data is saved. When set by
    [ReceiptCode] nvarchar(max),            ◄─┐        convention, this column holds
    CONSTRAINT [PK_CashPayments]              │        the name of the class as a string.
            PRIMARY KEY ([PaymentId])         │
);                                            │   The ReceiptCode column is used
                                                  only if it's a PaymentCredit.
```

As you can see, EF Core has added a Discriminator column, which it uses when returning data to create the correct type of class: PaymentCash or PaymentCard, based on what was saved. Also, the ReceiptCode column is filled/read only if the class type is PaymentCard.

Any scalar properties not in the TPH base class are mapped to nullable columns because those properties are used by only one version of the TPH's classes. If you have lots of classes in your TPH classes, it's worth seeing whether you can combine similar typed properties to the same column. In the Product TPH classes, for example, you might have a Product type "Sealant" that needs a double MaxTemp and another Product type, "Ballast", that needs a double WeightKgs. You could map both properties to the same column by using this code snippet:

```
public class Chapter08DbContext : DbContext
{
    //… other part left out

    Protected override void OnModelCreating
        (ModelBuilder modelBuilder)
    {
        modelBuilder.Entity<Sealant>()
```

```
        .Property(b => b.MaxTemp)
        .HasColumnName("DoubleValueCol");

    modelBuilder.Entity<Ballast>()
        .Property(b => b.WeightKgs)
        .HasColumnName("DoubleValueCol");
    }
}
```

USING THE FLUENT API TO IMPROVE OUR TPH EXAMPLE

Although the By Convention approach reduces the number of tables in the data
you have two separate DbSet<T> properties, and you need to use the right one to
the payment that was used. Also, you don't have a common Payment class that you
use in any other entity classes. But by doing a bit of rearranging and adding some
ent API configuration, you can make this solution much more useful.

Figure 8.12 shows the new arrangement. You create a common base class by h
an abstract class called Payment that the PaymentCash and PaymentCard inherit
This approach allows you to use the Payment class in another entity class called Sol

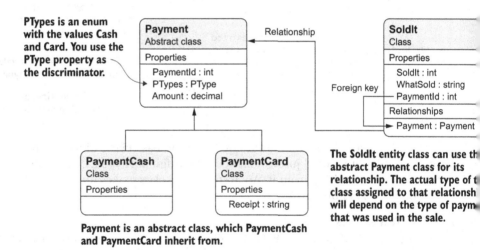

PTypes is an enum
with the values Cash
and Card. You use the
PType property as
the discriminator.

The SoldIt entity class can use th
abstract Payment class for its
relationship. The actual type of t
class assigned to that relationsh
will depend on the type of paym
that was used in the sale.

Payment is an abstract class, which PaymentCash
and PaymentCard inherit from.

**Figure 8.12 By using the Fluent API, you can create a more useful form of the TPH. Here, an abstr
class called Payment is used as the base, and this class can be used inside another entity class.
actual class type placed in the SoldIt payment property will be either PaymentCash or
PaymentCard, depending on what was used when the SoldIt class was created.**

This approach is much more useful because now you can place a Payment ab
class in the SoldIt entity class and get the amount and type of payment, whethe
cash or a card. The PType property tells you the type (the PType property is of
PTypes, which is an enum with values Cash or Card), and if you need the Rec
property in the PaymentCard, you can cast the Payment class to the type PaymentC

In addition to creating the entity classes shown in figure 8.12, you need to change the application's DbContext and add some Fluent API configuration to tell EF Core about your TPH classes, as they no longer fit the By Convention approach. This listing shows the application's DbContext, with the configuration of the Discrimination column.

Listing 8.24   Changed application's DbContext with Fluent API configuration added

```
public class Chapter08DbContext : DbContext
{
    //… other DbSet<T> properties removed
    public DbSet<Payment> Payments { get; set; }

    public DbSet<SoldIt> SoldThings { get; set; }

    public Chapter08DbContext(
        DbContextOptions<Chapter08DbContext> options)
        : base(options)
    { }

    protected override void OnModelCreating
        (ModelBuilder modelBuilder)
    {
        //… other configurations removed
        modelBuilder.Entity<Payment>()
            .HasDiscriminator(b => b.PType)
            .HasValue<PaymentCash>(PTypes.Cash)
            .HasValue<PaymentCard>(PTypes.Card);
    }
}
```

Defines the property through which you can access all the payments, both PaymentCash and PaymentCard

List of sold items, with a required link to Payment

The HasDiscriminator method identifies the entity as a TPH and then selects the property PType as the discriminator for the different types. In this case, it's an enum, which you set to be bytes in size.

Sets the discriminator value for the PaymentCash type

Sets the discriminator value for the PaymentCard type

NOTE This example uses an abstract class as the base class, which I think is more useful, but it could just as well keep the original PaymentCash, with the PaymentCard inheriting from it. An abstract base class makes it easier to alter the common TPH properties.

ACCESSING TPH ENTITIES

Now that you've configured a TPH set of classes, let's cover any differences in CRUD operations. Most EF database access commands are the same, but a few changes access the TPH parts of the entities. EF Core does a nice job (as EF6.x did) of handling TPH.

First, the creation of TPH entities is straightforward. You create an instance of the specific type you need. The following code snippet creates a PaymentCash type entity to go with a sale:

```
var sold = new SoldIt()
{
    WhatSold = "A hat",
    Payment = new PaymentCash {Amount = 12}
};
context.Add(sold);
context.SaveChanges();
```

Then EF Core saves the correct version of data for that type and sets the discrimi
so that it knows the TPH class type of the instance. When you read back the S₀
entity you just saved, with an Include to load the Payment navigational prop
the type of the loaded Payment instance will be the correct type (PaymentCa
PaymentCard), depending on what was used when you wrote it to the database.
in this example the Payment's property PType, which you set as the discriminator
you the type of payment: Cash or Card.

When you query TPH data, the EF Core OfType<T> method allows you to filte
data to find a specific class. The query context.Payments.OfType<PaymentCar
would return only the payments that used a card, for example. You can also filter
classes in Includes. See this article for more information: http://mng.bz/QmBj.

8.9.3 *Table per Type (TPT): Each class has its own table*

The EF Core 5 release added the table per type (TPT) option, which allows
entity class inherited from a base class to have its own table. This option is the c
site of the table per hierarchy (TPH) approach covered in section 8.9.2. TPT is a
solution if each class in the inherited hierarchy has lots of different information;
is better when each inherited class has a large common part and only a small am
of per-class data.

As an example, you will build a TPT solution for two types of containers: ship
containers used on bulk carrier ships and plastic containers such as bottles, jars
boxes. Both types of containers have an overall height, length, and depth, but c
wise, they are different. The following listing shows the three entity classes, with the
Container abstract class and then the ShippingContainer and PlasticContainer

Listing 8.25   The three classes used in the TPT example

```
public abstract class Container          ◁──┐   The Container class is marked
{                                               as abstract because it won't
    [Key]                                       be created.
    public int ContainerId { get; set; }

    public int HeightMm { get; set; }         Common part of each
    public int WidthMm { get; set; }          container is the overall
    public int DepthMm { get; set; }          height, width, and depth
}

public class ShippingContainer : Container
{
    public int ThicknessMm { get; set; }      These properties
    public string DoorType { get; set; }      are unique to a
    public int StackingMax { get; set; }      shipping container.
    public bool Refrigerated { get; set; }
}

public class PlasticContainer : Container
{
```

Becomes the primary key for each TPT table →

The class inherits the Container class. →

```
public int CapacityM1 { get; set; }          These properties are
public Shapes Shape { get; set; }            unique to a plastic
public string ColorARGB { get; set; }        container.
}
```

Next, you need to configure your application's DbContext, which has two parts: (a) adding a DbSet<Container> property, which you will use to access all the containers, and (b) setting the other container types, ShippingContainer and PlasticContainer, to map to their own tables. The following listing shows these two parts.

Listing 8.26 **The updates to the application's DbContext to set up the TPT containers**

```
public class Chapter08DbContext : DbContext
{
    public Chapter08DbContext(
        DbContextOptions<Chapter08DbContext> options)
        : base(options)
    { }
                                                      This single DbSet is
    //… other DbSet<T> removed for clarity            used to access all the
    public DbSet<Container> Containers { get; set; }  ◁──── different containers.

    protected override void OnModelCreating
        (ModelBuilder modelBuilder)
    {
        //… other configrations removed for clarity

        modelBuilder.Entity<ShippingContainer>()        These Fluent API methods
            .ToTable(nameof(ShippingContainer));        map each container to a
        modelBuilder.Entity<PlasticContainer>()         different table.
            .ToTable(nameof(PlasticContainer));
    }
}
```

The result of the update to the application's DbContext is three tables:

- A Containers table, via the DbSet, that contains the common data for each entry
- A ShippingContainer table containing the Container and ShippingContainer properties
- A PlasticContainer table containing the Container and PlasticContainer properties

You add a ShippingContainer and PlasticContainer in the normal way: by using the context.Add method. But the magic comes when you query the DbSet<Container> Containers in the application's DbContext, because it returns all the containers using the correct class type, ShippingContainer or PlasticContainer, for each entity returned.

You have a few options for loading one type of the TPT classes. Here are three approaches, with the most efficient at the end:

- *Read all query*—context.Containers.ToList()

  This option reads in all the TPT types, and each entry in the list will be of the correct type (ShippingContainer or PlasticContainer) for the type it returns. This option is useful only if you want to list a summary of all the containers.

- OfType query—context.Containers.OfType<ShippingContainer>().ToLi
  This option reads in only the entries that are of the type ShippingContain
- Set query—context.Set<ShippingContainer>().ToList()
  This option returns only the ShippingContainer type (just like the Of
  query), but the SQL is slightly more efficient than the OfType query.

8.9.4 Table splitting: Mapping multiple entity classes to the same table

The next feature, called *table splitting*, allows you to map multiple entities to the
table. This feature is useful if you have a large amount of data to store for one e
but your normal queries to this entity need only a few columns. Table splitting i
building a Select query into an entity class; the query will be quicker because y
loading only a subsection of the whole entity's data. It can also make updates qu
by splitting the table across two or more classes.

This example has two entity classes, BookSummary and BookDetail, both of v
map to a database table called Books. Figure 8.13 shows the result of configu
these two entity classes as a table split.

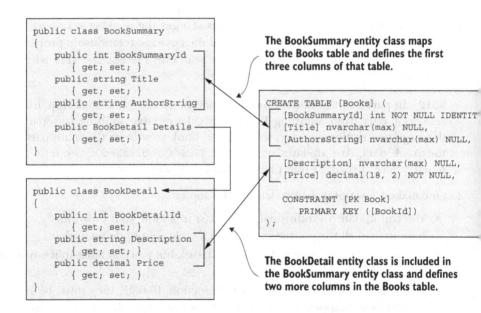

Figure 8.13   The result of using the table-splitting feature in EF Core to map two entity classes,
BookSummary **and** BookDetail, **to one table, Books. You do this because a book needs a lot o**
information, but most queries need only the BookSummary **part. The effect is to build a preselecte**
set of columns for faster querying.

Here's the configuration code.

Listing 8.27 Configuring a table split between `BookSummary` and `BookDetail`

```
public class SplitOwnDbContext : DbContext
{
    //… other code removed

    protected override void OnModelCreating
        (ModelBuilder modelBuilder)
    {
        modelBuilder.Entity<BookSummary>()
            .HasOne(e => e.Details)
            .WithOne()
            .HasForeignKey<BookDetail>
                (e => e.BookDetailId);
        modelBuilder.Entity<BookSummary>()
            .ToTable("Books");

        modelBuilder.Entity<BookDetail>()
            .ToTable("Books");
    }
}
```

Defines the two books as having a relationship in the same way that you'd set up a one-to-one relationship

case, the reignKey od must ence the ey in the il entity.

You must map both entity classes to the Books table to trigger the table splitting.

After you've configured the two entities as a table split, you can query the `BookSummary` entity on its own and get the summary parts. To get the `BookDetails` part, you can either query the `BookSummary` entity and load the `Details` relationship property at the same time (say, with an `Include` method) or read only the `BookDetails` part straight from the database.

> **NOTE** In part 3 of this book, I build a much more complex Book App, using real book data from Manning Publications. I use table splitting to separate the large descriptions used in the detailed book view from the main part of the Book data. Any updates of, say, the `Book`'s `PublishedOn` property are much quicker because I don't have to read in all the descriptions.

Let me make a few points before leaving this topic:

- You can update an individual entity class in a table split individually; you don't have to load all the entities involved in a table split to do an update.
- You've seen a table split to two entity classes, but you can table-split any number of entity classes.
- If you have concurrency tokens (see section 10.6.2), they must be in all the entity classes mapped to the same table to make sure that the concurrent token values are not out of data when only one of the entity classes mapped to the table is updated.

Property bag: Using a dictionary as an entity class

EF Core 5 added a feature called a *property bag* that uses a `Dictionary<string, object>` type to map to the database. A property bag is used to implement the direct many-to-many relationship feature, where the linking table had to be created at

configuration time. You can also use a property bag, but it is useful only in sp
areas, such as creating a property-bag entity in a table whose structure is defin
external data.

> **NOTE** A property bag uses two features that aren't described elsewhere in
> this book. The first feature is *shared entity types*, where the same type can be
> mapped to multiple tables. The second feature uses a C# indexer property in
> an entity class to access data, such as public object this[string key] … .

As an example, you map a property bag to a table whose name and column
defined by external data rather than by the structure of a class. For this exampl
table is defined in a TableSpec class, which is assumed to have been read i
startup, maybe from an appsettings.json file. The following listing shows the ap
tion's DbContext with the necessary code to configure and access a table via a pro
bag entity.

Listing 8.28 Using a property-bag Dictionary to define a table on startup

```
public class PropertyBagsDbContext : DbContext
{
    private readonly TableSpec _tableSpec;

    public PropertyBagsDbContext(
        DbContextOptions<PropertyBagsDbContext> options,
        TableSpec tableSpec)
        : base(options)
    {
        _tableSpec = tableSpec;
    }

    public DbSet<Dictionary<string, object>> MyTable
        => Set<Dictionary<string, object>>(_tableSpec.Name);

    protected override void OnModelCreating
        (ModelBuilder modelBuilder)
    {
        modelBuilder.SharedTypeEntity
            <Dictionary<string, object>>(
                _tableSpec.Name, b =>
        {
            foreach (var prop in _tableSpec.Properties)
            {
                var propConfig = b.IndexerProperty(
                    prop.PropType, prop.Name);
                if (prop.AddRequired)
                    propConfig.IsRequired();
            }
        }).Model.AddAnnotation("Table", _tableSpec.Name);
    }
}
```

You pass in a class containing the specification of the table and properties.

The DbSet MyTable I the Sharec entity buil OnModelC

Defines a SharedType entity type, which allows the same type to be mapped to multiple tables

You give this shared entity type a name so that you can refer to it.

Adds each property in t from the tab

Adds an index property to find the primary key based on its name

Sets the property to not being null (needed only nullable types such as st

Now you map to the table you want to access.

To be clear, the data in the `TableSpec` class must be the same every time because EF Core caches the configuration. The property-bag entity's configuration is fixed for the whole time the application is running. To access the property-bag entity, you use the `MyTable` property shown in the next listing. This listing shows adding a new entry via a dictionary and then reading it back, including accessing the property bag's properties in a LINQ query.

Listing 8.29 Adding and querying a property bag

```
var propBag = new Dictionary<string, object>      ◄───┤ The property bag is of type
{                                                      Dictionary<string, object>.
    ["Title"] = "My book",           For a shared type, such as a
    ["Price"] = 123.0                property bag, you must
};                                   provide the DbSet to Add to.
context.MyTable.Add(propBag);     ◄──┘
context.SaveChanges();                    ◄───┐ The property-bag entry is
                                                saved in the normal way.
var readInPropBag = context.MyTable     ◄───┐
    .Single(x => (int)x["Id"] == 1);    ◄───┤ To read back, you use the DbSet
                                              mapped to the property-bag entity.
var title = readInPropBag["Title"];  ◄───┐
                                           To refer to a property/column, you need
              You access the result by using    to use an indexer. You may need to cast
              normal dictionary access methods.  the object to the right type.
```

This listing is a specific example in which a property bag is a good solution, but you can configure a property bag manually. Here is some more information on the property bag:

- A property bag's property names follow By Convention naming. The primary key is `"Id"`, for example. But you can override this setting with Fluent API commands as usual.
- You can have multiple property bags. The `SharedTypeEntity` Fluent API method allows you to map the same type to different tables.
- A property bag can have relationships to other classes or property bags. You use the `HasOne`/`HasMany` Fluent API methods, but you can't define navigational properties in a property bag.
- You don't have to set every property in the dictionary when you add a property-bag entity. Any properties/columns not set will be set to the type's default value.

Summary

- If you follow the By Convention naming rules for foreign keys, EF Core can find and configure most normal relationships.
- Two Data Annotations provide a solution to a couple of specific issues related to foreign keys with names that don't fit the By Convention naming rules.
- The Fluent API is the most comprehensive way to configure relationships. Some features, such as setting the action on deletion of the dependent entity, are available only via the Fluent API.

- You can automate some of the configuration of your entity classes by ac code that is run in the DbContext's OnModelCreating method.
- EF Core enables you to control updates to navigational properties, inclu stopping, adding, or removing entries in collection navigational propertie:
- EF Core provides many ways to map entity classes to a database table. The ones are owned types, table per hierarchy, table per type, table splitting property bags.

For readers who are familiar with EF6:

- The basic process of configuring relationships in EF Core is the same EF6.x, but the Fluent API commands have changed significantly.
- EF6.x adds foreign keys if you forget to add them yourself, but they aren't a sible via normal EF6.x commands. EF Core allows you to access ther shadow properties.
- The EF Core 5 release added a similar feature as EF6.x's many-to-i relationship, with EF Core now automatically creating the linking table section 3.4.4), but EF Core's implementation is different from how EF6.x in ments this feature.
- EF Core has introduced new features, such as access to shadow properties, nate keys, and backing fields.
- EF Core's owned types provide features you would have found in EF6.x's plex types. Extra features include storing owned types in their own table.
- EF Core's TPH, TPT, and table-splitting feature are similar to the corresp ing features in EF6.x, but owned types and property bags aren't in EF6.x.

Handling
database migrations

9

This chapter covers

- Different ways to create commands to update a database's structure
- Three starting points from which you create database structure changes
- How to detect and fix database structure changes that would lose data
- How the characteristics of your application affect the way you apply a database change

This chapter covers ways of changing the structure of a database, referred to as migrating a database. The structure of the database is called the *database schema*; it consists of the tables, columns, constraints, and so on that make up a database. Creating and updating a database schema can seem to be simple because EF Core provides a method called Migrate to do it all for you: you create your entity classes and add a bit of configuration, and EF Core builds you a nice, shiny database.

The problem is that EF Core's Migrate method hides a whole series of database migration issues that aren't immediately obvious. Renaming a property in an entity class, for example, by default causes that property's database column to be deleted, along with any data it had! So in this chapter, in addition to detailing how to build apply database migrations, I cover the key issues that you must consider when u ing a database. No one wants to be the person who breaks your "live" database.

The EF Core documentation on migrations is excellent (see http://mn; XdR6), so this chapter doesn't try to duplicate that information. Instead. it d into the options and issues related to migrating a database, along with their and cons. You have many ways to create and apply database migrating, and chapter covers the various options. The chapter also contains examples of han the more complex issues, such as properly handing migrations that could lose and applying a migration to a database while the application is still running. knowledge will help you select the right approach to creating a migration and suc fully apply it to a database.

9.1 How this chapter is organized

This chapter starts with section 9.2, which introduces the topic of databases that migrating and the important issue of ensuring that no data is lost while migrat database. After that section, two parts cover creating and applying migrations:

- Part 1, creating a database migration, starts at section 9.3. This part cover three approaches to creating database migrations or creating your EF classes and configuration to match an existing database.
- Part 2, applying a migration to a database, starts at section 9.8. This part c the ways you can apply a migration to a production database, including complexities of updating a database while the application is still running.

These parts cover lots of approaches for you to consider. Each part has a table tha the pros, cons, and limitations of each given approach, which should help you the right choice for your project.

9.2 Understanding the complexities of changing your application's database

This section talks about the issues involved in migrating a database, especiall database that your live application is using. The topics covered in this section are eral to all relational databases and any software system. There are many ways to nize your database and application deployment, each with trade-offs of compl scalability, availability, and development/operations (DevOps) effort.

Combining the information in this chapter with your knowledge of your ap tion, you can decide which approach to use to create and migrate your databases. ing a thought-through plan or policy for creating and applying migrations will the migration process safer and quicker.

A view of what databases need updating

Before I describe how to update a database's schema, let's look at the databases that can be involved in an application being developed. Figure 9.1 shows a possible arrangement of a multiperson development team, with development, testing, preproduction, and production.

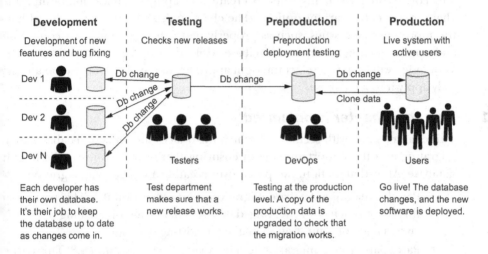

Figure 9.1 **Various databases can be used in an application's development, all of which will need database schema changes applied to them. The terms development, testing, preproduction, and production refer to different parts of the development, testing, and deployment of an application, and any associated database schema changes.**

Not all development projects have all these stages, and some have more or different stages. Also, this figure assumes that only one database is being used in production, but you may have multiple copies of the same database. You may also have developers sharing a single development database, but that approach has some limitations; see the following note. The permutations are endless. This chapter refers to the development and production databases, but be aware that database schema updates may be needed on other databases.

> **NOTE** Using a single shared database in the development environment can work, but it has limitations. A developer might apply a migration to the database before they merge the code into the main branch, for example, which could cause problems. Section 9.2.2 introduces the topic of migrations that might cause problems.

9.2.2 Handling a migration that can lose data

It's helpful to characterize migrations in two groups: a nonbreaking change or a loss breaking change. A *nonbreaking change* is one that doesn't remove tables o
umns that have useful data in them, and a *data-loss breaking change* removes
tables or columns. So if you don't want to lose important data, you need to ad
extra copy stage to a data-loss breaking change migration so that the data is prese

Fortunately, in applications that are being developed, many migrations ar
nonbreaking-change type because you are adding new tables and columns to
database. But at times, you want to restructure your database such that you nee
move columns in one table to another, possibly new table. Section 9.5 gives two e
ples of data-loss breaking changes and how to fix them:

- Renaming a property (section 9.5.1)
- Moving columns from one table to another (section 9.5.2)

NOTE   Section 9.8 discusses another type of breaking change: an application
breaking change, which refers to a migration that would cause errors in the
currently running application. This change matters if you are trying to migrate
a database while the current application is running.

9.3 Part 1: Introducing the three approaches to creating a migration

Section 9.2 applies to any form of database migration, but from now, on the foc
on EF Core. This focus is important because the job isn't only to change the
base; it's also to ensure that the changed database matches the entity classes an
EF Core configuration held by the application's DbContext. If you use EF C
migration tools, it's a given that the database will match the application's DbCor
but as you will see, that match isn't guaranteed in many other approaches to mi
ing a database.

You have three main ways to come up with an updated database that matches
application's DbContext. Each approach has a different starting point, which A
Vickers (engineering manager of the EF Core team) calls *the source of truth:*

- *Using EF Core's migration features*—This approach considers the entity cl
  and the EF Core configuration is the source of truth. This approach to
  dling migrations is the easiest one, but complex issues such as handling
  loss breaking changes require you to hand-edit migrations.
- *Using SQL scripts to build migrations*—In this approach, the source of truth i
  SQL commands used to build/migrate the database. You have complete co
  of your database schema and can include features that EF Core doesn't cc
  ure, such as column-level constraints. But the big challenge is matching
  SQL changes to EF Core's internal model.
- *Using EF Core's reverse-engineering tool*—In this approach, the database i
  source of truth. You re-create the entity classes and the application's DbCo

with all the required configurations. You'd use this approach mainly to build an EF Core application around an existing database.

Figure 9.2 gives you an overview of the five ways to migrate a database and their key attributes. Each section discussing a migration starts with a table summarizing the approach and including my views about when I think the approach is useful.

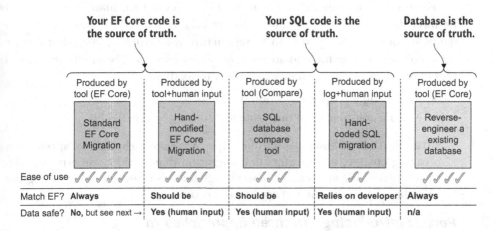

Figure 9.2   A simple summary of the five ways to migrate a database and make sure that the database matches EF Core's internal model of the database

Creating a migration by using EF Core's add migration command

EF Core's migration tools are the standard way to create and update a database from EF Core. This approach is easiest because it automatically builds the correct SQL commands to update the database, saving you from digging into databases and the SQL language to create and change the application's database.

You start by studying the standard migration produced by EF Core migration tools with no extra editing by you. A standard migration can handle most situations and forms the basis for altering the migration if you need to. Typically, you would need to edit a migration to handle things such as data-loss breaking changes (section 9.5) after you review what the standard can do.

You create a standard migration by using EF Core's migration tools—specifically, the add migration command. This command uses the entity classes and the application's DbContext, with its configuration code being the source of truth. But the add migration commands also needs to know the previous state of EF Core's model of the database to decide what needs changing. It does this by looking at a class created by the last run of the EF Core migration tools, which contain a snapshot of EF Core's model of the database. For the first migration, that class won't exist, so the migration

The process kicked off by the Add-Migration MyMigrate command

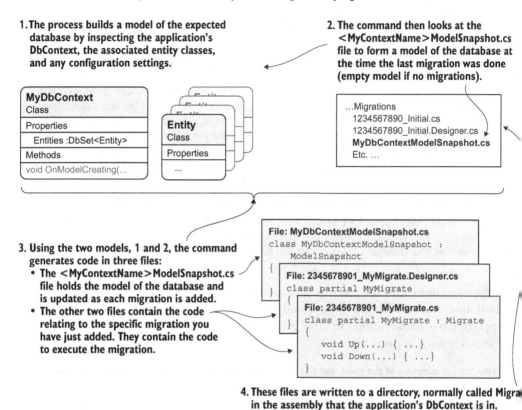

1. The process builds a model of the expected database by inspecting the application's DbContext, the associated entity classes, and any configuration settings.

2. The command then looks at the <MyContextName>ModelSnapshot.cs file to form a model of the database at the time the last migration was done (empty model if no migrations).

MyDbContext
Class

| Properties |
| Entities :DbSet<Entity> |
| Methods |
| void OnModelCreating(... |

Entity
Class

| Properties |
| ... |

...Migrations
  1234567890_Initial.cs
  1234567890_Initial.Designer.cs
  MyDbContextModelSnapshot.cs
  Etc. ...

3. Using the two models, 1 and 2, the command generates code in three files:
  - **The <MyContextName>ModelSnapshot.cs file holds the model of the database and is updated as each migration is added.**
  - **The other two files contain the code relating to the specific migration you have just added. They contain the code to execute the migration.**

File: MyDbContextModelSnapshot.cs
```
class MyDbContextModelSnapshot :
    ModelSnapshot
{

}
```
File: 2345678901_MyMigrate.Designer.cs
```
class partial MyMigrate
{
```
File: 2345678901_MyMigrate.cs
```
class partial MyMigrate : Migrate
{
    void Up(...) { ...}
    void Down(...) { ...}
}
```

4. These files are written to a directory, normally called Migra in the assembly that the application's DbContext is in.

Figure 9.3 **Running the** add migration **command to create a new EF Core migration. The command comp two models of the database. One model comes from our current application, with its DbContext, entity clas and EF Core configuration; the other is from the <MyContextName>ModelSnapshot.cs file (which is empty if mirgration is your first one). By comparing these two models, EF Core can create code that will update the database schema to match EF Core's current database model.**

tools assume that the database has an empty schema—that is, has no tables, ind and so on. So when you run the EF Core's add migration command, it compare snapshot class with your current entity classes and the application's DbContext wi configuration code. From that data, it can work out what has changed; then it b two classes containing the commands to add the changes to the database (figure

Don't build your entity classes the same way you build normal classes
EF Core is great at making your database look like normal classes, but you shouldr build your entity classes quite the same way that you would your normal classe In normal classes, for example, a good approach to stopping duplication is usir

(continued)

properties that access other properties, known as *expression body definitions*. Here's an example:

```
public string FullName => $"{FirstName} {LastName}";
```

That technique works for a normal class, but if you use it for an entity class, a query that filters or sorts on the `FullName` property would fail. In this case, you would need to provide a real property linked to a database column (possibly using the new, persisted computed column; see chapter 10) to make sure that EF Core can sort/filter on that data.

Also, you should think carefully about what properties and relational links you put in an entity class. Refactoring a normal class is easy, but refactoring an entity class requires a migration, possibly including a data-copying stage too.

Remember that your entity classes, with their navigational properties, define the database's structure. Just because EF Core makes it easy to define these things doesn't mean that you shouldn't think about the database structure and its performance.

Before you delve into the add migration command, table 9.1 summarizes using a standard migration to update your database's schema. Each section on a migration approach has a table similar to table 9.1 so that you can compare the features and limitations of each approach.

Table 9.1 A summary of the good, the bad, and the limitations of a standard migration created by the add migration command

	Notes
Good parts	■ Builds a correct migration automatically ■ Handles seeding of the databas ■ Doesn't require knowledge of SQL ■ Includes a remove migration feature (see section 9.4.4)
Bad parts	■ Only works if your code is the source of truth
Limitations	■ Standard EF Core migrations cannot handle breaking changes (but see section 9.5). ■ Standard EF Core migrations are database-specific (but see section 9.5.4).
Tips	Watch out for error messages when you run the add migration command. If EF Core detects a change that could lose data, it outputs an error message but still creates the migration files. You *must* alter the migration script; otherwise, you will lose data (see section 9.5.2).
My verdict	This approach is an easy way to handle migrations, and it works well in many cases. Consider this approach first if your application code is driving the database design.

TIP I recommend an EF Core Community Standup video that covers some EF Core 5's features and the philosophy behind EF Core's migration features; see http://mng.bz/yYmq.

9.4.1 Requirements before running any EF Core migration command

To run any of the EF Core migration tools' commands, you need to instal[ ] required code and set up your application in a certain way. There are two versio[ ] the EF Core migration tools: the `dotnet-ef` command-line interface (CLI) tools[ ] Visual Studio's Package Manager Console (PMC) version.

To install the CLI tools, you need to install them on your development [ ] puter via the appropriate command prompt. The following command will i[ ] the `dotnet-ef` tools globally so that you can use them in any directory:

```
dotnet tool install --global dotnet-ef
```

To use Visual Studio's PMC feature, you must include the NuGet package `Micro[ ]` `.EntityFrameworkCore.Tools` in your main application, and the correct EF Core [ ] base provider NuGet package, such as `Microsoft.EntityFrameworkCore.SqlSe[ ]` in the project that holds the application's DbContext you want to migrate.

These tools must be able to create an instance of the DbContext you wa[ ] migrate. If your startup project is an ASP.NET Core web host or .NET Core ge[ ] host, the tools can use it to get an instance of a DbContext set up in the startup c[ ]

If you aren't using ASP.NET Core, you can add a class that implement[ ] `IDesignTimeDbContextFactory<TContext>` interface. This class must be in the [ ] project as the DbContext you want to migrate. The following listing shows an exa[ ] taken from the `Part2` branch of the associated GitHub repo.

Listing 9.1 A class that provides an instance of the DbContext to the migration to[ ]

EF Core tools use this class to obtain an instance of the DbContext.

This interface defines a way that the EF Core tools find and create this class.

The interface requires this method, which returns a valid instance of the DbContext.

You need to provide a connection string to your local database.

You use the nor[ ] commands to s[ ] the database pr[ ] you are using.

```
public class DesignTimeContextFactory
    : IDesignTimeDbContextFactory<EfCoreContext>
{
    private const string connectionString =
        "Server=(localdb)\\mssqllocaldb;Database=..."

    public EfCoreContext CreateDbContext(string[] args)
    {
        var optionsBuilder =
            new DbContextOptionsBuilder<EfCoreContext>();
        optionsBuilder.UseSqlServer(connectionString);

        return new EfCoreContext(optionsBuilder.Options);
    }
}
```

Returns the DbContext for the EF Core tools to use

9.4.2 Running the add migration command

To create an EF Core migration, you need to run the `add migration` command fr[ ] command line (CLI tools) or in Visual Studio's PMC window. The two ways to mi[ ] a database, CLI tools and PMC, have different names and parameters. The follo[ ] list shows an add migration command that I used to create a migration in the Book App. Note that the CLI version was run in the directory of the BookApp ASP.NET Core project:

- *CLI*—dotnet ef migrations add Ch09Migrate -p ../DataLayer
- *PMC*—Add-Migration Ch09Migrate -Project DataLayer

NOTE There are lots of commands, with multiple parameters, and it would take many pages to reproduce the EF Core documentation. Therefore, I direct you to EF Core's command-line reference at http://mng.bz/MXEn.

Seeding your database via an EF Core migration

EF Core's migrations can contain data that will be added to the database, a process known as seeding the database. A good use of this feature is adding constants to your database, such as your product types and customer types for an e-commerce site. I should say that seeded data can be changed, so the data isn't a constant, but you can change it only via a migration, so it's best to use it for data that doesn't change (much).

NOTE As well as adding the seed data when a migration is applied, the context.Database.EnsureCreated() method (usually used in unit testing) seeds the created database. See chapter 17 for more on unit testing.

You add seed data via Fluent API configuration, using the HasData method. Listing 9.2 gives an example of ways you can link seed data via its primary and foreign keys. This example has seed data that is more complex than I usually have, but I'm providing it to show you the various ways that you can set up seed data. The classes used in this example are

- A Project entity class with a ProjectManager of type User
- The User entity class, which holds the user's Name and address
- The Address class, an owned type (see section 8.9.1) that holds the address part

Listing 9.2 An example of setting up seed data via the HasData Fluent API method

```
                                                          Seeding is configured
                                                          via the Fluent API.

protected override void OnModelCreating(ModelBuilder modelBuilder)   ◁──┘
{
        modelBuilder.Entity<Project>().HasData(            Adds two default projects.
            new { ProjectId = 1, ProjectName = "Project1"},   Note that you must
            new { ProjectId = 2, ProjectName = "Project2"});  provide the primary key.
        modelBuilder.Entity<User>().HasData(
            new { UserId = 1, Name = "Jill", ProjectId = 1 },   The User class has
            new { UserId = 2, Name = "Jack", ProjectId = 2 });  an owned type that
        modelBuilder.Entity<User>()                             holds the User's
            .OwnsOne(x => x.Address).HasData(                   address.
```

```
                    new {UserId = 1, Street = "Street1", City = "city1"},
                    new {UserId = 2, Street = "Street2", City = "city2"});
}
```
**Provide the user's addresses. Note that you use the
UserId to define which user you are adding data to.**

As you can see from listing 9.2, you must define the primary key, even if is usually
erated by the database, so that you can define relationships by setting foreign ke
the appropriate primary key. And if you change the primary key, the previous se
entry is removed. Also, if you keep the original primary key but change the da
that entry, the migration will update that entry.

NOTE The directory Chapter09Listings\SeedExample in the Test project of the
associated GitHub repo contains an example of what happens when you change
your seed data between migrations. The second migration contains code to
delete, update, and insert seed data due to changes in the HasData parts.

9.4.4 *Handling EF Core migrations with multiple developers*

When multiple developers are working on a project that uses EF Core's migratior
ture to update the database schema, you might bump into software merges in w
one developer's migration is in conflict with your migration. This section gives
some advice on what to do. I do assume that you are using source control and tha
have your own development database to try out a migration locally.

First, if your migration has no conflicts with a migration that you just merged
your software, you shouldn't have a source control conflict, because EF Core's m
tions are designed to be team-friendly (unlike EF6 migration code). You migh
migrations applied in a slightly different order; perhaps you created your migra
yesterday, and someone's else's migration was produced today and applied to
main database. That situation shouldn't cause a problem if there are no merge
flicts, because EF Core can handle out-of-order migrations.

You will know if you have a migration merge conflict because your source
trol system will show a conflict in the migration snapshot file, which has the n
<DbContextClassName>ModelSnapShot. If this conflict happens, here's the re
mended way to fix it:

1 Abort the source control merge that contained a migration change that
   flicted with your migration.
2 Remove the migration you created by using either of the following comm
   (*Note:* Keep the entity classes and configuration changes; you will need t
   later):
   a *CLI*—dotnet ef migrations remove
   b *PMC*—Remove-Migration
3 Merge the incoming migration you abandoned in step 1. A merge con
   should no longer appear in the migration snapshot file.
4 Use the add migration command to re-create your migration.

That migration conflict resolution process works in most cases, but it can get complex. My recommendation for projects in which migration conflicts can happen are

- Merge the main/production branch into your local version before you create a migration.
- Have only one migration in a source control merge into your main/production branch, because undoing two migrations is hard work.
- Tell your development team members if you think that your migration might affect their work.

Using a custom migration table to allow multiple DbContexts to one database

EF Core creates a table if you apply an EF Core migration to a database. EF Core uses this table to find out what migrations have been applied to the database so that it knows what migration should be applied to the database you are migrating. By default, that table is called __EFMigrationsHistory, but you can change the name via an option method called MigrationsHistoryTable.

There aren't many reasons for changing the migration history table, but sharing a database across multiple EF Core DbContexts is one of them. Here are two examples:

- Saving money by combining databases—You are building an ASP.NET Core application with individual user accounts that needs an accounts database. Your application's DbContext also needs a database. By using a custom migration table on your application's DbContext would allow both contexts to use the same database.
- Using a separate DbContext for each business group—In part 3 of this book, I want to make the project easier to extend as it gets bigger. Therefore, I have separate DbContexts: one for the book-display code and another for the order-processing code.

Both examples work, but using EF Core's migration system with either takes a bit more effort. The first migration example—saving money by combining databases—is easier because the two databases you are combining don't share any tables, views, and so on. But because both databases use EF Core's migration system, they need a different migration history table. ASP.NET Core's individual user account database uses the default name for the migration history table, so you need to change the name of your application's DbContext. The next listing shows how to do that when you are registering your application's DbContext in ASP.NET Core's startup class.

Listing 9.3 Changing the name of the migration history table for your DbContext

Registers your application's DbContext as a service in ASP.NET Core

The second parameter allows you to configure at the database provider level.

The MigrationsHistoryTable method allows you to change the migration table name and optionally the table's schema.

```
services.AddDbContext<EfCoreContext>(
    options => options.UseSqlServer(connection,
        dbOptions =>
            dbOptions.MigrationsHistoryTable("NewHistoryName")));
```

Next, of course, you must migrate each of the DbContexts—in this case, the ASP.
Core's individual user account context and your application's DbContext. Other
your job is done.

For the second example—having a separate DbContext for each business gro
you need a different migration history table name for each DbContext so that
migration is separate. You should also specify separate directories for the migra
classes for each DbContext, which you can do via an option in the add migra
command. That command will stop any clashes of class names if you use the
migration name in both DbContexts.

> **NOTE** You can also place the migration classes in a separate project if you
> want to. You need to tell the add migration command which project to place
> the migration in. Then you use the MigrationsAssembly method when you
> set up the database options. See http://mng.bz/aonB.

This example, however, has another problem for you to deal with: each DbCon
needs to access the table called Books, which would duplicate the migration of
table. The Books table is shared because both DbContexts must be able to read i
show the books and create an order for books, respectively).

You have several options to fix this problem, but the best is to use the Excl
FromMigrations Fluent API command, which stops that entity class from being incl
in a migration. In the BookDbContext/OrderDbContext example, you could remov
migration of the Book entity class in the OrderDbContext, as shown in this code snip

```
protected override void OnModelCreating(ModelBuilder modelBuilder)
{
    modelBuilder.Entity<Book>()
        .ToTable("Books",
            t => t.ExcludeFromMigrations());
}
```

If the Book entity class is mapped to a view, not to a table (see section 7.9.3), the m
tion tools will not include that view in a migration. For this example, that approa
a good one, as we want the BookDbContext to have read/write access, but the Or
DbContext should only have read access.

My approach to creating migrations

My approach to building migrations relies on having unit tests that can check thing
against a database. I realize that some developers don't like that approach, but I'
found that not being able to unit-test my code against a real database requires m
to build/apply a migration and then run the application to test my changes. Using un
tests against a real database makes me develop faster, and each unit test I wri
improves the coverage of the application I am working on.

Normally, I build a comprehensive set of unit tests across the whole applicatio
other than the final UI/WebAPI side. Many of my unit tests use the database becaus

(continued)

it's the quickest way to set up the test data; EF Core makes setting up a test database easy. Sure, for complex business logic I use a repository pattern (see section 4.2), which I can stub out, but for straightforward queries and updates, I can use test databases. As a result, I can implement a new feature in stages and check as I go by running my unit tests.

This approach does require the databases in unit tests to be up to date with the current EF Code Model; the schema must match your current entity classes and DbContext configuration. Many years of experience (and some suggestions from the EF Core team) have honed my approach, which I share with you in chapter 17. This approach allows me to build a complex feature in smaller steps, with the unit-test databases always in step with EF Core's current Model. Only after all the code is written and the unit tests pass do I finally create a migration.

Editing an EF Core migration to handle complex situations

EF Core migration tools are powerful and well thought out, but they can't handle every possible database migration, such as a data-loss breaking change. The EF Core team knows this, so it provided multiple ways to alter a migration class by hand. Let's look at the types of migrations that a standard migration can't handle without help:

- *Data-loss breaking changes,* such as moving columns from one table to a new table
- *Adding SQL features that EF Core doesn't create,* such as adding user-defined functions, SQL stored procedures, views, and so on
- *Altering a migration to work for multiple database types,* such as handling both SQL Server and PostgreSQL

You can fix these problems by editing the standard migration class created via the add migration command. To do this, you need to edit the migration class whose filename ends with the migration name and has a type of .cs, such as ..._InitialMigration.cs. In the following sections, you learn the different types of edits that can improve or fix your migrations, but table 9.2 provides a summary of the pros and cons of hand-editing a migration to achieve the required migration.

Table 9.2 A summary of the good, the bad, and the limitations of a migration created by the add migration command edited by you to handle situations that the standard migration can't handle on its own

	Notes
Good parts	- You start with most of the migration build via the add migration command. - You can customize the migration. - You can add SQL extra features, such as stored procedures.
Bad parts	- You need to know more about the database structure. - Some edits require SQL skills.

Table 9.2 A summary of the good, the bad, and the limitations of a migration created by the `migration` command edited by you to handle situations that the standard migration can't hand its own *(continued)*

	Notes
Limitations	Your edits aren't checked by EF Core, so you could get a mismatch between the upd database and your entity classes and application's DbContext.
Tips	Same as for standard migrations (see table 9.1)
My verdict	This approach is great for small alterations, but making big changes can be hard w as you are often mixing C# commands with SQL. If you expect to be editing lots of migrations to add SQL features, you should consider an SQL script approach (see tion 9.6.2) as an alternative.

9.5.1 Adding and removing MigrationBuilder methods inside the migration class

Let's start with a simple example of fixing a migration that contains a data-loss b ing change. This example looks at what happens if you change the name of a prop in an entity class, which causes a data-loss breaking change. This problem can be f by removing two commands and replacing them with `MigrationBuilder`'s Ren `Column` method inside the migration class.

This example comes from chapter 7, where you changed the `CustomerId` prop in the `Order` entity class to `UserId` to automate adding a Query Filter (see section 7.1 The standard migration sees this operation as being the removal of the `Custom` property and the addition of a new property called `UserId`, which would cause existing values in the CustomerId column to be lost. To fix this problem, make the lowing changes in the migration class generated by the standard migration gener in chapter 7:

- Remove the `AddColumn` command that adds the new `UserId` column.
- Remove the `DropColumn` command that removes the existing `CustomerId` col
- Add a `RenameColumn` command to rename the `CustomerId` column to `User`

The following listing shows the start of the altered migration class, the name of w is taken from the migration name, `Chapter07`. The methods that need to be rem are commented out, and the new `RenameColumn` method is added.

Listing 9.4 The updated migration class with old commands replaced

```
public partial class Chapter07 : Migration          ⊲——   Migration class created by the a
{                                                           migration command that has be

    protected override void Up(MigrationBuilder migrationBuilder)   ⊲—
    {
                                                           There are two methods in
        //migrationBuilder.AddColumn<Guid>(             migration class. Up applied th
        //    name: "UserId",                           migration, and another metho
        //    table: "Orders",                          called Down removed this migratio
```

The command to add the new UserId column should not run, so you comment it out.

```
//       type: "uniqueidentifier",
//       nullable: false,
//       defaultValue:
//           new Guid("00000000-0000-0000-0000-000000000000"));
```

```
//migrationBuilder.DropColumn(
//       name: "CustomerId",
//       table: "Orders");
```

```
migrationBuilder.RenameColumn(
    name: "CustomerId",
    table: "Orders",
    newName: "UserId");
```

The correct approach is to rename the CustomerId column to UserId.

```
//… rest of the migration code left out
    }
}
```

That code will change the Up migration from one that loses data to one that preserves the data held in the old CustomerId column. A migration class created by the add migration command also contains a Down method. This method undoes the migration if the Up migration has been applied to a database (see the remove command in section 9.4.4). Therefore, it is best practice to edit the Down method with the correct commands to undo the migration. The Down part that goes with listing 9.4 would also be edited do the reverse from the Up part. You would remove the AddColumn/Drop-Column commands in the Down part and replace them with RenameColumn, but now the rename is from UserId back to CustomerId.

> **NOTE** I haven't shown you the altered Down method, but you can find this migration class in the Migrations folder of the DataLayer project in the GitHub repo, branch Part2.

5.2 Adding SQL commands to a migration

There can be two main reasons for adding SQL commands to a migration: to handle a data-loss breaking change and to add or alter parts of the SQL database that EF Core doesn't control, such as adding views or SQL stored procedures.

As an example of adding SQL commands to a migration, you are going to handle a data-loss breaking change. In this case, you are going to start with a database with a User entity class that contains each user's Name and their address in the properties Street and City. As the project progresses, you decide that you want to copy the address part to another table and have the User entity class reference it via a navigational property. Figure 9.4 shows the before and after states of the database's schema and the content of the tables.

The best way to handle this situation with EF Core's migration is to add some SQL commands to copy over the data, but the process isn't trivial. Changing the migration requires adding SQL code.

Before—User's address in same table

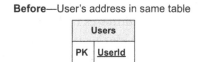

Userid	Name	Street	City
123	Jack	Jack Street	Jack City
456	Jill	Jill Street	Jill City

After—User's address in separate table

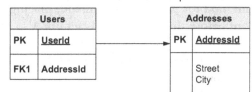

Userid	Name	AddressId
123	Jack	1
456	Jill	2

AddressId	Street	Cit
1	Jack Street	Jack
2	Jill Street	Jill Ci

Figure 9.4 The original (before) database schema and data, with one table called Users. The new (aft database schema has a new table, Addresses, and the address data in the original Users table has bee moved to the Addresses table. Also, the Users table address columns, Street and City, have been remov and a new foreign key, `AddressId`, has been added to link to the User's addresses.

NOTE You can see the whole migration in the associated GitHub repo at http://mng.bz/goME.

First, you change your User entity class to remove the address and link to the Address entity class to the DbContext. Then you create a new migration by usin add migration command, which will warn you that it may result in the loss of dat this point, you are ready to edit the migration.

The second step is adding a series of SQL commands, using the MigrationBui method Sql, such as migrationBuilder.Sql("ALTER TABLE..."). The following li shows you the SQL commands without the migrationBuilder.Sql so that the easier to see.

Listing 9.5 The SQL Server commands to copy over the addresses to a new table

```
ALTER TABLE [Addresses]
    ADD [UserId] [int] NOT NULL
```
Adds a temporary column to allow the correct foreign key to be set in the Users table

```
INSERT INTO [Addresses] ([UserId],[Street],[City])
    SELECT [UserId],[Street],[City] FROM [Users]
```
Copies over all the add data, with the User's p key, to the addresses t

```
UPDATE [Users] SET [AddressId] = (
    SELECT [AddressId]
        FROM [Addresses]
        WHERE [Addresses].[UserId] = [Users].[Userid])
```
Uses the temporary UserId column to mak sure that the right for keys are set up

```
ALTER TABLE [Addresses]
    DROP COLUMN [UserId]
```
Removes the temporary UserId column in the Addresses table, as it's not needed anymore

Sets the foreign key in the Users table back to the Addresses table

You add these SQL commands to the migration by using the `migrationBuilder.Sql` method for each SQL command, placing them after the Addresses table is created but before the foreign key is set up. Also, the `MigrationBuilder` methods that drop (remove) the address properties from the Users table must be moved to after the SQL code has run; otherwise, the data will have gone before your SQL can copy that data over.

> **NOTE** Section 9.8.1 covers a way to run C# code before and after a specific migration has been applied to a database. That approach is another way to copy data, but the SQL approach often performs better.

Adding your own custom migration commands

If you often add certain types of SQL commands to a migration, you can build some templating code to make your edits easier to write. Building templates, such as adding an SQL View to the database, is a good idea if you use an SQL feature often, because the cost of creating the template is less effort than handcoding the SQL feature multiple times. You have two ways to create a template:

- Create extension methods that take the `MigrationBuilder` class in and build commands with `MigrationBuilder`'s `Sql` method. These extension methods tend to be database-specific.
- A more complex but more versatile approach is to extend the `Migration-Builder` class to add your own commands. This approach allows you to access methods to build commands that work for many database providers.

In this section, I discuss only the first approach. The second is an advanced version that is well described in the EF Core documentation at http://mng.bz/xGBe.

As an example, you are going to create an extension method that will allow you to create SQL Views more easily. The extension method takes in the class that will be mapped to the View so that it can find the properties to map to the columns (assuming that you are using only properties and By Convention column naming). The following listing shows the extension method that will create a view within a migration.

Listing 9.6 Extension method to add/alter an SQL view in an EF Core migration

An extension method must be in a static class.

The method needs the class that is mapped to the view so that it can get its properties.

The MigrationBuilder provides access to the migration methods—in this case, the Sql method.

```
public static class AddViewExtensions
{
    public static void AddViewViaSql<TView>(
        this MigrationBuilder migrationBuilder,
        string viewName,
        string tableName,
        string whereSql)
        where TView : class
    {
```

needs use for nd the able it from.

Views have a Where clause that filters the results returned.

Ensures that the TView type is a class

<table>
<tr>
<td>

This method throws an exception if the database isn't Server because it uses an SQL Server view format.

</td>
<td>

```
if (!migrationBuilder.IsSqlServer())
    throw new NotImplementedException("warning...")
```

</td>
<td></td>
</tr>
<tr>
<td></td>
<td>

```
var selectNamesString = string.Join(", ",
    typeof(TView).GetProperties()
    .Select(x => x.Name));
```

</td>
<td>

Gets the names of the properties in the class mapped to the view ar uses them as column r

</td>
</tr>
<tr>
<td></td>
<td>

```
var viewSql =
    $"CREATE OR ALTER VIEW {viewName} AS " +
    $"SELECT {selectNamesString} FROM {tableName} " +
    $"WHERE {whereSql}";
```

</td>
<td>

Creates the SQL comman create/updat

</td>
</tr>
<tr>
<td></td>
<td>

```
    migrationBuilder.Sql(viewSql);
    }
}
```

</td>
<td>

Uses MigrationBuilder's method to apply the created SQL to the database

</td>
</tr>
</table>

You would use this technique in a migration by adding it to the Up method (and a VIEW command in the Down method to remove it). Here is a code snippet that crea view for the MyView class, which has the properties MyString and MyDateTime:

```
migrationBuilder.AddViewViaSql<MyView>(
    "EntityFilterView", "Entities",
    "MyDateTime >= '2020-1-1'");
```

The resulting SQL looks like this snippet:

```
CREATE OR ALTER VIEW EntityFilterView AS
SELECT MyString, MyDateTime
FROM Entities
WHERE MyDateTime >= '2020-1-1'
```

9.5.4 Altering a migration to work for multiple database types

EF Core migrations are database-provider-specific—that is, if you build a migratio SQL Server, it almost certainly won't work for a PostgreSQL database. You don't c need migrations for multiple database types, however. In fact, I don't recommend t multiple database types with the same EF Core code, as subtle differences between base types can catch you out (see chapter 16). But if you need to support migra for two or more types of databases, the recommended way is to build separate m tions for each database provider. If you want to use an SQLite database for a L version of your application and an SQL Server database for a Windows version of application, for example, you would need to execute the following steps.

The first step is creating a specific DbContext for each database type. The ea way is to create a main application's DbContext and inherit it in your other data types. The following listing shows two applications' DbContexts, with the second inheriting the first one.

Listing 9.7 Two DbContexts that have the same entity classes and configuration

```
public class MySqlServerDbContext : DbContext          ◁─┤ Inherits the normal
{                                                            DbContext class
    public DbSet<Book> Books { get; set; }          ┐
    // … other DbSets left out                      │  Adds all the DbSet properties
                                                    │  and Fluent APIs, which are
    protected override void OnModelCreating          │  used in both database types
        (ModelBuilder modelBuilder)                 ┘
    {
        //… your Fluent API code goes here                     The MySqliteDbContext
    }                                                          inherits the Sql Server
}                                                              DbContext class instead
                                                               of the normal
public class MySqliteDbContext : MySqlServerDbContext   ◁─┐   DbContext.
{
        ◁──────┐  The MySqliteDbContext inherits the
}               │  DbSet properties and Fluent APIs
                │  from the Sql Server DbContext.
```

The next step is creating a way for the migration tools to access each DbContext with the database provider defined. The cleanest way is to create an IDesignTimeDb-ContextFactory<TContext> class, as described in section 9.4.1. Alternatively, you can override the OnConfiguring method in each DbContext to define the database provider.

At this point, you can create a migration for each database type by using the Add-Migration command (see section 9.4.2). The important point is that each migration must be in a separate project so that when you create a migration, it can access the correct migration classes for the type of database to which the DbContext is linked. You tell EF Core where the migration classes can be found by using the Migrations-Assembly method when you create the database option. The following code snippet shows the AddDbContext method used to register an application's DbContext with its database provider and the migrations for that database in a project called Database .SqlServer:

```
services.AddDbContext<MySqlServerDbContext>(
    options => options.UseSqlServer(connection,
        x => x.MigrationsAssembly("Database.SqlServer")));
```

Alternatively, you have one migration and add if/then code inside the migration to change what the migration does based on the database provider. This approach isn't recommended because it's harder to maintain. If you want more information on this approach, I suggest looking at the EF Core documentation, which covers both approaches (http://mng.bz/pV08).

> **NOTE** Cosmos DB and NoSQL databases in general don't use EF Core migrations because they don't have a fixed schema, like SQL databases, and they're normally migrated by means of some form of upgrade script. Migrating a

Cosmos DB database accessed via EF Core does have some issues, which I discuss in chapter 16.

9.6 Using SQL scripts to build migrations

The next way to manage your database schema change is to produce SQL *change s* and then apply them to any of your databases. Change scripts contain SQL comm that update the schema of your database. This approach to handling database scl updates is more traditional and gives you much better control of the database fea and the schema update. You need good knowledge of SQL commands to write understand these migration scripts, but tools can generate these migration scrip you by comparing databases.

As with the migrations that EF Core can create, your aim is to create a migr that will alter the schema of your database to match the EF Core's internal mod the database. In this section, you will consider two approaches:

- Using SQL database comparison tools to produce migration from the cu: database schema to the desired database schema
- Handcoding a change script to migrate the database

Although option 1 should produce an exact match to EF Core's internal mod the database, option 2 relies on the developer to write the correct SQL to m what EF Core needs. If the developer makes a mistake (which I can testify is ea do), your application may fail with an exception; worse, it may silently lose dat at the end of this section, I describe a tool I have created that compares a datab schema with EF Core's current model of the database and tells you whether t are any differences.

9.6.1 Using SQL database comparison tools to produce migration

One approach to creating an SQL change script is to compare two databases: original database and a new database created by EF Core after you've updated th Core configuration. Tools can compare two databases and show the differenc their schemas. Many of these comparison tools can also create a script that will ch your original database to the same schema as the database you want to move to. you can create a database with the schema you want, a comparison tool can creat SQL change script needed to update a database to the required database. SQL parison tools make creating SQL change scripts quite easy, but like everything, have their own quirks. Before you look at the details, table 9.3 gives you an overvi this approach.

Several open source and commercial comparison tools are available for many base server types; they can compare database schemas and output SQL change sc: This example uses the SQL Server Object Explorer built into Visual Studio (an) sion), which you can find in the Data Storage and Processing workload of the V Studio installer. You can get the tool directly by choosing Tools > SQL Server > Schema Comparison.

Table 9.3 A summary of the good, the bad, and the limitations of using an SQL database comparison tool to build SQL change scripts to migrate a database

	Notes
Good parts	▪ Tools build the correct SQL migration script for you.
Bad parts	▪ You need some understanding of databases and SQL. ▪ SQL comparison tools often output every setting under the sun to make sure that they get everything right, which makes the SQL code output hard to understand. ▪ Not all SQL comparison tools produce a migration remove script.
Limitations	Tools do not handle breaking changes, so they need human input.
Tips	I use this approach only for complex/large migrations, and I strip out any extra settings to make the code easier to work with.
My verdict	This approach is useful and especially good for people who aren't comfortable with the SQL language. It's also useful for people who have written their own SQL migration code and want to check that their code is correct.

NOTE You can find a step-by-step guide to using SQL Server Object Explorer at http://mng.bz/OEDR.

Figure 9.5 shows how to compare the database in chapter 2 with the changes in chapter 4, where you add Order and LineItem entity classes. An SQL comparison tool relies on having two databases:

- The first database is the current state of the database, known as the Target database. You want to update to the new schema, which is shown as Chapter02Db in figure 9.5. This database is most likely your production database or some other database that matches the target schema.
- The second database, known as the Source database, must have a schema to which you want to update your database, shown as Chapter04Db.Test in figure 9.5. This database is most likely in your development environment. One nice feature I use to get a database like this one is EF Core's EnsureCreated method. This method, usually used in unit testing, creates a database based on the current entity classes and EF Core configuration.

By setting two databases as the Source and Target databases in the compare SQL schema tool, you can compare the two database schemas and then produce an SQL change script that transitions the schema of the Target database to the schema of the Source database.

This process initially tells you the differences; then you have an option to create an SQL change script that will migrate a database from the initial database schema to the required database schema. This option produces an SQL change script that will migrate a database from the initial database schema, Chapter02Db in figure 9.5, to the schema of the target database, Chapter04Db.Test in figure 9.5. I cover how to apply a change script in section 9.8.4.

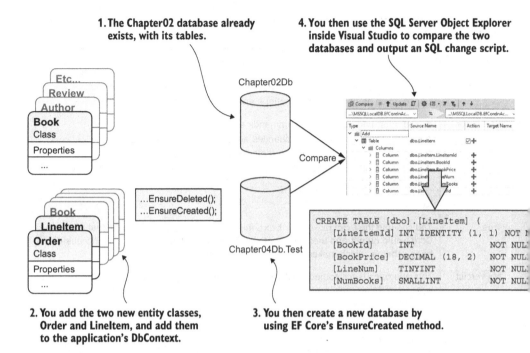

1. The Chapter02 database already exists, with its tables.

4. You then use the SQL Server Object Explorer inside Visual Studio to compare the two databases and output an SQL change script.

Chapter02Db

Compare

...EnsureDeleted();
...EnsureCreated();

Chapter04Db.Test

```
CREATE TABLE [dbo].[LineItem] (
    [LineItemId]  INT IDENTITY (1, 1) NOT N
    [BookId]      INT                 NOT NUL
    [BookPrice]   DECIMAL (18, 2)     NOT NUL
    [LineNum]     TINYINT             NOT NUL
    [NumBooks]    SMALLINT            NOT NUL
```

2. You add the two new entity classes, Order and LineItem, and add them to the application's DbContext.

3. You then create a new database by using EF Core's EnsureCreated method.

Figure 9.5 The process of building an SQL change script by comparing two databases. The important point is the second database, Chapter04Db.Test, is created by EF Core, so you know that it matches the current EF model. In this example, you use the SQL Server Object Explorer feature of Visual Studio to compare the two databases and build an SQL change script that will migrate the Chapter02 database to the correct level for software changes added in chapter 4.

9.6.2 Handcoding SQL change scripts to migrate the database

Another approach is to create the SQL commands needed for a migration you
This option is attractive to developers who want to define the database in ways th.
Core can't. You can use this approach to set more-rigorous CHECK constraints o
umns, add stored procedures or user-defined functions, and so on via SQL script

The only disadvantage for a software developer is that you need to know en
SQL to write and edit the SQL change scripts. This requirement might put off
developers, but it's not as bad as you think, because you can look at the SQL EF
outputs to create a database and then tweak that SQL with your changes. Tabl
gives you an overview of this approach.

The job of creating an SQL change script is made easier by the migration scr
dbcontext command, which outputs the SQL commands that EF Core would u
create a new database (equivalent to calling the context.Database.EnsureCre
method). The following listing shows a small part of the SQL produced by the Ens
Created method, with the focus on the Review table and its indexes.

Table 9.4 A summary of the good, the bad, and the limitations of handcoding the SQL change scripts to migrate a database

	Notes
Good parts	▪ You have total control of the database structure, including parts that EF Core won't add, such as user-defined functions and column constraints.
Bad parts	▪ You must understand SQL commands such as CREATE TABLE. ▪ You must work out what the changes are yourself (but see the Tip row). ▪ There's no automatic migration remove script. ▪ This approach is not guaranteed to produce a correct migration (but see CompareEfSql in section 9.6.3).
Limitations	None
Tips	You can use the Script-DbContext migration command to get the actual SQL that EF Core would output and then look for the differences in the SQL from the previous database schema, which makes writing the SQL migrations much easier.
My verdict	This approach is for someone who knows SQL and wants complete control of the database. It certainly makes you think about the best settings for your database, which can improve performance.

Listing 9.8 Part of SQL generated by EnsureCreated when creating a database

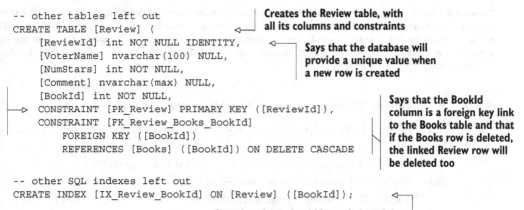

```
-- other tables left out
CREATE TABLE [Review] (
    [ReviewId] int NOT NULL IDENTITY,
    [VoterName] nvarchar(100) NULL,
    [NumStars] int NOT NULL,
    [Comment] nvarchar(max) NULL,
    [BookId] int NOT NULL,
    CONSTRAINT [PK_Review] PRIMARY KEY ([ReviewId]),
    CONSTRAINT [FK_Review_Books_BookId]
        FOREIGN KEY ([BookId])
        REFERENCES [Books] ([BookId]) ON DELETE CASCADE

-- other SQL indexes left out
CREATE INDEX [IX_Review_BookId] ON [Review] ([BookId]);
```

Creates the Review table, with all its columns and constraints

Says that the database will provide a unique value when a new row is created

Says that the BookId column is a foreign key link to the Books table and that if the Books row is deleted, the linked Review row will be deleted too

Says that there should be an index of the BookId foreign key to improve performance

Because you know what entity classes of EF Core configurations you have changed, you can find the appropriate part of the SQL that should reflect your changes. This information should help you write your SQL command, and you're more likely to write SQL change scripts that match what EF Core expects.

As with EF Core's migrations, you create a series of SQL change scripts that need to be applied to your database in order. To aid this process, you should name your

scripts with something that defines the order, such as a number or a sortable
Here are example SQL script names that I used for a client project:

```
Script001 - Create DatabaseRegions.sql
Script002 - Create Tenant table.sql
Script003 - TenantAddress table.sql
Script004 - AccountingCalenders table.sql
```

As well as being applied to the database in order, script names should be applied
once; I cover how in section 9.8.

Should I be writing a remove migrations for my SQL change scripts?

EF Core's migrations creates both the Up migration method and a Down migration
method. The Down method, which is known as a *reverting migration*, contains code
undo the Up migration. Some developers who move to SQL change scripts wo
about not having a remove migration feature.

The fact is that although it's great to have a way to remove a migration, you are
likely to use it much. EF Core can automatically produce a migration that reverts
migration, but when it comes to SQL change scripts, building a Down script isn't au
matic, so if you want a Down script, you have to write that SQL.

Therefore, I create a remove migration only if I need it, so any remove migration
another new SQL change script that reverts the last migration. But be warned: I
this only as a result of intensive testing of my migrations well before productio
because having to write a Down migration script because your production system
down due to a bad migration is a bit stressful!

9.6.3 *Checking that your SQL change scripts matches EF Core's database model*

I have used handcoded SQL change scripts in several projects, both in EF6 and EF (
and the main concern is making sure that my modifications to the database matc
Core's model of the database. So I created a tool, which I refer to as EfSchemaCom
that compares EF Core's model of the database with the schema of an actual data
Although EfSchemaCompare has some limitations, it provides good feedback or
ferences between a migrated database and EF Core's model of the database.

> **NOTE** I cover EF Core's model of the database, accessed by the Model prop-
> erty in your application's DbContext, in chapter 11.

Figure 9.6 shows how the EfSchemaCompare tool compares a database that has
updated by your SQL change scripts against EF Core's database model.

The EfSchemaCompare tool is available in my EfCore.SchemaCompare li
(see http://mng.bz/Yq2B). With this tool, I create unit tests that check my develop

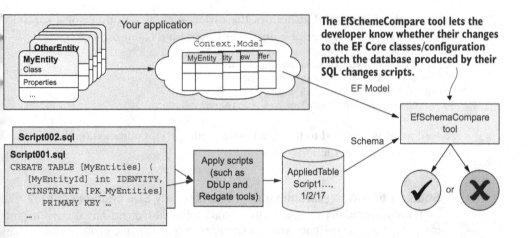

Figure 9.6 The EfSchemaCompare tool compares EF Core's model of the database, which it forms by looking at the entity classes and the application's DbContext configuration, with the database schema of a database that has been updated via your SQL change scripts. The tool outputs human-readable error messages if it finds a difference.

database—and, more important, my production database—to see whether the EF Core's database model has drifted away from the actual database schema.

Using EF Core's reverse-engineering tool

In some cases, you already have a database that you want to access via EF Core code. For this purpose, you need to apply the opposite of migrations and allow EF Core to produce your entity classes and application's DbContext by using your existing database as the template. This process is known as reverse engineering a database. This approach says that the database is the source of truth. You use EF Core's reverse-engineering tool, also known as scaffolding, to re-create the entity classes and the application's DbContext with all the required configurations. Table 9.5 gives you an overview of this approach, and figure 9.7 shows the process.

Table 9.5 A summary of the good, the bad, and the limitations of reverse-engineering a database as a way to access an existing database or continually update your entity classes and application DbContext to match a changed database

	Notes
Good parts	▪ The tool builds the EF Core code/classes from an existing database. ▪ The tool allows you to make the database the source of truth, and your EF Core code and classes are created and updated as the database schema changes.
Bad parts	▪ Your entity classes can't be edited easily, such as to change the way that the collections navigational properties are implemented. But see section 9.7.2 for a solution to this issue. ▪ The tool always adds navigational links at both ends of the relationship (see section 8.2).

Table 9.5 A summary of the good, the bad, and the limitations of reverse-engineering a databas‹ way to access an existing database or continually update your entity classes and application DbC to match a changed database *(continued)*

	Notes
Limitations	None
Tips	When you are going to repeatedly reverse engineer a database, I recommend usin‹ Visual Studio EF Core Power Tools extension, as it remembers the setting from the time you used the reverse-engineering feature.
My verdict	If you have an existing database that you need to access via EF Core, reverse engi‹ ing is going to save you a lot of time.

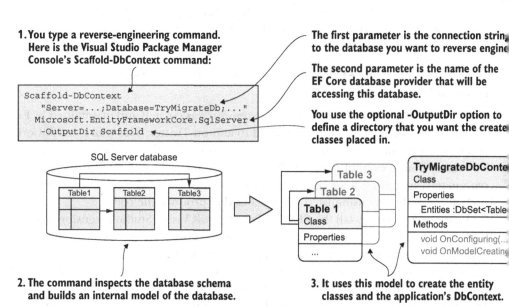

1. **You type a reverse-engineering command. Here is the Visual Studio Package Manager Console's Scaffold-DbContext command:**

```
Scaffold-DbContext
    "Server=...;Database=TryMigrateDb;..."
Microsoft.EntityFrameworkCore.SqlServer
    -OutputDir Scaffold
```

The first parameter is the connection strin‹ to the database you want to reverse engine‹

The second parameter is the name of the EF Core database provider that will be accessing this database.

You use the optional -OutputDir option to define a directory that you want the create‹ classes placed in.

2. **The command inspects the database schema and builds an internal model of the database.**

3. **It uses this model to create the entity classes and the application's DbContext.**

Figure 9.7 Typical use of EF Core's reverse-engineering command, which inspects the database found vi‹ database connection string and then generates the entity classes and the application's DbContext to matc‹ database. The command uses the foreign-key database relationships to build a fully defined relationship bet‹ the entity classes

You use this approach mainly when you want to build an EF Core application ar‹ an existing database, but I also describe a way to manage migrations. To start, look at how to run the reverse-engineering tool. You have two options:

- Run EF Core's reverse-engineering tool via a command line.
- Use the EF Core Power Tools Visual Studio extension.

Running EF Core's reverse-engineering command

You can reverse engineer a database from a command line (CLI tools) or Visual Studio's PMC window. CLI and PMC have different names and parameters. The following list shows the scaffold command to reverse engineer the BookApp database. Note that commands are run in the directory of the BookApp ASP.NET Core project and that the database connection string is in the appsettings.json file in that project:

- *CLI*—dotnet ef dbcontext scaffold name=DefaultConnection Microsoft
  .EntityFrameworkCore.SqlServer
- *PMC*—Scaffold-DbContext -Connection name=DefaultConnection -Provider
  Microsoft.EntityFrameworkCore.SqlServer

NOTE There are lots of commands, with multiple parameters, and it would take many pages to reproduce the EF Core's documentation. Therefore, I direct you to EF Core's command-line reference at http://mng.bz/MXEn.

Installing and running EF Core Power Tools reverse-engineering command

The EF Core Power Tools Visual Studio extension was created and maintained by Erik Ejlskov Jensen, known as @ErikEJ in GitHub and on Twitter. This tool uses EF Core's reverse-engineering service but provides a visual frontend to make it easier to use. This extension is helpful because the reverse-engineering code often needs lots of parameters, including long connection strings. Erik's tool also adds some features, such as the ability to customize the templates that produce the code.

First, you need to install the EF Core Power Tools Visual Studio extension. You can find the EF Core Power Tools at http://mng.bz/Gx0v. If you aren't familiar with installing Visual Studio extensions, see http://mng.bz/zxBB.

After you have installed the extension, right-click a project in Visual Studio's Solution Explorer. You should see a command called EF Core Power Tools, with a Reverse Engineering subcommand. Please read the EF Core Power Tools wiki in its GitHub repo (https://github.com/ErikEJ/EFCorePowerTools/wiki).

Updating your entity classes and DbContext when the database changes

One way to handle database changes is to migrate your database and then run the reverse-engineering tool to re-create your entity classes and application's DbContext. That way, you know that the database schema and EF Core's model are in step.

Using EF Core's reverse-engineering tool directly works, but you must remember all the settings for each run. The EF Core project has a feature on backlog (issue #831) that would try to preserve the current class and alter only the properties and relationships that changed. That sort of feature would be great, but it would be complex to implement, so it hasn't been considered for a while. Fortunately, EF Core Power Tools extension is a decent substitute.

EF Core Power Tools has been designed to make updating the entity classes application's DbContext easy, with nice features such as remembering your last ru adding a file to your project. I talked to Erik Ejlskov; he said he uses an SQL S database project (.sqlproj) to keep the SQL Server schema under source control the resulting SQL Server .dacpac files to update the database and EF Core P Tools to update the code.

For me, the downside of reverse engineering to handle migrations is that I easily change the design entity classes, such as to follow a DDD style (see chapter But you could use reverse engineering once to get the entity classes and DbCo and then swap over to use the EF Core code as the source of truth. Then you can the entity classes to the style you want, but after that, you would need to swap m ing your database via EF Core's migrations or SQL change scripts.

> **NOTE** Some of my experiments with reverse engineering show that EF Core's
> OnDelete configuration settings aren't quite what I expect; see EF Core issue
> #21252. When I asked Erik about this situation, his answer was along these
> lines: the database ON DELETE setting is right, and that's the important part.

9.8 Part 2: Applying your migrations to a database

Up to this point, you have been considering different ways to migrate a databas this section, you consider how to apply your migration to a database. The way tha create a migration influences how you can apply it. If you created your migratio using SQL change scripts, for example, you can't apply them by using EF C Migrate method. Here is a list of the techniques you will be evaluating in the re this chapter:

- Calling EF Core's Database.Migrate method from your main application
- Executing EF Core's Database.Migrate method from a standalone applic. designed only to migrate the database
- Applying an EF Core migration via an SQL change script and applying it database
- Applying SQL change scripts by using a migration tool

The other issue that affects how you migrate your database is the environment yo working in—specifically, the characteristics of the application that accesses the base being migrated, with special focus on your production system. The first ch teristic is whether you are running multiple instances of the application, suc multiple instances of an ASP.NET Core, which is known as scaled-out in Micr Azure. This characteristic is important because all the ways of applying a migratie a database rely on only one application's trying to change the database's schema. ing multiple instances running, therefore, rules out some of the simpler migr update techniques, such as running a migration when the application starts becau the multiple instances will try to run at the same time (but see @zejji's solution tc limitation in a note in section 9.8.1).

The second characteristic is whether the migration is applied while the current application is running. This situation happens if you have applications that need to be up all the time, such as email systems and sites that people want to access at any time, such as GitHub and Amazon. I refer to these types of applications as continuous-service applications.

Every migration applied to a database of a continuous-service application must not be an application-breaking change; the migrated database must still work with the currently running application code. If you add a non-nullable column with no default SQL value, for example, when the old application creates a new row, the database will reject it, as the old application didn't provide a value to fill in the new column. This application-breaking change must be split into a series of nonbreaking changes, as covered in section 9.9.2.

The following sections look at four ways to apply a migration to your database, with references to the application's characteristics. Some of the most complex issues related to database schema changes are covered in section 9.9.

Calling EF Core's Database.Migrate method from your main application

You saw this approach for ASP.NET Core in section 5.9.2, but to recap, you add some code that calls `context.Database.Migrate` before the main application starts. This approach is by far the easiest way to apply a migration, but it has a big limitation: you should not run multiple instances of the `Migrate` method at the same time. If your application has multiple instances running at the same time—the many app characteristic—you cannot use this approach. Table 9.6 provides an overview of this approach.

Table 9.6 A summary of the good, the bad, and the limitations of calling EF Core's `Database.Migrate` method from your main application

	Notes
Good parts	• This approach is relatively easy to implement. • It ensures that the database is up to date before your application runs.
Bad parts	• You must *not* run two or more `Migrate` methods in parallel. • There is a small period when your application isn't responding; see the note after this table. • If the migration has an error, your application won't be available. • It can be hard to diagnose startup errors.
Limitations	This approach does not work if multiple instances of the application are running (but see @zejji's solution to this limitation after this note).
Tips	For ASP.NET Core applications, I still recommend applying the migration in your CI/CD pipeline, even if you expect to run only one instance of the web app (see section 9.8.2), because your app won't be deployed if the migration fails, and you will be ready to scale out if you need to.
My verdict	If you can guarantee that only one instance of your application is starting up at any one time, this approach is a simple solution to migrating your database. Unfortunately, that situation isn't typical for websites and local applications.

NOTE This approach assumes that you are deploying your application without using any continuously running features, such as Azure Web App slots and swapping. In that case, the old application will be stopped before the new application starts. During that (brief) time, any accesses to the application will fail, possibly losing the data that they were editing.

The BookApp in the associated GitHub repo uses this approach, which means you can run the application on your development machine, and it will create the base for you automatically (if you have localdb installed), which shows how usefu. But for applications that you need to scale out, this approach isn't going to work.

NOTE The GitHub user @zejji posted an approach that ensures that the Migrate method is called only once in an application that has multiple instances running at the same time. This approach overcomes one of the problems of calling the Migrate method on startup; see http://mng.bz/VGw0.

FINDING WHAT MIGRATIONS THE DATABASE.MIGRATE METHOD WILL APPLY TO THE DATABASE

When you use the context.Database.Migrate method to migrate a database may want to run some C# code if a certain migration is applied. I used this techr to fill in a new property/column added in a certain migration. You can find what migrations are going to be applied to the database by calling the GetPend Migrations method before you call the Migrate method and the method called AppliedMigrations to get the migrations that have been applied to the database

Both methods return a set of strings of the filenames that hold the migra BookApp, for example, has a migration class called InitialMigration, which is file called something like 20200507081623_InitialMigration. The following listing s how you might detect that the InitialMigration had been applied so that you run your C# code on the migrated database.

Listing 9.9 Detecting what migrations have been applied to the database

You call the migration method to apply any missing migrations to the database.

You use the extension method to find whether the InitialMigration was added to the database.

```
context.Database.Migrate();
if (context.CheckIfMigrationWasApplied(nameof(InitialMigration)))
{
    //... run your C# code for this specific migration
}
//Extension method to detect a specific migration was applied
public static bool CheckIfMigrationWasApplied(
    this DbContext context, string className)
{
    return context.Database.GetAppliedMigrations()
        .Any(x => x.EndsWith(className));
}
```

Code that m run after the Migration h.

Simple extension me detect a specific mi from the class name

The GetAppliedMigrati method returns a filer for each migration app to the database.

All the filenames end with the class name, so we return true if any filename ends with className.

I have used this approach to good effect, but be warned that if your C# code takes too long in a ASP.NET Core application, your web server may time out the application, in which case your extra C# migration update code would be stopped in the middle of its work.

Executing EF Core's Database.Migrate method from a standalone application

Instead of running the migration as part of your startup code, you can create a standalone application to apply a migration to your databases. You could add a console application project to your solution, for example, using your application's DbContext to call the context.Database.Migrate method when it's run, possibly taking the database connection string as a parameter. Another option is calling the CLI command dotnet ef database update, which in EF Core 5 can take a connection string. This approach can be applied when the application is running or when it is stopped. This section assumes that the application is stopped. In section 9.9, I cover the approach to use while the application is running. Table 9.7 gives you an overview of this approach.

Table 9.7 A summary of the good, the bad, and the limitations of executing EF Core's Database.Migrate method from a standalone application

	Notes
Good parts	• If the migration fails, you get good feedback from the migration. • This approach overcomes the problem that the Migrate method isn't thread safe.
Bad parts	• Your application is down while the migration is applied. (But see section 9.9 for an example of migrating a database while the application is running.)
Limitations	None
My verdict	This option is a good one if you have multiple instances of your application. In your CI/CD pipeline, for example, you could stop the current applications, run one of EF Core's Migrate commands (such as dotnet ef database update), and then upload and start your new application.

If no applications are accessing the database, perhaps because they have all stopped, there are no issues involved in applying your migration to the database. This approach is what I call a *down for maintenance migration*; see figure 9.8 for details.

Applying an EF Core's migration via an SQL change script

In some cases, you want to use EF Core's migrations, but you want to check the migrations or apply them via SQL change scripts. You can get EF Core to create SQL change scripts, but watch out for a few things if you take this approach. The default SQL change script produced by EF Core, for example, contains only the script to update the database, with no check of whether a migration has already been applied. The reason is that developers normally apply SQL change scripts via some sort of deployment system that handles the job of working out what migrations need to be applied to the base being migrated. Table 9.8 gives you an overview of this approach.

NOTE There is also a way to output a script that checks whether the migration has been applied, which is covered at the end of this section.

Table 9.8 A summary of the good, the bad, and the limitations of applying an EF Core's migration an SQL change scripts

	Notes
Good parts	▪ EF Core will build your migrations for you and then give you the migration as SQL ▪ The SQL scripts generated by EF Core update the migration history table.
Bad parts	▪ You need an application to apply the migrations to your databases.
Limitations	None
Tips	▪ Be aware that the individual migrations don't check whether the migration has be applied to the database. This approach assumes that some other application is ing track of the migrations. ▪ If you need a migration that checks whether it has already been applied to the d base, you need to add the idempotent parameter to the command.
My verdict	If you want to check/sign off a migration or use a more comprehensive app/databa deployment system, such as Octopus Deploy or a RedGate product, this approach i way to go.

The basic command to turn the latest migration into an SQL script is

- *CLI*—dotnet ef migrations script
- *PMC*—Script-Migration

These two commands output the SQL for the last migration with no check of wh that migration has been applied to the database. But when you add the idempo parameter to these commands, the SQL code that they produce contains chec the migration history table and applies only migrations that haven't been appli the database.

NOTE There are lots of commands, with multiple parameters, and it would take many pages to reproduce the EF Core's documentation. Therefore, I direct you to EF Core's command-line reference at http://mng.bz/MXEn.

Since the EF Core 5 release, the SQL script created by the Script-Migration mand has applied a migration within an SQL transaction. The whole of the migr: will be applied to the database unless there is an error, in which case none o migration will be applied.

WARNING SQLite has some limitations on applying a migration in one transaction because some of the migration commands use transactions themselves, which means that a migration that fails may have applied part of the changes.

Applying SQL change scripts by using a migration tool

If you have gone for the SQL-change-scripts approach, it's likely that you already know how you will apply these change scripts to the database. You will need to use a migration tool such as DbUp (open source) or free or commercial tools such as RedGate's flyaway. Typically, these migration tools have their own version of EF Core migration history table. (DbUp calls this table SchemaVersions.)

How you implement the migration depends on the migration tool you use. DbUp, for example, is a NuGet package, so you can use it the same way as EF Core's `Migrate` method: call it on startup or as a separate application in your CI/CD pipeline, and so on. Other migration tools may not be callable from NET Core but use some form of command line or deployment pipeline integration. Table 9.9 gives you an overview of this approach.

Table 9.9 A summary of the good, the bad, and the limitations of applying SQL change scripts by using a migration tool

	Notes
Good parts	■ The tool works in all situations. ■ It works well with deployment systems.
Bad parts	■ You must manage the scripts yourself and make sure that their names define the order in which they will be applied.
Limitations	None
Tips	When I used this approach, I did a unit test to see whether a migrated test database matched EF Core's internal model by using my EfSchemaCompare tool (see section 9.6.3).
My verdict	I used SQL change scripts and DbUp in a couple of client projects, and they worked well. With some of the improvements in EF Core, I might be tempted back to using EF Core migrations.

Migrating a database while the application is running

Section 9.8 started a definition of two characteristics of the application that is accessing the database, and one of them was whether an application always needs to be available (a continuous-service application). Migrating a database while the application is running requires some extra work, which is covered in this section.

To start, let's compare the two types of applications: one that can be stopped for a migration or software update and one that must continue to provide a service while it's being updated (figure 9.8).

The rest of this section discusses how to migrate a database on a continuous-service application. There are two situations:

- The migration doesn't contain any changes that would cause the currently running application (referred to as the original app) to fail.
- The migration contains changes that would cause the original app to fail (application-breaking changes).

"Down for maintenance" approach

At some point the service is not available, and users will be rejected.

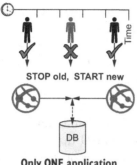

Continuous service approach

Even during a migration the service is still available.

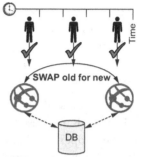

Figure 9.8   The example on the left is what happens if you replace the old application with a new application—in this case, also including a database migration. In this scenario, there is a period of time, known as *down time*, when neither the old or the new application is running, so there is a possibility of a user's request being lost or rejected. The example on the right has an existing application providing a service, and a new version of the application is run up, ready to take over. When the new application starts, it applies a migration to the database. When the new application is ready, a "swap" occurs, and it seamlessly takes over the service.

Things to consider when stopping an application for a database update

You need to consider what will happen if you stop an application abruptly. That eve could cause users to lose irretrievable data, or a user of an e-commerce site cou lose their order. For this reason, you should consider a warning or soft stop.

I had this problem on an e-commerce system I built some years ago and develop a "down for maintenance" approach. This approach provided an onscreen warning users, indicating that the site would close in a certain number of minutes. During t closing, I showed a "This site is down for maintenance" page and stopped users fro accessing any pages. You can read about this project at http://mng.bz/mXkN, but I warned: I built it in 2016 with ASP.NET MVC.

Another way to softly stop your application is to provide read-only access to the da base. You disable every method that could update the database. The application still reading the database, so you can't change the existing database structures, b you can add new tables and safely copy data into them. After you've loaded the ne application, you can apply another database schema update to remove the databa parts that are no longer needed.

Handling a migration that doesn't contain an application-breaking change

When I'm working on a new application with a new database, I tend to grow the database schema as the project progresses, perhaps by adding new tables that the previous versions of the software don't know about. These types of additions normally don't create migration, which breaks the application that is running in production. With a little bit of extra work, you can often make migrations that can be easily applied to a continuous-service application. Here are some issues to consider:

- If you're adding a new scalar property to an existing table, the old application won't set it. That's OK, because SQL will give it a default value. But what default do you want the property to have? You can control that setting by setting an SQL default value for the column (see chapter 10) or make it nullable. That way, the existing application running in production won't fail if you create a new row.
- If you're adding a new foreign-key column to an existing table, you need to make that foreign key nullable and have the correct cascade-delete settings. That approach allows the old application to add a new row to that table without the foreign-key constraint's reporting an error.

TIP Testing a (supposedly) nonbreaking database change that alters columns in existing tables is highly recommended, especially if you're going to a production database.

Some of these issues, such as making a column nullable when it would normally be non-nullable, might require a second migration to change the nullability of the database columns when your new application is in place. This situation leads to the multiple-step migration approach for dealing with application breaking changes.

Handling application-breaking changes when you can't stop the app

Applying an application breaking migration to a continuous-service application is one of the most complicated migrations there is. In fact, a couple of developers I talked to who work on continuous-service applications try hard to avoid an application-breaking migration. As I said in section 9.9.1, nonbreaking changes are the norm, so you might consider a "down for maintenance" approach for the (rare?) application-breaking changes. But if you really do need to apply an application-breaking change to your continuous-service application, read on.

As an example, you are going to consider to handle a database migration that moves columns from an Users table to a new Addresses table. In the original migration in section 9.5.2, this "move columns" issue was done by one migration, but it worked only because the original application was stopped, and after the migration finished, the new application ran.

For a continuous-service application, the move-columns task must be broken i series of stages so that each migration doesn't break the two applications that are ning at the same time. As a result, we end up with three migrations:

- ADD—The first migration is applied while App1 is currently running and new database features that the new interim application (App2) needs to ru
- COPY—The second migration is applied after App1 has stopped and b App3, the target application, has started. This migration copies the data final format.
- SUBTRACT—The last migration is a clean-up, which runs only when App stopped and App3 has taken over. At this point, it can remove the old table columns that are now redundant.

The ADD and then SUBTRACT migrations, with maybe a COPY in the middle, repr the common approach to applying breaking changes to continuous-service ap tions. At no time should the database be incorrect for two applications that are ning. In this example, you have five stages, as shown in figure 9.9.

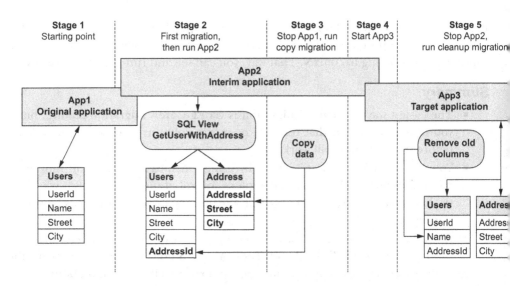

Figure 9.9 The five stages of turning an application-breaking migration so that the database isn't out of with the two applications that are running at the time. The first migration changes the database so that A can work with App1; the next changes the database so that App3 can work with App2; and the final migra cleans up the database.

Here is a detailed breakdown of these stages:

- *Stage 1*—This stage is the starting point, with the original application, A running.

- *Stage 2*—This stage is the most complex one. It does the following:
  - a Runs a migration that creates a new Addresses table and links it to the current user.
  - b Adds an SQL View that returns a User with their address from either the old Users' Street/City columns or from the new Address table.
  - c The interim application, App2, uses the SQL View to read the User, but if it needs to add or update a User's address, it will use the new Address table.
- *Stage 3*—App1 is stopped, so there is no possibility that new addresses will be added to the Users table. At this point, the second migration runs and copies any address data in the Users table to the new Addresses table.
- *Stage 4*—At this point, the target application, App3, can be run; it gets a User's address only from the new Addresses table.
- *Stage 5*—App2 is stopped, so nothing is accessing the address part of the old User's table. This stage is when the last migration runs, cleaning up the database by removing the Street and City columns from the Users table, deleting the SQL View needed by App2, and fixing the User/Address relationship as required.

I could list all the code and migrations for this example, but to save space, I emulated this multistage migration in an unit test called Ch09_FiveStepsMigration, which you can find at http://mng.bz/0m2N. That way, you can see and run the whole process.

Summary

- The easiest way to create a migration is via EF Core's migration feature, but if you have a migration that removes or moves columns, you need to hand-edit before the migration will work.
- You can build SQL change scripts by using a database comparison tool or by hand. This approach gives you complete control of the database. But you need to check that your SQL change scripts create a database that matches EF Core's internal model of the database.
- If you have an existing database, you can use EF Core's scaffold command or the more visual EF Core Power Tools Visual Studio extension to create the entity classes and the application's DbContext with all its configurations.
- Updating a production database is a serious undertaking, especially if data could be lost in the process. How you apply migration to a production system depends on the type of migration and certain characteristics of your application.
- There are several ways to apply a migration to a database. The simplest approach has significant limitations, but the complex approaches can handle all migration requirements.
- Applying migration to a database while the application is running requires extra work, especially if the migration changes the database schema to the point that the current application will fail.

For readers who are familiar with EF6:

- EF Core's migration feature is significantly changed and improved, but an who has done EF6 migrations shouldn't have a problem swapping to EF C migration system.
- There's no automatic migration in EF Core; you control when a migr happens.
- It's easier to combine EF Core's migrations in a multiperson team.

Configuring advanced features and handling concurrency conflicts

This chapter covers

- Using an SQL user-defined function in EF Core queries
- Configuring columns to have default values or computed values
- Configuring SQL column properties on databases not created by EF Core
- Handling concurrency conflicts

This chapter discusses several advanced configuration features that interact directly with your SQL database, such as using SQL *user-defined functions* (UDFs) and computed columns. These features allow you to move some of your calculations or settings into the SQL database. Although you won't use these features every day, they can be useful in specific circumstances.

The second half of this chapter is about handling multiple, near-simultaneous updates of the same piece of data in the database; these updates can cause problems known as *concurrency conflicts*. You'll learn how to configure one property/column or a whole entity/table to catch concurrency conflicts, as well as how to capture and then write code to correct the concurrency conflict.

10.1 DbFunction: Using user-defined functions (UDFs) with EF Core

SQL has a feature called UDFs that allows you to write SQL code that will be r
the database server. UDFs are useful because you can move a calculation from
software into the database, which can be more efficient because it can access the
base directly. UDFs can return a single result, which is referred to as *scalar-valued*
tion, and one that can return multiple data in a result, known as a *table-valued fun*
EF Core supports both types of UDFs.

> **DEFINITION** An SQL *user-defined function* (UDF) is a routine that accepts
> parameters, performs an SQL action (such as a complex calculation), and
> returns the result of that action as a value. The return value can be a scalar
> (single) value or a table. UDFs differ from *SQL stored procedures* (StoredProc)
> in that UDFs can only query a database, whereas a StoredProc can change the
> database.

UDFs are useful, especially when you want to improve the performance of an EF
query. I found some SQL (see https://stackoverflow.com/a/194887/1434764) t
quicker than EF Core at creating a comma-delimited string of authors' name
instead of having to convert the whole of the Book App's book list query to S
could replace only the part that returns the authors' names as a comma-delir
string. The steps for using a UDF in EF Core are as follows:

Configuration:

1 Define a method that has the correct name, input parameters, and output
   that matches the definition of your UDF. This method acts as a referen
   your UDF.
2 Declare the method in the application's DbContext or (optionally) in a
   rate class if it's a scalar UDF.
3 Add the EF Core configuration commands to map your static UDF refer
   method to a call to your UDF code in the database.

Database setup:

4 Manually add your UDF code to the database by using some form of
   command.

Use:

5 Now you can use the static UDF reference in a query. EF Core will conver
   method to a call to your UDF code in the database.

With that process in mind, let's detail the three stages: configuration, database s
and use.

> **NOTE** The configuration and database-setup stages can be applied in any
> order, but both must be applied before you can use your UDF in a query.

.1 Configuring a scalar-valued UDF

The configuration for a scalar-valued UDF consists of defining a method to represent your UDF and then registering that method with EF Core at configuration time. For this example, you're going to produce a UDF called AverageVotes that works out the average review votes for a book. AverageVotes takes in the primary key of the book you want to calculate for and returns a nullable double value—null if no reviews exist or the average value of the review votes if there are reviews.

You can define the UDF representation as a static or nonstatic method. Nonstatic definitions need to be defined in your application's DBContext; the static version can be placed in a separate class. I tend to use static definitions because I don't want to clutter the application's DBContext class with extra code. Figure 10.1 shows the static method that will represent the AverageVotes UDF in your software, with rules for forming this method.

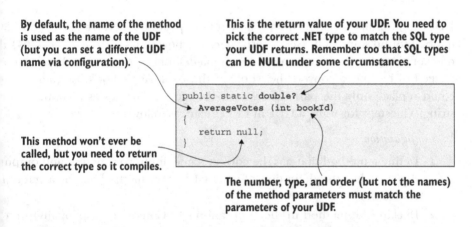

By default, the name of the method is used as the name of the UDF (but you can set a different UDF name via configuration).

This is the return value of your UDF. You need to pick the correct .NET type to match the SQL type your UDF returns. Remember too that SQL types can be NULL under some circumstances.

```
public static double?
    AverageVotes (int bookId)
{
    return null;
}
```

This method won't ever be called, but you need to return the correct type so it compiles.

The number, type, and order (but not the names) of the method parameters must match the parameters of your UDF.

Figure 10.1 An example static method that will represent your UDF inside your EF Core code. The callouts highlight the parts that EF Core will use to map any calls to your UDF code and the rules that you need to follow when building your own method to map to your UDF.

NOTE The UDF representation method is used to define the signature of the UDF in the database: it will never be called as a NET method.

You can register your static UDF representation method with EF Core by using either of the following:

- DbFunction attribute
- Fluent API

You can use the DbFunction attribute if you place the method representing the UDF inside your application's DbContext. In the example shown in the following listing, the DbFunction attribute and the static method are in bold.

Listing 10.1 Using a `DbFunction` attribute with a static method inside DbConte

```
public class Chapter08EfCoreContext : DbContext
{
    public DbSet<Book> Books { get; set; }
    //... other code removed for clarity

    public Chapter08EfCoreContext(
        DbContextOptions<Chapter08EfCoreContext> options)
        : base(options) {}
```
The DbFunction attribute defines the method as being a representation of your UDF.
```
    [DbFunction]
    public static double? AverageVotes(int id)
    {
        return null;
    }
```
The return value, the method name, and the number, type, and order of the method parameter must match your UDF c

The method is never called, but you need the right type for the code to compile.
```
    protected override void
        OnModelCreating(ModelBuilder modelBuilder)
    {
        //... no Fluent API needed
    }
}
```
If you use the DbFunction attribute, you don't need any Fluent API to register the static method.

The other approach is to use the Fluent API to register the method as a UDF r sentation. The advantage of this approach is that you can place the method in class, which makes sense if you have a lot of UDFs. This listing shows the Fluen approach for the same method, `AverageVotes`, but it's defined in a class called My Methods, as shown in figure 10.1.

Listing 10.2 Registering your static method representing your UDF using Fluent AF

```
protected override void
    OnModelCreating(ModelBuilder modelBuilder)
{
    //... other configuration removed for clarity

    modelBuilder.HasDbFunction(
        () => MyUdfMethods.AverageVotes(default(int)))
        .HasSchema("dbo");
}
```
Fluent API is placed inside th OnModelCreating method ins your application's DbContext

HasDbFunction w register your met as the way to acce your UDF.

Adds a call to your static method representation of your UDF code

You can add options. Here, you add HasSchema (not needed in this case); other options include HasName.

After you've used either of these configuration approaches, EF Core knows ho access your UDF in a query.

.2 Configuring a table-valued UDF

EF Core 5 has added support for table-valued UDFs, which allow you to return multiple values in the same way that querying a table returns multiple values. The difference from querying a normal table is that the table-valued UDF can execute SQL code inside the database, using the parameters you provide to the UDF.

The table UDF example returns three values: the Book's Title, the number of Reviews, and the average Review Votes for the Book. This example needs a class to be defined that will accept the three values coming back from the table-valued UDF, as shown in the following code snippet:

```
public class TableFunctionOutput
{
    public string Title { get; set; }
    public int ReviewsCount { get; set; }
    public double? AverageVotes { get; set; }
}
```

Unlike a scalar UDF, a table UDF can be defined in only one way—within your application's DbContext—because it needs access to a method inside the DbContext class called FromExpression (called CreateQuery before EF Core 5). What you are doing is defining the name and signature of the table-valued UDF: the name, the return type, and the parameters' type all must match your UTF. The following listing shows how you define the signature of your table UDF.

Listing 10.3 Defining a table-valued UDF within your application's DbContext

```
public class Chapter10EfCoreContext : DbContext
{
    public DbSet<Book> Books { get; set; }
    //… other code removed for clarity

    public Chapter10EfCoreContext(
        DbContextOptions<Chapter10EfCoreContext> options)
        : base(options) {}

    public IQueryable<TableFunctionOutput>
        GetBookTitleAndReviewsFiltered(int minReviews)
    {
        return FromExpression(() =>
            GetBookTitleAndReviewsFiltered(minReviews));
    }

    protected override void
        OnModelCreating(ModelBuilder modelBuilder)
    {

        modelBuilder.Entity<TableFunctionOutput>()
            .HasNoKey();
```

The return value, the method name, and the parameters type must match your UDF code.

The ssion e the vable sult.

You place the signature of the method within the FromExpression parameter.

You must configure the TableFunctionOutput class as not having a primary key.

```
modelBuilder.HasDbFunction(() =>
    GetBookTitleAndReviewsFiltered(default(int)));
//… other configurations left out
    }
}
```

You regist⟨
your UDF
method by⟨
the Fluent⟨

It might seem strange that you call the method within itself, but remember tha⟨
are only defining the signature of your UDF. EF Core will replace the inner me⟨
call with a call to your UDF when you use it in a query.

10.1.3 Adding your UDF code to the database

Before you can use the UDF you've configured, you need to get your UDF code⟨
the database. A UDF normally is a set of SQL commands that run on the databa⟨
you need to add your UDF code to the database manually before you call the UD⟨

The first way is by adding a UDF by using EF Core's migration feature. To do⟨
you use the migrationBuilder.Sql method described in section 9.5.2. In chapte⟨
I use two UDFs to improve the performance of the Book App; I added those UD⟨
the database by editing a migration and then added code to create the two UDFs⟨

Another approach is to add a UDF by using EF Core's ExecuteSqlRaw or Exec⟨
SqlInterpolated method, covered in section 11.5. This approach is more ap⟨
ble to unit testing than to production use where you aren't using migratio⟨
create your database, in which case you must add the UDFs manually. The follo⟨
listing uses EF Core's ExecuteSqlRaw command to add the SQL code that de⟨
the AverageVotes UDF.

Listing 10.4 Adding your UDF to the database via the ExecuteSqlRaw method

```
public const string UdfAverageVotes =
    nameof(MyUdfMethods.AverageVotes);

context.Database.ExecuteSqlRaw(
    $"CREATE FUNCTION {UdfAverageVotes} (@bookId int)" +
    @"  RETURNS float
    AS
    BEGIN
    DECLARE @result AS float
    SELECT @result = AVG(CAST([NumStars] AS float))
        FROM dbo.Review AS r
        WHERE @bookId = r.BookId
    RETURN @result
    END");
```

Captures the name of the static
method that represents your UDF
and uses it as the name of the
UDF you add to the database

Uses EF Core's
ExecuteSqlRaw
method to add
the UDF to the
database

The SQL code
that follows a⟨
a UDF to an S⟨
server databa⟨

This code should be executed before your EF Core queries call the UDF. As I⟨
chapter 9 gives more details on how to do this properly in a production environm⟨

> **NOTE** I have not listed the table UDF SQL code in this chapter. You can find⟨
> the method called AddUdfToDatabase in the repo at http://mng.bz/pJQz.

.4 Using a registered UDF in your database queries

Having registered the UDF as mapped to your method and added your UDFs to the database, you're ready to use UDFs in a database query. You can use this method as a return variable or as part of the query filter or sorting. The following listing has a query that includes a call to a scalar-values UDF that returns information about a book, including the average review votes.

Listing 10.5 Using a scalar-valued UDF in a EF Core query

```
var bookAndVotes = context.Books.Select(x => new Dto        ◁──┐  A normal EF Core
{                                                               │  query on the
    BookId = x.BookId,                                          │  Books table
    Title = x.Title,
    AveVotes = MyUdfMethods.AverageVotes(x.BookId)          ◁──   Calls your scalar
}).ToList();                                                       valued UDF by using its
                                                                  representing method
```

This listing produces the following SQL code to run on the database, with the UDF call in bold:

```
SELECT [b].[BookId], [b].[Title],
[dbo].AverageVotes([b].[BookId]) AS [AveVotes]
FROM [Books] AS [b]
```

> **NOTE** EF Core can calculate the average without using a UDF via the LINQ command x.Reviews.Average(q => (double?)q.NumStars). The calculation of the average votes is a running theme in this book, so you use it in the AverageVotes UDF example too.

A table-valued UDF requires a class to return the multiple values. The following code snippet shows a call to our GetBookTitleAndReviewsFiltered table-valued UDF:

```
var result = context.GetBookTitleAndReviewsFiltered(4)
    .ToList()
```

Scalar and table UDFs can also be used in any part of an EF Core query, as return values or for sorting or filtering. Here's another example, in which your scalar-valued UDF returns only books whose average review is 2.5 or better:

```
var books = context.Books
    .Where(x =>
        MyUdfMethods.AverageVotes(x.BookId) >= 2.5)
    .ToList();
```

10.2 Computed column: A dynamically calculated column value

Another useful SQL-side feature is a computed column (also known as a *generat* *umn*). The main reason for using computed columns is to move some of the ca tion—such as some string concatenations—into the database to improve perform Another good use of computed columns is to return a useful value based on othe umns in the row. An SQL computed column containing [TotalPrice] AS (NumB BookPrice), for example, would return the total price for that order, making yo code easier to write.

> **EF6** You can use computed columns in EF6.x, but EF6.x can't create them for you, so you have to add them via a direct SQL command. EF Core now provides a configuration method to define computed columns so that when EF Core creates or migrates a database, it'll add the computed column.

A *computed column* is a column in a table whose value is calculated by using othe umns in the same row and/or an SQL built-in function. You can also call syster UDFs (see section 10.1) with columns as parameters, which gives you a wide ran features.

There are two versions of SQL *computed columns:*

- One that does the calculation every time the column is read. I refer to this as a *dynamic computed column* in this section.
- One that does the calculation only when the entity is updated. This type called *persisted computed column* or *stored generated column.* Not all databases port persisted computed columns.

As an example of both types of SQL computed columns, you'll use a dynamic puted column to get only the year of the person's birth from a backing field that I the date of birth. This example mimics the code in section 7.14.3 that hides the birth date, but now the date-to-year code is done in the SQL database.

The second example of SQL computed columns is a persisted computed col that fixes the problem of not using lambda properties in entity classes (see section In that example, you had a FullName property, which was formed by combining FirstName and LastName properties, but you couldn't use a lambda property, a Core can't filter/order on a lambda property. When you use a persisted comp column, however, the computed column is updated whenever the row is upd and you can use the FullName column in any filter, order, search, and similar o tion. You declare the properties in the normal way in the class, as shown in the lowing listing, but because the computed columns are read-only, you make setter private.

Listing 10.6   `Person` entity class with two computed column properties

```
public class Person
{
    public int PersonId { get; set; }
    public int YearOfBirth { get; private set; }

    [MaxLength(50)]
    public string FirstName { get; set; }
    [MaxLength(50)]
    public string LastName { get; set; }
    [MaxLength(101)]
    public string FullName { get; private set; }

    //other properties/methods left out...
}
```

> Because you want to add an index to the FullName, you need make it and its parts fewer than 450 characters.

Then you need to configure the two computed columns and the index. The only way to configure columns is to use the Fluent API. This listing shows the various configurations for the `Person` entity class.

Listing 10.7   Configuring two computed columns, one persistent, and an index

```
public class PersonConfig : IEntityTypeConfiguration<Person>
{
    public void Configure
        (EntityTypeBuilder<Person> entity)
    {
        entity.Property<DateTime>("_dateOfBirth")
            .HasColumnName("DateOfBirth");

        entity.Property(p => p.YearOfBirth)
            .HasComputedColumnSql(
                "DatePart(yyyy, [DateOfBirth])");

        entity.Property(p => p.FullName)
            .HasComputedColumnSql(
                "[FirstName] + ' ' + [LastName]",
                stored:true);

        entity.HasIndex(x => x.FullName);
    }
}
```

> Configures the backing field, with the column name DateOfBirth

> Configures the property as a computed column and provides the SQL code that the database server will run

> Makes this computed column a persisted computed column

Figure 10.2 shows what happens when you update the Person table. EF Core knows that the table contains a computed column, so it reads the value back after an add or update.

NOTE To focus this figure on a single computed column, I show only the YearOfBirth column value, but in reality, the YearOfBirth and FullName column values are fed back because the `Person` entity class has two computed columns.

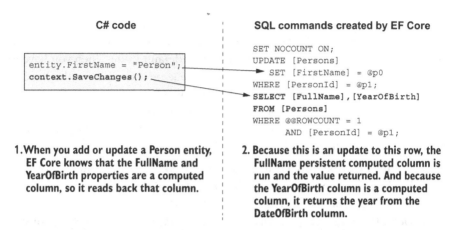

C# code

```
entity.FirstName = "Person";
context.SaveChanges();
```

SQL commands created by EF Core

```
SET NOCOUNT ON;
UPDATE [Persons]
    SET [FirstName] = @p0
WHERE [PersonId] = @p1;
SELECT [FullName],[YearOfBirth]
FROM [Persons]
WHERE @@ROWCOUNT = 1
        AND [PersonId] = @p1;
```

1. When you add or update a Person entity, EF Core knows that the FullName and YearOfBirth properties are a computed column, so it reads back that column.

2. Because this is an update to this row, the FullName persistent computed column is run and the value returned. And because the YearOfBirth column is a computed column, it returns the year from the DateOfBirth column.

Figure 10.2   Because EF Core knows that FullName and YearOfBirth are computed columns, it'll read back the values in these two columns into the entity that took part in an addition or update to the row. The FullName will have changed because this operation is an update to the row, and the YearOfBirth column is always recalculated, so it is also returned.

The dynamic computed column is recalculated on each read: for simple calcula† the compute time will be minimal, but if you call a UDF that accesses the database time taken to read the data from the database can increase. Using a persisted puted column overcomes this problem. Both types of computed columns can ha index in some database types, but each database type has limitations and restric† SQL Server doesn't allow an index on computed columns whose value came fr date function, for example.

10.3 Setting a default value for a database column

When you first create a .NET type, it has a default value: 0 for an int, null string, and so on. Sometimes, it's useful to set a different default value for a ɪ erty. If you asked someone their favorite color, but they didn't reply, you could vide the default string not given instead of the normal null value. You could se default value in .NET by using the C# 6.0 autoproperty initializer feature with such as this:

```
public string Answer { get; set; } = "not given";
```

But with EF Core, you have two other ways to set a default value. First, you can co ure EF Core to set up a default value within the database by using the HasDefa Value Fluent API method. This method changes the SQL code used to create table in the database and adds an SQL DEFAULT command containing your de value for that column if no value is provided. Generally, this approach is useful if are added to your database via raw SQL commands, as raw SQL often relies or SQL DEFAULT command for columns that the SQL INSERT doesn't provide value

The second approach is to create your own code that will create a default value for a column if no value is provided. This approach requires you to write a class that inherits the ValueGenerator class, which will calculate a default value. Then you have to configure the property or properties to use your ValueGenerator class via the Configure Fluent API method. This approach is useful when you have a common format for certain type of values, such as creating a unique string for a user's order of books.

Before exploring each approach, let's define a few things that EF Core's default value-setting methods have in common:

- Defaults can be applied to properties, backing fields, and shadow properties. We'll use the generic term *column* to cover all three types, because they all end up being applied to a column in the database.
- Default values (int, string, DateTime, GUID, and so on) apply only to scalar (nonrelational) columns.
- EF Core will provide a default value only if the property contains the CLR default value appropriate to its type. If a property of type int has the value 0, for example, it's a candidate for some form of provided default value, but if the property's value isn't 0, that nonzero value will be used.
- EF Core's default value methods work at the entity-instance level, not the class level. The defaults won't be applied until you've called SaveChanges or (in the case of the value generator) when you use the Add command to add the entity.

To be clear: default values happen only on new rows added to the database, not to updates. You can configure EF Core to add a default value in three ways:

- Using the HasDefaultValue method to add a constant value for a column
- Using the HasDefaultValueSql method to add an SQL command for a column
- Using the HasValueGenerator method to assign a value generator to a property

EF6 These three methods for setting a default value are new to EF Core. EF6.x has no equivalent commands.

.1 Using the HasDefaultValue method to add a constant value for a column

The first approach tells EF Core to add the SQL DEFAULT command to a column when it creates a database migration, providing a simple constant to be set on a column if a new row is created and the property mapped to that column has a default value. You can add the SQL DEFAULT command to a column only via a Fluent API method called HasDefaultValue. The following code sets a default date of 1 January 2000 to the column DateOfBirth in the SQL table called People.

Listing 10.8 Configuring a property to have a default value set inside the SQL database

```
protected override void OnModelCreating
    (ModelBuilder modelBuilder)
{
```
> You must configure the setting of a default value via Fluent API commands.

```
modelBuilder.Entity<DefaultTest>()
    .Property("DateOfBirth")
    .HasDefaultValue(new DateTime(2000,1,1));
//... other configurations left out
}
```

You add an SQL DEFAULT to a column via the **HasDefaultValue method**

If the SQL code that EF Core produces is asked to create/migrate an SQL Server base, it looks like the following SQL snippet, with the default constraint in bold:

```
CREATE TABLE [Defaults] (
    [Id] int NOT NULL IDENTITY,
    -- other columns left out
    [DateOfBirth] datetime2 NOT NULL
            DEFAULT '2000-01-01T00:00:00.000',
    CONSTRAINT [PK_Defaults] PRIMARY KEY ([Id])
);
```

If the column in a new entity has the CLR default value, EF Core doesn't prov value for that column in the SQL INSERT, which means that the database serve apply the default constraint of the column definition to provide a value to insert the new row.

> **NOTE** If you are working with a database not created by EF Core, you still need to register the configuration because EF Core must not set that column if the value in the related property contains the CLR default value for that type.

10.3.2 *Using the HasDefaultValueSql method to add an SQL command for a column*

Providing a constant default value at the database level doesn't add a lot over sett default value in your code unless your application, or another application, uses d SQL commands to create a new row. What is more useful is gaining access to of SQL's system functions that return the current date/time, which the HasDefa ValueSql method allows you to do.

In some situations, it's useful to get the time when a row is added to the data In such a case, instead of providing a constant in the SQL DEFAULT command can provide an SQL function that will provide a dynamic value when the row is a to the database. SQL Server, for example, has two functions—getdate and get date—that provide the current local datatime and the UTC datatime, respecti You can use these functions to automatically capture the exact time when the was inserted. The configuration of the column is the same as the constant exa in listing 10.8 except that the string used calls the SQL getutcdate functio shown in this code snippet:

```
protected override void
    OnModelCreating(ModelBuilder modelBuilder)
{
```

```
modelBuilder.Entity<DefaultTest>()
    .Property(x => x.CreatedOn)
    .HasDefaultValueSql("getutcdate()");
...
}
```

If you want to use this column to track when the row was added, you need to make sure that the .NET property isn't set by code (remains at the default value). You do this by using a property with a private setter. The following code snippet shows a property with a private setter and creates a simple tracking value that automatically tells you when the row was first inserted into the database:

```
public DateTime CreatedOn {get; private set;}
```

This feature is a useful one. In addition to accessing system functions such as getutcdate, you can place your own SQL UDFs in a default constraint. There's a limit to the SQL commands that you can place—you can't reference another column in the default constraint, for example—but the HasDefaultValue Fluent API method can provide useful features compared with setting a default in your code.

.3 Using the HasValueGenerator method to assign a value generator to a property

The third approach to adding a default value is executed not in the database, but inside your EF Core code. EF Core allows the class that inherits from the class Value-Generator or ValueGenerator<T> to be configured as a value generator for a property or backing field. This class will be asked for a default value if both of the following statements are true:

- The entity's State is set to Added; the entity is deemed to be a new entity to be added to the database.
- The property hasn't already been set; its value is at the .NET type's default value.

EF Core has a value generator that will provide unique GUID values for primary keys, for example. But for our example, the following listing shows a simple value generator that creates a unique string by using the Name property in the entity, the current date as a string, and a unique string from a GUID to create a value for the property OrderId.

Listing 10.9 A value generator that produces a unique string for the OrderId

```
public class OrderIdValueGenerator          The value generator needs
    : ValueGenerator<string> //             to inherit from EF Core's
{                                           ValueGenerator<T>.

    public override bool
        GeneratesTemporaryValues => false;  Set this to false if you want your
                                            value to be written to the database.

    public override string Next            This method is called when you Add
        (EntityEntry entry)                the entity to the DbContext.
```

The parameter gives you access to the entity that the value generator is creating a value for. You can access its properties.

```
{
    var name = entry.
        Property(nameof(DefaultTest.Name))
        .CurrentValue;
    var ticks = DateTime.UtcNow.ToString("s");
    var guidString = Guid.NewGuid().ToString();
    var orderId = $"{name}-{ticks}-{guidString}";
    return orderId;
}
}
```

Selects the property called "Name" and gets its curre

Provides th date in sort format

The method must return a value of the Type you have defined at T in the inherited ValueGenerator<T>.

The orderId combines these three parts to create a unique orderId containing useful info.

Provides a unique string

The following code configures the use of a value generator:

```
protected override void
    OnModelCreating(ModelBuilder modelBuilder)
{
    modelBuilder.Entity<DefaultTest>()
        .Property(p => p.OrderId)
        .HasValueGenerator((p, e) =>
            new OrderIdValueGenerator());
    ...
}
```

Note that the value generator's Next method is called when you Add the entity via text.Add(newEntity) but before the data is written to the database. Any data provided values, such as the primary key using SQL IDENTITY, won't be set whe Next method is called.

> **NOTE** You can use a NextAsync version if you need to implement an async version, such as using an async method to access the database while generating the default. In that case, you need to use the AddAsync method when adding the entity to the database.

The value generator is a specialized feature with limited applications, but one t worth knowing about. Chapter 11 shows you how to intercept writes to the databa add tracking or other information, which is more work but provides more capabi than the value generator.

10.4 Sequences: Providing numbers in a strict order

Sequences in a database enable you to produce numbers in strict order with no such as 1,2,3,4. Key values created by the SQL IDENTITY command aren't guarar to be in sequence; they might be like this: 1,2,10,11. Sequences are useful wher want a guaranteed known sequence, such as for an order number for purchases.

The way that sequences are implemented differs among database servers, b general, a sequence is assigned not to a specific table or column, but to a sch Every time a column wants a value from the sequence, it asks for that value. EF can set up a sequence and then, by using the HasDefaultValueSql method, set the value of a column to the next value in the sequence.

The following listing shows an Order entity class with an OrderNo that uses a sequence. The HasDefaultValueSql SQL fragment is for an SQL Server database and will be different for other database servers. This example adds an SQL sequence to a migration or to a database created via the context.Database.EnsureCreated() method and obtains the next value in the sequence by setting a default value on the OrderNo column.

Listing 10.10 The DbContext with the Fluent API configuration and the Order class

```
class MyContext : DbContext
{
    public DbSet<Order> Orders { get; set; }

    protected override void OnModelCreating
        (ModelBuilder modelBuilder)
    {
        modelBuilder.HasSequence<int>(
                "OrderNumbers", "shared")
            .StartsAt(1000)
            .IncrementsBy(5);

        modelBuilder.Entity<Order>()
            .Property(o => o.OrderNo)
            .HasDefaultValueSql(
                "NEXT VALUE FOR shared.OrderNumbers");
    }
}

public class Order
{
    public int OrderId { get; set; }
    public int OrderNo { get; set; }
}
```

Creates an SQL sequence OrderNumber in the schema "shared." If no schema is provided, it uses the default schema.

(Optional) Allows you to control the sequence's start and increments. The default is to start at 1 and increment by 1.

A column can access the sequence number via a default constraint. Each time the NEXT VALUE command is called, the sequence is incremented.

EF6 This feature is new in EF Core, with no corresponding feature in EF6.

.5 *Marking database-generated properties*

When working with an existing database, you may need to tell EF Core about specific columns that are handled differently from what EF Core expects. If your existing database has a computed column that you didn't set up by using EF Core's Fluent API (see section 10.2), EF Core needs to be told that the column is computed so that it handles the column properly.

I should say straightaway that marking columns in this way isn't the norm, because EF can work out the column attributes itself based on the configuration commands you provided. You *don't* need any of the features in this section if you use EF Core to do the following:

- Create or migrate the database via EF Core.
- Reverse-engineer your database, as described in chapter 9. (EF Core reads database schema and generates your entity classes and application DbCon

You might use these features if you want to use EF Core with an existing database out reverse engineering. In that case, you need to tell EF Core about columns don't conform to its normal conventions. The following sections teach you ho mark three different types of columns:

- Columns that change on inserting a new row or updating a row
- Columns that change on inserting a new row
- "Normal" columns—that is, columns that are changed only by EF Core

EF6 EF6 has the same Data Annotation for setting the database-generated properties, but EF Core provides Fluent API versions too.

10.5.1 Marking a column that's generated on an addition or update

EF Core needs to know whether a column's value is generated by the database, su a computed column, if for no other reason than it's read-only. EF Core can't "g that the database sets a column's value, so you need to mark it as such. You ca Data Annotations or the Fluent API.

The Data Annotation for an add-or-update column is shown in the following snippet. Here, EF Core is using the existing DatabaseGeneratedOption.Compute ting. The setting is called Computed because that's the most likely reason for a col to be changed on add or update:

```
public class PersonWithAddUpdateAttibutes
{
    …

    [DatabaseGenerated(DatabaseGeneratedOption.Computed)]
    public int YearOfBirth { get; set; }
}
```

This code snippet uses the Fluent API to set the add-or-update setting for the col

```
protected override void OnModelCreating(ModelBuilder modelBuilder)
{
    modelBuilder.Entity<Person>()
        .Property(p => p.YearOfBirth)
        .ValueGeneratedOnAddOrUpdate();
    …
}
```

2 Marking a column's value as set on insert of a new row

You can tell EF Core that a column in the database will receive a value via the database whenever a new row is inserted to the database. Two common situations are

- Via an SQL DEFAULT command, which provides a default value if no value is given in the INSERT command.
- By means of some form of key generation, of which SQL's IDENTITY command is the primary method. In these cases, the database creates a unique value to place in the column when a new row is inserted.

If a column has the SQL DEFAULT command on it, it will set the value if EF Core creates a new row and no value was provided with a value. In that case, EF Core must read back the value that the SQL DEFAULT command set for the column; otherwise, the data inside your entity class will not match the database.

The other situation in which EF Core needs to read back the value of a column is for a primary-key column when the database provides the key value, because EF Core won't know that the key was generated by SQL's IDENTITY command. This situation is most likely the reason why the annotation's DatabaseGeneratedOption is called Identity, as shown in the following code snippet:

```
public class MyClass
{
    public int MyClassId { get; set;}
    ...
    [DatabaseGenerated(DatabaseGeneratedOption.Identity)]
    public int SecondaryKey { get; set;}
}
```

The second example does the same thing but uses the Fluent API. For this example, you have a column with a default constraint. The following snippet of Fluent API code sets this constraint:

```
protected override void OnModelCreating(ModelBuilder modelBuilder)
{
    modelBuilder.Entity<Person>()
        .Property("DateOfBirth")
        .ValueGeneratedOnAdd();

    ...

}
```

3 Marking a column/property as "normal"

All scalar properties that aren't keys, don't have an SQL default value, and aren't computed columns are *normal*—that is, only you set the value of the property. In rare cases, you may want to set a property to be normal, and EF Core provides ways to do that. The one case in which this approach might be useful is for a primary key that uses a GUID; in that case, your software supplies the value.

DEFINITION A *GUID* is a *globally unique identifier*, a 128-bit integer that can be used safely anywhere. It makes a good key value in a few cases. In one case, the software wants to define the key, normally because some other part of the software needs the key before the row is inserted. In another case, you have replicated databases with inserts into both or all databases, which makes creating a unique key more difficult.

My tests show that if you use a GUID as a primary key, EF Core will automatically ate a GUID value if you don't supply one (EF Core provides a value generato GUID primary keys). Also, if the database provider is for SQL Server, EF Core u value generator called SequentialGuidValueGenerator, which is optimized for u Microsoft SQL server clustered keys and indexes. You can turn this value gene with a Data Annotation:

```
public class MyClass
{
    [DatabaseGenerated(DatabaseGeneratedOption.None)]
    public Guid MyClassId { get; set; }
    ...
}
```

You can also use the following Fluent API configuration:

```
protected override void OnModelCreating(ModelBuilder modelBuilder)
{
    modelBuilder.Entity<MyClass>()
        .Property("MyClassId")
        .ValueGeneratedNever();
    ...
}
```

10.6 Handling simultaneous updates: Concurrency conflicts

Concurrency conflicts represent a big topic, so let me start by explaining what sim neous updates look like before explaining why they can be problems and how can handle them. Figure 10.3 shows an example of simultaneous updates to PublishedOn column in a database. This update happens because of two sep pieces of code running in parallel, which read the column and then update it.

By default, EF Core uses an Optimistic Concurrency pattern. In figure 10.3 first update is lost because it's overwritten by the second. Although this situati often acceptable, in some cases, overwriting someone else's update is a problem. following sections explain unacceptable overwrites, known as *concurrency conflicts,* show how EF Core enables you to detect and fix such conflicts.

10.6.1 Why do concurrency conflicts matter?

If you think about it, a setting can be overwritten anyway. You could set the pub tion date of a book to 1/1/2020, and tomorrow you could change it to 1/1/204 why are concurrency conflicts such a big deal?

1. The first thread reads the book. The original
PublishedOn was 1/1/50, and it changes to 1/1/2051.

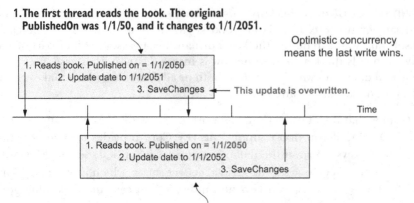

Optimistic concurrency
means the last write wins.

1. Reads book. Published on = 1/1/2050
 2. Update date to 1/1/2051
  3. SaveChanges ◄── This update is overwritten.

Time

1. Reads book. Published on = 1/1/2050
 2. Update date to 1/1/2052
  3. SaveChanges

2. The second thread reads the book and gets the original PublishedOn, which is 1/1/2050. It
then changes the PublishedOn date to 1/1/2052, which overwrites the first task's update.

Figure 10.3   Two pieces of code (say, in a web application) running in parallel that make
near-simultaneous updates of the same column (in this case, the publication date of the
same book). By default, EF Core allows the second write to win, and the first write is lost.
This situation is called optimistic concurrency, but the "last write win" rule may not be useful
in all cases.

In some cases, concurrent conflicts do matter. In financial transactions, for example, you can imagine that the purity and auditing of data are going to be important, so you might want to guard against concurrency changes. Another concurrent conflict exists in the example in section 8.7, where you calculated the average book review votes. In that case, if two people added reviews at the same time, that recalculation would be incorrect, so you need to detect and fix that conflict if that example is going to be robust.

Other human-level concurrent conflicts can occur. Instead of two tasks clashing on updates, two users looking at screens can clash, with the same default result: the second person to click the Submit button overwrites the update that the first person thought they had done. (Section 10.6.4 covers the details.)

Sometimes, you get around concurrency conflicts by design, by creating applications in such a way that dangerous concurrent updates can't happen. For an e-commerce website that I designed, for example, I had an order-processing system that used background tasks, which could've caused concurrent conflicts. I got around this potential problem by designing the order processing to remove the possibility of concurrent updates:

- I split the customer order information into an immutable order part that never changed. This part contained data such as what was ordered and where it should be sent. After that order was created, it was never changed or deleted.
- For the changing part of the order, which was the order status as it moved through the system, I created a separate table to which I added each new order status as it occurred, with the date and time. (This approach is known as *event*

sourcing.) Then I could get the latest order status by sorting by date/time c and picking the status with the newest date and time. This result would b of date if another status was added after I read the status, of course, but co rency handling would detect this addition.

This design approach meant that I never updated or deleted any order data, so current conflicts couldn't happen. It did make handling a customer change order a bit more complicated, but orders were safe from concurrent-conflict issu

But when concurrent conflicts *are* issues, and you can't design around them, EF provides two ways of detecting a concurrent update and, when the update is detect way of getting at all the relevant data so you can implement code to fix the issue.

10.6.2 *EF Core's concurrency conflict-handling features*

EF Core's concurrency conflict-handling features can detect a concurrency upda two ways, activated by adding one of the following to an entity class:

- A *concurrency token* to mark a specific property/column in your entity cla one to check for a concurrency conflict
- A *timestamp* (also known as a rowversion), which marks a whole entity class as one to check for a concurrency conflict

EF6 Concurrency-handling features are the same as in EF6.x but reimplemented in EF Core.

In both cases, when SaveChanges is called, EF Core produces database server co check for updates of any entities that contain concurrency tokens or timestamp that code detects that the concurrency tokens or timestamps have changed sin read the entity, it throws a DbUpdateConcurrencyException exception. At that p you can use EF Core's features to inspect the differing versions of the data and a your custom code to decide which of the concurrent updates wins. Next, you'll how to set up the two approaches—a concurrency token and a timestamp—and EF Core detects the change.

DETECTING A CONCURRENT CHANGE VIA CONCURRENCY TOKEN

The concurrency-token approach allows you to configure one or more properti concurrency tokens. This approach tells EF Core to check whether the current base value is the same as the value found when the tracked entity was loaded as pa the SQL UPDATE command sent to the database. That way, the update will fail loaded value and the current database value are different. Figure 10.4 shows an e ple of marking the PublishedOn property as a concurrency token, after which a currency conflict occurs.

To set up this example, you add the ConcurrencyCheck Data Annotation to PublishedOn property in our ConcurrencyBook entity class, shown in the follo listing. EF Core finds this Data Annotation during configuration and marks the p erty as a concurrency token.

**1. The first thread reads the book. The original
PublishedOn was 1/1/50, and it changes to 1/1/2051.**

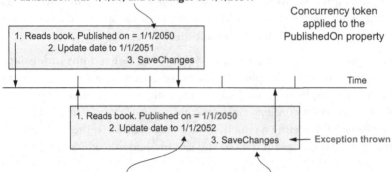

Concurrency token
applied to the
PublishedOn property

1. Reads book. Published on = 1/1/2050
2. Update date to 1/1/2051
3. SaveChanges

Time

1. Reads book. Published on = 1/1/2050
2. Update date to 1/1/2052
3. SaveChanges ← — Exception thrown

**2. The second thread reads the book
and gets the original PublishedOn,
which is 1/1/2050. It then changes
the PublishedOn date to 1/1/2052.**

**3. SaveChanges produces an UPDATE command that
checks that the PublishedOn column value is still
1/1/2050. This fails because the PublishedOn
column in the database has changed, so EF Core
throws a DbUpdateConcurrencyException.**

Figure 10.4 Two pieces of code—say, in a web application—running in parallel that make a near-simultaneous update of the PublishedOn column. Because you've marked the PublishedOn property as a concurrency token, EF Core uses a modified SQL UPDATE command that performs the update only if the database's PublishedOn column is the same as it was when it read in the Book entity. If it isn't the same, the UPDATE fails, and SaveChanges throws a DbUpdateConcurrencyException.

Listing 10.11 The `ConcurrencyBook` entity class, with a `PublishedOn` property

```
public class ConcurrencyBook
{
    public int ConcurrencyBookId { get; set; }
    public string Title { get; set; }

    [ConcurrencyCheck]
    public DateTime PublishedOn { get; set; }

    public ConcurrencyAuthor Author { get; set; }
}
```

Tells EF Core that the PublishedOn property is a concurrency token, which means that EF Core will check whether it has changed when you update it

In this case, you've used the `ConcurrencyCheck` Data Annotation to define the property as a concurrency token, which has the benefit of making it clear to anyone looking at the code that the `PublishedOn` property has special handling. Alternatively, you can define a concurrency token via the Fluent API, as shown in the next listing.

Listing 10.12 Setting a property as a concurrency token by using the Fluent API

```
protected override void
    OnModelCreating(ModelBuilder modelBuilder)
{
```

The OnModelCreating method is where you place the configuration of the concurrency detection.

```
modelBuilder.Entity<ConcurrencyBook>()
    .Property(p => p.PublishedOn)
    .IsConcurrencyToken();

//… other configuration removed
}
```

Defines the PublishedOn propert as a concurrency token, which means that EF Core checks whether it has changed when writing out an update

After either listing 10.11 or 10.12 is added, figure 10.4 shows that when SaveCha is called, instead of overwriting the first update, it detects that another task updated the PublishedOn column and throws an exception.

Listing 10.13 simulates a concurrent update by running an SQL command changes the PublishedOn column between the EF Core code that reads and updates the book. The SQL command represents another thread of the web applica or another application that has access to the same database, updating the Publishe column. In this case, a DbUpdateConcurrencyException exception is thrown v SaveChanges is called in the last line.

Listing 10.13   Simulating a concurrent update of the PublishedOn column

```
var firstBook = context.Books.First();

context.Database.ExecuteSqlRaw(
    "UPDATE dbo.Books SET PublishedOn = GETDATE()"+
    " WHERE ConcurrencyBookId = @p0",
    firstBook.ConcurrencyBookId);
firstBook.Title = Guid.NewGuid().ToString();
context.SaveChanges();
```

Loads the first book in the database as a tracked entity

Simulates another thread/application, changing the Publish column of the same

Changes the title in the bo cause EF Core to update th

This SaveChanges throws a DbUpdateConcurrencyException.

The important thing to note is that only the property marked as a concurrency t is checked. If your SQL-simulated update changed, say, the Title property, which marked as a concurrency token, no exception would be thrown.

You can see this effect in the SQL that EF Core produces to update the Tit the next listing. The SQL WHERE clause contains not only the primary key of the to update, but also the PublishedOn column.

Listing 10.14   SQL code to update Book where PublishedOn is a concurrency toke

```
SET NOCOUNT ON;
UPDATE [Books] SET [Title] = @p0
WHERE [ConcurrencyBookId] = @p1
    AND [PublishedOn] = @p2;
SELECT @@ROWCOUNT;
```

The test fails if the PublishedOn column has changed, which stops the update.

Returns the number of rows updated by this SQL command

When EF Core runs this SQL command, the WHERE clause finds a valid row to up only if the PublishedOn column hasn't changed from the value EF Core read in the database. Then EF Core checks the number of rows that have been updated b

SQL command. If the number of rows updated is zero, EF Core raises DbUpdate-ConcurrencyException to say that a concurrency conflict exists; it can catch a concurrency conflict caused by another task by changing the PublishedOn column or deleting the row when this task does an update.

The good thing about using a concurrency token is that it works on any database because it uses basic commands. The next way of detecting concurrency changes relies on a database server-side feature.

DETECTING A CONCURRENT CHANGE VIA TIMESTAMP

The second way to check for concurrency conflicts is to use what EF Core calls a timestamp. A timestamp works differently from a concurrency token, as it uses a unique value provided by the database server that changes whenever a row is inserted or updated. The whole entity, rather than specific properties or columns, is protected against concurrency changes.

Figure 10.5 shows that when a row with a property/column marked as a timestamp is inserted or updated, the database server produces a new, unique value for that column, which has the effect of detecting an update to an entity/row whenever Save-Changes is called.

The timestamp database type is database-type-specific: SQL Server's concurrency type is ROWVERSION, which maps to byte[] in .NET; PostgreSQL has a column called

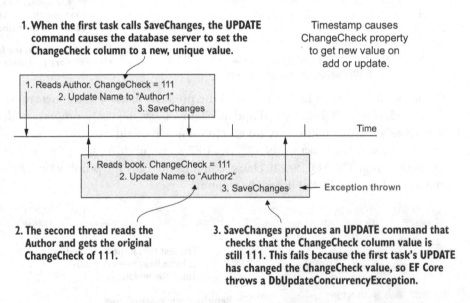

1. **When the first task calls SaveChanges, the UPDATE command causes the database server to set the ChangeCheck column to a new, unique value.**

Timestamp causes ChangeCheck property to get new value on add or update.

1. Reads Author. ChangeCheck = 111
2. Update Name to "Author1"
3. SaveChanges

Time

1. Reads book. ChangeCheck = 111
2. Update Name to "Author2"
3. SaveChanges ← Exception thrown

2. **The second thread reads the Author and gets the original ChangeCheck of 111.**

3. **SaveChanges produces an UPDATE command that checks that the ChangeCheck column value is still 111. This fails because the first task's UPDATE has changed the ChangeCheck value, so EF Core throws a DbUpdateConcurrencyException.**

Figure 10.5 Configuring a property as a timestamp means that the corresponding column in the table must be set to a database server type that will be set to a new, unique value every time an SQL INSERT or UPDATE command is applied to the row. (If you use EF Core to create your database, the database provider will ensure the use of the correct column type.) Then, when EF Core does an update, it checks that the timestamp column has the same value as when the entity was read in. If the value is different, EF Core will throw an exception.

xmin that is an unsigned 32-bit number; and Cosmos DB has a JSON property c _etag, which is a string containing a unique value. EF Core can use any of these via the appropriate database provider. For the examples of using a timestamp going to use SQL Server's timestamp; other databases will work in a similar way with a different .NET type.

The following listing adds a ChangeCheck property, which watches for any up to the whole entity, to an entity class called ConcurrencyAuthor. In this case ChangeCheck property has a Timestamp Data Annotation, which tells EF Co mark it as a special column that the database will update with a unique value. In case of SQL Server, the database provider will set the column as an SQL S rowversion; other databases have different approaches to implementing the T Stamp column.

Listing 10.15 The ConcurrencyAuthor class, with the ChangeCheck property

```
public class ConcurrencyAuthor
{
    public int ConcurrencyAuthorId { get; set; }
    public string Name { get; set; }
    [Timestamp]
    public byte[] ChangeCheck { get; set; }     ◀──
}
```

Marks the ChangeCheck pr as a timestamp, causing th database server to mark it SQL ROWVERSION. EF Core this property when updatin see whether it has change

---

Again, you use a Data Annotation, Timestamp, to mark the ChangeCheck property timestamp. This approach is my recommended way of configuring concurrency dling, because it makes obvious to anyone looking at the code that there's special currency handling of this entity. Alternatively, you can use the Fluent API to confi a timestamp, as shown in the following listing.

Listing 10.16 Configuring a timestamp by using the Fluent API

```
protected override void
    OnModelCreating(ModelBuilder modelBuilder)    ◀──
{
    modelBuilder.Entity<ConcurrencyAuthor>()
        .Property(p => p.ChangeCheck)
        .IsRowVersion();
}
```

OnModelCreating is where you place the configuration of the concurrency detectic

Defines an extra property calle ChangeCheck that will be chan every time the row is created/u EF Core checks whether this p has changed when it does an u

---

Both configurations create a column in a table that the database server will ch automatically whenever there's an INSERT or UPDATE to that table. For SQL Server base, the column type is set to ROWVERSION, as shown in the following listing. Other base servers can use different approaches, but they all provide a new, unique valu an INSERT or UPDATE.

Listing 10.17   The SQL to create the Authors table, with a `timestamp` column

```
CREATE TABLE [dbo].[Authors] (
    [ConcurrencyAuthorId] INT  IDENTITY (1, 1),
    [ChangeCheck]         TIMESTAMP NULL,
    [Name]                NVARCHAR (MAX) NULL
);
```

If the table is created by EF Core, sets the column type to TIMESTAMP if your property is of type byte[]. This column's value will be updated on each INSERT or UPDATE.

You simulate a concurrent change by using the code in listing 10.18, which consists of three steps:

1   You use EF Core to read in the Authors row that you want to update.

2   You use an SQL command to update the Authors table, simulating another task updating the same Author that you read in. EF Core doesn't know anything about this change because raw SQL bypasses EF Core's tracking snapshot feature. (See section 11.5 in chapter 11 for details about EF Core's raw SQL commands.)

3   In the last two lines, you update the Author's name and call `SaveChanges`, which causes a `DbUpdateConcurrencyException` to be thrown because EF Core found that the ChangeCheck column has changed from step 1.

Listing 10.18   Simulating a concurrent update of the `ConcurrentAuthor` entity

```
var firstAuthor = context.Authors.First();
context.Database.ExecuteSqlRaw(
    "UPDATE dbo.Authors SET Name = @p0"+
    " WHERE ConcurrencyAuthorId = @p1",
    firstAuthor.Name,
    firstAuthor.ConcurrencyAuthorId);
firstAuthor.Name = "Concurrency Name";
context.SaveChanges();
```

Loads the first author in the database as a tracked entity

Simulates another thread/application updating the entity. Nothing is changed except the timestamp.

Changes something in the author to cause EF Core to do an update to the book

Throws DbUpdateConcurrencyException

This code is like the case in which you used a concurrency token. The difference is that the timestamp detects an update of the row via the unique value in the property/column called ChangeCheck. You can see this difference in the following listing, which shows the SQL that EF Core produces to update the row with the check on the timestamp property, ChangeCheck.

Listing 10.19   The SQL code to update the author's name, with ChangeCheck check

```
SET NOCOUNT ON;
UPDATE [Authors] SET [Name] = @p0
WHERE [ConcurrencyAuthorId] = @p1
    AND [ChangeCheck] = @p2;
SELECT [ChangeCheck]
FROM [Authors]
```

Checks that the ChangeCheck column hasn't been changed since you read in the book entity

Because the update will change the ChangeCheck column, EF Core needs to read it back so that its in-memory copy is correct.

```
WHERE @@ROWCOUNT = 1
    AND [ConcurrencyAuthorId] = @p1;
```

Checks whether one row was updated in th command. If not, the ChangeCheck value w be returned, and EF Core will know that a concurrent change has taken place.

The UPDATE part checks whether the ChangeCheck column is the same value a copy it found when it first read the entity, and if so, it executes the update. The se part returns the new ChangeCheck column that the database server created the current update, but only if the UPDATE was executed. If no value is returned fo ChangeCheck property, EF Core knows that a concurrency conflict has happened throws a DbUpdateConcurrencyException.

Your choice between the two approaches—concurrency token and timestar depends on your business rules. The concurrency-token approach provides spe protection of the property/properties you place it on and is triggered only if a p erty marked as a concurrency token is changed. The timestamp approach catches update to that entity.

10.6.3 Handling a DbUpdateConcurrencyException

Now that you've seen the two ways that EF Core detects a concurrent change, yo ready to look at an example of catching DbUpdateConcurrencyException. The you write your code to fix a concurrency conflict depends on your business reason capturing it. The example in listing 10.20 shows how to capture the DbUpd ConcurrencyException and what data you have available for making your decisio fix this concurrency exception.

Listing 10.20 shows a method that you call after you've updated the Book e with your change. This method, BookSaveChangesWithChecks, calls SaveChanges captures any DbUpdateConcurrencyException exception if one happens; it also u method called HandleBookConcurrency, where you've put the logic to handle a currency exception on a Book entity.

```
public static string BookSaveChangesWithChecks
    (ConcurrencyDbContext context)
{
    string error = null;
    try
    {
        context.SaveChanges();
    }
    catch (DbUpdateConcurrencyException ex)
    {
        var entry = ex.Entries.Single();
        error = HandleBookConcurrency(
            context, entry);
        if (error == null)
            context.SaveChanges();
    }
```

Called after the Book entity has been updated in some way

Calls SaveChanges within a try...catch so that you can catch DbUpdateConcurrencyException if it occurs

Catches DbUpdateConcurrencyE and puts in your code to handle

Calls the HandleBookConcurrency m which returns null if the error was h or an error message if it wasn't

If the conflict was handled, you need to call SaveChanges to update the Book.

In this case, you know that only one Book will be updated. In other cases, you might need to handle multiple entities.

```
        return error;        ◄────┐  Returns the error message
}                                 │  or null if there's no error
```

The BookSaveChangesWithChecks method returns a string, which is null if successful or an error message if it can't handle this concurrency conflict. (In this example, you handle an update conflict, but you return an error message on a delete conflict; see the HandleBookConcurrency method in listing 10.21.) Note that you must call the SaveChanges method again, but only if you've fixed the concurrency problem. Otherwise, the method keeps looping around with the same exception.

The HandleBookConcurrency method handles a Book entity update concurrency conflict. You have at your disposal three versions of the database data, shown in the Exception Handler box in figure 10.6. In this example, you're looking at the PublishedOn property, which is protected by a concurrency token. Figure 10.6 shows the sequence of events and the value of the PublishedOn column at each stage.

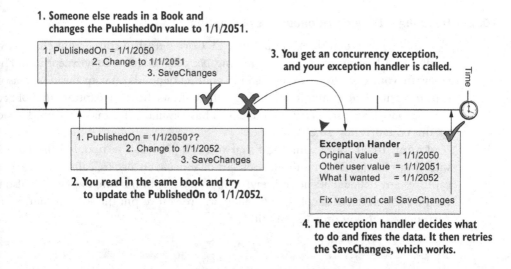

Figure 10.6 An overlap of two people accessing the same book can be caught by using a concurrency token in this example (but the stages would be the same if a timestamp were used). At stage 3, a concurrency exception happens, and your exception handler is called (see listing 10.21). Your exception handler gets a copy of the original PublishedOn date that your change read in, the value that the other user set the PublishedOn date to, and the actual value you wanted to set the PublishedOn date to.

Listing 10.21 shows the content of your exception hander called HandleBookConcurrency. The code names some of the variables, starting with originalValue, otherUserValue, and whatIWantedItToBe. These variables correspond to the three versions of the data shown in figure 10.6.

Listing 10.21 Handling a concurrent update on the book

```
private static string HandleBookConcurrency(          ⊲──    Takes in the application's
    DbContext context,                                       DbContext and the Change
    EntityEntry entry)                                       Tracking entry from the
{                                                            exception's Entities prope
    var book = entry.Entity
        as ConcurrencyBook;
    if (book == null)                                  ⊲──    Handles only ConcurrencyBook, so th
        throw new NotSupportedException(                       an exception if the entry isn't of type
"Don't know how to handle concurrency conflicts for " +
            entry.Metadata.Name);                                 Entity must be rea
                                                                  NoTracking; other
    var whatTheDatabaseHasNow =                                   it'll interfere with
        context.Set<ConcurrencyBook>().AsNoTracking()   ⊲──       same entity you're
            .SingleOrDefault(p => p.ConcurrencyBookId                 trying to write.
                == book.ConcurrencyBookId);
    if (whatTheDatabaseHasNow == null)
        return "Unable to save changes.The book was deleted by another
    user.";
                                                            You get the EntityEntry<T>
    var otherUserData =                                     version of the entity, which ha
        context.Entry(whatTheDatabaseHasNow);              all the tracking information.

    foreach (var property in entry.Metadata.GetProperties())     Holds the versic
    {                                                             property at the
        var theOriginalValue = entry                              you did the tra
            .Property(property.Name).OriginalValue;               read of the boo
        var otherUserValue = otherUserData
            .Property(property.Name).CurrentValue;            Holds the version of
        var whatIWantedItToBe = entry                         property as written t
            .Property(property.Name).CurrentValue;            database by someon

        // TODO: Logic to decide which value should be written to database
        if (property.Name ==
            nameof(ConcurrencyBook.PublishedOn))                  Business log
        {                                                         handle Publi
                                                                  sets to your
            entry.Property(property.Name).CurrentValue =          the other pe
            //… your code to pick which PublishedOn to use        value, or th
        }                                                         an exception

        entry.Property(property.Name).OriginalValue =
            otherUserData.Property(property.Name)                 Here, you set the
                .CurrentValue;                                    OriginalValue to t
    }                                                             value that someo
    return null;         ⊲──    You return null to say            set it to. This code
}                               that you handled this             for concurrency t
                                concurrency issue.                or a timestamp.
```

You want to get the data that someone else wrote into the database after your read.

Concurrency conflict method doesn't handle the case where the book was deleted, so it returns a user-friendly error message.

You go through all the properties in the book entity to reset the Original values so that the exception doesn't happen again.

Holds the version of the property that you wanted to set it to in your update

The main part you need to change is the section starting with the comment // T
You should put your code to handle the concurrent update there. What you put t
depends on the business rules in your application. In section 10.6.4, I show y
worked-through example with business logic, but in listing 10.21, the focus is or

three parts of the data: the original values, the other users' values, and what you want the PublishedOn value to be.

Note that your HandleBookConcurrency method also detects that a concurrency conflict caused by the original Book entity has been deleted. In that case, when your concurrency-handling method tries to reread the actual row in the database by using the Book's primary key, it won't find that row and will return null. Your current implementation doesn't handle that case and returns an error message to show the user.

Reference to more complex concurrency examples

Because concurrency handling is pretty hard to understand, I have made two simplifications on the descriptions in this chapter. They are as follows:

- HandleBookConcurrency shown in listing 10.21 handles only one entity.
- The BookSaveChangesWithChecks method shown in listing 10.20 assumes that a second concurrency issue isn't thrown when the HandleBook-Concurrency code has corrected the first concurrency issue.

In real applications, you might need to handle multiple entities in your concurrency handler, and you can't assume that you won't get another concurrency exception when you write the corrected entity that threw the first concurrency exception. Fortunately, chapter 15 provides examples of handling both of these issues.

In section 15.5, I describe a way to store values that contain preevaluated values, such as the average votes for a book, to improve the performance of the Book App when working with large amounts of data. These extra values have to be updated whenever the appropriate entities are changed, but of course, multiple updates would cause concurrency issues, so I had to solve both of these issues.

For simplification 1 (only one entity), have a look at listing 15.9, which handles multiple entities with concurrency issues and also different types of concurrency issues within one entity class.

For simplification 2 (concurrency within a concurrency), see listing 15.8, which adds a do / while loop around the call to SaveChanges. This loop means the code will catch a concurrency within a concurrency; the concurrency handles are designed for that possibility.

.4 *The disconnected concurrent update issue*

In applications such as websites, another concurrency-update scenario can occur that encompasses the user-interaction part of the system. The examples so far have covered simultaneous code updates, but if you bring in the human factor, the problem is more likely to occur and may be more business-relevant.

Figure 10.7 shows employee John Doe getting a pay raise set by both John's boss and human resources. The time between each entity's seeing the figure and deciding what to do is measured in minutes instead of milliseconds, but if you don't do anything

1. John Doe's boss gets an email saying it's time to review John's salary. The boss gives him a 10% raise for good work.

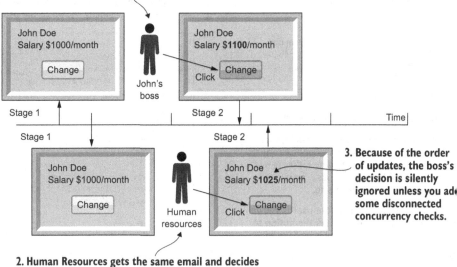

3. Because of the order of updates, the boss's decision is silently ignored unless you add some disconnected concurrency checks.

2. Human Resources gets the same email and decides to give John Doe the standard 2.5% raise.

Figure 10.7 A concurrency problem running in human time. John Doe's salary review is due, and two people—John's boss and a human resources employee—try to update his salary at the same time. Unless you add concurrency checks, the boss's update, which came first, is silently ignored, which most likely isn't the correct business outcome.

about it, you can have another concurrency conflict, potentially with the wrong s being set.

Although this example looks much like the concurrency-conflicts example in tion 10.6.2, the change is in the way that a disconnected concurrency conflict is fo To handle a disconnected update, the original value of the property you're prote (in this case, the Salary) must be passed from the first stage of the disconnect to second stage. Then your second stage must use that original Salary in the concurr conflict check during the update part of the process.

Also, the way that a concurrency conflict is dealt with is different. Typically, human-user case, the decision about what should happen is given back to the use a conflict occurs, the user is shown a new screen indicating what happened a given a choice about what should be done. This disconnected concurrent situa changes the code that handles DbUpdateConcurrencyException into more of a nostic role than code that fixes the problem.

If a concurrency conflict exists, the user is shown a new screen with an error sage indicating what happened. Then the user is invited to accept the current sta apply the update, knowing that this update will override the last user's update.

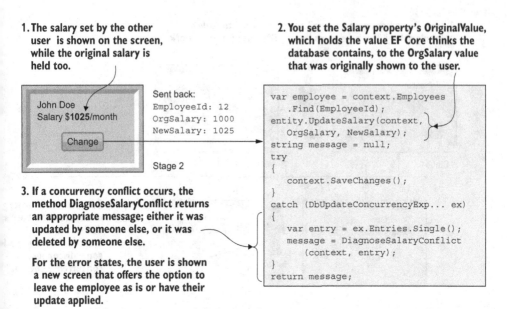

1. The salary set by the other user is shown on the screen, while the original salary is held too.

2. You set the Salary property's OriginalValue, which holds the value EF Core thinks the database contains, to the OrgSalary value that was originally shown to the user.

3. If a concurrency conflict occurs, the method DiagnoseSalaryConflict returns an appropriate message; either it was updated by someone else, or it was deleted by someone else.

   For the error states, the user is shown a new screen that offers the option to leave the employee as is or have their update applied.

Sent back:
```
EmployeeId: 12
OrgSalary: 1000
NewSalary: 1025
```

```
var employee = context.Employees
    .Find(EmployeeId);
entity.UpdateSalary(context,
    OrgSalary, NewSalary);
string message = null;
try
{
    context.SaveChanges();
}
catch (DbUpdateConcurrencyExp... ex)
{
    var entry = ex.Entries.Single();
    message = DiagnoseSalaryConflict
        (context, entry);
}
return message;
```

Figure 10.8 After the user has changed the salary and clicked the Change button, the new salary and the original salary values are sent back to the web application. Then the application calls the UpdateSalary method, shown in listing 10.24, which both updates the salary and sets the original value expected in the database when it does the update. If a concurrency conflict is found, a new screen with an appropriate error message is shown to the user, who can then accept the existing database state or apply their own update to the employee.

Figure 10.8 shows what happens when the user clicks the Change button after setting the new salary. As you can see, the original salary, which was displayed to the user on the first screen, is sent back with the other data and used in the concurrency check when the Salary is updated. (See the UpdateSalary method in listing 10.24.)

Listing 10.22 shows the entity class used for this example, with the Salary property set as a concurrency token. You also create a method called UpdateSalary that contains the code you need to execute to update the Salary property in such a way that DbUpdateConcurrencyException will be thrown if the Salary value has changed from the value originally shown on the user's screen.

Listing 10.22 Entity class used to hold an employee's salary with concurrency check

```
public class Employee
{
    public int EmployeeId { get; set; }

    public string Name { get; set; }

    [ConcurrencyCheck]
    public int Salary { get; set; }
}
```

Salary property set as a concurrency token by the ConcurrencyCheck attribute

```
public void UpdateSalary                    ◄──┐  Updates the Salary in
    (DbContext context,                          │  a disconnected state
     int orgSalary, int newSalary)
{
    Salary = newSalary;                   ◄─── Sets the Salary to the new value
    context.Entry(this).Property(p => p.Salary)
        .OriginalValue = orgSalary;                          ─┤
}
}                       Sets the OriginalValue, which holds the data read
                        from the database, to the original value that was
                        shown to the user in the first part of the update
```

After applying the `UpdateSalary` method to the `Employee` entity of the person w
salary you want to change, you call `SaveChanges` within a `try…catch` block to up
the `Employee`. If `SaveChanges` raises `DbUpdateConcurrencyException`, the job o
`DiagnoseSalaryConflict` method shown in the following listing isn't to fix the cor
but to create an appropriate error message so that the user can decide what to do.

Listing 10.23   Returns different errors for update or delete concurrency conflicts

```
private string DiagnoseSalaryConflict(       ◄──┐  Called if a DbUpdateConcurrencyExce
    ConcurrencyDbContext context,                │  occurs. Its job isn't to fix the proble
    EntityEntry entry)                           │  to form an error message and provi
{                                                │  options for fixing the problem.
    var employee = entry.Entity
        as Employee;                                 If the entity that failed wasn't an
    if (employee == null)               ◄───         Employee, you throw an exception,
        throw new NotSupportedException(             as this code can't handle that.
"Don't know how to handle concurrency conflicts for " +
            entry.Metadata.Name);
                                                     Must be read as NoTracking;
    var databaseEntity =                             otherwise, it'll interfere with the
        context.Employees.AsNoTracking()  ◄───       same entity you're trying to write.
            .SingleOrDefault(p =>
                p.EmployeeId == employee.EmployeeId);
                                                     Checks for a delete conflict:
    if (databaseEntity == null)         ◄───         employee was deleted becau
        return                                       the user attempted to upda
$"The Employee {employee.Name} was deleted by another user. " +
$"Click Add button to add back with salary of {employee.Salary}" +
" or Cancel to leave deleted.";     ◄──┐
                                        │  Error message to display to the use
    return                              │  with two choices about how to carry
$"The Employee {employee.Name}'s salary was set to " +
$"{databaseEntity.Salary} by another user. " +
$"Click Update to use your new salary of {employee.Salary}" +
$" or Cancel to leave the salary at {databaseEntity.Salary}.";  ◄──┐
}
                   Otherwise, the error must be an update conflict, so you return
                   a different error message with the two choices for this case.
```

You want to get the data that someone else wrote into the database after your read.

Listing 10.24 shows two methods: one for the update conflict case and one for
delete conflict. These methods are called depending on which sort of concurr

conflict was found (update or delete), and only if the user wants to apply an update to Employee.

The update conflict can be handled by using the same UpdateSalary method used for the normal update, but now the orgSalary parameter is the salary value as read back when the DbUpdateConcurrencyException was raised. The FixDeleteSalary method is used when the concurrent user deletes the Employee and the current user wants to add the Employee back with their new salary value.

Listing 10.24   Two methods to handle update and delete conflicts

```
public class Employee
{
    public int EmployeeId { get; set; }          Set as a concurrency token
                                                  by the ConcurrencyCheck
                                                  attribute
    public string Name { get; set; }

                                                  The same method used to update the Salary
    [ConcurrencyCheck]                            can be used for the Update conflict, but this
    public int Salary { get; set; }               time, it's given the original value that was
                                                  found when the DbUpdateConcurrency-
                                                  Exception occurred.
    public void UpdateSalary
        (DbContext context,
         int orgSalary, int newSalary)            Sets the Salary
    {                                             to the new value
        Salary = newSalary;
        context.Entry(this).Property(p => p.Salary)    Sets the OriginalValue,
            .OriginalValue = orgSalary;                which is now the value that
    }                                                  the database contained
                                                       when the DbUpdate-
    public static void FixDeletedSalary                ConcurrencyException
    (DbContext context,                                occurred
        Employee employee)
    {                                             The key must be at the CLR
        employee.EmployeeId = 0;                  default value for an Add to work.
        context.Add(employee);                    Adds the Employee because it was
    }                                             deleted from the database and
}                                                 therefore must be added back
```

NOTE These disconnected concurrency-conflict examples use a concurrency token, but they work equally well with a timestamp. To use a timestamp instead of passing the Salary concurrency token used in these examples, you'd pass the timestamp and set the timestamp's original value before any update.

Summary

- Using SQL user-defined functions (UDFs) with EF Core to move calculations into the database can improve query performance.
- Configuring a column as an SQL computed column allows you to return a computed value based on the other properties in the row.

- EF Core provides two ways to set a default value for a property/column entity; these techniques go beyond what setting a default value via .NET achieve.
- EF Core's `HasSequence` method allows a known, predictable sequence pro* by the database server to be applied to a column in a table.
- When the database is created/migrated outside EF Core, you need to conf columns that behave differently from the norm, such as telling EF Core t key is generated in the database.
- EF Core provides concurrency tokens and timestamps to detect concur conflicts.
- When a concurrency conflict is detected, EF Core throws `DbUpdateConcurre Exception` and then allows you to implement code to handle the conflict.

For readers who are familiar with EF6:

- The three default value methods, the `HasSequence` method, and the setting computed column aren't available in EF6.x.
- EF Core's handling of a concurrency conflict is identical to the way that F handles a concurrency conflict, but Microsoft suggests a few minor cha in the way that the `DbUpdateConcurrencyException` should be handled http://mng.bz/O1VE.

Going deeper into the DbContext

This chapter looks at the properties and methods available in the application's DbContext. You've seen a few of these properties and methods before, such as the Add, Update, and Remove methods covered in chapter 3, but in this chapter, you'll dig deeper into how they work. You'll also look at some other properties and methods that haven't been covered in earlier chapters. You will look at each method used to write to the database, ways to make saving data quicker, and ways to execute SQL commands directly on your database. You'll also look at accessing and using your EF Core configuration information.

This chapter discusses the DbContext properties for setting the State of an e class, including what to do if your call to SaveChanges is taking too long to run we'll start with an overview of the four properties in the DbContext class, with poi to coverage of their related features.

11.1 Overview of the DbContext class's properties

Your application's DbContext, which inherits EF Core's DbContext class, is the k accessing your database. Everywhere your application wants to use EF Core, it has t an instance of your application's DbContext.

This chapter focuses on the methods and data of the public properties that inherited from EFCore's DbContext class. These properties provide informatio methods that allow you to better manage your entity classes and their mapping to database:

- ChangeTracker—Provides access to EF Core's change tracking code. You the ChangeTracker property in chapter 4 to run data validation before S Changes. You'll spend quite a bit of time looking at an entity class's State in chapter, including the ChangeTracker property (section 11.4).
- ContextId—A unique identifier for the instance of the DbContext. Its r role is to be a correlation ID for logging and debugging so that you car what reads and writes were done from the same instance of the applicat DbContext.
- Database—Provides access to three main groups of features:
  - Transaction control, covered in section 4.7.2
  - Database creation/migration, covered in chapter 9
  - Raw SQL commands, covered in section 11.5
- Model—Provides access to the database model that EF Core uses when con ing to or creating a database. Section 11.6.2 covers this topic.

11.2 Understanding how EF Core tracks changes

EF Core uses a property called State that's attached to all tracked entities. The S property holds the information about what you want to happen to that entity v you call the application's DbContext method, SaveChanges.

> **DEFINITION** As you may remember from chapter 2, *tracked entities* are entity instances that have been read in from the database using a query that didn't include the AsNoTracking method. Alternatively, after an entity instance has been used as a parameter to EF Core methods—such as the Add, Update, Remove, or Attach method—it becomes tracked.

This State property, an enum of type EntityState, is normally set by the change t ing feature inside EF Core, and in this section, you're going to explore all the way State can be set. Chapter 3 gave you a brief introduction to State but skipped r of its features, especially those related to relationships, as well as extra comma which this section covers. The following list, repeated from chapter 3, lists possible values of the State property, which is accessed via the EF command context.Entry (myEntity).State:

- Added—The entity doesn't yet exist in the database. SaveChanges will insert it.
- Unchanged—The entity exists in the database and hasn't been modified on the client. SaveChanges will ignore it.
- Modified—The entity exists in the database and has been modified on the client. SaveChanges will update it.
- Deleted—The entity exists in the database but should be deleted. SaveChanges will delete it.
- Detached—The entity you provided isn't tracked. SaveChanges doesn't see it.

Figure 11.1 shows the change of State of the entity instance, without any relationships, as it's added, modified, and deleted from the database. The figure is a good overview of the values that the State of an entity can have.

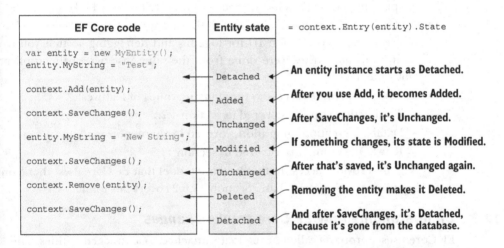

Figure 11.1 The code on the left uses all the standard ways of creating, updating, and deleting data in a database. The right column shows the EF Core state of the entity as it moves through each of these stages.

When you have an entity in the Modified state, another per-property boolean flag, IsModified, comes into play. This flag identifies which of the properties, both scalar and navigational, have changed in the entity. This IsModified property for a scalar property is accessed via

```
context.Entry(entity).Property("PropertyName").IsModified,
```

and the `IsModified` property for navigational properties is accessed via

```
context.Entry(entity).Navigation("PropertyName").IsModified
```

These two ways of setting the `IsModified` property provide a per property/bac field/shadow property flag to define what has changed if the entity's State is s `Modified`.

11.3 Looking at commands that change an entity's State

Figure 11.1 covers a simple entity, but when relationships are involved, the State tings get more complex. The following subsections present the commands that change the State of an entity and its relationships.

EF Core's approach to setting the State of an entity class has been finely tu based on feedback from the previous versions of EF (EF6.x and EF Core 1.x), t the State of related entities to the most "natural" State setting based on certain ria, especially when you are adding/updating an entity with relationships. To give an example, if you use the Add method to add a new entity with relationships to database, EF Core will decide whether any relationship entities' State should be s Added or Modified, depending on whether EF Core is tracking the entity. Gene this decision is the right one for most Add calls, but knowing how EF Core decides to set the State helps you when your needs fall outside normal use.

> **EF6** The setting for the State of an entity in EF Core differs from how EF6.x would set the State when you use methods such as Add and Remove. This chapter describes how EF Core sets the State of an entity. If you are interested in the changes from EF6.x, I recommend that you read this thread on the EF Core Git issues site: http://mng.bz/YA8A.

To start this section on an entity's State, table 11.1 lists the commands/actions change an entity's State.

Table 11.1 All the EF Core commands/actions that can change a tracked entity's State, showi example of each command/action and the final tracking State of the entity

Command/action	Example	Final Sta
Add/AddRange	context.Add(entity);	Added
Remove/RemoveRange	context.Remove(entity);	Deleted
Changing a property	entity.MyString = "hello";	Modified
Update/UpdateRange	context.Update(entity);	Modified
Attach/AttachRange	context.Attach(entity);	Unchange
Setting State directly	context.Entry(entity).State = …	Given Stat
Setting State via TrackGraph	context.ChangeTracker.TrackGraph(…	Given Stat

NOTE The SaveChange/SaveChangeAsync methods change the State of all the tracked entity classes to Unchanged. This topic is covered in section 11.4.

The table shows what happens for a single entity class with no relationships, but most of the commands also use a recursive search of any navigational properties to find any reachable entity classes. Any command that does a recursive search will track each reachable relational entity class and set its State.

You have already encountered most of these commands/actions, but a few commands, such as Attach and TrackGraph, haven't been covered so far. In this section, you visit each command/action. If the command/action has already been described, the section is short. New commands/actions are covered in more detail.

.1 The Add command: Inserting a new row into the database

The Add/AddRange methods are used to create a new entity in the database by setting the given entity's State to Added. Section 3.2 covers the Add method, and section 6.2.2 has a detailed, step-by-step look at adding an entity class with relationships. To summarize:

- The entity's State is set to Added.
- The Add method looks at all the entities linked to the added entity.
  - If a relationship isn't currently tracked, it is tracked, and its State is set to Added.
  - If a relationship is tracked, its current State is used unless there was a requirement to alter/set a foreign key, in which case its State is set to Modified.

Also, the AddAsync/AddRangeAsync methods are available for entities that use a value generator (see section 10.3.3) to set a property. If the value generator has a NextAsync method, you must use the AddAsync/AddRangeAsync methods when that entity is added.

.2 The Remove method: Deleting a row from the database

The Remove/RemoveRange methods delete the entity from the database by setting the given entity's State to Deleted. Section 3.5 covered the Remove method, and section 8.8.1 covers the different delete behaviors that EF Core supports. In this section, we are looking only at what happens to the State of the entity class you delete and the State of any of its relationships. If the removed entity has any relationships that are loaded/tracked, the value of the State for each relationship entities will be one of the following:

- State == Deleted—Typical for a required dependent relationship, such as a Review entity class linked to a Book entity class
- State == Modified—Typical for an optional dependent relationship in which the foreign key is nullable. In this case, the optional relationship is not deleted, but the foreign key that links to the entity that was deleted is set to null.
- State == Unchanged—Result of deleting a dependent entity class that is linked to a principal class. Nothing changes in the principal class keys/foreign keys when a dependent entity class is deleted.

NOTE You can get some odd State settings if you read in an entity class, add a required dependent relationship, and then delete the entity class. For a short time, the required dependent relationship will have a State of Added because it's the most logical State at that time.

But regardless of the State of relationships loaded with the entity class you del another stage takes precedence: the OnDelete behavior of the deleted entity cla the OnDelete behavior is set to Cascade, which is the default for a required depen relationship, it will delete any required dependent relationships of the deleted e class. Please see section 8.8.1 for a more detailed explanation.

11.3.3 Modifying an entity class by changing the data in that entity class

One clever thing that EF Core can do is automatically detect that you change data in an entity class and turn that change into an update of the database. This ture makes updates simple from the developer's point of view, but it requires qu bit of work on EF Core's part. The rules are

- For EF Core to detect a change, the entity must be tracked. Entities are tra if you read them in without an AsNoTracking method in the query or v you call a Add, Update, Remove, or Attach method with an entity class parameter.
- When you call SaveChanges/SaveChangesAsync, by default, EF Code execu method called ChangeTracker.DetectChanges, which compares the cur entity's data with the entity's tracking snapshot. If any properties, backing fi or shadow properties are different, the entity's State is set to Modified, an properties, backing fields, or shadow properties are set to IsModified.

Figure 11.2 gives you an idea of how EF Core can detect a change. In this example only change is to one of the properties in the first Book.

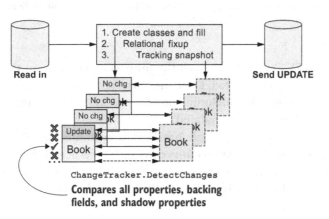

ChangeTracker.DetectChanges

Compares all properties, backing fields, and shadow properties

Figure 11.2 SaveChanges calls ChangeTracker .DetectChanges, which compares each tracked entit with its matching tracking snapshot to detect any differences between the two. ChangeTracker.Detect-Changes compares all data is mapped to the database. In example, only one property in first Book has been changed represented in the figure by c tick and the title Update abo the Book entity class.

4 *Modifying an entity class by calling the Update method*

Section 11.3.3 shows that EF Core can detect changes in an entity class for you. In chapter 3, however, you encountered an external application that returned a complete entity class in JSON form that had to be updated (see figure 11.3, which is taken from figure 3.3), but that entity class wasn't tracked. In this case, the Change-Tracker.DetectChanges method won't work because there is no tracking snapshot to compare. In cases like this one, you can use the Update and UpdateRange methods.

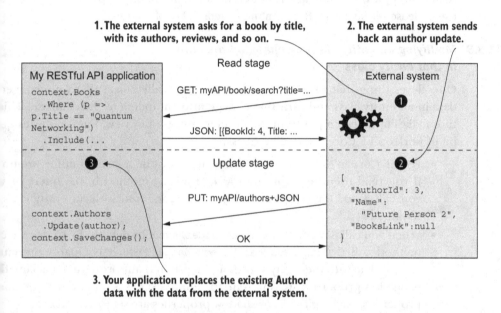

1. The external system asks for a book by title, with its authors, reviews, and so on.

2. The external system sends back an author update.

3. Your application replaces the existing Author data with the data from the external system.

Figure 11.3 An example of a disconnected update, in which you replace all the database information with the new data. The external system on the right returns the content of the Author class in JSON format. The ASP.NET Core application on the left converts the send JSON back to an Author entity class, and the receiving code uses EF Core's Update command to update the Authors table in the database. The Update command updates all the properties, backing fields, and shadow properties in the reconstituted entity class.

The Update method tells EF Core to update all the properties/columns in this entity by setting the given entity's State to Modified and sets the IsModified property to true on all nonrelational properties, including any foreign keys. As a result, the row in the database will have all its columns updated.

If the entity type using the Update call has loaded relationships, the Update method will recursively look at each related entity class and set its State. The rules for setting the State on a related entity class depend on whether the relationship entity's primary key is generated by the database and is set (its value isn't the default value for the key's .NET type):

- Database-generated key, not the default value—In this case, EF Core will ass
  that the relationship entity is already in the database and will set the Sta
  Modified if a foreign key needs to be set; otherwise, the State will be Unchan
- Not database-generated key, or the key is the default value—In this case, EF
  will assume that the relationship entity is new and will set its State to Added.

All that sounds quite complicated, but EF Core generally sets the State to the
appropriate setting. If you add an existing entry to an entity class's relationship
example, its State will be Updated, but if you add a new entry to an entity class's
tionships, its State will be Added.

11.3.5 The Attach method: Start tracking an existing untracked entity class

The Attach and AttachRange methods are useful if you have an entity class with
ing valid data and want it to be tracked. After you attach the entity, it's tracked, an
Core assumes that its content matches the current database state. This behavior v
well for reconstituting entities with relationships that have been serialized and
deserialized to an entity, but only if the entities are written back to the same data
as the primary and foreign keys need to match.

> **WARNING** Serializing and then deserializing an entity class instance that uses
> shadow properties needs special handling with the Attach method. The
> shadow properties aren't part of the class, so they'll be lost in any serializa-
> tion. Therefore, you must save/restore any shadow properties, especially for-
> eign keys, after the Attach method has been called.

When you Attach an entity, it becomes a normal tracked entity, without the cost of
ing it from the database. The Attach method does this by setting the entity's Sta
Unchanged. As with the Update method, what happens to the relationships of
updated entity depends on whether the relationship entity's primary key is generate
the database and is set (its value isn't the default value for the key's .NET type):

- *Database-generated key, and key has a default value*—EF Core will assume tha
  relationship entity is already in the database and will set the State to Added
- *Not a database-generated key, or the key is the not default value*—EF Core will ass
  that the relationship entity is new and will set its State to Unchanged.

If you are unsure whether to use Attach or Update in your code, I recommend
read Arthur Vickers's article "Make sure to call Update when it is needed!" (htt
mng.bz/G68O).

11.3.6 Setting the State of an entity directly

Another way to set the State of an entity is to set it manually to whatever state
want. This direct setting of an entity's State is useful when an entity has many
tionships, and you need to specifically decide which state you want each relation
to have. Section 11.3.7 shows a good example.

Because the entity's State is read/write, you can set it. In the following code snippet, the myEntity instance's State is set to Added:

```
context.Entry(myEntity).State = EntityState.Added;
```

You can also set the IsModified flag on the property in an entity. The following code snippet sets the MyString property's IsModified flag to true, which sets the entity's State to Modified:

```
var entity = new MyEntity();
context.Entry(entity).Property("MyString").IsModified = true;
```

> **NOTE** If the entity wasn't tracked before you set the State, it'll be tracked afterward.

.7 TrackGraph: Handling disconnected updates with relationships

The TrackGraph method is useful if you have an untracked entity with relationships, and you need to set the correct State for each entity. The TrackGraph method will traverse all the relational links in the entity, calling an action you supplied on each entity it finds. This method is useful if you have a group of linked entities coming from a disconnected situation (say, via some form of serialization), and you want to change only part of the data you've loaded.

> **EF6** The TrackGraph method is a welcome addition to EF Core. There's no equivalent command in EF6.x.

Let's expand on the simple example of a RESTful API in chapter 3, in which an author's Name property was updated. In that case, the external system sent back only the Author entity data. In this example, the external system will send back the whole book, with all its relationships, but it still wants you to update only the author's Name property in every Author entity class in the relationship.

Listing 11.1 shows the code you'd need to traverse a Book entity instance, which you've reconstituted from a JSON copy (not a tracked entity). The TrackGraph method will call your lambda Action method, given as the second parameter, for every entity, starting with the Book entity instance; then it will work through all the relational navigational property's entity instances it can reach.

Listing 11.1 Using TrackGraph to set each entity's State and IsModified flags

Expects an untracked book with its relationships

Calls ChangeTracker.TrackGraph, which takes an entity instance and an Action, which, in this case, you define via a lambda. The Action method is called once on each entity in the graph of entities.

If the method sets the state to any value other than Detached, the entity will become tracked by EF Core.

```
var book = … untracked book with all relationships
context.ChangeTracker.TrackGraph(book, e =>
{
    e.Entry.State = EntityState.Unchanged;
```

```
        if (e.Entry.Entity is Author)
        {
            e.Entry.Property("Name").IsModified = true;
        }
    });
    context.SaveChanges();
```

Here, you want
only the Name p
of the Author en
Modified, so you
whether the ent
type Author.

Sets the IsModified flag
on the Name property;
also sets the State of the
entity to Modified

**Calls SaveChanges, which finds that only the Name
property of the Author entity has been marked as
changed; creates the optimal SQL to update the
Name column in the Authors table**

TrackGraph traverses the entity provided as its first parameter and any entities tha
reachable by traversing its navigation properties. The traversal is recursive, so the
igation properties of any discovered entities will also be scanned. The Action me
you provide as the second parameter is called for each discovered untracked (S
== Detached) entity and can set the State that each entity should be tracked in. I
visited entity's State isn't set, the entity remains in the State of Detached (that is
entity isn't being tracked by EF Core). Also, TrackGraph will ignore any entities it
that are currently being tracked.

Although you could still use the Update command for this purpose, doin
would be inefficient because the command would update every table and colum
the book's relationships instead of only the authors' names. EF Core's ChangeTra
.TrackGraph method provides a better approach.

Figure 11.4 shows the "change only the Author's Name" example with an exte
system returning a serialized version of a Book entity. Using TrackGraph allows yc
target the specific entity and property you want to set the State to a new value; ir
case, you set the property called Name to IsModified in any Author entity class ir
relationships of the Book entity.

The result of running this code is that only the Author entity instance's State
to Modified, whereas the State of all the other entity types is set to Unchange
addition, the IsModified flag is set only on the Author entity class's Name prop
In this example, the difference between using an Updated method and using
TrackGraph code reduces the number of database updates: the Updated me
would produce 20 column updates (19 of them needlessly), whereas the TrackG
code would change only one column.

11.4 *SaveChanges and its use of ChangeTracker.DetectChanges*

Section 11.3 was about setting the State of the tracked entities so that when you
the SaveChanges (or SaveChangesAsync) method, the correct updates are applie
the database. In this section, you look at

- How SaveChanges finds any updates by using the ChangeTracker.DetectCha
  method
- What to do if ChangeTracker.DetectChanges is taking too long
- How to use the State of each tracked entity to log any changes
- How to tap into EF Core's StateChanged events

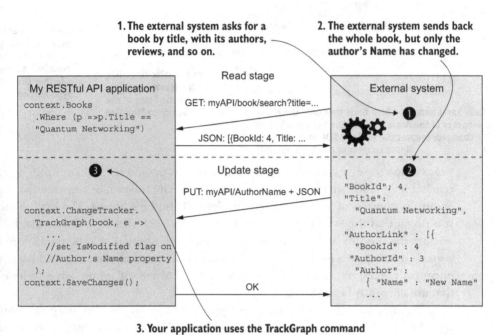

1. The external system asks for a book by title, with its authors, reviews, and so on.

2. The external system sends back the whole book, but only the author's Name has changed.

3. Your application uses the TrackGraph command to update only the author's Name property.

Figure 11.4 An external system that asks for a specific book and gets the JSON containing the book and all its relationships. When the external system wants to update each author's name, it sends back *all* the original JSON, with the changed names, but tells your application that it needs to change only the author's name. Your application uses EF Core's `ChangeTracker.TrackGraph` method to set all the classes to `State Unchanged` but sets the `IsModified flag` on the `Name` property in the `Author` entity class.

.1 How SaveChanges finds all the State changes

Whereas states such as `Added` and `Deleted` are set by the EF Core commands, the "change a property" approach (section 11.3.3) to updates relies on code to compare each entity class with its tracking snapshot. To do so, `SaveChanges` calls a method called `DetectChanges` that is accessed via the `ChangeTracker` property.

Figure 11.5 (repeated from section 11.3.3) shows an example in which four `Book` entities have been read in and one property, the `PublishedOn` property, was changed in the first `Book` entity instance.

This process makes updates easy for you, the developer; you update only the property, backing field, or shadow property, and the change will be detected. But if you have a lot of entities with lots of data, the process can become slow. Section 11.4.2 shows you a solution to use when `ChangeTracker.DetectChanges` is taking too long.

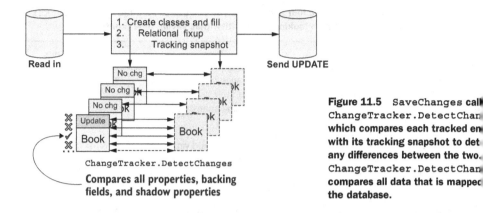

Figure 11.5 `SaveChanges` call `ChangeTracker.DetectChan` which compares each tracked en with its tracking snapshot to det any differences between the two. `ChangeTracker.DetectChan` compares all data that is mapped the database.

11.4.2 What to do if ChangeTracker.DetectChanges is taking too long

In some applications, you may have a large number of tracked entities loaded. V you're executing mathematical modeling or building artificial intelligence apption, for example, holding a lot of data in memory may be the only way to achieve level of performance that you require.

The problem is if you have a large amount of tracked entity instances and/or entities have a lot of data in them. In that case, a call to `SaveChanges/SaveChan Async` can become slow. If you are saving a lot of data, the slowness is most caused by the database accesses. But if you are saving only a small amount of data slowdown is likely due to the time the `ChangeTracker.DetectChanges` takes to pare each entity class instance with its matching tracking snapshot.

EF Core offers you a few ways to replace `ChangeTracker.DetectChanges` wit alternative way to detect changes. These features work by detecting individual up to the data in your entity classes, cutting out any comparisons of data that hasn't changed. A rather unscientific test of saving 100,000 tiny entities that had no cha took 350 ms with the normal `ChangeTracker.DetectChanges` method, for exam whereas the approach that detects changes via the class took 2 ms for the same da

You have four ways to replace the `ChangeTracker.DetectChanges`; each appr has different features and different levels of effort to implement. Table 11.2 sun rizes these approaches, with their pros and cons.

Table 11.2 A comparison of the four approaches you can use to stop the ChangeTracker .DetectChanges method from looking at an entity, thus saving time

What	Pros	Cons
`INotifyPropertyChanged`	■ Can change only the entities that are slow ■ Handles concurrency exceptions	■ Need to edit every pro

Table 11.2   A comparison of the four approaches you can use to stop the `ChangeTracker`
`.DetectChanges` method from looking at an entity, thus saving time *(continued)*

What	Pros	Cons
`INotifyPropertyChanged` and `INotifyPropertyChanging`	▪ Can change only the entities that are slow ▪ No tracking snapshot, so uses less memory	▪ Need to edit every property
Proxy change tracking (EF Core 5 feature) `INotifyPropertyChanged`	▪ Easy to code; add virtual to every property ▪ Handles concurrency exceptions	▪ Must change *all* entity types to use proxy
Proxy change tracking (EF Core 5 feature) `INotifyPropertyChanged` and `INotifyPropertyChanging`	▪ Easy to code; add virtual to every property ▪ No tracking snapshot, so uses less memory	▪ Must change *all* entity types to use proxy ▪ Have to create a new entity class via the `CreateProxy<T>` method

Overall, the proxy change tracking feature is easier to code but requires you to change all your entity classes to use proxy change tracking. But if you find a `SaveChanges` performance issue in an existing application, changing all your entity classes might be too much work. For this reason, I focus on the first approach, `INotifyPropertyChanged`, which is easy to add to a few entity classes that have a problem, and the last approach, proxy changed/changing tracking, which is easier but requires you to use it across the whole application.

FIRST APPROACH: INOTIFYPROPERTYCHANGED

EF Core supports the `INotifyPropertyChanged` interface on an entity class to detect whether any property has changed. This interface notifies EF Core that a property has changed, but you have to raise a `PropertyChanged` event, which means the `Change-Tracker.DetectChanges` method isn't used.

To use the `INotifyPropertyChanged` interface you need to create a `Notification-Entity` helper class, shown in the following listing. This class provides a `SetWith-Notify` method that you call when any property in your entity class changes.

Listing 11.2   `NotificationEntity` helper class that `NotifyEntity` inherits

```
public class NotificationEntity : INotifyPropertyChanged
{
    public event PropertyChangedEventHandler PropertyChanged;

    protected void SetWithNotify<T>(T value, ref T field,
        [CallerMemberName] string propertyName = "")
    {
        if (!Object.Equals(field, value))
        {
            field = value;
```

Automatically gets the propertyName by using System.Runtime .CompilerServices

Only if the field and the value are different do you set the field and raise the event.

s the
o the
value

```
            PropertyChanged?.Invoke(this,
                new PropertyChangedEventArgs(propertyName));
        }
    }
}
```

... with the name
of the property

**Invokes the PropertyChanged event, but using ?.
to stop the method from failing when the new
entity is created and the PropertyChangedEvent-
Handler hasn't been filled in by EF Core...**

The following listing shows an entity class called `NotifyEntity`, which inherit
`NotificationEntity` shown in listing 11.2. You must call the `SetWithNotify` me
whenever a noncollection property changes. For collections, you have to u
`ObservableCollection` to raise an event when a navigational collection pro
is changed.

Listing 11.3 `NotifyEntity` using `NotificationEntity` class for events

```
public class NotifyEntity : NotificationEntity
{
    private int _id;
    private string _myString;
    private NotifyOne _oneToOne;

    public int Id
    {
        get => _id;
        set => SetWithNotify(value, ref _id);
    }

    public string MyString
    {
        get => _myString;
        set => SetWithNotify(value, ref _myString);
    }

    public NotifyOne OneToOne
    {
        get => _oneToOne;
        set => SetWithNotify(value, ref _oneToOne);
    }

    public ObservableCollection<NotifyMany>
        Collection { get; }
        = new ObservableCollection<NotifyMany>();
}
```

**Each noncollection
property must have
a backing field.**

**If a noncollection
property is changed
you need to raise a
PropertyChanged
event, which you do
via the inherited
method SetWithNot**

**Any collection naviga
property must be an
Observable collection
you need to predefin
Observable collection**

**You can use any Observable collection, but for performance
reasons, EF Core prefers ObservableHashSet<T>.**

After you've defined your entity class to use the `INotifyPropertyChanged` i
face, you must configure the tracking strategy for this entity class to `Chan
Notifications` (listing 11.4). This configuration tells EF Core not to detect cha
via `ChangeTracker.DetectChanges` because it will be notified of any change

INotifyPropertyChanged events. To configure INotifyPropertyChanged events for one entity class, you use the Fluent API command.

Listing 11.4 Setting the tracking strategy for one entity to ChangedNotifications

```
protected override void OnModelCreating(ModelBuilder modelBuilder)
{
    modelBuilder
      .Entity<NotifyEntity>()
      .HasChangeTrackingStrategy(
          ChangeTrackingStrategy.ChangedNotifications);
}
```

APPROACHES 2 AND 3

I am not covering approach 2 (change and changing events), but the differences from approach 1 are

- The NotificationEntity class must create change and changing events.
- You use a different ChangeTrackingStrategy setting, such as ChangingAnd-ChangedNotifications.

Also not covered is approach 3 (proxy change tracking, INotifyPropertyChanged), which works in a similar way to how lazy loading proxy works with virtual properties. Instead, I cover the last approach (described next), which handles both INotify-PropertyChanged and INotifyPropertyChanging. The main difference is that in approach 3, you can create an instance of an entity class by using the normal constructor approach, whereas the last approach requires you to use the CreateProxy<TEntity> method to create an entity class.

LAST APPROACH: PROXY CHANGE TRACKING

The last approach uses proxy change tracking via the INotifyPropertyChanged and INotifyPropertyChanging events introduced in EF Core 5. These change-tracking events are added to the lazy-loading proxy approach with the virtual properties described in section 2.4.4. To use this approach, you need to do five things:

- Change all your entity classes to have virtual properties.
- Use an Observable collection type for navigational collection properties.
- Change your code that creates a new instance of an entity class to use the Create-Proxy<TEntity> method.
- Add the NuGet library Microsoft.EntityFrameworkCore.Proxies.
- Add the method UseChangeTrackingProxies when building the application's DbContext options.

Let's start by looking at the structure of the entity class you need to use the proxy change tracking approach, as shown in the following listing.

Listing 11.5   An example entity class set up to use proxy change tracking

```
public class ProxyMyEntity
{
    public virtual int Id { get; set; }
    public virtual string MyString { get; set; }                   All propertie
    public virtual ProxyOptional ProxyOptional { get; set; }       must be virt

    public virtual ObservableCollection<ProxyMany>
        Many { get; set; }                            For navigational collection
        = new ObservableCollection<ProxyMany>();      properties, you need to use
}                                                     an Observable collection ty
```

If you read in an entity class via a query, the proxy change tracking will add its code to create the INotifyPropertyChanged and INotifyPropertyChanging e when a property is changed. But if you want to create a new entity class, you can' the normal new command, such as new Book(). Instead, you must use the Cre Proxy<TEntity> method. If you wanted to add a new version of the ProxyMyEn class shown in listing 11.5, for example, you would write

```
var entity = context.CreateProxy<ProxyMyEntity>();
entity.MyString = "hello";
context.Add(entity);
context.SaveChanges();
```

You must use the CreateProxy<TEntity> method (first line of the preceding code pet); otherwise, EF Core won't be able to detect the changing event. (Don't worry; i forget, EF Core throws an exception with a useful message.)

The final part is making sure that the Microsoft.EntityFrameworkCore.Pro NuGet package is loaded and then updating your DbContext configuration to inc the UseChangeTrackingProxies method, as shown in the following code snippet:

```
var optionsBuilder =
    new DbContextOptionsBuilder<EfCoreContext>();
optionsBuilder
    .UseChangeTrackingProxies()
    .UseSqlServer(connection);
var options = optionsBuilder.Options;

using (var context = new EfCoreContext(options))
```

> **NOTE**   For the third approach, you can turn off the INotifyPropertyChanging part of the proxy change tracking by setting the first parameter, useChange-TrackingProxies, in the UseChangeTrackingProxies method to false. Then EF Core would start using the tracking snapshot for comparison.

.3 Using the entities' State within the SaveChanges method

So far, you've learned how to set the State of an entity and heard about how Change-Tracker can be used to find out what has changed. Now you are going to use the State data within the SaveChanges/SaveChangesAsync to do some interesting things. Here are some of the possible uses of detecting what's about to be changed in the database:

- Automatically adding extra information to an entity—for instance, adding the time when an entity was added or updated
- Writing a history audit trail to the database each time a specific entity type is changed
- Add security checks to see whether the current user is allowed to update that particular entity type

The basic approach is to override the SaveChanges/SaveChangesAsync methods inside your application's DbContext and execute a method before the base SaveChanges/SaveChangesAsync is called. We check the States before the base SaveChanges is called because a) the State of every tracked entity will have a value of Unchanged once SaveChanges is called and b) you want to add/alter some of the entities before they are written to the database. What you do with the State information is up to you, but next is an example that logs the last time the entity was added or updated, with the UserId of the user who did the add/update.

The following listing provides an interface you can add to any entity class. This defines the properties that you want filled in when the entity is added or updated, and a method that can be used to set the properties to the right values.

> Listing **11.6** The ICreatedUpdated interface defining four properties and a method

Add this interface to any entity class where you want to log when/who it was created or updated.

Holds the datetime when the entity was first added to the database

```
public interface ICreatedUpdated
{
    DateTime WhenCreatedUtc { get; }
    Guid CreatedBy { get; }
    DateTime LastUpdatedUtc { get; }
    Guid LastUpdatedBy { get; }

    void LogChange(EntityState state, Guid userId = default);
}
```

Holds the UserId who created the entity

Holds the datetime when the entity was last updated

Called when the entity's state is Added or Modified State. Its job is to update the properties based on the state.

Holds the UserId who last updated the entity

The following listing shows an entity class called CreatedUpdatedInfo that implements the ICreatedUpdated interface that you'll detect when your modified SaveChanges method is called (see listing 11.8). The LogChange method, which you'll call in your modified SaveChanges method, sets the various properties in the entity class.

Listing 11.7   Automatically setting who and when a entity was updated

Entity class inherits ICreatedUpdated, which
means any addition/update of the entity is logged.

```
public class CreatedUpdatedInfo : ICreatedUpdated    ◁─┘
    {
        public DateTime WhenCreatedUtc { get; private set; }      These properties h
        public Guid CreatedBy { get; private set; }               private setters so
        public DateTime LastUpdatedUtc { get; private set; }      only the LogChang
        public Guid LastUpdatedBy { get; private set; }           method can chang

        public void LogChange(EntityEntry entry,                  Its job is to update the
            Guid userId = default)                                created and updated
        {                                                         properties. It is passed
            if (entry.State != EntityState.Added &&               the UserId if available.
                entry.State != EntityState.Modified)
                return;                                           Obtains the current time s
                                                                  that an add and update tin
            var timeNow = DateTime.UtcNow;              ◁─┘       will be the same on create
            LastUpdatedUtc = timeNow;
            LastUpdatedBy = userId;
            if (entry.State == EntityState.Added)                 If it's an add, then you update
            {                                                     the WhenCreatedUtc and the
                WhenCreatedUtc = timeNow;                         CreatedBy properties.
                CreatedBy = userId;
            }
            else
            {
                entry.Property(                                   For performance
                    nameof(ICreatedUpdated.LastUpdatedUtc))       reasons you turne
                    .IsModified = true;                           off DetectChanges
                entry.Property(                                   you must manual
                    nameof(ICreatedUpdated.LastUpdatedBy))        mark the propert
                    .IsModified = true;                           as modified.
            }
        }
    }
}
```

This method only
handles Added or
Modified States.

It always sets the
LastUpdatedUtc
and LastUpdatedBy.

The next step is to override all versions of the SaveChanges method inside your a
cation's DbContext and then precede the call to the base SaveChanges with a c
your AddUpdateChecks method shown in listing 11.8. This method looks for en
with a State of Added or Modified and inherits the ICreatedUpdated interface. I
method finds an entity (or entities) that fits that criteria, it calls the entity's LogCh
method to set the two properties to the correct values.

The following listing shows your application's DbContext, called Chapter1
Context, which implements that code. (To keep the code shorter, you only ove
the SaveChanges method. Normally, you'd also override the SaveChangesAsync me
with two parameters.) Notice too that the code ensures the ChangeTracker.Det
Changes method is only called once, because, as you have seen, that method can
some time.

Listing 11.8 Your DbContext looks for added or modified `ICreatedUpdated` entities

This private method will be called from
SaveChanges and SaveChangesAsync.

It calls DetectChanges to
make sure all the updates
have been found.

```
private void AddUpdateChecks()
{
    ChangeTracker.DetectChanges();
    foreach (var entity in ChangeTracker.Entries()
        .Where(e =>
            e.State == EntityState.Added ||
            e.State == EntityState.Modified))
    {
        var tracked = entity.Entity as ICreatedUpdated;
        tracked?.LogChange(entity);
    }
}

public override int SaveChanges(bool acceptAllChangesOnSuccess)
{
    AddUpdateChecks();
    try
    {
        ChangeTracker.AutoDetectChangesEnabled = false;
        return base.SaveChanges(acceptAllChangesOnSuccess);
    }
    finally
    {
        ChangeTracker.AutoDetectChangesEnabled = true;
    }
}
```

It loops through all
the tracked entities
that have a State of
Added or Modified.

So we call the LogChange
command. In this example we
don't have the UserId available.

You override SaveChanges (and
SaveChangesAsync—not shown).

You call the base.SaveChanges
that you overrode

Because
DetectChanges
has been called
we tell
SaveChanges not
to call it again
(for performance
reasons).

Finally to turn the
AutoDetectChangesEnabled
back on

You call the AddUpdateChecks,
which contains a call to
ChangeTracker.DetectChanges().

This is only one example of using `ChangeTracker` to take actions based on the `State` of tracked entities, but it establishes the general approach. The possibilities are endless.

NOTE In chapter 16 I have another example of detecting the `State` of certain entities to update a separate database when a `Book` or its related entities change.

.4 Catching entity class's State changes via events

EF Core 2.1 added two events to EF Core: `ChangeTracker.Tracked`, which is triggered when an entity is first tracked, and `ChangeTracker.StateChanged`, which is triggered when the `State` of an already tracked entity is changed. This feature provides a similar effect to calling `ChangeTracker.Entries()`, but by producing an event when something changes. The `ChangeTracker` events are useful for features such as logging changes or triggering actions when a specific entity type's `State` changes. But to start, let's look at the basics of these two events.

The `Tracked` event, which is simpler, is triggered when an entity class is tracked and tells you whether it came from a query via its `FromQuery` property. event could occur when you execute an EF Core query (without the `AsNoTrac` method) or start tracking an entity class via an `Add` or `Attach` method. The follo listing is a unit test that captures a `Tracked` event when an entity class is `Add`ed t context.

Listing 11.9 Example of a `ChangeTracker.Tracked` event and what it contain:

Holds a log of any tracked events →

```
var logs = new List<EntityTrackedEventArgs>();
context.ChangeTracker.Tracked += delegate(
    object sender, EntityTrackedEventArgs args)
{
    logs.Add(args);
};
//ATTEMPT
var entity = new MyEntity {MyString = "Test"};
context.Add(entity);

//VERIFY
logs.Count.ShouldEqual(1);
logs.Single().FromQuery.ShouldBeFalse();
logs.Single().Entry.Entity.ShouldEqual(entity);
logs.Single().Entry.State
    .ShouldEqual(EntityState.Added);
```

You register your event handl the ChangeTracker.Tracked ev

This event handler simply logs the EntityTrackedEventArgs.

Creates an entity class

Adds that entity class to context

There is one event.

This event wasn't tracking during a query

You can access the entity that triggered the event.

You can also get the current State of that entity.

This listing shows you what information is available in the event data. For a Tra event, you get the `FromQuery` flag, which is `true` if the query was tracked duri query. The `Entry` property gives you information about the entity.

One thing to note in this example is that the `context.Add(entity)` method gers an `Tracked` event but doesn't trigger a `StateChanges` event. If you want to d a newly added entity class, you can do so only via the `Tracked` event.

The `StateChanges` event is similar but contains different information. The follo listing captures the `StateChanges` event when `SaveChanges` is called. The event con the entity's `State` before `SaveChanges` was called in the property called `OldS` and the entity's `State` after `SaveChanges` was called in the property called `NewStat`

Listing 11.10 Example of a `ChangeTracker.StateChanges` event and what it cont

Holds a log of any StateChanged events

```
var logs = new List<EntityStateChangedEventArgs>();
context.ChangeTracker.StateChanged += delegate
    (object sender, EntityStateChangedEventArgs args)
{
    logs.Add(args);
};
```

You register your event handler to the ChangeTrack .StateChanged ev

This event handler simply logs the EntityTrackedEventArgs.

```
//ATTEMPT
var entity = new MyEntity { MyString = "Test" };          Adds that entity
context.Add(entity);                                       class to context
context.SaveChanges();           ◄─────── SaveChanges will change the State to
                                          Unchanged after the database update.
//VERIFY
logs.Count.ShouldEqual(1);                                         The State before
logs.Single().OldState.ShouldEqual(EntityState.Added);    ◄─────── the change was
logs.Single().NewState.ShouldEqual(EntityState.Unchanged); ◄────── Added
logs.Single().Entry.Entity.ShouldEqual(entity);  ◄────────
                                                                The State after the
                    You get access to the entity                change is Unchanged
                    data via the Entry property.
```

The listing shows that you get the before and after States of the entity by using the OldState and NewState properties, respectively. Now that you have seen the two ChangeTracker events, let's use them for logging changes to some other form of storage. But in the following listing, I show a class that will turn the two ChangeTracker events into logs via NET's ILogger interface.

> **Listing 11.11 Class holding the code to turn `ChangeTracker` events into logs**

```
public class ChangeTrackerEventHandler    ◄──── This class is used in your
{                                                DbContext to log changes.
    private readonly ILogger _logger;

                                                         You will log
    public ChangeTrackerEventHandler(DbContext context,  to ILogger.
        ILogger logger)
    {                                                          Adds a Tracked
        _logger = logger;                          ◄───────── event handler
        context.ChangeTracker.Tracked += TrackedHandler;    ◄──
        context.ChangeTracker.StateChanged += StateChangeHandler;
    }

    private void TrackedHandler(object sender,      Handles
        EntityTrackedEventArgs args)                Tracked events
    {
        if (args.FromQuery)       We do not want to log
            return;               entities that are read in.

        var message = $"Entity: {NameAndPk(args.Entry)}. " +     Forms a useful
            $"Was {args.Entry.State}";                           message on Add
        _logger.LogInformation(message);                         or Attach
    }

    private void StateChangeHandler(object sender,
        EntityStateChangedEventArgs args)
    {                                                            The
        var message = $"Entity: {NameAndPk(args.Entry)}. " +     StateChanged
            $"Was {args.OldState} and went to {args.NewState}";  event handler
        _logger.LogInformation(message);                         logs any changes.
    }
}
```

Now add this code to the constructor of your application DbContext, as shown i■
following listing.

Listing 11.12 Adding the `ChangeTrackerEventHandler` to your application DbCon■

```
public class Chapter11DbContext : DbContext         ◁──┐  Your application DbContext
{                                                         you want to log changes fro■
    private ChangeTrackerEventHandler _trackerEventHandler;  ◁──  You need■
                                                                 instance
    public Chapter11DbContext(                                   event ha■
        DbContextOptions<Chapter11DbContext> options,           class whi■
        ILogger logger = null)                                  DbContex■
        : base(options)           ┌─ If an ILogger is
    {                             │  available, you register
        if (logger != null)    ◁──┘  the handlers.
            _trackerEventHandler = new                    ─┐  Creates the ev■
                ChangeTrackerEventHandler(this, logger);   │  handler class,
    }                                                      │  which register■
    //… rest of code left out                              ─┘  event handlers■
}
```

You add a
ILogger to the
constructor.

This example is a simple one, but it does show how powerful the `ChangeTra`■
events are. My logged messages are rather simple (see the next listing), but you c■
easily expand these messages to detail what properties have been modified, inc■
the `UserId` of the user who changed things, and so on.

Listing 11.13 Example output of `ChangeTrackerEventHandler` event logging

Code that triggered that event: context.Add(new MyEntity)

Code that
triggered
context.Sa■

```
Entity: MyEntity {Id: -2147482647}. Was Added           ◁──┘
Entity: MyEntity {Id: 1}. Was Added and went to Unchanged      ◁──┘
Entity: MyEntity {Id: 1}. Was Unchanged and went to Modified
Entity: MyEntity {Id: 1}. Was Modified and went to Unchanged    ◁──┐
```

**Code that triggered that event: entity.MyString
= "New string" + DetectChanges**

**Code that triggered that
event: context.SaveChanges()**

11.4.5 Triggering events when SaveChanges/SaveChangesAsync is called

EF Core 5 introduced `SavingChanges`, `SavedChanges`, and `SaveChangesFailed` ev■
which are called before the data is saved to the database, after the data has been■
cessfully saved to the database, and if the save to the database failed, respecti■
These events allow you to tap into what is happening in the `SaveChanges`■
`SaveChangesAsync` methods. You could use these events to log what was written t■
database or alert someone if there was a certain exception inside `SaveChange`■
`SaveChangesAsync`.

To use these events, you need to subscribe to the `SavingChanges` and `Sa`■
`Changes` events. The following listing shows you how.

Listing 11.14 How to subscribe to the `SavingChanges/SavedChanges` **events**

This event will trigger when SaveChanges is
called but before it updates the database.

```
context.SavingChanges +=              ◄─┘
─▷ delegate(object dbContext,
       SavingChangesEventArgs args)   ◄─┘
{
     var trackedEntities =
        ((DbContext)dbContext)        ◄─┤
        .ChangeTracker.Entries();
     //… your code goes here
};

context.SavedChanges +=               ◄─┘
─▷ delegate(object dbContext,
            SavedChangesEventArgs args) ◄─┤
{
     //… your code goes here
};

context. SaveChangesFailed+=          ◄─┘
─▷ delegate(object dbContext,
            SaveChangesFailedEventArgs args) ◄─┐
{
     //… your code goes here
};
```

The SavingChangesEventArgs contains
the SaveChanges Boolean parameter
acceptAllChangesOnSuccess.

The first parameter is the instance
of the DbContext, but you need to
cast the object to use it.

This event will trigger when
SaveChanges successfully
updates the database.

The SavedChangesEventArgs
contains the count of entities
that were saved to the database.

This event will trigger when
SaveChanges has an exception
during an update to the database.

The SavingChangesEventArgs
contains the exception that
happened during the update
to the database.

To use these events, you need to know a few things about them:

- Like all C# events, the subscription to these events lasts only as long as the instance of the DbContext exists.
- The events are triggered by both the `SaveChanges` and `SaveChangesAsync` methods.
- The `SavingChanges` event is called before the `ChangeTracker.DetectChanges` method is called, so if you want to implement the code shown in section 11.4.3 to update entities by using their `State`, you need to call the `ChangeTracker` `.DetectChanges` method first. This approach isn't a good idea, however, because `DetectChanges` would be called twice, which could cause a performance issue.

.6 *EF Core interceptors*

EF Core 3.0 introduced interceptors that enable you intercept, modify, and/or suppress EF Core operations, including low-level database operations, such as executing a command, as well as higher-level operations, such as calls to `SaveChanges`. These interceptors have some powerful features, such as altering commands being sent to the database.

This feature is advanced, so this section simply signposts the fact that it is available. Also, the EF Core documentation for interceptors is good, provides lots of useful

examples, and is about 15 pages long. I refer you to the Microsoft documentatio
more information (http://mng.bz/zGJQ).

11.5 *Using SQL commands in an EF Core application*

EF Core has methods that allow raw SQL commands to be used, either as part
LINQ query or a database write, such as an SQL UPDATE. These commands are
ful when the query you want to perform can't be expressed with LINQ—when it
an SQL stored procedure, for example, or when a LINQ query results in ineffi
SQL being sent to the database.

> **DEFINITION** An SQL stored procedure is a set of SQL commands—which may
> or may not have parameters—that can be executed. These commands typi-
> cally read and/or write to the database. The set of SQL commands is stored in
> the database as a stored procedure and given a name. Then the stored proce-
> dure can be called as part of an SQL command.

EF Core's SQL commands are designed to detect SQL injection attacks—attac
which a malicious user replaces, say, a primary-key value with some SQL commands
extract extra data from your database. EF Core provides two types of SQL comman

- Methods ending in `Raw`, such as `FromSqlRaw`. In these commands, you pro
  separate parameters, and those parameters are checked.
- Methods ending in `Interpolated`, such as `FromSqlInterpolated`. The s
  parameter provided to these methods used C#6's string interpolation with
  parameters in the string, such as `$"SELECT * FROM Books WHERE Book
  {myKey}"`. EF Core can check each parameter within the interpolated string

> **WARNING** If you build an interpolated string outside the command—such as
> `var badSQL = $"SELECT … WHERE BookId = {myKey}"`—and then use it in a
> command like `FromSqlRaw(badSQL)`, EF Core can't check SQL injection
> attacks. You should use `FromSqlRaw` with parameters or `FromSqlInterpolated`
> with parameters embedded in a string interpolation.

You can include SQL commands in EF commands in several ways. In addition to s
ing each group, I will use a mixture of ...Raw and ...Interpolated sync versions in
examples. Every command I show has an async version other than the `GetDbConnec`
method. The groups of SQL commands that are covered are

- `FromSqlRaw`/`FromSqlInterpolated` sync/async methods, which allow yo
  use a raw SQL command in an EF Core query
- `ExecuteSqlRaw`/`ExecuteSqlInterpolated` sync/async methods, which exe
  a nonquery command
- `AsSqlQuery` Fluent API method, which maps an entity class to an SQL quer
- `Reload`/`ReloadAsync` command, used to refresh an EF Core-loaded entity
  has been changed by an `ExecuteSql…` method

- EF Core's GetDbConnection method, which provides low-level database access libraries to access the database directly

EF6 The commands in EF Core for SQL access are different from the way that EF6.x provides SQL access to the database.

.1 FromSqlRaw/FromSqlInterpolated: Using SQL in an EF Core query

The FromSqlRaw/FromSqlInterpolated methods allow you to add raw SQL commands to a standard EF Core query, including commands that you wouldn't be able to call from EF Core, such as stored procedures. Here's an example of calling a stored procedure that returns only books that have an average review vote of the given value.

Listing 11.15 Using a FromSqlInterpolated method to call an SQL stored procedure

You start the query in the normal way, with the DbSet<T> you want to read.

The FromSqlInterpolated method allows you to insert an SQL command.

```
int filterBy = 5;
var books = context.Books
    .FromSqlInterpolated(
        $"EXECUTE dbo.FilterOnReviewRank @RankFilter = {filterBy}")
    .IgnoreQueryFilters()
    .ToList();
```

Uses C#6's string interpolation feature to provide the parameter

You need to remove any query filters; otherwise, the SQL won't be valid.

There are a few rules about an SQL query:

- The SQL query must return data for all properties of the entity type (but there is a way around this rule; see section 11.5.5).
- The column names in the result set must match the column names that properties are mapped to.
- The SQL query can't contain related data, but you can add the Include method to load related navigational properties (see listing 11.16).

You can add other EF Core commands after the SQL command, such as Include, Where, and OrderBy. The following listing shows an SQL command that filters the results by the average star rating with an Include of the book's Reviews and AsNoTracking command added.

Listing 11.16 Example of adding extra EF Core commands to the end of an SQL query

```
double minStars = 4;
var books = context.Books
    .FromSqlRaw(
        "SELECT * FROM Books b WHERE " +
        "(SELECT AVG(CAST([NumStars] AS float)) " +
        "FROM dbo.Review AS r " +
```

The SQL calculates the average votes and uses it in an SQL WHERE.

```
            "WHERE b.BookId = r.BookId) >= {0}", minStars)
        .Include(r => r.Reviews)
        .AsNoTracking()
        .ToList();
```

In this case, you use the normal sql parameter check and substitution method— {0}, {1}, {2}, and so on.

The Include method works with the FromSql because you are not executing a store procedure.

You can add other EF Core commands after the SQL command.

WARNING If you're using model-level query filters (see section 6.1.7), the SQL you can write has limitations. ORDER BY won't work, for example. The way around this problem is to apply the IgnoreQueryFilters method after the Sql command and re-create the model-level query filter in your SQL code.

11.5.2 ExecuteSqlRaw/ExecuteSqlInterpolated: Executing a nonquery command

In addition to putting raw SQL commands in a query, you can execute nonq SQL commands via EF Core's ExecuteSqlRaw/ExecuteSqlInterpolated meth Typical commands are SQL UPDATE and DELETE, but any nonquery SQL comm can be called. The following listing shows an SQL UPDATE command, which two parameters.

Listing 11.17 The ExecuteSqlCommand method executing an SQL UPDATE

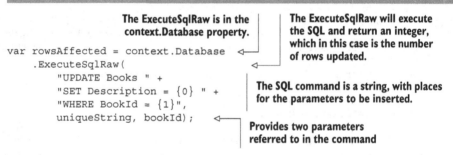

The ExecuteSqlRaw is in the context.Database property.

The ExecuteSqlRaw will execute the SQL and return an integer, which in this case is the number of rows updated.

```
var rowsAffected = context.Database
    .ExecuteSqlRaw(
        "UPDATE Books " +
        "SET Description = {0} " +
        "WHERE BookId = {1}",
        uniqueString, bookId);
```

The SQL command is a string, with places for the parameters to be inserted.

Provides two parameters referred to in the command

The ExecuteSqlRaw method returns an integer, which is useful for checking tha command was executed in the way you expected. In this example, you'd expec method to return 1 to show that it found and updated a row in the Books table had the primary key you provided.

11.5.3 AsSqlQuery Fluent API method: Mapping entity classes to queries

EF Core 5 provided a way to map an entity class to an SQL query via a the AsSqlQ Fluent API method. This feature allows you to hide your SQL code inside the app tion's DbContext's configuration, and developers can use this DbSet<T> proper queries as though it were a normal entity class mapped to an entity. It's a read entity class, of course, but see the following note if you need a read/write version

NOTE EF Core 5 added the ability to configure an entity class to be mapped to both a table (for create, update, and delete) and a view (for read). See http://mng.bz/0rY6.

As an example, you will create an entity class called BookSqlQuery that returns three values for a Book entity class: BookId, Title, and the average votes for this Book in a property called AverageVotes. This class is shown in the following listing.

Listing 11.18 The `BookSqlQuery` class to map to an SQL query

```
public class BookSqlQuery
{                                          The primary key of
    [Key]                                  the book that is
    public int BookId { get; set; }    ◁─┘ returned

    public string Title { get; set; }  ◁─┘ The title of the book

    public double? AverageVotes { get; set; }  ◁─┤ The average votes for this
}                                                  Book based on the Review's
                                                   NumStars property
```

Now you need to configure this entity class to an SQL query, using the AsSqlQuery Fluent API method, as shown in the following listing.

Listing 11.19 Configuring the `BookSqlQuery` entity class to an SQL query

```
public class BookDbContext : DbContext          You add a DbSet<T> for the
{                                               BookSqlQuery entity class to
    //… other DbSets removed for clarity        make querying easy.

    public DbSet<BookSqlQuery> BookSqlQueries { get; set; }    ◁─┘

    protected override void
        OnModelCreating(ModelBuilder modelBuilder)
    {                                                           The ToSqlQuery
        //… other configrations removed for clarity            method maps the
                                                                entity class to an
        modelBuilder.Entity<BookSqlQuery>().ToSqlQuery(  ◁─┘    SQL query.
        @"SELECT BookId
            ,Title
            ,(SELECT AVG(CAST([r0].[NumStars] AS float))    Returns the
        FROM Review AS r0                                    three values
        WHERE t.BookId = r0.BookId)  AS AverageVotes         for each Book
        FROM Books AS t");
    }
}
```

You can add LINQ commands, such as Where and OrderBy, in the normal way, but the returned data follows the same rules as the FromSqlRaw and FromSqlInterpolated methods (section 11.5.1).

11.5.4 Reload: Used after ExecuteSql commands

If you have an entity loading (tracked), and you use an ExecuteSqlRaw/Exec SqlInterpolated method to change the data on the database, your tracked ent out of date. That situation could cause you a problem later, because EF Core do know that the values have been changed. To fix this problem, EF Core has a me called Reload/ReloadAsync, which updates your entity by rereading the database

In the following listing, you load an entity, change its content via the Execute Command method, and then use the Reload method to make sure that the entity's tent matches what's in the database.

Listing 11.20 Using the `Reload` method to refresh the content of an existing enti

```
var entity = context.Books.
    Single(x => x.Title == "Quantum Networking");
var uniqueString = Guid.NewGuid().ToString();
```
⟵ Loads a Book entity in the normal way

```
context.Database.ExecuteSqlRaw(
        "UPDATE Books " +
        "SET Description = {0} " +
        "WHERE BookId = {1}",
        uniqueString, entity.BookId);
```
Uses ExecuteSqlRaw to change the Description column of that same Book entity

```
context.Entry(entity).Reload();
```
⟵ When calling the Reload method, EF Core rereads that entity to make sure that the local copy is up to date.

At the end of this code, the entity instance will match what's in the database.

11.5.5 GetDbConnection: Running your own SQL commands

When EF Core can't provide the query features you want, you need to drop ba another database access method that can. A few low-level database libraries requ lot more code to be written but provide more-direct access to the database, so you do almost anything you need to do. Normally, these low-level database librarie database-server-specific. In this section, you use a NuGet library called Dapper https://github.com/StackExchange/Dapper). Dapper is a simple object mappe .NET, sometimes known as a micro-ORM. Dapper is simple but fast. It uses the ADO. library to access the database and adds autocopying of columns to class propertie

The following listing uses Dapper to read specific columns into a nonentity called RawSqlDto that has properties called BookId, Title, and AverageVotes, sc can load only the columns you want. In this example, you use Dapper to query same database that your application's DbContext is linked to. The Dapper q returns a single RawSqlDto class with data in the three properties for the Books where the BookId column (the primary key) has a value of 4.

Listing 11.21 Obtaining a `DbConnection` from EF Core to run a Dapper SQL query

Gets a DbConnection to the database, which
the micro-ORM called Dapper can use

```
var connection = context.Database.GetDbConnection();
string query = "SELECT b.BookId, b.Title, " +
    "(SELECT AVG(CAST([NumStars] AS float)) " +
    "FROM dbo.Review AS r " +
    "WHERE b.BookId = r.BookId) AS AverageVotes " +
    "FROM Books b " +
    "WHERE b.BookId = @bookId";
```

Creates the SQL
query you want
to execute

```
var bookDto = connection
    .Query<RawSqlDto>(query, new
    {
        bookId = 4
    })
    .Single();
```

Calls Dapper's Query method with
the type of the returned data

Provides parameters to Dapper to
be added to the SQL command

PERFORMANCE TIP `FromSqlRaw`/`FromSqlInterpolated` methods must return all the columns mapped to the entity calls, and even if you add a LINQ `Select` after the `FromSqlRaw`/`FromSqlInterpolated` method, it still returns all the columns. As a result, Dapper is likely to be faster at loading a few columns from the database than any of the EF Core `RawSql...` methods.

Don't be afraid to mix EF Core and Dapper, especially if you have a performance problem. I use Dapper with EF Core in part 3 to get a performance improvement because I wrote an improved SQL query that sorted on average review stars. The downside of Dapper is that it doesn't know anything about navigational properties, so working with linked entities takes more code in Dapper than it does in EF Core.

Accessing information about the entity classes and database tables

Sometimes, it's useful to get information about how the entity classes and properties are mapped to the database tables and columns. EF Core provides two sources of information, one that emphasizes the entity classes and one that focuses more on the database:

- `context.Entry(entity).Metadata`—Has more than 20 properties and methods that provide information on the primary key, foreign key, and navigational properties
- `context.Model`—Has a set of properties and methods that provides a similar set of data to the `Metadata` property, but focuses more on the database tables, columns, constraints, indexes, and so on

Here are some examples of how you might use this information to automate certain services:

- Recursively visiting an entity class and its relationships so that you can apply some sort of action in each entity class, such as resetting its primary-key values

- Obtaining the settings on an entity class, such as its delete behavior
- Finding the table name and column names used by an entity class so tha can build raw SQL with the correct table and column names

EF6 EF6.x provided some model information, but it was complex to use and incomplete. EF Core has a comprehensive, easy-to-use set of Model information, but there isn't much documentation other than the methods' comments.

The following sections provide examples of using these sources.

11.6.1 *Using context.Entry(entity).Metadata to reset primary keys*

In section 6.2.3, you learned how to copy an entity class with certain relationshi resetting the primary keys manually. I needed a similar feature for a client's ap tion, so I built a service that resets the primary keys automatically as a good exa of using context.Entry(entity).Metadata.

The example in section 6.2.3 copied an Order entity with two LineItem ent but the Book entity class shouldn't be copied. The following listing is a copy of the ing from section 6.2.3.

Listing 11.22 Creating an Order with two LineItems ready to be copied

Create an Order with two LinItems that you want to copy.

For this test, add four books to use as test data.

```
var books = context.SeedDatabaseFourBooks();
var order = new Order
{
    CustomerId = Guid.Empty,
    LineItems = new List<LineItem>
    {
        new LineItem
        {
            LineNum = 1, ChosenBook = books[0], NumBooks = 1
        },
        new LineItem
        {
            LineNum = 2, ChosenBook = books[1], NumBooks = 2
        },
    }
};
context.Add(order);
context.SaveChanges();
```

Set CustomerId to the default value so that the query filter lets you read the order back.

Adds the fir LineNum lin to the first I

Adds the second LineNum linked to the second book

Writes this Order out to the database

In the version in chapter 6, you read in the Order and LineItems entity classes, then reset the primary keys manually. But in this example, you build a class c PkResetter to perform this task automatically. The following listing shows this co the PkResetter class.

Listing 11.23 Using metadata to visit each entity and reset its primary key

```
public class PkResetter
{
    private readonly DbContext _context;
    private readonly HashSet<object> _stopCircularLook;

    public PkResetter(DbContext context)
    {
        _context = context;
        _stopCircularLook = new HashSet<object>();
    }

    public void ResetPksEntityAndRelationships(object entityToReset)
    {
        if (_stopCircularLook.Contains(entityToReset))
            return;

        _stopCircularLook.Add(entityToReset);

        var entry = _context.Entry(entityToReset);
        if (entry == null)
            return;

        var primaryKey = entry.Metadata.FindPrimaryKey();
        if (primaryKey != null)
        {
            foreach (var primaryKeyProperty in primaryKey.Properties)
            {
                primaryKeyProperty.PropertyInfo
                    .SetValue(entityToReset,
                    GetDefaultValue(
                        primaryKeyProperty.PropertyInfo.PropertyType));
            }
        }

        foreach (var navigation in entry.Metadata.GetNavigations())
        {
            var navProp = navigation.PropertyInfo;

            var navValue = navProp.GetValue(entityToReset);
            if (navValue == null)
                continue;

            if (navigation.IsCollection)
            {
                foreach (var item in (IEnumerable)navValue)
                {
                    ResetPksEntityAndRelationships(item);
                }
            }
            else
            {
                ResetPksEntityAndRelationships(navValue);
            }
```

Used to stop circular recursive steps

This method will recursively look at all the linked entities and reset their primary keys.

If the method has already looked at this entity, the method exits.

mbers at this ty has visited y this ethod

Deals with an entity that isn't known by your configuration

Gets the primary-key information for this entity

sets every rty used in ary key to fault value

all the tional erties entity

Gets a property that contains the navigation property

Gets the avigation rty value

If null, skips the navigation property

e navigation property is ection, visits every entity

Recursively visits each entity in the collection

If a singleton, visits that entity

```
            }
        }
    }
```

That listing might seem to be a lot of code to reset the three primary keys, but i
work with any entity-class configuration, so you can use it anywhere. Here is a l
the various Metadata properties and methods used in listing 11.23:

- *Find the entity's primary key*—entry.Metadata.FindPrimaryKey()
- *Get the primary key's properties*—primaryKeyProperty.PropertyInfo
- *Find the entity's navigational relationships*—Metadata.GetNavigations()
- *Get a navigational relationship's property*—navigation.PropertyInfo
- *Checking whether the navigational property is a collection*—navigation.IsCollec

NOTE The PkResetter class assumes that the primary keys and the navigational properties are stored in a property, but in fact, these values could be in
backing fields or shadow properties. This simplification was used to make the
code shorter and easier to read.

11.6.2 *Using context.Model to get database information*

The context.Model property gives you access to the Model of the database tha
Core builds on first use of an application's DbContext. The Model contains some
similar to context.Entry(entity).Metadata, but it also has specific informatic
the database schema. Therefore, if you want to do anything with the database
context.Model is the right information source to use.

I used the context.Model source to build the EfCore.EfSchemaCompare li
that I mentioned in section 9.5.3. But for a smaller example, you'll produce a me
that returns an SQL command to delete a collection of entities with a commor
eign key. The reason for doing this is to improve the delete performance of a grou
dependent entities.

If you deleted a group of dependent entities via EF Core, you would typically re
all the entities to delete, and EF Core would delete each entity with a separate SQL
mand. The method in the following listing produces a single SQL command that de
all the dependent entities in one SQL command without the need to read them in.
process, therefore, is much quicker than EF Core, especially on large collections.

Listing 11.24 Using context.Model to build a quicker dependent delete

Gets the Model information for the given type,
or null if the type isn't mapped to the database

This method provides a
quick way to delete all
the entities linked to a
principal entity.

```
public string BuildDeleteEntitySql<TEntity>
    (DbContext context, string foreignKeyName)
    where TEntity : class
{
    var entityType = context.Model.FindEntityType(typeof(TEntity));
```

```
var fkProperty = entityType?.GetForeignKeys()          Looks for a foreign
    .SingleOrDefault(x => x.Properties.Count == 1       key with a single
        && x.Properties.Single().Name == foreignKeyName) property with the
    ?.Properties.Single();                              given name

if (fkProperty == null)                                 If any of those things
    throw new ArgumentException($"Something wrong!");    doesn't work, the code
                                                        throws an exception.
```

The full name, schema uired

```
var fullTableName = entityType.GetSchema() == null
    ? entityType.GetTableName()
    : $"{entityType.GetSchema()}.{entityType.GetTableName()}";

return $"DELETE FROM {fullTableName} " +                Forms the main part
    $"WHERE {fkProperty.GetColumnName()}"               of the SQL code
    + " = {0}";        ←
}                              Adds a parameter that the
                              ExecuteSqlRaw can check
```

Having found the right entity/table and checked that the foreign key name matches, you can build the SQL. As the listing shows, you have access to the table's name and schema, plus the column name of the foreign key. The following code snippet shows the output of the BuildDeleteEntitySql method in listing 11.24 with a Review entity class for the TEntity and a foreign-key name of BookId:

```
DELETE FROM Review WHERE BookId = {0}
```

The SQL command is applied to the database by calling the ExecuteSqlRaw method, with the SQL string as the first parameter and the foreign-key value as the second parameter.

> NOTE The BuildDeleteEntitySql class assumes that the foreign key is singular, but a foreign key could be a composite key with multiple values. This simplification was used to make the code shorter and easier to read.

Although this example is simple, it does show that using the Model methods allows you to obtain information entity classes with its relationships and match those entity classes to the database's schema.

Dynamically changing the DbContext's connection string

EF Core 5 makes it easier to change the connection string in an instance of an application's DbContext. Now it provides a method called SetConnectionString that allows you to change the connection string at any time so that you can change the database you are accessing at any time. I typically use this feature to pick different databases based on the person who is logged in, where the user is located, and so on. This process is known as *database sharding*, and it offers better performance because the user's data is spread over multiple databases. It can also add some security by placing all the data for one group of users in one database. Figure 11.6 shows the SetConnectionString method used to implement a database sharding system with EF Core.

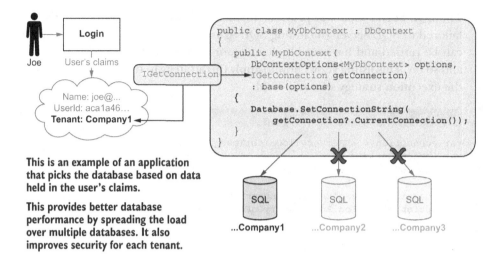

This is an example of an application that picks the database based on data held in the user's claims.

This provides better database performance by spreading the load over multiple databases. It also improves security for each tenant.

Figure 11.6 A user logging in to an ASP.NET Core application. The application uses the user's details to work out what database they should access and adds a claim called `Tenant` to hold that information. This works because when the application's DbContext is created, its constructor code runs to set the database connection string. This code uses the injected `IGetConnection` class, which returns a connection string based on the `Tenant` claim that maps the user to the correct database.

EF Core 5 made one other important change: the connection string can be null v you first create the application's DbContext. (Before EF Core 5 the connection s could not be null.) The connection string can be null until you need to acces database. This feature is useful because on startup, there would be no tenant info tion, so the connection string would be null. With the EF Core 5 change, how your EF Core configuration code can run without needing a connection st Another example is my EfCore.GenericServices library, which needs to scar entities used in a database on startup. Now that library works even if the conne string is null.

11.8 Handling database connection problems

With relational database servers, especially in the cloud, a database access car because the connection times out or certain transient errors occur. EF Core ha execution strategy feature that allows you to define what should happen when a out occurs, how many timeouts are allowed, and so on. Providing an execution egy can make your application less likely to fail due to connection problem transient internal errors.

EF6 EF Core's execution strategy is an improvement on the EF6.x execution strategy, as EF Core can handle retries in a transaction.

The SQL Server database provider includes an execution strategy that's specifically tailored to SQL Server (including SQL Azure). It's aware of the exception types that can be retried and has sensible defaults for maximum retries, delay between retries, and so on. This listing shows how to apply this strategy to the setup of SQL Server, with the execution strategy shown in bold.

Listing 11.25 Setting up a DbContext with the standard SQL execution strategy

```
var connection = @"Server=(localdb)\mssqllocaldb;Database=… etc.";
var optionsBuilder =
    new DbContextOptionsBuilder<EfCoreContext>();

optionsBuilder.UseSqlServer(connection,
    option => option.EnableRetryOnFailure());
var options = optionsBuilder.Options;

using (var context = new EfCoreContext(options))
{
    … normal code to use the context
```

Normal EF Core queries or SaveChanges calls will automatically be retried without your doing anything. Each query and each call to SaveChanges is retried as a unit if a transient failure occurs. But database transactions need a little more work.

1 Handling database transactions with EF Core's execution strategy

Because of the way that an execution strategy works, you need to adapt any code that uses a database transaction in which you have multiple calls to SaveChanges within an isolated transaction. (See section 4.7.2 for information on how transactions work.) The execution strategy works by rolling back the whole transaction if a transient failure occurs and then replaying each operation in the transaction; each query and each call to SaveChanges is retried as a unit. For all the operations in the transaction to be retried, the execution strategy must be in control of the transaction code.

The following listing shows both the addition of the SQL Server EnableRetryOnFailure execution strategy and the use of the execution strategy (in bold) with a transaction. The transaction code is written in such a way that if a retry is needed, the whole transaction is run again from the start.

Listing 11.26 Writing transactions when you've configured an execution strategy

```
var connection = @"Server=(localdb)\mssqllocaldb;Database=… etc.";
var optionsBuilder =
    new DbContextOptionsBuilder<EfCoreContext>();          Configures the database to use
                                                           the SQL execution strategy, so
optionsBuilder.UseSqlServer(connection,                    you have to handle transactions
    option => option.EnableRetryOnFailure());    ◁───────  differently
var options = optionsBuilder.Options
```

```
using (var context = new Chapter09DbContext(options))
{
    var strategy = context.Database              Creates an
        .CreateExecutionStrategy();              IExecutionStrategy
    strategy.Execute(() =>                       instance, which uses
    {                                            the execution strategy
        try                                      you configured the
        {                                        DbContext with
            using (var transaction = context     The important thing is to m
                .Database.BeginTransaction())    whole transaction code inte
            {                                    Action method it can call.
                context.Add(new MyEntity());
                context.SaveChanges();           The rest of the transaction
                context.Add(new MyEntity());     setup and running your
                context.SaveChanges();           code are the same.
                transaction.Commit();
            }
        }
        catch (Exception e)
        {
            //Error handling to go here
            throw;
        }
    });
}
```

WARNING The code in listing 11.26 is safe when it comes to a retry. By *safe*, I mean that the code will work properly. But in some cases, such as when data outside the execution strategy retry action is altered, the retry could cause problems. An obvious example is an int count = 0 variable defined outside the scope of the retry action that's incremented inside the action. In this case, the value of the count variable would be incremented again if a retry occurred. Bear this warning in mind when you design transactions if you're using the execution strategy retry facility.

11.8.2 Altering or writing your own execution strategy

In some cases, you might need to change the execution strategy for your databa. there's an existing execution strategy for your database provider (such as SQL Ser you can change some options, such as the number of retries or the SQL errors t retried.

If you want to write your own execution strategy, you need to implement a that inherits the interface IExecutionStrategy. I recommend that you look at th Core internal class called SqlServerExecutionStrategy as a template. You can this template at http://mng.bz/A1DK.

After you've written your own execution strategy class, you can configure it your database by using the ExecuteStrategy method in the options, as shown in in the next listing.

Listing 11.27 Configuring your own execution strategy into your DbContext

```
var connection = this.GetUniqueDatabaseConnectionString();
var optionsBuilder =
    new DbContextOptionsBuilder<Chapter09DbContext>();

optionsBuilder.UseSqlServer(connection,
    options => options.ExecutionStrategy(
        p => new MyExecutionStrategy()));

using (var context = new Chapter09DbContext(optionsBuilder.Options))
{
    … etc.
```

Summary

- You can use EF Core's entity State property, with a little help from a per-property IsModified flag, to define what will happen to the data when you call SaveChanges.

- You can affect the State of an entity and its relationships in several ways. You can use the DbContext's methods Add, Remove, Update, Attach, and Track-Graph; set the State directly; and track modifications.

- The DbContext's ChangeTracker property provides several ways to detect the State of all the entities that have changed. These techniques are useful for marking entities with the date when an entity was created or last updated, or logging every State change for any of the tracked entities.

- The Database property has methods that allow you to use raw SQL command strings in your database accesses.

- You can access information about the entities and their relationships via the Entry(entity).Metadata and the database structure via the Model property.

- EF Core contains a system that allows you to provide a retry capability. This system can improve reliability by retrying accesses if there are connection or transient errors in your database.

For readers who are familiar with EF6:

- EF Core has changed the ways that the entity's State is set based on lessons learned from EF6.x. Now, it is more likely to set the entity's State to the correct value for the action you're using.

- EF Core introduces a new method called TrackGraph, which will traverse a graph of linked entities and call your code to set each entity's State to the value you require.

- The way you use raw SQL commands in EF Core is different from the way it's done in EF6.x.

- EF Core's `Entry(entity).Metadata` and `Model` properties are a tremen**
  improvement over EF6.x's access to the model metadata. Now you can a
  every aspect of the database model.
- EF Core's execution strategy is an improvement on the EF6.x execution
  egy, as EF Core can handle retries in a database transaction.

Part _

Using Entity Framework Co in real-world applicatio

I n parts 1 and 2, you learned about EF Core in some detail, and at every I tried to provide examples of using each feature or approach. Now, in pa you are going to build a more complex version of the Book App and performance-tune it. There will be some new information, such as lookii Cosmos DB in chapter 16 and unit testing in chapter 17, but the focus of p is on using EF Core rather than learning about it.

I am a freelance contractor. My clients want their requirements turned robust, secure, high-performance applications—and they want them quickl provide these applications, I use approaches and libraries that are ro secure, and high-performance. The first two chapters in part 3 cover va approaches I have learned over the years that allow me to build applica quickly. As Kent Beck said, "Make it work, make it right, make it fast."

Having built an application in chapters 12 and 13, we move on to perform tuning. The initial Book App has around 700 real books in it, but for perform testing, we clone that data to 100,000 books and more. That number of b exposes some database performance issues, and over two and a half chapters will improve the Book App's performance by using several techniques.

Chapter 16 is about using Cosmos DB to add a final performance tune o Book App. This chapter exposes the differences between a relational (S database and a NoSQL database so that you are better informed about w and how to use either type of database.

Finally, chapter 17 covers unit testing, with the focus on EF Core. Unit testing when a database is involved requires careful thought, especially if you don't want the unit test to run slowly. I share several techniques and approaches, and I provide a NuGet package that I built, called EfCore.TestSupport. This library contains setup methods that help you unit test EF Core applications safely and quickly.

Using entity events
to solve business problems

This chapter covers

- Understanding the types of events that work well with EF Core
- Using domain events to trigger extra business rules
- Using integration events to synchronize two parts of your application
- Implementing an Event Runner and then improving it

In software, the term *event* covers a wide range of architectures and patterns. erally, it means "Action A triggers action B." You saw some C# events in chapte such as events in which an entity state changes (section 11.4.4). But this chap about another, quite different type of event, which I call an *entity event* because held in your entity classes. Using an entity event is like putting a message in entity class for someone to read later.

The purpose of entity events is to trigger business logic when somet changes in an entity class. In section 12.1.1 I show an example where a chang an address's details causes the sales tax on a quote to be updated. This examp implemented by detecting a change to the address details and sending an entity event (message) that runs some business logic that updates the sales tax for quotes at that address.

In addition to the entity events, you need parts that make them work. At the heart of the entity-event approach is code that I call the *Event Runner*, whose job is to read in all the entity events and run the specific business code (referred to as *event handlers*) associated with each entity event. Each event handler contains the specific business logic for that entity event, and each entity-event message provides the data that the event handler needs.

The Event Runner runs before the SaveChanges and SaveChangesAsync methods are called. The best way is to override the SaveChanges and SaveChangesAsync methods and then run the Event Runner into the methods. I refer to these SaveChanges and SaveChangesAsync methods as being event-enhanced.

Using events to solve business problems

I came up with the name entity events, but much cleverer people coined the terms *domain events* and *integration events* to define two uses of entity events. In this chapter, you'll learn about domain events and integration events, as well as the situations in which they can be used. Then you will implement event-enhanced SaveChanges and SaveChangesAsync methods that you can use in your applications.

.1 *Example of using domain events*

I was introduced to domain events by one of my clients. The client had used an event system discussed by Jimmy Bogard in his article "A better domain events pattern" (see http://mng.bz/oGNp), which described how to add domain events to EF Core. I had read this article some years before and didn't get it, but my client did and used domain events successfully. Seeing entity events being used in a real application persuaded me of their usefulness, and I went on to use domain events to solve several business requirements and performance issues in the client's application. The following example is taken from one of those business requirements.

My client's company sells bespoke constructions in the United States, and every project starts with a quote to send to the client. The construction could be anywhere in the United States, and the state where the work is done defines the sales tax. As a result, the sales tax had to be recalculated when any of the following things happened:

- *A new quote was created.* By default, a new quote doesn't have a location, so the business rule was to give it the highest sales tax until the location was specified.
- *The job location was set or changed.* The sales tax had to be recalculated, and it was the sales team's job to select a location from a list of known locations.
- *A location's address changed.* All the quotes linked to that location had to be recalculated to make sure that the sales tax was correct.

Now, you could add business logic for all these actions, but doing that would make the frontend more complex, and you might miss one area where a location changed and then the sales tax was wrong. The solution was to use events that triggered if a qu location was added or updated, and it worked well. A change in the Location e class created a domain event to trigger an event handler that recalculated the sale for a quote (or quotes). Each domain event needed a slightly different piece of ness logic, plus a common service to calculate the tax. Figure 12.1 shows an exa of what might happen if the address of a location changes.

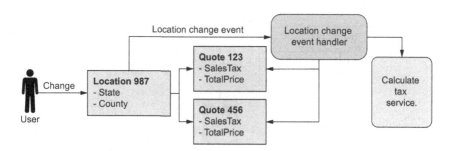

Figure 12.1 **Rather than add code at the frontend to run some business logic when a location changes, you can catch the change in the entity class and add a domain event to the entity class. When** SaveChanges **is called, a piece of code added to** SaveChanges **looks at any domain events and runs the appropriate event handler to make sure that all the open** Quotes **have their** SalesTax **recalculated.**

I won't delve into how this example works now, as this section describes where why events are useful. Suffice it to say that in section 12.4, you write code to ha entity events and improve that code as you go deeper into this approach.

12.1.2 *Example of integration events*

The second use of an entity event is a more complex situation. In chapter 13, yo learn multiple ways to improve the performance of your EF Core database acce One of these approaches is to precalculate the data you need to show to the user store it in another database used only for displaying data to the user. This appr improves read performance and scalability.

The normal SQL commands for the Book App, for example, calculate the ave star rating of a book by dynamically calculating the average across all the Bo Reviews. That technique works fine for a small number of Books and Reviews, with large numbers, sorting by average review ratings can be slow. In chapter 16, will use a Query Responsibility Segregation (CQRS) database pattern to store the calculated data in a separate, read-side database. The problem is making sure tha write-side SQL database and the read-side Cosmos DB database are always in step.

I use this solution in chapter 16: when writing the SQL database, run a transac that contains both the update to the SQL database and the update to the read Cosmos DB database. If either database fails, both databases will fail, which means they can't get out of step. Figure 12.2 shows how this solution might work.

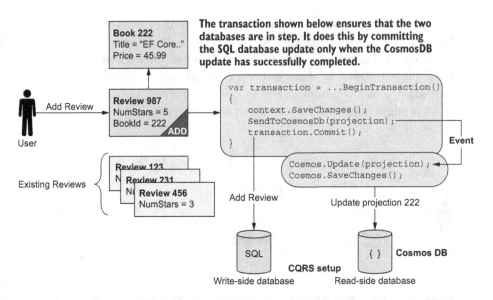

Figure 12.2 A CQRS database using a relational database as the primary data store, with a Cosmos DB database acting as a read-side database to improve performance. The issue is how to ensure that the two databases are in step—in this case, the `Book` projection in the Cosmos DB matches what the SQL database has. This figure is an example of using integration events to cross the boundary of the code handling the relational database and the code handling the Cosmos DB database.

Defining where domain events and integration events are useful

The two examples you have seen use events in different ways; the sales-tax event example is focused within a specific part of the code relating to customers and quotes, and the CQRS example is linking two quite different parts of an application. These two types of events have been given names, primarily by the Domain-Driven Design (DDD) community, but you will see that events can be used in normal, non-DDD entity types too.

> **NOTE** I cover how to apply a DDD approach to EF Core entity classes in chapter 13. But in this chapter, you will learn how to use events in non-DDD entity types.

DDD talks a lot about a bounded context, which represents a defined part of software where particular terms, definitions, and rules apply in a consistent way. A bounded context is about applying the Separation of Concerns (SoC) principle at the macro level. The part 3 Book App, for example, is broken into different bounded contexts: one handles displaying the books by using a SQL database, another provides a way to display the books by using a NoSQL database, and yet another handles processing a user's order. So using the term bounded context, you can categorize the two event types as follows:

- The sales-tax example is referred to as a domain event because it is wor
exclusively within a single bounded context.
- The CQRS example is referred to as an integration event because it cr
from one bounded context to another.

NOTE I cover bounded contexts in more detail in chapter 13.

12.3 *Where might you use events with EF Core?*

I don't want to suggest that you should do everything by using entity events, but
think that entity events are a good approach to learn. Where would you use e
events? The answer is best provided by some examples:

- Setting or changing an Address triggers a recalculation of the sales-tax co
a Quote.
- Creating an Order triggers a check on reordering Stock.
- Updating a Book triggers an update of that Book's Projection on anc
database.
- Receiving a Payment that pays off the debt triggers the closing of the Accou
- Sending a Message to an external service.

Each example has two entity class names in an italic monospace font. These entity cl
are different but not tightly linked: Address/Quote, Order/Stock, Book/Project
Payment/Account, and Message/external service. When I say that the classe:
not tightly linked, I mean that the second class isn't dependent on the first class. I
Address entry were deleted, for example, the Quote entry wouldn't be deleted.

NOTE A good indication that domain events could help is when your business logic is going to be working on two different groups of data.

In all these cases, the first class could be handled in the standard way (that is,
using entity event), and a domain event could trigger an event handler to handle
update to the second class. Conversely, events aren't useful when the entity classe:
already closely linked. You wouldn't use events to set up each LineItem in an O1
for example, because the two classes are closely linked to each other.

Another time where events can be useful is when you want to add a new featu
some existing code and don't want to alter the existing methods and business log
the new feature doesn't change the existing code, you might have a case for t
events even if the two entity classes are closely linked. Chapter 15 has a good exai
that improves the performance of the existing Book App. I don't want to change
existing code, which works, but I want to add some cached values to the Book e
class, and using domain events is a great solution.

Having said all that, it's likely that you won't use lots of domain events. There
only 20 domain events in the system from which the sales-tax example came, for e:
ple, but some of these events were critical to the features and especially the pe
mance of the application.

Integration events are even rarer; they are useful only when you have two bounded contexts that need to work together. But if you need to synchronize two different parts of your application, integration events are among the best approaches you can use.

Overall, I find events like these to be so useful that I have built a library, `EfCore .GenericEventRunner`, to easily add entity events (both domain and integration) to an application when I need them. But before I get into how to implement such a system, consider the pros and cons of using domain and integration events.

1 Pro: Follows the SoC design principle

The event systems already described provide a way to run separate business rules on a change in an entity class. In the location-change/sales-tax example, the two entities are linked in a nonobvious way; changing the location of a job causes a recalculation of the sales tax for any linked quotes. When you apply the SoC principle, these two business rules should be separated.

You could create some business logic to handle both business rules, but doing so would complicate a simple update of properties in an address. By triggering an event if the `State`/`County` properties are changed, you can keep the simple address update and let the event handle the second part.

2 Pro: Makes database updates robust

The design of the code that handles domain events is such that the original change that triggers the event and the changes applied to entity classes via the called event handler are saved in the same transaction. Figure 12.3 shows this code in action.

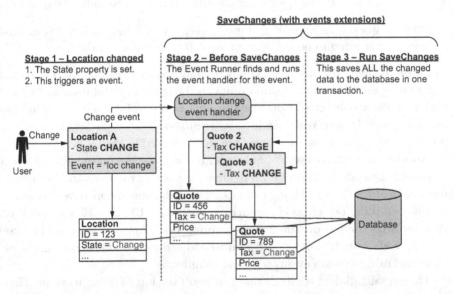

Figure 12.3 The domain events system saves both the initial `Location` update that triggered the event and the changes made to `Quote` entity classes in one transaction. The database will contain all the changes in one go, so the two types of updates can't get out of date.

As you will see in section 12.5, the integration event implementation is robust tc the integration event fails, the database update will be rolled back, ensuring tha local database and the external service and different database are in step.

12.3.3 Con: Makes your application more complex

One of the downsides of using events is that your code is going to be more coɪ cated. Even if you use a library such as EfCore.GenericEventRunner to manage events, you will still have to create your events, add the events to your entity cla and write your event handlers, which requires more code than building service your business logic, as covered in chapter 4.

But the trade-off of events that need more code is that the two business logic ɪ are decoupled. Changes to the address become a simple update, for example, v the event makes sure that the tax code is recalculated. This decoupling reduces business complexity that the developer has to deal with.

12.3.4 Con: Makes following the flow of the code more difficult

It can be hard to understand code that you didn't write or wrote a while back. helpful VS/VS Code feature that I use is Go to Implementation, which lets me j to a method's code so that I can dig down through the code to understand how part works before I change it.

You can do the same thing when you use events, but that technique does add more level of indirection before you get to the code. For the sales-tax-change exaɪ in figure 12.1, you would need to click the LocationChangedEvent class to finc LocationChangedEventHandler that has the business code you're looking for— one more step, but a step you don't need if you don't use events.

12.4 Implementing a domain event system with EF Core

In this section, you are going to implement a domain event system in EF Core. ᛁ you'll add the ability to hold entity events in your entity classes. Then you'll oveɪ the DbContext's SaveChanges so that you have extra logic to extract the entity eᵥ and to find and run each corresponding event handler.

Figure 12.4 shows the code and steps needed to implement a domain eventᵢ tem, using the example described in figure 12.1, where a Location's State proɪ changes. In this example, two Quotes are linked to that location, so their Sale property should be updated to the correct sales tax at that location.

To implement this domain event system, add the following code to your applicaɪ

1 You create some domain events classes to be triggered.
2 Add code to the entity classes to hold the domain events.
3 Alter the code in the entity class to detect a change on which you want to ger an event.

STAGE 1: The Location entity class State property is set to "NewState."

STAGE 1a: The setting of the State property adds a domain event to the entity class.

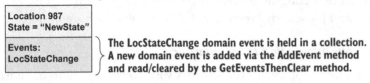

Location 987
State = "NewState"

Events:
LocStateChange

The **LocStateChange** domain event is held in a collection.
A new domain event is added via the **AddEvent** method
and read/cleared by the **GetEventsThenClear** method.

STAGE 2: Overridden SaveChanges is called.

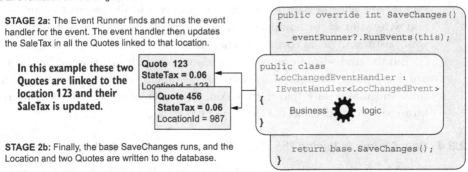

STAGE 2a: The Event Runner finds and runs the event
handler for the event. The event handler then updates
the SaleTax in all the Quotes linked to that location.

**In this example these two
Quotes are linked to the
location 123 and their
SaleTax is updated.**

Quote 123
StateTax = 0.06
LocationId = 123

Quote 456
StateTax = 0.06
LocationId = 987

```
public override int SaveChanges()
{
    _eventRunner?.RunEvents(this);
```

```
public class
    LocChangedEventHandler :
    IEventHandler<LocChangedEvent>
{
    Business    logic
}
```

STAGE 2b: Finally, the base SaveChanges runs, and the
Location and two Quotes are written to the database.

```
    return base.SaveChanges();
}
```

Figure 12.4   **Stage 1 shows that a change of a** `Location`'s `State` **property will cause a domain event to
be added to the** `Location` **entity class. In stage 2, when the overridden** `SaveChanges` **method is called, it
will read in any domain events in the tracked entities and then find and run the appropriate event handler for
each domain event. In this example, the event handler updates the** `SalesTax` **property in all the** `Quotes`
linked to that `Location`.

4 Create some event handlers that are matched to the events. These event handlers may alter the calling entity class or access the database or business logic to
execute the business rules it is designed to handle.

5 Build an Event Runner that finds and runs the correct event handler that
matches each found event.

6 Add the Event Runner to the DbContext, and override the SaveChanges (and
SaveChangesAsync) methods in your application's DbContext.

7 When the Event Runner has finished, run the base SaveChanges, which updates
the database with the original changes and any further changes applied by the
event handlers.

8 Register the Event Runner and all the event handlers.

Next, you will follow these steps to build each part of this approach.

.1   *Create some domain events classes to be triggered*

There are two parts to creating an event. First, an event must have an interface that
allows the Event Runner to refer to it. This interface can be empty, representing an
event. (I call this interface IDomainEvent in this example.) I use this interface to represent a domain event inside the Event Runner.

Each application event contains data that is specific to the business needs. The following listing shows the `LocationChangedEvent` class, which needs only the `Loca` entity class.

Listing 12.1   The `LocationChangedEvent` class, with data that the event handler ne

```
public class LocationChangedEvent : IDomainEvent
{
    public LocationChangedEvent(Location location)
    {
        Location = location;
    }

    public Location Location { get; }
}
```

The event class must i
the IDomainEvent. Th
Event Runner uses th
IDomainEvent to repr
every domain event.

The event handler needs Location
to do the Quote updates.

Each event should send over the data that the event handler needs to do its job. 1 it is the event handler's job to run some business logic, using the data provide the event.

12.4.2 Add code to the entity classes to hold the domain events

The entity class must hold a series of events. These events aren't written to the base but are there for the Event Runner to read via a method. The following li shows a class that an entity can inherit to add the event feature to its capabilities.

Listing 12.2   The class that entity classes inherit to create events

```
public class AddEventsToEntity : IEntityEvents
{
    private readonly List<IDomainEvent>
        _domainEvents = new List<IDomainEvent>();

    public void AddEvent(IDomainEvent domainEvent)
    {
        _domainEvents.Add(domainEvent);
    }

    public ICollection<IDomainEvent>
        GetEventsThenClear()
    {
        var eventsCopy = _domainEvents.ToList();
        _domainEvents.Clear();
        return eventsCopy;
    }
}
```

The IEntityEvents defines
GetEventsThenClear meth
for the Event Runner.

The list of IDomainEvent
events is stored in a field.

The AddEvent is used to
add new events to the
_domainEvents list.

This method is called by
the Event Runner to get
the events and then
clear the list.

The entity class can call the `AddEvent` method, and the Event Runner can get domain events via the `GetEventsThenClear` method. Getting the domain events clears the events in the entity class, because these messages will cause an event han to be executed, and you want the event handler to run only once per domain event. Remember that domain events are nothing like C# events; domain events are messages passed to the Event Runner via the entity classes, and you want a message to be used only once.

.3 Alter the entity class to detect a change to trigger an event on

An event is normally something being changed or something reaching a certain level. EF Core allows you to use backing fields, which make it easy to capture changes to scalar properties. The following listing shows the Location entity class that creates a domain event when the State property changes.

Listing 12.3 The Location entity class creates a domain event if the State is changed

```
public class Location : AddEventsToEntity
{
    public int LocationId { get; set; }
    public string Name { get; set; }

    private string _state;

    public string State
    {
        get => _state;
        set
        {
            if (value != _state)
                AddEvent(
                    new LocationChangedEvent(this));
            _state = value;
        }
    }

}
```

This entity class inherits the AddEventsToEntity to gain the ability to use events. →

These normal properties don't generate events when they are changed.

The backing field contains the real value of the data. ←

The setter is changed to send a Location-ChangedEvent if the State value changes. ←

This code will add a LocationChangedEvent to the entity class if the State value changes.

NOTE Collection navigational properties are a little harder to check for changes, but DDD-styled entity classes (covered in chapter 13) make this check much simpler.

.4 Create event handlers that are matched to the domain events

Event handlers are key to using events in your application. Each event handler contains some business logic that needs to be run when the specific event is found. For the Event Runner to work, every event handler must have the same signature, which is defined by an interface I created for this example, called IEventHandler<T> where T : IDomainEvent. The following listing shows the event handler that updates the Sales-Tax in every Quote that is linked to the Location that changed.

Listing 12.4   The event handler updates the sales tax on `Quotes` linked to this `Locat`

This class must be registered as a service via DI.

Every event handler must **
the interface IEventHandle**
where T is the event class t

```
public class LocationChangedEventHandler
    : IEventHandler<LocationChangedEvent>
{
    private readonly DomainEventsDbContext _context;
    private readonly
        ICalcSalesTaxService _taxLookupService;

    public LocationChangedEventHandler(
        DomainEventsDbContext context,
        ICalcSalesTaxService taxLookupService)
    {
        _context = context;
        _taxLookupService = taxLookupService;
    }

    public void HandleEvent
        (LocationChangedEvent domainEvent)
    {
        var salesTaxPercent = _taxLookupService
            .GetSalesTax(domainEvent.Location.State);

        foreach (var quote in _context.Quotes.Where(
            x => x.WhereInstall == domainEvent.Location))
        {
            quote.SalesTaxPercent = salesTaxPercent;
        }
    }
}
```

This specific event
handler needs two class**
registered with DI.

The Event Runner will use
DI to get an instance of
this class and will fill in
the constructor
parameters.

The method from the
IEventHandler<T> that
Event Runner will execut**

Uses another service
calculate the right s**

Sets the SalesT**
every Quote tha**
linked to this L**

The key point here is that the event handler is registered as a service so that the E
Runner can get an instance of the event handler class via dependency injection (
The event handler class has the same access to DI services that normal busi
logic does. In this case, the LocationChangedEventHandler injects the applicati**
DbContext and the ICalcSalesTaxService service.

12.4.5   *Build an Event Runner that finds and runs the correct event handler*

The Event Runner is the heart of the event system: its job is to match each event **
event handler and then invoke the event handler's method, providing the event
parameter. This process uses NET Core's ServiceProvider to get an instance o**
event handler, which allows the event handlers to access other services. Figure
provides a visual representation of what the Event Runner does.

> **NOTE** If you don't have NET Core's DI feature available in your application,
> you could replace the DI by handcoding a switch statement with code to cre-
> ate each event manager. This technique is harder to manage, but it will work.

① Get all events from all tracked entities. This also clears
the events in each entity to make sure it is run only once.

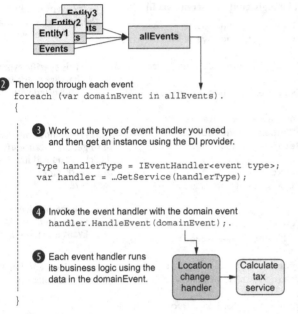

② Then loop through each event
```
foreach (var domainEvent in allEvents).
{
```

③ Work out the type of event handler you need
and then get an instance using the DI provider.

```
Type handlerType = IEventHandler<event type>;
var handler = …GetService(handlerType);
```

④ Invoke the event handler with the domain event
```
handler.HandleEvent(domainEvent);.
```

⑤ Each event handler runs
its business logic using the
data in the domainEvent.

**Figure 12.5   The Event Runner
gathers the events from each tracked
entity that has the `IEntityEvents`
interface; then, for each event, it gets
an instance of the matching event
handler class and invokes the handler
with the event as a parameter.
Finally, each event handler runs its
business logic, using the data found
in the event.**

The following listing shows the Event Runner code. This code is fairly complex, because
the design of the Event Runner requires the use of generic classes.

Listing 12.5   The Event Runner that is called from inside the overridden `SaveChanges`

The Event Runner needs an interface
so that you can register it with the DI.

```
public class EventRunner : IEventRunner        ◄─┘
{
    private readonly IServiceProvider _serviceProvider;

    public EventRunner(IServiceProvider serviceProvider)
    {
        _serviceProvider = serviceProvider;
    }

    public void RunEvents(DbContext context)
    {
        var allEvents  = context.
            ChangeTracker.Entries<IEntityEvents>()
            .SelectMany(x => x.Entity.GetEventsThenClear());

        foreach (var domainEvent in allEvents)
        {
            var domainEventType = domainEvent.GetType();
            var eventHandleType = typeof(IEventHandler<>)
                .MakeGenericType(domainEventType);
```

The Event Runner needs
the ServiceProvider to
get an instance of the
event handlers.

**Loops
through
h event
found**

Reads in all the
events and clears the
entity events to stop
duplicate events

Gets the interface
type of the matching
event handler

Uses the DI provider to create an instance of the event handler and returns an error if one is not found

```
var eventHandler =
    _serviceProvider.GetService(eventHandleType);
if (eventHandler == null)
    throw new InvalidOperationException(
        $"Could not find an event handler")
```

Creates the EventHandlerRunner that you need to run the event handler

```
var handlerRunnerType = typeof(EventHandlerRunner<>)
    .MakeGenericType(domainEventType);
var handlerRunner = ((EventHandlerRunner)
    Activator.CreateInstance(
        handlerRunnerType, eventHandler));

handlerRunner.HandleEvent(domainEvent);     ⟵
        }
    }
}
```

Uses the EventHandlerRunne run the event hand

The following listing shows the EventHandlerRunner and EventHandlerRunne classes. You need these two classes because the definition of an event handl generic, so you can't call it directly. You get around this problem by creating a that takes the generic event handler in its constructor and has a nongeneric me (the abstract class called EventHandlerRunner) that you can call.

Listing 12.6 The EventHandlerRunner class that runs the generic-typed event han

```
internal abstract class EventHandlerRunner          ⟞  By defining a nongeneric
{                                                       method, you can run the
    public abstract void HandleEvent                    generic event handler.
        (IDomainEvent domainEvent);
}
```

Uses the Ev Runner<T: the type of HandlerRu

```
internal class EventHandlerRunner<T> : EventHandlerRunner   ⟵
    where T : IDomainEvent
{
    private readonly IEventHandler<T> _handler;
```

The EventHandler class is created wi instance of the eve handler to run.

```
    public EventHandlerRunner(IEventHandler<T> handler)
    {
        _handler = handler;
    }

    public override void HandleEvent
        (IDomainEvent domainEvent)
    {
        _handler.HandleEvent((T)domainEvent);
    }
}
```

Method that overrides the abstract class's HandleEvent method

.6 Override SaveChanges and insert the Event Runner before SaveChanges is called

Next, you override SaveChanges and SaveChangesAsync so that the Event Runner is run before the base SaveChanges and SaveChangesAsync run. Any changes the event handlers make to entities are saved with the original changes that caused the events. This point is really important: both the changes made to entities by your nonevent code are saved with any changes made by your event handler code. If a problem occurs with the data being saved to the database (a concurrency exception was thrown, for example), neither of the changes would be written to the database, so the two types of entity changes—nonevent code changes and event-handler code changes—won't become CQRS out of step. The following listing shows how you inject the Event Runner via your application's DbContext constructor and then use that Event Runner inside the overridden SaveChanges method.

Listing 12.7 Your application's DbContext with `SaveChanges` overridden

```
public class DomainEventsDbContext : DbContext
{
    private readonly IEventRunner _eventRunner;          ◁──┐  Holds the Event Runner
                                                              that is injected by DI via
                                                              the class's constructor

    public DomainEventsDbContext(
        DbContextOptions<DomainEventsDbContext> options,        The constructor now has
        IEventRunner eventRunner = null)                        a second parameter DI
        : base(options)                                         fills in with the Event
    {                                                           Runner.
        _eventRunner = eventRunner;
    }

    //… DbSet<T> left out


    public override int SaveChanges              │ You override SaveChanges so that you can run
        (bool acceptAllChangesOnSuccess)         │ the Event Runner before the real SaveChanges.
    {
        _eventRunner?.RunEvents(this);           ◁──┘  Runs the Event Runner
        return base.SaveChanges(acceptAllChangesOnSuccess);   ◁──┐  Runs the
    }                                                              base.SaveChanges

    //… overridden SaveChangesAsync left out
}
```

NOTE There are two version of SaveChanges and SaveChangesAsync, but you need to override only one of each of them. You need to override only the int SaveChanges(bool acceptAllChangesOnSuccess), for example, because the SaveChanges with no parameters calls the SaveChanges with the acceptAllChangesOnSuccess parameter set to true.

12.4.7 Register the Event Runner and all the event handlers

The last part is registering the Event Runner and the event handlers with the DI vider. The Event Runner relies on the DI to provide an instance of your event dlers, using their interfaces; also, your application's DbContext needs the E Runner injected by DI into the `IEventRunner` parameter of its constructor. W Event Runner and the event handlers are registered, along with any services tha event handlers need (such as the sales tax calculator service), the Event Runner work. In this simple example, you can register the few classes and interfaces man by using the following NET Core DI provider, as shown in the following listing.

Listing 12.8   Manually registering the Event Runner and event handlers In ASP.NET C

Registers the Event Runner, which will be injected into your application's DbContext

You register interfaces/classes with the NET dependency injection provider—in this case, in a ASP.NET Core app.

```
public void ConfigureServices(IServiceCollection services)
{
    //… other registrations left out

    services.AddTransient<IEventRunner, EventRunner>();

    services.AddTransient<IEventHandler<LocationChangedEvent>,
            LocationChangedEventHandler>();
    services.AddTransient<IEventHandler<QuoteLocationChangedEvent>,
        QuoteLocationChangedEventHandler>();

    services.AddTransient<ICalcSalesTaxService,
        CalcSalesTaxService>();
}
```

Re; all eve ha

You need to register any ser that your event handlers wil

Although manual registration works, a better way is to automate finding and regi ing the event handlers. Listing 12.9 shows an extension method that will registe Event Runner and all the event handlers in each assembly you provide. The follo code snippet shows how it is called:

```
services.RegisterEventRunnerAndHandlers(
    Assembly.GetAssembly(
        typeof(LocationChangedEventHandler)));
```

The following listing shows the `RegisterEventRunnerAndHandlers` code.

Listing 12.9   Automatically registering the Event Runner and your event handlers

The method needs the NET Core's service collection to add to.

Registers the Event Runner

```
public static void RegisterEventRunnerAndHandlers(
    this IServiceCollection services,
    params Assembly[] assembliesToScan)
{
    services.AddTransient<IEventRunner, EventRunner>();
```

You provide one or r assemblies to scan.

```
    foreach (var assembly in assembliesToScan)          Calls a method to find
    {                                                    and register event
        services.RegisterEventHandlers(assembly);        handler in an assembly
    }
}
```

```
private static void RegisterEventHandlers(          Finds and registers all
    this IServiceCollection services,               the classes that have the
    Assembly assembly)                              IEventHandler<T> interface
{
    var allGenericClasses = assembly.GetExportedTypes()      Finds all the classes
        .Where(y => y.IsClass && !y.IsAbstract              that could be an event
            && !y.IsGenericType && !y.IsNested);            handler in the assembly
    var classesWithIHandle =
        from classType in allGenericClasses
        let interfaceType = classType.GetInterfaces()       Finds all the classes
            .SingleOrDefault(y =>                           that have the
                y.IsGenericType &&                          IEventHandler<T>
                y.GetGenericTypeDefinition() ==             interface, plus the
                    typeof(IEventHandler<>))                interface type
        where interfaceType != null
        select (interfaceType, classType);

    foreach (var tuple in classesWithIHandle)
    {                                                   Registers each
        services.AddTransient(                          class with its
            tuple.interfaceType, tuple.classType);      interface
    }
}
```

> **NOTE** The RegisterEventRunnerAndHandlers code won't register the Calc-
> SalesTaxService service because it looks only for event handlers. But the
> CalcSalesTaxService class is a normal service—that is, a class with a non-
> generic interface, like any other service. Chapter 5, especially section 5.7.3,
> shows how to register these types of services.

And that's it! You have added the domain events feature to your application, and you
are ready to go. You will use domain events in chapter 15 as one way to improve database query performance by updating cache values when Reviews are added or removed.
You can also see this feature in action in the Book App by clicking the SQL (cached)
menu link.

5 Implementing an integration event system with EF Core

Now that you've seen how domain events work, we'll move on to integration events.
Integration events are simpler to implement than domain events but harder to design
because they work across bounded contexts (see section 12.2).

There are many ways to implement integration events, but this book is about EF
Core, so this section concentrates on using an integration event within a database

transaction in the SaveChanges method. The purpose is to ensure that the databa
updated only if the integration event was successful.

I provided one example in section 12.2: combining the update of a SQL data
with the corresponding update of a CQRS read-side database. This example w
because the core tries to update a CQRS read-side database only if the SQL up
succeeded, and it commits the SQL update only if the CQRS read-side database
successful; that way, the two databases contain the same data. You can generalize
example into two parts, both of which must work for the action to be successful

- Don't send the integration event if the database update didn't work.
- Don't commit the database update unless the integration event worked.

Now let's implement some code that follows the integration event approach. As a
ple example, suppose that you are building a new service that sends customers
orders of Lego bricks by courier on the same day. You don't want to disappoint
customers, so you must be sure that your warehouse has the items in stock and
courier that can deliver the order immediately. The overall system is depicted ir
ure 12.6.

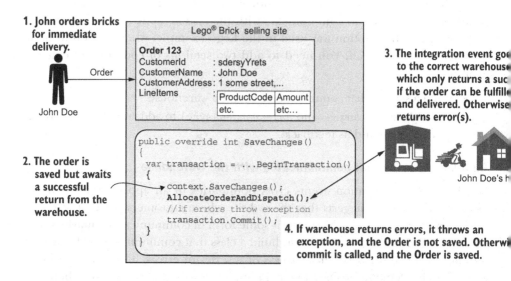

1. John orders bricks for immediate delivery.

John Doe

Order

Lego® Brick selling site

Order 123
CustomerId   : sdersyYrets
CustomerName   : John Doe
CustomerAddress: 1 some street,...
LineItems

ProductCode	Amount
etc.	etc...

2. The order is saved but awaits a successful return from the warehouse.

```
public override int SaveChanges()
{
    var transaction = ...BeginTransaction()
    {
        context.SaveChanges();
        AllocateOrderAndDispatch();
        //if errors throw exception
        transaction.Commit();
    }
}
```

**3. The integration event go
to the correct warehouse
which only returns a suc
if the order can be fulfille
and delivered. Otherwise
returns error(s).**

John Doe's h

**4. If warehouse returns errors, it throws an exception, and the Order is not saved. Otherwi
commit is called, and the Order is saved.**

**Figure 12.6   Using an integration event to make sure that you can deliver an order before you save it. T
implement this event, you override SaveChanges in your application's DbContext and handle any new
Order by using a transaction. The Order is validated and saved; then an integration event sends the
content of the order to the warehouse. If the warehouse has all the items needed and has a courier availabl
to get the order to the customer, it returns a success message, which causes the Order to be committe
to the database. If errors occur, the Order is not written to the database, and the errors are shown to th
customer.**

You have two options for detecting and handling your integration event in your application's DbContext:

- You inject the service directly into your application's DbContext, which works out for itself whether a specific event has happened by detecting the State of the entities. A second part is called only if the first method says that it needs to be called.
- You could use an approach similar to the Event Runner that you used for domain events, but a different event type is run within a transaction after the base SaveChanges is called.

In most cases, you won't have many integration events, so the first option is quicker; it bypasses the event system you added to the entity for the domain events and does its own detection of the event. This approach is simple and keeps all the code together, but it can become cumbersome if you have multiple events to detect and process.

The second option is an expansion of the Event Runner and domain events, which uses a similar creation of an integration event when something changes in the entity. In this specific case, the code will create an integration event when a new Order is created.

Both options require an event handler. What goes in the event handler is the business logic needed to communicate with the system/code and to understand its responses. The first option was used in the Lego example, where the event handler detected the event itself. You need to add two sections of code to implement this example:

- Build a service that communicates with the warehouse.
- Override SaveChanges (and SaveChangesAsync) to add code to create the integration event and its feedback.

.1 Building a service that communicates with the warehouse

You know that integration events cross boundaries in an application. In the Lego example, the design suggests that the website where customers place orders is separate from the warehouse, which means some form of communication, maybe via some RESTful API. In this case, you would build a class that communicates with the correct warehouse and returns either a success or a series of errors. The following listing is one way to implement the code that communicates with the external warehouse.

Listing 12.10 The Warehouse event handler that both detects and handles the event

```
public class WarehouseEventHandler : IWarehouseEventHandler
{
    private Order _order;

    public bool NeedsCallToWarehouse(DbContext context)
    {
```

This method detects the event and returns true if there is an Order to send to the warehouse.

```
        var newOrders = context.ChangeTracker
            .Entries<Order>()                              Obtains all the
            .Where(x => x.State == EntityState.Added)      newly created
            .Select(x => x.Entity)                         Orders
            .ToList();

        if (newOrders.Count > 1)                           The business logi
            throw new Exception(                           handles only one
                "Can only process one Order at a time");   per SaveChanges

        if (!newOrders.Any())          If there isn't a new
            return false;              Order, returns false

        _order = newOrders.Single();       If there is an Order,
        return true;                       retains it and returns true
    }

    public List<string> AllocateOrderAndDispatch()              This method will
    {                                                           communicate wit
        var errors = new List<string>();                        warehouse and r
                                                                any errors the w
        //... code to communicate with warehouse               sends back.

        return errors;            Returns a list of errors.     Adds the code to
    }                             If the list is empty, the     communicate with
}                                 code was successful.          the warehouse
```

12.5.2 Overriding SaveChanges to handle the integration event

As stated earlier, you are using an integration event implementation that detects
event itself, rather than adding an event to the entity class, so the code inside the
ridden SaveChanges and SaveChangesAsync is specific to the integration event.
following code listing shows the code to implement the Lego example.

Listing 12.11 DbContext with overridden SaveChanges **and** Warehouse **event han**

```
public class IntegrationEventDbContext : DbContext       Holds the instance of the
{                                                         code that will communicat
    private readonly IWarehouseEventHandler               with the external
        _warehouseEventHandler;                           warehouse

    public IntegrationEventDbContext(
        DbContextOptions<IntegrationEventDbContext> options,
        IWarehouseEventHandler warehouseEventHandler)       ◁
        : base(options)
    {                                                         Injects the ware
                                                              event handler w
        _warehouseEventHandler = warehouseEventHandler;     ◁
    }

    public DbSet<Order> Orders { get; set; }
    public DbSet<Product> Products { get; set; }
                                                          Overrides SaveChanges to
    public override int SaveChanges                       include the warehouse
        (bool acceptAllChangesOnSuccess)                  event handler
```

```
    {
        if (!_warehouseEventHandler.NeedsCallToWarehouse(this))
            return
                base.SaveChanges(acceptAllChangesOnSuccess);

        using(var transaction = Database.BeginTransaction())
        {
            var result =
                base.SaveChanges(acceptAllChangesOnSuccess);

            var errors = _warehouseEventHandler
                .AllocateOrderAndDispatch();

            if (errors.Any())
            {
                throw new OutOfStockException(
                    string.Join('.', errors));
            }

            transaction.Commit();
            return result;
        }
    }

    //… overridden SaveChangesAsync left out
}
```

he event doesn't n event, a normal changes.

There is an integration event, so a transaction is opened.

s the base Change to the Order

Calls the warehouse event handler that communicates with the warehouse

If the warehouse returned errors, throws an OutOfStockException

urns the lt of the Changes

If there were no errors, the Order is committed to the database.

NOTE When you use transactions in which the retry-on-failure option is enabled, you need to wrap the transaction in an execution strategy (see section 11.7.1).

Improving the domain event and integration event implementations

The code shown so far implements a fully running domain events and integration-events system that you can use, but it omits several features that would be useful. Async event handlers would be important features to add, for example. In this section, you explore some extra features that you might like to add to your event handling. Here are some of the additional features I found when I created a generalized event library called EfCore.GenericEventRunner:

- Generalizing events (events running before, during, and after the call to SaveChanges)
- Adding support for async event handlers
- Handling multiple event handers for the same event
- Handling event sagas, in which one event kicks off another event

The following sections add the features in this list to the domain and integration designs you have worked on so far. The aim is to build a generalized event library that you can use in any application that events would help.

NOTE Full implementations of the new features are not provided due to space constraints. The aim is to show what sort of improvements you could add to the Event Runner. Links to the implementation in the `EfCore.Generic-EventRunner` library are provided where appropriate.

12.6.1 Generalizing events: Running before, during, and after the call to SaveChanges

If you are going to build a library to handle events, it's worth looking at all the typ events you might want to handle. You have already seen the domain event and an gration event, but for the integration event example, you handcoded an integra event system because doing that was easier. But when you are willing to write a lib it's worth putting in the work to handle integration events too.

Another event type might be useful—one that runs when SaveChanges or S ChangesAsync has finished successfully. You could send an email when you are that an Order has been checked and successfully added to the database. That exan uses three event types, which I call *Before* (domain events), *During* (integration eve and *After* events (figure 12.7).

The three types of events:

1. **Before events (domain events)**
   These are run before SaveChanges is called.

2. **During events (integration events)**
   These are run within a transaction and after SaveChanges is called.

3. **After events**
   These are run after the SaveChange has finished successfully.

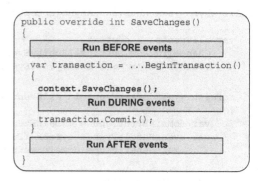

```
public override int SaveChanges()
{
    Run BEFORE events
    var transaction = ...BeginTransaction()
    {
        context.SaveChanges();
        Run DURING events
        transaction.Commit();
    }
    Run AFTER events
}
```

Figure 12.7 A study of the various events around the call to SaveChanges or SaveChangesAsync suggests three important positions: 1. Before SaveChanges is called, which allows you to alter entities before they are saved; 2. within a transaction where SaveChanges has been called but the transaction hasn't been committed yet, allowing you to roll back the saved data if the outgoing event fails; and 3. after SaveChanges/SaveChangesAsync finishes successfully, which allows you to run code that is valid only if the data was successfully saved.

To implement the Before, During, and After event system, you must add two n Event Runners (see listing 12.5): one called within a transaction to handle the inte tion events, and one after SaveChanges/SaveChangesAsync has finished success (figure 12.7). You also need three event-handler interfaces—Before, During, After—so that the correct event handler is run at the same time.

The full implementation is rather long and not repeated here. You can find the code in the `RunEventsBeforeDuringAfterSaveChanges` method that implements the Before, During, and After event system in the `EfCore.GenericEventRunner` library. See http://mng.bz/K4A0.

.2 Adding support for async event handlers

In many of today's multiuser applications, async methods will improve scalability, so you need to have async versions of the event handlers. Adding an async method requires an extra event handler interface for an async event handler version. Also, the Event Runner code must be altered to find an async version of the event handler when the `SaveChangesAsync` is called. Listing 12.12 shows the updated `RunEvents` method in the Event Runner from listing 12.5 updated as an async `RunEventsAsync` method.

NOTE To help you see the changes added to the version from listing 12.5, I've added comments for only the changed code.

Listing 12.12 The original `RunEvents` method updated to run async event handlers

```
public async Task RunEventsAsync(DbContext context)          ◁──┐  The RunEvent
{                                                                │  becomes an
    var allEvents = context.                                     │  async method,
        ChangeTracker.Entries<IEntityEvents>()                   │  and its name is
        .SelectMany(x => x.Entity.GetEventsThenClear());         │  changed to
                                                                 └─ RunEventAsync.
    foreach (var domainEvent in allEvents)
    {
        var domainEventType = domainEvent.GetType();
        var eventHandleType = typeof(IEventHandlerAsync<>)   ◁──┐
            .MakeGenericType(domainEventType);                  │  The code is now
                                                                │  looking for a
                                                                │  handle with an
        var eventHandler =                                      └─ async type.
            _serviceProvider.GetService(eventHandleType);
        if (eventHandler == null)
            throw new InvalidOperationException(
                "Could not find an event handler");
                                           ┌─ Needs a async
        var handlerRunnerType =            │  EventHandlerRunner to
            typeof(EventHandlerRunnerAsync<>)  ◁──┘  run the event handler
            .MakeGenericType(domainEventType);
        var handlerRunner = ((EventHandlerRunnerAsync)   ◁──┐  Is cast to a
            Activator.CreateInstance(                        └─ async method
                handlerRunnerType, eventHandler));

        await handlerRunner.HandleEventAsync(domainEvent);   ◁──┐  Allows the code
    }                                                            │  to run the async
}                                                                └─ event handler
```

12.6.3 Handling multiple event handers for the same event

You might define more than one event handler for an event. Your LocationChan
Event, for example, might have one event handler to recalculate the tax code
another event handler to update the company's map of ongoing projects. In the
rent implementations of the Event Runners, the .NET Core DI method GetSer
would throw an exception because it can return only one service. The solution is
ple. Use the .NET Core DI method GetServices method and then loop through
event handler found:

```
var eventHandlers =
    _serviceProvider.GetServices(eventHandleType);
if (!eventHandlers.Any())
    throw new InvalidOperationException(
        "Could not find an event handler");
foreach(var eventHandler in eventHandlers)
{
    //... use code from listing 12.5 that runs a single event handler
```

12.6.4 Handling event sagas in which one event kicks off another event

In my client's system, we found that one event could cause a new event to be crea
The LocationChangedEvent event updated the SalesTax, which, in turn, caus
QuotePriceChangeEvent. These updates are referred to as *event sagas* because
business logic consists of a series of steps that must be executed in a certain orde
the business rule to be completed.

Handling event sagas requires you to add a looping arrangement that look
events being created by other events. The following listing shows the updated :
Events method in the Event Runner from listing 12.5, with only the new looping •
having comments.

Listing 12.13 Adding looping on events to the RunEvents method in the Event Run

```
public void RunEvents(DbContext context)        Controls whether the code should
{                                               loop around again to see whether
    bool shouldRunAgain;                    ◁── there are any new events
    int loopCount = 1;
    do                                  ◁──  Counts how many times the
    {                                        Event Runner loops around
        var allEvents = context.             to check for more events
            ChangeTracker.Entries<IEntityEvents>()
            .SelectMany(x => x.Entity.GetEventsThenClear());

        shouldRunAgain = false;             ◁── shouldRunAgain is set to
        foreach (var domainEvent in allEvents)   false. If there are no event
        {                                        it will exit the do/while loc
            shouldRunAgain = true;

            var domainEventType = domainEvent.GetType();
            var eventHandleType = typeof(IEventHandler<>)
                .MakeGenericType(domainEventType);
```

This do/while code keeps looping while shouldRunAgain is true.

There are events, so shouldRunAgain is set to true.

```
        var eventHandler =
            _serviceProvider.GetService(eventHandleType);
        if (eventHandler == null)
            throw new InvalidOperationException(
                "Could not find an event handler");

        var handlerRunnerType = typeof(EventHandlerRunner<>)
            .MakeGenericType(domainEventType);
        var handlerRunner = ((EventHandlerRunner)
            Activator.CreateInstance(
                handlerRunnerType, eventHandler));

        handlerRunner.HandleEvent(domainEvent);
    }
    if (loopCount++ > 10)
        throw new Exception("Looped to many times");
} while (shouldRunAgain);
}
```

> **This check catches an event handler that triggers a circular set of events.**

> **Stops looping when there are no events to handle**

Summary

- A domain event class carries a message that is held inside an entity class. The domain event defines the type of event and carries event-specific data, such as what data has changed.
- Event handlers contain business logic that is specific to a domain event. Their job is to run the business logic, using the domain event data to guide what it does.
- The domain events version of the SaveChanges and SaveChangesAsync methods captures all the domain events in the tracked-entities classes and then runs matching event handlers.
- The integration events versions of the SaveChanges and SaveChangesAsync methods use a transaction to ensure that both the database and integration event handler succeed before the database is updated. This requirement allows you to synchronize two separate parts of your application.
- In section 12.4, you implemented a domain events system by creating domain event classes, event handlers, and an Event Runner. Using these three parts and overriding the SaveChanges and SaveChangesAsync methods allows you to use domain events in your applications.
- In section 12.5, you updated the domain events system in section 12.4 to handle integration events, which requires calling an external service within a database transaction.
- In section 12.5, you added enhancements to the Event Runner, such as supporting event handlers that use async methods.

Domain-Driven Design
and other architectur
approach

This chapter covers

- Three architectural approaches applied to the part 3 Book App
- The differences between normal and DDD-styled entity classes
- Eight ways you can apply DDD to your entity classes
- Three ways to handle performance problems when using DDD

Although this book is about EF Core, I want to include something about soft architecture, as readers of the first edition of this book found it useful. You introduced to the layered architecture in part 1. Now, in part 3, in which we building a much more complex Book App, I'll change the Book App's soft architecture to improve the separation of parts of the code and make the e classes' data more secure.

The most important of these architectural changes is swapping to the us Domain-Driven Design (DDD), from Eric Evan's book of the same name (Add Wesley Professional, 2003). The first version of EF Core added one new feature

EF6 didn't have—backing fields—and that new feature makes following the DDD approach possible. Since the first edition of this book came out, I have used DDD a lot, both in client applications and in building libraries to handle DDD entity classes.

I share my experiences and code to help you learn how DDD can help you with developing applications. The use of DDD on entity classes is broken into eight sections so that you can understand how each part of DDD helps improve the application. Finally, I cover ways to deal with slow performance on updates when there are lots of entries in a relationship using DDD-styled entities.

A good software architecture makes it easier to build and maintain your application

One problem with building software applications is that they can become harder and harder to develop as they get bigger because you need to alter the existing code to add a new feature. All sorts of issues arise, such as finding and understanding the existing code, deciding on the best way to add the new feature, and making sure that you haven't broken anything.

The architecture you choose for your application is one of the ways you can make it easier to write and update the code. Software principles, such as Separation of Concerns (SoC) and DDD, also play a part in making the application easier to fix and extend. A good application design provides a pattern that guides your coding, as well as some rules that encourage you down a good development route.

Neal Ford coined the term *evolutionary architecture* in *Building Evolutionary Architectures* (O'Reilly, 2017) to recognize the fact that, nowadays, applications need to grow and change to keep providing the user the right features and the best experience. In section 13.2, I describe the architecture/software principles I chose for the Book App in part 3—principles that make adding features much easier.

The Book App's evolving architecture

In parts 1 and 2, the Book App uses one database containing about 50 books. Its purpose is to provide a simple application to show how various EF Core features can be used in a real application. Therefore, the layered architecture (see section 5.2) is a good fit.

The part 1 and 2 Book App is small enough that I could have put all the code inside the ASP.NET Core application, but I didn't. Instead, I used a layered architecture with most of the interesting code in the data layer and the service layer. Here is why I didn't put all the code in the ASP.NET Core application:

- It would be harder to find something inside the single ASP.NET Core project.
- It would be harder to test because the code would be hardcoded to ASP.NET Core.

In addition to using the layered architecture, I used the SoC software principle (see section 2.7) to break the software into smaller parts because I knew that I would be adding features. Here are two of many examples that show why SoC is so useful:

- I build the main Book App query in sections (Select, Filter, Sort, Page) to r it easier to understand, test, and refactor.
- In part 2, I moved the EF Core Fluent API code into per-entity configu classes to made it easier to find, show, and refactor a configuration for a spe entity class.

The layered architecture works well in parts 1 and 2, where the focus is on how Core works, but part 3 focuses on performance-tuning your EF Core applicat This part uses multiple databases (SQL and Cosmos DB), two ways to access the base (EF Core and Dapper), and multiple performance-tuning techniques. This m there are different versions of the code to display the books in the Book App's base. To manage all these different query approaches and to show you some new wa design applications, I am adopting three new architectural/software principles to t part 3's Book App:

- A *modular monolith* approach, which enforces SoC by using .NET projects
- DDD principles, both architecturally and on the entity classes
- A *clean architecture*, as described by Robert C. Martin (known as Uncle Bob)

I provide introductions to these three architectural/software principles in sections 1 through 13.2.3. Figure 13.1 provides an overall view of the part 3 Book App architec

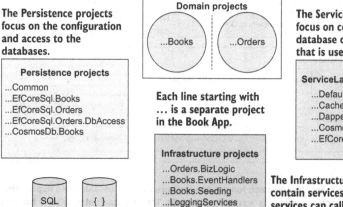

Figure 13.1 An overview of how the part 3 Book App is constructed, with five groups: Domain, Persiste Infrastructure, ServiceLayer, and the ASP.NET Core BookApp.UI. This structure is designed to enforce SoC rules by limiting what the developer can access from a project. The aim is to break the code into disc "features" to make it easier to understand and refactor the code.

.1 Building a modular monolith to enforce the SoC principles

My goal is to make the application modular. By *modular,* I mean that the code for a specific feature, such as displaying the books, is easy to identify, and has no links to feature code that it doesn't need. I achieve this goal by creating small projects that implement code for a specific job and link only to projects that contain the code required for a specific feature (see figure 13.2).

The layered architecture in parts 1 and 2 has a service layer project containing code for lots of Book App features mixed together, including code for displaying books, creating an order, seeding the database, and running background services. This architecture becomes a mass of interconnected code (known as a *ball of mud*) and is hard to refactor. In part 3's modular monolith design, each of these features has its own project, which makes it (nearly) impossible for features to share code except via a lower layer.

It's not obvious in figure 13.1, but various projects are linked to create features that are as self-contained as possible. Figure 13.2 shows two features, one for handling books and one for handling user's orders. These two features are separate (apart from the Persistence.Common project) and have only one shared project.

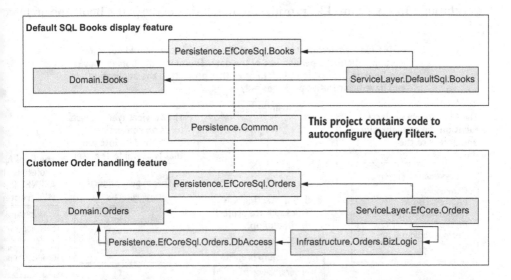

Figure 13.2 The modular monolith approach follows the SoC principle by breaking the application's code into small projects, each of which has a specific job to do. This approach also follows the clean architecture layer approach with four layers: Domain, Persistence, Infrastructure, and ServiceLayer, as shown in the names in each project. Some of the project names, such as ServiceLayer.DefaultSql .Books, may not make sense now, but they will become clear when you get to chapters 15 and 16.

The main aim of applying a modular approach to a monolith is to overcome the typical "ball of mud" monolith structure. If it helps, you can think of features in a modular monolith architecture as being the same as microservices, but the fea communicate by means of simple method calls, whereas microservices commun over some sort of protocol, with possible failures.

DEFINITION The *microservices architecture* arranges an application as a collection of loosely coupled services that communicate by using some form of message passing, such as HTTP messages.

Using a modular approach provides numerous benefits:

- It's easy to see all the code involved in a certain command, such as displa a book.
- A change in a feature should have no effect, or minimal effect, on other feat
- You should be able to move a feature to another application, such as a m service, with minimal problems for the rest of the application.

At the same time, you want your code to be DRY (don't repeat yourself), so there be some shared code, such as the Persistence.Common project shown in figure But I recommend that you don't create lots of generic code that is used in lots of ects, because changing that generic code could break code in another feature. If generic code is that good, turn it into a library. (That's what I do.)

This section ends our overview of the overall architecture of the part 3 Book The rest of this chapter looks at DDD, because DDD can profoundly affect how build and use your EF Core code and entity classes.

NOTE Because I made significant changes in chapters 15 and 16, I added a new section 13.8 to this chapter to share my experiences of using the three architectural approaches as I added new features that doubled the size of the Book App from its chapter 13 start.

13.2.2 Using DDD principles both architecturally and on the entity classes

DDD details many approaches for defining, building, and managing software app tions. But I want to point out three DDD principles in particular:

- The part 3 Book App's entity classes follow the DDD rules for what DDD *entities* (and what EF Core calls *entity classes*). The main rule is that a DDD e is in total control of the data in that entity: all the properties are made r only, and there are constructors/methods to create/update the entities' Giving the entity total control of its data makes your entity classes much r powerful; each entity class has clearly defined constructors/methods for developer to use.
- DDD says that entities, which contain both data and domain (business) l should not know anything about how the entities are persisted to a data (mentioned in section 4.3.1). I talk more about that topic in section 13 which covers the use of clean architecture.

- DDD talks about *bounded contexts*, which separate your application into distinct parts. The idea is to create bounded contexts that are separate so that they are easier to understand, and then set up clearly defined communication between the bounded contexts. In the part 3 Book App, I created a bounded context around the display and editing of books, and another bounded context covering the ordering of books.

.3 Applying a clean architecture as described by Robert C. Martin

Clean architecture is a software design approach that separates the different parts of your code into layers, arranged as a series of rings like those of an onion. These layers, plus some rules, are there to organize your code so that your entity classes and business logic are kept isolated from higher layers in the rings. I couldn't get all the projects into figure 13.1 by using a series of rings, but the arrangement of the Book App does follow the clean-architecture approach.

NOTE Here is a link to the clean architecture definition written by Robert C. Martin (Uncle Bob): http://mng.bz/9N71.

Clean architecture incorporates several other architectures, including hexagonal and onion. The purpose of this architecture is to define rules that state how different layers communicate. Clean architecture has a dependency rule, for example, stating that code in inner rings can't explicitly link to outer rings. Clean architecture matches DDD's rule to separate the entities from the database (DDD persistence) code and helps keep the code separated in rings, which I have defined as Domain, Persistence, Infrastructure, ServiceLayer, and the ASP.NET Core BookApp.UI.

Introduction to DDD at the entity class level

DDD is a massive topic with many facets, but this book is about EF Core. Therefore, I focus on EF Core entity classes, keeping the database parts out of DDD entities and using DDD's bounded context pattern to define how your code accesses the database.

With its focus on patterns and designs that make building applications better and more relevant, Eric Evans's 2003 *Domain-Driven Design* is a pivotal book in software development. What *Domain-Driven Design* doesn't do is give you a detailed set of steps on how you should implement with DDD. I think that is good, because if the book had given detailed steps, it would be outdated by now, but the principles are just as relevant today.

Because the Evans book didn't include detailed implementation plans, however, lots of people have come up with different ways to implement DDD. At one end, the entity classes are carefully crafted to contain only business code; all database parts, such as primary and foreign keys, are hidden. At the other end are designs in which—due to the developer's desire to move all the business code inside the entity class—the entity class contains reads and writes to the database. I'm going to describe the approach that most people take to DDD, plus some code to reduce the code you must write. (I don't show the strict DDD style, with all keys hidden, but you can follow approach with shadow properties.)

First, however, let's look at the major changes between a normal entity class a DDD entity class, which will help you understand the differences between wha been shown in this book so far and how DDD works. We'll start with a simple up to a `Book`'s `PublishedOn` property as an example of updating the database; you saw this update in section 3.3. The code is trivial, making it easier to see the di ences in the two approaches. Figure 13.3 shows the original, non-DDD design or left and the DDD design on the right.

The DDD version in figure 13.3 requires slightly more code, but as you will se section 13.4, that extra code lets these DDD entity classes become much more able parts of your code. Nevertheless, with potentially hundreds of creates and upd those few extra lines add up, which is why I am always trying to find ways to reduce code I need to write (see section 13.5).

13.4 Altering the Book App entities to follow the DDD approach

In this section, you are going to change the `Book` entity class and associated e classes to follow the DDD approach. You will make these changes in stages so tha can understand how and why you are making them. Here are the steps in the pro of changing your code to the DDD approach:

- Changing the properties in the `Book` entity to read-only
- Updating the `Book` entity properties via methods in the entity class
- Controlling how the `Book` entity is created
- Understanding the differences between an entity and a value object
- Minimizing the relationships between entity classes
- Grouping entity classes (DDD name: *aggregates*)
- Deciding when the business logic shouldn't be run inside an entity
- Applying DDD's bounded context to your application's DbContext

13.4.1 Changing the properties in the Book entity to read-only

DDD says that the entity class is in charge of the data it contains; therefore, it control how the data is created or changed. For the entity class to control its data, make all the properties in the entity read-only. After that, a developer can set the in the entity class only via the class's constructor (section 13.4.3) or via the methoc the entity class (section 13.4.2). The entity can ensure that it is always in a valid s With a non-DDD `Book` entity class, I could create a `Book` without an `Author`, bu business rules state that a valid book has at least one `Author`. To get this level of trol, you need to make all the properties read-only so that a developer must use defined methods/constructors. Listing 13.1 shows the `Book` entity class with the p erties changed to read-only.

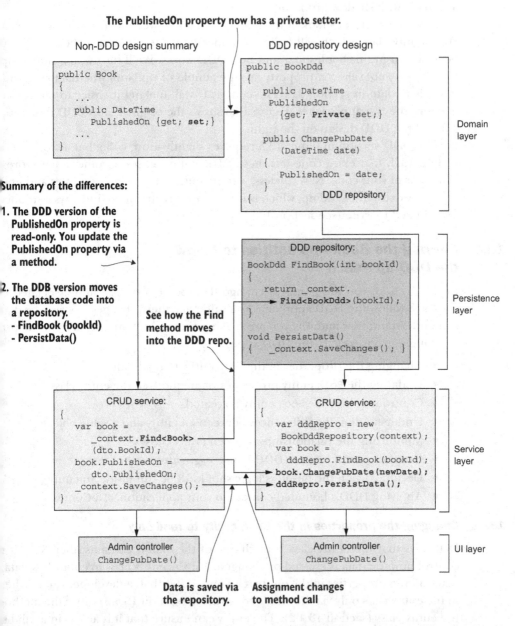

The PublishedOn property now has a private setter.

Non-DDD design summary   DDD repository design

```
public Book
{
    ...
    public DateTime
        PublishedOn {get; set;}
    ...
}
```

```
public BookDdd
{
    public DateTime
    PublishedOn
        {get; Private set;}

    public ChangePubDate
        (DateTime date)
    {
        PublishedOn = date;
    }
{                       DDD repository
```

Summary of the differences:

1. The DDD version of the PublishedOn property is read-only. You update the PublishedOn property via a method.

2. The DDB version moves the database code into a repository.
- **FindBook (bookId)**
- **PersistData()**

See how the Find method moves into the DDD repo.

```
DDD repository:
BookDdd FindBook(int bookId)
{
    return _context.
        Find<BookDdd>(bookId);
}

void PersistData()
{   _context.SaveChanges(); }
```

Domain layer

Persistence layer

```
CRUD service:
{
    var book =
        _context.Find<Book>
        (dto.BookId);
    book.PublishedOn =
        dto.PublishedOn;
    _context.SaveChanges();
}
```

```
CRUD service:
{
    var dddRepro = new
        BookDddRepository(context);
    var book =
        dddRepro.FindBook(bookId);
    book.ChangePubDate(newDate);
    dddRepro.PersistData();
}
```

Service layer

```
Admin controller
ChangePubDate()
```

```
Admin controller
ChangePubDate()
```

UI layer

Data is saved via the repository.   **Assignment changes to method call**

Figure 13.3 Comparing the non-DDD design for updating a `Book`'s publication date in the Book App (left) with the DDD design (right). The code required for the update has the same parts, but the DDD version moves all the EF Core code to the Persistence layer. If you also "hide" the application's DbContext in the DDD version, you can ensure that the developer can access the database only via the DDD repository.

Listing 13.1 Making the `Book` **entity class's properties read-only**

```
public class Book
{
    public int BookId { get; private set; }
    public string Title { get; private set; }
    //… other non-collection properties left out

    private HashSet<Review> _reviews;
    public IReadOnlyCollection<Review>
        Reviews => _reviews?.ToList();

    private HashSet<BookAuthor> _authorsLink;
    public IReadOnlyCollection<BookAuthor>
        AuthorsLink => _authorsLink?.ToList();
    //… other collection properties left out
}
```

Noncollection properties have **their setter set to private.**

A collection **is stored in a** **backing field.**

The property collection **returns the appropriate** **backing fields as read-** **only collections.**

WARNING If you are using AutoMapper, it will ignore the private access scope on your setter and update the property, which is *not* what you want to happen when using DDD. To stop this update, you need to add the `IgnoreAll-PropertiesWithAnInaccessibleSetter` method after the call to AutoMapper's `CreateMap<TSource,TDestination>` method.

13.4.2 Updating the Book entity properties via methods in the entity class

With all the properties converted to read-only, you need another way to update data inside an entity. The answer is to add methods inside the entity class that update the properties. I call these methods *access methods*. Creating access metho extra work, so why does DDD say you should do this? Here are the main benefits:

- You can use an entity like a black box. The access methods and constructor its API: it's up to the entity to make sure that the data inside the entity is al in a valid state.
- You can put your business rules in the access method. The method can re errors to users so that they can fix the problem and retry, or for a software p lem, you can throw an exception.
- If there isn't a method to update a specific property, you know that you're allowed to change that property.

Some simple methods only change a property, but many methods contain the ness rules for your application. One example in the Book entity is adding and rei ing a promotional price. In the part 3 Book entity class, you replace the PriceO entity class with two methods that run the business rules for adding and removi promotional price. The rules are

- The sale price of a book is contained in the ActualPrice property.
- The full price of a book is contained in the OrgPrice property.

- The PromotionalText property should be null if there is no promotion, but it must have the promotion message if there is a promotion.

It would be easy for someone to disobey these rules, but turning the rules into an access method means that no one can get them wrong. Also, the rules are in one place, so they're easy to change if necessary. These access methods are some of DDD's most powerful techniques.

Listing 13.2 shows the AddPromotion and RemovePromotion access methods in the Book entity. These methods ensure that the rules for adding and removing a promotional price are followed.

NOTE The IStatusGeneric interface and StatusGenericHandler class come from a small open source NuGet library called GenericServices.Status-Generic, which I use in many of my own libraries and applications.

Listing 13.2 Example of a DDD access method that contains business logic/validation

The AddPromotion returns a status.
If that status has errors, the
promotion is not applied.

The parameters came
from the input.

```
public IStatusGeneric AddPromotion(          ←
    decimal actualPrice, string promotionalText)   ←
{
    var status = new StatusGenericHandler();    ←
    if (string.IsNullOrWhiteSpace(promotionalText))
    {
        return status.AddError(                  ←
            "You must provide text to go with the promotion.",
            nameof(PromotionalText));
    }

    ActualPrice = actualPrice;
    PromotionalText = promotionalText;

    return status;      ←
}

public void RemovePromotion()       ←
{
    ActualPrice = OrgPrice;
    PromotionalText = null;
}
```

Creates a status that is
successful unless errors
are added to it

The AddError method adds an
error and returns immediately.

The error contains a user-
friendly message and the
name of the property that
has the error.

The status, which is
successful, is returned.

This removes an existing promotion. Because
there are no possible errors it returns void.

Removes the promotion by resetting the
ActualPrice and the PromotionalText

NOTE The name of the property in the AddError method in listing 13.2 is PromotionalText, not promotionalText, because we are providing the name of the property that the ASP.NET Core frontend was using when it called the AddPromotion method.

13.4.3 Controlling how the Book entity is created

In line with the DDD approach, in which the entity controls the setting of data
you need to think about the creation of an entity. As far as I know, Eric E
doesn't define this process, but creating an entity class is an important issue, c
cially as all the properties are read-only. Therefore, you need to provide at least
constructor or a static create factory method for a developer to use to create a
instance of the entity.

In the Book entity class, it's possible to create an invalid instance, because the
ness rules state that a Book's Title must not be empty and that there should be at
one Author. A constructor can't return errors, so you create a static create fac
method that returns a status containing errors if the Book's Title is empty or i
Author is provided. If there aren't any errors, the status contains a Result prop
containing the newly created Book, as shown in the following listing.

Listing 13.3 The static create factory to create a valid Book or return the errors

Creating a private constructor means that people can't create the entity via a constructor.

The static CreateBook method returns a status with a valid Book (if there are no errors).

```
private Book() { }

public static IStatusGeneric<Book> CreateBook(
    string title, DateTime publishedOn,
    decimal price,
    ICollection<Author> authors)
{
    var status = new StatusGenericHandler<Book>();
    if (string.IsNullOrWhiteSpace(title))
        status.AddError(
            "The book title cannot be empty.");

    var book = new Book
    {
        Title = title,
        PublishedOn = publishedOn,
        OrgPrice = price,
        ActualPrice = price,
    };
    if (authors == null)
        throw new ArgumentNullException(nameof(authors));

    byte order = 0;
    book._authorsLink = new HashSet<BookAuthor>(
        authors.Select(a =>
            new BookAuthor(book, a, order++)));

    if (!book._authorsLink.Any())
        status.AddError(
            "You must have at least one Author for a book.");

    return status.SetResult(book);
}
```

These parameters are all that are needed to create a valid Book.

Creates a status that can return a result—in this case, a Book

Adds an error. Note that it doesn't return immediately that other errors can be ad

Sets the properties

The authors pa which is null, is considered to b software error throws an exce

Creates the BookAuthor in the order in which the Authors have been provi

If there are Authors, ad an error.

Sets the status's Result to the new Book instance. If there are errors, the value is null.

For simple entity classes, you can use a public constructor with specific parameters, but any entities that have business rules and return error messages should use a static factory in the entity class.

4 Understanding the differences between an entity and a value object

DDD talks about an *entity* (the Book entity being an example), but it also talks about a *value object*. The difference is what uniquely defines an instance of each. Eric Evans says, "Tracking the identity of entities is essential," but "Make [value objects] express the meaning by the attributes [properties] it conveys" (*Domain-Driven Design*, p. 98–99). Here are two examples that might help:

- An entity isn't defined by the data inside it. I expect that more than one person named John Smith has written a book, for example. Therefore, the Book App would need a different Author entity for each author named John Smith.
- A value object is defined by the data inside it. If I have an address to send an order to, and another address with the same road, city, state, zip code, and country, was created, the two instances of the address are said to be equal.

From an EF Core perspective, a DDD entity is an EF Core entity class, which is saved to the database with some form of primary key. The primary key ensures that the entity is unique in the database, and when EF Core returns a query including entity classes (and the query doesn't include any form of the AsNoTracking method), it uses a single instance for each entity class that has the same primary key (see section 6.1.3).

You can implement a value object by using EF Core's owned type (see section 8.9.1). The main form of an owned type is a class with no primary key; the data is added to the table it is included in.

> **NOTE** The Book App doesn't include any value objects, so I can't use it as an example. Please look at listing 8.15 for a good example of using owned types in an entity class.

5 Minimizing the relationships between entity classes

Eric Evans says, "It is important to constraint relationships as much as possible" (*Domain-Driven Design*, p. 83). He goes on to say that added two-way relationships between entities mean you need to understand both entities when working on either entity, which makes the code harder to understand. His recommendation (and mine) is to minimize the relationships. A Book, for example, has a navigational property of all the Reviews for a Book, but the Review does not have a navigational property back to the Book (see section 8.2).

It's easy to minimize navigational relationships between entity classes. In section 8.2, I look at the relationships between the Book entity class and the Review entity class. I concluded that the Book entity needed a navigational collection of Reviews linked to it, but the Review entity didn't need a navigational link back to the Book entity. In

other words, understanding the Book entity requires some idea of what the Re
entity does, but when dealing with the Review entity, I had to understand only
the Review entity does.

13.4.6 Grouping entity classes

Another important DDD pattern called *aggregates* offers some guidance on hand
related entities. The aggregates principle says that you should group entities tha
be considered to be "one unit for the purpose of data changes" (*Domain-Driven D*
p. 126). One of the entities in an aggregate is the *root aggregate*, and any changes i
other aggregates are made via this root aggregate.

Figure 13.4 shows aggregate entities around the DDD version of the Book e
class used in the Book App. Any changes to the Review or BookAuthor entities li
to a Book entity can be changed only via access methods or constructors in the
entity. The Author entity is outside the Book aggregate because it can be linked to
tiple Books.

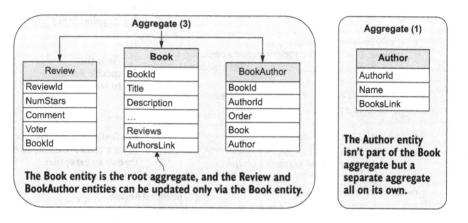

**Figure 13.4   DDD's aggregates concept groups entities that can be managed as though they
were one group of data. One of the entities is the root aggregate (the Book entity in the left
aggregate and Author in the right aggregate). All updates to the Book's Reviews or
BookAuthor entities are done via the Book entity. This technique reduces the amount of
entities you need to deal with and allows the root entity to ensure that all the other aggregates
are set up correctly (that a Book has at least one BookAuthor link, for example).**

> **NOTE** The BookAuthor entity in figure 13.4 breaks Evans's DDD aggregate
> rule because a nonroot aggregate should not be referenced from outside the
> aggregate. (The Author entity has a backlink to the BookAuthor entity.) But
> the BookAuthor entity contains book-specific data: the Order property, which
> defines the order in which the Authors should be cited. These features of the
> BookAuthor entity make it an aggregate of the Book entity.

The aggregate rule simplifies the handling of entities classes because one root e
can handle multiple aggregates in its group. Also, the root entity can validate tha

other, nonroot aggregates are set up correctly for the root aggregate, such as the Book create factory's checking that there is at least one Author for a Book entity.

This rule also calls for using an access method in the Book entity to add, update, or remove Review entities' links to the Book entity instance. The following listing shows the two access methods for adding or removing Reviews.

Listing 13.4 The access methods that control the aggregate entity `Review`

```
public void AddReview(int numStars,            Adds a new review with
    string comment, string voterName)          the given parameters
{
    if (_reviews == null)                       This code relies on the _reviews
        throw new InvalidOperationException(     field to be loaded, so it throws
            "Reviews collection not loaded");    an exception if it isn't.

    _reviews.Add(new Review(                     Creates a new Review, using
        numStars, comment, voterName));          its internal constructor
}

public void RemoveReview(int reviewId)      ◄───┤ Removes a Review,
{                                                 using its primary key
    if (_reviews == null)
        throw new InvalidOperationException(
            "Reviews collection not loaded");           Finds the
                                                         specific Review
    var localReview = _reviews.SingleOrDefault(          to remove
        x => x.ReviewId == reviewId);

    if (localReview == null)                     Not finding the Review is considered
        throw new InvalidOperationException(     to be a software error, so the code
            "The review wasn't found");          throws an exception.

    _reviews.Remove(localReview);   ◄───┐ The found Review
}                                         is removed.
```

One additional change you make is marking the Review entity class's constructor as internal. That change stops a developer from adding a Review by creating an instance outside the Book entity.

.7 Deciding when the business logic shouldn't be run inside an entity

DDD says that you should move as much of your business logic inside your entities, but the DDD aggregates rule says that the root aggregate should work only with other entities in the aggregate group. If you have business logic that includes more than one DDD aggregate group, you shouldn't put (all) the business logic in an entity; you need to create some external class to implement the business logic.

An example of a situation that requires more than one aggregate group in the business logic is processing a user's order for books. This business logic involves the Book entity, which is in the Book/Review/BookAuthor aggregate group, and the Or LineItem aggregate group.

You saw a solution to the order-for-books problem in section 4.4.3. The DDD sion uses similar code, but the final stage of building the Order is carried in a factory inside the Order entity because the Order is the root aggregate in the Or LineItem aggregate group. The following listing shows the external business called PlaceOrderBizLogic.

> **NOTE** Because you saw some of this code in listing 4.2, I left out similar parts of the code. The purpose is to focus on the changes in the DDD parts, especially creating the Order via an Order static factory.

Listing 13.5 PlaceOrderBizLogic **class working across** Book **and** Order **enti**

This method returns a status with the created
Order, which is null if there are no errors.

The PlaceOrderInDto
contains a TandC bool,
a collection of BookIds
and number of books.

```
public async Task<IStatusGeneric<Order>>
    CreateOrderAndSaveAsync(PlaceOrderInDto dto)
{
    var status = new StatusGenericHandler<Order>();

    if (!dto.AcceptTAndCs)
    {
        return status.AddError("accept T&Cs...");
    }
    if (!dto.LineItems.Any())
    {
        return status.AddError("No items in your basket.");
    }

    var booksDict = await _dbAccess
        .FindBooksByIdsAsync
            (dto.LineItems.Select(x => x.BookId));

    var linesStatus = FormLineItemsWithErrorChecking
        (dto.LineItems, booksDict);
    if (status.CombineStatuses(linesStatus).HasErrors)
        return status;

    var orderStatus = Order.CreateOrder(
        dto.UserId, linesStatus.Result);

    if (status.CombineStatuses(orderStatus).HasErrors)
        return status;

    await _dbAccess.AddAndSave(orderStatus.Result);

    return status.SetResult(orderStatus.Result);
}
```

Validate the user's input

This status is used t
gather errors, and i
there are no errors,
code returns an Orc

This method creates a list of bookIds and numbers of books (see end of listing 4.2).

The _dbAccess contains
the code to find each
book (see listing 4.3)

If any errors were
found while checki
each order line, ret
the error status

Calls the Order static factory. It is the Order's job to form the Order with LineItems.

Again, any errors w
the Order and retu

The _dbAccess
contains the code
add the Order and
SaveChangesAsyn

Returns a successful status with
the created Order entity

The biggest change from the code in chapter 4 is that the Order entity takes over the final stage of building the Order. The following listing shows the Order static factory method.

Listing 13.6   This static factory creates an Order with the LineItems, with error checks

The OrderBookDto lives in the Order domain and carries the info that the Order needs.

This static factory creates the Order with lineItems.

The Order uses the UserId to show orders only to the person who created it.

```
public static IStatusGeneric<Order> CreateOrder
    (Guid userId,
    IEnumerable<OrderBookDto> bookOrders)
{
    var status = new StatusGenericHandler<Order>();
    var order = new Order
    {
        UserId = userId,
        DateOrderedUtc = DateTime.UtcNow
    };

    byte lineNum = 1;
    order._lineItems = new HashSet<LineItem>(
        bookOrders
        .Select(x => new LineItem( x, lineNum++)));

    if (!order._lineItems.Any())
        status.AddError("No items in your basket.");

    return status.SetResult(order);
}
```

Creates a status to return with an optional result of Order

Sets the standard properties in an order

Creates each of the LineItems in the same order in which the user added them

Double-checks that the Order is valid

Returns the status with the Order. If there are errors, the status sets the result to null.

8   Applying DDD's bounded context to your application's DbContext

In section 13.2.2, I said that bounded contexts "separate your application into distinct parts" and that bounded contexts have "clearly defined communication." In figure 13.1, you saw two Persistence projects, Persistence.EfCoreSql.Books and Persistence.EfCoreSql.Orders, which are independent. But code previously described for placing a user's order needed information about the Book, so how do we manage this situation?

In this specific case, the solution is to use an SQL View in the Order's DbContext that maps to the Books table in the Book's DbContext, as shown in figure 13.5. That way, you can make the Persistence.EfCoreSql.Books and Persistence.EfCoreSql.Orders independent while letting both access the database data.

Using an SQL View is an excellent solution in this case because it follows many of the DDD rules. First, the BookView contains only the data that the Orders side needs, so the developer isn't distracted by irrelevant data. Second, when an entity class is configured as a View, EF Core marks that entity class as read-only, enforcing the DDD rule that only the Books entity should be able to change the data in the Books table.

NOTE   Another benefit is that a class mapped to an SQL View won't add migration code to alter that table. You can apply EF Core migrations from both the

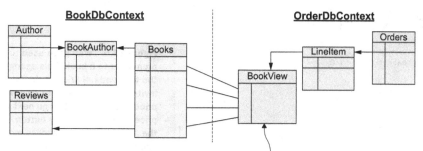

The OrderDbContext has a class called BookView, which is configured
as an SQL View mapped to specific columns in the Books table.

Figure 13.5 To follow the DDD bounded-context approach, the Domain.Books should be
independent of the Domain.Orders. But at the database level, both Domains need a `Book`
entity. The solution in this case is to create a `BookView` entity in the Domain.Orders that
contains only the specific properties to create and display an order. Then we configure the
`BookView` class as an SQL View mapped to the Books table.

BookDbContext and the OrderDbContext contexts to the database, and only
the BookDbContext's Book entity will affect the Books table (see section 9.4.3).

Although the SQL View works well for this purpose, it creates a link between the
bounded contexts. Be careful if you change the Book entity and then migrate
database.

> **NOTE** Passing data between bounded contexts is a big topic that I can't cover
> here. I recommend the old but still-relevant article "Strategies for Integrating
> Bounded Contexts," in which Philip Brown gives a good overview of many
> ways to communicate between bounded contexts (http://mng.bz/96Bg).

13.5 *Using your DDD-styled entity classes in your application*

The DDD approach is to keep the focus on the domain mode—that is, on the en
and their relationships. Conversely, it doesn't want the database (DDD persiste
parts to distract the developer who is working on the domain design. The idea is
the entity and its relationships (navigational properties in EF Core terms) are al
developer needs to consider when solving domain issues.

Having updated the design of your entity classes to one that follows the I
approach, now you want to use these classes in your application. Querying the
hasn't changed, but how you create and update your DDD-styled entity classes
changed. In section 13.4, you altered your entity classes to use constructors or s
create factories to create and access methods to update. In this section, you are g
to look at how you would use these new approaches in an application. The exan
come from the Book App (which is an ASP.NET Core MVC application) in part 3
ure 13.6 shows the page that the admin user uses to add a promotion to a book.

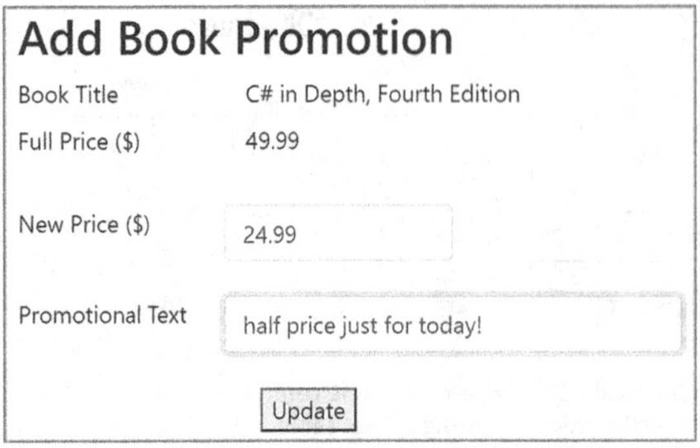

Add Book Promotion

Book Title	C# in Depth, Fourth Edition
Full Price ($)	49.99
New Price ($)	24.99
Promotional Text	half price just for today!

Update

Figure 13.6   Web page used to add a promotion to a book. This example shows the title and full price of the book, and invites the admin user to give the new price and some text to go next to the price. When the Update button is clicked, the `AddPromotion` access method is called with the new data, and if there are no errors, `SaveChanges` is called to update the `Book`.

Next, you will implement the code to put in an ASP.NET Core controller to display the page shown in figure 13.6 and update the `Book` entity when the user has provided their input and clicked the Update button. You will use two approaches: the standard approach described by Evans and a library designed to work directly with DDD access methods (which I refer to as a *class-to-method-call* library). The following list allows you to compare the two approaches:

- Calling the `AddPromotion` access method via a repository pattern
- Calling the `AddPromotion` access method via a class-to-method-call library

You will build code that adds a new `Review` to the `Book` entity class. Updates to relationships require you to decide how to handle the update. You will implement the `AddReview` example in two ways so that you can compare the two approaches:

- Adding a `Review` to the `Book` entity class via a repository pattern
- Adding a `Review` to the `Book` entity class via a class-to-method-call library

.1   Calling the AddPromotion access method via a repository pattern

Evans's book uses a repository pattern to handle the database accesses. Microsoft's definition of the repository pattern says, "Repositories are classes or components that encapsulate the logic required to access data sources. They centralize common data access functionality, providing better maintainability and decoupling the infrastructure or technology used to access databases from the domain model layer."

There are many ways to build a repository pattern. I have chosen to use a generic repository, which will work with any entity. The following listing shows the generic repository that you need for the `AddPromotion` example.

Listing 13.7   A generic repository that handles some basic database commands

```
public class GenericRepository<TEntity>
    where TEntity : class
{
```
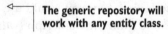
The generic repository will work with any entity class.

```
        protected readonly DbContext Context;                          ◄─┐   The repository needs
                                                                         │   the DbContext of the
        public GenericRepository(DbContext context)            ◄─┐      │   database.
        {                                                        │      │
            Context = context;                                   │      │
        }                                                      ◄─┘

        public IQueryable<TEntity> GetEntities()
        {                                                          Returns an
            return Context.Set<TEntity>();                         IQueryable query
        }                                                          of the entity type
```

Finds an entity via its single, integer primary key →

```
        public async Task<TEntity> FindEntityAsync(int id)     ◄─   This method find
        {                                                           returns a entity
            var entity = await Context.FindAsync<TEntity>(id);      integer primary

            if (entity == null)                                     A rudimentary
                throw new Exception("Could not find entity");       the entity was
```

The found entity is returned. →

```
            return entity;
        }

        public Task PersistDataAsync()                         Calls SaveChanges
        {                                                      to update the
            return Context.SaveChangesAsync();                 database
        }
    }
```

Using this repository, you can find a specific Book entity and call that Book's Promotion access method, using the data provided by the admin user. The following ing shows the code using the GenericRepository<Book> that would go in the ASP. Core AdminController. This controller has two methods, both named AddPromot but with different parameters and attributes. The first AddPromotion method is call display the page shown in figure 13.6. The second AddPromotion method is called v the user clicks the Update button and handles the update of the Book entity with promotion.

NOTE If you aren't familiar with ASP.NET Core, please look at section 5.7, which gives you a step-by-step look at how ASP.NET Core controllers work.

The following listing shows the AdminController with its constructor and the methods. Note that only the new code that uses the repository has comments.

Listing 13.8 Handling the AddPromotion update by using a repository pattern

```
public class AdminController : Controller
{
    private readonly GenericRepository<Book> _repository;

    public AdminController(                                     The Generic-
        GenericRepository<Book> repository)                    Repository<Bool
    {                                                           is injected into th
        _repository = repository;                              Controller.
    }
```

```
public async Task<IActionResult> AddPromotion(int id)
{
    var book = await _repository.FindEntityAsync(id);

    var dto = new AddPromotionDto
    {
        BookId = id,
        Title = book.Title,
        OrgPrice = book.OrgPrice
    };

    return View(dto);
}

[HttpPost]
[ValidateAntiForgeryToken]
public async Task<IActionResult> AddPromotion(AddPromotionDto dto)
{
    if (!ModelState.IsValid)
    {
        return View(dto);
    }

    var book = await _repository
        .FindEntityAsync(dto.BookId);
    var status = book.AddPromotion(
        dto.ActualPrice, dto.PromotionalText);

    if (!status.HasErrors)
    {
        await _repository.PersistDataAsync();
        return View("BookUpdated", "Updated book...");
    }

    //Error state
    status.CopyErrorsToModelState(ModelState, dto);
    return View(dto);
}
}
```

Annotations:
- **Copies over the parts of the Book you need to show the page**
- **Calls the AddPromotion access method with the two properties from the dto**
- **The access method returned no errors, so you persist the data to the database.**

Left margin: **...s the ...sitory ...ad in Book ...entity**

.2 Calling the AddPromotion access method via a class-to-method-call library

Although calling DDD access methods by using a repository system works, this approach has some repetitious code, such as in the first stage, where you copy properties into a DTO/ViewModel (referred to as the DTO from now on) to show to the user, and in the second stage, where returned data in the DTO is turned into an access method call. What would happen if you had a way to automate this process?

Well, in early 2018, after I had finished the first edition of this book, I found a way to automate both parts of the DDD CRUD and built an open source library called EfCore.GenericServices (referred to as GenericServices from now on). The GenericServices library automates most CRUD operations from normal entity classes with settable properties and DDD entity classes with their constructors access methods.

One benefit of using this library is that it reduces the amount of code you ha write in comparison to the repository approach. The library saves you about five in ASP.NET Core, and you don't have to write the repository. Another benefit is the code you use is the same for every update; only the DTO is different. The li allows you to copy/paste frontend code and then change only the DTO type to to another access method, constructor, or static factory.

> **NOTE** I designed `GenericServices` to deal with most, but not all, CRUD code. It's great at dealing with simple to moderate CRUD situations, but it can't cover every circumstance. For more complex CRUD code, I write the code by hand. You can learn more about this library at http://mng.bz/jBoP.

The rest of this section shows how you can implement the `AddPromotion` examp using `GenericServices`. First, you will look at the DTO in figure 13.7, which de what entity the library needs to load, what properties to load for the read part, what access method to call.

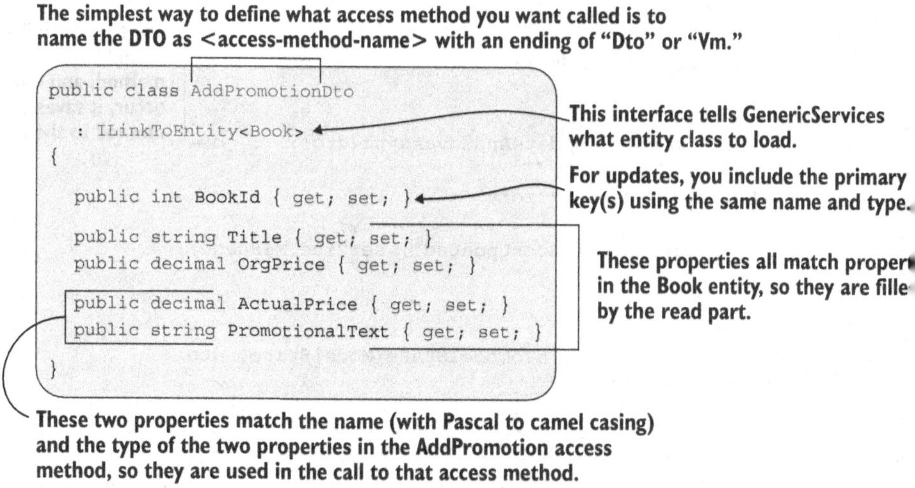

The simplest way to define what access method you want called is to
name the DTO as <access-method-name> with an ending of "Dto" or "Vm."

```
public class AddPromotionDto
    : ILinkToEntity<Book>
{
    public int BookId { get; set; }

    public string Title { get; set; }
    public decimal OrgPrice { get; set; }
    public decimal ActualPrice { get; set; }
    public string PromotionalText { get; set; }
}
```

This interface tells GenericServices what entity class to load.

For updates, you include the primary key(s) using the same name and type.

These properties all match propert in the Book entity, so they are fille by the read part.

These two properties match the name (with Pascal to camel casing) and the type of the two properties in the AddPromotion access method, so they are used in the call to that access method.

Figure 13.7 The DTO defines what entity class is read and updated by using the `ILinkToEntity<T>` interface. On a read, it will fill in all the properties in the DTO that have the same name/type as the linked entity class—in this case, the `Book` entity. The name of the DTO is used to find the access method to call, and the properties are found by matching names (with Pascal to camel casing) and their types.

The following listing shows the use of the `GenericServices` library instead of a re itory (listing 13.8). Note that I've commented only the new code that uses Gene Services.

Listing 13.9   Handling the AddPromotion update by using GenericServices

```
//public class AdminController : Controller
{
    private readonly ICrudServicesAsync _service;

    public AdminController(
        ICrudServicesAsync service)
    {
        _service = service;
    }

    public async Task<IActionResult> AddPromotion(int id)
    {
        var dto = await _service
            .ReadSingleAsync<AddPromotionDto>(id);

        return View(dto);
    }

    [HttpPost]
    [ValidateAntiForgeryToken]
    public async Task<IActionResult> AddPromotion(AddPromotionDto dto)
    {
        if (!ModelState.IsValid)
        {
            return View(dto);
        }

        await _service.UpdateAndSaveAsync(dto);

        if (!_service.HasErrors)
        {
            return View("BookUpdated", service.Message);
        }

        //Error state
        _service.CopyErrorsToModelState(ModelState, dto);
        return View(dto);
    }
}
```

The ICrudServicesAsync service comes from GenericServices and is injected via the Controller's constructor.

The ReadSingleAsync<T> reads into the DTO, using the given primary key.

The UpdateAndSaveAsync method calls the access method, and if no errors occur, it saves the access method to the database.

As you can see, the code is much smaller, with only one line in each ASP.NET Core action method. My own before-and-after analysis suggests that the GenericServices library reduces the time it takes to build a backend ASP.NET Core application by 10–20%.

.3   *Adding a Review to the Book entity class via a repository pattern*

When you're updating navigational properties, you need to handle another step: preloading the navigational property. In listing 13.4, the access methods to add a Review to or remove a Review from the Book entity require the _reviews backing field to be filled before the addition or removal, so you need to update the repository that reads

in the Book entity with its Reviews collection included. Because this task is specific t
Book entity, you create a BookRepository class that inherits the GenericReposi
The following listing shows this new BookRepository.

Listing 13.10   Add the `LoadBookWithReviewsAsync` method to the repository

The book repository inherits the generic repository to get the general commands.

```
public class BookRepository : GenericRepository<Book>       ◄─┘
{
    public BookRepository(DbContext context)                │  The GenericRepository
        : base(context)                                     │  needs the application's
    { }                                                     │  DbContext.

    public async Task<Book>
        LoadBookWithReviewsAsync(int bookId)                   Uses the GenericRepository's
    {                                                          GetEntities to get a
        var book = await GetEntities()          ◄─────         IQueryable<Book> query
            .Include(b => b.Reviews)
            .SingleOrDefaultAsync(                             Selects the Book with
                b => b.BookId == bookId);                      the given BookId
        if (book == null)
            throw new Exception("Could not find book");        A rudimentary
        return book;    ◄──────┐                               check that the
    }                          │ Returns the book              entity was
}                              │ with the Reviews              found
                               │ collection loaded
```

Loads a
Book with
Reviews └─▷

Makes sure that
the Review
collection is
loaded with
the book

This repository replaces the `GenericRepository<Book>` in listing 13.9. This code
pet shows how you would call the `LoadBookWithReviewsAsync` method in ASP.
Core's POST action method:

```
var book = await _repository
    .LoadBookWithReviewsAsync(dto.BookId);
book.AddReview(
    dto.NumStars, dto.Comment, dto.VoterName);
await _repository.PersistDataAsync();
```

13.5.4   Adding a Review to the Book entity class via a class-to-method-call library

For preloading navigational properties, the GenericServices library provide
IncludeThen attribute that you add to the DTO. This attribute allows you to de
the name of navigational properties to Include or ThenInclude. The following li
shows the AddReviewDto class with its IncludeThen attribute.

Listing 13.11   The `AddReviewDto` class with an attribute to load the Reviews

The IncludeThen attribute includes the
Book's Reviews navigational property.

```
[IncludeThen(nameof(Book.Reviews))]   ◄─
public class AddReviewDto             ◄─
```

The name of the DTO shows
that it should call the
AddReview access method.

```
   : ILinkToEntity<Book>
{
    public int BookId { get; set; }

    public string Title { get; set; }

    public string VoterName { get; set; }
    public int NumStars { get; set; }
    public string Comment { get; set; }
}
```

The primary key of the Book is filled in by the read and used by the update method.

The Title is read in on a read and used to confirm to the user what book they are adding a Review to.

These three properties are used as parameters in the AddReview access method.

After you add the IncludeThen attribute, any read of an entity will include the navigational properties. You use GenericServices' ReadSingleAsync<T> and UpdateAndSaveAsync(dto) methods the same way that you would access methods that do not have navigational properties to update.

The downside of DDD entities: Too many access methods

Matthew Krieger read one of my articles about using DDD with EF Core and left this comment: "Here is the big thing I cannot get my head around: Won't you end up with lots of access methods?" He was right. In real applications, you can end up with lots of access methods. When you are building a large application, the time it takes to write an access method grows if you have hundreds to write.

Two of my clients used DDD, and both went for an approach that allowed some properties to be updated directly—that is, not using access methods. One client wanted to use JSON Patch to update the entities because it sped up the building of the frontend pages. Another client was using DDD but updating some properties by letting AutoMapper "punch through" the private setter and set the value. (See my warning in section 13.4.1.)

DEFINITION   JSON Patch is a way to send alterations to data by using a JSON object that conforms to the IETF RFC 6902 specification. See http://jsonpatch .com for more information.

Both clients were attempting to speed up development, and saying "That's not the right way to use DDD" wasn't the right suggestion. We agreed on this approach: if the property has no business rules (other than validation attributes), the setter on that property could be made public. I refer to entity classes that use this approach as *hybrid* DDD entities.

As an example, if you look at the Book entity class, the Title property and the Publisher property have no business logic but should not be empty, so the setter of these two properties could be made public without having any effect on the business rules. Making the properties' setter public would save you from writing two more access methods and allow JSON Patch or AutoMapper to update these properties. Some DDD practitioners might criticize this hybrid DDD suggestion as not following the DDD pattern, but I call it a pragmatic solution. 😊

> **NOTE** My `GenericServices` library can detect and use hybrid DDD classes. If a DDD class has properties with public setters, it registers the entity class as a hybrid DDD class. Hybrid DDD classes enable `GenericServices` to use JSON Patch or AutoMapper to set these properties directly without needing an access method to be written. See my article at http://mng.bz/Wrj1.

13.7 Getting around performance issues in DDD-styled entities

So far, you have looked at the ways to apply the DDD approach to entity classes i Core. But when you start building real applications, you sometimes need to imp performance. Typically, the performance issues in an application involve queries DDD doesn't affect them at all. But if you have database write performance issues might feel the need to bypass DDD. Instead of ditching DDD, you have three wa keep using DDD with minimal bending of the rules.

As an example, we look at the performance of adding or removing a Revie far, you have loaded all the reviews before running add/remove access metho you have only a few Reviews, you have no problem, but if your site is like Am where products can have thousands of reviews, loading all of them to add one Review is going to be too slow.

In section 3.4.3, I describe a way to add a single Review to a Book by creating Review and setting its BookId foreign key to the primary key of the Book. This appr means that you don't have to include all the Reviews, so the update will be quick. B the solutions in this section break the DDD rule that the entity classes shouldn't anything about the database code. So in this section, you look at three solutions.

Each solution requires one change: a way to set the BookId foreign key ir Review entity. This change immediately breaks the rule that DDD entities shou know about the database, but I can't see any way around this part, although the approach I describe is close.

We start with the following listing, which shows the updated Review constru Note that the Review has an internal access modifier, which means that it can be cre only in the Domain.Books project. The use of an internal access modifier and optional BookId parameter in the constructor will become clearer as we solve this is

Listing 13.12 The updated `Review` public constructor with optional foreign key

A new, optional property is added for setting the Review foreign key.

The Review constructor is internal, so only entity classes can create a Review.

Standard properties

```
internal Review(
    int numStars, string comment, string voterName,
    int bookId = 0)
{
    NumStars = numStars;
    Comment = comment;
    VoterName = voterName;
```

Sets the standard properties

```
if (bookId != 0)                    If a foreign-key parameter
    BookId = bookId;                was provided, the BookId
}                                   foreign key is set.
```

ALTERNATIVE   The other option is to expose a navigational property linking the Review back to the Book entity. This option keeps the entity from knowing about foreign keys but breaks the DDD rule on minimizing relationships. Pick which rule you want to break.

After you have changed the Review entity, you can use any of three options:

- Allow database code into your entity classes.
- Make the Review constructor public and write nonentity code to add a Review.
- Use domain events to ask an event handler to add a Review to the database.

.1   Allow database code into your entity classes

One solution is for the AddReview access method to have access to the application's DbContext. You can provide the application's DbContext by adding an extra parameter to the AddReview/RemoveReview access methods or using EF Core's service injection as shown in section 6.1.10. Listing 13.13 shows the two access methods to add/remove a Review. The DbContext is provided in the access methods via a parameter.

NOTE   I couldn't use this solution in the part 3 Book App because clean architecture bans adding any substantial libraries, especially anything having to do with databases, to the Domain projects. But I have used this solution in other applications.

Listing 13.13   Providing the application's DbContext to the access methods

```
public void AddReview(                              The access method takes the
    int numStars, string comment, string voterName, normal AddReview inputs ...
    DbContext context)
{
    if (BookId == default)                          This method works only on a Book
        throw new Exception("Book must be in db");   that is already in the database.

    if (context == null)
        throw new ArgumentNullException(            This method works
            nameof(context),                        only if an DbContext
            "You must provide a context");          instance is provided.

    var reviewToAdd = new Review(                   Creates the Review
        numStars, comment, voterName,               and sets the Review
        BookId);                                    BookId foreign key

    context.Add(reviewToAdd);        ◀───┐ Uses the DbContext Add method to mark the
}                                         new Review to be added to the database

public void RemoveReview (                The access method takes
    int reviewId,                        the normal RemoveReview
    DbContext context)                   input of the ReviewId.
```

```
{
    if (BookId == default)                              This method works only
        throw new Exception("Book must be in db");      that is already in the da◼

    if (context == null)                                This method works
        throw new ArgumentNullException(                only if an DbContext
            nameof(context),                            instance is provided.
            "You must provide a context");

    var reviewToDelete = context.Set<Review>()          Reads in the
        .SingleOrDefault(x => x.ReviewId == reviewId);  review to delete

    if (reviewToDelete == null)                         A rudimentary check that
        throw new Exception("Not found");               the review entity was found
    if (reviewToDelete.BookId != BookId)
        throw new Exception("Not linked to book");      If not linked to
                                                        this Book, throw
    context.Remove(reviewToDelete);    ◄──┐             an exception.
}
                            Deletes the review
```

This solution breaks the following DDD rules:

- The add/remove review access methods contain database features.
- The Review entity knows about a database feature: the BookId foreign key

NOTE GenericServices supports injection of a DbContext via a parameter. When GenericServices calls DDD constructors, static factories, or access methods, it looks for parameters of type DbContext or the type of the application's DBContext and fills them in with the DBContext that GenericServices was registered with.

13.7.2 *Make the Review constructor public and write nonentity code to add a Review*

This solution removes the database features introduced in section 13.7.1 from Book's access methods and places them in another project (most likely BizLogic). solution makes the Book entity cleaner, but it does require the Review construc access modifier to be changed to public. The downside is that anyone can cre Review entity instance.

The code to add/remove a Review is the same as shown in listing 13.4, but no in its own class. This solution breaks the following DDD rules:

- The Book entity isn't in charge of the Review entities linked to it.
- The Review has a public constructor, so any developer can create a Review
- The Review entity knows about a database feature: the BookId foreign key.

.3 Use domain events to ask an event handler to add a review to the database

The last solution is to use a domain event (see chapter 12) to send a request to event handlers that add or remove a `Review`. Figure 13.8 shows the `AddReviewViaEvents` access method in the `Book` entity on the left and the `AddReviewHandler` being run by `SaveChanges` (or `SaveChangesAsync`) on the right.

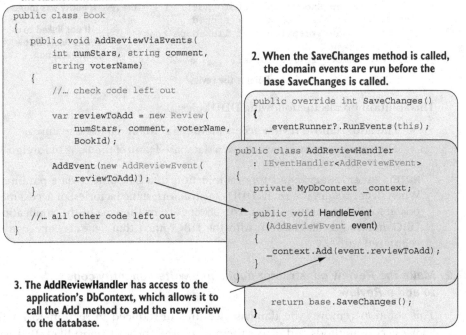

1. The **AddReviewViaEvents** access method creates the Review and sends it via an event to the **AddReviewHandler**.

```
public class Book
{
    public void AddReviewViaEvents(
        int numStars, string comment,
        string voterName)
    {
        //... check code left out

        var reviewToAdd = new Review(
            numStars, comment, voterName,
            BookId);

        AddEvent(new AddReviewEvent(
            reviewToAdd));
    }

    //... all other code left out
}
```

2. When the SaveChanges method is called, the domain events are run before the base SaveChanges is called.

```
public override int SaveChanges()
{
    _eventRunner?.RunEvents(this);
```

```
public class AddReviewHandler
    : IEventHandler<AddReviewEvent>
{
    private MyDbContext _context;

    public void HandleEvent
        (AddReviewEvent event)
    {
        _context.Add(event.reviewToAdd);
    }
}
```

3. The **AddReviewHandler** has access to the application's DbContext, which allows it to call the Add method to add the new review to the database.

```
    return base.SaveChanges();
}
```

Figure 13.8 A solution using events to add a single `Review` without loading all the `Reviews` in a `Book` entity. The `Book` entity has an access method called `AddReviewsViaEvents`, which creates the review and sends it in a domain event to an event handler. When your event-enhanced `SaveChanges/SaveChangesAsync` method is called, it finds and runs the `AddReviewHandler` while providing the domain event as a parameter. The event handler can access the application's DbContext, so it can call the `Add` method to add that new `Review` to the database. Then the base `SaveChanges/SaveChangesAsync` updates the database with the changes.

Figure 13.8 shows only the `AddReview` example, but `RemoveReview` would send the `ReviewId` to a `RemoveReviewHandler`, whose job is to find and delete that `Review`. This approach has the least divergence from the DDD approach because it leaves the `Book` entity in charge of managing the `Reviews` linked to the `Book`. Also, the `Review` entity can keep its internal access modifier so that no code outside the entity classes project

can create a `Review`. But it still has the downside that all the solutions have: the Re
entity knows about a database foreign key.

13.8   Three architectural approaches: Did they work?

The experience of building and enhancing part 3's Book App was a great test of a
ing the three architectural approaches during development. The Book App st
with 9 projects, but by the end of chapter 16, it had 23 projects—a big change,
lots of refactoring to support new features. This section summarizes my experien
using these approaches on the initial part 3 Book App up to the end of chapter 1

13.8.1   A modular monolith approach that enforces SoC by using projects

I was aware of the modular monolith approach but hadn't used it in an applic
before. My experience was that it worked well; in fact, it was much better than I tho
it would be. I would use this approach again for any medium-size to large applica
Following the modular monolith approach meant each project was small and foc
and giving the project a name that said what it did made navigating the code easy.

Having used the layered architecture (see section 5.2) for some time, I know
the service layer can get really big and hard to work on (sometimes referred to a
big ball of mud problem). I try to mitigate this problem by grouping related code
folders, but I'm never quite sure whether the code in folder A links to code i
other folders. When I'm using a layered architecture, if I'm in a hurry, I tend to
something new instead of refactoring the old code. I can't take the time to wor
whether code is used elsewhere or uses something I don't know about.

By contrast, the modular monolith approach provides small, focused proje
know that all the code in the project is doing one job, and the only links are to
projects that are relevant to this project. That approach makes the code easi
understand, and I'm much more inclined to refactor the old code, as I'm less like
break something else.

One lazy thing I found myself doing was referring to the book display projec
contained the original Book App code from part 1. That layer has some useful cl
and enums that could be used in other book-display projects. I was breaking the m
lar monolith rules by referring to a project that had a lot of code that wasn't rele
to the linked project. I should have pulled those common classes into a separate
ect, but I was racing to finish my book, and it was easy to reference the first boo
play project (as on a real job!). The modular monolith approach helps separat
code, but it relies on the developer to follow the rules.

> **NOTE**   I had to go back to the Book App in chapter 16 to add new versions of
> some display features, so I took the opportunity to create a project called
> `BookApp.ServiceLayer.DisplayCommon.Books`, which holds all the common
> code. That project removes the linking between query features and makes the
> code much easier to understand and refactor.

Here are a few tips for using the modular monolith approach:

- Use a hierarchal naming rule for your projects. A name like `BookApp.Persistence.EfCoreSql.Books`, for example, makes it easier to find things.
- Don't end a project name with the name of a class. Instead, use something like ...Books, not ...Book. I named some projects ...Book, which required me to prefix each `Book` class with its complete namespace—in this case, `BookApp.Domain.Books.Book`.
- You're going to get project names wrong. I called one project `BookApp.Infrastructure.Books.EventHandlers`, but as the Book App grew and the project expanded, I had to change it to `BookApp.Infrastructure.Books.CachedValues`.
- If you change the name of a project in Visual Studio by selecting the project and typing the new name, you don't change the folder name. I found that situation confusing in GitHub, so I made sure to rename the folder as well, which meant editing the solution file (there is a nice tool that can do this for you; see https://github.com/ModernRonin/ProjectRenamer).
- You need Visual Studio 16.8.0 or later if you are going to have lots of projects in your application because Visual Studio 16.8 is much quicker than older versions at dealing with lots of projects in a solution. (VS Code has always been fast with lots of projects.)

.2 DDD principles, both architecturally and on the entity classes

I am familiar with using DDD, and as I expected, it worked well. Here is a list of DDD features that made the development of the Book App easier:

- Each entity class contained all the code needed to create or update that entity and any aggregate entities. If I needed to change anything, I knew where to look, and I knew that there wasn't another version of this code elsewhere.
- The DDD access methods were especially useful when I used domain events in chapter 15.
- The DDD access methods were even more useful when I used integration events in chapter 16 because I had to capture every possible change to the `Book` entity and its aggregates, which was easy to do by adding integration events to every access method and static create factory method in the `Book` entity. If I couldn't capture all changes in that way, I would have to detect changes by using the entities' `State`, and I know from experience that detecting changes is hard to implement.
- The DDD bounded context that allowed two different EF Core DbContexts, `BookDbContext` and `OrderDbContext`, also worked well. Migrating the two parts of the same database (see section 9.4.5) worked fine.

13.8.3 *Clean architecture as described by Robert C. Martin*

It wasn't my first time using clean architecture, as I had worked on a client's a
cation that used a clean architecture approach, but it was the first time I'd st
from scratch with this approach. I was much more aware of where I should
the different parts of the application. Overall, I found the clean architecture l
to be useful, but I had to change one thing, which I will describe at the end o
section.

By the end of chapter 16, the part 3 Book App consisted of five layers, starti
the center and working out:

- *Domain*—Holding entity classes
- *Persistence*—Holding the DbContexts and other database classes
- *Infrastructure*—Holding a mixture of projects, such as seeding the database
  event handlers
- *ServiceLayers*—Holding code to adapt the lower layers to the frontend
- *UI*—Holding the ASP.NET Core application

Figure 13.9 shows these five layers, with the number of projects in each layer aft
the chapters were written.

The five layers in the final Part 3 Book App

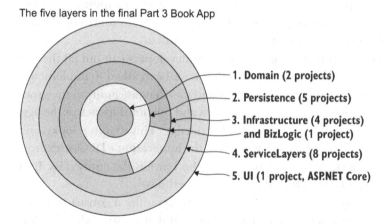

1. Domain (2 projects)
2. Persistence (5 projects)
3. Infrastructure (4 projects)
   and BizLogic (1 project)
4. ServiceLayers (8 projects)
5. UI (1 project, ASP.NET Core)

**Figure 13.9 The five layers of the Book App in part 3, with the number of
projects in each layer after chapter 16 was finished. See the `Part3` branch
of the associated GiHub repo for each project.**

The main problem was fitting the EF Core DbContext into the clean architec
Clean architecture says that the database should be on the outer ring, with inter
for the access. The problem is that there is no simple interface you can use fo
application's DbContext. Even if I were using a repository pattern (which I wasn

would still have a problem because the application's DbContext has to be defined deep in the onion.

One rule of the clean architecture approach that I didn't like, but stuck to, is that the Domain layer shouldn't have any significant external package (such as a NuGet library) added to it. This clean-architecture rule required me to do more work in a few places. In chapter 15, for example, I had code that marked every Book entity when it was added or updated. It would have been easier to pass EF Core's EntityEntry class to the LogAddUpdate method in the Domain level. Also, in chapter 16, I wanted to use an owned type with Cosmos DB, and I had to use Fluent API configuration commands to set that up. I would rather have added the [Owned] attribute to the class, which would save me from adding a OnModelCreating method to the CosmosDbContext class to add extra Fluent API configuration commands. Next time, I might add the EF Core base NuGet package to handle these features.

Summary

- The architecture you use to build an application should help you focus on the feature you are adding while keeping the code nicely segregated so that it's easier to refactor.
- DDD provides lots of good recommendations on how to build an application, but this chapter focuses on EF Core entity classes and application DbContexts.
- DDD-styled entities control how they are created and updated; it's the job of an entity to ensure that the data inside it is valid.
- DDD has lots of rules to make sure that developers can put all their effort into the domain (business) needs that they have been asked to implement.
- DDD groups entities into aggregates and says that one entity in the group, known as the root aggregate, manages the data and relationships across the aggregate.
- Bounded context is a major DDD concept. This chapter looks only at how bounded context might be applied to the application's DbContext.
- To update a DDD entity, you call a method within the entity class. In this book, these methods are referred to as access methods.
- To create a new instance of an DDD entity, you use a constructor with specific parameters or a static create factory method that returns validation feedback.
- To update a DDD entity, first load the entity so that you can call the access method. You can do this via normal EF Core code, a repository, or the EFCore.GenericServices library.
- The EFCore.GenericServices library saves you development time. It removes the need to write a repository, and it can find and call access methods by using the name and properties in the DTO.
- Updating collection relationships can be slow if there are lots of existing entries in the collection. You have three ways to improve performance in these cases.

- A review of applying the three architectural approaches through chapt
  shows that all three made enhancing and refactoring the Book App easie
  approaches worked, but the standouts were modular monolith and DDD.

For readers who are familiar with EF6.x:

- In EF6.x, you can't fully create DDD entities in EF6.x because you can't
  navigational collection properties read-only. EF Core has solved that pro
  with its backing fields feature.

14

EF Core
performance tuning

This chapter covers

- Deciding which performance issues to fix
- Employing techniques that find performance issues
- Using patterns that promote good performance
- Finding patterns that cause performance issues

This chapter is the first of three addressing performance-tuning your database accesses. Covering what to improve, as well as where and how to improve your EF Core database code, this chapter is divided into three parts:

- *Part 1*—Understanding performance, the difference between speed and scalability, deciding what to performance-tune, and determining the costs of performance tuning
- *Part 2*—Techniques you can use to find performance issues and the use of EF Core's logging to help you spot problems
- *Part 3*—A whole range of database access patterns, both good and bad, to help you diagnose and fix many EF Core performance issues

In chapter 15, you'll apply the approaches shown in this chapter to the Book App's book list query. You'll start by tuning EF Core code and then progress to

438

more complex techniques, such as adding SQL commands to squeeze the best
formance out of the database accesses.

14.1 Part 1: Deciding which performance issues to fix

Before describing how to find and fix performance issues, I want to provide an
view of the subject of performance. Although you can ignore performance at the
of a project, some concepts might help you later, when someone says, "The ap
tion is too slow; fix it."

When people talk about an application's *performance*, they're normally ta
about how fast an application deals with requests—how long it takes an API to re
a specific request, for example, or how long a human user has to wait when searc
for a specific book. I call this part of the application's performance *speed* and
terms such as *fast* and *slow* to describe it.

The other aspect is what happens to the speed of your application when it ha
of simultaneous requests. A fast website with a few users might become slow wh
has many simultaneous users, a situation that is referred to as the *scalability* o
application—the ability of the application to feel fast even when it has a high lo
users. Scalability is often measured via *throughput*—the number of requests an ap
tion can handle per second.

14.1.1 "Don't performance-tune too early" doesn't mean you stop thinking

Pretty much everyone says you shouldn't performance-tune early; the number
goal is to get your application working properly first. A saying attributed to Kent
is "Make it Work. Make it Right. Make it Fast," which gets across the progressive
in building an application, with performance tuning coming last. I totally agree
with three caveats:

- Make sure that any software patterns you use don't contain inherent pe
  mance problems. Otherwise, you'll be building in inefficiencies from day
  (See section 14.4.)
- Don't write code that makes it hard to find and fix performance problems. I
  mix your database access code with other code, such as frontend code, for e
  ple, performance changes can get messy and difficult to test. (See section 14.
- Don't pick the wrong architecture. Nowadays, the scalability of web applica
  is easier to improve by running multiple instances of the web application. I
  you have an application that needs high scalability, a Command and C
  Responsibility Segregation (CQRS) architecture might help. I cover this
  in chapter 16.

It's often hard to predict what performance problems you're going to hit, so wa
until your application is starting to take shape is sensible. But a bit of up-front tho
can save you a lot of pain later if you find that your application is too slow.

2 How do you decide what's slow and needs performance tuning?

The problem with terms such as *fast, slow,* and *high load* is that they can be subjective. You might think your application is fast, but your users may think it's slow. Sticking with subjective views of an application's performance isn't going to help, so the key questions are these: Does the speed matter in this case, and how fast should it be?

You should remember that in human-facing applications, the raw speed matters, but so do the *user's expectations* of how fast a certain feature should be. Google search has shown how blindingly fast a search can be, for example; therefore, we expect all searches to be fast. Conversely, paying for an online purchase—with the need to fill in your address, credit card number, and so on—isn't something that we expect to be fast (although if it's too slow or too difficult, we'll give up!).

When you think about what needs to be performance-tuned, you need to be selective; otherwise, you're in for a lot of work for little gain. I once developed a small e-commerce site that had a little more than 100 different queries and updates to 20 database tables. More than 60% of the database accesses were on the admin side, and some were rarely used. Maybe 10% of the database accesses affected paying users. That analysis helped me decide where to put my effort.

Figure 14.1 shows what happens when you apply the same analysis of the user's expectations against the speed of the database access for the Book App. This analysis covers the book listing/search; the placing of an order; and the few admin commands, ranging from updating the publication date of a book (fast) to wiping and inputting all the books again (quite slow).

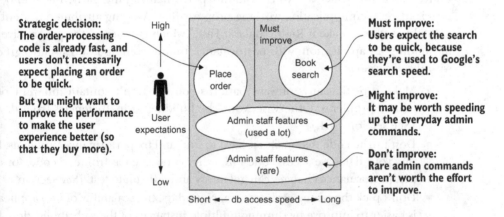

Figure 14.1 Various features from the Book App graded with the user's expectations of speed on the vertical access and the actual complexity/speed of the database access part of the feature. The type of user and user expectations have a big impact on what needs performance-tuning.

After you've done some analysis of your application, you should get a list of features that are worthy of performance tuning. But before you start, you need clear metrics:

- *Define the feature.* What's the exact query/command that needs improving under what circumstances is it slow (number of concurrent users, for examp

- *Get timings.* How long does the feature take now, and how fast does it need to

- *Estimate the cost of the fix.* How much is the improvement worth? When sh you stop?

- *Prove that it still works.* Do you have a way to confirm that the feature is wo properly before you start the performance tuning and that it still works the performance change?

TIP You can find an old but still-useful article on general performance tuning at http://mng.bz/G62D.

14.1.3 *The cost of finding and fixing performance issues*

Before diving into finding and fixing performance issues, I want to point out there's a cost to performance-tuning your application. It takes development time effort to find, improve, and retest an application's performance. As figure 14.1 trates, you need to be picky about what you plan to improve.

Many years ago, I wrote an article in which I measured the gain in performan an EF6.x database access against the time it took me to achieve that improvement ure 14.2 shows the results of that work. I started with an existing EF6.x query (1 o

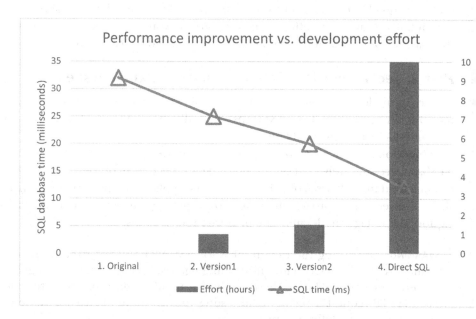

Figure 14.2 The trade-off between database performance and development effort for three stage of improvement of an EF database access. Development time is shown as a bar chart (hours: left sca and the speed of the database access is shown as a line (milliseconds: right scale). An almost-exponential increase occurs in development effort against an almost-linear reduction in database access time.

horizontal scale) and then applied two steps (2 and 3) of improvement, still using EF6.x. Finally, I estimated the time it would take to write a raw SQL version (4 on the horizontal scale).

The point of figure 14.2 is to show that extreme performance improvements aren't easy. I had an exponential increase in development effort against an almost-linear reduction in database access time. Therefore, it's worth thinking about the problem holistically. Although it might be that the database access is slow, the solution might come from changing other parts of the application. For web/mobile applications, you have a few other possibilities:

- *HTTP caching*—Caching allows you to remember a request in memory and return a copy if the same URL is presented, thus saving any need to access the database. Caching takes work to get right, but it can have a big effect on perceived performance.
- *Scaling up/out*—Cloud hosting allows you to pay for more-powerful host computers (known as *scaling up* in Azure) and/or running more instances of the web application (known as *scaling out* in Azure). This approach might solve a lot of small performance problems quickly, especially if scalability is the problem.

I'm not suggesting sloppy programming. I certainly try to show good practices in this book. But by choosing EF Core over writing direct SQL commands, you've already opted for quicker development time with (possibly) slower database access times. In the end, it's always about effort against reward, so you should performance-tune only the parts of your application that need the extra speed or scalability.

Part 2: Techniques for diagnosing a performance issue

In part 1, you decided which parts of your application need improving and how much improvement you want. The next steps are finding the code involved in the slow feature and diagnosing the problem.

This book is about EF Core, so you'll concentrate on the database code, but those database accesses rarely exist on their own. You need to drill down through your application to find the database code that's hitting the application's performance. Figure 14.3 shows a three-step approach that I use to pinpoint performance bottlenecks. You'll explore these stages in detail in the next three subsections.

> **WARNING** Measuring the time it takes for ASP.NET Core to execute a command in debug mode can give misleading figures, because some slow logging methods may be enabled. These methods can add significant extra time to each HTTP request. I recommend testing your software in Release mode to get more-representative figures.

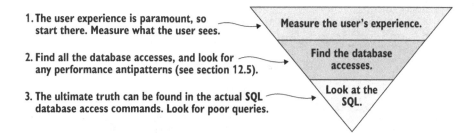

1. The user experience is paramount, so start there. Measure what the user sees. → Measure the user's experience.

2. Find all the database accesses, and look for any performance antipatterns (see section 12.5). → Find the database accesses.

3. The ultimate truth can be found in the actual SQL database access commands. Look for poor queries. → Look at the SQL.

Figure 14.3 Finding database performance issues requires you to start with what the user sees and then drill down to the database code. After finding the database code, you check whether it uses the optimal strategies outlined in this chapter. If this step doesn't improve the situation, you need to look at the actual SQL commands sent to the database and consider ways to improve them.

14.2.1 Stage 1: Get a good overview, measuring the user's experience

Before you go digging to find a performance problem, you need to think abou user's experience, because user experience is what matters. You might improve the s of a database access by 500%, but if speed is a small part of the whole picture, improvement won't help much.

First, you need to find a tool that measures how long a specific request/fe takes. What you use will depend on the type of application you're using. Here's of free tools that are available for looking at the overall time a request takes:

- For Windows applications, you can use the Performance Profiler in Visual St
- For websites, you can use your browser in developer mode to obtain timir use Google Chrome).
- For the ASP.NET Core Web API, you can use Azure Application Insights lc in debug mode.
- And don't forget logging output. ASP.NET Core and EF Core's logging o include timings.

NOTE All the tools I listed are free, but plenty of commercial (paid) tools are available for testing and profiling all manner of systems.

Figure 14.4 shows the timeline for the Book App before any performance tunir measured by the Google browser, Chrome, in developer mode (F12), but mos browsers contain the same features. The figure shows only one timing, but you sh take multiple timings for a query, as timings will differ. Also, to get an overvie where the performance issues exist, you should try different sort/filter combina in the book list feature. See chapter 15 for an example of timings for multiple so ter combinations.

NOTE The Book App in branch Part3 captures ASP.NET Core's Request-Finished log, which contains the total time for the HTTP request. If you

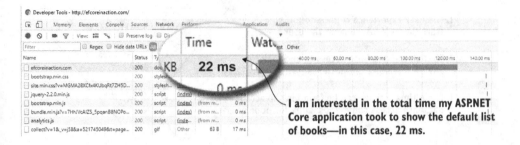

Figure 14.4 Using the Google Chrome browser in development mode to find out how long the Book App takes to display 700 books when using EF Core 5, before you start any performance tuning. This feature is already quick, but in chapter 15, when we take it up to 100,000 books, it starts to have problems.

repeat the same query, this feature will provide max, min, and average timings. You can access this timing feature via the Admin > Timings last URL menu command.

.2 Stage 2: Find all the database code involved in the feature you're tuning

Having identified the part of the application you want to performance-tune, you need to locate all the database access code involved in that feature. After you've found the database code, run your eye over the code, looking for performance antipatterns (see sections 14.5 and 14.6), which is a quick way to find and fix issues. It's not foolproof, but after a while, you'll get a feel for what might be causing a problem.

When you look at the listing of books in your Book App, for example, the most obvious performance bottleneck is calculating the average review votes. Average review votes are used not only for displaying to the user, but also for sorting and filtering the books to be displayed. Running various timing tests showed that sorting or filtering on average votes was slow, but it wasn't until I looked at the EF Core logging output (section 14.2.3) that I saw the problems.

The Book App doesn't have a lot of writes, only adding a review or adding or removing a promotion, and they are fast, but in many applications, writes can be a bit of a bottleneck. Write-performance issues can be more complex to diagnose, as there are two parts to consider: the time EF Core takes to detect and link changes to the data and the time it takes to write to the database. For writes, the overall timing is important, as it contains both parts (see section 14.6).

.3 Stage 3: Inspect the SQL code to find poor performance

The ultimate source of database query performance is the SQL code, and the EF Core logs will list the SQL sent to the database, along with the time that query took. I'll cover how you can use this information to look for performance issues, but first, let

me describe how to access the logging information that EF Core produces. The
in obtaining the EF Core logging output are

1 Understanding the logging output produced by EF Core
2 Capturing the logging output
3 Extracting the SQL commands sent to the database

UNDERSTANDING THE LOGGING OUTPUT PRODUCED BY EF CORE

.NET Core defines a standard logging interface that any piece of code can use
Core produces a substantial amount of logging output, which is normally collect
the application it's running in. Logging information is categorized by a LogL
which ranges from the most detailed information at the Trace (0) level, right t
Critical (5). In production, you'd limit the output to Warning (3) and above
when running in debug mode, you want Information level, as EF Core (and ASP.
Core) have useful information and timings at this level.

CAPTURING THE LOGGING OUTPUT

One way to access the logs is to use what is known as a *logging provider*. Logging
useful that most applications include code to set up the logging providers. I
ASP.NET Core application, for example, a logging provider(s) is configured d
startup (see http://mng.bz/KH6W), so you can obtain the logs as your applicati
running either in debug mode or from your live application.

Another way to capture logging information is to use EF Core 5's new LogT
ture inside your unit tests. This feature provides a simple way to capture the log
put by EF Core. Listing 14.1 shows you one way to use this feature, but I recomm
that you also read chapter 17, which is all about unit-testing your EF Core code.

NOTE Because you're using the xUnit unit-tests library (see https://xunit
.net), you can't output by using the Console.Writeline method, as xUnit
runs tests in parallel. Therefore, you'll log to a list. Chapter 17 covers this
topic in detail in section 17.11.1, including how to output to a console from
xUnit.

Listing 14.1 Capturing EF Core's logging output in a unit test

Holds all the logs that
EF Core outputs

The DbContextOptionsBuilde
is the way to build the optio
needed to create a context.

The log
string is
captured
and added
to the log.

```
var logs = new List<string>();
var builder =
    new DbContextOptionsBuilder<BookDbContext>()
    .UseSqlServer(connectionString)
    .EnableSensitiveDataLogging()
    .LogTo(log => logs.Add(log),
        LogLevel.Information);
using var context = new BookDbContext(builder.Options);
//... your query goes here
```

Says you are using a S
Server database and ta
in a connection string

By default, exceptions don't cont
data. This code includes sensitive

Sets the log level. Information
level contains the executed SQL.

Creates the application's
DbContext—in this case, the
context holding the books data

WARNING The `EnableSensitiveDataLogging` method in listing 14.1 will include any parameters in the logging. This method is helpful for debugging but should *not* be used in your live application, as the parameters may contain private data that should not be logged for security and/or privacy reasons.

We've covered how to capture EF Core's logging; next, you'll see how to use this information to find performance issues.

EXTRACTING THE SQL COMMANDS SENT TO THE DATABASE

EF Core logs what it is doing, and these logs can be useful. If you set the log level to `Information` in your application, you'll get a complete list of the SQL commands generated by EF Core and sent to the database. The following listing shows an example of an `Information` message containing the SQL code from the part 1 or 2 Book App context.

> **Listing 14.2 An `Information` log showing the SQL command sent to the database**

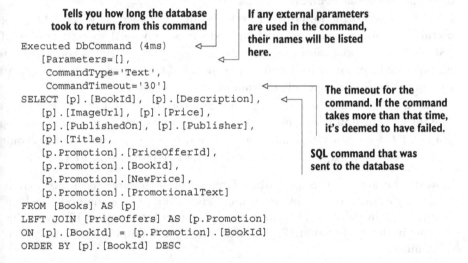

```
                Tells you how long the database        If any external parameters
                took to return from this command       are used in the command,
                                                        their names will be listed
Executed DbCommand (4ms)      ◄─┐                       here.
   [Parameters=[],          ◄─────
    CommandType='Text',
    CommandTimeout='30']                      ◄────────  The timeout for the
SELECT [p].[BookId], [p].[Description],       ◄───────   command. If the command
   [p].[ImageUrl], [p].[Price],                          takes more than that time,
   [p].[PublishedOn], [p].[Publisher],                   it's deemed to have failed.
   [p].[Title],
   [p.Promotion].[PriceOfferId],                         SQL command that was
   [p.Promotion].[BookId],                               sent to the database
   [p.Promotion].[NewPrice],
   [p.Promotion].[PromotionalText]
FROM [Books] AS [p]
LEFT JOIN [PriceOffers] AS [p.Promotion]
ON [p].[BookId] = [p.Promotion].[BookId]
ORDER BY [p].[BookId] DESC
```

For those of you who are happy working with SQL, you can copy the SQL code from the logging output and run it in some form of query analyzer. Microsoft SQL Server Management Studio (SSMS) allows you to run a query and look at its execution plan, which tells you what each part of the query is made up of and the relative cost of each part. Other databases have a query analyzer, such as MySQL Query Analyzer and the PostgreSQL plprofiler.

Part 3: Techniques for fixing performance issues

The rest of this chapter provides a list of good and bad EF Core patterns for database access. These patterns are here both to teach you what can help or hurt performance and to act as a reference on database performance issues. This section consists of four parts:

- *Good EF Core patterns*—"Apply always" patterns that you might like to a They aren't foolproof but give your application a good start.
- *Poor database query patterns*—EF Core code *antipatterns*, or patterns you shou adopt, because they tend to produce poor-performing SQL queries.
- *Poor software patterns*—EF Core code antipatterns that make your database code run more slowly.
- *Scalability patterns*—Techniques that help your database handle lots of data accesses.

Chapter 15 walks you through an example of the performance-tuning appro shown in this chapter. Chapter 15 starts with tuning the EF Core commands in Book App, but then goes into deeper techniques, such as replacing EF Core code direct SQL and changing the database structure to provide better performance. C ter 16 takes the discussion to the next level with a CQRS approach using the Co DB database, which has excellent performance and scalability.

14.4 Using good patterns makes your application perform well

Although I'm not a fan of early performance tuning, I do look at the perform aspects of any patterns I adopt. It's silly to create a pattern that's going to bake in performance right from the start. Many of the patterns and practices described i book do have some effect on performance or make performance tuning easier. H a list of the patterns that help with performance issues that I always apply right the start of a project:

- Using `Select` loading to load only the columns you need
- Using paging and/or filtering of searches to reduce the rows you load
- A warning that using lazy loading will affect database performance
- Always adding the `AsNoTracking` method to read-only queries
- Using the async version of EF Core commands to improve scalability
- Ensuring that your database access code is isolated/decoupled, so it's read performance tuning

14.4.1 Using Select loading to load only the columns you need

In section 2.4, you learned about the four ways of loading related data, one of v was to use the LINQ `Select` command. For database queries that require inform from multiple tables, the `Select` method often provides the most efficient data access code for queries. (See section 14.5.1 for more on minimizing database acce Figure 14.5 illustrates this process.

Creating a `Select` query with a DTO does take more effort than using eager ing with the `Include` method (see section 2.4.1), but benefits exist beyond hi database access performance, such as reducing coupling between layers.

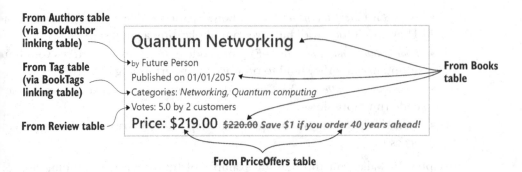

From Authors table
(via BookAuthor
linking table)

From Tag table
(via BookTags
linking table)

From Review table

Quantum Networking

by Future Person
Published on 01/01/2057
Categories: *Networking, Quantum computing*
Votes: 5.0 by 2 customers
Price: $219.00 $220.00 *Save $1 if you order 40 years ahead!*

From Books
table

From PriceOffers table

Figure 14.5 Select **queries provide the best-performing database access, in which the final result consists of a mixture of columns from multiple tables.**

TIP Section 6.1.9 describes how you can use AutoMapper to automate the building of a Select query and thus speed your development.

.2 Using paging and/or filtering of searches to reduce the rows you load

Because EF Core's queries use LINQ commands, you can sometimes forget that one query can pull in thousands or millions of rows. A query that works fine on your development system, which might have only a few rows in a table, may perform terribly on your production system, which has a much larger set of data. You need to apply commands that will limit the amount of data returned to the user. Typical approaches are as follows:

- *Paging*—You return a limited set of data to the user (say, 100 rows) and provide the user commands to step through the "pages" of data (see section 2.7.3).
- *Filtering*—If you have a lot of data, a user will normally appreciate a search feature, which will return a subset of the data (see section 2.7.2).

Remember not to write open-ended queries, such as context.Books.ToList(), because you might be shocked when it runs on your production system, especially if you're writing code for Amazon's book site.

.3 Warning: Lazy loading will affect database performance

Lazy loading (see section 2.4.4) is a technique that allows relationships to be loaded when read. This feature is in EF6.x and was added to EF Core in version 2.1. The problem is that lazy loading has a detrimental effect on the performance of your database accesses, and after you've used lazy loading in your application, replacing it can require quite a bit of work.

This instance is one in which where you bake in poor performance, and you might regret doing that. When I understood the effects of lazy loading in EF6.x, I didn't use it anymore. Sure, it can make development easier in some cases, but each lazy load is going to add another database access. Considering that the first performance antipattern

I list is "Not minimizing the number of calls to the database" (section 14.5.1), i have too many lazy loads, your query is going to be slow.

14.4.4 Always adding the AsNoTracking method to read-only queries

If you're reading in entity classes directly and aren't going to update them, inclu the AsNoTracking method (see section 6.1.2) in your query is worthwhile. It tel Core not to create a tracking snapshot of the entities loaded, which saves a bit of and memory use. It also helps when saving data, as it reduces the work that Det Changes method has to do (see section 14.6.2).

The query in listing 14.3 is an example of one for which the AsNoTrac method, in bold, will improve performance. The simple performance test of loa 100 Books with Reviews and Authors in chapter 6 said that using AsNoTrackin 50% quicker—an extreme case, because the query had 5,000 Reviews in it; fewer tionships will provide less performance savings. See table 6.1 for detailed timings

---

Listing 14.3   Using the `AsNoTracking` method to improve the performance of a q

```
var result = context.Books
    .Include(r => r.Reviews)
    .AsNoTracking()          <-
    .ToList();
```

Returns a Book entity class and a collection of Review entity classes

Adding the AsNoTracking method tells EF Core not to create a tracking snapshot, which saves time and memory use.

If you use a Select query in which the result maps to a DTO, and that DTO do contain any entity classes, you don't need to add the AsNoTracking method. I your DTO contains an entity class, adding the AsNoTracking method will help.

14.4.5 Using the async version of EF Core commands to improve scalability

Microsoft's recommended practice for ASP.NET applications is to use async mands wherever possible. (Section 5.10 explains async/await.) This practice imp the scalability of your website by releasing a thread while the command is waitin the database to respond; this freed-up thread can run another user's request.

Nowadays, using async/await has a small performance cost, so for applications handle multiple simultaneous requests, such as a website, you should async/a Section 14.7.2 covers this topic in more detail.

14.4.6 Ensuring that your database access code is isolated/decoupled

As I said earlier, I recommend that you get your EF Core code working first, wit any performance tuning—but you should be ready to make that code faster if need to later. To achieve isolation/decoupling, make sure that your code

- *Is in a clearly defined place (isolated).* Isolating each database access into its method allows you to find the database code that's affecting performance.

- *Contains only the database access code (decoupled).* My advice is to not mix your database access code with other parts of the application, such as the UI or API. That way, you can change your database access code without worrying about other, nondatabase issues.

Throughout this book, you've seen lots of examples of this approach. Chapter 2 introduced the Query Object pattern (see section 2.6), and chapter 4 showed the use of a separate project to hold the database access code for the business logic (see section 4.4.4). These patterns make performance-tuning your database access code easier, as you have a clearly defined section of code to work on.

Performance antipatterns: Database queries

The previous patterns are worth using all the time, but you'll still bump into issues that require you to tune up your LINQ. EF doesn't always produce the best-performing SQL commands, sometimes because EF didn't come up with a good SQL translation, and sometimes because the LINQ code you wrote isn't as efficient as you thought it was.

This section presents some of the performance antipatterns that affect the time it takes to get data to and from the database. I use the negative antipattern terms, as that's what you're looking for—places where the code can be improved. Here's a list of potential problems, followed by how to fix them, with the ones you're most likely to hit listed first:

- Not minimizing the number of calls to the database
- Missing indexes from a property that you want to search on
- Not using the fastest way to load a single entity
- Allowing too much of a data query to be moved into the software side
- Not moving calculations into the database
- Not replacing suboptimal SQL in a LINQ query
- Not precompiling frequently used queries

1 Antipattern: Not minimizing the number of calls to the database

If you're reading an entity from the database with its related data, you have four ways of loading that data: select loading, eager loading, explicit loading, and lazy loading. Although all three techniques achieve the same result, their performance differs quite a lot. The main difference comes down to the number of separate database accesses they make; the more separate database accesses you do, the longer your database access will take.

Since EF Core 3.0, the default way to handle any collections found in a query has been to load the collection with the base entity. context.Books.Include(b => b.Reviews), for example, would load the Book entity and the related Review entities in one database access. Select and eager loading queries will load the collections to the database in one call. The example queries in the following code snippets take only one database access:

```
var bookInclude = context.Books.Include(b => b.Reviews).First();

var bookSelect = context.Books.Select(b => new
{
    b.Title,
    Reviews = b.Reviews.ToList()
}).First();
```

On the other hand, explicit or lazy loading would take two database accesses. T the effect of the different approaches on performance, load the Book entity wi Reviews, BookAuthor, and Authors (two authors) by using select/eager loading, (loading with AsSplitQuery (see section 6.1.4), and explicit/lazy loading. Table shows the results.

Table 14.1 Comparing the four ways to load data, which tells you that the more trips to the dat the query makes, the longer the query will take

Type of query	#Database accesses	EF 5 time (ms) / %
Select and eager loading	1	1.95 / 100%
Eager loading with AsSplitQuery	4	2.10 / 108%
Explicit and lazy loading	6	4.40 / 225%

> **WARNING** Queries that include multiple collections with large amounts of entries will not perform well when you use the default query approach. Loading an entity with three collections, each containing 100 entries, would return 100*100*100 = 1,000,000 rows. In these cases you should add the AsSplit-Query method to your query. See section 6.1.4 for details.

> **NOTE** The figures in table 14.1 were so different from the first edition of the book that I ran the old code to check my results, and EF Core 2.1 was much slower. EF Core 3.0 improved loading of collections, and NET 5 improved the time taken to access the SQL Server database.

With the improvements in EF Core, the differences between Select/eager, eager AsSplitQuery, and explicit/lazy loading are smaller, but multiple accesses to the base still have a cost. So the rule is to try to create one LINQ query that gets al data you need in one database access. Select queries are the best-performing i need only specific properties; otherwise, eager loading, with its Include methc better if you want the entity with its relationships to apply an update.

14.5.2 Antipattern: Missing indexes from a property that you want to search on

If you plan to search on a property that isn't a key (EF Core adds an index automat to primary, foreign, or alternate keys), adding an index to that property will imp search and sort performance. It's easy to add an index to a property; see section 6.9

There's a small performance cost to updating an index when the value of a property (column) is changed, but often, update performance cost is far smaller than the performance gain when sorting or filtering on that property. Even so, adding indexes works best if you have lots of entries to sort/filter by a property, and reads are more important than update times.

3 Antipattern: Not using the fastest way to load a single entity

When I learned EF Core, I thought that the best way to load a single entity was to use the EF Core's Find method. I used that method until I saw Rick Anderson, who works for Microsoft, using FirstOrDefault. I asked why, and he said it was quicker. At that point, I measured performance, and he was right.

Table 14.2 gives you the timings for each of the methods you could use to load a single entity, in these cases via the entity's primary key, with the timing.

Table 14.2 Time taken to read in a single book using different methods. The timing was taken by averaging the time taken to load 1,000 books. Note that there are two versions of loading via the Find method.

Method	Time	Ratio to single
context.Books.Single(x => x.BookId == id)	175 us.	100%
context.Books.First(x => x.BookId == id)	190 us.	109%
context.Find<Book>(id) (entity not tracked)	610 us.	350%
context.Find<Book>(id) (entity already tracked)	0.5 us.	0.3%

> **NOTE** I couldn't find any significant performance difference between the sync and async versions or First or FirstOrDefault methods I show.

The table shows that Single (and SingleOrDefault) was fastest for a database access, and also better than using First, as Single will throw an exception if your Where clause returns more than one result. Single and First also allow you to use Includes in your query.

You should use the Find method if the entity is being tracked in the context, in which case Find will be super-fast; see the last row of table 14.2. Find is fast because it scans the tracked entities first, and if it finds the required entity, it returns that entity without any access to the database. The downside of this scan is that Find is slower if the entity isn't found in the context.

> **NOTE** The Find method will return a tracked entity that hasn't yet been added or updated in the database. I use this capability in a concurrency handler (see listing 15.11) to recalculate a cached value, using the new author name that hasn't been written out to the database yet.

14.5.4 Antipattern: Allowing too much of a data query to be moved into the software side

It's all too easy to write LINQ code that moves part of the database evaluation o
the database and into the software, often with a big impact on performance. Let's
with a simple example.

This query would perform well, as the Where part would be executed in the database.	This query would per badly, as all the book would be returned (w takes time), and then Where part would be executed in software.
`context.Books.Where(p => p.Price > 40).ToList();` ←	
`context.Books.ToList().Where(p => p.Price > 40);` ←	

Although most people would immediately spot the mistake in listing 14.4, it's pos
for code like this listing to be hidden in some way. So if you find a query that's ta
a long time, check the parts of the query.

One big change in EF Core 3 was to use only client vs. server evaluation (see
tion 2.3) at the last `Select` level of a query. This situation caused problems when
ple updated to EF Core 3, but it exposed only LINQ queries that were running sl
Since that change, if EF can't translate your query to database commands, you
could not be translated exception, so many bad LINQ queries are caught.
exception goes on to say

```
… or switch to client evaluation explicitly by inserting a call
to 'AsEnumerable', 'AsAsyncEnumerable', 'ToList', or 'ToListAsync'
```

This exception message is helpful, but sometimes EF Core throws a could no
translated exception because you didn't get the LINQ query quite right. Aggre
LINQ methods (that is, `Sum`, `Max`, `Min`, and `Average`; see section 14.5.5) require a
lable version of the type to work, and if you don't provide it, you will get the coul
be translated exception. See "Aggregates need a null (apart from count)" in
tion 6.1.8. So before you add `'AsEnumerable'`, `'AsAsyncEnumerable'`, and so on
should check for a way to make the query translate to database commands.

14.5.5 Antipattern: Not moving calculations into the database

One of the reasons why the Book App is fast is that you moved part of the calcula
into the database—specifically, the count of `Reviews` and the average of the votes
the `Reviews`. If you hadn't moved these calculations into the database, the Book
might work, but it would be slow, especially on sorting or filtering of average votes.

Typically, you won't be able to move many calculations into the database, bu
ones you do get can make a big difference, especially if you want to sort or filte
the calculated value. Here are a couple of examples of what you can do:

- Count a collection navigational property, such as `Book.Reviews`. This approa
  useful if you need the count but don't need the content of the collection typ

- Sum a value in a collection, such as summing the price of all the LineItems in an Order. This approach is useful if you want to sort the Orders by price.

NOTE See section 6.1.8 for LINQ commands that require special attention to make the LINQ queries translate to database commands.

.6 Antipattern: Not replacing suboptimal SQL in a LINQ query

Sometimes, you know something about your data that allows you to come up with a piece of SQL code that's better than EF Core. But at the same time, you don't want to lose the ease of creating queries with EF Core and LINQ. You have several ways to add SQL calculations to the normal LINQ queries:

- *Add user-defined functions to your LINQ queries.* A scalar-valued user-defined function (UDF; see section 10.1) returns a single value that you can assign to a property in a query, whereas a table-valued UDF returns data as though it came from a table. In section 15.3, I use a scalar-valued UDF 3 to build the list of author names for a book.
- *Create an SQL View in your database that has the SQL commands to compute values.* Map an entity class to that View (see section 7.9.3) and then apply LINQ queries to that mapped entity class. This approach gives you room to add some sophisticated SQL inside the View while using LINQ to access that data.
- *Use EF Core's raw SQL methods* FromSqlRaw *and* FromSqlInterpolated. These methods allow you to use SQL to handle the first part of the query. You can follow with other LINQ commands, such as sort and filter, but read section 11.5 for the limitations of the FromSqlRaw and FromSqlInterpolated methods.
- *Configure a property as a computed column.* Use this approach if that property calculation can be done with other properties/columns in the entity class and/or SQL commands. (See listing 10.7 for some examples, and see section 10.2 for more on computed columns.)

Clearly, you need to understand and write SQL, but if you can, these techniques provide a simpler experience than using a library that works with SQL, such as ADO.NET or Dapper (see section 11.5.4).

.7 Antipattern: Not precompiling frequently used queries

When you first use an EF Core query, it's compiled and cached, so if you use it again, the compiled query can be found in the cache, which saves compiling the query again. But there's a (small) cost to this cache lookup, which the EF Core method EF.CompiledQuery can bypass. If you have a query that you use a lot, it's worth trying, but I don't think that precompiled queries improve performance much. The other issue is that precompiled queries have some limitations that can make them hard to use:

- You can use a compiled query only if the LINQ command isn't built dynamically, with parts of the LINQ being added or removed. The BookListFilter

method, for example, builds the LINQ command dynamically by using a s᠁
statement, so you couldn't turn that LINQ into a compiled query.

- The query returns a single entity class—an IEnumerable<T> or an IAs᠁
  Enumerable<T>—so you can't chain query objects as you did in chapter 2.

The EF.CompiledQuery method allows you to hold the compiled query in a static᠁
able, which removes the cache lookup part. The LINQ queries can have variabl᠁
the LINQ methods, and you pass the values for these variables with the applicat᠁
DbContext, as shown in the following listing.

Listing 14.5 Creating a compiled query and holding it in a static variable

```
private static Func<EfCoreContext, int, Book>
    _compiledQueryComplex =           f
    EF.CompileQuery(
        (EfCoreContext context, int i) =>
            context.Books
                .Skip(i)
                .First()
    );
```

You define a static function
your compiled query—in th
the function with two input
the type of the returned qu᠁

Defines the query to
hold as compiled

Expects a DbContext, one or two
parameters to use in your query,
the returned result (an entity clas᠁
IEnumerable<TEntity>)

The EF.CompiledQuery method is for taking a specific query and compiling it. I᠁
case of the book query, you'd need to build a separate compiled query for each᠁
and sort option to allow each one to be compiled, as follows:

- Query books, no filter, no sort
- Query books, filter on votes, no sort
- Query books, filter on votes, sort on votes
- Query books, filter on votes, soft on publication date

The EF.CompiledQuery method is useful, but it's best to apply it when the query᠁
want to performance-tune is stable because it may take some work to reformat᠁
query in the correct form to fit the EF.CompiledQuery method.

14.6 Performance antipatterns: Writes

Now that you've learned about performance antipatterns that apply to queries,᠁
look at performance antipatterns that apply to writes. These performance issues᠁
mixture of patterns that produce poor performance from either the database or᠁
pute time in your application. I've listed the problems with the most likely ones f᠁

- Calling SaveChanges multiple times
- Making DetectChanges work too hard
- Not using HashSet<T> for navigational collection properties
- Using the Update method when you want to change only part of the entity
- Startup issue: Using one large DbContext

.1 Antipattern: Calling SaveChanges multiple times

If you have lots of information to add to the database, you have two options:

- *Add one entity and call* SaveChanges. If you're saving 10 entities, call the Add method followed by a call to the SaveChanges method 10 times.
- *Add all the entity instances, and call* SaveChanges *at the end.* To save 10 entities, call Add 10 times (or, better, one call to AddRange) followed by one call to Save-Changes at the end.

Option 2—calling SaveChanges only once—is a *lot* faster, as you can see in table 14.3, because EF Core will batch multiple data writes on database servers that allow this approach, such as SQL Server. As a result, this approach generates SQL code that's more efficient at writing multiple items to the database. Table 14.3 shows the difference in time for the two ways of writing out 100 new entities to an SQL Server database on my development system.

Table 14.3 A comparison of calling SaveChanges after adding each entity, and adding all the entities and then calling SaveChanges at the end. Calling SaveChanges at the end is about 15 times faster than calling SaveChanges after every Add.

One at a time	All at once (batched in SQL Server)
| ```
for (int i = 0; i < 100; i++)
{
    context.Add(new MyEntity());
    context.SaveChanges();
}

Total time = 160 ms
``` | ```
for (int i = 0; i < 100; i++)
{
    context.Add(new MyEntity());
}
context.SaveChanges();

Total time = 9 ms
``` |

The difference between the two ways of saving multiple entities can be large. In the extreme example in table 14.3 where SaveChanges is called 100 times (left side), the time taken is more than 15 times slower than calling SaveChanges once (right side).

Some of the performance loss of the "one at a time" approach is due to extra database accesses. The "all at once" approach taps EF Core's batching capability, which produces SQL that performs well when adding lots of data to a database. For a detailed look at this topic, see http://mng.bz/ksHg.

> NOTE It's also not a good practice to call SaveChanges after each change, because what happens if something goes wrong halfway through? The recommendation is to do all your additions, updates, and removals and then call SaveChanges at the end. That way, you know that all your changes were applied to the database or that if there was an error, none of the changes were applied.

14.6.2 *Antipattern: Making DetectChanges work too hard*

Every time you call SaveChanges, by default it runs a method inside your applicat
DbContext called ChangeTracker.DetectChanges to see whether any of the tra
entities has been updated. (See section 9.3.3 for details.) The time DetectChanges
to run depends on how many tracked entities are loaded—that is, the number of
ties you read in without the AsNoTracking or AsNoTrackingWithIdentityResolu
method (see section 6.1.2) that don't implement the INotifyPropertyChanged i
face (see section 11.4.2).

Table 14.4 shows the time taken for different levels of tracked entities. In this
the entities are small, with a few properties; if the tracked entities were more com
the time would be larger.

**Table 14.4 Time taken by the SaveChanges method, which contains the call to the DetectCha
.Detect method, to save one entity for different levels of tracked entities. Note that the tracked e
used in this table are small.**

Number of tracked entities	How long SaveChanges took	How much slower?
0	0.2 ms.	n/a
100	0.6 ms.	2 times slower
1,000	2.2 ms.	11 times slower
10,000	20.0 ms.	100 times slower

This sort of problem has various solutions, depending on the design of your app
tion. Here are ways to solve this sort of performance issue:

- Do you need all these tracked entities loaded? If SaveChanges is taking a
  time, did you forget to use the AsNoTracking/AsNoTrackingWithIdent
  Resolution method when you made read-only queries?
- Can you break a big insert into smaller batches? I do this in chapter 15, wh
  build a class to create large test data sets for performance tests. In that
  I write out in batches of ~700 Books and use a new instance of the applicat
  DbContext so that there aren't any tracked entities.
- When you need a lot of entities loaded that are ready to be modified, con
  changing your entity classes to use the INotifyPropertyChanged ch
  tracking strategy. This change requires extra coding of your entity classes to
  the INotifyPropertyChanged and configure the entity class's change trac
  strategy (see section 11.4.2). The result is that your entities will report
  changes to EF Core, and DetectChanges doesn't have to scan your loaded
  ties for changes.

.3 Antipattern: Not using HashSet<T> for navigational collection properties

In section 6.2.2, you learned that when you call the Add method to add a new entity to the database, EF Core runs a series of steps to ensure that all the relationships are set up correctly. One of the steps EF Core runs, called *relational fixup*, checks whether any of the entities in the added entity are already tracked. (See section 6.2.2 for details.)

From a performance point of view, the relational fixup stage can cost you compute time because it must compare all the tracked entities that are used in the added entity and its relationships. It's hard to get reliable timings because the first few uses of the application's DbContext are slow, but here are some observations:

- When you're loading collection navigational properties in a query—say, by using the Include method—HashSet<T> for collections is quicker than collection navigational properties using ICollection<T> / IList<T>. Adding an entity with 1,000 entities in a collection navigational property, for example, took 30% longer with ICollection<T> than using HashSet<T> because it is easier to detect/find instances in a HashSet<T>.
- The more tracked entities of the same type found in the entity (and its relationships) that was added, the more time it takes to check them all. The performance hit is hard to measure but seems to be small. But if you have issues with an Add taking a long time, it's worthwhile to check for a lot of tracked entities, which may be part of the slowness of your Add method call.
- As I said in section 2.1.3, the downside of using HashSet<T> is that it does not guarantee the order of the entries in the collection. So if you are using EF Core 5's ability sort entries in an Include method, you can't use HashSet<T>.

.4 Antipattern: Using the Update method when you want to change only part of the entity

EF Core is great at detecting changes to individual properties in an entity class using the DetectChanges.Detect method. If you change one property, such as the publication date of a book, and then call SaveChanges, the DetectChanges.Detect method will find that property change, and EF Core will create some SQL to update that single column in the correct row of the Books table.

On the other hand, if you use the Update method on the Book entity, all the properties are marked as changes, and the SQL becomes bigger and takes (a bit) longer to execute. The Update method should be used only when the whole entity has changed; see section 11.3.4 for an example.

.5 Antipattern: Startup issue—Using one large DbContext

The first time you create your application's DbContext, it'll take some time, perhaps several seconds. There are many reasons for this slowness, but one of them is that EF Core needs to scan all the entity classes in the application's DbContext to configure itself and build a model of the database you want to access. Normally, this problem isn't a big one, because after your application is running, the configuration and base model information is cached by EF Core. But if your application is const being started and stopped—say, in a serverless architecture (see https://martinfc .com/articles/serverless.html)—this startup time could matter.

You can help speed the building of the first application's DbContext by redu the number of entity classes it includes. The only reasonable way to do that is to duce multiple application DbContexts, with each one covering a subset of the t in the database. Section 13.4.8 covers splitting a database across multiple DbCon based on the DDD approach bounded contexts. Figure 14.6 illustrates how a database could be split across multiple applications' DbContexts.

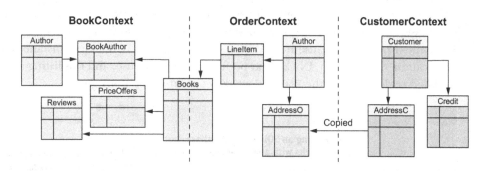

Figure 14.6 A large database can be split into multiple applications' DbContexts. In this case, the database is split along business lines. If you need to minimize application startup costs, you could create specific DbContexts for each application containing only the entities that the application needs to access.

Figure 14.6 splits the database across different applications' DbContexts based on business domains, which might be an appropriate split for some applications. If yo building small, self-contained applications, such as in a serverless architecture microservices architecture (see https://martinfowler.com/articles/microservices .h you could build an application's DbContext, including only the entities/tables cific to each application.

14.7 *Performance patterns: Scalability of database accesses*

Scalability of an application (the number of simultaneous accesses that the app tion can handle) is a big topic. Even when limiting the scope to database access ability, you still have a lot of things to think about. Scalability issues typically can tracked to a poorly written piece of code, because scalability is more about de This section covers

- Using pooling to reduce the cost of creating a new application's DbContex
- Adding scalability with little effect on overall speed

- Helping your database scalability by making your queries simple
- Scaling up the database server
- Picking the right architecture for applications that need high scalability

.1 Using pooling to reduce the cost of a new application's DbContext

If you're building an ASP.NET Core application, EF Core provides a method called AddDbContextPool<T> that replaces the normal AddDbContext<T> method. The Add-DbContextPool<T> method uses an internal pool of an application's DbContext instances, which it can reuse. This method speeds your application's response time when you have lots of short requests.

But be aware that you shouldn't use it in some situations. When you're passing in data based on the HTTP request, such as the logged-in user's ID, you shouldn't use DbContext pooling because it would use the wrong user ID in some instances of the application's DbContext. DbContext pooling is simple to use, and this listing shows an updated registration of the EfCoreContext context in the Book App.

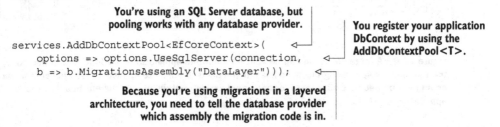

Listing 14.6 Using `AddDbContextPool` to register the application's DbContext

You're using an SQL Server database, but pooling works with any database provider.

You register your application DbContext by using the AddDbContextPool<T>.

```
services.AddDbContextPool<EfCoreContext>(
    options => options.UseSqlServer(connection,
    b => b.MigrationsAssembly("DataLayer")));
```

Because you're using migrations in a layered architecture, you need to tell the database provider which assembly the migration code is in.

Whether DbContext pooling makes a significant difference to the scalability of your application depends on the type of concurrent traffic you have. But you should get at least a small improvement in speed, as the AddDbContextPool<T> method will be quicker at returning a fresh application's DbContext instances.

.2 Adding scalability with little effect on overall speed

In section 14.4.5, I said that you should use the async versions of the database access methods in an application that must handle multiple simultaneous requests because async/await releases a thread to allow other requests to be handled while the async part is waiting for the database to respond (see figure 5.8). But using an async method instead of the normal, synchronous method does add a small amount of overhead to each call. Table 14.5 lists performance figures for a few types of database accesses.

The differences between sync and async in table 14.5 are small, but there is a difference: the slow queries need async, as it releases a thread for a long time. But the fact that the fastest queries have the smallest sync/async difference says that using async won't penalize the small queries. Overall, you have plenty to gain and little downside from using async/await.

Table 14.5 Performance for a mixture of types of database access returning books, using syn async versions. The database contains 1,000 books.

Type of database access	#DB trips	Sync	Async	Differer
Read book only, simple load	1	0.7 ms.	0.8 ms.	112%
Read book, eager-load relationships	1	9.7 ms.	13.7 ms.	140%
Read book, eager-load relation-ships+sort and filter	1	10.5 ms.	14.5 ms.	140%

14.7.3 Helping your database scalability by making your queries simple

Creating SQL commands that have a low cost on the database server (they're ea execute and return a minimal amount of data) minimizes the load on the datal Performance-tuning your key queries to be simple and return only the data ne not only improves the speed of your application, but also helps with the scalabili your database.

14.7.4 Scaling up the database server

With the move to using cloud databases, you can increase the performance of database with the click of a button (and a credit card!). You have are so many op (Azure has more than 50 options for SQL Server) that it's not hard to balance pe mance and cost.

14.7.5 Picking the right architecture for applications that need high scalability

Section 5.2 details how a web application can have multiple instances to provide i scalability. Running multiple instances of your web application is helpful for ware/compute performance, but if all the web application instances are acce only one database, it doesn't necessarily help the database scalability.

Although software/compute performance is normally the bottleneck in scalal for applications that make high demands on the database, extra instances of the application won't help much. At this point, you need to think about other arcl tures. One approach, called *sharding*, spreads your data across multiple datab which can work for certain types of multitenant applications. In chapters 15 an you will explore two architectural approaches—caching and the CQRS pattern— improve performance and scalability.

Because most applications read the database more than they write to the data the CQRS architecture can help with database performance. In addition, by spli out the read-only queries to a NoSQL database called Cosmos DB, you can mak replication of the read-only databases easier, which gives you more database k width. I implement such an architecture by using a CQRS approach in chapte with impressive performance gains.

Summary

- Don't performance-tune too early; get your application to work properly first. But try to design your application so that if you need to performance-tune later, it's easier to find and fix your database code.
- Performance tuning isn't free, so you need to decide what performance issues are worth the development effort to fix.
- EF Core's log output can help you identify database access code that has performance issues.
- Make sure that any standard patterns or techniques you use in writing your application perform well. Otherwise, you'll bake in performance issues from day one.
- Avoid or fix any database performance antipatterns (database accesses that don't perform well).
- If scalability is an issue, try simple improvements, but high scalability may need a fundamental rethinking of the application's architecture.
- Chapter 15 provides an example of applying the recommendations in this chapter to improve the performance of the Book App.

For readers who are familiar with EF6:

- Some EF6.x performance issues, such as using the `AddRange` method over repeated `Add` method calls, have been fixed in EF Core.

Master class performance-tunir database queri

This chapter covers

- Understanding four different approaches to performance-tuning EF Core queries
- Comparing the different performance gains each approach provides
- Extracting the good practices from each approach to use in your applications
- Evaluating the skills and development effort needed to implement each approach
- Understanding what database scalability is and how to improve it

Chapter 14 provided lots of information on how to performance-tune an app tion. In this chapter and part of chapter 16, you are going to see how quickly can make the part 3 Book App display books. This information will expose to various ways to performance-tune an EF Core application; each appr involves a balance between better performance and extra development time learning a range of approaches, you'll be ready to decide what you need in own applications.

You will apply different performance-tuning approaches that progressively increase the speed of the Book App while taking more and more development effort to achieve these performance gains. Although the specific performance code in the Book App may not apply to your application, each of the performance changes uses a different methodology, so you can adapt the approach that works for you.

This chapter focuses on read-only queries, which are often the main performance problem areas in applications. For database writes, see section 14.6.

The test setup and a summary of the four performance approaches

Before we can performance tune an application, we need some example data to test against. Sometimes, the data comes from an existing application that is showing performance problems, or maybe your design/management team has set some performance targets. But to improve performance, you need test data that's representative of the real data that you would encounter in the real world.

For part 3 of this book, I reached out to Manning Publications (this book's publisher), which provided a set of real data containing about 700 real books. Figure 15.1 shows this book's information in the Book App. (Clicking the book title takes you to a details page with further data and an image of the cover.)

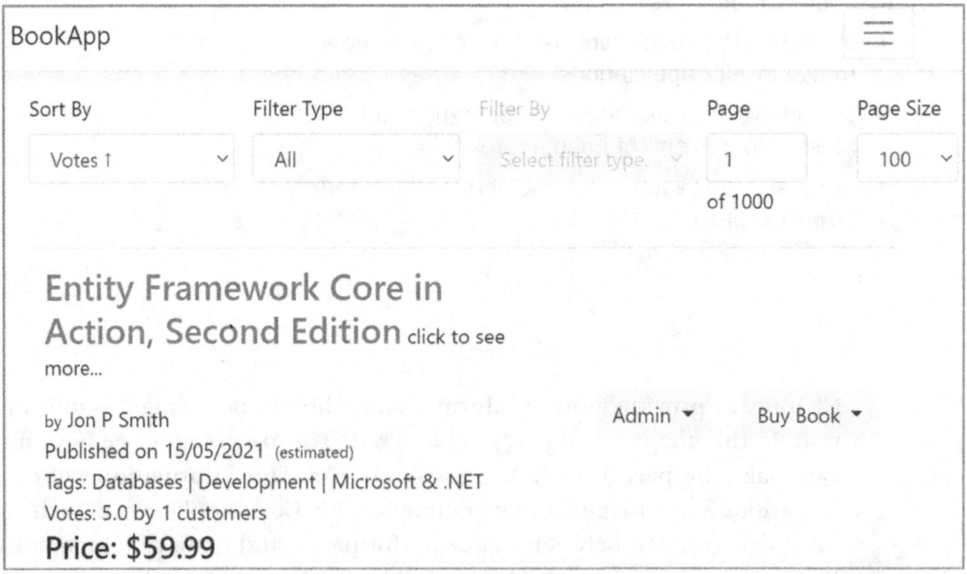

BookApp					≡
Sort By	Filter Type	Filter By	Page		Page Size
Votes ↑ ∨	All ∨	Select filter type. ∨	1		100 ∨
			of 1000		

Entity Framework Core in Action, Second Edition click to see more...

by Jon P Smith
Published on 15/05/2021 (estimated)
Tags: Databases | Development | Microsoft & .NET
Votes: 5.0 by 1 customers

Admin ▼   Buy Book ▼

Price: $59.99

Figure 15.1 The upgraded BookApp.UI, using real book data from Manning Publications. This figure shows an example of the Book App using real book data provided by Manning, which has been duplicated so that there are 100,000 Books in the database, as well as more than a half-million Reviews.

NOTE You can try this example yourself by downloading the GitHub repo associated with this book (http://mng.bz/XdlG) and then selecting the Part3 branch. The BookApp.UI project contains the ASP.NET Core application. When you run this application, see the Things to Do section of the home page for a link to information on configuring the app to show the four approaches used in this chapter.

The four approaches used in this chapter to performance-tune are

- *Good LINQ*—Uses the same approach shown in section 2.6 and follows the gestions in chapter 14. This approach is our base performance.
- *LINQ+UDFs*—Combines LINQ with SQL UDFs (user-defined functions; see tion 10.1) to move concatenations of Author's Names and Tags into the data
- *SQL+Dapper*—Creates the required SQL commands and then uses Dapp execute that SQL to read the data.
- *LINQ+caching*—Precalculates some of the costly query parts, such as the ages of a Review's NumStars (referred to as *votes*).

To provide a more demanding set of data to test these approaches, use the Book A BookGenerator to duplicate the initial 700 books to get as many as you like. Fo tests in this chapter, I used 100,000 books. Table 15.1 shows the full list of the da the database.

Table 15.1 The test data used in this chapter to test the four performance approaches

Table	Books	Review	BookAuthor	Authors	BookTags	T.
Number of rows	100,000	546,023	156,958	868	174,405	35

In this chapter, you are going to compare the performance of these four q approaches with that of three different book-display queries. The three queries r from the simple sort-by-date query to the complex sort-by-votes query. Figure shows the time taken for each query approach for each of the three queries, using data detailed in table 15.1.

Here is a detailed explanation of the three types of queries shown in figure 15

- *Sort by votes*—Sorts by average votes, which is calculated by averaging the Stars property in the Reviews linked to a book. This query shows that so on the average votes, which is a sort that users would use a lot, has a large am of variation across all four approaches, for reasons explained in the section each approach.
- *Filter votes+sort price*—Filters out all books with fewer than 4 for its average (which leaves about 3,000 books) and then sorts on price. This query shows the first three approaches take a similar amount of time. The cached versi fast because the average vote is precalculated and has an SQL index.

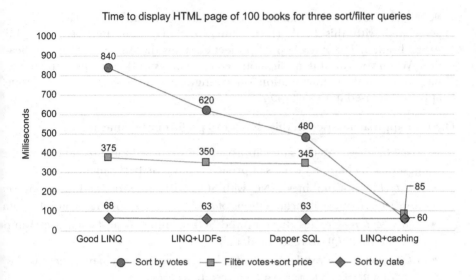

Figure 15.2 **The chart shows the time it took to display a page containing 100 books for three different sorts/filters. The database contains 100,000 books and a half-million reviews (see table 15.1 for full details). The timings were done on my local PC, using a localdb SQL Server running on the same PC; all the queries are async.**

- *Sort by date*—Sorts by the date of publication of the book, which is a sort on a known property that has an SQL index. All the approaches provide good performance, with some subtle differences between the Good LINQ approach and the SQL+UDFs and Dapper SQL approaches.

Although these four approaches are applied to the Book App, they define four general approaches to performance-tuning EF Core database queries. The explanation of each approach details the application of the performance improvements in the Book App, but then pulls out the learning from each approach so that you can decide whether it would work in your EF Core application.

Good LINQ approach: Using an EF Core Select query

This approach is close to the book query you created in chapter 2. The great thing about this approach is that it's simple: the query uses only LINQ to build this version, whereas the LINQ+SQL and Dapper versions require you to use raw SQL, and the cached SQL requires some serious code to make it work.

First, I should say that the current LINQ query is fast enough with only 700 books; it takes about 70 ms to sort on votes and displays 100 books. The reason is that the query from chapter 2 already uses some good practices. I didn't call out these good practices in chapter 2 because that chapter was early in the book, but now we can explore this query in detail.

NOTE If you download and run the Part3 branch Book App, you can see the SQL generated by each approach by selecting the approach and type of filter/sort and then clicking the Logs menu item, which will show you the SQL as used in the query you executed.

The following listing shows the part of the query that gathers all the data needed, comments on various parts that make this query a good LINQ query.

Listing 15.1 MapBookToDto method that selects what to show in the book display qu

```
public static IQueryable<BookListDto>
public static IQueryable<BookListDto>
    MapBookToDto(this IQueryable<Book> books)
{
    return books.Select(p         => new BookListDto
    {
        BookId                    = p.BookId,
        Title                     = p.Title,
        PublishedOn               = p.PublishedOn,
        EstimatedDate             = p.EstimatedDate,
        OrgPrice                  = p.OrgPrice,
        ActualPrice               = p.ActualPrice,
        PromotionText             = p.PromotionalText,
        AuthorsOrdered            = string.Join(", ",
            p.AuthorsLink
                .OrderBy(q     => q.Order)
                .Select(q      => q.Author.Name)),
        TagStrings                = p.Tags
            .Select(x => x.TagId).ToArray(),
        ReviewsCount              = p.Reviews.Count(),
        ReviewsAverageVotes       =
            p.Reviews.Select(y =>
                (double?)y.NumStars).Average(),
        ManningBookUrl            = p.ManningBookUrl
    });
}
```

Good practice: Load only the properties you need.

Good practice: Use ind properties to sort/filte (in this case, the Actua

Good practice: Don't load the whole entity of each relationships, only the parts you need.

Good practice: The ReviewsCount and ReviewsAverageVotes a calculated in the datab

Next, let's look at what is going in the MapBookToDto extension method so that can understand and apply these good practices to your own applications.

LOADING ONLY THE PROPERTIES YOU NEED FOR THE QUERY

You could have loaded the whole Book entity, but that would mean loading data didn't need. The Manning Publications book data contains large strings summar the book's content, what technology it covers, and so on. The book display do need that data, however, and loading it would make the query slower, so you c load it.

In line with the recommendation that you don't performance-tune too early might start with a simple query that reads in the entity classes, and performance- later. In the Book App, it was obvious that the book display query was a key q especially with respect to sorting by votes, so I started with a Select query. But for if a query is slow and you are loading the whole entity class, consider changing to the LINQ Select method and loading only the properties you need.

DON'T LOAD WHOLE RELATIONSHIPS—ONLY THE PARTS YOU NEED

There are many ways to load relationships, including eager loading, explicit loading, and lazy loading. The problem is that these three approaches to reading relationships load the whole entity class of each relationship. Typically, you don't need to load the relationship's whole entity classes.

In listing 15.1, you see that the AuthorLink collection is used to select only the Author's Name, which minimizes the data returned from the database. Similarly, the Tags are stripped to return only an array of the TagIds. So to improve the performance of a query, if you need data from relationships, try to extract the specific parts from any relationships. An even better idea is to move calculations into the database if you can, which I cover next.

IF POSSIBLE, MOVE CALCULATIONS INTO THE DATABASE

If you want good performance, especially for sorting or filtering on values that need calculating, it's much better for the calculation to be done inside the database. Calculating data inside the database has two benefits:

- The data used in the calculation never leaves the database, so less data needs to be sent back to the application.
- The calculated value can be used in a sort or filter, so you can execute the query in one command to the database.

If you didn't calculate the ReviewsAverageVotes value in the database, for example, you would need to read in *all* the Reviews NumStars and BookId properties, and work out the ReviewsAverageVotes value for every book. Only then could you work out which Books you should read in. That process is going to be slow and take up a lot of memory because it would have to read in all the Reviews from the database and then work out the average votes in software before it could read in the Books to display.

I have to say that getting these types of calculations right wasn't obvious! When I wrote the first edition of this book, I couldn't get the ReviewsAverageVotes value query correct, and it took raising an issue on the EF Core GitHub issues page to get the right answer. In section 6.1.8, I cover some of the LINQ commands that must be written in a specific way to work.

IF POSSIBLE, USE INDEXED PROPERTIES TO SORT/FILTER ON

In part 1, I applied a promotion to a Book by adding a PriceOffer entity class. I did that not only because I wanted to show how one-to-one relationships worked, but also because using a PriceOffer entity class made it obvious what I was doing. The downside of this approach is that the query had to include code to look for the PriceOffer entity class. The following code snippet is from the part 1 version of the MapBookToDto method:

```
ActualPrice = book.Promotion == null
    ? book.Price
    : book.Promotion.NewPrice,
```

```
PromotionPromotionalText =
    book.Promotion == null
    ? null
    : book.Promotion.PromotionalText,
```

That code has two negative effects on sorting on price: the LINQ is converted t
SQL JOIN to find the optional PriceOffers row, which takes time, and you can't a
SQL index to this calculation. In part 3, the Book App moved to using DDD, so
could add or remove a price promotion by using access methods in the Book e
(see section 13.4.2). The access methods hide the business logic of the promo
which means that the ActualPrice property always contains the price that the bo
sold for. Changing the code to not use the PriceOffer entity removes the SQL J
and you can add an SQL INDEX to the ActualPrice column in the database, sig
cantly improving the sort-on-price feature.

So if you need to query some data, especially if you're sorting or filtering on
data, try to precompute the data in your code. Or use a persisted computed col
(see section 10.2) if the property is calculated based on other properties/colum
the same entity class, such as [TotalPrice] AS (NumBook * BookPrice). That way
will get a significant improvement in any sort or filter because of the SQL inde
that column.

15.3 LINQ+UDFs approach: Adding some SQL to your LINQ code

In the Good LINQ approach, both the LINQ that forms the book display rea
Authors Names and the Tag's TagId return collections, because there can be r
Authors and Tags. Before EF Core 3.0, these collections were read in by using an e
query per collection, so reading in 100 books with Author's Name alone would cu
101 accesses to the database (one for the main query and then one per bool
Author's Name) and take about 230 ms.

Since EF Core 3.0, this query has been reduced to one access to the databas
returning multiple rows per book and extra columns to make sure that the rows a
the right order. With lots of Books, Author's Names, and TagIds, the end of the
produced by the Good LINQ book display with the default ordering (order on Bo
descending) looks like this:

```
SELECT [t].[BookId],…
-- other parts of the SQL
ORDER BY [t].[BookId] DESC
    , [t0].[Order]
    , [t0].[BookId], [t0].[AuthorId], [t0].[AuthorId0]
    , [t2].[BookId], [t2].[TagId0], [t2].[TagId]
```

I'm not going to explain the various tables and columns in ORDER BY (you can se
whole SQL query by running the Book App and clicking the Logs menu item)
you can see that there are a lot of ORDER BY parameters. It turns out that if you add

sort-on-average-votes LINQ query at the top of the existing ORDER BYs, performance starts to drop, which is one reason why the Good LINQ book display is so bad (840 ms, as shown in figure 15.2).

NOTE Before you say that having all those ORDER BY parameters is bad SQL, I can tell you that without that code, the query would take about twice the time and would go from one database access to five separate database accesses. The EF Core 3.0 change has improved most, but not all (see section 6.1.4) queries containing collections.

Some time ago, I found some SQL code on Stack Overflow that concatenated a series of strings into a single string inside the database. In section 14.5.6, I described four ways to enhance a LINQ query by providing SQL that is custom-made for your specific situation. In this case, I used a scalar UDF to access this code, as shown in the following code snippet:

```
CREATE FUNCTION AuthorsStringUdf (@bookId int)
RETURNS NVARCHAR(4000)
AS
BEGIN
-- Thanks to https://stackoverflow.com/a/194887/1434764
DECLARE @Names AS NVARCHAR(4000)
SELECT @Names = COALESCE(@Names + ', ', '') + a.Name
FROM Authors AS a, Books AS b, BookAuthor AS ba
WHERE ba.BookId = @bookId
      AND ba.AuthorId = a.AuthorId
      AND ba.BookId = b.BookId
ORDER BY ba.[Order]
RETURN @Names
END
```

NOTE You should add raw SQL only if you have code that does something better than EF Core. Merely adding SQL that is the same as what EF Core would have created won't improve performance.

To use the UDF code AuthorsStringUdf and TagsStringUdf to concatenate the TagIds, I had to define it (see section 10.1) and add the UDFs to a database by editing a migration (see section 9.5.2). Then I needed to create a new mapping from the Book entity to a book-display DTO, as shown in the next listing. See the lines with comments for the calls to the two UDFs.

Listing 15.2 MapBookUdfsToDto using UDFs to concatenate Name/Tag names

```
public static IQueryable<UdfsBookListDto>
    MapBookUdfsToDto(this IQueryable<Book> books)       ◁───┐  Updated MapBookToDto
{                                                           │  method, now called
    return books.Select(p       => new UdfsBookListDto      │  MapBookUdfsToDto
    {
        BookId          = p.BookId,
        Title           = p.Title,
```

```
    PublishedOn    = p.PublishedOn,
    EstimatedDate  = p.EstimatedDate,
    OrgPrice       = p.OrgPrice,
    ActualPrice    = p.ActualPrice,
    PromotionText  = p.PromotionalText,
    AuthorsOrdered = UdfDefinitions             The AuthorsOrdered
        .AuthorsStringUdf(p.BookId),            and TagsString are set
    TagsString     = UdfDefinitions             to the strings from
        .TagsStringUdf(p.BookId),               the UDFs.
    ReviewsCount = p.Reviews.Count(),
    ReviewsAverageVotes =
        p.Reviews.Select(y =>
            (double?)y.NumStars).Average(),
    ManningBookUrl = p.ManningBookUrl
});
}
```

When you change the MapBookToDto extension method to use the AuthorsStrin
and the TagsStringUdf UDFs, each book returns only one row, and there is no O
BY other than the default ordering on BookId, descending. This change has a s
effect on a nonsorted display of 100 books (improving it by a few milliseconds)
the big effect is on the sort by average votes, which comes down from 840 ms ir
Good LINQ approach to 620 ms in the LINQ+SQL approach—an improveme:
about 25%.

15.4 SQL+Dapper: Creating your own SQL

The ultimate SQL approach is to stop using EF Core and write your own SQL que
you want to do this, you need a library that can execute your SQL code for you.
best one I have found is Dapper (covered in section 11.5.4). The issue is comin
with better SQL than EF Core.

I studied the SQL that EF Core produced and did some digging, and found
place where I could improve the SQL over EF Core. It turns out that you can sort
parameter in a SQL SELECT command; see https://stackoverflow.com/a/38750
1434764. According to this Stack Overflow page, "ORDER BY is solved after the SE
(which means you can use a calculated column from the SELECT), unlike WHEF
FROM, which are solved before the SELECT and therefore can't refer to column a
in SQL Server."

EF Core doesn't take advantage of this feature, so its SQL computes average v
twice: once in the SELECT and again in the ORDER BY. My tests showed that compu
average votes only once significantly improved the performance in the sort-by-v
query, so I set about rewriting the various sort, filter, and paging features used by
Book App, which involved selecting and concatenating SQL strings to form the co
SQL query. Converting the LINQ features to SQL was quite complicated. Figure
shows a flow chart depicting how the SQL query was built.

NOTE The SQL that I created uses the two UDFs used in the LINQ+UDFs
approach; otherwise, it would be slower than LINQ+UDFs. If you want to see

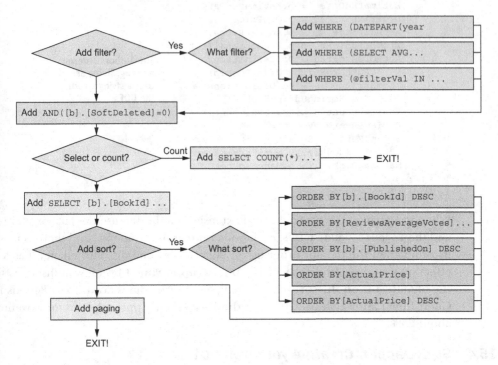

Figure 15.3 The Dapper code consists of a series of string concatenations that produce the final SQL query. This code isn't as elegant as the EF Core version, with its four Query Objects, but when you're performance-tuning, you often must accept some loss of cleanness from your original code to achieve the performance you need.

the code that builds and runs the SQL, you can find it at http://mng.bz/ n2Q2.

The performance improvement for the sort-by-votes query is impressive: the Dapper version is nearly twice as fast as the Good LINQ version (Dapper: 480 ms, Good LINQ: 840 ms). But on every other query that didn't include a sort on votes, the Dapper version wasn't much faster than LINQ version, especially against LINQ+UDFs. To understand this result, I looked at the simplest query—sort by the date of publication—to see where the time was going. Figure 15.4 breaks down the time into three parts:

- (Bottom) *Database time* (important)—Time taken for the SQL to run
- (Middle) *HTML time*—Time it took to send the HTML page to the browser
- (Top) *Software time*—Rest of the time, mostly ASP.NET Core

NOTE The SQL timing came from EF Core's logging, which includes the time the execution took. For Dapper, I used a stopwatch, starting it before the call to Dapper and stopping it when the data was returned.

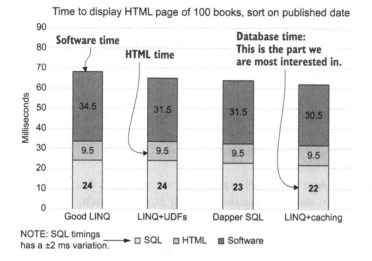

Time to display HTML page of 100 books, sort on published date

Figure 15.4 Breakdown of the sort by the date of publication of the book with a page of 100 books. The important part to look at is the bottom timings, which cover the time taken to execute the SQL: ±2 ms on the SQL part, with some outliers that I left out. The other parts have larger variations. The overall variation is 10 ms for the Good LINQ version and smaller (say, 5 ms).

As you can see from figure 15.4, the differences in the SQL are small, and becau the ±2 ms variations in the timings, they are essentially the same. The quick pe mance of the Dapper library becomes less and less a factor when the SQL used ir query takes many milliseconds to execute. And because the only queries you nee performance-tune typically take many milliseconds to run, ½ or 1 ms saved by Da doesn't make much of a difference. (It helps that EF Core is getting quicker.)

The takeaway from figure 15.4 is that it's worth converting your slow queri Dapper only if you can find some SQL that is better than what EF Core produc took me quite a bit of time to build and debug the complex book display, ane hadn't had another way to improve the performance, the effort would have worthwhile. The cached SQL approach (section 15.5) provides a much bigger pe mance improvement, but it's a lot more work.

NOTE To be clear, other than the sort-by-votes issue, I didn't find any other part of the EF Core that would be improved by using Dapper, and EF Core already had issue #16038 to solve this problem.

15.5 LINQ+caching approach: Precalculating costly query parts

The final approach in this chapter is precalculating the parts of the query that ta long time to calculate and storing them in extra properties/columns in the entity class. This technique is known as *caching* or *denormalization*. Caching works with data that is expensive to generate, such as the average votes for a Book. As you saw in figure 15.2, caching has the biggest effect on the sort-by-votes query, making it about 14 times faster than the Good LINQ approach and 8 times faster than the Dapper approach.

But when you're thinking about using caching, you also need to think about how often the cached value is updated and how long it takes to update the cache. If the data that is cached is updated a lot, the cost of updating the cache may move the performance problem from running the query to updating entities. As you will see in section 15.5.2, the design of the caching algorithms used in the Book App is quick when it comes to handling updates.

But the main problem with caching is that it's really hard to make sure your cached values are up to date. Under the caching SQL approach, for example, you must update the cached ReviewsAverageVotes property every time a Review is added, updated, or deleted. And what happens if two Reviews are applied to a Book entity simultaneously, or when the database update of the cached ReviewsAverageVotes property fails? Here's a quote from the 1990s stating that cache updates have always been a problem:

There are only two hard things in computer science: cache invalidation and naming things.

—Phil Karlton (while at Netscape)

I can attest that building a caching system is hard. I built a caching system for the first edition of the book, and it was good, but now I know about one rare situation in which it would fail to update a cached properly. (I fixed this problem in the new version for this book.)

Studying the SQL query shows that caching the average votes (the average of the NumStars in all Reviews linked to a specific Book entity) would improve performance on sort/filter on average votes. You could stop there, but caching the number of Reviews, the Book, and the concatenation of Author's Names would provide a small boost for all displays of books (about a 5 ms performance gain for displaying 100 books).

Adding a caching system isn't trivial to implement. Here are the steps:

1 Add a way to detect changes that affect the cached values.
2 Add code to update the cached values.
3 Add the cache properties to the Book entity and provide concurrency code to handle simultaneous updates of the cached values.
4 Build the book display query to use the cached values.

At the end of the description of this caching system, section 15.5.4 describes a checking/healing system that checks whether the cached values are set properly.

15.5.1 Adding a way to detect changes that affect the cached values

I have had good results from a domain events approach (see chapter 12) to in
ment caching, so this design uses that approach. One positive feature of the do
events approach is that the change that triggers an update of a cached value is s
in the same transaction that saves the cached value (see figure 12.3). As a result,
changes are applied to the database, or if anything fails, none of the update
applied to the database. That approach prevents the real data and cached data
getting out of step (known as a dirty cache).

As for detecting a change of properties or relationships, we can take advanta
the fact that the part 3 Book App uses the DDD design approach. So, to updat
two cached values related to the Reviews, you can add code to the Book's AddRe
and RemoveReview access methods.

For the cached property called AuthorsOrdered, we are going to use a non-
approach to trigger a domain event in which an Author's Name is changed.
example shows how you would handle domain events and caching when you're
using DDD.

To speed the development, you are going to use my EfCore.GenericEventRu
library. This library is well tested and contains other features that will speed dev
ment. So let's see what the code would look like, starting with the event-enha
BookDbContext, as shown in the following listing.

Listing 15.3 `BookDbContext` updated to use `GenericEventRunner`

```
                                          ┌── The BookDbContext handles
public class BookDbContext        ◄───┘    the Books side of the data.
    : DbContextWithEvents<BookDbContext>   ◄──┐ Instead of inheriting EF Core's
  {                                            │ DbContext, you inherit the clas
                                               │ from GenericEventRunner.
      public BookDbContext(
          DbContextOptions<BookDbContext> options,
          IEventsRunner eventRunner = null)   ◄──┐ DI will provide GenericEventRur
    ├─▷    : base(options, eventRunner)           │ EventRunner. If null, no events
          { }                                     │ used (useful for unit tests).

      //… rest of BookDbContext is normal, so left out
}
```

The constructor
of the DbContext-
WithEvents class
needs the Event-
Runner.

The next stage is adding the events to the Book's AddReview and RemoveReview a
methods. The following listing shows how these methods create an event.

Listing 15.4 The `Book` entity with the `AddReview` and `RemoveReview` methods

```
public class Book : EntityEventsBase,    ◄──┐ Adding the EntityEventsBase
    ISoftDelete                              │ will provide the methods to
  {                                          │ send an event.

      //… other code left out for clarity
```

```
public void AddReview(int numStars,                  The AddReview is the
    string comment, string voterName)                only way to add a Review
{                                                    to this Book.
    if (_reviews == null)
        throw new InvalidOperationException(
            "The Reviews collection must be loaded");

    _reviews.Add(new Review(                          Adds a BookReview-
        numStars, comment, voterName));               AddedEvent domain
                                                      event with the NumStars
    AddEvent(new BookReviewAddedEvent(numStars,   ←   of the new Review
        UpdateReviewCachedValues));
}
                                                      The RemoveReview
                                                      method is the only way
public void RemoveReview(int reviewId)          ←     to remove a Review
{                                                     from this Book.
    if (_reviews == null)
        throw new InvalidOperationException(
            "The Reviews collection must be loaded");

    var localReview = _reviews.SingleOrDefault(
        x => x.ReviewId == reviewId);
    if (localReview == null)
        throw new InvalidOperationException(
            "The review was not found.");
                                                      Adds a BookReview-
                                                      AddedEvent domain
    _reviews.Remove(localReview);                     event with the review
                                                      that has been deleted
    AddEvent(new BookReviewRemovedEvent(localReview, ←
        UpdateReviewCachedValues));
}

private void UpdateReviewCachedValues        ←        This private method can
    (int reviewsCount, double reviewsAverageVotes)    be used by the event
{                                                     handlers to update the
    ReviewsCount = reviewsCount;                      cached values.
    ReviewsAverageVotes = reviewsAverageVotes;
}
}
```

To catch a change of an Author's Name, we will use a non-DDD approach and intercept the setting of a property. This approach uses EF Core's backing-field feature so that we can detect a change in the Author's Name. The modified Author entity class is shown in the following listing.

Listing 15.5 Author **entity sending an event when the** Name **property is changed**

```
public class Author : EntityEventsBase        ←       Adding the EntityEventsBase
{                                                     will provide the methods to
    private string _name;    ←   The backing field for the   send an event.
                                 Name property, which EF
    public string Name           Core will read/write
    {
```

```
    get => _name;              ←——|  You make the setting public and override
    set                            |  the setter to add the event test/send.
    {
        if (value != _name &&                    If the Name has
            AuthorId != default)                 changed, and it's not
            AddEvent(                            a new Author, sends
                new AuthorNameUpdatedEvent());    a domain event
        _name = value;
    }
}

//… other code left out for clarity
}
```

Note that the test of whether the event should be sent includes a test of whethe
Author's primary key, AuthorId, is set. Because the Author entity class doesn't fc
the DDD style, you can't be sure how the developer might create a new instance o
Author entity, so you add the extra primary-key test to ensure that events are sent
when a Author's Name is updated.

15.5.2 Adding code to update the cached values

Now you will create some event handlers to update the cached values when the ap
priate domain event comes in. These event handlers will be called before SaveChan
SaveChangesAsync, so the changes that triggered the events and the subsequent cha
applied by the event handlers will be saved in the same transaction. I am goir
show two styles of updating the cached values within the event handlers:

- The fast delta updates, which work with numeric changes to cached values. V
  the AddReview event is received, for example, the event handler will increr
  the ReviewsCount cache property. This option is fast, but it needs careful co
  to make sure that it produces the correct result in every situation.

- The more-normal recalculate updates, in which you run a query to recalc
  the cached value. This option is used to update the AuthorsOrdered c
  property.

UPDATING THE REVIEWS CACHED VALUES USING THE DELTA UPDATE STYLE

Adding, updating, or removing Reviews causes specific events, which in turn caus
event handle linked to each event type to run. In this example, you are going to l
the event handler code that will update the two cached values, ReviewsCount
ReviewsAverageVotes, in the Book entity. Figure 15.5 shows the stages in the pro
of adding a new Review to a Book that already has one Review.

The main part of the process is in the event handler, which uses a delta sty
update the two Review cached values. Listing 15.6 shows the ReviewAddedHan
class, which the GenericEventRunner library will run before calling SaveChan
SaveChangesAsync.

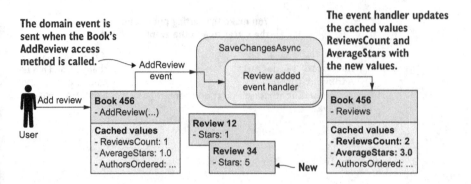

The domain event is sent when the Book's AddReview access method is called.

AddReview event

SaveChangesAsync

Review added event handler

The event handler updates the cached values ReviewsCount and AverageStars with the new values.

User | Add review

Book 456
- AddReview(...)

Cached values
- ReviewsCount: 1
- AverageStars: 1.0
- AuthorsOrdered: ...

Review 12
- Stars: 1

Review 34
- Stars: 5

New

Book 456
- Reviews

Cached values
- ReviewsCount: 2
- AverageStars: 3.0
- AuthorsOrdered: ...

Figure 15.5 When a user adds a new `Review`, the `AddReview` access method creates a domain event, which is picked up by the `GenericEventRunner` when `SaveChanges/SaveChangesAsync` is called. The `GenericEventRunner` runs the `ReviewAddedHandler`, which updates the `Review` cached values using a delta update-style approach.

Listing 15.6 Linking `ReviewAddedHandler` class to the `BookReviewAddedEvent`

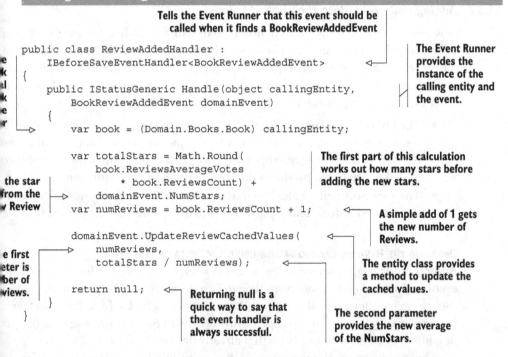

Tells the Event Runner that this event should be called when it finds a **BookReviewAddedEvent**

```
public class ReviewAddedHandler :
    IBeforeSaveEventHandler<BookReviewAddedEvent>
{
    public IStatusGeneric Handle(object callingEntity,
        BookReviewAddedEvent domainEvent)
    {
        var book = (Domain.Books.Book) callingEntity;

        var totalStars = Math.Round(
            book.ReviewsAverageVotes
                * book.ReviewsCount) +
            domainEvent.NumStars;
        var numReviews = book.ReviewsCount + 1;

        domainEvent.UpdateReviewCachedValues(
            numReviews,
            totalStars / numReviews);

        return null;
    }
}
```

The Event Runner provides the instance of the calling entity and the event.

the star from the Review

The first part of this calculation works out how many stars before adding the new stars.

A simple add of 1 gets the new number of Reviews.

first parameter is number of reviews.

The entity class provides a method to update the cached values.

Returning null is a quick way to say that the event handler is always successful.

The second parameter provides the new average of the NumStars.

This event handler doesn't access the database and therefore is quick, so the overhead of updating the `ReviewsCount` and `ReviewsAverageVotes` cached values is small.

NOTE The `RemoveReview` event handler isn't shown here but works the same way as the `AddReview` event handler.

UPDATING THE BOOK'S AUTHORS' NAME CACHED VALUE BY RECALCULATION

There are many ways that an `Author` or `Author`'s `Name` could be changed in a Boo
`Book` level, someone might have left an `Author` out. At `Author` entity level, som
might have misspelled the author's name (as *John P Smith* instead of *Jon P Smith*
example). For any of these changes, the affected `Book` entity or entities should up
the `Book`'s `AuthorsOrdered` cache value. This string isn't used in a filter or sort, l
saves some time for the display of author names. For this example, you are goir
implement the update of the `Author`'s `Name` property, which requires looping thre
all the `Books` that contain that `Author` entity, as shown in figure 15.6.

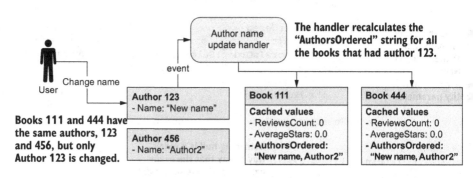

Figure 15.6 An admin user changes the `Name` of an `Author` that is used in two `Books`. In this
example, `Books` `111` and `444` have two `Authors`—`123` and `456`—linked to them. Changing the
`123` `Author`'s `Name` requires the event handler to loop through all the `Books` that the `123`
`Author` is used in and recalculate the correct `AuthorsOrdered` string.

The following listing shows the `AuthorNameUpdatedHandler` that the `GenericEv`
`Runner` calls when it finds the domain event that was created when an `Author`'s
property was changed. This event handler loops through all the `Books` that have
`Author` and recalculates each `Book`'s `AuthorsOrdered` cache value.

Listing 15.7 The event handler that manages a change of an `Author`'s `Name` prop

> Tells the Event Runner that this event should be
> called when it finds a AuthorNameUpdatedEvent

```
public class AuthorNameUpdatedHandler :
    IBeforeSaveEventHandler<AuthorNameUpdatedEvent>       ◁─┐
{
    private readonly BookDbContext _context;

    public AuthorNameUpdatedHandler              The event handler
        (BookDbContext context)                  needs to access
        {                                        the database.
            _context = context;
        }
}
```

ent
ner
the
the
tity
ent.

```
public IStatusGeneric Handle(object callingEntity,
    AuthorNameUpdatedEvent domainEvent)
{
    var changedAuthor = (Author) callingEntity;

    foreach (var book in _context.Set<BookAuthor>()
        .Where(x => x.AuthorId == changedAuthor.AuthorId)
        .Select(x => x.Book))
    {
        var allAuthorsInOrder = _context.Books
            .Single(x => x.BookId == book.BookId)
            .AuthorsLink.OrderBy(y => y.Order)
            .Select(y => y.Author).ToList();

        var newAuthorsOrdered =
            string.Join(", ",
                allAuthorsInOrder.Select(x =>
            x.AuthorId == changedAuthor.AuthorId
                ? changedAuthor.Name
                : x.Name));

        book.ResetAuthorsOrdered(newAuthorsOrdered);
    }

    return null;
}
}
```

Casts the object back to its actual type of Author to make access easier

through ne books tain the that has changed

Gets the Authors, in the correct order, linked to this Book

eturns the list of uthor names, but aces the changed 's Name with the e provided in the Entity parameter

Creates a comma-delimited string with the names from the Authors in the Boo

Updates each Book's AuthorsOrdered property

Returning null is a quick way to say that the event handler is always successful.

As you can see, the `Author's Name` event handler is much more complex and accesses the database multiple times, which is much slower than the `AddReview/RemoveReview` event handler. Therefore, you need to decide whether caching this value will provide an overall performance gain. In this case, the likelihood of updating an `Author's Name` is small, so on balance, it is worthwhile to cache the list of author names for a book.

.3 Adding cache properties to the Book entity with concurrency handling

Adding the three cached value properties—`ReviewsCount`, `ReviewsAverageVotes`, and `AuthorsOrdered`—is easy to do. But an issue may occur if two `Reviews` are added simultaneously (or nearly simultaneously) to the same `Book`, which could cause the `Review`-related cached values to be out of date.

Working out the best way to handle simultaneous updates took the most time to think through and design. I spent days thinking about all the concurrency issues that could cause a problem and then even more days coming up with the best way to handle those issues. This part of the caching design is the most complex and needs careful thought.

First, I considered updating the cache values inside a transaction, but the isolation level needed for totally accurate cache updating required locking a lot of data. Even

using direct SQL commands to calculate and update the cache wasn't safe. (Se‹
fascinating Stack Overflow question/answer "Is a single SQL Server statement at‹
and consistent?" at https://stackoverflow.com/q/21468742/1434764.)

I found that the best way to handle the simultaneous-updates problem w‹
configure the three cache values as concurrency tokens (see section 10.6.2).
simultaneous updates of a cache value will throw a DbUpdateConcurrencyExcept‹
which then calls a concurrency handler written to correct the cache values to
right values.

Figure 15.7 shows what happens if two Reviews are added simultaneously, w‹
causes a DbUpdateConcurrencyException to be thrown. Then the concurrency
dler comes in to fix the ReviewsCount and ReviewsAverageVotes cache values.

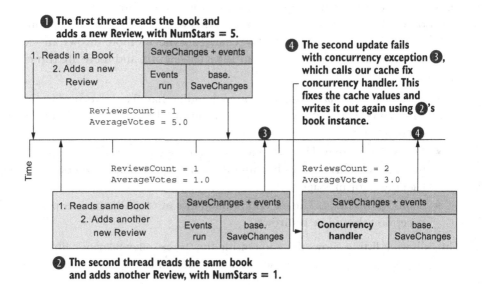

Figure 15.7 This figure shows how two simultaneous updates could cause an incorrect cached value, which is detected by making the ReviewsCount and ReviewsAverageVotes cache properties configured as concurrency tokens. This example would throw a DbUpdate-ConcurrencyException, which would be caught and directed to the concurrency handler. The concurrency handler is designed to handle this type of concurrency issue and correct the cache values.

This section shows the following parts of the concurrency handler:

- Code to capture any exception thrown by SaveChanges/SaveChangesAsync
- The top-level concurrency handler that finds the Book(s) that caused‹ DbUpdateConcurrencyException
- The concurrency handler for a problem with the Review's cached values
- The concurrency handler for a problem with the AuthorsString cached va‹

CODE TO CAPTURE ANY EXCEPTION THROWN BY SAVECHANGES/SAVECHANGESASYNC

To capture DbUpdateConcurrencyException, you need to add a C# try/catch around the call to the SaveChanges/SaveChangesAsync methods. This addition allows you to call an exception handler to try to fix the problem that caused the exception or rethrow the exception if it can't fix the problem. If your exception handler managed to fix the exception, you call SaveChanges/SaveChangesAsync again to update the database with your fix.

In this specific case, you need to consider another issue: while you were fixing the first concurrency update, another concurrency update could have happened. Sure, this scenario is rather unlikely, but you must handle it; otherwise, the second call to SaveChanges/SaveChangesAsync would fail. For this reason, you need a C# do/while outer loop to keep retrying the call to the SaveChanges/SaveChangesAsync method until it is successful or an exception that can't be fixed occurs.

Also, the GenericEventRunner library allows you to register an exception handler to be called if the SaveChanges/SaveChangesAsync method throws an exception. Your exception handler must return an IStatusGeneric, and there are three possible options:

- *Status has no errors.* Your exception handler has fixed the problem, and the SaveChanges/SaveChangesAsync method should be called again to update the database
- *Status returns errors.* The exception handler has converted the exception to error message(s). This approach is useful for turning database exceptions into user-friendly error messages.
- *Status returns* null. The exception handler can't handle the exception, and the exception should be rethrown

The following listing shows the code inside the GenericEventRunner library that calls SaveChanges, showing the outer do/while and the inner try/catch of the exception.

Listing 15.8 A simplified version of the GenericEventRunner's SaveChanges call

```
private IStatusGeneric<int>                                    The returned value is a
    CallSaveChangesWithExceptionHandler                        status, with int returned
    (DbContext context,                                        from SaveChanges.
        Func<int> callBaseSaveChanges)
{                                                              The base SaveChanges is
    var status = new StatusGenericHandler<int>();             provided to be called.

    do                    The call to the
    {                     SaveChanges is done
        try               within a do/while.
        {                                                      If no exception occurs,
            int numUpdated = callBaseSaveChanges();            sets the status result
            status.SetResult(numUpdated);                      and breaks out of the
            break;                                             do/while
        }
```

Calls the base Changes

The catch caches any exceptions that SaveChanges throws.

```
catch (Exception e)
{
    IStatusGeneric handlerStatus
        = … YOUR EXCEPTION HANDLER GOES HERE;
    if (handlerStatus == null)
        throw;
    status.CombineStatuses(handlerStatus);
}
} while (status.IsValid);

return status;
}
```

Your exception ha is called here, and returns null or a s

If the exception hanc returns null, it rethr the original exceptio

If the exception handler was successful, it loops back to try calling SaveChanges again.

…otherwise, any error from your exception handler are added to the main status.

Returns the status

TOP-LEVEL CONCURRENCY HANDLER THAT FINDS THE BOOK(S) THAT CAUSED THE EXCEPTION
Handling a concurrency issue involves several common parts, so you build a top-concurrency handler to manage those parts. The following listing shows the level concurrency handler method `HandleCacheValuesConcurrency`.

Listing 15.9 The top-level concurrency handler containing the common exception c

If the exception isn't a Db.UpdateConcurrencyException, we return null to say that we can't handle that exception

This extension method handles the Reviews and Author cached values concurrency issues.

```
public static IStatusGeneric HandleCacheValuesConcurrency
    (this Exception ex, DbContext context)
{
    var dbUpdateEx = ex as DbUpdateConcurrencyException;
    if (dbUpdateEx == null)
        return null;

    foreach (var entry in dbUpdateEx.Entries)
    {
        if (!(entry.Entity is Book bookBeingWrittenOut))
            return null;

        var bookThatCausedConcurrency = context.Set<Book>()
            .IgnoreQueryFilters()
            .AsNoTracking()
            .SingleOrDefault(p => p.BookId
                == bookBeingWrittenOut.BookId);

        if (bookThatCausedConcurrency == null)
        {
            entry.State = EntityState.Detached;
            continue;
        }

        var handler = new FixConcurrencyMethods(entry, context);
```

Casts the exce DbUpdateCon Exception

Should be only one entity, but we handle many entities in case of bulk loading

Casts the entity Book. If it isn't a we return null t the method can handle it.

Reads a nor version of t from the da (Note the Ig QueryFilter it might hav soft-deleted

If no book was deleted, marks the current book as detached so it won't be updated

Creates the class containing the Reviews and AuthorsOrdered cached values

```
       handler.CheckFixReviewCacheValues(
           bookThatCausedConcurrency, bookBeingWrittenOut);

       handler.CheckFixAuthorOrdered(
           bookThatCausedConcurrency, bookBeingWrittenOut);
   }

   return new StatusGenericHandler();
}
```

Fixes any concurrency issues with the AuthorsOrdered cached value

Returns a valid status to say that the concurrency issue was fixed

CONCURRENCY HANDLER FOR A PROBLEM WITH THE REVIEW'S CACHED VALUES

The CheckFixReviewCacheValues concurrency handler method deals only with the Review cached values. Its job is to combine the Review cached values in the entity that is being written out and the Review cached values that have been added to the database. This method uses the same delta update style used in the Review cached values event handler. The following listing shows the CheckFixReviewCacheValues concurrency handler.

NOTE If you aren't familiar with EF Core concurrency handling, I recommend that you look at section 10.6.3, which describes the different types of data that are involved in handling a concurrency exception.

Listing 15.10 The code to fix a concurrent update of the Review cached values

```
public void CheckFixReviewCacheValues(
    Book bookThatCausedConcurrency,
    Book bookBeingWrittenOut)
{
    var previousCount = (int)_entry
        .Property(nameof(Book.ReviewsCount))
        .OriginalValue;
    var previousAverageVotes = (double)_entry
        .Property(nameof(Book.ReviewsAverageVotes))
        .OriginalValue;

    if (previousCount ==
        bookThatCausedConcurrency.ReviewsCount
        && previousAverageVotes ==
            bookThatCausedConcurrency.ReviewsAverageVotes)
        return;

    var previousTotalStars = Math.Round(
        previousAverageVotes * previousCount);

    var countChange =
        bookBeingWrittenOut.ReviewsCount
        - previousCount;
    var starsChange = Math.Round(
        bookBeingWrittenOut.ReviewsAverageVotes
        * bookBeingWrittenOut.ReviewsCount)
        - previousTotalStars;
```

This method handles concurrency errors in the Reviews cached values.

This parameter is the Book from the database that caused the concurrency issue.

Holds the count and votes in the database before the events changed them

If the previous count and votes match the current database, there is no Review concurrency issue, so the method returns.

Works out the stars before the new update is applied

Gets the change that the event was trying to make to the cached values

```
    var newCount =
        bookThatCausedConcurrency.ReviewsCount
        + countChange;
    var newTotalStars = Math.Round(
            bookThatCausedConcurrency.ReviewsAverageVotes
            * bookThatCausedConcurrency.ReviewsCount)
        + starsChange;

    _entry.Property(nameof(Book.ReviewsCount))
        .CurrentValue = newCount;
    _entry.Property(nameof(Book.ReviewsAverageVotes))
        .CurrentValue = newCount == 0
        ? 0 : newTotalStars / newCount;

    _entry.Property(nameof(Book.ReviewsCount))
        .OriginalValue = bookThatCausedConcurrency
        .ReviewsCount;
    _entry.Property(nameof(Book.ReviewsAverageVotes))
            .OriginalValue =
        bookThatCausedConcurrency
            .ReviewsAverageVotes;
}
```

Works out the combined chan[ge] from the curre[nt] book and the o[ther] updates done t[o] the database

Sets the Reviews cached values with the recalculated values

Sets the OriginalValues for the Review cached values to the current database

Yes, this code is quite complicated, which is why I give the variables good names. I can get lost in this code if I come back to it months later.

Concurrency handler for a problem with the AuthorsString cached value

The `CheckFixAuthorsOrdered` concurrency handler method has the same form [as] the `CheckFixReviewCacheValues` method, but it deals with the `AuthorsOrd[ered]` cached value. Its job is to combine the `AuthorsOrdered` cached value in the entity [that] is being written out and the `AuthorsOrdered` cached value that has been added t[o the] database. As a result, the `CheckFixAuthorsOrdered` concurrency handler, show[n in] the next listing, must use the recalculate update style, because you can't use the [delta] update approach.

Listing 15.11 The code to fix a concurrent update of the `AuthorsOrdered` cached va[lue]

```
public void CheckFixAuthorsOrdered(
    Book bookThatCausedConcurrency,
    Book bookBeingWrittenOut)
{
    var previousAuthorsOrdered = (string)_entry
        .Property(nameof(Book.AuthorsOrdered))
        .OriginalValue;

    if (previousAuthorsOrdered ==
        bookThatCausedConcurrency.AuthorsOrdered)
        return;
```

This method handles concurrency errors in the AuthorsOrdered cached value.

This parameter is the Book from the database that caused the concurrency issue.

This parameter is the Book you were trying to update.

Gets the previous AuthorsOrdered string before the event updated it

If the previous AuthorsOrdered match the current database AuthorsOrdered, there is no AuthorsOrdered concurrency issue, so the method returns.

```
var allAuthorsIdsInOrder = _context.Set<Book>()
    .IgnoreQueryFilters()
    .Where(x => x.BookId ==
            bookBeingWrittenOut.BookId)
    .Select(x => x.AuthorsLink
        .OrderBy(y => y.Order)
        .Select(y => y.AuthorId)).ToList()
    .Single();

var namesInOrder = allAuthorsIdsInOrder
    .Select(x => _context.Find<Author>(x).Name);

var newAuthorsOrdered =
    string.Join(", ", namesInOrder);

_entry.Property(nameof(Book.AuthorsOrdered))
    .CurrentValue = newAuthorsOrdered;

_entry.Property(nameof(Book.AuthorsOrdered))
    .OriginalValue =
        bookThatCausedConcurrency.AuthorsOrdered;
}
```

Gets the AuthorIds for each Author linked to this Book in the correct order

Gets the Name of each Author, using the Find method

Creates a comma-delimited list of authors

From this, you can set the AuthorsOrdered cached value with the combined values.

the
lues
the
ered
e to
rent
ase

The important part to point out is that you must read in the Author entity classes by using the Find method because the Author that created the update to the Authors-Ordered cached value hasn't yet been written to the database. Find is the only query method that will first inspect the current application's DbContext for tracked entities to find the entity you want. The Find will load the tracked entity with that AuthorId instead of loading the version in the database that hasn't been updated yet.

.4 Adding a checking/healing system to your event system

Since the first edition, I have performance-tuned several client systems and created a caching system that covers all eventualities I can think of. But I may have missed something, so I added a separate checking/healing system to run alongside my caching system to tell me if there is a problem. That system lets me sleep at night, and my clients like the fact that they can be certain their data is up to date.

You may think this approach is overkill, but if you are adding a caching system to an existing system, you need some way to fill in the cached values of existing data anyway. Typically, I build some code to add the cached values to the current application's production database before releasing a new version of the application that uses the cached values in a query. It takes only a bit more effort to make that update-cache code into a useful service that can be used to check and fix cached values.

As an example, I have built a checking/healing system into the Book App. This service, called CheckFixCacheValuesService, is available in the ASP.NET Core app. This service can be used in checking/healing as required. Rather than detailing the code, I provided figure 15.8, which shows an overview of what the CheckFixCacheValues-Service class does.

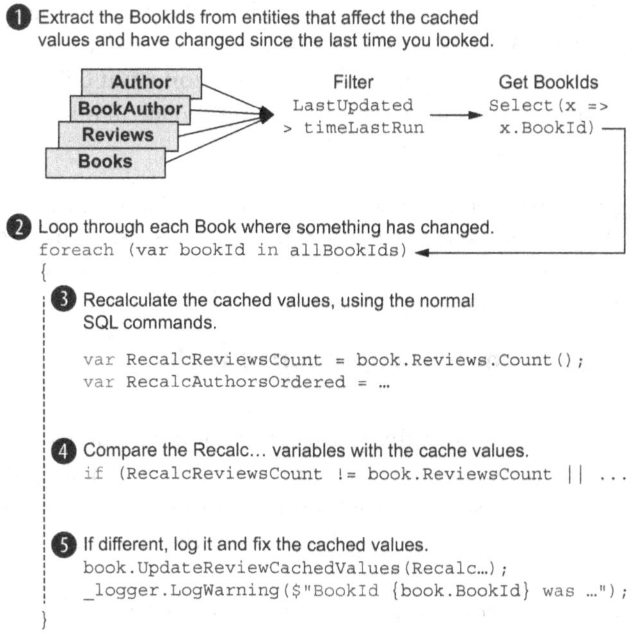

1 Extract the BookIds from entities that affect the cached
values and have changed since the last time you looked.

```
 ┌──────────────┐                  Filter            Get BookIds
 │   Author     │                LastUpdated        Select(x =>
 │  BookAuthor  │ ──────►         > timeLastRun ───►   x.BookId) ──┐
 │   Reviews    │ ──────►                                          │
 │    Books     │ ──────►                                          │
 └──────────────┘                                                  │
```

2 Loop through each Book where something has changed.
```
foreach (var bookId in allBookIds) ◄──────────────────────────────┘
{
```
    3 Recalculate the cached values, using the normal
       SQL commands.

```
    var RecalcReviewsCount = book.Reviews.Count();
    var RecalcAuthorsOrdered = …
```

    4 Compare the Recalc… variables with the cache values.
```
    if (RecalcReviewsCount != book.ReviewsCount || ...
```

    5 If different, log it and fix the cached values.
```
    book.UpdateReviewCachedValues(Recalc…);
    _logger.LogWarning($"BookId {book.BookId} was …");
}
```

Figure 15.8 The five stages of the `CheckFix` service in the `Part3` Book
App. This code is run from a background service, which periodically checks
the database for entities that have changed and could potentially change
the cached values. Because this code uses a different way to find and
calculate the cached values, it will find any cached values that are out of
date and correct them for you.

NOTE The `CheckFixCacheValuesService` class and its related classes are in
the GitHub repo associated with this book, inside the folder called CheckFix-
Code in the project called BookApp.Infrastructure.Books.EventHandlers.
You can also find a background service in the project called BookApp.Back-
groundTasks.

The downside of the checking/healing code shown in figure 15.8 is that it adds
database accesses, which could affect the performance of your system. In the
App, for example, an update to an entity class causes a `LastUpdatedUtc` property
updated (see section 11.4.3). The checking/healing code can find all the entities
were changed in, say, the past 24 hours quite quickly (the test database has 70
entities and takes only about 10 ms to scan), but each check of a changed entity
5 ms. So if your application has lots of changes per day, the checking/healing co
going to take some time.

For that reason, this sort of checking/healing system is run at a time when
aren't many users on the system—at night or on the weekend, or manually by an a
person when they suspect a problem. The system isn't likely to find anything, bu
does find a bad cache value setting, you know that there is a bug in your cache cod

The Part3 Book App has an example of the overnight and manual triggering of its checking/healing system. An ASP.NET Core background service runs CheckFix-CacheValuesService at 1:00 every morning (was GMT time zone, but failed on Linux, so now uses UTC), and you can run the checking/healing service manually by choosing the Admin > Check Cached Vals menu item.

> **WARNING** The design of the Book App's CheckFixCacheValuesService service assumes that no database updates are happening when it is fixing incorrect cache values. If concurrency exceptions arise, the CheckFixCacheValues-Service service would need its own concurrency exception handler.

Comparing the four performance approaches with development effort

At the start of this chapter, I compared the performance improvements of the four approaches. Although the improvements in performance are undeniable, there are other factors to consider when considering each performance-tuning approach, such as how much development effort each approach took, whether any of them needed specific skills, and how complex the solutions were.

In this section, I look at these considerations and provide some extra information to try to answer some development questions. To start, figure 15.9 provides a quick summary of the four ways to improve your application in terms of performance, skills, and development time.

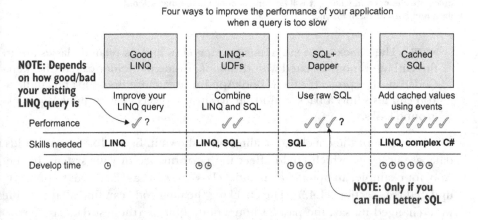

Figure 15.9 Four approaches to improving the performance of a query. Each approach is scored for performance improvement (more check marks mean better performance), the skills you need to apply that approach, and the amount of development time needed to implement the code associated with the approach.

Table 15.2 provides a textual summary of the four approaches in terms of effort and skills required.

Table 15.2 The amount of effort needed to apply the four approaches to the Book App

Approach	Effort+skills	Comments
Good LINQ	Time: Low (built in chapter 2) Skills: LINQ, DDD	The `Select` query is the same one I used in chapter ? and it works well. The key part was working out how to age the `Review`'s `NumStars` properties inside the da base (see section 6.1.8).
		Also, the change to a DDD-styled entity class meant th the price was available as a single property that could an SQL index added to it.
LINQ+UDFs	Half a day LINQ + SQL	I have found that UDFs (see section 10.1) are good wa keep a LINQ approach but replace part of a LINQ query isn't working as well as I would like. But UDFs are use only if you can find some better SQL to put into a UDF
SQL+Dapper	Half-day of study, half-day to write SQL	This approach required studying the SQL generated by Core and working out whether I could do anything to improve it. I found only one thing to improve (sort on vo but that feature is a key one. Rewriting the SQL to hav the filters, sorts, and paging was a bit tedious—much harder than using LINQ.
LINQ+caching	LINQ+caching: about a week, but quicker next time. Check/heal: 1.5 days Complex C#, concurrency	This approach is definitely hard work but also provides fantastic result. It took a lot of time to work out the be way to handle concurrent updates and testing, but hav implemented this approach once, I'd be quicker next t The checking/healing code took a bit more time, but a said, I'd normally have to write it anyway if I was perfo mance-tuning an existing application that already had user data.
		Another source of time taken to implement a caching s tem was work I did for a client. I took 11 hours to buil single delta cached values system, but I didn't need to the concurrency handling, as the client's app stopped duplicate user updates of data.

Overall, I'm pleased with the process. EF Core produces great SQL code from get-go, but only because you made sure that your LINQ queries were written in a that is sympathetic to how EF Core works. The methods and approaches introd in the first six chapters are a good starting point for writing good LINQ queries.

As I said in chapter 14, make sure that your standard patterns for queries well; otherwise, you'll be building inefficiencies into your application from the But at some point, you'll need to performance-tune an EF Core application; this c ter provides lots of ideas and approaches that can help.

15.7 *Improving database scalability*

The four performance-tuning approaches are all about speed: how fast you can re the result to the user. But the other aspect to consider is *scalability*: handling numbers of concurrent users. To end this chapter, let's look at database scalabili

Section 14.7 talks about database scalability in terms of the ability to buy more-powerful hardware to run your database server on, because this book is about EF Core. But the overall scalability of the application is what matters most. For that reason, I always show the performance of the whole application, as that's what the end user is going to see. Focusing on overall application performance stops you from spending a lot of time shaving a few milliseconds off database access timings when the frontend code is taking more than 100 ms to display the data.

The first thing you should do to improve scalability is use async database accesses. Async commands used in an ASP.NET Core application will release a thread that can be used by another user, thus saving the ASP.NET Core thread pool from being used up (see section 5.10.1). Async commands have a small downside—they take a bit longer to run (see section 14.7.2 for detailed timings)—but overall, async is the way to go in any application that has lots of simultaneous users. The Part3 Book App uses async commands throughout.

The other helpful whole-application changes you can make with applications such as ASP.NET Core are running more-powerful instances of the application (known as *scaling up*) and running more instances of the application (known as *scaling out*). You might like to pay for more-powerful hardware to run your database server on, too.

> **NOTE** All the approaches used in this chapter will work on an application using multiple instances of ASP.NET Core, including the LINQ+caching approach. The overnight check/heal service, however, would need to be run on a single WebJob instead of as a ASP.NET Core background service.

One basic fact about database scalability is that the quicker you make the database accesses, the more concurrent accesses the database can handle. Reducing the number of round trips to the database also reduces the load on the database (see section 14.5.1). Fortunately, since EF Core 3, the default query type has loaded any collections within one database access. Also, lazy loading might feel like a great time-saver, but it adds all those individual database accesses back in, and both scalability and performance suffer.

But some large applications will have high concurrent database accesses, and you need a way out of this situation. The first, and easiest, approach is to pay for a more powerful database. If that solution isn't going to cut it, here are some ideas to consider:

- *Split your data over multiple databases: Sharding your data*
  If your data is segregated in some way (if you have a financial application that many small businesses use, for example), you could spread each business's data over a different database—that is, one database for each business. This approach is called sharding (see http://mng.bz/veN4). Section 11.7 shows a simple way to implement sharing by using EF Core.

- *Split your database reads from your writes: CQRS architecture*
  Command and Query Responsibility Segregation (CQRS) architecture (see https://martinfowler.com/bliki/CQRS.html) splits the database reads from the

database writes. This approach allows you to optimize your reads and possibl‍
a separate database, or multiple read-only databases, on the CQRS read side.‍

- *Mix NoSQL and SQL databases: Polyglot persistence*

  The cached SQL approach makes the `Book` entity look like a complete d‍
  tion of a book that a JSON structure would hold. With a CQRS architecture‍
  could have used a relational database to handle any writes, but on any write‍
  could build a JSON version of the book and write it to a read-side NoSQL‍
  base or multiple databases. This approach, which might provide higher‍
  performance, is one form of polyglot persistence (see http://mng.bz/K4‍
  In section 16.3, you'll implement a mixed SQL/NoSQL application to‍
  even more performance, especially in terms of scalability.

Summary

- If you build your LINQ queries carefully and take advantage of all its feat‍
  EF Core will reward you by producing excellent SQL code.
- You can use EF Core's `DbFunction` feature to inject a piece of SQL code he‍
  an SQL UDF into a LINQ query. This feature allows you to tweak part of a‍
  Core query that's run on the database server.
- If a database query is slow, check the SQL code that EF Core is producing‍
  can obtain the SQL code by looking at the `Information` logged messages‍
  EF Core produces.
- If you feel that you can produce better SQL for a query than EF Core is pr‍
  ing, you can use several methods to call SQL from EF Core, or use Dapp‍
  execute your SQL query directly.
- If all other performance-tuning approaches don't provide the performance‍
  need, consider altering the database structure, including adding properti‍
  hold cached values. But be warned: you need to be careful.
- In addition to improving the time that a query takes, consider the scalabil‍
  your application—that is, supporting lots of simultaneous users. In many ap‍
  tions, such as ASP.NET Core, using async EF Core commands can improve‍
  ability. Chapter 16 provides another way to improve scalability and perform‍
  by adding a Cosmos DB database to the Book App.

For readers who are familiar with EF6:

- EF6.x doesn't have EF Core's `DbFunction` feature, which makes calling a‍
  so easy in EF Core.

Cosmos DB, CQRS,
and other database types

16

This chapter covers

- Introducing NoSQL databases and how they differ from relational databases

- Exploring the features that the NoSQL database called Cosmos DB

- Performance-tuning the Book App using EF Core Cosmos DB database provider

- Considering the differences between and limitations of using Cosmos DB with EF Core 5

- Knowing what issues you might hit when swapping from one database type to another

The Book App has been a constant theme throughout this book, and up until now, it has used an SQL Server database to store the books data. In this chapter, we are going to performance-tune the Book App by combining the original SQL Server database with another database called Cosmos DB. In chapter 14, we performance-tuned the Book App to handle 100,000 books. In this chapter, we take the number of books to 500,000 with the same or better performance by using Cosmos DB. Cosmos DB is relatively new (it came out in 2017), and some readers won't have used it

yet. So in addition to using this database to improve performance and scalabil
point out the differences between Cosmos DB, which is a NoSQL database, and
more traditional relational databases such as SQL Server.

Cosmos DB and relational databases differ a lot, but there are also some s
changes between various relational databases that EF Core supports. So at the e
the chapter, there is a list of things to check and change if you're swapping from
relational database type to another.

16.1 The differences between relational and NoSQL databases

TIME-SAVER Skip this section if you already know about NoSQL databases.

Cosmos DB isn't like the databases described so far in the book, such as SQL Se
PostgreSQL, and SQLite. Cosmos DB is what is referred to as a NoSQL data
whereas SQL Server, PostgreSQL, and SQLite (along with many others) are refe
to as relational databases.

As you have already read, relational databases use primary keys and foreign ke
form links between tables, which EF Core turns into navigational properties.
tional databases excel at relationships with lots of database rules (called constra
to make sure that these relationships follow the design you decided on for your
base, which is why they are called relational databases.

Relational databases have been around for decades, and nearly all of them us
SQL language, which means that each implementation of a relational database is
ilar to every other. So swapping from, say, SQL Server to PostgreSQL isn't too l
especially if you are using EF Core, which hides some of the differences. The lon
of relational databases also means that you can find many relational implementat
lots of tools, and expertise on relational databases.

On the other hand, NoSQL databases are designed to be high-performan
terms of speed, scalability, and *availability* (the ability to swap to another datab
one fails). There is no common language, such as SQL, so each implementation
its own way to maximize the features it wants to focus on. To achieve these pe
mance goals, the NoSQL databases give up some of the rules that the relational
bases apply.

Many NoSQL databases allow multiple instances of the same database to pr
scalability and availability, for example. To do so, NoSQL databases drop the
tional rule that the data is always consistent—that is, you will always get the latest
NoSQL databases are *eventually consistent*, which means that an update to one data
instance may take some time (ideally, seconds or less) to be applied to another
base instance.

MORE INFORMATION If you want to look into the types of and differences
between relational and NoSQL databases, I recommend the Microsoft article
"Relational vs. NoSQL data" at http://mng.bz/9Nzj.

Introduction to Cosmos DB and its EF Core provider

As I've already said, Cosmos DB doesn't follow the way that relational databases work. Sure, it has a database, and it even has some pseudo-SQL commands, but otherwise, it's quite different from relational databases. EF Core's support of Cosmos DB, however, provides a common frontend that makes it easier for someone who already knows EF Core to use Cosmos DB.

In this chapter, you are going to look at features of both Cosmos DB itself and EF Core's current Cosmos DB database provider. You should note that I say *current* Cosmos DB database provider because the EF Core 5 Cosmos DB database provider is far from finished, as I cover in detail in this chapter.

To understand why EF Core's Cosmos DB database provider hasn't been improved, you need only look at this statistic: the number of Cosmos DB downloads is only 1% of all SQL Server downloads. The EF Core team is driven by what the developers need, and being a small team, it can't do everything. Therefore, the Cosmos DB database provider hasn't been improved in EF Core 5. But as you will see, I successfully used the EF Core 5 Cosmos DB database provider to improve the Book App's performance.

So why am I dedicating this chapter to Cosmos DB if EF Core's database provider has limitations, and why should you read it? Fundamentally, for some applications, using a NoSQL database is going to provide better performance and scalability than a similarly priced relational database. Also, the plan for EF Core 6 (see http://mng.bz/Wreg) has a section on improving EF Core's support of Cosmos DB, so I am hopeful that some (if not many) of the limitations in this chapter will be removed.

Because EF Core's current Cosmos DB database provider is likely to improve, I am careful to separate the differences between the Cosmos DB and a relational database and the limitations of the EF Core Cosmos DB database provider. This convention ensures that this chapter will still be useful when improved versions of the Cosmos DB database provider are released.

> **NOTE** This SQL/NoSQL comparison *doesn't* say that one is better than the other; each has its own strengths and weaknesses. Also, Cosmos DB is one implementation of a NoSQL database, so its limitations are going to be different from other NoSQL implementations. The comparison is here to point out the parts of the Cosmos DB that work differently from the relational databases that have been around for years.

The other reason for looking at the differences between a Cosmos DB database and relational databases is to give you some pointers about when you could use Cosmos DB instead of an SQL database. Section 16.6.1 covers many of the differences between Cosmos DB and relational databases, with a few other differences identified by notes starting with COSMOS DB DIFFERENCE; see the following example.

> **COSMOS DB DIFFERENCE** This feature of the Cosmos DB database doesn't work the same way as relational databases.

The other area I want to highlight is the limitations of the EF Core 5 Cosmos DB base provider. These are areas where EF Core 5 doesn't implement code to advantage of all the features of Cosmos DB (but be aware that future releases of Core may well remove some of these limitations). Section 16.6.3 covers many of limitations of the EF Core 5 Cosmos DB database provider, with a few other limitations identified by notes starting with EF CORE 5 LIMITATION; see the following example.

> **EF CORE 5 LIMITATION** This limitation applies to the current EF Core 5 Cosmos DB database provider.

16.3 Building a Command and Query Responsibility Segregation (CQRS) system using Cosmos DB

To get a good feel for Cosmos DB, we need to build something real; that's the way learn. I suggested in section 15.7 that a CQRS architecture could provide better ability performance. Adding a CQRS system that uses Cosmos DB isn't trivial, so example will reveal many differences between the NoSQL Cosmos DB and relational databases. I hope that it will also provide another technique you can use to performance tune your own applications.

In this section, you are going to build a CQRS architecture by using a polyglot database structure that will provide better performance and scalability.

> **DEFINITION** A CQRS architecture segregates query operations from operations that update data by using separate interfaces. This architecture can maximize performance, scalability, and security, and supports the evolution of the system over time through higher flexibility. See http://mng.bz/Ix8D.

> **DEFINITION** A polyglot database structure uses a combination of storage types: relational databases, NoSQL databases, flat files, and so on. The idea is that each database type has strengths and weaknesses, and by using two or more, you can obtain a better overall system. See http://mng.bz/6r1W.

The CQRS architecture acknowledges that the read side of an application is different from the write side. Reads are often complicated, drawing in data from multiple places whereas in many applications (but not all), the write side can be simpler and less serious. You can see in the current Book App that listing the books is complex but adding review is fairly trivial. Separating the code for each part can help you focus on the specific features of each part—another application of the SoC software principle.

In chapter 15, you produced the performance version, in which you cached values (see section 15.5). It struck me then that the final query didn't access any relationships and could be stored in a simpler database, such as a NoSQL database. In this example, you'll use a polyglot database structure, with a mixture of SQL and NoSQL databases, for the following reasons:

- Using an SQL write-side database makes sense because business applications often use relational data. Think about a real book-selling site, which would a lot of complex, linked data to handle business aspects such as suppliers, inventory, pricing, orders, payment, delivery, tracking, and audits. I think that a well-known relational/SQL database, with its superior level of data integrity, would be a good choice for many business problems.

- But those relationships and some aspects of an SQL database, such as the need to dynamically calculate some values, can make it slow in retrieving data. So a NoSQL database with precalculated values such as average review votes can improve performance considerably over an SQL database. The CQRS read-side projection is what Mateusz Stasch calls "a legitimate cache" in his article at http://mng.bz/A7eC.

As a result of these design inputs, you'll develop what I refer to as a two-database CQRS architecture, as shown in figure 16.1.

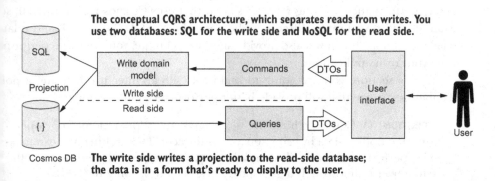

The conceptual CQRS architecture, which separates reads from writes. You use two databases: SQL for the write side and NoSQL for the read side.

Cosmos DB   The write side writes a projection to the read-side database; the data is in a form that's ready to display to the user.

Figure 16.1   A conceptual view of a CQRS architecture: an SQL database for the write side and a NoSQL database for the read side. A write takes a bit more work because it writes to two databases: the normal SQL database and the new NoSQL read-side database. In this arrangement, the read-side database is writing in the exact format needed by the user, so reads are fast.

Because the CQRS architecture separates read and write operations, using one database for read operations and another for write operations is a logical step. The write side holds the data in a relational form, with no duplication of data—a process known as *normalization*—and the read side holds the data in a form that is appropriate for the user interface.

In the Book App, the read side would contain the data already converted to match what the book display needs; these prebuild entities are known as *projections*. These projections are built with the same code as the MapBookToDto method in section 2.6. What you are doing is prebuilding the views you need and writing them to the read-side database.

This design creates good performance gains for reads but a performance cost on writes, making the two-database CQRS architecture appropriate when your business application has more reads of the data than writes. Many business applications have

more reads than writes (e-commerce applications are good examples), so this a
tecture fits our Book App well.

16.4 The design of a two-database CQRS architecture application

The fundamental issue in building any CQRS system is making sure that any chang
the data change the associated projection in the read-side CQRS database. If yo
that part wrong, you will show the wrong data to the user. This issue is the same c
invalidation issue I worked so hard to get right in the cached SQL approach descr
in section 15.5. The trick is to capture every change to the SQL Book entity and its
ciated entities and to make sure that the read-side CQRS database is updated.

In the first edition of this book, I detected changes to Book and associated en
by looking at the State of tracked entities within the call to the SaveChan
SaveChangesAsync methods. These States and entities were decoded to d
whether a projection to the NoSQL database should be added, updated, or del
That approach is valid (I show an example in section 12.5), but using the Sta
multiple entities can be quite complex.

Another approach is using integration events (section 12.1.2) triggered b
DDD access methods (see section 13.4.2). Here are some benefits of this approac

- *More robust*—Using integration events ensures that the SQL databa
  updated only when the Cosmos DB database has successfully updated its
  base. Applying both database updates within a transaction reduces the p
  bility that the Cosmos DB database will get out of step with the SQL write
  (The design in the first edition of this book could get out of step if a Rave
  update failed.)
- *More obvious*—You trigger integration events inside the DDD methods
  change the data. Each event tells the event handler whether it's an Add, Up
  or Delete (soft delete, in this case) of a Book. Then it's easy to write the e
  handler to Add, Update, or Delete a Book projection in the Cosmos DB.
- *Simpler*—As already stated, sending integration events is much simpler
  making detected changes via the State of the tracked entities. (See section
  for a description of that approach.)

Figure 16.2 shows what happens when an admin person adds a new Book and how
new Book gets added to the Cosmos DB database so that the user can see it.

To implement the CQRS system shown in figure 16.2, you must take the fo
ing steps:

1. Create an event to trigger when the SQL Book entity changes.
2. Add events to the Book entity to send Add, Update, or Delete integration eve
3. Use the EfCore.GenericEventRunner to override your BookDbContext.
4. Create the Cosmos entity classes and DbContext.
5. Create the Cosmos Add, Update, and Delete event handlers.

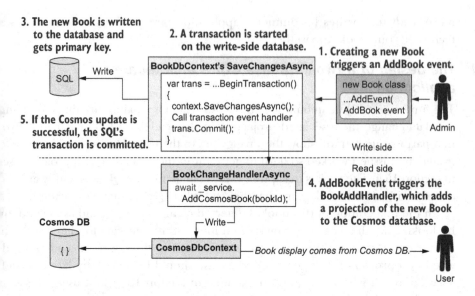

3. The new Book is written to the database and gets primary key.

2. A transaction is started on the write-side database.

1. Creating a new Book triggers an AddBook event.

5. If the Cosmos update is successful, the SQL's transaction is committed.

4. AddBookEvent triggers the BookAddHandler, which adds a projection of the new Book to the Cosmos datatbase.

Figure 16.2 Adding a new `Book` entity. The `Book`'s static factory adds an `Add Book` integration event; this event is picked up by the `BookDbContext`, which handles access to the SQL database. `SaveChanges/SaveChangesAsync` has been overridden by the `EfCore.GenericEvent-Runner`. Because the event is an integration event, the library starts a transaction and writes out the new `Book`, which obtains the SQL primary key. Then the `Add Book` integration event calls the `BookChange` event handler, which creates a projection of the new `Book` and adds it to the Cosmos DB database. If the write to the Cosmos DB database is successful, the transaction is committed, and both databases are in step. If the Cosmos DB fails, the SQL transaction is rolled back, and the admin person is alerted that the add of the new `Book` failed.

1 Creating an event to trigger when the SQL Book entity changes

In this design, you want to update the Cosmos DB database when an `Add`, `Update`, or `Delete` integration event is found. But it's possible that when you add a `Book`, which creates an `Add` event, you may trigger an `Update` event too (that happens when seeding the database). Also, some complex updates, such as changing multiple parts of the entity, might trigger multiple `Update` events. At minimum, multiple events are inefficient, as you would update the Cosmos DB database multiple times, and, in certain cases, make your code more complex. The problem is that the event handler has no knowledge of other events, so you can't detect that the update is not needed. How do you reduce multiple events to one?

For this type of problem, the `GenericEventRunner` provides the `RemoveDuplicate-Events` attribute to remove duplicate events that are the same event type, and linked to the same class instance (as determined by the `ReferenceEquals` method). The following listing shows the `BookChangedEvent` with the `RemoveDuplicateEvents` attribute added.

Listing 16.1 The `BookChangedEvent` sending `Add`, `Update`, and `Delete` chan

This attribute causes the **GenericEventRunner** to remove duplicate events from the same **Book** instance.

The three types of changes that need mapping to the **Cosmos DB database**

When an ever created, you say what type change the Bo gone through

```
public enum BookChangeTypes { Added, Updated, Deleted } ◁──┘

[RemoveDuplicateEvents]
public class BookChangedEvent : IEntityEvent              ◁──────────
{
    public BookChangedEvent(BookChangeTypes bookChangeType)
    {
        BookChangeType = bookChangeType;
    }

    public BookChangeTypes BookChangeType { get; }        ◁──┐
}
```

Used by the eve to work out wr add, update, or the CosmosBoo

Holds the type of chan the event handler to u

As well as being more efficient, this listing makes the code that updates the Co
DB simpler, because an `Add` followed by an `Update` would cause problems with u
ing an entity with the same key that is already being tracked. This problem cou
solved in the `Add`/`Update` Cosmos code, but removing duplicate events is easier,
cially as that feature is built into the `GenericEventRunner` library.

16.4.2 Adding events to the Book entity send integration events

Because you are using DDD-styled entity classes, it is reasonably easy to spot al
places where a `Book` entity is created or updated. You simply add an `Added` eve
the `Book`'s static factory and lots of `Update` events in any DDD access methods.
following listing shows an `Update` event being added via the `AddEvent` method
section 12.4.2) if the update isn't rejected because of a user input error.

Listing 16.2 Adding a `BookUpdate` to a Book's `AddPromotion` method

```
public IStatusGeneric AddPromotion(
    decimal actualPrice, string promotionalText)
{
    var status = new StatusGenericHandler();
    if (string.IsNullOrWhiteSpace(promotionalText))
    {
        return status.AddError(
            "You must provide text to go with the promotion.",
            nameof(PromotionalText));
    }

    ActualPrice = actualPrice;
    PromotionalText = promotionalText;

    if (status.IsValid)                          ◁────
        AddEvent(new BookChangedEvent(
            BookChangeTypes.Updated),
            EventToSend.DuringSave);
```

You don't want to trigger unnecessary updates, so you trigger only if the change was valid.

Adds a **BookChangedEvent** event with the **Update** setting as a **During** (integration) event

```
        return status;
}
```

For the delete event, you are using a soft delete, so you capture a change to the Soft-Deleted property via its access method. The options are

- If the SoftDeleted value isn't changed, no event is sent.
- If the SoftDeleted value is changed to true, a Deleted event is sent.
- If the SoftDeleted value is changed to false, an Added event is sent.

The following listing shows this example.

Listing 16.3 A change of SoftDeleted that triggers an AddBook or DeleteBook event

```
public void AlterSoftDelete(bool softDeleted)        You don't trigger unnecessary updates,
{                                                    so you trigger only if there was a
    if (SoftDeleted != softDeleted)          ◁────   change to the SoftDeleted property.
    {
        var eventType = softDeleted              The type of event to
            ? BookChangeTypes.Deleted            send depends on the
            : BookChangeTypes.Added;             new SoftDelete setting.

        AddEvent(new BookChangedEvent(eventType)       Adds the BookChangedEvent
            , EventToSend.DuringSave);                 event as a During
    }                                                  (integration) event
    SoftDeleted = softDeleted;
}
```

---

3 Using the *EfCore.GenericEventRunner* to override your *BookDbContext*

In section 15.5.1, you used the Cached SQL performance-tuning approach. The SQL (+cache) approach uses domain events, but this CQRS approach uses integration events. The Cached SQL approach and this CQRS approach can coexist, with each part having no knowledge of the other—another example of applying the SoC principle.

4 Creating the *Cosmos entity classes and DbContext*

The projection of the SQL Book needs to contain the normal properties, such as Title and AcualPrice, plus the values that take a lot of time to calculate, such as the count of the Reviews linked to the Book. The idea of the CQRS read side is to build a ready-to-display version, known as a *projection*, of the SQL Book so that it's quick to display. The following two listings show the CosmosBook class and the CosmosTag class that are used to hold the projection of the SQL Book.

Listing 16.4 The CosmosBook that holds the projection of the SQL Book

```
public class CosmosBook                    We use the BookId used in the
{                                          SQL database to link this entity
    public int BookId { get; set; }   ◁──  to the SQL entity.
```

```
    public string Title { get; set; }
    public DateTime PublishedOn { get; set; }
    public bool EstimatedDate { get;  set; }
    public int YearPublished { get; set; }
    public decimal OrgPrice { get; set; }
    public decimal ActualPrice { get; set; }
    public string PromotionalText { get; set; }
    public string ManningBookUrl { get; set; }

    public string AuthorsOrdered { get; set; }
    public int ReviewsCount { get; set; }
    public double? ReviewsAverageVotes { get; set; }

    public List<CosmosTag> Tags { get; set; }
    public string TagsString { get; set; }
}
```

Normal properties that are needed to display the Book

Precalculated values used for display and filtering

To allow filtering on TagIds we provide a list of CosmosTags, which are configured as Owned Type

This string is used later to overcome a limitation of EF Core's current Cosmos DB provider.

Listing 16.5 The `CosmosTag` class that holds the `TagId` from the SQL `Book`

```
public class CosmosTag
{
    public string TagId { get; set; }
}
```

As you can see in listing 16.5, the CosmosTag class contains one property: TagId.
class mimics the Tag class used in the SQL database, but it will be added as an ov
type (see section 8.9.1). Then the CosmosBook's Tags collection holds each Tag s
for the Book, allowing you to filter Books by a Tag, such as Books about "Databa
The CosmosTag class is registered as an owned type (see section 8.9.1), so it is en
ded in the data sent to Cosmos DB (see listing 16.10).

In fact, a common way to save data to Cosmos DB is to contain collections of c
classes within the main class (Cosmos DB calls this approach *nesting*), which is wh
Core's owned types do. Consider using nested owned type classes when building
to be stored in a Cosmos DB.

The EF Core Cosmos DbContext is small and simple, as shown in listing
because many of the EF Core configuration commands don't work with a Cosmo
database. You can't set the type of the data stored, as each property is converted
JSON key/value, and other settings, such as indexing, are handled by Cosmos its

Listing 16.6 The `DbContext` class needed to access the Cosmos DB database

```
public class CosmosDbContext : DbContext
{
    public CosmosDbContext(
        DbContextOptions<CosmosDbContext> options)
        : base(options)
    { }

    public DbSet<CosmosBook> Books { get; set; }
}
```

The Cosmos DB DbContext has the same structure as any other DbContext.

For this use, you nee to read/write only th CosmosBooks.

```
protected override void OnModelCreating(
    ModelBuilder modelBuilder)
{
    modelBuilder.Entity<CosmosBook>()
        .HasKey(x => x.BookId);

    modelBuilder.Entity<CosmosBook>()
        .OwnsMany(p => p.Tags);
}
```

`.HasKey(x => x.BookId);`	**BookId doesn't match the By Convention rules, so you need to configure it manually.**
`.OwnsMany(p => p.Tags);`	**The collection of CosmosTags is owned by the CosmosBook.**

```
}
```

NOTE For a full list of Cosmos DB-specific Fluent API commands, please see the EF Core documentation on the Cosmos database provider at http://mng .bz/8WyK.

5 Creating the Cosmos event handlers

The `BookChangedEvent` integration event comes into the `BookDbContext`, and you need a matching event handler. A `BookChangeType` property says whether the event is an `Add`, `Update`, or `Delete`, so it uses a C# switch to call the correct code. Because adding, updating, and deleting entries in the Cosmos database use similar code, you build a service that contains three methods, one for each type of update. Putting all the update code in a service makes the event handler simple, as the following listing shows.

Listing 16.7 An example Cosmos event handler that handles an Add event

```
public class BookChangeHandlerAsync
    : IDuringSaveEventHandlerAsync<BookChangedEvent>
{
    private readonly IBookToCosmosBookService _service;

    public BookChangeHandlerAsync(
        IBookToCosmosBookService service)
    {
        _service = service;
    }

    public async Task<IStatusGeneric> HandleAsync(
        object callingEntity, BookChangedEvent domainEvent,
        Guid uniqueKey)
    {
        var bookId = ((Book)callingEntity).BookId;
        switch (domainEvent.BookChangeType)
        {
            case BookChangeTypes.Added:
                await _service.AddCosmosBookAsync(bookId);
                break;
            case BookChangeTypes.Updated:
                await _service.UpdateCosmosBookAsync(bookId);
                break;
            case BookChangeTypes.Deleted:
                await _service.DeleteCosmosBookAsync(bookId);
                break;
```

Annotations:
- **Defines the class as a During (integration) event for the BookChanged event**
- **This service provides the code to Add, Update, and Delete a CosmosBook.**
- **The event handler uses async, as Cosmos DB uses async.**
- **Extracts the BookId from the calling entity, which is a Book**
- **The ...eType ...dded, ...ed, or ...leted.**
- **Calls the Add part of the service with the BookId of the SQL Book**
- **Calls the Update ...lls the Update of the service the BookId of the SQL Book**
- **Calls the Delete part of the service with the BookId of the SQL Book**

```
        default:
            throw new ArgumentOutOfRangeException();
    }

    return null;        <----
}
}
```

> **Retuning null tells the
> GenericEventRunner
> that this method is
> always successful.**

Remember that if the update to the Cosmos database fails, the SQL update, which
executed in a transaction, is rolled back so the databases are kept in step. Bu
want to minimize throwing an exception if the service can fix the problem itself,
ing some extra checks to catch states that it can fix.

The following listing shows the MapBookToCosmosBookAsync method that ha
updating a Book. It's unlikely to happen, but in the time it took the Update event
dler to trigger that SQL, Book might have been (soft-) deleted. Therefore, if the
BookToCosmosBookAsync method returns null, it assumes that the Book has
deleted and will delete any existing CosmosBook with that BookId. Note the use
Core's Update in the code.

Listing 16.8 Creating a projection of the SQL Book and adding it to the Cosmos datab

> **This method is called by the BookUpdated event
> handler with the BookId of the SQL book.**

```
public async Task UpdateCosmosBookAsync(int bookId)    <----
{
    if (CosmosNotConfigured)
        return;

    var cosmosBook = await MapBookToCosmosBookAsync(bookId);    <----

    if (cosmosBook != null)            <----
    {
        _cosmosContext.Update(cosmosBook);
        await CosmosSaveChangesWithChecksAsync(
            WhatDoing.Updating, bookId);
    }
    else
    {
        await DeleteCosmosBookAsync(bookId);    <----
    }
}
```

> **This met▌
> a Select ▌
> similar to
> in chapte
> CosmosB▌
> entity cla▌**

> **The Book App can be run without
> access to Cosmos DB, in which
> case it exits immediately.**

> **If the CosmosBook is successfully filled,
> the Cosmos update code is executed.**

> **Updates the CosmosBook to
> cosmosContext and then call
> method to save it to the data▌**

> **If the SQL book wasn't foun▌
> we ensure that the Cosmos
> database version was remov▌**

COSMOS DB DIFFERENCE The Cosmos DB database always updates the whole
of the entry for the given key in one go, unlike a relational database, which
can change individual columns in a row. The EF Core Update method is more
efficient because it saves a read of the Cosmos database.

The CosmosSaveChangesWithChecksAsync method is also designed to capture an
any states that it might find. An update that doesn't find a CosmosBook to updat▌

example, will be turned into a new CosmosBook instead. These situations are rare but could happen due to concurrent updates to the same CosmosBook entity.

Listing 16.9 shows part of the CosmosSaveChangesWithChecksAsync method that detects errors, possibly caused by concurrency issues, making sure that the Cosmos database is up to date. The catch part of the code in the listing covers the following situations:

- CosmosException:
  - An Update in which the corresponding entity has been Deleted, turning the Update into an Add.
  - A Delete in which the corresponding entity was already Deleted (job done).
  - If not fixed, rethrow the exception.
- DbUpdateException:
  - An Add of a new entity when a corresponding entity already exists there, turning the Add into an Update.

This code shows another useful difference when using the Cosmos DB provider.

Listing 16.9   Part of the handling of SaveChanges exceptions with Cosmos DB

```
private async Task CosmosSaveChangesWithChecksAsync          ◁── Calls SaveChanges and
    (WhatDoing whatDoing, int bookId)           ◁──              handles certain states
{                                                    The whatDoing parameter tells
    try                                              the code whether this is an Add,
    {                                                Update, or Delete.
        await _cosmosContext.SaveChangesAsync();
    }
    catch (CosmosException e)   ◁──┤ Catches any
    {                                CosmosExceptions          Catches an attempt to
        if (e.StatusCode == HttpStatusCode.NotFound           update a CosmosBook
            && whatDoing == WhatDoing.Updating)               that wasn't there
        {
            var updateVersion = _cosmosContext           You need to remove
                .Find<CosmosBook>(bookId);               the attempted update;
            _cosmosContext.Entry(updateVersion)          otherwise, EF Core will
                .State = EntityState.Detached;           throw an exception.
            await AddCosmosBookAsync(bookId);
        }
        else if (e.StatusCode == HttpStatusCode.NotFound
            && whatDoing == WhatDoing.Deleting)          Catches the
        {                                                state where the
            //Do nothing as already deleted              CosmosBook was
        }                                                already deleted...
        else
        {          ...otherwise, not an
            throw;    exception state you can
        }          handle, so rethrow the
    }              exception                             If you try to add a new CosmosBook
    catch (DbUpdateException e)   ◁──                    that's already there, you get a
                                                         DbUpdateException.
```

Turns the Update to an Add → `await AddCosmosBookAsync(bookId);`

```
                        {
The inner        ┌──▷    var cosmosException = e.InnerException as CosmosException;
exception contains│      if (cosmosException?.StatusCode == HttpStatusCode.Conflict
the CosmosException.│        && whatDoing == WhatDoing.Adding)
                  │      //… rest of code left out as nothing new there
                        }
                        }
```

Catches an Add where there is already a CosmosBook with the same key

> **COSMOS DB DIFFERENCE** I found the CosmosException to be helpful for diagnosing Cosmos database issues. The CosmosException contains a StatusCode property that uses HTTP status codes, such as NotFound and Conflict, to describe what went wrong.

16.5 *Understanding the structure and data of a Cosmos DB account*

Before moving on to the query of the CosmosBook class, it is worth looking at how mos DB is organized and what the data looks like when EF Core writes to a data These sections explain how to use a Cosmos DB database account to access a Co database in your application and look at the JSON data stored in the Cosmos datab

> **NOTE** The EF Core Cosmos DB provider uses the Cosmos SQL API. which presents a traditional NoSQL document store using JSON. But Cosmos DB has multiple ways to handle data, such as column store; key-value and graph; and multiple APIs, such as MongoDB, Cassandra, Azure Table, and Gremlin (graph).

16.5.1 *The Cosmos DB structure as seen from EF Core*

This section provides a quick summary of the various parts of the Cosmos DB s ture. It isn't a detailed explanation (the Azure documentation offers one), but it vides the terms you need to use Cosmos DB with EF Core.

Azure provides an Azure Cosmos DB account, which is like a database serve you can have multiple databases in one Azure Cosmos DB account. This accoun be accessed via a connection string, made up of two parts: the URI to access the mos DB account and an account key. This combination allows you to access Azure Cosmos DB account.

> **NOTE** An Azure Cosmos DB Emulator provides a local (and free) version of the Cosmos DB account. It also contains a feature that allows you to read and manage databases that it has stored locally. I cover Azure Cosmos DB Emulator in section 17.8.

A Cosmos DB account can have many Cosmos DB databases; each database can many Cosmos DB containers; and containers are where the data is held. Figure shows how the EF Core code maps onto the Cosmos DB structure.

Having configured the DbContextOptionsBuilder<T> class (or registered the mos DbContext via the AddDbContext method), you can obtain an instance o application's DbContext and are ready to access the Cosmos DB database.

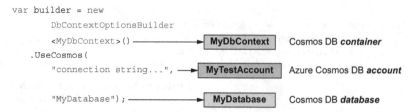

```
var builder = new
      DbContextOptionsBuilder
      <MyDbContext>() ──────────►  MyDbContext      Cosmos DB container
   .UseCosmos(
      "connection string...", ──►  MyTestAccount    Azure Cosmos DB account

      "MyDatabase"); ──────────►   MyDatabase       Cosmos DB database
```

Figure 16.3 Mapping the EF Core setup of a Cosmos DB database provider to the three levels in the Cosmos DB system. The Azure Cosmos DB account can have many Cosmos databases, but this figure shows only one. The database's name is defined in the UseCosmos method. A Cosmos DB database can have many containers, but when used by EF Core, it allows only one container per EF Core application DbContext. By default, the container is given the name of the application DbContext's class.

2 *How the CosmosClass is stored in Cosmos DB*

When you have a correctly configured application DbContext for a Cosmos DB database, you can read and write to its database—strictly, the Cosmos DB's container, but to keep the discussion EF Core-centric I'm going to use the word *database.* For normal read/writes, you don't need to know how the data is stored in the Cosmos database, but sometimes that information is useful, as it gives you an idea of what is being stored.

The next listing shows the data stored when you write a CosmosBook to the database. As you will see, extra properties at the end aren't in the CosmosBook class but are critical for making Cosmos DB work.

> **Listing 16.10   The CosmosBook data stored as JSON in Cosmos DB**

```
{
    "BookId": 214,
    "ActualPrice": 59.99,
    "AuthorsOrdered": "Jon P Smith",
    "EstimatedDate": true,
    "ManningBookUrl": "https://www.manning.com...",          The standard
    "OrgPrice": 59.99,                                        properties from
    "PromotionalText": null,                                  the CosmosBook
    "PublishedOn": "2021-05-15T05:00:00+01:00",               class
    "ReviewsAverageVotes": 5,
    "ReviewsCount": 1,
    "Title": "Entity Framework Core in Action, Second Edition",

    "Tags": [
        {
            "TagId": "Databases"          Holds the
        },                                collection of
        {                                 Tags, which are
            "TagId": "Microsoft & .NET"   configured as an
        }                                 owned type
    ],
```

```
    "YearPublished": 2021,                                          These two properties
    "TagsString": "| Databases | Microsoft & .NET |",              added to overcome s
                                                                    limitations in the EF
    "Discriminator": "CosmosBook",                                 Cosmos provider.

    "id": "CosmosBook|214",

    "_rid": "QmRlAMizcQmwAg…",                                     Cosmos-specific
    "_self": "dbs/QmRlAA==/colls/QmRlAMizcQk=…",                   properties; see
    "_etag": "\"1e01b788-0000-1100-0000-5facfa2f0000\"",           the following
    "_ts": 1605171759,                                             notes
    "_attachments": "attachments/"
}
```

The id is the database's primary key and must be unique. This id is set by EF Core, using the EF Core designated primary key and the discriminator.

EF Core adds the discriminator to differentiate this class from other classes saved In the same Cosmos container.

The first set of JSON key/values comes from the properties and relationships i▮ CosmosBook class, including the Tags collection:

- The id key/value is the unique key used to define this data. EF Core fill▮ unique key with a value—by default, a combination of the Discriminator ▮ and the value from the property(s) that you told EF Core is the primary k▮ this entity class.

- The _etag key/value can be used with the UseETagConcurrency Fluen▮ method to provide a concurrency token covering any change in the data.

- The _ts key/value contains the time of the last Add/Update in Unix forma▮ is useful for finding when an entry last changed. The _ts value can be ▮ verted to C# DateTime format by using the UnixDateTimeConverter class.

- The _rid and _self key/value are unique identifiers used internally for na▮ tion and resources.

- The _attachments key/value is depreciated and is there only for old syste▮

16.6 *Displaying books via Cosmos DB*

Having built a system that copies changes in the SQL Book entity class to a Co▮ database, we are ready to implement the book-display features of the original ▮ App by getting data from the Cosmos DB database. Implementing all the book-di▮ features exposes several interesting Cosmos DB differences from the way a relat▮ database works.

In the end, I could match the original book display, but it is interesting to u▮ stand the differences, which tell me what I can achieve by using a Cosmos DB ▮ base. I also built the display with direct Cosmos DB commands by using its .NET ▮ (software development kit), which I refer to as Cosmos (Direct). The Cosmos (Di▮

code allowed me to differentiate between EF Core 5 Cosmos database provider limitations and differences in the way that Cosmos DB natively queries a database.

EF CORE 5 LIMITATION EF Core's raw SQL commands, such as `FromSqlRaw` and `FromSqlInterpolated`, don't work. But you can get a `CosmosClient` instance via `var cosmosClient = context.Database.GetCosmosClient()`. This technique allows you to use the Cosmos DB .NET SDK commands.

Here are the variations from relational databases and the EF Core 5 limitations that I found while implementing the two-database CQRS architecture:

- *Cosmos DB differences from relational databases*
- *Cosmos DB/EF Core difference: Migrating a Cosmos database*
- *EF Core 5 Cosmos DB database provider limitations*

NOTE If you want to try running the Book App with Cosmos DB, download the associated GitHub repo (http://mng.bz/XdlG), run the BookApp.UI project, and look for the Chapter 16 Setup link on the home page for more info.

1 Cosmos DB differences from relational databases

This section covers the differences between a Cosmos DB (NoSQL) database and a relational (SQL Server) database. This information is useful for developers who haven't worked with NoSQL and, more specifically, a Cosmos DB database before. Here is a summary of the various differences:

- The Cosmos DB provides only async methods.
- There are no database-created primary keys.
- Complex queries may need breaking up.
- Skip is slow and expensive.
- By default, all properties are indexed.

THE COSMOS DB PROVIDES ONLY ASYNC METHODS

Because Cosmos DB uses HTTP to access databases, all the methods in the Cosmos DB .NET SDK use async/await, and there are no sync versions. EF Core does provide access to Cosmos DB via EF Core's sync methods, such as `ToList` and `SaveChanges`, but these methods currently use the `Task`'s `Wait` method, which can have deadlock problems.

I strongly suggest that you use only async EF Core methods when working with the Cosmos database provider. In addition to getting a more robust application, you will get better scalability in multiuser situations, such as ASP.NET Core.

COSMOS DIFFERENCE: THERE ARE NO DATABASE-CREATED PRIMARY KEYS

With a relational database, you are used to having the database provide a unique value for its primary key when a new row is added to a table. But in Cosmos and many other NoSQL databases, by default, the key for an item (item is Cosmos's name for each JSON entry) must be generated by the software before you add an item.

NOTE The Cosmos DB has a way to create a unique key for you, but this key will be stored in the `id` key/value.

The key for an item must be unique, and Cosmos will reject (with the HTTP `Conflict`) a new item if its key was already used. Also, after you have added an with a key, you can't change the key.

One easy choice for a Cosmos DB key is a C# `Guid` type, which is designed unique. EF Core also makes using a `Guid` type as a key simple, as it has a built-in generator (see section 10.3.2) that will provide a new `Guid` value if the designate mary key is a `Guid` and its value is `default`. You can configure composite keys wit Core, which will combine their values into a string that Cosmos DB needs for i key/value. When using Cosmos in the Book App, I used an `int` as the key fo `CosmosBook` entity, but the `int`'s value came from the primary key that the SQL side database created.

> **NOTE** Cosmos DB talks about a partition key and logical and physical partitions. I'm not covering these topics here, as they're big topics, and I'm not sure I understand them well enough. EF Core 5 defaults to not having a partition key, but you can change that setting.

COMPLEX QUERIES MAY NEED BREAKING UP

In the filter-by-year option in the book display, the `FilterDropdownService` fin the years when books were published. This task requires a series of steps:

1 Filter out any books that haven't yet been published.
2 Extract the `Year` part of the `Book`'s `PublishedOn` `DateTime` property.
3 Apply the LINQ `Distinct` command to obtain the years for all the published b
4 Order the years.

This complex query works in SQL, but Cosmos DB can't handle it. Figure 16.4 sh side-by-side view of the two queries.

This shows the two versions of the FilterDropdownService
that finds all the years when books were published.

Cosmos DB example	SQL Server example

```
var nextYear = DateTime.UtcNow.AddYears(1).Year
var allYears = await _db.Books
    .Select(x => x.YearPublished)
    .Distinct().ToListAsync();

var result = allYears
    .Where(x => x < nextYear)
    .OrderByDescending(x => x)
    .Select(x => new DropdownTuple
    {
        Value = x.ToString(),
        Text = x.ToString()
    }).ToList();
```

```
var nextYear = DateTime.UtcNow.AddYears(1).
var result = _db.Books
    .Where(x => x.PublishedOn <= DateTime.T
    .Select(x => x.PublishedOn.Year)
    .Distinct()
    .Where(x => x < nextYear)
    .OrderByDescending(x => x)
    .Select(x => new DropdownTuple
    {
        Value = x.ToString(),
        Text = x.ToString()
    }).ToList();
```

Figure 16.4 Two versions of the `FilterDropdownService` that finds all the years when books were published. The Cosmos DB example simplifies the query that is run in the Cosmos DB, with the second done in the software. This example shows that Cosmos DB doesn't have the wide range of query features relational databases have.

When I ran the code I was using in SQL Server (see the right side of figure 16.4), I got an exception in Cosmos DB, with a link to EF Core issue #16156, which says that Cosmos DB has some limitations on queries. Cosmos doesn't have the massive depth of query features that relational databases have gained over decades of improvement, so you may have to alter some of your more complex queries when dealing with Cosmos DB. Here is what I did to make the filter drop-down query work in Cosmos DB:

- I added a new property called `YearPublished` that had the year as an integer. (I tried using a Cosmos DB user-defined function to extract the year, but it wouldn't work with the `Distinct` command.) This property is filled in during the projection of the SQL `Book` entity by the `Year` part of the `DateTime PublishedOn` property.
- I ran the `Distinct` query by using the `YearPublished` value in Cosmos and then ordered the returned years in software.

My two changes to the code makes the Cosmos query work, but it's slow (section 16.7.2). But the takeaway from this section is that you shouldn't be applying queries with multiple parts to the Cosmos DB database whether you're using EF Core or not. The strength of a Cosmos DB database is its scalability and availability, not its ability to handle complex queries.

SKIP IS SLOW AND EXPENSIVE
In the Book App, I used paging to allow the user to move through the books display. This type of query uses the LINQ `Skip` and `Take` methods to provide paging. The query `context.Books.Skip(100).Take(10)`, for example, would return the 101st to 111th books in a sequence. Cosmos DB can do this too, but the `Skip` part gets slower as the skip value gets bigger (another difference from relational databases) and is expensive too.

> **COSMOS REQUEST UNITS**   Azure's Cosmos DB database uses *request units* (RUs) to manage provisioning the throughput of a container. You have various ways to provision your Cosmos DB container: fixed provisioning (fixedish price), serverless (pay as you use), and autoscale (scales to use). In the end, however, you are going to pay for every access to the Cosmos DB service.

It seems that if you `Skip` 100 items, Cosmos still reads them. But even though Cosmos doesn't send the `Skip`ped items to the application, there is a time and cost in RUs. In the Book App, you can see performance go down as the user goes farther down the list of books (see figure 16.8).

Whether the `Skip` performance is a problem depends on your application. In the Book App, I doubt that people would read much past the first 100 books. But this example suggests that showing 100 books at a time is better than showing 10 books and having the user page, as paging isn't free.

BY DEFAULT, ALL PROPERTIES ARE INDEXED
We know that adding an index to a property in a relational database significantly improves the time it takes to filter or sort on that property, with a (small) performance

cost when you update the indexed property. Cosmos DB's default setup is to inde
the key/values, included nested key values. (The CosmosBook entity has the Tags.T
key/values indexed too, for example.) You can change the Cosmos DB indexing
icy, but "index all" is a good starting point.

> **NOTE** EF Core's indexing configuration features, including a unique index,
> don't work in Cosmos DB. But you can define indexes via the Cosmos DB
> setup section of the container.

You should also remember that Cosmos DB saves data by using JSON string for
and Cosmos indexes knows about only three index types: numbers, strings, and
raphy. C#'s DateTime and TimeSpan types are stored in a string format that ca
sorted or filtered by means of a string, so date and time are stored with the mor
nificant time parts first, as in YYYY-MM-DDTHH:MM:SS. EF Core handles time-to-s
conversions for you, but if you use EF Core's value converters (see section 7.8) o
SQL queries, you need to understand the various JSON formats that Cosmos DB

16.6.2 Cosmos DB/EF Core difference: Migrating a Cosmos database

Cosmos DB is a *schemaless* database, meaning that each item doesn't have to hav
same properties or nested data in each item. Each item is a JSON object, and it's
you what keys/values you put in the JSON object. This database is different fr
relational database, in which the schema is important and requires some effo
change (see chapter 9).

At some point, you are going to change or add properties to an entity
mapped to a Cosmos DB database. You must be careful, though; otherwise, you c
break some of your existing Cosmos DB queries. This example shows what ca
wrong and how to fix it:

1 You have a CosmosBook entity class, and you have written data to a Cosmo
   database.
2 You decide that you need an additional property called NewProperty of
   int (but it could be any non-nullable type).
3 You read back old data that was added before the NewProperty property
   added to the CosmosBook entity class.
4 At this point, you get an exception saying something like object must ha
   value.

Cosmos DB doesn't mind your having different data in every item, but EF Core
EF Core expects a NewProperty of type int, and it's not there. The way arounc
problem is to make sure that any new properties are nullable; then reading the
data will return a null value for the new properties. If you want the new prope
be non-nullable, start with a nullable version and then update *every* item in the
base with a non-null value for the new property. After that, you can change the
property back to a non-nullable type, and because there is a value for that prope
every item, all your queries will work.

Another point is that you can't use the Migrate command to create a new Cosmos DB database, because EF Core doesn't support migrations for a Cosmos DB database. You need to use the EnsureCreatedAsync method instead. The EnsureCreatedAsync method is normally used for unit testing, but it's the recommended way to create a database (Cosmos DB container) when working with Cosmos DB.

3 EF Core 5 Cosmos DB database provider limitations

This section covers the limitations of the EF Core 5 Cosmos DB database provider. This information is useful if you want to use EF Core 5 to access a Cosmos DB database; it'll also be useful when future releases of EF Core remove some of these limitations, making the workarounds I had to apply to the part 3 Book App unnecessary. Here is a summary of the various limitations:

- Counting the number of books in Cosmos DB is *slow!*
- Many database functions are not implemented.
- EF Core 5 cannot do subqueries on a Cosmos DB database.
- There are no relationships or Includes.

COUNTING THE NUMBER OF BOOKS IN COSMOS DB IS SLOW

Almost the first thing I noticed when I added a Cosmos version to the Book App was that counting the CosmosBooks, which I used for paging, was extremely slow via EF Core. I built a mini version of this Book App in late 2019, and there were two reasons for the poor performance:

- Cosmos DB's aggregates (Count, Sum, and so on) were slow and took a lot of RUs to run.
- EF Core didn't use Cosmos DB's aggregates, so I needed to read every Cosmos-Book in to count them (a EF Core 5 limitation).

Fortunately, the first issue was fixed in April 2020. Cosmos DB's aggregates are much quicker and uses a lot less resources. (Example: the original Cosmos Count took 12,000 RUs, whereas the new Count used only 25 RUs.) But EF Core 5 didn't get any quicker, because it was reading all the books in the Cosmos database to count them. Not to be thwarted, I changed the way the Cosmos EF book display worked and moved over to using a Next/Previous approach to paging. Figure 16.5 shows this format.

Changing to the Next/Previous approach was trivial; the main problem was setting up the ASP.NET Core Razor page. Many e-commerce sites, including Amazon, use this approach, so this change might be a good one to make anyway.

In the Cosmos (Direct) version, I kept the normal paging, with its count of all filtered books. It turns out that the direct Cosmos Count command, SELECT value COUNT(c) FROM c, is fast (~25 ms to count 500,000 Cosmos books) even compared with the SQL version (90 ms to count 500,000 SQL books).

Cosmos (EF) - using EF Core access Cosmos DB holding pre-built read version.

Sort By	Filter Type	Filter By	Paging			Page Size
sort by... ⌄	All ⌄	Select filter ⌄	Prev	Page 1	Next	100 ⌄

Introducing Data Science click to see more...

by Davy Cielen, Arno D. B. Meysman, Mohamed Ali
Published on 02/05/2016
Tags: Data | Data Science

Because the EF Core 5 Count of books in a Cosmos database is so slow, the paging was changed to use a Next/Previous approach.

Figure 16.5 The page where the Cosmos DB is accessed via EF Core 5. To overcome the slow speed of counting the number of books, I changed the controls to use a **Next/Previous** approach.

MANY DATABASE FUNCTIONS ARE NOT IMPLEMENTED

EF Core 5 has mapped LINQ to a small set of five Cosmos functions, so you may to alter your LINQ to work around these issues. One filter I tried failed becaus Core knew that it should convert the method `DateTime.UtcNow` to a UTC date the database server, but that Cosmos DB function hadn't been mapped in EF Co The problem was easy to fix: I created a variable to hold the value given by D Time.UtcNow. Figure 16.6 shows the failed (left) and the fixed (right) query, with differences in **bold**.

FAILED Cosmos DB query	**FIXED Cosmos DB query**

```
var filterYear = int.Parse(filterValue);
var result = _db.books.Where(x =>
    x.PublishedOn.Year == filterYear &&
    x.PublishedOn <= DateTime.UtcNow);
```

```
var now = DateTime.UtcNow;
var filterYear = int.Parse(filterValue)
var result = _db.books.Where(x =>
    x.PublishedOn.Year == filterYear &&
    x.PublishedOn <= now);
```

Figure 16.6 The original query on the right failed, because EF Core 5 knew that it should convert th DateTime.UtcNow method (left, in bold) to the UTC time provided by the database server, but tha part of the mapping had not been done. The solution was to put the value from the DateTime.UtcNc method in a variable (top right, in bold) and feed that variable into the query.

EF CORE 5 CANNOT DO SUBQUERIES ON A COSMOS DB DATABASE

The Book App provides a way to filter books by their Tags, such as looking or books with a Tag called "Databases". This solution requires a subquery in the query, like the Cosmos DB SQL command shown in the following code snippet:

```
SELECT DISTINCT value f.TagId FROM c JOIN f in c.Tags
```

This EF Core 5 limitation precludes querying any nested parts of the Cosmos J such as any owned types that are saved with the main entity class. You can get that by reading the entity, of course, but you can't filter, sort, or select nested parts on their own via EF Core. In section 16.7.2, I show you a way to get around this problem.

THERE ARE NO RELATIONSHIPS OR INCLUDES

The EF Core 5 Cosmos database provider doesn't support relationships between entity classes (other than via owned types embedded in the main entity class). Although this lack of support seems to be a big missing feature, when it comes to Cosmos entities, owned types are the way to go, so maybe this feature doesn't matter so much.

The design approach of a Cosmos DB item is more about embedding (Cosmos calls it *nesting*), which you can do with owned types, such as the Tags collection in CosmosBook. In fact, the Cosmos DB documentation (http://mng.bz/EVnq) says

> *Because there is currently no concept of a constraint, foreign-key or otherwise, any inter-document relationships that you have in documents are effectively "weak links" and will not be verified by the database itself.*

Most NoSQL databases are like Cosmos DB in not supporting relationships between items. Personally, I'm not sure that EF Core should add relationships across different items in a Cosmos database, as they aren't going to work in the way we expect with relational databases, but we will see.

Was using Cosmos DB worth the effort? Yes!

You built a CQRS two-database system to improve the performance and scalability of the Book App. Also, implementing the CQRS system with Cosmos DB taught you a lot about what Cosmos can and can't do, as well as the limitations of the EF Core 5 Cosmos provider. In this section, you are going to look at three topics:

- The performance of the two-database CQRS in the Book App
- The features that the EF Core 5 Cosmos DB database provider can't handle
- How difficult it would be to use this two-database CQRS design in your application

To compare performance and features, you use four types of queries:

- *Cosmos (EF)*—Uses EF Core's Cosmos DB database provider
- *Cosmos (Direct)*—Uses the Cosmos DB .NET SDK
- *SQL (+cache)*—Uses the cached values in the SQL database (see section 15.5)
- *SQL (Dapper)*—Uses the best SQL to access the SQL database (see section 15.4)

NOTE I left out the original book-display code developed in chapter 2 because it was so slow that it wasn't useful. Also, it threw an exception on queries that exceeded the database timeout of 30 seconds.

The aim is to compare the performance, features, and development effort, as I did in section 15.6 for four levels of SQL performance tuning.

16.7.1 Evaluating the performance of the two-database CQRS in the Book App

To compare the performance of the SQL approaches in chapter 15 and the Co CQRS system in this chapter, I had two types of Cosmos DB queries, using EF and direct via the Cosmos SQL API, and two SQL queries from chapter 15, using (+cache) and SQL (Dapper). Having these four ways of displaying the books alle me to compare the performance of the two types of databases.

To make the comparison fair, the two databases need to be

- *Located in the same place* so that the travel time (latency) is the same. I achi this by creating both databases on the Azure site in London, which is abor miles from my location.

- *Similar in price* because price defines the performance of the two databases. databases are close in price and cheap enough to test without spending lc money. Table 16.1 shows details on the two databases.

Table 16.1 The two databases used to compare the performance of an SQL database and a Cosme database

Database type	Azure service name	Performance units	Price/month
Azure SQL Server	Standard	20 DTUs	$37
Cosmos DB	Pay as you go	Manual scale, 800 RUs	$47

NOTE Both Azure SQL Server and Cosmos DB have a serverless version, in which the performance of the database can rise and fall based on demand. That version might have been cheaper for me, but I wanted specific perfor-mance to compare SQL queries with Cosmos DB queries.

The following list shows the levels of Books (both SQL Book and CosmosBook) ir databases that were used in the performance tests. It also shows the numbe Reviews in the database, as sorting or filtering by votes is one of the most challer queries:

- 100,000 Books, which has 546,000 Reviews
- 250,000 Books, which has 1,365,000 Reviews
- 500,000 Books, which has 2,740,000 Reviews

My first attempt at measuring the performance at different sizes of databases incl the SQL (+cache) and SQL (Dapper) queries described in chapter 15. But it turn that performance in counting the number of Books in a query is slow. At 50(Books, a simple display of the first 100 books took 230 ms. I felt that this evalu. between Cosmos (EF) and SQL (EF) wasn't fair, so I created SQL (+cacheNC) SQL (DapperNC) versions. (*NC* stands for *no count.*) The first performance c which looks at performance as the database grows, contains only Cosmos DB (EF) Cosmos DB (Direct), as shown in figure 16.7.

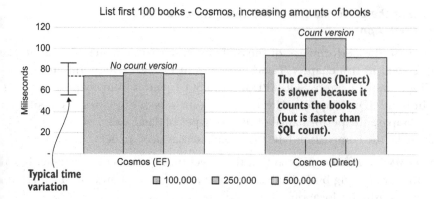

Figure 16.7   **Time taken to display an HTML page containing the first 100 books (ordered by primary key, descending) in the Cosmos DB container for three sizes of the database. This figure shows that the size of the database has little effect on the time taken. Note that these timings were done days apart, and the variation is fairly large (~ 35 ms), so this chart might look different if I ran the test again.**

NOTE   All timings were taken from the ASP.NET Core's RequestFinished log, which contains the total time to the HTTP request. The time for a query is obtained by running the query at least seven times and taking the average of the last five times. To access this data, choose the Admin > Timings command in the Book App.

The main feature difference between Cosmos DB (EF) and Cosmos DB (Direct) is that the Cosmos DB (Direct) uses the original paging approach, which means that it had to count the number of Books in the overall query. Figure 16.7 shows that Cosmos DB is fast at counting—in fact, about twice as fast as SQL for 500,000 Books. In this case, speed doesn't matter too much, but in some applications, Cosmos's fast counting could make a big difference. The next performance tests were on most of the key sorts and filters across the four types of queries: Cosmos DB (EF), Cosmos DB (Direct), SQL (+cacheNC), and SQL (DapperNC) at 500,000 Books, as shown in figure 16.8.

NOTE   I discuss the effect of extracting the tags from 500,000 CosmosBooks in section 16.7.2, in the sidebar titled "Interesting things happen when you overload a Cosmos DB database."

Figure 16.8 and the SQL count information provide the information to make some conclusions, which are presented in the following list with the important facts first.

- Even the best SQL version, SQL (DapperNC), doesn't work in this application because any sort or filter on the Reviews took so long that the connection timed out at 30 seconds.
- The SQL (+cacheNC) version was at parity or better with Cosmos DB (EF) on the first two queries, but as the query got more complex, it fell behind in performance.

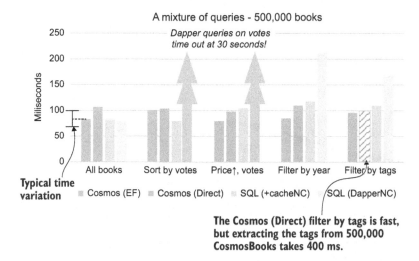

A mixture of queries - 500,000 books

Figure 16.8 Time taken for five key queries on databases containing 500,000 Books. The four types of database access are Cosmos DB (EF), Cosmos DB (Direct), SQL (+cacheNC), and SQL (DapperNC).

- The Cosmos DB (Direct), with its Book count, was ~25% slower than the mos DB (EF) with no count, but it's still about twice as fast as an SQL coun

Overall, I think this test shows a good win for Cosmos DB, especially when you add fact that implementing this CQRS was easier and quicker than building the orig SQL (+cache) version. Also, Cosmos DB's concurrency handling (see section 16 is easier than the SQL (+cache) version.

The CQRS/Cosmos DB approach has some downsides, of course. First, adding updating a book take a bit longer because the CQRS requires four database acce two to update the SQL database and two to update the Cosmos database. These up add up to about 110 ms, which is more than double the time a single SQL data would take. So if your application does lots of writes to the database, this approac its own might not work for you.

ADVANCED NOTE   There are several ways to improve the write performance of the CQRS approach at the expense of more-complex code. I describe some of these approaches in one of my articles; see http://mng.bz/N8dE.

The second downside is a feature of Cosmos DB: using the LINQ Skip method is and expensive (see section 16.6.4). Figure 16.9 shows that the more books you s the more time the process takes. Time shouldn't be a problem with the Book Ap many people would give up after a few pages, but if your application needs deep ping through data, Cosmos DB is not a good fit.

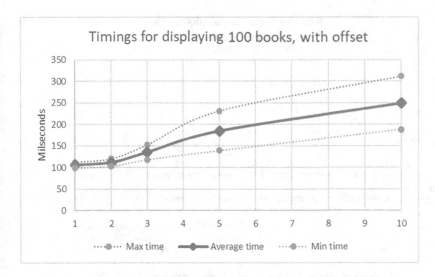

Figure 16.9 The more books you Skip, the more execution time increases. The chart shows the maximum and minimum ranges of the five timings that were used. As you can see, the more items Skipped, the more the variation increased.

.2 Fixing the features that EF Core 5 Cosmos DB database provider couldn't handle

In creating the original implementation of querying the Cosmos DB via the EF Core 5 Cosmos DB database provider, I limited myself to using only the features that EF Core 5 provided. But when you are building a real application, you use what you have and then improvise, because making the application work is what you are paid for. In this section, you are going to fix the problems already highlighted in this chapter:

- Couldn't count the number of books in Cosmos DB quickly
- Couldn't create the By Years Published drop-down filter in a reasonable time
- Couldn't create the By Tags drop-down filter
- Couldn't filter by TagIds because EF Core 5 Cosmos doesn't support the IN command

NOTE This section is only about handling limitations in the EF Core 5 Cosmos DB database provider. It does not cover Cosmos DB limitations, such as the need to break up complex queries (see section 16.6.3).

COULDN'T COUNT THE NUMBER OF BOOKS IN COSMOS DB QUICKLY

This issue is covered in section 16.6.8. Swapping to a Next/Previous form of paging is quite acceptable in many places. Amazon uses the Next/Previous paging approach, so it should work for selling books.

COULDN'T CREATE THE BY YEARS PUBLISHED DROP-DOWN FILTER IN A REASONABLE TIME

When you select the By Years Published drop-down filter, the code must look thro
all the books to find the YearPublished property and use the Distinct metho
obtain all the years. The problem here wasn't that the LINQ query couldn't be
but it was quite slow (25 seconds on 500,000 books). I suspect that it was slow bec
the Distinct method is run in software, but I can't be sure.

But I do know that using direct Cosmos SQL commands can work. In fact
direct Cosmos SQL is quicker than the SQL version. For 500,000 books, Cosmos
took ~400 ms, whereas SQL took ~2.5 seconds. So the solution is to use a direct
mos SQL command to get the distinct years, which requires getting the Cosmo
container via the Cosmos DB context, as shown in the following listing.

Listing 16.11 The Filter Drop-down service showing the use of direct Cosmos S

This code covers only the section that
handles filtering by publication year.

```
//… other parts of the switch removed for clarity
case BooksFilterBy.ByPublicationYear:                      ⟵

    var container = _db.GetCosmosContainerFromDbContext(
        _settings.CosmosDatabaseName);

    var now = DateTime.UtcNow;
    var comingSoonResultSet =
        container.GetItemQueryIterator<int>(
        new QueryDefinition(
            "SELECT value Count(c) FROM c WHERE" +
            $" c.YearPublished > {now:yyyy-MM-dd} " +
            "OFFSET 0 LIMIT 1"));
    var comingSoon = (await
        comingSoonResultSet.ReadNextAsync())
        .First() > 0;

    var resultSet = container.GetItemQueryIterator<int>(
        new QueryDefinition(
            "SELECT DISTINCT VALUE c.YearPublished FROM c" +
            $" WHERE c.YearPublished > {now:yyyy-mm-dd}"));

    var years = (await resultSet.ReadNextAsync()).ToList();   ⟵

    //… the code turns the 'years' into a drop-down tuple
```

Obtains a Cosm
container via th
DB context plus
name of the dat

This query is desig
to see whether the
are any publication
that aren't out yet.

The coming-
SoonResultSet is
executed, and its
ingle value tells us
whether there are
uture publications
in the list.

This query g
distinct yea
all books al
published.

Executes
query an
a list of
when bo
were pu

But be warned: the query shown in listing 16.11 is another high-RUs query, co
out about the same as TagIds at 2,321 RUs. This chapter may be a place for a stati
as technical books more than five years old normally aren't useful (except for
Evan's *Domain-Driven Design*, of course!).

COULDN'T CREATE THE BY TAGS DROP-DOWN FILTER

EF Core 5 couldn't get a distinct set of `TagIds` from the `Tags` collection of each `CosmosBook` because EF Core 5's Cosmos database provider doesn't support subqueries. Again, you can use direct Cosmos SQL commands instead—Cosmos (Direct) takes only ~350 ms—but doing so is costly. Getting the list of `TagIds` from the SQL database is simple because it has a table called Tags, with only 35 rows. So instead of looking through 500,000 `CosmosBooks` and extracting all the `TagIds`, we can simply run the following SQL code, which takes only ~30 ms:

```
var drop-down = _sqlContext.Tags
    .Select(x => new Drop-downTuple
    {
        Value = x.TagId,
        Text = x.TagId
    }).ToList();
```

> ### Interesting things happen when you overload a Cosmos DB database
> In building the Cosmos (Direct) to filter by tags, I decided to extract the `TagIds` by using a Cosmos SQL command:
>
> ```
> SELECT DISTINCT value f.TagId FROM c JOIN f in c.Tags
> ```
>
> This command works but takes a long time (~400 ms) and costs a lot of RUs—2,445 RUs, to be exact. Because that command exceeds the 800 RUs provisioned for my database (Cosmos container), Cosmos penalizes any queries that come after it.
>
> In this case, Cosmos seemed to go slow for a few seconds, and I was charged more money for going over the 800 RUs I paid for. Try to keep the cost of your queries within the allocated provision if you don't want subsequent queries to be slow.
>
> I should say that asking Cosmos DB to extract all the `TagIds` from all 500,000 `CosmosBooks` and returning the 35 distinct `TagIds` isn't a good design, but it did uncover what happens if you exceed your allotted RUs.

COULDN'T FILTER BY TAGIDS BECAUSE EF CORE 5 COSMOS DOESN'T SUPPORT THE IN COMMAND

The last issue to overcome is filtering the books by their `TagIds` because EF Core 5's Cosmos DB database provider doesn't support the `IN` command. Although you could use a direct Cosmos SQL command, EF Core 5 supports the LINQ `Contains` method for strings.

> **EF CORE 5 LIMITATION** EF Core 5 doesn't support the Cosmos equivalent of the SQL `IN` command to filter on the `Tags` collection. The LINQ query `Books.Where(x => x.Tags.Any(y => y == "some tag name"))` would throw a could not be translated exception. I get around this problem by using string `Contains`.

By adding a string called `TagsString` and putting in each `TagId`, plus extra delim▪ characters, we can use string `Contains` to filter by `TagIds`. The following code sni▪ shows the `TagsString` key/value taken from the `CosmosBook` JSON in listing 16.1▪

```
"TagsString": "| Databases | Microsoft & .NET |"
```

> **NOTE** The delimiting | character in `TagsString` ensures that the filter-by-tag feature matches the whole `TagId` string; otherwise, the `Tag` "Data" would match "Data" and "Databases".

This technique makes filtering by `Tag` easy. To select all the `Books` with `Tag` "C#"▪ example, you would write

```
context.Books
    .Where(x => x.TagsString.Contains("| C# |"))
    .ToListAsync();
```

This approach is quite acceptable in Cosmos DB, which has a page about `Cont`▪ and strings. In fact, the `Contains` string method is faster than the `IN/subq`▪ method. For 500,000 books, the string `Contains` took ~125 ms, whereas the J▪ `WHERE` version had a large variation in timings, up to 3 seconds.

16.7.3 How difficult would it be to use this two-database CQRS design in your application?

There is no doubt that the Cosmos DB version provides an excellent performanc▪ the Book App when the numbers of `Books` and `Reviews` increase. But how hard w▪ it be to add this approach to an existing application, and would doing that have a ▪ ative effect on further development of the application? I added this CQRS desig▪ the existing Book App, so I am in a good position to answer these questions.

On reflection, most of the time was taken up by understanding how the Co▪ DB worked and adjusting things to fit its style. Looking at the GitHub commits, it ▪ me about two weeks to add the two-database CQRS enhancement to the existing I▪ App, but that time included a lot of research and building the extra Cosmos (Di▪ version. As I said earlier, I think that the two-database CQRS design was a bit easi▪ build and test than the SQL (+cache) version.

> **NOTE** The two-database CQRS enhancement was implemented as an addi- tional query approach while leaving all the original book-display systems; also, I altered the SQL (+cache) and SQL (Dapper) code to have a no-count ver- sion. Building all these versions allowed me to compare the performance of the two-database CQRS system with the original SQL book-display systems.

Here is a breakdown of the parts, with my views on how difficult they were:

- *Detecting changes to an SQL* `Book`—This part was made easy by the use of ▪ classes, as I could add an event to each access method in the `Book` entity cla▪

you aren't using DDD classes, you would need to detect changes to entities during SaveChangesAsync, but as I say in section 16.4, that approach is harder.

- *Running the event code within a transaction*—My GenericEventRunner library made this part significantly quicker to write. You don't need to use this library, but it would take longer to develop.

- *Writing to the Cosmos DB database*—That part was fairly easy, with some straightforward Add, Update, and Delete methods. (See listing 16.8 for an example.) I spent some time making the write more robust by handing possible causes by concurrent updates.

- *Querying the Cosmos DB database*—This part took the most time, mainly because there are limitations in EF Core and in Cosmos DB.

When it came to the effects of adding the CQRS design to the existing Book App, I would say that the Cosmos DB part had little effect on the Book App's structure. Here are the changes I needed to make to the existing code:

- Registering the Cosmos DbContext on startup
- Adding integration events to the Book entity class
- Altering the SQL (+cache) and SQL (Dapper) code to have no-count versions

All the existing code still works the same way that it always did. Clearly, changes to the Book entity could require changes to the CosmosBook entity and its associated Map-BookToCosmosBook extension method. Except for changes to the Book entity, a change to the SQL code should have no effect on the Cosmos DB code, and a change to the Cosmos DB code should have no effect on the SQL code of the application.

Differences in other database types

Most of this chapter is about Cosmos DB, which is different from the relational databases that this book covers. But at the end of this chapter, we look at relational databases again. Different types of relational databases are similar, mainly because there is an official standard for the SQL language, but many small differences exist. This section is useful if you want to move from one relational database to another, such as SQL Server to PostgreSQL.

EF Core will handle many of the differences between relational database types, such as how table names should be wrapped in the SQL commands, but you have to handle some things yourself, such as the different formats of UDFs (see section 10.1). Here is a list of typical things to check and change if you are moving from one relational database to another:

1 Download the NuGet database provider, and change the registration of your DbContext.

The first thing you need to do is install the specific EF Core database provider via NuGet, such as Microsoft.EntityFrameworkCore.SqlServer or Npgsql.EntityFrameworkCore.PostgreSQL. Then you need to change the way you

register that database provider to your DbContext. In ASP.NET Core, you w
have something like this for a MySQL database provider:

```
services.AddDbContext<MyDbContext>(
    options => options.UseMySql(connection));
```

2 Rerun the Add-Migration command for the new database provider.

EF Core migrations are database-provider-specific and are *not* transfer
between databases. You need to throw away your old migrations and rur
Add-Migration command, using your new database provider.

NOTE You can have migrations for multiple database types as long as you
keep them in different projects. You must add the MigrationsAssembly
method to the registration of each DbContext to tell EF Core where the
migrations are located.

3 Fix any type mapping between .NET and the database that has changed.

You need to rerun your LINQ queries and see whether anything
changed. In the first edition of this book, I converted the Book App from
Server to MySQL, and the main Select book display query (see listing ‽
threw an exception. It turns out that the returned type of the SQL AVG comm
in MySQL is a nullable decimal rather than the nullable double in SQL Se
To overcome this problem, you need to change the BookListDto's Aver
ReviewVotes property .NET type to decimal? to match the way MySQL work

Other, subtler type differences exist between database servers that migh
unnoticed. Typical things to look at are

a *Concurrency timestamp types*—In SQL Server, it's a byte[] type; in Postgre‽
you use a uint type (and you need to configure it when your register
DbContext); and MySQL uses a DateTime type, so check that you have
correct type for your database type.

b *String queries and collation* (see section 2.8.3)—By default, SQL Server
MySQL use a case-insensitive match between strings, and PostgreSQL
default case-sensitive. Setting a Collation on the database, table, or col
has different names and effects.

c DateTime *precision*—Most databases have moved to DateTime2, with its
precision at 100 ns, but it's worth checking. SQLite stores DateTime
string, using ISO8601 format: "YYYY-MM-DD HH:MM:SS.SSS".

4 Check and change any raw SQL that you are using.

This step is where things get more complex, because EF Core isn't cove
any changes in the way that the database type uses SQL. Standard SQL ⸱
should work, but the way of referring to tables and columns might cha
More-complex SQL such as UDFs and stored procedures seem to have sli
different formats between database types.

Summary

- A NoSQL database is designed to be high-performance in terms of speed, scalability, and availability. It achieves this performance by dropping relational-database features such as strongly linked relationships between tables.

- A CQRS architecture separates the read operations from the write operations, which allows you to improve the read side's performance by storing the data in a form that matches the query, known as a projection.

- The Book App has been augmented by the ability to store a projection of the SQL Book on the read side of the CQRS architecture, which uses a Cosmos DB database. This approach improves performance, especially with lots of entries.

- The design used to implement the SQL/Cosmos DB CQRS architecture uses an integration event (see chapter 12).

- The Cosmos DB database works differently from relational databases, and the process of adding this database to the Book App exposes many of these differences.

- The EF Core 5 Cosmos DB database provider has many limitations, which are discussed and overcome in this chapter. But it is still possible to implement a useful app with Cosmos DB.

- The updated Book App shows that the Cosmos DB database can provide superior read performance over a similarly priced SQL Server database.

- The SQL/Cosmos DB CQRS design is suitable for adding to an existing application where read-side performance needs a boost, but it does add a time cost to every addition or update of data.

- Relational databases are more like one another than they are like NoSQL databases, due to the standardization of the SQL language. But you need to make some changes and checks if you change from one type of relational database to another.

Unit testin
EF Core applicatio

This chapter covers

- Simulating a database for unit testing
- Using the database type as your production app for unit testing
- Using an SQLite in-memory database for unit testing
- Solving the problem of one database access breaking another part of your test
- Capturing logging information while unit testing

This chapter is about unit testing applications that use EF Core for database ac
You'll learn what unit testing approaches are available for working with EF
and how to choose the correct tools for your specific needs. I also describe nu
ous methods and techniques to make your unit testing both comprehensive
efficient. Personally, I think unit testing is useful, and I use it a lot. It makes
better developer because I can catch bugs both when I develop the code and, r
important, when I refactor the code.

But although I really like unit testing, I'm also aware that writing unit tests
development effort, including refactoring unit tests as the application grows.

the years, I have learned a lot of tips and techniques for unit testing, and I have built a library called EfCore.TestSupport to help me, and you, write unit tests quickly and efficiently.

Unit testing is a big subject, with whole books dedicated to the topic. I focus on the narrow but important area of unit testing applications that use EF Core for database accesses. To make this chapter focused, I don't explain the basics of unit testing, but leap right in. Therefore, I recommend skipping this chapter if you're new to unit testing and coming back to it after you've read up on the subject. This chapter won't make any sense without that background, and I don't want to discourage you from unit testing because I make it look too hard.

> **MORE INFO** For an introduction to unit testing in .NET, try this video: http:// mng.bz/K44E. For much more in-depth coverage of unit testing, I recommend Vladimir Khorikov's *Unit Testing Principles, Practices, and Patterns* (Manning, 2020; https://www.manning.com/books/unit-testing).

OK, if you're still with me, I assume that you know what unit testing is and have at least written some unit tests. I'm not going to cover the differences between unit tests and integration tests, acceptance tests, and so on. I'm also not here to persuade you that unit tests are useful; I assume that you're convinced of their usefulness and want to learn tips and techniques for unit testing an EF Core application.

> **NOTE** I call all of my tests *unit tests*, but some people use the term *integration tests* for tests that use a real database.

As I said, I use unit tests a lot. I have more than 700 unit tests in this book's GitHub repo, some to check that my Book App works and some to check that what I say in the book is correct. Those tests make me much more confident that what the book says is correct and that the Book App runs properly. Some of the code in the part 3 Book App is pretty complex, which is where unit tests become most useful.

> **NOTE** Arthur Vickers, who is the engineering manager of EF Core, put out a tweet to say that EF Core has more than 70,000 unit tests (using xUnit). See http://mng.bz/D18y for the facts and timings.

One other thing I have learned is that I want my unit tests to run as quickly as possible, because a quick test-debug cycle makes developing and refactoring an application a much nicer experience. Also, I'm much more likely to run all my unit tests if those tests are quick, which might catch bugs in places I didn't think would be affected by my new code. I summarize these two aspects of unit testing in figure 17.1.

The rest of the chapter starts with the basics, looks at ways you could write your unit tests, and finally presents specific tips and problems you might have when testing your EF Core code. The sections in this chapter are

- An introduction to the unit test setup
- Getting your application's DbContext ready for unit testing

The two aspects of efficiency in unit testing

Fast to develop

Of course you want to develop unit tests quickly, but that needs planning. Think about:
- What tools can you find to make you more efficient?
- Will the way you simulate your database still work as your application grows?

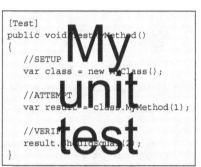

```
[Test]
public void TestMyMethod()
{
    //SETUP
    var class = new MyClass();

    //ATTEMPT
    var result = class.MyMethod(1);

    //VERIFY
    result.ShouldEqual(2);
}
```

Fast to run

The quicker your unit tests run, the more you will use unit tests.
- When developing a class, you may run one set of unit tests 10 or 20 times.
- The faster the whole test suite runs, the more likely you are to run it after a change.

Figure 17.1 I believe wholeheartedly in unit tests, but that doesn't mean I want to spend a lot of time developing or running them. My approach is to try to be efficient at using them, which splits into developing quickly and not having to hang around while the tests run.

- Three ways to simulate the database when testing EF Core applications
  - Using a production-type database in your unit tests
  - Using an SQLite in-memory database for unit testing
  - Stubbing or mocking an EF Core database
- Unit testing a Cosmos DB database
- Seeding a database with test data to test your code correctly
- Solving the problem of one database access breaking another part of your
- Capturing the database commands sent to a database

17.1 An introduction to the unit test setup

Before I start explaining the techniques, I need to introduce our unit test setup; erwise, the examples won't make any sense. I use a fairly standard approach, b you'll see, I've also created tools to help with the EF Core and database side of testing. Figure 17.2 shows a unit test that uses some of the features and methods ered in this chapter.

> **NOTE** All the unit tests in this chapter (apart from the Cosmos DB section, 17.8) use sync methods; they call SaveChanges, not SaveChangesAsync, for example. I do that partly because the code is a little bit easier to understand without the await code, but in real life, I use sync methods whenever I can because sync code provides better exception StackTrace results and is easier to debug when using breakpoints.

This section covers

- The test environment you'll be using: the xUnit unit test library
- A NuGet package I created to help with unit testing EF Core applications

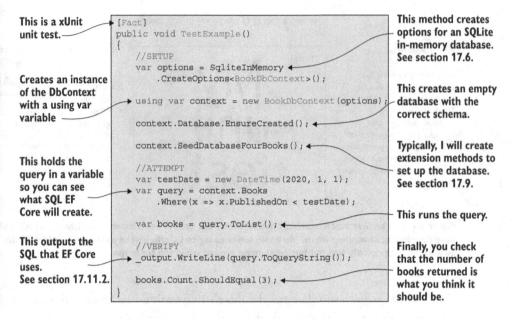

Figure 17.2 A unit test with three parts: Setup, Attempt, and Verify (also known as Arrange, Act, and Assert). The figure also shows some EF Core techniques that will be explained in this chapter.

1 The test environment: xUnit unit test library

I'm using the xUnit unit test library (see https://xunit.net) because Microsoft supports it well and because the EF Core team uses it. Also, xUnit is quicker than some other unit test frameworks, such as NUnit (which I used to use), because xUnit can run unit test classes in parallel. Running tests in parallel has a downside, which I show you how to get around, but it does mean that you can run your complete unit test suite a lot quicker.

I also use *fluent validation, which uses a series of extension methods that flow one after another*; see row 1 in table 17.1. I find the fluent validation style to be much easier to work with than the static Assert methods approach; it's slightly shorter, and Intellisense can suggest the fluent validation methods that are appropriate.

Table 17.1 Two approaches to checking that two books were loaded by the previous query that was under test. The static Assert methods are built into XUnit; the fluent validation style has to be added as an extra step.

Type	Example code
Fluent validation style	`books.Count().ShouldEqual(2);`
Static Assert method style	`Assert.Equal(2, books.Count());`

You can find these fluent validation extension methods at http://mng.bz/l2Ej, but you can create your own; they are normal C# extension methods. I've included the

sample xUnit fluent validation extension methods, plus a few extra fluent validat
in the NuGet package called EfCore.TestSupport that I've built. See section 17.1.

The following listing shows a simple unit test that employs the xUnit unit test p
age and the fluent validation extensions. This example uses a three-stage patte
Setup, Attempt, and Verify, shown as //SETUP, //ATTEMPT, and //VERIFY in the
test code in this chapter. Setup, Attempt, and Verify are also known as Arrange,
and Assert, but because I'm dyslexic, I prefer //SETUP, //ATTEMPT, and //VERIFY i
code because they look quite different.

> **Listing 17.1 A simple example xUnit unit test method**

The [Fact] attribute tells the unit test runner that
this method is an xUnit unit test that should be run.

```
[Fact]
public void DemoTest()
{
    //SETUP
    const int someValue = 1;

    //ATTEMPT
    var result = someValue * 2;

    //VERIFY
    result.ShouldEqual(2);
}
```

This line is where you run the code you want to test.

The method must be public. It
should return void or, if you're
running async methods, a Task.

Typically, you put code here
that sets up the data and/or
environment for the unit test.

Here is where you put the
test(s) to check that the
result of your test is correct.

You can run your unit tests by using Visual Studio's built-in Test Explorer, which
access from the Test menu. If you're using Visual Studio Code (VS Code), the test
ner is also built in, but you need to set up the build and test tasks in the VS (
tasks.json file, which allows you to run all the tests via the Task > Test command.

17.1.2 A library I created to help with unit testing EF Core applications

I learned a lot about unit testing EF Core applications as I built the software that
with the first edition of this book. As a result, I built an open source library c
EfCore.TestSupport (see https://github.com/JonPSmith/EfCore.TestSupport)
contains lots of methods that are useful in the Setup stage of a unit test method.

The EfCore.TestSupport library differentiate between EF Core 2 and EF Co
using the netstandard they used, but now that EF Core 5 is out, that differenti
doesn't work anymore. Therefore, I aligned the EfCore.TestSupport library t
Core via the first part of the version number. For EF Core 5, for example, you
EfCore.TestSupport version 5.

> **NOTE** Readers who are already using my EfCore.TestSupport library should
> be aware that I also took the opportunity to tidy up the EfCore.TestSupport
> library, which introduced breaking changes. The SqliteInMemory has changes
> (see section 17.6), some methods are now obsolete, and I moved the EfSchema-
> Compare code to another library. See http://mng.bz/BK5v for more details.

This chapter uses many of the methods in the EfCore.TestSupport library, but I don't detail their signatures because the EfCore.TestSupport wiki (see http://mng.bz/dmND) contains documentation for this library. But I'll explain the how and why of unit testing by using some of the methods from my EfCore.TestSupport library and showing some of the code I developed too.

Getting your application's DbContext ready for unit testing

Before you can unit test your application's DbContext with a database, you need to ensure that you can alter the database connection string. Otherwise, you can't provide a different database(s) for unit testing. The technique you use depends on how the application's DbContext expects the options to be set. The two approaches that EF Core provides for setting the options are as follows:

- The application's DbContext expects the options to be provided via its constructor. This approach is recommended for ASP.NET Core and .NET Generic Host applications.
- The application's DbContext sets the options internally in the OnConfiguring method. This approach is recommended for applications that don't use dependency injection.

The application's DbContext options are provided via its constructor

If the options are provided via the application's DbContext constructor, you don't need any changes to the application's DbContext to work with the unit test. You already have total control of the options given to the application's DbContext constructor; you can change the database connection string, the type of database provider it uses, and so on. The following listing shows the format of an application's DbContext that uses a constructor to obtain its options. The constructor is shown in bold.

Listing 17.2 An application DbContext that uses a constructor for option setting

```
public class EfCoreContext : DbContext
{
    public EfCoreContext(
        DbContextOptions<EfCoreContext> options)
        : base(options) {}

    public DbSet<Book> Books { get; set; }
    public DbSet<Author> Authors { get; set; }

    //… rest of the class left out
}
```

For this type of application's DbContext, the unit test can create the options variable and provide that value as a parameter in the application's DbContext constructor. The

next listing shows an example of creating an instance of your application's DbCo
in a unit test that will access an SQL Server database, with a specific connection st

Listing 17.3 Creating a DbContext by providing the options via a constructor

**Defines that you want to use the
SQL Server database provider**

**Holds the connection string
for the SQL Server database**

```
const string connectionString
    = "Server= … content removed as too long to show";
var builder = new
    DbContextOptionsBuilder<EfCoreContext>();
builder.UseSqlServer(connectionString);
var options = builder.Options;
using (var context = new EfCoreContext(options))
{
    //… unit test starts here
```

**You need to create the
DbContextOptionsBuild
<T> class to build the
options.**

**Builds the final DbContext
<EfCoreContext> option
the application's DbConte**

**Allows you to create an instance
for your unit tests**

17.2.2 Setting an application's DbContext options via OnConfiguring

If the database options are set in the OnConfiguring method inside the applicat
DbContext, you must modify your application's DbContext before you can use
unit testing. But before you change the application's DbContext, I want to show
the normal arrangement of using the OnConfiguring method to set the options
the bold text in the following listing).

Listing 17.4 A DbContext that uses the OnConfiguring method to set options

```
public class DbContextOnConfiguring : DbContext
{
    private const string connectionString
        = "Server=(localdb)\\... shortened to fit";

    protected override void OnConfiguring(
        DbContextOptionsBuilder optionsBuilder)
    {
        optionsBuilder.UseSqlServer(connectionString);
        base.OnConfiguring(optionsBuilder);
    }
    // … other code removed
}
```

The next listing shows Microsoft's recommended way to change a DbContext that
the OnConfiguring method to set up the options. As you'll see, this technique
the same sort of constructor setup that ASP.NET Core uses while making sure tha
OnConfiguring method still works in the normal application.

Listing 17.5 An altered DbContext allowing the connection string to be set by the unit test

```
public class DbContextOnConfiguring : DbContext
{
    private const string ConnectionString
        = "Server=(localdb)\\ … shortened to fit";

    protected override void OnConfiguring(
        DbContextOptionsBuilder optionsBuilder)
    {
        if (!optionsBuilder.IsConfigured)
        {
            optionsBuilder
                .UseSqlServer(ConnectionString);
        }
    }

    public DbContextOnConfiguring(
        DbContextOptions<DbContextOnConfiguring>
        options)
        : base(options) { }

    public DbContextOnConfiguring() { }
    // … other code removed
}
```

Changes the OnConfigured method to run its normal setup code only if the options aren't already configured

Adds the same constructor-based options settings that the ASP.NET Core version has, which allows you to set any options you want

Adds a public, parameterless constructor so that this DbContext works normally with the application

To use this modified form, you can provide options in the same way you did with the ASP.NET Core version, as shown in the following listing.

Listing 17.6 A unit test providing a different connection string to the DbContext

Holds the connection string for the database to be used for the unit test

```
const string connectionString
    = "Server=(localdb)\\... shortened to fit";
var builder = new
    DbContextOptionsBuilder
        <DbContextOnConfiguring>();
builder.UseSqlServer(connectionString);
var options = builder.Options;
using (var context = new
    DbContextOnConfiguring(options)
{
    //… unit test starts here
```

Sets up the options you want to use

Provides the options to the DbContext via a new, one-parameter constructor

Now you're good to go for unit testing.

Three ways to simulate the database when testing EF Core applications

If you unit test your application, and it includes accesses to a database, you have several ways to simulate the database. Over the years, I've tried several approaches to simulating the database in a unit test, ranging from a library that mocks the DbContext in

EF6 called Effort (see https://entityframework-effort.net/overview) to using real ·
bases. This chapter covers some of those approaches and a few new tactics tha·
Core offers.

NOTE I cover stubbing and mocking in much more detail in section 17.7.

Early consideration of how to unit test with a database can save you a lot of pain l·
especially if you're using EF Core. When I started writing the first edition of this b·
I found that the unit testing approach I used at the start didn't work with the r·
SQL-based parts of the book, so I had to refactor some of my early unit tests, and·
was a bit of a pain.

But that experience wasn't new. In some of my projects, I later regretted my ·
decisions on unit testing, as the tests started to fall apart as the projects grew. Altho·
some reworking of early unit tests is inevitable, you want to minimize rework, bec·
it slows you down. Therefore, I want to describe different ways to unit test code·
EF Core so that you can make an informed decision about how to write your·
tests. Figure 17.3 summarizes the three main ways you can test code that con·
database accesses.

Three ways unit test your EF Core code, with pros and cons

	Use same db type as production	Use SQLite in-memory db	Stubbing the database
PROS:	• Perfect match to production db • Handles SQL features	• Quick to run • Has correct schema • Starts empty	• Gives total control of the data access • Quick to run
CONS:	• Needs unique db per unit test class • Takes time to create schema/empty db	• Doesn't support some SQL commands • Doesn't work like the production db	• Can't test some db code, like relationships • You need to write more code.
BEST FOR:	When your code includes raw SQL features	When your code uses only LINQ commands	When you want to test complex business logic

Figure 17.3 **You have three main ways to provide access to a database when you are testing your code. Each approach has pros and cons, and the main ones are listed in the figure.**

DEFINITION The term *production database* refers to the database type/provider used by your application in production. If you are running an ASP.NET Core web application using EF Core, for example, and that application uses an SQL Server database, a production database type is SQL Server. In that case, using the same database type as production means that SQL Server databases will be used in your unit tests.

There is no right answer as to which approach is best for you—only a series of trade-offs between your unit tests running in the same way as your production application and the time to write and run your unit tests. The safe solution is to use a database that is the same as your production database type. But I often use a mixture of all three of these approaches when I am unit testing some applications.

Before I describe the three approaches to simulating the database, section 17.4 digs deeper into the differences between the first two approaches. This section gives you more information to help you decide whether you can test your application with the SQLite in-memory database or need to use unit test databases of the same type as your production database.

Choosing between a production-type database and an SQLite in-memory database

In this section, I give you the information you need to decide whether to use a production-type database or an SQLite in-memory database. You should consider using an SQLite in-memory database because it is easier for unit testing, creating a new database every time. As a result

- The database schema is always up to date.
- The database is empty, which is a good starting point for a unit test.
- Running your unit tests in parallel works because each database is held locally in each test.
- Your unit tests will run successfully in the Test part of a DevOps pipeline without any other settings.
- Your unit tests are faster.

The downside is that the SQLite database doesn't support and/or match some SQL commands in your production database, so your unit tests will fail or, in a few cases, give you incorrect results. If this possibility worries you, you should ignore SQLite and use the same database type as your production database for unit testing (see section 17.5).

If you want to consider using SQLite for unit testing, you need to know how different it might be from your production database. The simple answer is "a lot," but to help you understand what might cause problems, I've prepared table 17.2. This table lists the features that could cause problems when you use SQLite for unit testing. The far-right column lists the possible outcome of using the feature:

- *Wrong answer*—The feature might work but give you the wrong answer (which, in unit testing, is the worst result). You must be careful to run the test with a production-type database or make sure that you understand the limitations and work around them.
- *Might break*—The feature might work correctly in your unit test code, but in some cases, it might throw an exception. You can test this feature with SQLite, but you might have to change to a production-type database if a unit test fails.

- *Will break*—The feature is likely to fail when the database is set up (but m
  work if the SQL is basic). This result rules out using an SQLite in-mer
  database.

Table 17.2 The SQL features that EF Core can control but that aren't going to work with S
because SQLite doesn't support the feature or because SQLite uses a different format from SQL S
MySQL, and so on

SQL feature	See section	SQLite support?	Breaks
String compare and collations	2.8.3	Works but provides different results	Wrong ans
Different schemas	7.12.2	Not supported; ignores config	Wrong ans
SQL column default value	10.3	C# constants work; SQL is likely to fail	Might brea
SQL computed columns	10.2	SQL is different; likely to fail	Will break
Any raw SQL	11.5	SQL is different; very likely to fail	Will break
SQL sequences	10.4	Not supported exception	Will break

Also, the following C# types aren't natively supported by SQLite, so they could
duce the wrong value:

- `Decimal`
- `UInt64`
- `DateTimeOffset`
- `TimeSpan`

EF Core will throw an exception if you sort/filter on a property that is of type Dec
while running on SQLite, for example. If you still want to unit test with SQLite,
can add a value converter to convert the `Decimal` to a `double` (see section 7.13)
that approach might not return the exact `Decimal` value you saved to the database

So if you use any of the features in table 17.2 that will break, you definitely c
want to use SQLite for unit testing. But you also need to consider what you pla
add to your application, because if you add code that uses "will break" features,
are going to have to change all your unit tests to use a database of the same typ
your production database, which can be a real pain.

If you're not using, and are unlikely to use, the "will break" features shown in
17.2, SQLite could be a good choice for most of your unit tests. You can switc
using a production-type test database for the "might break" features, which is w
do for EF Core applications that don't use much raw SQL features.

> **NOTE** I haven't yet covered the pros and cons of the third option in figure 17.3:
> stubbing the database (see section 17.7). Stubbing the database is a different
> approach from using SQLite or a production-type database because stub-
> bing tries to remove all the database code from the unit test. For that reason,

stubbing the database doesn't test any of your EF Core code. Therefore, I start with the two approaches that do include EF Core: using an SQLite in-memory database and using a production-type database.

Using a production-type database in your unit tests

This section covers using a production-type database for your unit testing, which is the best way to unit test because your unit test databases are fully compatible with your production database. The downside is that the database is more complex to set up than in the SQLite in-memory database approach (see section 17.6), as well as slightly slower to run. You need to solve four issues to use a production-type database in your unit tests:

- Providing a connection string to the database to use for the unit test
- Providing a database per test class to allow xUnit to run tests in parallel
- Making sure that the database's schema is up to date and the database is empty
- Mimicking the database setup that the EF Core's migrations would deliver

Interestingly, the SQLite in-memory approach overcomes the first three items in the list by its design alone, and the last item, which deals with SQL embedded in your migrations, is something that the SQLite in-memory approach can't handle because the SQL code is likely to be different. The list of four issues you must meet to run a unit test is a good indication of the extra work involved in finding the best way to unit test code that includes database accesses. But help is on hand via my EfCore.TestSupport library, which provides extension methods that help you set up the database options, deal with the "database per test class" problem, and make sure that the database schema is up to date and empty of data.

NOTE The following examples use an SQL Server database, but the approaches work equally well with database types other than Cosmos DB, which has its own section (17.8).

Providing a connection string to the database to use for the unit test

To access any database, you need a connection string (see section 5.4.1). You could define a connection string as a constant and use that, but as you'll see, that approach isn't as flexible as you'd want. Therefore, in this section you'll mimic what ASP.NET Core does by adding to your test project a simple appsettings.json file that holds the connection string. Then you'll use some of the .NET configuration packages to access the connection string in your application. The appsettings.json file looks something like this:

```
{
  "ConnectionStrings": {
    "UnitTestConnection": "Server=(localdb)\\mssqllocaldb;Database=... etc"
  }
}
```

WARNING You should not put a connection string that contain private keys, passwords, and so on in the appsetting.json file, as those elements may leak when you store your code in source control. .NET has a feature called *user secrets* that is built into ASP.NET Core (see http://mng.bz/rmYg), and you can use user secrets in your unit tests by using the AddUserSecrets method.

Listing 17.7 shows the GetConfiguration method from my EfCore.TestSup library. This method loads an appsettings.json file from the top-level directory o assembly that calls it, which would be the assembly in which you're running your tests.

> **Listing 17.7** GetConfiguration **method allowing access to the appsettings.json**

Returns IConfigurationRoot, from which you can use methods
such as GetConnectionString("ConnectionName") to access
the configuration information

In the TestSupport librar
method returns the absc
path of the calling assem
top-level directory (the
assembly that you're
running your tests in).

```
public static IConfigurationRoot GetConfiguration()
{
    var callingProjectPath =
        TestData.GetCallingAssemblyTopLevelDir();
    var builder = new ConfigurationBuilder()
        .SetBasePath(callingProjectPath)
        .AddJsonFile("appsettings.json", optional: true);
    return builder.Build();
}
```

Uses ASP.NET Core's ConfigurationBuilder
to read that appsettings.json file. It's
optional, so no error is thrown if the
configuration file doesn't exist.

Calls the Build method, which
returns the IConfigurationRoot type

You can use the GetConfigration method to access the connection string and use this code to create an application's DbContext:

```
var config = AppSettings.GetConfiguration();
config.GetConnectionString("UnitTestConnection");
var builder = new DbContextOptionsBuilder<EfCoreContext>();
builder.UseSqlServer(connectionString);
using var context = new EfCoreContext(builder.Options);
// … rest of unit test left out
```

That code solves the problem of getting a connection string, but you still have problem of having different databases for each test class because by default, x runs unit tests in parallel. This topic is covered in section 17.5.2.

17.5.2 Providing a database per test class to allow xUnit to run tests in parallel

Because xUnit can run each class of unit tests in parallel, using one database fo your tests wouldn't work. Good unit tests need a known starting point and sh return a known result, which rules out using one database, as different tests will si taneously change the database.

NOTE You can run xUnit sequentially (see the "Changing Default Behavior" section of this xUnit documentation at https://xunit.net/docs/running-tests-in-parallel), but I don't recommend doing that because it will slow the running of your unit tests.

One common solution is to have separately named databases for each unit test class or possibly each unit test method. The EfCore.TestSupport library contains methods that produce an SQL Server DbContextOptions<T> result in which the database name is unique to a test class or method. Figure 17.4 shows the two methods. The first method creates a database with a name unique to this class, and the second one produces a database with a name that's unique to that class and method.

The result of using either of these classes is that each test class or method has its own uniquely named database. So when unit tests are run in parallel, each test class has its own database to test against.

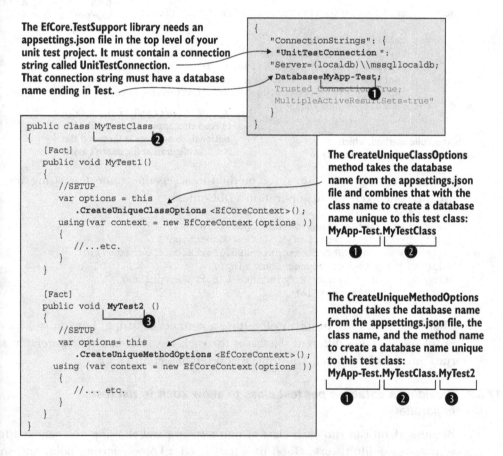

Figure 17.4 Two methods that set up the database options for an SQL Server database but alter the database name to be class-unique or class-and-method-unique. When you run multiple unit test classes, they have their own databases, so they won't interfere with each other.

TIP   xUnit runs each test class in parallel; but within a class, it runs each test serially. For this reason, I normally use a class-unique database. I use a class-and-method-unique database rarely, but it's there if I need it.

The next listing shows the code inside the CreateUniqueClassOptions exten method. This code encapsulates all the settings of the DbContext options to save from having to include them in every unit test.

> **Listing 17.8**   `CreateUniqueClassOptions` extension method with a helper

It's expected that the object instance provided will be this—the class in which the unit test is running.

Returns options for an SQL Server database w a name starting with the database name in th original connection string in the appsettings.j file, but with the name of the class of the instance provided in the first parameter

```
public static DbContextOptions<T>
    CreateUniqueClassOptions<T>(
        this object callingClass,
        Action<DbContextOptionsBuilder<T>> builder = null)
    where T : DbContext
{
    return CreateOptionWithDatabaseName<T>
        (callingClass, builder);
}

private static DbContextOptions<T>
    CreateOptionWithDatabaseName<T>(
        object callingClass,
        Action<DbContextOptionsBuilder<T>> extraOptions,
        string callingMember = null)
    where T : DbContext
{
    var connectionString = callingClass
        .GetUniqueDatabaseConnectionString(callingMember);
    var builder = new DbContextOptionsBuilder<T>();
    builder.UseSqlServer(connectionString);
    builder.ApplyOtherOptionSettings();
    extraOptions?.Invoke(builder);
    return builder.Options;
}
```

Calls a private ethod shared between this thod and the reateUnique-ethodOptions options

Builds the SQL Server part of the options, with the correct database name

This par allows y add mor methods building options.

These paramete passed from Cr UniqueClassOpt CreateUniqueCla the calling meth as null.

Returns the connection tring from the ppsetting.json e, but with the latabase name nodified to use the calling-Class's type ame as a suffix

Sets up OptionsB and creates an S database provide the connection st

Returns the DbContextOptions<T> to configure the application's DbContext

Calls a general method used on a option builders, enabling sensitiv logging and better error messag

Applies any extra option methods that the caller provided

xUnit's parallel-running feature has some other constraints. The use of static varia (static constants are fine) to carry information causes problems, for example, as d ent tests may set a static variable to different values in parallel. Nowadays, we d use statics much because dependency injection fills that gap. But if you use static ables in your code, you should turn off parallel running in xUnit so that you run tests serially.

3 Making sure that the database's schema is up to date and the database is empty

Section 17.5.2 shows how to create unique databases for your tests, but you still have the problem of making sure that a database's schema is up to date and empty when you rerun a test. When I say that the "database's schema is up to date," I mean that the database's schema matches the database model that EF Core creates by scanning your entity classes and any EF Core configuration code you have applied to your application's DbContext.

Unlike your application, which will use some form of migration to update the entity classes or EF Core configuration, your unit tests will use EF Core's Ensure-Create/EnsureCreatedAsync methods to make sure that you have a database to work with. These methods create a database with an up-to-date schema using the current entity classes and configuration of your application's DbContext, but only if there isn't an existing database of the same name. After the first run of the unit test, the database's schema is fixed, so its schema will be out of date if you change the EF Core configuration or any of the entity classes. Therefore, you need a way to make sure that the database has an up-to-date schema and, at the same time, provide an empty database as a starting point for a unit test.

Let's start with a foolproof but slow method. Listing 17.9 shows Microsoft's recommended way to create an empty database with the correct schema without using migrations. These two EF Core methods delete and create databases; the create-database method builds the database schema up by using the current EF Core configuration and entity classes. The following listing shows a call to the EnsureDeleted method first to delete the database and then calls EnsureCreated to build the correct schema with no data in it.

> **Listing 17.9 The foolproof way to create a database that's up to date and empty**

```
[Fact]
public void TestExampleSqlDatabaseOk()
{
    //SETUP
    var options = this
        .CreateUniqueClassOptions<EfCoreContext>();
    using (var context = new EfCoreContext(options))
    {
        context.Database.EnsureDeleted();        ← Deletes the current
        context.Database.EnsureCreated();        database (if present)
        //... rest of test removed                ← Creates a new database, using
                                                  the configuration inside your
                                                  application's DbContext
```

Because listing 17.9 uses EfCore.testSupport's CreateUniqueClassOptions method, each unit test in that class uses the same database, but each unit test method deletes and re-creates the database in the Setup stage of the test.

This approach used to be slow (~10 seconds) for an SQL Server database, but since the new SqlClient library came out in .NET 5, it's been much quicker (~ 1.5 seconds),

which makes a big difference in how long a unit test would take to run with
EnsureDeleted/EnsureCreated version.

> **NOTE** How long EnsureDeleted/EnsureCreated takes depends on the data-
> base. When I was writing the first edition of this book, a delete/create of an
> SQL Server database used to take about 10 seconds, but a MySQL database
> took only 1 second. You need to test your own database types to see how long
> it takes to delete and re-create the database.

Another approach, suggested by Arthur Vickers of the EF Core team, is a method
the team uses in its unit tests: EnsureClean. This clever method removes the cur
schema of the database by deleting all the SQL indexes, constraints, tables, seque
UDFs, and so on in the database. Then, by default, it calls the EnsureCreated me
to return a database that has the correct schema and is empty of data.

The EnsureClean method is deep inside EF Core's unit tests, but I extracted
code and built the other parts needed to make it useful; it is available in
EfCore.TestSupport version 5. The following listing shows how to use this metho
your unit tests.

Listing 17.10 Using the `EnsureClean` method to update the database's schema

```
[Fact]
public void TestExampleSqlServerEnsureClean()
{
    //SETUP
    var options = this.
        CreateUniqueClassOptions<BookDbContext>();

    using var context = new BookDbContext(options);

    context.Database.EnsureClean();      ⟵  Wipes the data and schema in the
                                             database and then calls EnsureCreated
    //... rest of test removed               to set up the correct schema
}
```

EnsureClean approach is faster, maybe twice as fast as the EnsureDeleted/Ens
Created version, which could make a big difference in how long your unit tests ta
run. It's also better when your database server doesn't allow you to delete or c
new databases but does allow you to read/write a database, such as when your
databases are on an SQL server on which you don't have admin privileges.

> **NOTE** At the moment, the EnsuredClean method works only for SQL Server,
> but the method could be improved to handle other database types. If a data-
> base type already has a quick EnsureDeleted/EnsureCreated run time, how-
> ever, it's not worth extending.

The final approach to obtaining a database for use in a unit test is unusual but ca
useful in some situations. It works by applying changes to the database only with

transaction. This approach works because when the transaction is disposed, if you haven't called the `transaction.Commit` method, it rolls back all the changes made in a database while the transaction is active. As a result, each unit test starts with the same data every time.

This approach is useful if you have an example database, maybe copied from the production database (with personal data anonymized, of course), that you want to test against, but you don't want the example database to be changed. I used this approach for a client who had an example database (1 TB in size and held in Azure). Using the transaction version allowed me to run some of the client's code to understand what it changed in the database without changing the database's content.

To use this transaction version, you must create a transaction immediately after you create the application's DbContext, and you must hold the transaction in a variable that will be disposed at the end of the unit test. In the following listing, I achieve that effect via the using var keywords.

Listing 17.11 Using a transaction to roll back any database changes made in the test

```
[Fact]
public void TestUsingTransactionToRollBackChanges()
{
    //SETUP
    var builder = new
        DbContextOptionsBuilder<BookDbContext>();      You most likely
    builder.UseSqlServer(_connectionString);           will link to a
    using var context =                                database via a
        new BookDbContext(builder.Options);            connection string.

    using var transaction =                            The transaction is held in a user
        context.Database.BeginTransaction();           var variable, which means that it
                                                       will be disposed when the current
    //ATTEMPT                                          block ends.
    var newBooks = BookTestData
        .CreateDummyBooks(10);        Run your
    context.AddRange(newBooks);      test ...
    context.SaveChanges();

    //VERIFY
    context.Books.Count().ShouldEqual(4+10);    ◄─────  ... and check
                                                        whether it worked.
}   ◄─────  When the unit test method ends, the
            transaction will be disposed and will roll back
            the changes made in the unit test. In this case,
            four books were already in the database.
```

4 Mimicking the database setup that EF Core migration would deliver

One problem I came across in unit testing occurred when my database had extra SQL commands that EF Core didn't add. If you use a UDF in your code, for example, how do you get that SQL into your unit test database? You have three solutions:

- For simple SQL, such as a UDF, you can execute a script file after the Ens
  Created method.
- If you've added your SQL to the EF Core migration files (see section 9.5.2)
  should call context.Database.Migrate instead of ....EnsureCreated.
- If you're using script-based migrations (see section 11.4), instead of ca
  EnsureCreated, you should execute the scripts to build the database.

The last two items have the solution detailed in the list, but the first item needs s
code. I created a method called ExecuteScriptFileInTransaction in my Efe
.TestSupport library. This method executes the SQL inside an SQL script file or
database that the application's DbContext is connected to. The format of the scr
in a Microsoft SQL Server Management Studio format: a set of SQL commands,
ending with a single line containing the SQL command GO. The following li
shows an SQL change script file that adds a UDF to a database.

Listing 17.12 An example SQL script file with GO at the end of each SQL command

Removes existing version of the UDF you want to add.
If you don't do this, the create function will fail.

```
IF OBJECT_ID('dbo.AuthorsStringUdf') IS NOT NULL
    DROP FUNCTION dbo.AuthorsStringUdf
GO
```

Adds a
er-defined
function to
e database

```
CREATE FUNCTION AuthorsStringUdf (@bookId int)
RETURNS NVARCHAR(4000)
-- … SQL commands removed to make the example shorter
RETURN @Names
END
GO
```

ExecuteScriptFileInTran
looks for a line starting
GO to split out each SQ
command to send to th
database.

The ExecuteScriptFileInTransaction extension method can apply an SQL scri
a database by using the format in listing 17.12. Listing 17.13 shows a typical wa
apply this script to a unit test database.

> **NOTE** The TestData.GetFilePath method in the following listing is another
> EfCore.TestSupport library method; it allows you to access files in a top-level
> directory called TestData in your Test project.

Listing 17.13 An example of applying an SQL script to a unit test database

```
[Fact]
public void TestApplyScriptExampleOk()
{
    var options = this
        .CreateUniqueClassOptions<EfCoreContext>();
    var filepath = TestData.GetFilePath(
        "AddUserDefinedFunctions.sql");
    using (var context = new EfCoreContext(options))
    {
        context.Database.EnsureDeleted();
        context.Database.EnsureCreated();
```

Gets the file path of th
SQL script file via your
TestData's GetFilePath
method

```
        context                                  Applies your script to the database by
            .ExecuteScriptFileInTransaction(     using the ExecuteScriptFileInTransaction
            filepath);                           method

    //… the rest of the unit test left out
    }
}
```

Using an SQLite in-memory database for unit testing

SQLite has a useful option for creating an in-memory database. This option allows a
unit test to create a new database in-memory, which means that it's isolated from any
other database. This approach solves all the problems of running parallel tests, having
an up-to-date schema, and ensuring that the database is empty, and it's fast. But see
section 17.4 for potential problems.

To make an SQLite database in-memory, you need to set DataSource to ":memory:",
as shown here. The code in listing 17.14 comes from the SqliteInMemory.Create-
Options method in my EfCore.TestSupport library.

NOTE The CreateOptions method in listing 17.14 returns a class called
DbContextOptionsDisposable<T>. This class implements the DbContext-
OptionsBuilder<T> type needed for creating an instance of your application's DbContext, and the IDisposable interface, which is used to dispose
the SQLite connection when the application's DbContext is disposed. I cover
this topic toward the end of this section.

Listing 17.14   Creating SQLite in-memory database `DbContextOptions<T>` options

This parameter allows you to add more   A class containing the SQLite in-memory
option methods while building the options.   options, which is also disposable

```
public static DbContextOptionsDisposable<T> CreateOptions<T>
    (Action<DbContextOptionsBuilder<T>> builder = null)
    where T : DbContext
{
    return new DbContextOptionsDisposable<T>          Gets the
        (SetupConnectionAndBuilderOptions<T>(builder)  DbContextOptions<T> and
            .Options);                                 returns a disposable version
}

private static DbContextOptionsBuilder<T>                Contains any extra
    SetupConnectionAndBuilderOptions<T>                  option methods the
    (Action<DbContextOptionsBuilder<T>> applyExtraOption)  user provided
    where T : DbContext
{
    var connectionStringBuilder =            Creates an SQLite connection
        new SqliteConnectionStringBuilder    string with the DataSource set
            { DataSource = ":memory:" };     to ":memory:"
    var connectionString = connectionStringBuilder.ToString();
```

**Turns the SQLiteConnectionStringBuilder
into a connection string**

Forms an SQLite connection by using the connection string

```
var connection = new SqliteConnection(connectionString);
connection.Open();

// create in-memory context
var builder = new DbContextOptionsBuilder<T>();
builder.UseSqlite(connection);
builder.ApplyOtherOptionSettings();
applyExtraOption?.Invoke(builder);

return builder;
}
```

You must open the SQ┃ connection. If you don'┃ the in-memory databa┃ won't work.

Builds a DbContextOption┃ with the SQLite database provider and the open connection

Returns the DbContextOptions<T> to use in the creation of your application's DbContext

Adds any extra options the user added

Calls a general method used on all your option builders, enabling sensitive logging and better error messages

Then you can use the SQLiteInMemory.CreateOptions method in one of your tests, as shown in the next listing. You should note that in this case, you need to only the EnsureCreated method, because no database currently exists.

Listing 17.15 Using an SQLite in-memory database in an xUnit unit test

```
[Fact]
public void TestSQLiteOk()
{
    //SETUP
    var options = SQLiteInMemory
        .CreateOptions<EfCoreContext>();

    using var context = new BookDbContext(options);

    context.Database.EnsureCreated();

    //ATTEMPT
    context.SeedDatabaseFourBooks();

    //VERIFY
    context.Books.Count().ShouldEqual(4);
}
```

The SQLiteInMemory.CreateOptions provides the options for an in-memory database. The options are also IDisposable.

ses that option to create your application's DbContext

You call context.Database .EnsureCreated to create the database.

Runs a test method you've written that adds four test books to the database

Checks that your SeedDatabaseFourBooks worked and adds four books to the database

At the end of the unit test, the context is disposed because you used a using var s ment to hold the application's DbContext instance. Disposing the context in disposes the options variable, which deletes the database by disposing the Sql Connection connection. Disposing the SqliteConnection connection follows the ommended practice in the EF Core documentation; see http://mng.bz/VG7X.

NOTE If you are using multiple instances of the application's DbContext, you need to postpone disposing the SqliteConnection connection by using the options.StopNextDispose or options.TurnOffDispose method (see section 17.10.2 for one way).

> ### What about EF Core's in-memory database provider for unit testing?
>
> EF Core has an in-memory database provider that the team uses in its testing, but the documentation states that this database is "not suitable for testing applications that use EF Core" (http://mng.bz/xGO8). Therefore, the team was surprised to get feedback that lots of people are using the in-memory database provider for unit testing.
>
> When I wrote the first edition of this book, I used the in-memory database provider and quickly found its limitations. For one thing, it doesn't work like a real relational database; therefore, it doesn't catch all the problems. When I found that SQLite had an in-memory mode, I swapped over to that database. It's not perfect, but it's *much* better than the EF Core in-memory database provider.

Stubbing or mocking an EF Core database

Moving away from using an actual database, let's look at the third approach depicted in figure 17.3: stubbing or mocking the database. Here are the definitions of the two approaches:

- *Stubbing* a database means creating some code that replaces the current database. Stubbing works well when you are using a repository pattern (see section 13.5.1).
- *Mocking* usually requires a mocking library such as Moq (see https://github .com/moq/moq4), which you use to take control of the class you are mocking. This task is basically impossible for EF Core; the closest library to mocking EF Core is EF Core's in-memory database provider.

NOTE This article provides more information on stubbing and mocking: http://mng.bz/A1Wp.

Having said that mocking isn't going to work, now I'll show an example that I use with the complex business logic described in section 4.2. In this pattern, I use a per-business logic repository pattern. Because business logic can be complex, often with complicated validation rules, I find stubbing to be a useful approach to replacing the database access. The stub provides a lot more control of the database access, and you can more easily simulate various error conditions, but it does take longer to write the mocking and unit tests.

As an example of this approach, I am going to stub the database when testing the business logic that handles orders for books. The book-order business logic method uses the repository pattern to separate database access code from the business logic because it makes the business logic code simpler; it also helps with unit testing because I can replace the database access code with a test class that can replace the database with a stub that matches the repository interface. I find that stubbing gives me much better control of the data going into, and out of, the method I'm testing.

This next example is taken from my unit tests in the book's GitHub repo; here, you want to test the PlaceOrderAction method developed in chapter 4. The PlaceOrder-Action class's constructor requires one parameter of type IPlaceOrderDbAccess,

which is normally the `PlaceOrderDbAccess` class that handles the database acce
But for testing, you replace the `PlaceOrderDbAccess` class with our test class—
stub that implements the same `IPlaceOrderDbAccess` interface. This stub class a
you to control what the `PlaceOrderAction` class can read from the database and
ture what it attempts to write to the database. The following listing shows a uni
that uses this mock, which captures the order that the `PlaceOrderAction` method
duces so that you can check whether the user's ID was set properly.

Listing 17.16 A unit test providing a stub instance to the `BizLogic`

Creates an instance of the mock database access code. This instance
has numerous controls, but in this case, you use the default settings.

```
[Fact]
public void ExampleOfStubbingOk()
{
    //SETUP
    var lineItems = new List<OrderLineItem>
    {
        new OrderLineItem {BookId = 1, NumBooks = 4}
    };
    var userId = Guid.NewGuid();
    var input = new PlaceOrderInDto(true, userId,
        lineItems.ToImmutableList());

    var stubDbA = new StubPlaceOrderDbAccess();
    var service = new PlaceOrderAction(stubDbA);

    //ATTEMPT
    service.Action(input);

    //VERIFY
    service.Errors.Any().ShouldEqual(false);
    mockDbA.AddedOrder.CustomerId
        .ShouldEqual(userId);
}
```

Creates the
input to the
PlaceOrderAction
method

Creates your
PlaceOrderAction
instance, providing
mock of the databas
access code

Checks that the order
placement completed
successfully

Your mock database access code
has captured the order that the
PlaceOrderAction's method "wrote"
to the database, so you can check
whether it was formed properly.

Runs the PlaceOrderAction's method
called Action, which takes in the input
data and outputs an order

The stub class, `StubPlaceOrderDbAccess`, doesn't access the database, but it has p
erties or methods that you can use to control every part of the reading of data
the database. This class also captures anything the `PlaceOrderAction` method tri
write to the database, so you can check that too. Listing 17.17 shows the stub data
class, `StubPlaceOrderDbAccess`. Note that I created a static method called Cre
DummyBooks to generate a known set of Books to use in this test (see section 17.9).

Listing 17.17   The stub database access code used for unit testing

Mock MockPlaceOrderDbAccess implements the IPlaceOrderDbAccess, which allows it to replace the normal PlaceOrderDbAccess class.

```
public class StubPlaceOrderDbAccess
    : IPlaceOrderDbAccess
{
    public ImmutableList<Book> DummyBooks
        { get; private set; }

    public Order AddedOrder { get; private set; }

    public StubPlaceOrderDbAccess(
        bool createLastInFuture = false,
        int? promoPriceFirstBook = null)
    {
        var numBooks = createLastInFuture
            ? DateTime.UtcNow.Year -
                EfTestData.DummyBookStartDate.Year + 2
            : 10;
        var books = EfTestData.CreateDummyBooks
            (numBooks, createLastInFuture);
        if (promotionPriceForFirstBook != null)
            books.First().Promotion = new PriceOffer
            {
                NewPrice = (int) promoPriceFirstBook,
                PromotionalText = "Unit Test"
            };
        DummyBooks = books.ToImmutableList();
    }

    public IDictionary<int, Book>
        FindBooksByIdsWithPriceOffers
        (IEnumerable<int> bookIds)
    {
        return DummyBooks.AsQueryable()
            .Where(x => bookIds.Contains(x.BookId))
            .ToDictionary(key => key.BookId);
    }

    public void Add(Order newOrder)
    {
        AddedOrder = newOrder;
    }
}
```

Holds the dummy books that the mock uses, which can be useful if the test wants to compare the output with the dummy database

In this case, you set up the mock via its constructor.

Allows you to check that a book that hasn't been published yet won't be accepted in an order

Allows you to add a PriceOffer to the first book so you can check that the correct price is recorded on the order

Adds a PriceOffer to the first book, if required

Creates a method to create dummy books for your test

Called to get the books that the input selected; uses the DummyBooks generated in the constructor

Called by the PlaceOrderAction's method to write the Order to the database. In this case, you capture the Order so that the unit test can inspect it.

As I said earlier, the stubbing code is long and a bit complicated to write, but because you copied the real PlaceOrderDbAccess class and then edited it, the job isn't too hard.

17.8   Unit testing a Cosmos DB database

Unit testing a Cosmos DB database doesn't fit any of the three approaches descri
in section 17.4, but it's closest to mocking the database because Microsoft has cre
an application called Azure Cosmos DB Emulator, which you can run on your d
opment PC and test against. Microsoft's documentation at http://mng.bz/RK8j s

> *The Azure Cosmos DB Emulator provides a high-fidelity emulation of the Azure Cosmos
> DB service. It supports equivalent functionality as the Azure Cosmos DB, which includes
> creating data, querying data, provisioning and scaling containers, and executing stored
> procedures and triggers.*

You need to download the Azure Cosmos DB Emulator from http://mng.bz/4
and run it locally. When you run the emulator, it provides a URL that takes yo
the emulator's quick-start web page, which contains details on accessing this Co
DB service. The emulator's website also has a useful Explorer (see figure 17.5)
provides full access and configuration of the databases, containers, and items w
a container.

NOTE   The Azure Cosmos DB Emulator is available only for Windows.

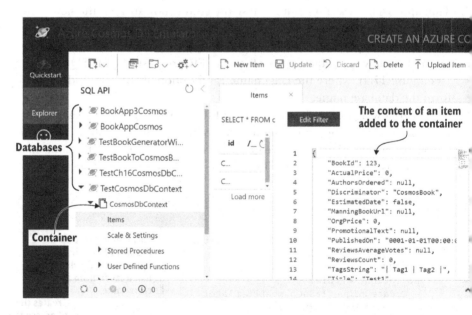

**Figure 17.5   When you run the Azure Cosmos DB Emulator, it gives you a URL to access information
about the Cosmos DB emulator settings on the quick-start page, as well as access to the emulated
Cosmos DB databases and containers via the Explorer page, as shown in this figure. The Explorer
page provides full access to and configuration of the databases, containers, and items within a
container.**

In section 16.5, you learned that to access a Cosmos DB service, you need a connection string, and the Emulator's quick-start page provides the connection string for you. The following listing shows how.

Listing 17.18   Setting up EF Core to access a Cosmos DB database

```
public async Task AccessCosmosEmulatorViaConnectionString()          The connection
{                                                                     string taken from
    //SETUP                                                           the quick-start
    var connectionString =                                           page of the
        "AccountEndpoint=https://localhost... rest left out"         emulator' website
    var builder = new
        DbContextOptionsBuilder<CosmosDbContext>()
    .UseCosmos(                                                       The connection string
        connectionString,                                            is provided first.
        "MyCosmosDatabase");
    using var context = new CosmosDbContext(builder.Options);

    //... rest of the unit test left out                            Creates an instance of the
}                                                                   application's DbContext
```

UseCosmos method is found in the   The name you want
Microsoft.EntityFrameworkCore.Cosmos   for the database
NuGet package.

That approach works fine, but because the connection string is the same wherever you run the emulator, you can build a method to set up the options automatically. I added methods of that type to the EfCore.TestSupport version 5 NuGet packages. These methods follow the same approach as the EfCore.TestSupport SQL Server methods (see figure 17.4), where the class name (and optionally the method name) is used to form the database name.

The following listing shows the use of EfCore.TestSupport's CreateUniqueClass-CosmosDbEmulator method to set up the options for an application DbContext called CosmosDbContext. This code creates a Cosmos database with the same name as the unit test class type, which makes the database unique in your project.

Listing 17.19   Unit testing Cosmos DB code by using the Cosmos DB Emulator

```
[Fact]
public async Task TestAccessCosmosEmulator()                This method sets up the
{                                                            Cosmos DB database
    //SETUP                                                  options with the database
    var options = this.                                      name taken from the
        CreateUniqueClassCosmosDbEmulator                   class name.
        <CosmosDbContext>();
                                                            Creates the DbContext
                                                            to access that
    using var context = new CosmosDbContext(options);      database

    await context.Database.EnsureDeletedAsync();           Creates an empty database
    await context.Database.EnsureCreatedAsync();           with the correct structure
```

```
    //… rest of unit test left out
}
```

As I stated in section 16.6.6, the `EnsureCreatedAsync` method is the recomme:
way to create an empty Cosmos DB database. Therefore, using the `EnsureDele`
`Async` and then `EnsureCreatedAsync` method is the correct way to delete and re-c
a Cosmos DB database. Fortunately, the process is quick.

17.9 Seeding a database with test data to test your code correctly

Often, a unit test needs certain data in the database before you can run a tes
test the code that handles orders for books, for example, you need some `Boo`
the database before you run the test. In cases like this one, you would add s
code in the Setup stage of the unit test to add those books before you test the c
code in the Verify stage.

My experience is that setting up the database with data to test some feature
real application can quite complex. In fact, setting up the database with the right
can be much harder than running and verifying the test's results. Here are some
on seeding a unit test database:

- It's OK at the start to write the setup code in the unit test, but as soon as
  find yourself copying that setup code, it's time to turn that code into a met
- I created two types of help methods in my Test project to help me set up
  data, and I gave them good names so I can quickly identify what they do.
  two types are
  - Ones that return the test data, with names such as `CreateFourBooks()`
    `CreateDummyBooks(int numBooks = 10)`. I use these methods when I wa
    test adding these types to the database.
  - Ones that write the test data to the database, with names such as `SeedD`
    `baseFourBooks()` and `AddDummyBooksToDb()`. These methods write the
    data to the database and normally return the added data so that I ca
    their primary keys to use in a test.
- Keep your test-data setup methods up to date, refactoring them as you c
  across different scenarios.
- Consider storing complex test data in a JSON file. I created a method to s
  ize data from a production system to a JSON file and have another method
  will deserialize that data and write it to the database. But make sure that
  anonymize any personal data before you save the JSON.
- The `EnsureCreated` method will also seed the database with data configure
  the `HasData` configuration (see section 9.4.3).

0 Solving the problem of one database access breaking another stage of your test

In section 17.9, I describe how to add data to the test database, referred to as *seeding* your database, before you run your test. But a problem can arise in your test because of EF Core's relational fixup stage (see section 6.1.1) in a database query. Every tracked database query (that is, a query without the AsNoTracking method in it) will try to reuse the instances of any the entities already tracking by the unit test's DbContext. The effect is that any tracked query can affect any tracked query after it, so it can affect the Attempt and Verify parts of your unit test.

An example is the best way to understand this concept. Suppose that you want to test your code for adding a new Review to a Book, and you wrote the code shown in the following snippet:

```
var book = context.Books
    .OrderBy(x => x.BookId).Last();
book.Reviews.Add( new Review{NumStars = 5});
context.SaveChanges();
```

But there's a problem with this code: it has a bug. The code should have Include(b => b.Reviews) added to the first line to ensure that the current Reviews are loaded first. But if you're not careful, your unit test will work as it does in the following listing.

> Listing 17.20 An INCORRECT simulation of a disconnected state, with the wrong result

```
[Fact]
public void INCORRECTtestOfDisconnectedState()
{
    //SETUP
    var options = SqliteInMemory
            .CreateOptions<EfCoreContext>();
    using var context = new EfCoreContext(options);

    context.Database.EnsureCreated();          | Sets up the test database with test
    context.SeedDatabaseFourBooks();           | data consisting of four books

    //ATTEMPT
    var book = context.Books                    | Reads in the last book from your test
        .OrderBy(x => x.BookId).Last();         | set, which you know has two reviews
    book.Reviews.Add(new Review { NumStars = 5 });
    context.SaveChanges();                       ←⌐ Saves the Review
                                                   | to the database
    //VERIFY
    //THIS IS INCORRECT!!!!!
    context.Books                               | Checks that you have three Reviews,
        .OrderBy(x => x.BookId).Last()          | which works, but the unit test should
        .Reviews.Count.ShouldEqual(3);          | have failed with an exception
}
```
Adds another Review to the book, which shouldn't
work but does because the seed data is still being
tracked by the DbContext instance

In fact, this unit test has two errors because of tracked entities:

- *Attempt* stage—Should have failed because the Reviews navigational pro was null, but works because of relational fixup from the Setup stage
- *Verify stage*—Should fail if a context.SaveChanges call was left out, but v because of relational fixup from the Attempt stage

To my mind, the worst outcome—even worse than not having a unit test—is a uni that works when it shouldn't so that you think something is fine when it isn't. look at ways to change the incorrect unit test in listing 17.20 so that it will fail prop Previously, there was only one way to handle this problem, but another approacl been possible since EF Core 5. The two approaches are

- Use EF Core 5's ChangeTracker.Clear method to clear the tracked entitie
- Use multiple instances within using scopes (original approach)

I find the EF Core 5's ChangeTracker.Clear approach to be quicker to write shorter, so I show it first, but I also show the original multiple-instances approac comparison purposes.

17.10.1 Test code using ChangeTracker.Clear in a disconnected state

The following listing solves the problem of the seeding data affecting the Att stage and the Attempt stage affecting the Verify stage. In this case, an excepti thrown, as the Reviews collection is null (assuming that you followed my recom dation in section 6.1.6). If the Attempt stage was fixed, the code in the Verify would be able to detect that SaveChanges wasn't called.

Listing 17.21 Using ChangeTracker.Clear to make the unit test work properly

```
[Fact]
public void UsingChangeTrackerClear()
{
    //SETUP
    var options = SqliteInMemory
        .CreateOptions<EfCoreContext>();
    using var context = new EfCoreContext(options);

    context.Database.EnsureCreated();          │ Sets up the test database
    context.SeedDatabaseFourBooks();           │ with test data consisting
                                               │ of four books

    context.ChangeTracker.Clear();

                                               │ Reads in the last book from
    //ATTEMPT                                  │ your test set, which you
    var book = context.Books                   │ know has two reviews
        .OrderBy(x => x.BookId).Last();
    book.Reviews.Add(new Review { NumStars = 5 });   ◄─────
```

Calls
ChangeTracker
.Clear to stop
tracking all
entities

When you try to add the new Review, EF Core throws a NullReferenceException because the Book's Review collection isn't loaded and therefore is null.

```
    context.SaveChanges();                    ◄──┐  Saves the Review
                                                  │  to the database
    //VERIFY
    context.ChangeTracker.Clear();

    context.Books.Include(b => b.Reviews)        Reloads the book with its
        .OrderBy(x => x.BookId).Last()           Reviews to check whether
        .Reviews.Count.ShouldEqual(3);           there are three Reviews
}
```

If you compare listing 17.21 with listing 17.22, you see that the code is shorter by nine lines, mainly because you don't need all the scoped using blocks in listing 17.22. I also find this approach to be slightly easier to read without all the scoped blocks.

0.2 Test code by using multiple DbContext instances in a disconnected state

The following listing uses two instances of the application's DbContext: one to set up the database and one to run the test. The test fails because an exception is thrown, as the Reviews collection is null (assuming that you followed my recommendation in section 6.1.6).

Listing 17.22   Three separate DbContext instances that make the test work properly

```
[Fact]
public void UsingThreeInstancesOfTheDbcontext()
{
    //SETUP                                       Creates the in-memory SQLite
    var options = SqliteInMemory                  options in the same way as the
        .CreateOptions<EfCoreContext>();          preceding example
    options.StopNextDispose();
    using (var context = new EfCoreContext(options))   ◄──┐  Creates the first instance
    {                                                      │  of the application's
                                                           │  DbContext
        context.Database.EnsureCreated();            Sets up the test database with test data
        context.SeedDatabaseFourBooks();        ◄──  consisting of four books, but this time
    }                                                in a separate DbContext instance
    options.StopNextDispose();
    using (var context = new EfCoreContext(options))
    {
        //ATTEMPT                                     Reads in the last book
        var book = context.Books                     from your test set, which
            .Include(x => x.Reviews)                  you know has two Reviews
            .OrderBy(x => x.BookId).Last();
        book.Reviews.Add(new Review { NumStars = 5 });   ◄─────────────────────┐

        context.SaveChanges();    ◄──┐  Calls SaveChanges to         When you try to
    }                                │  update the database          add the new Review,
    using (var context = new EfCoreContext(options))                 EF Core throws a
    {                                                                 NullReferenceException
                                                                      because the Book's
    Closes that last instance and opens a new instance of the        Review collection isn't
    application's DbContext. The new instance doesn't have            loaded and therefore
    any tracked entities that could alter how the test runs.         is null.
```

```
//VERIFY
context.Books.Include(b => b.Reviews)        Reloads the Book with its
    .OrderBy(x => x.BookId).Last()           Reviews to check whether
    .Reviews.Count.ShouldEqual(3);           there are three Reviews
    }
}
```

17.11 Capturing the database commands sent to a database

Sometimes, it's helpful to see what EF Core is doing when it accesses a real data
and EF Core provides a couple of ways to do that. Inspecting the EF Core log
from your running application is one way, but it can be hard to find the exac
among all the other logs. Another, more focused approach is to write unit tests
test specific parts of your EF Core queries by capturing SQL commands that EF
would use to query the database.

The EF Core logs often contain the SQL commands but also carry other info
tion, such as warnings of possible problems and timings (how long the database a
took). Also, even if you don't know the SQL language well, it's not hard to c
whether the configuration changes you made created the expected changes in
database. EF Core 5 added two new features that make capturing database comm
much easier than in previous versions:

- The `LogTo` option extension, which makes it easy to filter and capture EF
  logging
- The `ToQueryString` method, which shows the SQL generated from a I
  query

17.11.1 Using the LogTo option extension to filter and capture
EF Core logging

Before EF Core 5, getting logs out of EF Core required you to build an ILog
Provider class and register that logger provider via the UseLoggerFactory op
extension method. This technique wasn't easy. The EF Core 5's LogTo option e
sion method makes it much easier to get log output and adds some features that
the logs you want to see.

The LogTo method typically returns each log via an Action<string> type, and
can add the logs to a List<string> variable or output to some console. In xUnit
would use the xUnit ITestOutputHelper's WriteLine method, as shown in the fc
ing listing.

Listing 17.23 Outputting logs from an xUnit test by using the `LogTo` method

```
public class TestLogTo                           The class holding your
{                                                unit tests of LogTo
    private readonly ITestOutputHelper _output;

                                    An xUnit interface that allows
                                    output to the unit test runner
```

```
public TestLogTo(ITestOutputHelper output)
{
    _output = output;
}


[Fact]
public void TestLogToDemoToConsole()
{
    //SETUP
    var connectionString =
        this.GetUniqueDatabaseConnectionString();
    var builder =
        new DbContextOptionsBuilder<BookDbContext>()
        .UseSqlServer(connectionString)
        .EnableSensitiveDataLogging()
        .LogTo(_output.WriteLine);

    using var context = new BookDbContext(builder.Options);
    // … rest of unit test left out
}
}
```

xUnit will inject the ITestOutputHelper via the class's constructor.

This method contains a test of LogTo.

Provides a database connection where the database name is unique to this class

the option to an SQL r database

Adds the simplest form of the LogTo method, which calls an Action<string> method

d to turn on ensitiveData in your unit tests.

The default has the following format:

- LINE1: <loglevel(4 chars)> <DateTime.Now> <EventId> <Category>
- LINE2: <the log message>

The following code snippet shows one of the logs in this format:

- LINE1: warn: 10/12/2020 11:59:38.658 CoreEventId.SensitiveDataLogging-
  EnabledWarning[10400] (Microsoft.EntityFrameworkCore.Infrastructure)
- LINE2: Sensitive data logging is enabled. Log entries and exception messages may include sensitive application data; this mode should only be
  enabled during development.

As well as outputting the logs, the LogTo method can filter by the following types:

- LogLevel, such as LogLevel.Information or LogLevel.Warning
- EventIds, which define a specific log output, such as CoreEventId.Context-
  Initialized and RelationalEventId.CommandExecuted
- Category names, which EF Core defines for commands in groups, such as
  DbLoggerCategory.Database.Command.Name
- Functions that take in the EventId and the LogLevel and return true for the
  logs you want to be output

This method is great, but there are so many options to choose from for adding the
LogTo feature to the EfCore.TestSupport library that I built a class called LogTo-
Options to handle all the settings (along with code to throw an exception if the com-
bination you picked isn't supported). The LogToOptions class also includes some

different defaults from LogTo's defaults, which are based on my experience with ging in unit tests. The changes are

- The default LogLevel should be Information. (I find Debug LogLevel lo be useful only if I am trying to find a bug.)
- I don't want a DataTime in a log, because that means I can't compare a log a constant string, so I set the DbContextLoggerOptions parameter to (The DbContextLoggerOptions controls the log output and can add information to the log string.)
- Most times, I don't want to see logs of the Setup stage of the unit test, so I a a bool ShowLog property (defaults to true) to allow you to control when Action<string> parameter is called.

Here is a listing of the LogToOptions class with comments on each property.

Listing 17.24   The LogToOptions class with all the settings for the LogTo meth

```
public class LogToOptions
{
    public bool ShowLog { get; set; }
        = true;

    public LogLevel LogLevel { get; set; }
        = LogLevel.Information;

    public string[] OnlyShowTheseCategories
        { get; set; }

    public EventId[] OnlyShowTheseEvents
        { get; set; }

    public Func<EventId, LogLevel, bool>
        FilterFunction { get; set; }

    public DbContextLoggerOptions
        LoggerOptions { get; set; }
            = DbContextLoggerOptions.None;
}
```

If false, your Action<string> method isn't called; defaults to true

Only logs at or higher than the LogLevel property will be output defaults to LogLevel.Information

If not null, returns only logs with a Category name in this array; defaults to null

If not null, returns only logs with an EventId in this array; defaults to null

If not null, this function is called, a logs only where this function retur true are returned; defaults to null

Controls the format of the EF Core I The default setting does not prefix log with extra information, such as LogLevel, DateTime, and so on.

Now let's use the LogToOptions class with EfCore.TestSupport's SqliteInMe .CreateOptionsWithLogTo method. In the following listing, you use the Sho property in the LogToOptions class to display the logs only after the Setup stage of unit test has finished.

Listing 17.25   Turning off log output until the //SETUP stage of the unit test is finis

```
[Fact]
public void TestEfCoreLoggingCheckSqlOutputShowLog()
{
    //SETUP
```

```
var logToOptions = new LogToOptions
{
    ShowLog = false
};
var options = SqliteInMemory
    .CreateOptionsWithLogTo
    <BookDbContext>(
        _output.WriteLine,
        logToOptions);

using var context = new BookDbContext(options);
context.Database.EnsureCreated();
context.SeedDatabaseFourBooks();

//ATTEMPT
logToOptions.ShowLog = true;
var book = context.Books.Count();

//VERIFY
}
```

In this case, you want to change the default LogToOptions to set the ShowLog to false.

This method sets up the SQLite in-memory options and adds LogTo to those options.

This setup and seed section doesn't produce any output because the ShowLog property is false.

Turns on the logging output by setting the ShowLog property to true

This query produces one log output, which will be sent to the xUnit runner's window.

The second parameter is optional, but in this case, you want to provide the logToOptions to control the output.

The result is that instead of wading through the logs from creating the database and seeding the database, you see only one log output in the xUnit runner's window, as shown in the following code snippet:

```
Executed DbCommand (0ms) [Parameters=[],
        CommandType='Text', CommandTimeout='30']
SELECT COUNT(*)
FROM "Books" AS "b"
WHERE NOT ("b"."SoftDeleted")
```

17.2 Using the ToQueryString method to show the SQL generated from a LINQ query

The logging output is great and contains lots of useful information, but if you simply want to see what your query looks like, you have a much simpler way. If you have built a database query that returns an IQueryable result, you can use the ToQueryString method. The following listing incorporates the output of the ToQueryString method in the test.

> **Listing 17.26 A unit test containing the** ToQueryString **method**

```
[Fact]
public void TestToQueryStringOnLinqQuery()
{
    //SETUP
    var options = SqliteInMemory.CreateOptions<BookDbContext>();
    using var context = new BookDbContext(options);
```

```
context.Database.EnsureCreated();
context.SeedDatabaseFourBooks();

//ATTEMPT
var query = context.Books.Select(x => x.BookId);
var bookIds = query.ToArray();

//VERIFY
_output.WriteLine(query.ToQueryString());
query.ToQueryString().ShouldEqual(
    "SELECT \"b\".\"BookId\"\r\n" +
    "FROM \"Books\" AS \"b\"\r\n" +
    "WHERE NOT (\"b\".\"SoftDeleted\")");
bookIds.ShouldEqual(new []{1,2,3,4});
}
```

You provide the LINQ query without an execution part.

Then you run the LINQ query by adding ToArray on the end.

Outputs the SQL for your LINQ query

Tests whether the SQL is what you expected

Tests the output of the query

Summary

- Unit testing is a way to test a *unit* of your code—a small piece of code that be logically isolated in your application.

- Unit testing is a great way to catch bugs when you develop your code and, important, when you or someone else refactors your code.

- I recommend using xUnit because it is widely used (EF Core uses xUnit an ~70,000 tests), well supported, and fast. I also have built a library called EF .TestSupport that provides methods to make testing EF Core code in x easier.

- An application's DbContext designed to work with an ASP.NET Core app tion is ready for unit testing, but any application's DbContext that use OnConfiguring method to set options needs to be modified to allow unit te

- There are three main ways to simulate a database when unit testing, each its own trade-offs:
  - *Using the same type of database as your production database*—This approach safest, but you need to deal with out-of-date database schemas and man; databases to allow parallel running of unit test classes.
  - *Using an SQLite in-memory database*—This approach is the fastest and ea but it doesn't mimic every SQL feature of your production database.
  - *Stubbing the database*—When you have a repository pattern for accessin database, such as in business logic (see section 4.4.3), stubbing that re tory gives you fast and comprehensive control of the data for unit testin it typically needs more test code to be written.

- Cosmos DB has a handy Azure Cosmos DB Emulator that you can dow and run locally. This application allows you to unit test Cosmos DB wi needing an Azure Cosmos DB service.

- Many unit tests need the test database to contain some data to be used i test, so it's worth spending time to design a suite of test methods that will c test data to use in your unit tests.

- Your unit tests might say that the code under test is correct when it's not. This situation can happen if one section of your unit test is picking up tracked instances from a previous stage of the test. You have two ways to ensure that this problem doesn't happen: use separate DbContext instances or use `Change-Changer.Clear`.
- EF Core 5 has added two methods that make capturing the SQL produced from your code much easier: the `LogTo` option to capture logging output and the `ToQueryString` method to convert LINQ queries to database commands.

appendix
A brief introductic
to LIN

This appendix is for anyone who is new to Microsoft's Language Integrated Q (LINQ) feature or anyone who wants a quick recap of how LINQ works. The I language bridges the gap between the world of objects and the world of data, a used by EF Core to build database queries. Understanding the LINQ language to using EF Core to access a database.

This appendix starts with the two syntaxes you can use to write LINQ You'll also learn the types of commands available in LINQ, with examples of those commands can manipulate collections of in-memory data.

Then you'll explore the related .NET type IQueryable<T>, which holds I code in a form that can be executed later. This type allows developers to split plex queries into separate parts and change the LINQ query dynamically. IQueryable<T> type also allows EF Core to translate the LINQ code into mands that can be run on the database server. Finally, you'll learn what an EF query, with its LINQ part, looks like.

A.1   *An introduction to the LINQ language*

You can manipulate collections of data by using LINQ's methods to sort, select, and so on. These collections can be in-memory data (such as an arr integers, XML data, or JSON data) and of course databases, via libraries su EF Core. The LINQ feature is available in Microsoft's languages C#, F#, Visual Basic; you can create readable code by using LINQ's functional prog ming approach.

> **TIP** If you haven't come across functional programming, it's worth taking a look at it. See http://mng.bz/97CY or, for a more in-depth, .NET-focused

book, Enrico Buonanno's *Functional Programming in C#* (Manning, 2017; http://mng.bz/Q2Qv).

The two ways you can write LINQ queries

LINQ has two syntaxes for writing LINQ queries: the *method* syntax and the *query* syntax. This section presents the two syntaxes and points out which one is used in this book. You'll write the same LINQ query, a filter, and a sort of array of integers in both syntaxes.

Listing A.1 uses what is known as the LINQ *method*, or *lambda*, syntax. This code is a simple LINQ statement. Even if you haven't seen LINQ before, the names of the LINQ methods, such as `Where` and `OrderBy`, provide a good clue to what's going on.

Listing A.1   Your first look at the LINQ language using the method/lambda syntax

```
int[] nums = new[] {1, 5, 4, 2, 3, 0};          ◁──────┐   Creates an array of
                                                        │   integers from 0 to 5,
int[] result = nums          ◁──────┐   Applies LINQ commands │   but in a random order
    .Where(x => x > 3)       ◁──────┤   and returns a new array
 ┌─▷ .OrderBy(x => x)                │   of integers
 │   .ToArray();    ◁───┐
 │                      │   Filters out all the
ns the query back into an array.    integers 3 and below
 result is an array of ints { 4, 5 }.
```

The *lambda* name comes from lambda syntax, introduced in C# 3. The lambda syntax allows you to write a method without all the standard method definition syntax. The `x => x > 3` part inside the `Where` method is equivalent to the following method:

```
private bool AnonymousFunc(int x)
{
    return x > 3;
}
```

As you can see, the lambda syntax can save a significant amount of typing. I use lambdas in all of my EF Core queries and in lots of other code I wrote for this book.

The next listing shows the other way of writing LINQ code, called the *query* syntax. This code achieves the same result as listing A.1 but returns a slightly different result type.

Listing A.2   Your first look at the LINQ language using the query syntax

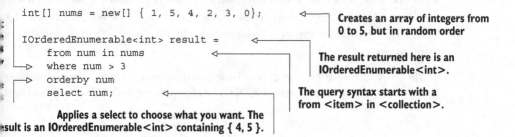

```
int[] nums = new[] { 1, 5, 4, 2, 3, 0};          ◁──────┐   Creates an array of integers from
                                                        │   0 to 5, but in random order
IOrderedEnumerable<int> result =        ◁──────┐
    from num in nums                    ◁──────┤   The result returned here is an
 ┌─▷ where num > 3                              │   IOrderedEnumerable<int>.
 ├─▷ orderby num
 │   select num;    ◁───────┐           The query syntax starts with a
 │                          │           from <item> in <collection>.
    Applies a select to choose what you want. The
sult is an IOrderedEnumerable<int> containing { 4, 5 }.
```

You can use either syntax; the choice is up to you. I use the method syntax beca involves slightly less typing and because I like the way that commands are cha together, one after the other. The rest of the examples in this book use the me syntax.

Before I leave the topic of the LINQ syntax, I want to introduce the concept o calculating values in a LINQ query. The query syntax has a feature specifically to dle this task: the `let` keyword. This keyword allows you to calculate a value onc then use that value multiple times in the query, making the query more efficient. listing shows code that converts an integer value to its word/string equivalen then uses that string in both the sort and filter parts of the query.

Listing A.3   Using the `let` keyword in a LINQ query syntax

Creates an array of integers from
0 to 5, but in random order

```
int[] nums = new[] { 1, 5, 4, 2, 3, 0 };
string [] numLookop = new[]
    {"zero","one","two","three","four","five"};
```

A lookup to convert a
number to its word form

The result returned her
an IEnumerable<int>

Orders the
number by
the word
form

```
IEnumerable<int> result =
    from num in nums
    let numString = numLookop[num]
    where numString.Length > 3
    orderby numString
    select num;
```

The query syntax starts with a
from <item> in <collection>.

The let syntax allows you to
calculate a value once and use
it multiple times in the query.

Applies a select to choose what you want.
The result is an IEnumerable<int>
containing { 5,4,3,0 }.

Filters out all the numbers indicating that
the word is shorter than three letters

The equivalent in the method syntax is the LINQ `Select` operator earlier i query, as shown in the following listing. (Section A.1.2 provides more details a the LINQ `Select` operator.)

Listing A.4   Using the LINQ `Select` operator to hold a calculated value

Applies another Select to choose what you want. The
result is an IEnumerable<int> containing { 5,4,3,0 }.

Creates an array of integers from
0 to 5, but in random order

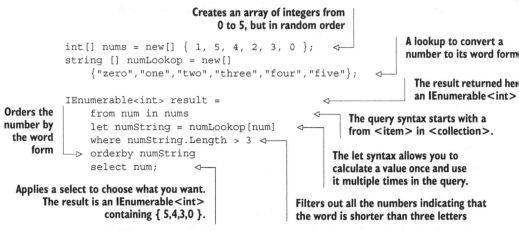

```
int[] nums = new[] { 1, 5, 4, 2, 3, 0 };
string[] numLookop = new[]
    {"zero","one","two","three","four","five"};
```

A lookup to convert a
number to its word form

The result returned he
an IEnumerable<int>

```
IEnumerable<int> result = nums
    .Select( num => new
```

Orders the
number by
the word
form

```
    {
        num,
        numString = numLookop[num]
    })
    .Where(r => r.numString.Length > 3)
    .OrderBy(r => r.numString)
    .Select(r => r.num);
```

Uses an anonymous type to hold
the original integer value and
your numString word lookup

Filters out all the numbers indicatin
the word is shorter than three lette

EF6   EF6.x used the `let` or the `Select` as a hint to precalculate a value only once in the database. EF Core doesn't have that performance feature, so it recalculates every occurrence of a value.

The data operations you can do with LINQ

The LINQ feature has many methods, referred to as *operators*. Most operators have names and functions that clearly indicate what's going on. Table A.1 lists some of the most common LINQ operators; similar operators are grouped to help you see where they might be used. The list is not exhaustive; the aim is to show you some of the most common operators to give you a feel for what LINQ can do.

Table A.1   Examples of LINQ operators, grouped by purpose

Group	Examples (not all operators shown)
Sorting	`OrderBy, OrderByDescending, Reverse`
Filtering	`Where`
Select element	`First, FirstOrDefault`
Projection	`Select`
Aggregation	`Max, Min, Sum, Count, Average`
Partition	`Skip, Take`
Boolean tests	`Any, All, Contains`

Listing A.4 shows a LINQ query that sorts and filters an array of `int` numbers. Now we are going to look at some examples in which the LINQ query works on a C# class. First, you need to define a new class called `Review` with data to help with the examples, as shown in the following listing.

Listing A.5   A `Review` class and a `ReviewsList` variable containing two Reviews

```
class Review
{
    public string VoterName { get; set; }
    public int NumStars { get; set; }
    public string Comment { get; set; }
}

List<Review> ReviewsList = new List<Review>
{
    new Review
    {
        VoterName = "Jack",
        NumStars = 5,
        Comment = "A great book!"
    },
    new Review
```

```
    {
        VoterName = "Jill",
        NumStars = 1,
        Comment = "I hated it!"
    }
};
```

The ReviewsList field in LINQ code is shown in table A.2. This table should give a feel for how various LINQ operators work.

Table A.2 Four uses of LINQ on the ReviewsList field as data. The result of each LINQ opera shown in the Result value column.

LINQ group	Code using LINQ operators	Result value

Projection	`string[] result = ReviewsList`
	`.Select(p => p.VoterName)`
	`.ToArray();`
		`string[]{"Jack", "Jil`

Aggregation	`double result = ReviewsList` `.Average(p => p.NumStars);`	3 (average of 5 and 1)
Select element	`string result = ReviewsList` `.First().VoterName;`	`"Jack"` (first voter)
Boolean test	`bool result = ReviewsList` `.Any(p => p.NumStars == 1);`	true (Jill voted 1)

A.2   *Introduction to IQueryable<T> type, and why it's useful*

Another important part of LINQ is the generic interface IQueryable<T>. LIN rather special, in that whatever set of LINQ operators you provide isn't exec straightaway but is held in a type called IQueryable<T>, awaiting a final comma execute it. This IQueryable<T> form has two benefits:

- You can split a complex LINQ query into separate parts by using the IQu able<T> type.
- Instead of executing the IQueryable<T>'s internal form, EF Core can tran it into database access commands.

A.2.1   *Splitting up a complex LINQ query by using the IQueryable<T> type*

In the book, you learn about Query Objects (see section 2.6), and you build a plex book list query by chaining together three Query Objects. This operation v because of the IQueryable<T> type's ability to hold the code in a specialized called an *expression tree*, so that other LINQ operators can be appended to it.

As an example, you're going to improve the code from listing A.1 by adding own method that contains the sorting part of the query, allowing you to alter the order of the final LINQ query. You'll create this method as an extension me which allows you to chain the method in the same way that the LINQ operators do. (LINQ operators are extension methods.)

> **DEFINITION** An *extension method* is a static method in a static class; the first parameter of the method has the keyword this in front of it. To allow chaining, the method must also return a type that other methods can use as an input.

Listing A.6 shows the extension method MyOrder, which takes in an IQueryable<int> type as its first parameter and returns an IQueryable<int> result. It also has a second boolean parameter called ascending that sets the sort order to ascending or descending.

Listing A.6 Your method encapsulates part of your LINQ code via IQueryable<int>

Provides a second parameter that allows you to change the order of the sorting

Extension method needs to be defined in a static class

Static method Order returns an IQueryable<int> so other extension methods can chain on

```
public static class LinqHelpers
{
    public static IQueryable<int> MyOrder
        (this IQueryable<int> queryable,
        bool ascending)
    {
        return ascending
            ? queryable
                .OrderBy(num => num)
            : queryable
                .OrderByDescending(num => num);
    }
}
```

Extension method's first parameter is of IQueryable and starts with the this keyword

Uses the Boolean parameter ascending to control whether you add the OrderBy or OrderByDescending LINQ operator to the IQueryable result

...ending ...eter is ...ou add ...y LINQ to the ...e input

Ascending parameter is false, so you add the OrderByDescending LINQ operator to the IQueryable input

This listing uses this IQueryable<int> extension method to replace the OrderBy LINQ operator in the original code in listing A.1.

Listing A.7 Using the MyOrder IQueryable<int> method in LINQ code

```
var numsQ = new[] { 1, 5, 4, 2, 3 }
    .AsQueryable();
```

Turns an array of integers into a queryable object

```
var result = numsQ
    .MyOrder(true)
    .Where(x => x > 3)
    .ToArray();
```

Calls the MyOrder IQueryable<int> method, with true, giving you an ascending sort of the data

Executes the IQueryable and turns the result into an array. The result is an array of ints { 4, 5 }.

Extension methods, such as the MyOrder example, provide two useful features:

- *They make your LINQ code dynamic.* By changing the parameter into the MyOrder method, you can change the sort order of the final LINQ query. If you didn't have that parameter, you'd need two LINQ queries—one using OrderBy and

one using `OrderByDescending`—and then you'd have to pick which one
wanted to run by using an `if` statement. That approach isn't good software
tice, as you'd be needlessly repeating some LINQ code, such as the `Where` pa

- *They allow you to split complex queries into a series of separate extension methods th.*
  can chain. This approach makes it easier to build, test, and understand con
  queries. In section 2.9, you split your Book App's book list query, which is r
  complicated, into separate *Query Objects.* The following listing shows this pr
  again, with each Query Object highlighted in bold.

Listing A.8   The book list query with select, order, filter, and page Query Objects

```
public IQueryable<BookListDto> SortFilterPage
    (SortFilterPageOptions options)
{
    var booksQuery = _context.Books
        .AsNoTracking()
        .MapBookToDto()
        .OrderBooksBy(options.OrderByOptions)
        .FilterBooksBy(options.FilterBy,
                       options.FilterValue);

    options.SetupRestOfDto(booksQuery);

    return booksQuery.Page(options.PageNum-1,
                           options.PageSize);
}
```

The book list query uses both features I've mentioned: it allows you to chang
sorting, filtering, and paging of the book list dynamically, and it hides some c
complex code behind an aptly named method that tells you what it's doing.

A.2.2   *How EF Core translates IQueryable<T> into database code*

EF Core translates your LINQ code into database code that can run on the data
server. It can do this because the `IQueryable<T>` type holds all the LINQ code
expression tree, which EF Core can translate into database access code. Figure
shows what EF Core is doing behind the scenes when it translates a LINQ query
database access code.

EF Core provides many extra extension methods to extend the LINQ oper
available to you. EF Core methods add to the LINQ expression tree, such as `Inc`
`ThenInclude` (see section 2.4.1), and so on. Other EF methods provide async ver
(see section 5.10) of the LINQ methods, such as `ToListAsync` and `LastAsync`.

A.3   *Querying an EF Core database by using LINQ*

Using LINQ in an EF Core database query requires three parts, as shown in figure
The query relies on an application's DbContext, which is described in section
This section concentrates on only the format of an EF Core database query, wit
LINQ operators shown in bold.

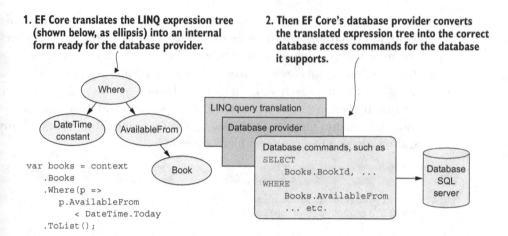

Figure A.1   Some book query code (bottom left) with its expression tree above it. EF Core takes the expression tree through two stages of translation before it ends up in the right form for the database that the application is targeting.

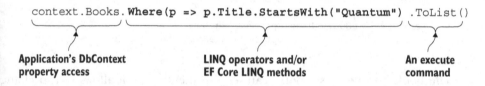

Figure A.2   An example database access, with the three parts

These three parts of an EF Core database query are as follows:

- *Application's DbContext property access*—In your application's DbContext, you define a property by using a `DbSet<T>` type. This type returns an `IQueryable<T>` data source to which you can add LINQ operators to create a database query.

- *LINQ operators and/or EF Core LINQ methods*—Your database LINQ query code goes here.

- *The execute command*—Commands such as `ToList` and `First` trigger EF Core to translate the LINQ commands into database access commands that are run on the database server.

In chapter 2 and onward, you'll see much more complex queries, but they all use the three parts shown in figure A.2.

ind

A

ASP.NET Core in Action, Second Edition
by Andrew Lock

ISBN 9781617298301
832 pages, $69.99
March 2021

Blazor in Action
by Chris Sainty

ISBN 9781617298646
400 pages (estimated), $59.99
July 2021 (estimated)

Code like a Pro in C#
by Jort Rodenburg

ISBN 9781617298028
391 pages (estimated), $59.99
Summer 2021 (estimated)

C# in Depth, Fourth Edition
by Jon Skeet
Foreword by Eric Lippert

ISBN 9781617294532
528 pages, $49.99
March 2019

For ordering information go to www.manning.com

the United States
Taylor Publisher Services